D1490363

GERMANIC GENEALOGY

A Guide to Worldwide Sources
and Migration Patterns

Edward R. Brandt, Ph. D.

Mary Bellingham

Kent Cutkomp

Kermit Frye

Patricia A. Lowe

with a chapter on Jewish genealogy
by George E. Arnstein, Ph. D.

Germanic Genealogy Society
P.O. Box 16312
St. Paul, MN 55116

Published by the Germanic Genealogy Society, P.O. Box 16312, St. Paul, MN 55116.

Library of Congress Catalog Card Number: 95-76669.

Second printing, November 1995, slightly revised.

Cataloging-in-Publication Data.

Germanic genealogy: A guide to worldwide sources and migration patterns /
Edward R. Brandt <et al.>
  370p maps
  Bibliography: p.274-291.
  Includes index.

1. Genealogy—Germany—Handbooks, manuals, etc. 2.Genealogy—United States—Handbooks, manuals, etc. I. Brandt, Edward R.
929'.1072

95-76669

To order this book, send $24.00 plus $3.00 ($5.00 for surface delivery if outside the United States) shipping and handling to:

Germanic Genealogy Society, P.O. Box 16312, St. Paul, MN 55116.

Minnesota residents, add another $1.56 Minnesota sales tax.

TABLE OF CONTENTS

Germanic Genealogy: A Guide to Worldwide Sources and Migration Patterns

TABLES

PREFACE

Perspective of This Guide

James N. Bade, in his book, *The German Connection: New Zealand and German-Speaking Europe in the Nineteenth Century*, concluded that "the basic criterion for the term 'German' should be that the person or people in question be German-speaking." This guide is based on the same premise. The bond shared by all humankind is the summit of civilization. The family, where the sense of linkage is much deeper, is its foundation.

Between these two, however, are intermediate levels of kinship. What is it that causes people to identify more closely with some of their fellow human beings than with others, beyond the degree of consanguinity? What makes them feel they share a tradition?

The notion of race has, of course, been proven to be totally incompatible with historical fact. The strongest ties are likely to be based on religion, a common homeland, territorial proximity, or language.

For our German-speaking immigrant ancestors, it could not have been religion, because nowhere else in contemporary Europe (with the exception of Bosnia) do you see such an even denominational cleavage as in Germany and Switzerland. Our ancestors were even more diverse, because members of small denominations emigrated in disproportionately large numbers, often because of religious intolerance.

Nor could the feeling of sharing be based on a common homeland. Today there are five German-speaking countries in Europe, although two have more than one official language. Before 1871 the number of sovereign entities was much larger.

There never has been a united "Germany" which included nearly all German-speakers and few other people. The closest parallels are Ludwig the German's ninth-century Austrasia and the Holy Roman Empire of the German Nation, which ceased to have more than symbolic significance in the thirteenth century. However, both included non-Germanic territory and excluded large areas which were, or became, Germanic.

Nor can it be explained by proximity, since German-speaking people were scattered throughout most of Europe long before they became trans-oceanic migrants. Having been neighbors historically can explain a lot of migration patterns of different ethnic groups from the same general area. It can explain the affinity which Germans and Slavs often (though certainly not always) had for each other before the virus of nationalism hit the world and increasingly among their descendants into the post-nationalistic era ushered in by the incredible horrors of World War II. It can not explain, however, why certain groups of subjects of so many different countries shared a feeling that they were all part of "Our People" — a concept which has its identical equivalent, in terminology and importance, among a great many other peoples.

Thus the only thing our ancestors had in common was a language. We have used the term "Germanic" to denote this and to distinguish it from any particular former or present political entity.

While it is easy to exaggerate the relationship between a common language and a common culture, an important connection exists nevertheless. A shared language is certainly by far the greatest facilitator of communication. This makes a common culture possible, although the various sub-cultures (national, regional, religious) often had a more profound impact on people than the common culture.

Does this have any relevance for the scores of millions of descendants scattered throughout the world, most of whom have lost all knowledge of the ancestral mother tongue and become almost fully assimilated into the cultures of their respective countries of residence?

It certainly does. They have a common heritage. And heritage matters. As Hodding Carter put it, there are only two lasting bequests which parents can give to their children: roots and wings.

The molding effect of the past has an impact on everyone. The difference between genealogists and most non-genealogists is simply that the former tend to be more conscious of their heritage and more inquisitive about it.

This consciousness is, of course, shared by other historians, whether professionals or amateurs — "other," because family history is but a branch of history, even though it often does not get proper academic recognition.

These are the reasons why this guide has expanded so greatly in scope, not merely in the number of pages (which has increased by about two-thirds).

The more significant changes are listed in the Introduction.

Because this book deals primarily with research on Germans, we have used the German *Umlaut* mark (*ä, ö, ü*) throughout the book. However, in the case of the many varying diacritical marks in other languages, we have generally shown them only in the case of actual addresses, but not in the text, with such exceptions as seemed appropriate.

Clarification of Key Acronym

The Family History Library (FHL) in Salt Lake City, under the auspices of The Church of Jesus Christ of Latter-day Saints (LDS), is by far the largest repository of genealogical records in the world. All of its microfilms, but not its unfilmed books, are available through any Family History Center (FHC). Such centers, formerly called branch libraries, exist in every large American city (and in many small ones), as well as in dozens of countries throughout the world. The actual filming is done by the Genealogical Society of Utah (GSU), also an arm of the church.

Since the Mormons have been extremely generous in sharing the genealogical information they have gathered, at considerable cost, and the vast majority of people who use its resources are not Mormons, we have substituted the more appropriate acronym, "FHL," for the better known "LDS."

November 1995

Edward R. Brandt
Mary Bellingham
Kent Cutkomp
Kermit Frye
Patricia A. Lowe

INTRODUCTION

Germanic Genealogy: A Guide to Worldwide Sources and Migration Patterns is a successor to the *Research Guide to German-American Genealogy*, but has been greatly expanded and totally revised to include 140 additional pages of information. It is a comprehensive, well-indexed and easy-to-use reference work.

This book is intended as a guide to help beginning and advanced genealogists successfully search for their Germanic ancestors throughout the world. It provides detailed information on research using European records as well as a global focus on the migration of Germanic people. We have incorporated and provided background on the major aspects of genealogy research to aid you in your search. These aspects include: migration patterns, history and geography, religion, German genealogical terms, sample German letters, the Gothic script, historical and regional maps, background and how-to-hints for each country with up-to-date addresses on where to write for more information. An extensive bibliography and chapter references provide other sources for further research on each topic.

In addition, the book shows how to: begin your research, find the place of your ancestor's origin, access church records, civil records and passenger lists, correspond abroad and use the Family History Library and its centers.

Among the new or expanded features are:

(1) Considerably more comprehensive and detailed information concerning the European countries in which ethnic Germans lived. In particular, the book provides you with revised and up-to-date information concerning the contents of and access to archives in Eastern Europe following the collapse of the closed Communist societies and the reunification of Germany.

(2) An expanded and thoroughly revised chapter on religion with narratives on each religious group.

(3) A new chapter on the genealogical sources for German Jewish ancestry.

(4) Updates to the German postal codes for all German addresses.

(5) Global coverage with detailed information on the records in the countries where German-speaking people settled. This expansion of material includes Australia, New Zealand, Latin America, Africa, Asia and other areas throughout the world. This global coverage complements the material on records in the United States, Canada and Europe.

(6) A list of hard to identify, but commonly used, references to geographic and historical areas.

(7) Expanded material concerning geography and history as it pertains to Germanic people to assist you in tracing your ancestors.

(8) Greatly expanded material on migration of Germanic people throughout the world.

(9) Revised and expanded information on the Family History Library and its centers.

(10) Additional information on using American and German sources.

(11) Expanded and updated bibliography and chapter references for further research. These references provide you with descriptions of other books where you may find more information.

No book is perfect and the more information it contains the greater the chance that some inaccuracies and errors crept in. Moreover, the world of genealogy is constantly changing. Hence, periodic revisions are essential. We welcome any corrections and comments as to what should be clarified or expanded in future endeavors.

This research guide provides you with the information and answers to make tracing your Germanic ancestors more successful and enjoyable. We wish you the best of luck in your search.

ACKNOWLEDGMENTS AND CREDITS

This book could not have been as comprehensive or up-to-date without the assistance of many other individuals and institutions. We especially thank the following for providing substantive information or making it available to us:

Ken V. André of the **South African-German Cultural Association** (German immigration to South Africa, and genealogy).

Sharon Anno of *Historic Harmony* (history and settlements of the Harmonists).

David Armstrong of the **European Interest Group of the Western Australian Genealogical Society** (donated a book on the Germans in that state and helped in obtaining the leading Australian genealogical guide).

Dr. George E. Arnstein, contacted through *Avotaynu*, who generously contributed the chapter on Jewish genealogy.

Roy Bernard of the **Anglo-German Family History Society** (German immigration to England).

Jessie L. Daraska of the **Balzekas Museum of Lithuanian Culture** (Lithuania).

Patricia A. Eames of the **National Archives Volunteer Association** (Russian-American Genealogical Archival Service).

Irmgard Hein Ellingson of the **Bukovina Society of the Americas** (Bukovina German history and bibliography).

The European Interest Group of the New Zealand Society of Genealogists (donated a book on German-speaking immigrants to that country).

Dr. Duncan B. Gardiner of the **Czechoslovak Genealogical Society International** (nearly all of the historical and genealogical information on the Germans in Slovakia and most of that on the Czech Republic, in addition to proofreading and correcting our drafts).

Prof. Ayrton Gonçalves Celestino of Brazil, contacted through the **Bukovina Society of the Americas** (donated a manuscript on the Bukovina Germans in Brazil).

Ginger Hamer and **John Hamer** (cover design).

Marianne Hauser (review and revision of the German form letters).

Vernon Kading of **GGS** (reviewing back issues of *Die Zeitung*, published by the German Interest Group of the Genealogical Society of Queensland, and proofreading our entire draft).

Nelson Kickhoefel, mayor of Pomerode, Santa Catarina, Brazil (donated a booklet on the history of that heavily German area).

Dr. Lawrence Klippenstein, director of the **Mennonite Heritage Centre** (Soviet Mennonite refugees who fled to the Americas via Harbin, China), and along with **Henry N. Fast** (1835 Russian Molochna Mennonite revision list).

Jo Ann Kuhr of the **American Historical Society of Germans from Russia** (update on the Commonwealth of Independent States after reviewing our semi-final draft).

Brian J. Lenius of the **East European Branch of the Manitoba Genealogical Society** (genealogical resources in Western Canada).

Virginia Less of the **Northern Illinois Chapter of the American Historical Society of Germans from Russia** (archival records on the Soviet German Lutheran refugees quartered in Harbin, China, pending travel to Latin America).

Zella Mirick of **GGS** (patronymic naming practices in northern Germany).

Jill Robinson of Reefton, New Zealand (list of German pioneers on the west coast of South Island; help in getting a free copy of a book on the New Zealand Germans).

David F. Schmidt (Volga German research, organizational arrangement of collections in the Russian archives, and his experiences with various channels for genealogical research in the Commonwealth of Independent States).

Vladislav Yevgyenevich Soshnikov, formerly of the **Archives of Russia Society, Ltd.,** and founder of the **Genealogy and Family History Society, Moscow** (current overview of the records of the former Russian Empire, supplementing information previously available here).

Liz Twigden of the **South Australian Genealogical and Historical Society** (South Australian resources and recent Australian books).

Karen Whitmer of GGS, who played a major role in the preparation of our first book, *Beginning Research in Germany*, out of which this guide eventually developed.

Judith Williams of Puhoi, New Zealand, identified through the *AGoFF-Wegweiser* (copy of the local *Homeland News* for the New Zealand members of the **Bohemian Association Originating in Puhoi - Ohaupo**).

The staff of the **Family History Library** was most helpful in reviewing our drafts and providing additional information and corrections where needed: **Kahlile B. Mehr, Thomas Kent Edlund** and volunteer **Gwen B. Pritzkau** (successor states to the Soviet Union), **Eva T. Liptak** (Hungary), **Daniel Schlyter** (gazetteers), and **Tab Thompson** and **Tom Daniels** (Family History Library).

Help with bibliographical information, annotation and library research was received from **Margaret Freeman** of the **Glückstal Colonies Research Association** (Germans in the Lower Danubian region, some of whom migrated onward to the Russian Empire), **Jan Frye** (publication data and citations), **Carol O'Brien** and **Stephanie Frame** (German-language books), **Horst A. Reschke,** *Heritage Quest* columnist (Jews), and **Sophia Stalzer Wyant,** editor of *The Gottscheer Connection,* published by the **Gottscheer Research and Genealogy Association** (history of the Gottschee Germans in Slovenia).

We appreciate the assistance in translating titles or letters by **Korkut Gurkanlar** (Turkish); **W. Kornel Kondy** and **Bernie Szymczak** of the **Polish Genealogical Society of Minnesota, Chester Rog** (*Pol-Am Newsletter*) and **Roma Kehne** (Polish); and **Linda Watson** of the **Immigration History Research Center** (Italian). This is a better book because of the work of **Michael Haase, Douglas Lowe, Alonna Tunstead** (proofreading and editing); and **Charles Bellingham** (map-making).

We obtained important addresses from **Myron Gruenwald,** editor of *Die Pommerschen Leute,* and **Maxwell O. Andrae** (South Africa and Brazil); **Gail Hermann** (New Zealand); **Richard Rye** of the **American Historical Society of Germans from Russia, Michael Krannaweitter,** and **Carlos Windler** (Argentina); and **Ewald Wuschke,** editor of *Wandering Volhynians* (Brazil).

The list of institutional or societal connections is obviously incomplete, since many of these genealogists belong to numerous societies.

SOCIETIES, AUTHORS, EDITORS, PUBLISHERS, SPEAKERS AND LIBRARIANS

Much of our information, of course, comes from numerous books, articles, periodicals and conference presentations. We have tried to give proper credit to these authors, editors and speakers in the text.

Although we relied heavily on numerous German-oriented sources, periodicals of various **other ethnic and multi-ethnic societies** that focus on non-Germanic countries where Germans lived were a very useful supplement. Genealogists with ancestors from countries where German-speakers constituted a minority of the population would be well advised to examine what such societies have to offer.

The multi-continental **Federation of East European Family History Societies (FEEFHS)** deserves special mention. It enabled us to establish connections with genealogists of many other ethnic groups, which made it possible for us to tap their expertise with respect to genealogical resources pertaining to non-Germanic countries where Germans lived. Ten of the individuals mentioned above spoke without reimbursement at the first FEEFHS convention in 1994, or were contacted as a result of membership in FEEFHS. Other convention speakers included Germanic experts **Larry O. Jensen** of the *German Genealogical Digest*, **Charles M. Hall**, founding president of FEEFHS, and **John D. Movius**, vice-president of FEEFHS and of the **Sacramento German Genealogical Society**. **John C. Alleman**, editor of the *FEEFHS Newsletter*, was instrumental in our gaining access to information not previously known to us.

Librarians and staff members, including those at the **University of Minnesota, Concordia College (St. Paul)**, local **Family History Centers**, the **North Star Chapter of the American Historical Society of Germans from Russia**, and the **Germans from Russia Heritage Collection at the North Dakota Institute for Regional Studies, North Dakota State University**, facilitated the preparation of this book.

ARCHIVES AND DIPLOMATIC ESTABLISHMENTS

Valuable information was received, often on very short notice, from the **Manitoba Provincial Archives (Ken Reddig)**, the **National Archives of New Zealand (Vicky Fabian)**, the **State Archives and Heraldic Services of South Africa (Letitia Coetzee** and others), the **Ottoman Archives (Necati Gültepe)**, the **Consulate General of the Netherlands, Chicago (Olga Burgerhout Tipton)**, and the **Brazilian Embassy**.

We have continued to use information provided for our 1991 guide by the **Hungarian National Archives (Dr. Imre Ress** and others), the **Polish National Archives**, the **Yugoslavian National Archives**, the **Austrian National Archives (Dr. Kammerhofer)**, the **German Central Office for Genealogy in Leipzig**, the **Tyrolean State Archives, Innsbruck**, and the **German Cultural Archives in Bozen, Italy**.

Other **governmental offices** that helped us at the time were the **Czechoslovakian, Yugoslavian and German embassies**.

The following **societies and institutions** provided us with information in 1991: the **Society for Genealogy and Heraldry in Poznan, Poland (Rafal T. Prinke)**; the **Mennonite Historical Library in Goshen, Indiana (John D. Roth)**; and the **Max Kade Institute for German-American Studies in Madison, Wisconsin**.

Dozens of other societies and individuals contributed to the genealogical education of the authors and thus indirectly to the book.

Minneapolis, Minnesota
November 1995

Edward R. Brandt, Ph.D.
Mary Bellingham
Kent Cutkomp
Kermit Frye
Patricia A. Lowe

About the Authors

Germanic Genealogy: A Guide to Worldwide Sources and Migration Patterns is the co-operative endeavor of five members of the Germanic Genealogy Society, who have volunteered their time and pooled their knowledge to produce this guide. Cumulatively, they have over 150 years of experience in Germanic genealogical research. We are thankful for the many outside experts listed in our acknowledgments who have generously provided important supplementary information for the 1995 global edition.

Of the five primary authors, four are charter members of the Germanic Genealogy Society, founded as the German Interest Group in December 1979, or joined it in its first year; three had been active in its parent society, the Minnesota Genealogical Society, prior to that; four have served GGS as president; and four have served as research chair or research project director.

The authors have done personal or professional research in, or relating to, the United States, Canada, Germany, Luxembourg, Switzerland, Austria, France, Poland, Ukraine, England, Norway and Sweden. Their publications also pertain to Hungary and the successor states to the Soviet Union in particular, and to Eastern Europe in general. Organizations to which they belong are also concerned with Germans in the Czech and Slovak Republics, Slovenia, Romania and, peripherally, Latin America, Ireland, Croatia and Yugoslavia. In addition, they have relatives or ancestral roots in the Netherlands, Belgium, Mexico, and Belize.

Their experience includes deciphering and translating the Gothic script, on-site European research, cartography, working as a Family History Center director, hunting lost relatives for the probate process, giving genealogical seminars, working as an accredited genealogist, teaching history, and an active role in non-Germanic societies.

About the Publisher

The Germanic Genealogy Society is a non-profit organization. Proceeds from the sale of this guide and other publications are used exclusively to fund further publications relating to Germanic genealogy, broadly defined, and to expand library resources. Authors seeking a publisher are welcome to contact GGS to discuss contractual arrangements.

Chapter I

BEGINNING YOUR SEARCH

This chapter provides some suggestions for beginning your genealogical research. Some basic considerations are: questioning family members and relatives; following good rules of organization; using proper research procedures; visiting libraries, court houses and archives; finding original source material; and getting the most out of each record.

Begin with your family sources. Gather as much information as possible from your memory and by questioning your parents and relatives. Ask about full names, dates and places of birth, marriage and death. Don't forget to ask about interesting stories and family traditions as to where relatives came from. Ask for names and addresses of other relatives who may help. Ask to see old photos, the family Bible, old letters and passports.

Now it is time to get organized. Make use of available forms to help organize your information. These include ancestor charts, family group sheets, individual ancestor data sheets, and correspondence and research logs. These forms are available through many genealogical societies and book distributors. You should maintain a careful record-keeping system. Some elements of that system are:

- Keep all notes on paper of consistent size (8½ by 11 inch paper is recommended).

- Photocopy original documents for use and leave the originals at home in a file.

- Create a separate 3-ring binder for each major surname you are searching. This should contain all known details about that surname as it pertains to your family.

- Number each page and file it by surname. Create indexes as needed.

- Create a small traveling notebook of duplicate copies and blank forms.

William Dollarhide has developed a record keeping system that works well. See his book entitled *Managing a Genealogical Project*.

Follow good research techniques:

- Trace one generation back at a time. Do not attempt to jump generations.

- Keep a full citation of where each piece of information was found.

- When photocopying pages from a book, always copy the title page to remind you where you found the information.

- Record <u>all</u> information found for each record. This can save time if you need to re-examine the information in the record at a later time.

- Record information on a separate page for each surname. This makes it easier when you file your notes.

Record sources can be divided into two general categories: primary sources and secondary sources. **Primary sources** are original documents pertaining to a particular event: for example, birth certificates, census records, family Bible entries or passenger lists. They are primary sources only for that specific event. **Secondary sources** include any other sources, such as indexes to files, extracts of original documents, or a book written about your family. Many sources contain both primary and secondary information. For example, a census record is primary for the place of residence on a specific date, but secondary for peoples' ages. Some sources may be primary or secondary depending upon when the information was written. For example, family information in a family Bible may be considered primary if it appears to be written on or near the date of an event, but should be considered secondary if entered at a much later date. Primary sources are generally considered to be more reliable, although not always.

Federal, state and local census records (available on microfilm) and various vital records (births, marriages and deaths) recorded at county court houses are among the most helpful types of records. Chapter II contains more about these and other records. You can access public records at libraries, state historical libraries, county court houses or archives; each place might have some records but not others. You can rent census records at public libraries. Regional libraries or genealogical libraries contain many genealogical reference works. You can access microfilm copies of original records from around the world by visiting any of the Church of Jesus Christ of Latter-day Saints (LDS) Family History Centers. You can also visit the main LDS library, known as the Family History Library, in Salt Lake City, UT. Chapter III contains additional information about the Family History Library and Family History Centers.

Use a variety of sources to find out information about each generation. This is important to verify the information you have and to fill in missing details about names, events, dates, or places. Inevitably there will be inconsistencies in the data, and you must evaluate the accuracy and reliability of each source to decide which is most probable. Periodically go through your research notes to see if information on older documents has new meaning when compared with more recently acquired information.

For additional help and ideas, look in Chapter II, join a genealogy society, and read the following references or other beginning genealogy books.

REFERENCES (See bibliography for full citations if not shown)

Fredrick H. Barth and Kenneth F. Thomsen, comps. *The Beginner's Guide to German Genealogical Research*. Bountiful, UT: Thomsen's Genealogical Center. 1988. 34 pp.
> Good short, simple starter for genealogical newcomers.

William Dollarhide. *Managing a Genealogical Project: A Complete Manual for the Management and Organization of Genealogical Materials*. Baltimore: Genealogical Publishing Co. 1988. 80 pp.
> A carefully presented system to organize your family research materials. Contains helpful terms and excellent discussion of their usage.

Family History Library. *Research Outline: Germany*. Salt Lake City: Family History Library. 1994.

F. Wilbur Helmbold. Edited by Karen Phillips. *Tracing Your Ancestry: A Step-by-step Guide to Researching Your Family History*. Birmingham, AL: Oxmoor House. 1976. 210 pp.
> Guide to beginning genealogy.

Diane J. Wandler and Prairie Heritage Chapter members. *Handbook for Researching Family Roots: With Emphasis on German-Russian Heritage*. B.H.G., Inc., P.O. Box 309, Garrison, ND 58540. 1992. 250 pp.

Richard S. Lackey. *Cite Your Sources: A Manual for Documenting Family Histories and Genealogical Records*. Jackson, MS: University Press of Mississippi. 1980. 94 pp. Indexed.

Chapter II

USING AMERICAN RECORDS TO FIND YOUR ANCESTOR'S PLACE OF ORIGIN

Are you *really* ready to "cross the ocean" with your German research?

If you can't answer "yes" to all of the following questions, you aren't fully prepared to start German research from German sources, and you will probably end up wasting a lot of time, effort and money . . . unless you get lucky.

- Do you know which town or village your immigrant came from in Germany? Be aware there are some towns with the same name as a larger district, province or state. Also, there are often many towns with the same name, even in the same province. The great majority of people who immigrated came from small towns or villages. Have you located your German town or village on a map? If your information shows the place of origin as "Prussia," this generally means very little, since Prussia at one time covered about two thirds of Germany. See Chapters VIII and IX for further information.

- Have you prepared a list of family members with pertinent vital record data (called a family group sheet) for the family of your immigrant? Is it complete regarding events that took place in the United States? This includes all children in the family, whether they were born in Germany, the United States, or elsewhere. Sometimes tracing a sibling helps in gathering information about your ancestor. See Chapter XVI for more information.

- Do you have dates or fairly narrow time periods so you can place some reasonable limits on your search?

- Do you know the political jurisdictions in which your German town is located? See Chapter IX for more information.

- Do you know the religion of your German ancestor? This is very important in German research. See Chapter XI for more information.

- Are you sure you have the German name of your immigrant, keeping in mind there may be more than one "correct" spelling? Name changes often occurred, particularly spelling changes and Anglicizing of names. You may have to look under more than one spelling or version of a name. See Chapter VII for more information.

FINDING THE PLACE OF ORIGIN

If you do not know the origin or place of birth of your ancestor, documents showing this can probably be found, but the key is to know where to begin looking. Remember that German immigration was very often a group effort. Friends and family left a German town or area, traveled together, and settled together in the United States. It is important to look carefully at the community situation and see if there is an old-world connection between your ancestor and others in the area.

If you can learn the origin of some of the others in the community, it may serve as a clue to the locale from which your ancestor originated. Look also for family ties among community members.

You may want to use some lesser-known sources like coroner or mortician files, medical records, or school and university records to see if your ancestor's origin is given in any of them. Look for local membership records of German-American immigrants who belonged to athletic clubs, musical societies, trade and benevolent groups, and mutual aid or church societies, which may give information on your ancestor. A visit to the area where your ancestor lived may also turn up more information.

If you cannot find any connection with the local people and area, you may want to investigate some of the following sources to see if you can find your ancestor's name.

FAMILY SURNAME ASSOCIATIONS

Family associations will be another place to look for origins. Many groups collect data on all people with the same surname and may publish newsletters, etc. This can be helpful for all but the most common names.

QUERIES IN GERMAN GENEALOGICAL PUBLICATIONS

There are two major German genealogical periodicals that are widely read in Germany and run queries. One is the *Familienkundliche Nachrichten [Genealogical News]*, known as *FaNa*. The other is *Praktische Forschungshilfe [Practical Research Help]*, known as *PraFo*, which is a quarterly supplement to the *Archiv für Sippenforschung [Archive for Genealogical Research]*. American sources are likely to identify them as FANA and PRAFO.

The German Genealogical Society of America has published the surnames listed in both of these publications in its *GGSA Bulletin*. It has complete indexed files of both, dating back to 1956. You can obtain entries relating to the surname(s) you are researching for a modest sum by sending a self-addressed, stamped envelope to GGSA, but you must know the date, volume, and number of the issue in which the entry appears. You may also wish to send your own query for publication.

FaNa is published by:

Verlag Degener & Co.
Postfach 1360
D-91403 Neustadt/Aisch
Germany

PraFo is published by:

C. A. Starke Verlag
Postfach 1310
D-65549 Limburg/Lahn
Germany

You may submit your query in English and ask the publisher to translate it. The cost depends on the length of the query, but a $20-$30 fee is common.

GLENZDORFS INTERNATIONALES GENEALOGEN-LEXIKON

This directory is similar to *FaNa*, but is in book form. There are three volumes that list German names being researched by genealogists all over the world. It is known in English as *Glenzdorf's International Directory of Genealogists*.

LIBRARIES AND GENEALOGICAL SOCIETIES

Some larger public libraries and libraries of genealogical and historical societies in the United States may have German phone books, German-language newspapers, books about emigrants to America, and published emigration lists. Check the indexes for your surname. Also look at newsletters and publications of societies that are located near your ancestor's residence.

German genealogical societies publish periodicals that contain various queries and surname exchange information. There are many ethnic genealogical societies in the United States that publish similar information. See Chapter XIX for addresses of some of them.

The Family History Library has many German lineage books and family histories, guild records and population lists, biographies and town histories. While generally arranged by German area, you may want to take a look at some of these to see if any contain your family name. Don't overlook the resources at the Family History Library discussed in Chapter III and the related books by Jensen, Dearden, and Hall mentioned and listed in the bibliography because there is no other comparably comprehensive genealogical resource in the world.

USING THE RECORDS

Develop a strategy for completing your research. Has someone else already done the research? There probably is someone who is researching the same family line. All you have to do is find them. Place a query in a genealogical periodical published by a United States or German genealogical society. The *Genealogical Helper* is a popular genealogical periodical published in the United States. Its German equivalent is *Familienkundliche Nachrichten* (see above). Another similar German publication is the *Praktische Forschungshilfe* (see above). You may also find another genealogist researching your surname or town in *Glenzdorfs Internationales Genealogen-Lexikon* (see above). Also check the Family History Library indexes for your surname.

Contact relatives here and in Germany. Find possible relatives there by using a query in a German genealogical periodical, by looking in Glenzdorfs, or by checking in German phone books, which are available in some major libraries. You may also purchase specific phone books from AT&T and German post offices. Phone books are now also available on CD-ROM for use by computer users.

Possibly there has been a village lineage book (*Dorfsippenbuch* or *Ortssippenbuch*) written about your village or a family history (*Familiengeschichte*) written about your family, or maybe someone can share family group sheets or ancestor charts with you.

There are also a great variety of indexes and guides that can help you in your research of a specific region or with a specific problem. Once your search is narrowed and targeted, these can be very useful.

Be sure to check these sources early in your research.

STEPS TO FURTHER YOUR RESEARCH

To find the person, place and date, you need the immigrant's name with the correct spelling, specific place of origin, and a date associated with an event such as a birth, marriage or death that occurred there. Finding the place of origin has been covered on the preceding page. For spelling possibilities and information about names see Chapter VII on Personal Names and Chapter VIII on Place Names.

Once you know the exact location your ancestors came from, you will want to locate it on a map. Try using *Der Grosse Shell Atlas* [*The Large Shell Atlas*] if the town is not extremely small. You can find helpful information about specific contemporary German towns by using the gazetteer, *Müllers Grosses Deutsches Ortsbuch* [*Mueller's Large Gazetteer of German Places*]. It shows the nearest government offices, archives, churches, and the German postal code of your ancestor's town. *Meyers Orts- und Verkehrs-Lexikon des Deutsches Reichs* [*Meyer's Dictionary of Places and Commerce in the German Empire*] has similar information about each town, no matter how small, for the period from 1871 until World War I. *Meyers Orts* is very complete but is in Gothic typescript. Both of these books are in German.

The purpose of checking these gazetteers is to help you determine where to find public and church records related to your ancestors. If you know the state or province, you may wish to consult a regional gazetteer first. You will find it helpful to use a guide to abbreviations for these two gazetteers.

Fay Dearden and Douglas Dearden, in *The German Researcher: How to Get the Most Out of an LDS Family History Center*, do a superb job of listing abbreviations commonly found in *Meyers Orts* and have instructions on how to read the entries.

Which parish church might your family have attended? Many communities were too small to have their own church. These gazetteers tell whether a place had its own church or churches, where the local court house (*Amtsgericht*) and local civil registrar (*Standesamt*) were, as well as help determine which city archive (*Stadtarchiv*) and which regional archive (*Staatsarchiv*) may have the relevant records. Larry O. Jensen's *Genealogical*

Handbook for German Research is particularly good in describing how to conduct area searches for information.

FINDING PROFESSIONAL GENEALOGISTS

Most likely you will prefer to do your own research, because doing it is half the fun. But at some point you may want to get the assistance of a professional genealogist in North America or Europe.

There are two major organizations through which an American genealogist can establish professional credentials. One is the Board for Certification of Genealogists, P.O. Box 19165, Washington, DC 20036. Through it, a person with proven credentials can become a Certified Genealogical Record Specialist (C.G.R.S.) or a Certified Genealogist (C.G.). The difference is that the latter must have additional expertise in helping to solve difficult research problems. You should be able to obtain a list of people with these qualifications from your state genealogical society.

The other organization is the Accreditations Committee, Family History Library, 35 North West Temple St., Salt Lake City, UT 84150. Those who pass its examination are known as Accredited Genealogists (A.G.). These examinations are based on specialization in a given country or area, and require a good knowledge of a foreign language, where applicable. A list of genealogists who have qualified is available at any Family History Center or it may be ordered from the Family History Library in Salt Lake City. This list includes some European genealogists with a knowledge of English.

Many German-American genealogical societies publish such information in their newsletters from time to time. Palatines to America is one good source. In addition, there is a genealogical association of English-speaking researchers in Europe. See **OTHER SPECIALIZED GENEALOGICAL RESOURCE CENTERS** under **GERMANY** in Chapter XV for more information.

Two major sources identifying experienced genealogists are the *Directory of Professional Genealogists*, published by the Association of Professional Genealogists, and *Who's Who in Genealogy and Heraldry*, edited by Mary Keysor Meyer and P. William Filby.

For a modest fee, many genealogical organizations provide record-searching and other specified research services that are not necessarily limited to members. They generally do not function as professional genealogists with respect to problem-solving. An organization with particularly extensive services is the Immigrant Genealogical Society, which has large German-oriented holdings. See **GENEALOGY-RELATED GERMANIC SOCIETIES** in Chapter XIX.

The *FEEFHS Resource Guide to East European Genealogy* lists a large number of professional genealogists for East and Central Europe, including Germany and Austria.

CHECKLIST OF RESEARCH SOURCES

The following is a checklist of the most promising sources for further research in the United States (or, with a few variations, in other immigrant countries). Please feel free to use it if you are not yet ready for research in German records. Refer to standard genealogical books if you need ideas for other sources. Some of these books are listed in the references for this chapter and Chapter I, and others in the accompanying bibliography in Chapter XVIII. Your local public library is likely to have books to help you get started.

FAMILY SOURCES

Relatives. Maybe you haven't yet contacted the person who can help you or you haven't jogged the memory of someone you have contacted. Give them time to think about your questions and contact them again. Ask about old papers or letters that might be stored away somewhere. Be careful to note dates and places of events. Try advertisements in newspapers when seeking current but unknown relatives.

Family Bibles, prayer books and funeral cards. These and other family papers may give pertinent information about various family members. Note the information given and try to determine if it was recorded near the time of the event or if it was recorded at a later time. Information recorded at or near the time of the event is almost always more reliable.

CHURCH AND OTHER PRIVATE RECORDS

Church records, especially the first church your immigrant ancestor joined after coming to the United States, will have information concerning baptisms, confirmations, marriages, funerals, communicants, members, and church histories. Note names of baptismal sponsors since they are probably related to the child being baptized. Don't overlook records of children born or married in the United States; sometimes church records give valuable information about their parents. These records may give the previous place of residence or place of birth of your ancestor. Occasionally, a baptismal record of a child will even give information about the place of birth of the parents or the location the parents lived before they emigrated to the United States.

Mortuary records contain information about death and burial dates and place of burial. They may also contain information about relatives, church membership, and place of residence. They also often have an obituary of the deceased person.

Tombstones carry inscriptions that may include birth and death dates, place of origin, immigration date, and family relationships. Tombstones in many cemeteries have been recorded by historical or genealogical societies and some of this information is available in published form.

Cemetery associations have record books with burial dates, and may also have birth and death dates, church membership, and family relationships. These records may be especially helpful for unmarked burials. Cemeteries can be either public or privately owned. Public cemeteries are usually administered by the township that contains the cemetery, and record books are kept by a township official. Sometimes townships are incorporated into cities and their records are transferred to city administration. Private cemeteries are owned by churches or private cemetery associations. Records should be maintained by the owning organization. Some cemeteries have been abandoned or destroyed and records may be difficult or impossible to find.

Private school records give information about student records and alumni of the school.

Lodge records have names of lodge members and can help establish new or old residences.

Professional associations have names and addresses of people in particular professions, such as nurses, doctors, teachers, ministers, priests and nuns.

Orphanage records have varied contents but may give the child's name, the time period the child was at the orphanage, where and when the child went to school, personal information such as physical description and attitude, and placement information. There were also numerous state schools for boys and private schools (for example, Father Flanagan's Boys Town in Nebraska).

From about 1854-1929 there were about 150,000 immigrant and other orphans who were taken from various institutions (especially the New York Children's Aid Society) and transported by trains to homes throughout the rural Midwest and Upper Midwest. The Orphan Train Heritage Society of America, Route 4, Box 565, Springdale, AZ 72764, seeks information about orphan train riders and their descendants.

NEWSPAPERS AND OTHER PUBLICATIONS

City directories will give the address of a person living within a specified city or suburban area. Usually only the head of household of a family is listed, but a spouse, the occupation of the head of household, and any boarders may also be shown. The older directories may give a date of death for a previously listed individual or a new address if the person moved out of the area covered by the directory. More current directories have three categories: alphabetical name, street address, and telephone listing. These later categories can be reversed to find the name of the owner of the property. City directories can be found at many libraries, genealogical societies, and some local historical societies. They may also be available as books or on microfilm.

County atlases, county plat books, and insurance maps. These maps help identify the location where a family was living if they were property owners. Brief sketches of residents are also sometimes included. Check census records to see if a person owned the property.

Newspapers, especially obituaries, anniversary articles, vital records listings, and local news columns, may give information about your ancestor's family. Many newspapers have been microfilmed and are available at many state and local historical societies and genealogical societies, and at some libraries.

German-language newspapers in the United States contained information about people in the area in which they were published, as well as those areas in which they were sold, both in the United States and abroad. Many of these newspapers have been microfilmed and are available at many state and local historical societies and genealogical societies, and at some libraries. See Karl R. Arndt and May Olson, *German-American Newspapers and Periodicals, 1732-1955*, for more information about German-American newspapers.

Printed genealogies and family histories should be helpful in case you haven't already tried them. Many of these are available, both privately and in libraries. They can be extremely helpful if well written and documented, but the quality of research varies.

Local histories, especially if they contain biographical information, may have helpful information. These are usually county and town histories. Look for them at historical societies, genealogical societies and local libraries.

Genealogical magazines, such as the *German Genealogical Digest*, contain many articles of general genealogical interest, book advertisements, genealogical information exchange columns, and other information such as how to hire researchers. Chapter XIX contains a short list of periodicals.

PUBLIC RECORDS

Civil court records include probate records and related records such as conservatorships, guardianships and commitments. These records are kept by the county courts and are usually found at the county courthouses. It is important to know that different counties may have differing terminology for these records and may keep them in different county offices. Ask at the county offices to find out where the records are kept in that county.

Probate records are filed by the name of the deceased person, and consist of testate and intestate proceedings. **Testate proceedings** include the deceased person's will, which lists the devisees. Heirs may be listed. **Intestate proceedings** have no associated will, but all the heirs to the decedent are listed, along with their relationship to the decedent, and their addresses. Older wills may be found in books located at the probate office. The probate file may also contain the real estate description of property the decedent owned (which may be where the person lived), birth date and place, death date and place, and address of decedent. Occasionally other records can be found in the file, such as birth and death certificates for the decedent, birth (and sometimes, death) certificates of the heirs, and references to other files.

A **Conservator** is appointed to make decisions for a legally incapacitated person and a **Guardian** is appointed to make decisions for a legally incompetent person. In both of these files, the commencing petition is the document that will provide you with the most family history information. You will find the age, date of birth and last address of the proposed conservatee or ward; along with names, addresses and maybe the ages of the known family members; and the name, address and occupation of the proposed conservator or guardian. A guardianship or Conservatorship of the estate will provide you with an Inventory of the assets, personal property and real estate, owned by the conservatee or ward on the date the conservator or guardian was appointed.

Commitments consist of the confinement of an incapacitated person. This may be due to such things as inebriation, drugs, mental deficiency, senility, etc. Commitments may also be voluntary or involuntary. The file contains personal information such as date and place of birth, parents, spouse, family members, length of time residing in county or state, church membership, schooling and occupation.

Other records that may be found at county offices are adoptions, divorce files (including the divorce decree), judgments regarding what a person may owe to others, lawsuits in civil disagreements, paternity actions, name changes and naturalizations. Note that adoption records are generally not available to the public.

Criminal court records consist mainly of criminal cases. Some paternity actions are also found here.

Land records are usually kept at the county courthouses. In order to search land records, one should have the legal description of the property, although this is not necessary. Land records are of two types: abstract and Torrens. For **abstract property**, an abstract (or history) of the title to a particular tract of land summarizes all material parts of recorded legal instruments affecting the title of the property. The abstract provides a lengthy history of the real estate, usually in one bound document. It contains a record of previous owners, together with a report of all judgments, mortgages and similar claims against the property that have been recorded. For **Torrens property**, or registered property as it is sometimes called, there is a certificate of title documenting transactions during a particular ownership period. Registration creates a judicial determination of the status of the title at the time of the registration. Abstract property can be converted into Torrens property through the registration process. Access to these records can be gained through use of the tract index, which is a consecutive listing of the owners of a particular piece of property.

Land records contain the document number of the property, the names of the buyer and seller, and may also contain references to births, marriages, deaths and other court proceedings. Name changes, divorces, satisfactions, mortgages, taxes levied, and liens may also be included. When heirs sell property owned by a decedent, the file can be quite extensive.

Land records for land issued by the United States government are also found at the county offices. This includes so-called **homestead property** (which was given to a person by the United States government per the Morrill Act of 1862) and **bounty land property** (given to a person by the government for some service to the government, such as military service in a war). These records are the same as other land transactions, except that the government is the grantor of the property.

Some counties have **grantor and grantee indexes** to assist in finding the property if only the name of the person owning the land is known. These indexes are usually organized alphabetically by first letter of the surname. Other systems are also in use. Ask at the county office as to how the records are organized and what finding aids are available.

Tax records can be used to trace ownership of land. Older tax records can sometimes be used in lieu of census and other records to show a person resided in a given area.

Vital records. Births, marriages, and deaths are recorded at county court houses. Older birth and death records are also usually available through state agencies. Privacy laws exist in most states that limit access to these records. These laws vary widely and usually make exceptions for family members.

Civil registration was introduced at an early time but was not mandatory until 1850-1930 depending on the state. Even when it was made mandatory, events were not well-recorded for some time after that, even for years. As for all records, there are also errors in vital records, and in certified and non-certified copies of those records (even if the original was accurate). See *The Handy Book for Genealogists* by Everton Publishers for information about dates of introduction of vital registration in counties, names and organization dates of counties and whether they were formed from other counties, and other information of use when looking for vital records. This is especially true of older records and records for counties that no longer exist.

Birth records give the name, date and place of birth of the child, the name, age and residence of the mother and usually the name, age, residence and occupation of the father. Delayed birth records occasionally occur if the birth was not recorded near the time of birth; many times this happens when a person approaches retirement age and wants to file for Social Security benefits, but discovers that his or her birth was not recorded. The county requires other proofs of birth for a person to obtain a delayed registration of birth.

Marriage records consist of marriage banns, marriage applications, marriage licenses, and certificates of marriage. Marriage banns were public announcements of an upcoming marriage and were still in use in the early 1800s, especially in the New England states. They are no longer in use today. A marriage application is recorded when the future bride and groom apply for a marriage license. A marriage license is issued to the couple being married and is usually kept by them. The certificate of marriage is recorded after the marriage occurs. Occasionally a marriage application is recorded without a corresponding certificate of marriage. A marriage application by itself is not proof that the marriage occurred. Marriage records give the names of the bride and groom, their places of residence, the date and place of marriage, the name and residence of the person who married them, names of witnesses to the marriage, and sometimes the names of the parents of the bride and groom and the religions of the bride and groom.

Death records give the name, date and place of death of the decedent and the cause of death. Also usually included are the residence, age at death, and name of spouse. Sometimes the place of birth and names of parents are also given. Check the name of the informant for the record to get a clue as to the reliability of the information given on the record. Information for death records was sometimes given by children, relatives or friends who may not have had a first-hand knowledge of the event or were confused while giving the information, or the record keeper did not correctly understand them. The information was sometimes passed down orally over a span of time before being recorded. Occasionally the record keeper did not ask all of the questions required to fill out the record, even though the informant knew the information.

Military records give a record of military service for a person. These records include information pertinent to the person's tour of duty, including such things as dates and places of service, battles, regiments, honors awarded, etc. A physical description of the person is also included in many cases, and information about the person's death is included if killed in service.

Military pension files give information about the person after military service has ended and covers the time period when a pension is awarded. This usually continues until the person dies. The person's residence and occupation are shown, as well as any disabilities pertinent to the pension. These records can sometimes have information of surprising genealogical value, especially when the person dies and the spouse claims a pension continuation, since proof of relationship is required in this case.

Passenger departure lists for ports of embarkation may provide information about a town of origin or an emigrant destination. See Chapter IV for more information.

Ship arrival lists for ports in United States (and other immigrant countries as well) may help find previous residences if you know when your immigrant arrived in that country. See Chapter IV for more information.

Naturalization records give information about an immigrant who wishes to become a United States citizen. The **Declaration of Intention** to become a citizen (sometimes called the "first paper"), is generally the most important record for genealogists, and is commonly filed in the county where your immigrant first settled in the United States, but might be in any county through which your immigrant traveled. Naturalizations could and did occur in any jurisdiction, whether it be county, state or federal. After a waiting period, usually about five years, the person could then petition to complete the naturalization process. The place where this occurred may or may not have been the place where the Declaration of Intention was obtained. Once the court decreed the person to become a citizen, a **naturalization paper** (sometimes call the "second paper") was issued to the person and the event was recorded by the court. In many states, naturalization records have been transferred from the counties to a central state archives or historical society. Contents of naturalization records vary greatly from time to time and place to place.

Federal census records are used for locating where people lived in the United States and who was living within each family unit. Federal censuses have been taken every ten years starting in 1790. Before 1850, only the heads of household are named, along with a tally of the number of people of various age groups and gender living in the same household. Beginning with the 1850 census, all household members are named. Places of birth are shown beginning with the 1880 census. The 1890 federal census was almost completely destroyed by fire but a small number of schedules still exist. The year of immigration to the United States was first indicated in the 1900 federal census. The 1910 and 1920 federal census records are also currently available for use. Soundex indexes exist for the 1880, 1900 and later federal censuses.

A special 1885 Federal census was taken by some states. Mortality schedules listing deaths of persons in the twelve months immediately preceding the census were taken along with the census during the 1850-1885 time period. Revolutionary War pensioners were also recorded in the 1840 census. A special 1890 census of Union veterans of the Civil War and widows of Union veterans exists, which is arranged alphabetically by state beginning with Kentucky and continues through the remainder of the alphabet of states existing in 1890. Other kinds of Federal census schedules also exist, such as agricultural schedules and Indian censuses.

Soundex index to federal census records was designed to assist in finding an individual name among the millions listed in the 1880, 1900, 1910 and 1920 census records and some passenger list records. The 1880 Soundex index only shows households in which there were children of age ten years or younger. The Soundex is a coded surname index based on the way a surname sounds rather than the way it is spelled, so surnames that sound alike but are spelled differently—like Schmidt, Schmied, Smith, and Smythe—have the same Soundex code and are filed together. The Soundex was developed so you can find a surname even though it may have been recorded under different spellings.

To search for a particular surname in the Soundex, you must first work out its Soundex code. Every Soundex code consists of a letter followed by three numbers (e.g., S650). The letter is always the first letter of the surname. The numbers are assigned to the remaining letters of the surname according to the following Soundex coding guide.

Table 1: Soundex Coding Guide

The number:	Represents the letters:
1	B, P, F, V
2	C, S, K, G, J, Q, X, Z
3	D, T
4	L
5	M, N
6	R
Disregard the letters A, E, I, O, U, W, Y and H.	

Most surnames can be coded using the following five steps.

1. Write out the surname you are coding.

2. Save the first letter of the surname as the letter part of the Soundex code for the surname.

3. For the remaining letters, cross out all letters A, E, I, O, U, W, Y, and H.

4. Assign numbers from the above Soundex coding guide to the letters still remaining.

   If the surname has any side-by-side letters that have the same number, these letters should be treated as one letter, e.g., in the surname Pfennig, the F should be crossed out since P and F both have 1 as their code number - also in Jackson, the C, K, and S all have code number 2 so the K and S should be crossed out. As a special case of this rule, if the surname has any doubled letters, they should be treated as a single letter, e.g., in the surname Lloyd, the second L should be crossed out.

5. If you now have three numbers, they are the ones to use in the Soundex code for the surname, e.g., Brandt = B653. If you have less than three numbers, add enough zeros at the right end so there are three numbers, e.g., Frye = F600. If you have more than three numbers, just use the leftmost three numbers and ignore the rest, e.g., Bellingham = B452 and Cutkomp = C325.

If your surname of interest has a prefix - like Van, Von, De, Di or Le - you should code it both with the prefix and without the prefix because it might be listed under either code. For example, the surname Von Grossman should be coded both as V526 and as G625. Mac and Mc are not considered to be prefixes. If your surname could have its first letter misspelled, you should code the surname other ways, e.g., Cutkomp (coded C325) could also be spelled Kutcomp (coded as K325). Catholic nuns are usually indexed as "Sister" being the surname. The side-by-side rule can sometimes be confusing, e.g., the surname Suess is indexed as S200 rather than S000 since the last two S's are doubled but are not next to the first one. Also be aware of possible misspellings in original documents and look-alike letters that may be incorrectly coded, e.g., Pfennig may be misspelled as Fennig, and Sanders may be mistaken for Landers. Surname coding errors do occasionally occur in the Soundex. So if you cannot find the name you are seeking, be creative in how the surname might have been coded.

Once you have coded your ancestor's name, you are ready to use the microfilmed Soundex card indexes. They are organized by state, then by Soundex code, and then alphabetically by first name or initial.

Some states, such as Minnesota, incorporate Soundex coding into automobile drivers license numbers, so you may be able to check the coding of your own surname by looking at your drivers license number.

State census records are similar to federal census records, except state censuses were authorized by individual state governments. State censuses were usually collected midway between federal censuses, or in special situations such as a territory preparing for statehood. State census records generally give the names of persons in a household and the county and township where the household was, and may give other information as well, such as age and occupation. Check for the state censuses that may exist for a particular state. See *The Source* for more information about state census records.

Alien registrations. All non-United States citizens are required to register their residence annually. These records are maintained by the counties. Alien registration was required from 1802 to 1828 and was again made mandatory in 1929 and continues to the present. A Special Alien Registration and Declaration of Holdings was required of all—particularly new—alien residents in the state of Minnesota in February 1918 by the State Commission of Public Safety. This record gives extensive and valuable information about each alien registration, such as full name, address, length of residence, age, data and place of birth, data of arrival in the United States and port of entry, occupation, names and ages of all living children, names of male relatives involved in World War I, date of "first papers," legal description of land holdings, etc. These records are organized by county and then by city or township. This registration may also have been required in other states as well.

Miscellaneous public records. These records include such things as voter registrations, military draft registrations, drivers license registrations, Social Security registrations, public school records (student records and names of alumni), licenses (justices of the peace, ministers, school teachers, morticians, steam fitters, etc.), and building permits. Also included are bond and oath records of officials of state and local governments, burial records for state hospitals, correctional facilities records, and coroner's records.

USING COMPUTERS IN YOUR RESEARCH

The personal computer has become an increasingly valuable tool for genealogists, because computers complement the hobby of genealogy very well. Many computer software packages and other computerized services have been developed for genealogy. This section is a brief introduction to what is available for the genealogist who owns a computer.

There are many **software packages and databases** to assist you in your record keeping. This software allows you to record names, dates, and sources. It can print a great variety of charts and reports and will allow you to quickly search your records for someone. You can use it to index your files and to create mailing lists.

Computers can be used to print a family history book or to exchange information with other researchers. **Genealogy programs** range greatly in price and capabilities. Among the more popular ones are Family Tree Maker™ by Banner Blue, Personal Ancestry File™ (PAF) available from the Family History Library through the Salt Lake Distribution Center, and Roots IV™ by Commsoft, Inc. See the next chapter about the Family History Library for more information about PAF. Read reviews about genealogy programs before purchasing any. If possible, see or get demo versions to decide which one best fits your needs.

Any genealogy program you purchase should have a capability called **GEDCOM**™. GEDCOM allows researchers with different software programs to share their computerized research with other researchers. Using GEDCOM, you can also extract data from the CD-ROM diskettes at Family History Centers.

The *Guide to Genealogy Software* by Donna Przecha and Joan Lowrey, which is a guide to over 100 genealogy programs and utilities, is a good place to start.

Some well-known **computer bulletin board services** you can subscribe to for access with a modem include National Genealogy Conference (sponsored by the Computer Interest Group of the National Genealogical Society), Internet, America Online®, GEnie®, CompuServe® and Prodigy®. These services allow genealogical queries and the exchange of information between fellow researchers. You will also find tips on using genealogical software and will have access to copies of genealogical "shareware" programs.

Shareware programs are user-supported software. The authors authorize you to copy the programs to share with your friends and request that each person send a nominal fee if the programs are used after a period of evaluation. You are encouraged to register the program if it is valuable to you. Many authors offer technical support and updated versions. In contrast to shareware, software that users can legally copy without charge is called **"public domain" software**. Authors of public domain software allow these programs to be copied freely and do not expect payment.

Major libraries throughout the United States have computerized their card catalogs. You can access these library catalogs with a computer modem attached to your phone. The Library of Congress card catalog is now available on **CD-ROM diskettes**. These are high capacity, read-only diskettes similar in appearance to audio compact discs. Libraries are also beginning to put some of their books on CD-ROM. CD-ROM disk drives are now available for personal computers. A good-sized library could be stored on 200 CD-ROM diskettes.

Also available are computer programs that show maps. One example is Centennia, which is a guide to the history of Europe and the Middle East from the year 1000 A.D. to the present. These maps show year-by year changes in the boundaries in Europe. The program is available from:

> Clockwork Software, Inc.
> P.O. Box 148036
> Chicago, IL 60614
> (*phone: 312-281-3132*)
> (*e-mail: clockwk@delphi.com*)

When using a computer, you need to do some planning to maximize the benefit and minimize your effort. You need to decide what information you want to keep on the computer and what formats you want to use. What reports, charts, and printed output do you want to have? How do you want to organize the information on the computer?

The use of computers is a growing and changing field, so it is important to use current sources of information related to it. There are many books and articles written to help you learn how to use computers for genealogy. Joining a computer user group can help you meet others with whom to share and exchange information about genealogy and computers.

REFERENCES (See bibliography for full citations if not shown)

Karl R. Arndt and May Olson, *German-American Newspapers and Periodicals*, 1732-1955.

Elizabeth Petty Bentley. *County Courthouse Book*. Baltimore: Genealogical Publishing Co. 1993. 400 pp.

Elizabeth Petty Bentley. *Directory of Family History Associations*. Baltimore: Genealogical Publishing Co. 1993.

Elizabeth Petty Bentley. *Genealogist's Address Book*. 3rd ed. Baltimore: Genealogical Publishing Co. 1995.

Johni Cerny and Arlene Eakle. *Ancestry's Guide to Research: Case Studies in American Genealogy*. Salt Lake City, UT: Ancestry, Inc. 1985. 364 pp.
> This companion to *The Source* (see below) provides many problem-solving examples of how to trace your ancestors, including a section on tracing a German immigrant family.

Elizabeth Powell Crowe. *Genealogy Online: Researching Your Roots*. New York: Windcrest/ McGraw-Hill, Inc. 1995. 280 pp.
> How to access computer genealogy bulletin boards and library card catalogs online.

Directory of Professional Genealogists. Washington: Association of Professional Genealogists. 1995. 110 pp.

> Lists some specialists for Germanic and other European countries, as well as Australia and Israel.

Arlene Eakle and Johni Cerny, eds. *The Source: A Guidebook of American Genealogy*. Salt Lake City, UT: Ancestry Publishing Co. 1984. 786 pp.

> This collection, written by 16 of the nation's top genealogists, covers every phase of American genealogy, from colonial times to the present. It shows how to locate records and how to use them, and covers questions a genealogist might have on all levels of genealogical research.

Alice Eichholz, ed. *Ancestry's Red Book: American State, County and Town Sources*. Rev. ed. With maps by William Dollarhide. Salt Lake City, UT: Ancestry Publishing Co. 1992. 858 pp.

George B. Everton, Sr., ed. *The Handy Book for Genealogists*. Logan, UT: Everton Publishers, Inc. 8th ed. 1991. 382 pp. maps.

> Illustrated with outline maps of each state of the United States, showing boundaries and history of each county and the location of the county seat. Gives location of important reference sources, location of archives, libraries, historical and genealogical societies and other information for each state. Also contains some information about European countries.

Family History Library. *Tracing Immigrant Origins*. #34111. 31 pp.

P. William Filby. *A Bibliography of American County Histories*. Baltimore: Genealogical Publishing Co. 1985. Reprinted 1987. 449 pp.

> Standard work on U.S. county histories, often helpful for tracing immigrants and ancestors.

Val D. Greenwood. *The Researcher's Guide to American Genealogy*. 2nd ed. Baltimore: Genealogical Publishing Co., Inc. 1990. 609 pp. Revised 1992. 568 pp.

> Official textbook for correspondence course of the National Genealogical Society. Comprehensive guide to American research, especially land and probate records.

Estelle M. Guzik, ed. *Genealogical Resources in the New York Metropolitan Area*. NY: Jewish Genealogical Society, Inc. P.O. Box 6398, NY, NY 10128. 1989. 404 pp.

Marion Kaminkow, ed. *United States Local Histories in the Library of Congress: A Bibliography*. Baltimore: Magna Carta Book Co. 1975.

Thomas Jay Kemp. *International Records Handbook*. 3rd ed. Baltimore: Genealogical Publishing Co. 1994. 417 pp.

> Contains addresses for civil records in every country in the world, with forms used to request birth, marriage and death records for English-speaking and some other countries.

E. Kay Kirkham. *The Handwriting of American Records for a Period of 300 Years*. Logan, UT: Everton Publishers. 1973. 108 pp.

> Examines a variety of handwriting in American records at various times in history. Heavily illustrated.

Mary K. Meyer, ed. *Meyer's Directory of Genealogical Societies in the U.S.A. and Canada*, 9th ed. Mt. Airy, MD: Mary Keysor Meyer. 1992. 123 pp.

> Also lists special interest organizations (ethnic, religious, geographic, adoptees).

Mary Keysor Meyer and P. William Filby, eds. *Who's Who in Genealogy and Heraldry, 1990*. Savage, MD: Who's Who in Genealogy and Heraldry. 1990. 331 pp.

Donna Przecha and Joan Lowrey. *Guide to Genealogy Software*. Baltimore: Genealogical Publishing Co. 1993. 206 pp.

> A guide to over 100 genealogy computer programs and utilities.

United States. National Archives and Records Service. *Guide to Genealogical Research in the National Archives*. Washington, DC:National Archives & Records Service. 1982. 304 pp.

> A highly acclaimed and easy to use genealogical overview of the holdings of the National Archives. Gives inventory and ordering information to obtain photocopies of records, etc.

Chapter III

FAMILY HISTORY LIBRARY AND ITS CENTERS

Before you make any trip to Europe looking for your ancestors, you should take advantage of the world's largest genealogical library, the Family History Library in Salt Lake City, UT. The Family History Library is affiliated with The Church of Jesus Christ of Latter-day Saints (Mormons). In this book we usually refer to it as the Family History Library (or FHL), but it is also popularly known as the LDS Library. It is free and open to the public, Monday 7:30am-6:00pm, Tuesday through Saturday 7:30am-10:00pm. Microfilming for the FHL is done under the auspices of the Genealogical Society of Utah.

The Family History Library was organized in 1894 and has been characterized by a steady acquisition of family history material. Since the late 1930s the library has pursued an aggressive records preservation program, microfilming in over 150 countries of the world. Presently the library operates 250 cameras in 46 countries to film birth, marriage, death, land, tax, probate, immigration, census, military and many other types of records. The collection presently includes over 1.8 million reels of microfilm, 385,000 microfiche, and 250,000 books.

Each year the library adds over 100 million new pages of microfilmed documents to its collection. This is approximately equivalent to 70,000 microfilm reels. It also acquires some 25,000 microfiche and 12,000 books each year.

The Germanic collection itself is extensive, with over 114,000 microfilm reels preserving Catholic, Lutheran and Jewish registers and civil records of birth, marriage, death, and emigration records. There are over 42,000 additional microfilm reels for Austria and Switzerland. In recent years the library has also been able to microfilm in many areas of eastern Europe including the former East Germany, Poland, Hungary, Slovenia, Croatia, Yugoslavia, the Baltic states, Russia, Ukraine, and Belarus. The table below gives more detail about the size of the microfilm collection.

Table 2: Germanic Microfilm Collection at the Family History Library

Country	Number of Reels	Country	Number of Reels
Germany	114,000	Croatia	1,223
Austria	32,000	Estonia	963
Poland	22,284	Slovak Republic	655
Hungary	12,880	Slovenia	185
Switzerland	10,662	Bulgaria	178
Russia	1,627	Czech Republic	99

MAIN LIBRARY IS WEST OF TEMPLE SQUARE

The main library is conveniently located west of historic Temple Square in downtown Salt Lake City. Materials in the five-story library building are geographically arranged, with microfilms, microfiche and books and experienced reference librarians on each floor. The staff are trained to give research advice on specific localities. There are many microfilm and microfiche readers, but be advised to get there early in the day to use one. There are nearly 3,000 patrons using the library each day.

There are also self-service copy centers equipped with microfilm, microfiche, and paper copiers, change machines, various publications, blank charts and forms for sale. The publications are designed to help in using the collection more effectively.

PLAN AHEAD FOR MICROFILM USE

Because of the huge collection and limited space, the library has recently made some changes so a majority of their microfilms are stored off site. The library is arranged by geographic regions: United States and Canada, British (currently includes Australia and

New Zealand), and International (includes all other countries). The main and second floors contain the entire collection of the United States and Canada. However, this may change as space runs out. The other localities have already experienced this space crunch. Level B-1 is the International floor where the core collection of all continental European, Asian, and African materials is housed. Level B-2 holds the core collection of the British Isles, Australia and New Zealand. Each area determines which films are used heavily and forms a core collection that remains in the main library. The rest of the microfilms are stored off site, but are retrievable.

Consult the table below to determine if the films you need will be at the main library or stored off-site. If stored off-site, you must request them ahead of time — preferably one month. The best advice is to send a list of the requested films in NUMERICAL ORDER to the Film Attendant's Office - Floor B1 (European). Be sure to include the date of your arrival and how long you will use the films. Three weeks are normally allotted for use.

If only a few numbers are needed you may telephone the Film Attendant's office. Ask how long it will take to get the films to the main library. This call-ahead process is also helpful for group visits. Guided tours are NOT provided, but orientation classes for groups of 15-60 people can be arranged by calling 801-240-2331 or writing the Library in advance:

Family History Library
35 North West Temple St.
Salt Lake City, Utah 84150

GERMANIC MICROFILMS USUALLY STORED AT MAIN LIBRARY

COUNTRIES	RECORD TYPES IN CORE COLLECTION
Germany, Luxembourg, Poland, Slovak Republic	Church, civil registration, Jewish records, emigration, census records
Belarus, Romania, Russia, Ukraine	Roman Catholic & Protestant church records (including those of many Russian Germans), civil registration, Jewish records, emigration and immigration records
Austria	Emigration records
Hungary	Jewish records, emigration records, census records. Also for Budapest: church records.

COMPUTER TECHNOLOGY AIDS FAMILY HISTORY

The Family History Library has developed a computer software program designed to help personal computer users at home to document their ancestry and to print charts and forms. It is called the Personal Ancestral File®, or PAF. It includes a standard feature called GEDCOM, which allows for data exchange with other software programs. This means you can share data with other genealogists on diskette if both have GEDCOM capability, with no retyping of the data. That's why GEDCOM has become a standard feature of all good software programs. Personal Ancestral File is available through the church's distribution center for either MS-DOS™ or Macintosh® machines. For information inside the United States and Canada, call 800-537-5950. Outside the United States and Canada, call 801-240-1174. The address for mail orders is:

Salt Lake Distribution Center
1999 West 1700 South
Salt Lake City UT 84104-4233

FAMILY SEARCH CENTER

The Family History Library now has computers available on each floor to search the library's catalog, and other data files on an "umbrella" program called FamilySearch™. However, due to the enormous popularity of their FamilySearch computer data files, the library has recently opened the FamilySearch Center, located one block to the east in the

Joseph Smith Memorial Building. The FamilySearch Center hours are 8:00am-10:00pm during the summer and 9:00am-9:00pm after the first weekend in September.

The FamilySearch Center is equipped with 133 computer terminals that are served by an on-line network. This center is staffed mainly by volunteers who have been trained to help beginners. Information from FamilySearch can be printed out on paper or down-loaded to diskette and taken with you.

If you need further help, you may go to the fourth floor where 60 additional computers workstations are located, or to the main library. Also on the fourth floor are meeting rooms reserved for computer research by family groups or other organizations.

The FamilySearch computer program currently contains five different data files:

> Ancestral File™
> International Genealogical Index™
> Family History Library Catalog™
> U.S. Social Security Death Index
> Korean and Vietnam War Death Index

Each data file contains millions of names of individuals and can be easily accessed in seconds. No previous computer experience is necessary. You don't even need to know how to type. If you can only hunt-and-peck, you can still search millions of records by simply typing in a name.

ANCESTRAL FILE

Ancestral File now contains 15 million names and is designed to work with the previously mentioned Personal Ancestral File for home computer users. Data from your personal computer can be sent via diskette to the Family History Library for inclusion in the Ancestral File. In fact, this sharing of data is the theme of the Library's centennial year just celebrated in 1994. Write for the free pamphlet "Submitting Names to Ancestral File."

Ancestral File links family members by pedigree charts and family group sheets with dates and places of birth or christening, marriage, death and burial. It also lists the names and addresses of submitters. You can then correspond with them to learn details of documentation. Any of the data found can be printed in paper or diskette form. When data is down-loaded to a diskette, it is put into GEDCOM format by the program.

INTERNATIONAL GENEALOGICAL INDEX

The International Genealogical Index (IGI) is a large data file that contains over 200 million records worldwide. These records are organized by locality, then by name, then by birth/christening date or marriage date. The section for Germany contains over 25 million records and the section for Central Europe contains over 12 million records. Be sure to search this data base. Unfortunately, these names are not linked in relationships as in the Ancestral File. Usually a birth/christening entry of a child gives date and place and names of parents. A typical marriage entry gives date and place, and names of spouses. Most German entries come from the indexing or extraction of early Lutheran or Catholic registers. This is due to the thousands of microfilms from Germanic areas of the world. So if you find an ancestor listed in the IGI, be sure to trace the source of the data: either the name and address of a member of the LDS Church who submitted it, or Family History Catalog entry for the microfilm involved. Many details on the original records were not included in the IGI and extraction errors do occasionally occur, so always look at the microfilm source.

The IGI is also available in a microfiche version that is subdivided into geographical regions. It is available for sale for 15 cents per sheet through the Distribution Center listed above. Regional sets must be ordered together. Contact the Acquisitions Department for an order form.

FAMILY HISTORY LIBRARY CATALOG

Learning to use the Family History Library Catalog (FHLC) is the key to the collection's immense records. Here are some hints to help you find what you want. There are two versions: CD-ROM and microfiche. They are accessed differently. The CD-ROM version can be searched by surname or by microfilm number or by locality (then subject). The microfiche version is separated into 4 sets: Surname, Author/Title, Subject, Locality (then subject).

It helps to understand what jurisdiction held the record you need. For example, if you want to use the church records of a small village in Germany you must first learn how it is filed in the catalog. Church records are kept by the parish, so you must first determine if the place you want is a parish. One quick way is to look at the beginning of the microfiche of the country you need. There is an alphabetical listing of all entries. If the place is a parish (and in the catalog) it will be listed. If that quick method does not work, try to use a German gazetteer that describes geographic places. One of the best, though not the easiest to use, is commonly called *Meyers Orts*.

The German collection is cataloged according to the 1871-World War I boundaries found in *Meyers Orts- und Verkehrs-Lexikon des Deutsches Reichs*, a locality and business gazetteer. (See Chapter VIII for a more complete discussion of *Meyers Orts*.) This includes the states of Elsass-Lothringen (Alsace-Lorraine), Anhalt, Baden, Bayern (Bavaria), Braunschweig (Brunswick), Hessen (Hesse), Lippe, Mecklenburg, Oldenburg, Sachsen (Kingdom of Saxony), Waldeck, Württemberg, and Prussia. The cities of Hamburg, Bremen and Lübeck are cataloged separately.

Cataloging for Prussia is subdivided into the provinces of Brandenburg, Ostpreussen (East Prussia), Hannover (Hanover), Hessen-Nassau (Hesse-Nassau), Hohenzollern, Pommern (Pomerania), Posen, Rheinland (Rhineland), Sachsen (Saxony Province), Schlesien (Silesia), Schleswig-Holstein, Westfalen (Westphalia), and Westpreussen (West Prussia). The Pfalz (Palatinate) is cataloged as part of Bavaria, and Birkenfeld is cataloged as part of Oldenburg.

Thüringen (Thuringia) is not listed as a state in *Meyers Orts*, but it can be found on the International Genealogical Index described later in this chapter. However, the individual duchies and principalities within Thuringia when the German Empire existed are listed in *Meyers Orts*. The FHLC lists the localities in Thuringia separately, but the duchies and principalities of Sachsen-Altenburg, Sachsen-Coburg-Gotha, Sachsen-Meiningen, Sachsen-Weimar-Eisenach, Schwarzburg-Rudolstadt and Schwarzburg-Sondershausen are also combined and listed alphabetically under Thüringen. See Chapter IX for more information about Thuringia.

Remember that only localities that generated records or have some publication written about them are cataloged in the FHLC. If the locality you are seeking is not listed, it may be because no records were generated there (for example, no church parish was there), no books or other articles have been written about the place, or no information was available when microfilming was done.

See the pamphlet *Research Outline: Germany*, by the Family History Library, for more detailed information about the collection. See end of chapter references for ordering details.

There are gazetteers for each province or state; these are helpful in determining correct localities. See Larry Jensen's *A Genealogical Handbook of German Research*, Vol. 1, and Fay Dearden's *The German Researcher: How to Get the Most Out of an LDS Family History Center*.

The FHLC is also available for sale in microfiche version. Like the IGI it is 15 cents a fiche and regional sets are sold together. Write to the FHL Acquisitions Department for an order form.

U.S. SOCIAL SECURITY DEATH INDEX

The United States Social Security Death Index includes some 39 million names of deceased individuals who received social security benefits, who died between 1938-1988. The majority of the file is from after 1962. Like the other data files it is searched easily by name. The typical information found is the deceased person's name, social security number, state of issue, birth date, death date and residence at death. With the name and social security number you may write for a copy of that person's original application, which may contain more information, to: Officer, 4HB Annex Bldg, 6401 Security Bl, Baltimore, MD 21235, or telephone 410-965-3962. Cost is $7.00 if a social security number is supplied, $16.50 otherwise.

KOREAN & VIETNAM WAR DEATH INDEX

The U.S. Military Death Index covers individuals who died or were declared dead in the Korean War from 1950 to 1957, or the Vietnam War from 1957 to 1975. It is also searched by name. It contains birth and death dates, home residence, military rank, service number and branch of service, race, start date of tour of duty, religious affiliation and marital status (Vietnam only), country where died (casualty locations include Cambodia, Communist China, Laos, North Vietnam, South Vietnam and Thailand).

REFERENCE SERVICES AVAILABLE

Like most libraries, the library's staff does not do research for you. However, each floor has a reference desk staffed with experts in reading old handwriting in each foreign language used. The staff librarians know the collections well and will steer you to the most effective use of your time at the library. These reference people handle hundreds of different questions daily with grace, skill and enthusiasm. Please learn all you can beforehand so you are prepared when you ask for their help. Ask for their publications and list of language helps.

ACCREDITED GENEALOGISTS

If you would like to consult a professional researcher for hire, the library maintains a list of "Accredited Genealogists." These are persons who have passed a rigorous test showing proficiency and the ability to perform professional quality work in a specific geographical area of expertise. Ask for or write for a list of these "Accredited Genealogists." Other organizations, such as the National Genealogical Society in Washington, DC, provide a similar service. See Chapter II for details.

ON-LINE COMPUTER SERVICES

With the advent of the computer, the Reference staff has found yet another way to accommodate patron inquiry through on-line commercial computer services. Many of these services already have a Genealogy Question and Answer (Q&A) session, so check that before asking the library staff. Identification numbers to contact the FHL are:

CompuServe	75300,3123
GEnie (research questions)	F.H.Library
GEnie (FamilySearch questions)	FamilySearch
America Online	FamHIstLib
Prodigy	FHLS97C to F, and FHLS99B to F

FAMILY HISTORY CENTERS ARE WORLDWIDE

The Family History Library operates over 2,000 branch libraries, called Family History Centers, in the United States and Canada and 62 other countries. They are usually located in Latter-day Saint church buildings, but mail is not delivered to the Family History Centers. Check in your local telephone books under "Church of Jesus Christ of Latter-day Saints—Family History Center" or Stake Center. A list of center locations and phone numbers is available upon request from the Family History Library in Salt Lake City. All Family History Centers are free and open to the public. However, since each center is staffed by volunteers, hours of operation vary. Call ahead before traveling long distances to reach them.

The concept of Family History Centers gives local researchers access to practically the entire microfilm and microfiche collection. Because each center is a satellite of the main library you may, for a small fee, borrow any microfilm for a loan period of 3 weeks, or 6 months, or indefinitely. Borrowed microfilm/fiche must be used at the local center. Most centers are classroom size and are pressed for space; therefore they limit the number of microfilms kept there on "indefinite" loan. Ask to speak to the director about the center's indefinite loan policy, which is set locally according to space and patron research needs. There may be some records the local center is trying to acquire, but hasn't yet, due to lack of funds. Generally a microfilm that has broad value to many people can be termed indefinite. Indexes to records generally qualify.

Because microfiche take up so little space, generally anything you are willing to pay for can be borrowed on indefinite loan. The price is pennies per fiche, but the entire set must be borrowed. Check the FHLC to determine the number of fiche in the set.

All centers are equipped with microfilm and microfiche readers and printers. Each have sets of reference books and microfiche. Usually they have some blank forms and charts for sale. Each center has the microfiche version of the Family History Library catalog and the International Genealogical Index. They may have also compiled a catalog of their local holdings.

There is also a way to gain access to the unmicrofilmed books in the Family History Library collection. You may ask for a free "Request to Microfilm" form. For a small copying fee the pages you need will be sent to you via mail.

Each center has the FamilySearch computer program discussed above. But because of heavy use, most centers may limit the time each patron spends on the computer. If you phone ahead you can ask if you can be given an appointment to use the computer. Each data file can be printed on paper or diskette for a small charge. Also most centers have diskettes for sale or you can bring your own.

The staff at Family History Centers are volunteers. Many have their own geographic area of expertise after years of personal research and volunteer service. However, if they are not equipped to answer your specific questions, they may telephone, e-mail, or fax questions to the Family History Library's reference staff. There is also a free "Reference Questionnaire" form that you may fill out and send to the Family History Library, but it will get the slowest response due to the heavy volume of mail.

REFERENCES (See Bibliography for full citation if not shown)

Family History Library. *Accredited Genealogists in U.S. & Canada.* #32749. 3 pp.
Family History Library. *Accredited Genealogist: International.* #32750. 3 pp.
Family History Library. *Ancestral File: Contributing to Ancestral File.* #34029. 4 pp.
Family History Library. *Ancestral File: Correcting the Ancestral File.* #34030. 4 pp.
Family History Library. *Ancestral File: Using the Ancestral File.* #34113. 4 pp.
Family History Library. *Family History Library Catalog on CD-ROM.* #34052. 4 pp.
Family History Library. *Family History Library Catalog on Microfiche.* #32916. 4 pp.
Family History Library. *Family History Publications List.* #34085. 3 pp. (free)
Family History Library. *FamilySearch Military Index.* #34540. 1 p.
Family History Library. *FamilySearch Social Security Death Index.* #34446. 4 pp.
Family History Library. *Germany: Research Outline.* #34061. 52 pp.
Family History Library. *Guide to Research: Family History Centers.* #30971. 16 pp.
Family History Library. *Guide to Research: Family History Library.* #30967. 16 pp.
Family History Library. *Hamburg Passenger Lists.* #34047. 4 pp. (free)
Family History Library. *How to Use the Family History Catalog.* #53191. 4 pp. (video).
Family History Library. *Finding an IGI Source.* #31024. 4 pp.
Family History Library. *IGI CD-ROM User's Guide.* #31025. 4 pp.

Family History Library. *IGI on Microfiche.* #31026. 4 pp.

Family History Library. *PAF Brochure.* #30969. 2 pp. Includes 1 p. order form.

Family History Library. *Hiring a Professional Genealogist.* #34548. 4 pp.

Family History Library. *Using a Family History Center.* #53041.

Family History Library. *Where Do I Start?* Research Paper #32916. 4 pp.

The above FHL publications are available at a nominal charge (or free where indicated) and may be ordered from the Salt Lake Distribution Center at the address indicated earlier in this chapter.

Johni Cerny and Wendy Elliot. *The Library.* Salt Lake City, UT: Ancestry, Inc. 1988. 763 pp.

> Reference to the Family History Library collection at Salt Lake City. Somewhat out of date but still very descriptive.

Fay Dearden and Douglas Dearden. *The German Researcher: How to Get the Most Out of an LDS Family History Center.* May be ordered from the authors, 5700 Oakview Lane North, Plymouth, MN 55442. Telephone 612-557-7138.

Chapter IV

PASSENGER DEPARTURE AND ARRIVAL LISTS

Both departure and arrival lists usually include the names, ages and (for adults) the occupations of all passengers. Departure lists are more likely to include the specific place of origin.

DEPARTURE LISTS

A large majority of German-speaking trans-oceanic emigrants left from one of five ports: **Le Havre, Antwerp, Rotterdam, Bremen,** and **Hamburg**.

Those who left in the eighteenth century generally embarked at Le Havre (the shortest route) or sailed down the Rhine to Rotterdam. Later Antwerp, Bremen and then Hamburg became the leading points of departure. Only the Hamburg and Le Havre records are intact. The Hamburg records have been microfilmed by the Family History Library (FHL).

There are two Hamburg passenger lists: direct and indirect. The **direct list** covers those who sailed directly from Hamburg to an overseas port. The **indirect list** includes passengers on ships that (1) stopped at another European port (e.g., Southhampton) en route, or (2) sailed to Hull (or a few other ports, but infrequently), then took the train across northern England and sailed to their destination from **Liverpool, Glasgow,** or other British ports. The indirect route was actually cheaper, so it was widely used by the poorer emigrants. The British passenger lists have not been preserved.

If attempting to read the FHL microfilms seems to be too much of an obstacle, you can get the Hamburg records searched for $60 per year by the:

Historic Emigration Office
Holstenwall 24
D-20355 Hamburg
Germany

This is the only place in Europe that will accept personal checks in United States dollars.

The Bremen records were routinely destroyed after a few years because of lack of space, although Clifford Neal Smith has published some monographs on the 1846-1850 departures. The lists are now being reconstructed, using United States port arrival lists, in the series, *German Immigrants: Lists of Passengers Bound from Bremen to New York, with Places of Origin*, begun by Gary J. Zimmerman and Marion Wolfert and now continued by the latter. But these include only the small minority of passengers for whom a specific place of origin is mentioned in the New York lists.

For an explanation of omissions in the two major series of volumes published in the United States, see Michael Palmer's critique, "Published Passenger Lists: A Review of *German Immigrants* and *Germans to America*" (*GGSA Bulletin*, May/August 1990). There are also reports that some boats sailed into international waters before boarding trans-Atlantic ships; these illegal passengers would not be listed in the Hamburg records.

The Le Havre records have not been microfilmed. You can get information from them by writing to:

Archive nationale de France
60, rue des Frances-Bourgeois
F-75141 Paris
France

If you know the date of embarkation, the name of the ship and the name(s) of the passengers, Jacques de Guise, director of the Centre for Genealogical Research in Grand Saconnex, Switzerland, will search the Le Havre records for $90 per family and send you information (and evidence, whenever possible) from those records in English. It is also helpful to provide the following, if known: ages of passengers, place of origin or birth, destination, and any other significant information. Checks should be made payable to the Centre or to de Guise, but may be sent to 2845 North 72nd St., Milwaukee, WI 53210.

The FHL has microfilmed the 1817-66 typewritten in-transit records in Strasbourg for emigrants bound for Le Havre.

Except for fragments, the Antwerp and Rotterdam records were destroyed. Charles Hall has published a monograph on the Antwerp lists for 1855 and some for 1854.

Could your ancestor have left from another European port? Yes, although the chances are slim. For example, single young men might have worked for their passage on cargo ships, which sailed from a much larger number of ports.

A few passenger ships left from various minor ports, e.g., **Copenhagen**, **Danzig** (Gdansk), **Riga** and **Libau** (now Liepäja, Latvia). The latter two had passenger service to England. We are not aware of any of these records having been preserved. However, as the archives of the former Communist countries become more accessible, it is possible that embarkation records could surface. Latvian ports were used mostly by Baltic Germans and the legal Soviet emigrants of the 1920s. Most Russian Germans sailed from western ports, chiefly Hamburg.

Immigrants from the southern parts of the former Austro-Hungarian Empire could have left from Adriatic ports, mainly **Trieste**. No passenger records for these ports are known to have been preserved.

Many people emigrated from Germany without registering their intent to depart, but if they did register, a helpful source (if you can find it) is the Emigrant's Lists (*Auswandererlisten*) kept by the various German State Archives (*Staatsarchiv*) and by the local church parishes. They usually give name of emigrant, date and place of birth, place of residence, occupation, country of destination, and given names of the wife and children. See Chapter XV for the addresses of state archives in Germany and elsewhere in Europe.

PASSENGER ARRIVAL LISTS

Port arrival lists are much more likely to provide only a general place of origin (e.g., France, Posen province, or Russian Poland) than the departure lists. However, the village of origin and/or the destination are sometimes recorded.

American Lists

The vast majority of German-speaking immigrants landed in **New York**. **New Orleans** was of secondary importance for the Mississippi River basin, including the Midwest, until 1860, since riverboat fares were very cheap. This was because the boats carried agricultural and other exports downriver to New Orleans, but had little cargo on the way back. Thus boat owners crammed the boats with passengers, charging a low fare, but also leading to tragedies in some cases, e.g., if a fire broke out.

Those who landed at New Orleans are most likely to have left from Le Havre, but they could have come from other ports as well. **Baltimore** had especially good connections with Bremen. **Galveston** was also used as a minor port of entry.

During the colonial era, New York was not in such a dominant position. **Philadelphia**, Baltimore and **Boston** were also important ports of arrival during the earlier period. An example of the numerous published books on these arrivals is Carl Boyer's 289-page, indexed *Ship Passenger Lists, Pennsylvania and Delaware (1641-1825)*, 3rd edition, 1980. Philadelphia and Baltimore continued to be important throughout the nineteenth century.

A major reference series for German immigration to the United States has recently been published by Ira A. Glazier and P. William Filby, called *Germans to America: Lists of Passengers Arriving at United States Ports, 1850-1893*. This work is still in progress and is a list of passenger arrivals at United States ports between 1850 and 1893, including all ports of embarkation. (For example, many people who arrived from Bremen are also in

Germans to America.) So far, 46 volumes covering January 1850 to June 1883 have been published. Information for the series is taken from original ship manifest schedules, or passenger lists, that were prepared by shipping agents and ship's officers, and filed by all vessels entering United States ports. These lists are now deposited at Temple-Balch Institute for Immigration Research in Philadelphia.

What makes this series such a great help is that the former place of residence is commonly included, as well as the name, age, sex and occupation of the passengers. One drawback is that the index for 1850-55 includes only ships that had 80% or more of their passengers with German surnames (all passengers on those ships are included in the index). From 1856 on, all passengers with Germanic surnames are included, regardless of the number on each ship, but non-Germans are not included in the index. However, many "German" passengers were actually from France, Switzerland and Luxembourg.

Since there is other information in the original records not included in the index, such as deaths on board, they should be consulted once you have determined the ship name and arrival date. Microfilms of the original passenger lists are available at the National Archives and for loan by various organizations, such as the American Genealogical Lending Library and Family History Centers.

The National Archives has microfilms of passengers arriving at more than 60 Atlantic and Gulf of Mexico ports, but with many gaps and only a few records for most of the minor ports. Microfilmed indexes for Baltimore (1820-97), Boston (1848-1940), New Orleans (before 1850 to 1952), New York (1820-46, 1897-1902), and Philadelphia (1800-1906) are available from the National Archives or the FHL. For further information, see the *Guide to Genealogical Research in the National Archives*, which also describes many other records, or *Immigrant & Passenger Arrivals: A Select Catalog of National Archives Microfilm Publications*, both published by the National Archives and Records Administration.

Canadian Lists

The chief Canadian ports of entry were **Quebec** and **Halifax**, but some ships landed at **Montreal** or **North Sydney**. Microfilms are at the National Archives of Canada and can be borrowed under the inter-library loan program. Provincial archives also have copies of some of these records. A major problem is that the ink on many of these arrival lists has faded so badly as to be illegible or even invisible.

Both Canadian and American genealogists should be aware that at least prior to 1867, most passengers who landed in Canada headed for the United States, while most Canadian immigrants landed in New York.

Australian and New Zealand Lists

Nick Vine Hill, *Tracing Your Family History in Australia: A Guide to Sources*, has copious information about Australian passenger arrival lists. He indicates that some records can be found for nearly all European immigrants, despite gaps and faded pages, but many of the pre-1860 records appear to have sparse genealogical information. Many pre-1900 lists have been microfilmed.

The major ports were **Moreton Bay-Brisbane** (Queensland), **Sydney** and **Newcastle** (New South Wales), **Port Philip-Melbourne** (Victoria), **Port Adelaide** (South Australia) and later **Fremantle** (Western Australia).

There are numerous published and unpublished indexes and guides, but generally each one deals with only a certain port and a certain time period. In some cases, records for assisted passengers (whose fare was paid by others) are more detailed than for unassisted passengers.

The most valuable publication for Germanic research appears to be the 7-volume series, *Emigrants from Hamburg to Australia, 1860-69*, by Eric and Rosemary Kopittke (Indooroopilly: Queensland Family History Society, 1991-93).

Andrew G. Peake, *National Register of Shipping Arrivals: Australia and New Zealand* (Sydney: Australasian Federation of Family History Organizations, 3rd ed., 1992), covers both countries.

The 6-volume *M. Hodge Index* lists passenger traffic between South Australia and New Zealand, as well as with other Australian ports, for 1837-1859, which would include the Gold Rush years.

Olga K. Miller, *Migration, Emigration, Immigration*, lists quite a few publications on passenger lists and other immigrant and German emigrant records, including records for 1836-1918, with some gaps, for South Australia (mostly by the State Archives, Adelaide); Queensland (*Register of Overseas Arrivals in Queensland, 1848-1923*); Victoria (*German Emigrants to Victoria, 1849*); New South Wales (*Assisted Immigrants to Sydney, 1828-1890*); and Tasmania (*Lists of Free Arrivals, Tasmania, 1816-1871*). Some of these have been microfilmed by the Family History Library. She also lists a number of publications concerning immigrants who landed at **Canterbury** (1855-1871), **Christchurch** (1855-1864), **Otago** (1843-1950), and unspecified ports in New Zealand. **Auckland** and **Wellington** were also important.

South African and Namibian Lists

See R. T. J. Lombard, *Handbook for Genealogical Research in South Africa* (listed in Chapter VI), for information about records relating to South Africa and Namibia.

Most German immigrants to South Africa would have landed in **Cape Town** or **Port Elizabeth**. According to *Meyers Konversations-Lexikon* [*Meyer's (Small) Conversational Encyclopedia*], Vol. 2 (listed in Chapter VIII), the chief German port in what used to be German South-West Africa was **Swakopmund**.

Latin American Lists

The principal immigration ports in Latin America were **Rio de Janeiro, Santos, Salvador, Buenos Aires** and **Valparaiso**. Relatively few Germans are likely to have landed at Salvador. **Porto Alegre, Montevideo** and **Ensenada** (La Plata) were also ports of entry. Port arrival records have been kept since the mid-nineteenth century. Check the Family History Library's *Research Outlines* and *Research Papers* for further details.

REFERENCES (See Bibliography for full citation if not shown)

Arlene Eakle and Johni Cerny, eds. *The Source: A Guidebook of American Genealogy*. Salt Lake City, UT: Ancestry Publishing Co. 1984. 786 pp.

> See Table 15-2 (Availability of Emigration Lists) and Table 15-6 (Printed Immigration Sources) for references too numerous to mention here.

Family History Library. *Hamburg Passenger Lists*. Order #34047. 4 pp.

Ira A. Glazier and P. William Filby. *Germans to America: Lists of Passengers Arriving at United States Ports, 1850-1893*.

National Archives Trust Fund Board. *Immigrant & Passengers Arrivals: A Select Catalog of National Archives Microfilm Publications*. Washington: National Archives Trust Fund Board. 1983.

> U.S. port arrival lists of the U.S. Customs Service (1820-ca. 1891) and the Immigration and Naturalization Service (1891-1954) for over 60 Atlantic, Gulf of Mexico and Great Lakes ports.

Michael H. Tepper. *American Passenger Arrival Records: A Guide to the Records of Immigrants Arriving at American Ports by Sail and Steam*. Baltimore: Genealogical Publishing Co. 1988. 134 pp. 8-page bibliography.

Michael Tepper, ed. *Emigrants to Pennsylvania: A Consolidation of Ship Passenger Lists from The Pennsylvania Magazine of History and Biography*. Baltimore: Genealogical Publishing Co. 1975; reprinted 1992. 302 pp.

> Information on some 6,000 (mostly British and German) immigrants who arrived at the port of Philadelphia, 1641-1819, transcribed from manuscripts in the Historical Society of Pennsylvania. Most of the names come from two extensive lists of indentured servants. Indexed. One of the few works to cover German immigration during the early post-colonial era.

Michael H. Tepper, gen. ed. *Passenger Arrivals at the Port of Baltimore, 1820-1834: From Customs Passenger Lists*. (transcribed by Elizabeth P. Bentley). Baltimore: Genealogical Publishing Co. 1982. 768 pp.

> Details on all family members. About three-fourths of the 50,000 immigrants are estimated to have been Germans.

Michael H. Tepper, gen. ed. *Passenger Arrivals at the Port of Philadelphia, 1641-1819: The Philadelphia Baggage Lists*. (transcribed by Elizabeth P. Bentley). Baltimore: Genealogical Publishing Co. 1986. 913 pp.

United States. National Archives and Records Administration. *Immigrant & Passenger Arrivals: A Select Catalog of National Archives Microfilm Publications*, 2nd ed. Washington, DC: National Archives Trust Fund Board. 1991. 171 pp.

Gary J. Zimmerman and Marion Wolfert. *German Immigrants: Lists of Passengers Bound from Bremen to New York, with Places of Origin*. 1985-93 and ongoing. Currently 4 vols., covering 1847-1871.

Chapter V

RESEARCHING GERMANIC ANCESTORS IN CANADA

Researching in Canada is much like researching in the United States. Most types of records found in the United States also exist in Canada. Canada has national repositories that can be compared to the United States National Archives and Library of Congress. Each province, county or rural municipality, and local area also maintains its own designated records. Those of genealogical importance include births, baptisms, marriages, deaths, census records (currently available through 1911), church records, court records, land records, immigration and naturalization records, military records, newspapers, etc.

After compiling information from your family members and learning that your ancestors immigrated to Canada, you are ready to begin researching Canadian records. First you need to locate the place in Canada where your ancestors lived. Next determine the county or rural municipality, the town or township, and the time period they were at that locale. Keep in mind that many place names have changed over the years, especially in Ontario. Questions regarding this will be answered by the Archives of Ontario. See Chapter XIII for more information about immigration to Canada.

If your ancestors came to Canada between 1764 and 1867, a unique index is available to help you locate where they lived: the "Computerized Land Records Index." See under **PROVINCIAL ARCHIVES** later in this chapter for land records of Ontario. Since the Canadian government advertised for settlers to come to eastern Canada and land was offered free until 1826 to those willing to improve the property, most settlers of this time period owned land. After 1826, land was purchased at a minimal cost. This index summarizes the original land grants from the Crown (government) dating from the earliest settlement in Upper Canada/Canada West/Ontario (1791-1867), and Quebec/Lower Canada (1764-1841). The index is alphabetized by surname of the applicant and/or by township name and is available on microfiche through Family History Centers. When using the index, remember to search every spelling variation of your surname. Data on the index includes: surname, given name, town or township, lot number, concession number, date identity code, issue date, transaction type, type of free grant, type of lease/sale, and archival reference (registry, series, volume and page number). Based on information from this index, photocopies of the actual records can be obtained. For more complete information, see *Genealogy in Ontario: Searching the Records*, by Brenda Dougall Merriman and *Families* (Vol. 25, No. 2, 1986) published by the Ontario Genealogical Society.

Once you have located the exact place of residence, many city and county directories from the 1840s to the present are available. See Dorothy E. Ryder's *Checklist of Canadian Directories, 1790-1950* (National Library of Canada, 1979).

Another unique aid to locating your Canadian ancestor is the useful *Directory of Canada* of 1857. This directory includes people from all parts of Canada although it does not list every household. Land owners and business people are most likely to be found. The Ontario section of this directory has been alphabetized and reprinted in *Directory of the Province of Ontario, 1857, with a Gazetteer*, by Thomas B. Wilson and Emily S. Wilson (1987), published by the Ontario Genealogical Society.

CHURCH RECORDS

Since registration of vital events did not begin in Canada until 1869, church registers should be consulted for baptisms, marriages, deaths or burials prior to this time. Many churches have their own cemetery and keep their own burial and sexton records. Additional records found in church registers may include communicants, membership and confirmation lists. Many churches kept records of arrival of church members as well as removal of members to other congregations. Vestry records can include lists of donors to the church, sometimes biographical material on members, records of orphans, illegitimate births, and lists of the poor.

Churches kept their own individual registers, but over time some churches merged, separated or disbanded. Census records can be used to determine a family's religious affiliation. The location of some church records can be a problem since many baptisms were performed in the "nearest" church, regardless of religious affiliation, and during particular periods of history only certain denominations were allowed to perform marriages. This means that marriages of various denominations can be found within one register. Some records were kept by circuit (traveling) ministers, and may be found miles from the area of the event, or were lost entirely. The following short dateline can help explain why it may be difficult to locate your ancestor's marriage record in Canada:

1754-1793   Only Anglican and Roman Catholic clergy could perform marriages.

1793-1798   District clerks were allowed to perform marriages if the couple lived more than 18 miles from an Anglican minister. Anglican and Roman Catholic clergy also performed marriages.

1798-1831   Anglican, Roman Catholic, Calvinist, Church of Scotland and Lutheran clergy could perform marriages.

1831-1858   All above denominations as well as Baptists, Methodists and Presbyterians were allowed to perform marriages. Marriage registers were required to be kept by law.

1858-Present All denominations can perform marriages.

Individual church archives can help in locating where the records are for a particular congregation. Before writing to Canada, check with a Family History Center to see if microfilming has been done in the area. Many church registers have also been published. The following are useful addresses pertaining to research in Canadian records. See the *Yearbook of American and Canadian Churches* (referenced in chapter XI) for more addresses.

Organization: Address	Holdings
• Amish Historical Library RR 4 Aylmer, ON N5H 2R3	Has older order Amish records. Records of other Amish sects are kept at the University of Waterloo.
• Anglican Church of Canada General Synod Archives 600 Jarvis St. Toronto, ON M4Y 9Z9	Can help you locate which diocesan archives to contact for names and addresses of Anglican churches in the area your family lived. Records are kept in the local churches.
• Archdiocese of Toronto 355 Church St. Toronto, ON M5B 1Z8 *(Roman Catholic)*	All records are in local churches. You can contact your local archdiocese or diocese to locate individual churches, diocese or archdiocese in Canada.
• Canadian Baptists Archives McMaster Divinity College Hamilton, ON L8S 4K1	The Baptist denomination has its roots in the Anabaptist movement.
• Canadian Jewish Congress Central Region Archives 150 Beverly St. Toronto, ON M5T 1Y6	May be helpful with questions concerning ancestry of Canadian Jews.

- Kitchener Public Library
  Grace Schmidt Room of Local History
  85 Queen St. N.
  Kitchener, ON N2H 2H1

  Has extensive newspaper indexes and family histories in a heavily German area.

- Leo Baeck Institute
  129 E. 73rd St.
  New York, NY 10021

  May be helpful for German Jewish genealogical research in both Canada and the United States.

- Mennonite Archives of Ontario
  Conrad Grebel College
  University of Waterloo
  Waterloo, ON N2L 3G6

  This is the central repository for Mennonite church records in Ontario.

- United Church of Canada Archives
  Birge Carnegie Library
  Victoria University
  73 Queen's Park Crescent East
  Toronto, ON M5S 1K7

  This is a unity of the Congregationalists, Methodists, and some Presbyterians, including the United Brethren in Christ and German Methodists.

- Waterloo Lutheran Seminary
  75 University Ave. W.
  Waterloo, ON N2L 3C6

  Records are kept in congregations. Some records are shared with synod archives at seminaries. German language is predominant in early Lutheran records.

GENEALOGICAL SOCIETIES

Genealogical societies can provide a variety of help in locating the records you need, but do not expect them to do your research for you. Many organizations have extensive indexes, obituary files, printed genealogies and local histories that they will check for you. See also chapter XIII for more information.

Alberta Family History Societies
P.O. Box 30270, Sta. B
Calgary, AB T2M 4P1
(library in Red Deer)

Alberta Genealogical Society
P.O. Box 12015
Edmonton, AB T5J 3L2

Manitoba Genealogical Society
P.O. Box 2066
Winnipeg, MB R3B 0T6
(East European Branch:
P.O. Box 2536
Winnipeg, MB R3C 4A7)
(library at 885 Notre Dame Ave.)

British Columbia Genealogical Society
P.O. Box 88054
Richmond, BC V6X 3T6

Genealogical Association of Nova Scotia
P.O. Box 641, Station "M"
Halifax, NS B3J 2T3

Ontario Genealogical Society
40 Orchard View Blvd., Suite 253
Toronto, ON M4R 1B9

Saskatchewan Genealogical Society
P.O. Box 1894
Regina, SK S4P 3E1
(library at 1870 Lorne St.)
(has many branches)

Waterloo-Wellington Branch of
    Ontario Genealogical Society (OGS)
Box 603
Kitchener, ON N2G 4A2
(center of German settlement)

The Ontario Genealogical Society is the largest genealogical society in Canada with 27 branches and over 6,000 members. OGS is recording all cemeteries in Ontario and is indexing the 1871 census for the Province of Ontario. It offers an extensive list of publications.

NATIONAL ARCHIVES AND LIBRARY

Canada's national record repository collects and preserves records of national importance. This includes all national government records and sizable collections of provincial, local and private records from all of Canada. This national collection includes census records, vital statistics, Crown Land records, wills and estate records, some early marriage bonds, military records and immigration records. The staff is permitted to provide limited photocopying of original documents and copies from microfilm. The archive is open for private research but an appointment should be arranged in advance. They also offer an inexpensive booklet, *Tracing Your Ancestors in Canada*, as a brief guide to using the archive for genealogical research. The National Library of Canada can be compared to the U.S. Library of Congress. Write to:

National Archives of Canada
395 Wellington St.
Ottawa, ON K1A 0N3

National Library of Canada
395 Wellington St.
Ottawa, ON K1A 0N3

Many of the above records, including census records, have been microfilmed by the Family History Library (FHL) in Salt Lake City and are available at local Family History Centers.

Estate records may include wills, inventories of property, petitions for and letters of administration, trusteeships and guardianships, as well as miscellaneous correspondence. These are located at the local court in which the estate was probated. Many of these documents have been microfilmed by the FHL.

Newspapers, school records, and military records are also found at the National Archives of Canada, and many have been microfilmed. These can be ordered through Family History Centers. See chapter III.

PROVINCIAL ARCHIVES

The **Ontario Provincial Archives** has recently made many of its records available through inter-library loan. These records include some vital events before 1869, court records, and pre-1900 publications on microfilm. Births from 1869-96, marriages from 1869-1911 and deaths from 1819-1921 have been transferred to the archives and are being microfilmed. District marriage registers dating from 1831 (a few dating back to the early 1800s) of the minority denominations (i.e., other than Catholic and Anglican) are indexed and available on microfilm. Copies of the county marriage registers from 1858-69 have been microfilmed.

Among the most genealogically important holdings are the applications or petitions for **land grants**. The Ontario abstract records (1764-1867) were filmed by the FHL. A copy was given to the archives and can be borrowed. An index by surname provides an easy search for the appropriate petition. The **computerized land records index** mentioned earlier in this chapter is available through the FHL. This is an index for the Crown Land, Canada Company, and Peter Robinson papers (companies providing land settlement) and also to the land grants of the United Empire Loyalists and veterans of the South African War.

They also have a **card index** of 43,000 personal names from 1780-1869 extracted from family histories, marriages, land records, wills and cemetery records. This index has been microfilmed by the FHL.

Homestead records and **land purchase records** of various kinds are available in the provincial archives of the western provinces. Homesteading was available there much later than in the United States, which is a major reason why many German-Americans migrated onward to Western Canada. In Manitoba, homesteading occurred in the 1870-1930 period. In northern British Columbia, it is still continuing on a small-scale basis.

The **Manitoba Provincial Archives** also has the records listed below, according to information received from archivist Ken Reddig and Brian Lenius of the Manitoba Genealogical Society. It is likely that similar records exist in most other provincial archives.

- Tax assessment and collectors rolls
- Probate (formerly surrogate) and estate records (beginning in 1871 in Winnipeg; later elsewhere)

- Many Canadian passenger arrival lists (microfilm copies)

- Census records (microfilm copies)

- Voters or electors lists (in Canada, as in most other countries, the government prepares a list of eligible voters, so these lists include almost all adults)

- Semi-annual school attendance reports, listing the name of the teacher and the names, ages, grades and attendance of students (beginning in 1915)

Selected Manitoba Government Records: Family & Community History itemizes the records produced at the provincial level (but not microfilms of federal records) in considerable detail. However, the referenced records, while useful for genealogical purposes, are not family and local histories as we usually think of them. *Tracing Your Ancestors in Alberta*, by Victoria Lemieux and David Leonard, is available from the Provincial Archives of Alberta. *Exploring Local History in Saskatchewan* can be obtained from the Saskatchewan Provincial Archives. The Regina Public Library is noted for its collection of local histories for the three Prairie Provinces.

The following provincial archives contain material of particular importance for Germanic research:

Provincial Archives of Alberta
12845 - 102nd Avenue
Edmonton, Alberta T5N 0M6

British Columbia Archives and
   Records Service
655 Belleville St.
Victoria, BC V8V 1X4

Manitoba Provincial Archives
200 Vaughan St.
Winnipeg, MB R3C 1T5

Public Archives of Nova Scotia
6016 University Ave.
Halifax, NS B3H 1W4

Archives of Ontario
77 Grenville St.
Toronto, ON M7A 2R9

Saskatchewan Provincial Archives
Murray Memorial Building
3 Campus Drive
University of Saskatchewan
Saskatoon, SK S7N 0W0

Saskatchewan Provincial Archives
3303 Hillsdale Street
University of Regina
Regina, SK S4S 0A2

Addresses of provincial archives are also listed in other sources, including Thomas Jay Kemp, *International Vital Records Handbook*, 3rd ed. (Baltimore: Genealogical Publishing Co., 1994).

PROVINCIAL LIBRARIES

Published materials, including many family, local and church histories, can be found in the provincial libraries. Some provinces have requirements that a copy of each copyrighted book published in that province must be deposited with the provincial or legislative library on request. The addresses of these and other libraries can be found in Lynn Fraser (managing ed.), *Directory of Libraries in Canada*, published annually by Micromedia, Ltd., in Toronto. Alternatively, you can call 800-387-2689 to get the address you want.

State and local libraries house vast amounts of genealogical information and have formed local archive sections. See Angus Baxter, *In Search of Your Canadian Roots*, for a list of some of these libraries and a synopsis of their genealogical collections.

CIVIL RECORDS

There are ten Canadian provinces (similar to states in the U.S.), as well as the Yukon Territory and the Northwest Territories. The latter territories are in a state of transition. Previously they have consisted of Mackenzie, Keewatin and Franklin districts, but this administrative subdivision had no real significance. The eastern part of the Northwest Territories is to become Nunavut, a self-governing territory for the Inuit (previously known as Eskimos), who speak Inuktitut. Few Caucasians live there permanently, although quite a few work there for a while as government officials, business representatives, teachers, etc.

Each province and territory has the responsibility to collect and record events within its own jurisdiction. However, all past vital records for the Northwest Territories are in Yellowknife. No equivalent archive has as yet been set up in what will become Nunavut.

These records include births, marriages, deaths, civil and criminal court records, probate records, wills, guardianships, etc. Each province began civil registration at a different time period. Services and fees to obtain searches and copies of these records vary considerably from one province to another.

Alberta

Complete records from 1898, with some birth records from 1853 and some death records from 1893.

Division of Vital Statistics
Dept. of Social Services and
    Community Health
10405 - 100th Ave., 4th Floor
Edmonton, AB T5J 0A6

British Columbia

Civil registrations began in 1872 but early records are incomplete.

Division of Vital Statistics
Ministry of Health
655 Belleville St.
Victoria, BC V8V 1X4

Manitoba

Almost complete records since 1882 and also some incomplete church records prior to 1882.

Office for Vital Statistics
Dept. of Community Services and
    Corrections
254 Portage Ave.
Winnipeg, MB R3C 0B6

New Brunswick

Incomplete records from 1888-1920 and complete records from 1920.

The Registrar General
Vital Statistics Division
PO Box 6000
Fredericton, NB E3B 5H1

Newfoundland

Began civil registration in 1892.

Registrar General
Vital Statistics Division
Department of Health
Confederation Building
St. John's, Newfoundland A1C 5I7

Newfoundland *(continued)*

The Provincial Archives of Newfoundland has numerous church records for the period 1860-1891.

Provincial Archives of Newfoundland
and Labrador
Colonial Building
Military Road
St. John's, Newfoundland A1C 5T7

Northwest Territories

Complete records from 1925.

Registrar of Vital Statistics
P.O. Box 1320
Yellowknife, Northwest Terr. X1A 2L9

Nova Scotia

Records of births and deaths from 1865-1908 and marriages from the late 1700s.

Public Archives of Nova Scotia
6016 University Ave.
Halifax, NS B3H 1W4

Records of births and deaths after 1 Oct. 1908 and marriages after 1907-1918:

Deputy Registrar General
Department of Health
PO Box 157
Halifax, NS B3J 2M9

Ontario

Civil registration began 1 July 1869. (Some records are available through the Ontario Provincial Archives.)

Deputy Registrar General
MacDonald Block
Queen's Park
Toronto, ON M7A 1Y5

Prince Edward Island

Civil registration began in 1906, but some marriage records date back to 1787.

Director, Division of Vital Statistics
Dept. of Health and Social Services
PO Box 3000
Charlottetown, PEI C1A 7P1

Quebec

Church records have been kept since 1621 by the priests of the Catholic Church. A duplicate of the church registry was sent to the office of one of the 34 district protonotaries. These are deposited in 9 regional offices of the Archives nationales du Quebec.

Archives nationales du Quebec
PO Box 10450
Sainte-Foy, Quebec G1V 4N1

Write to this archive to obtain addresses of the regional offices. Extracts can also be made directly from the parish records. Many of the parish records have been indexed and printed as well as filmed by the Family History Library.

Saskatchewan

Complete records since 1920 and incomplete records for 1878-1920.

Vital Statistics, Dept. of Health
1919 Rose St.
Regina, SK S4P 3V7

Yukon Territory

Some birth records for 1898, an index of births about 1900-24 and complete records from 1924.

Vital Statistics
Government of the Yukon Territory
PO Box 2703
Whitehorse, YT Y1A 2C6

REFERENCES (See bibliography for full citations if not shown)

Angus Baxter. *In Search of Your Canadian Roots.* Baltimore, MD: Genealogical Publishing Co. 1994. 350 pp.

Virginia Easley DeMarce. *German Military Settlers in Canada after the American Revolution.* Sparta, WI: Joy Reisinger. 1984. 350 pp. Available from Joy Reisinger, 1020 Central Ave., Sparta, WI 54656.
> Roster of 2,000 men who remained in Canada after the American Revolution, with Anglicized and Gallicized names. Historical background on the formation of German mercenary units.

Eric Jonasson. *A Canadian Genealogical Handbook.* Winnipeg, Manitoba: Wheatfield Press. 1978. 352 pp.

Janine Roy. *Tracing Your Ancestors in Canada.* 9th ed., revised 1987. Ottawa: National Archives of Canada. 1988. 47 pp.

Heinz Lehmann. *The German Canadians, 1750-1937.*

Brenda Dougall Merriman. *Genealogy in Ontario, Searching the Records.* Toronto, Ontario: Ontario Genealogical Society. 1988. 168 pp.

Leonard H. Smith, Jr., and Norma H. Smith. *Nova Scotia Immigrants to 1867.* Baltimore: Genealogical Publishing Co. 1992. 560 pp.
> Comprehensive index of immigrants, including many who came to the U.S., based on extensive research in Canadian, American, British and French archival sources.

Ryan Taylor. *Family Research in Waterloo and Wellington Counties.* Kitchener, Ontario: Waterloo-Wellington Branch of Ontario Genealogical Society. 1986. 106 pp.
> Exceptionally well-done guide for the German areas of Ontario.

Chapter VI

RESEARCHING GERMANIC ANCESTORS OUTSIDE THE UNITED STATES AND CANADA

LATIN AMERICA

The principal aids to genealogical research in Latin America are the *Research Outlines* published by the Family History Library (FHL), although they contain very few explicit references to Germans in those countries. The FHL has published Spanish-language *Research Outlines* for Argentina (1975), Chile (1974), Mexico (1970), Paraguay (1977) and Uruguay (1974).

In 1992 the FHL published an English-language *Research Outline: Latin America*, which is the main source for the information in this section. We have used Thomas Jay Kemp, *International Vital Records Handbook*, 3rd ed. (Baltimore: Genealogical Publishing Co., 1994) as a supplemental source. The FHL *Research Outline* contains many useful tips for beginners who have had no, or only limited, experience in researching their ancestors.

Addresses of some multi-purpose Germanic societies and useful genealogical contacts are listed at the end of this section.

Family History Library Holdings

The Family History Library has over 190,000 microfilm and microfiche records, including some from almost every Latin American country. The largest collections are for Mexico, Guatemala, Chile, Argentina and Brazil. The number of Germans in Guatemala was small, but nevertheless they were the largest non-Hispanic, non-native group. There are a large number of Germans in the other four mentioned countries.

The Family History Library has microfilm copies of records in government archives, church archives, and private collections, including:

- birth, baptism, marriage and death records
- census records
- notarial records
- Immigration records

The library's books also include family histories, as well as atlases, gazetteers, and national and local histories. Copies of some of these books are on microfilm.

Church and Cemetery Records

The original German immigrants included Catholics (apparently a majority in Argentina and possibly in Brazil, and minorities in other countries), Lutherans (apparently a majority in Chile and possibly in Brazil, with a sizable minority in Argentina and other countries), and Mennonites (a majority of Germans in Mexico and, at least among the unassimilated, in Paraguay, as well as several other countries with only a small number of Germans).

A small number of Seventh-Day Adventists and Baptists appear to have been among the original immigrants. Various other denominations (e.g., Congregationalists and members of the United Church of Christ) are now represented, but this appears to be the result of later North American missionary activities.

Ernst Wagemann, in his article, "Die deutschen Kolonisten im brasilianischen Staate Espirito Santo" ["The German Colonists in the Brazilian State of Espirito Santo"] (in *Schriften des Vereins für Sozialpolitik* [*Publications of the Society for Social Betterment*], Vol. 147, Part 5 (Munich/Leipzig: Verlag von Duncker & Humblot, 1915), indicates that parish registers in this small state, northeast of Rio de Janeiro, date back to the 1850s. It seems likely that earlier registers can be found in southern Brazil, an area to which many

Germans had already immigrated in the 1820s. These registers include the same kind of data as in other countries.

To what extent any of these German parish records have been microfilmed is uncertain. However, if they are kept at the parish level, they probably have not been filmed. Those kept at the state, and possibly diocesan, archives are more likely to be on microfilm.

The Catholic Church took ecclesiastical censuses every 10-15 years or so. *Censo* or *padrón* is the Spanish word for "census"; *rol*, the Portuguese one. Presumably the censuses were universal and included the German Catholics. Furthermore, German Catholics were more likely to live in multi-ethnic parishes than the Lutherans were, not only because of their religious affinity with the long-time residents, but also because most of the other non-Iberian immigrants came from Catholic countries, especially Italy and Poland.

In case you visit the ancestral parish in person, you may find local cemetery records and gravestones to be useful.

Civil Registers

Civil registration was introduced in the following years in the various countries, but these records often are not complete. However, information is less likely to be missing for European immigrants and their descendants than for the native population.

Table 3: Civil Registers in Latin American Countries

Country	Year of Introduction
Argentina	1886
Belize	1881-1885
Bolivia	1898-1940*
Brazil	1870
Chile	1885
Costa Rica	1881
Guatemala	1877
Mexico	1859
Paraguay	1880
Uruguay	1879

* Civil registration was authorized in 1898, but modern civil records (which are incomplete) begin in 1940.

Civil registers are in the local towns in Brazil, Guatemala and Mexico. They are kept in the provincial civil registry offices in Argentina. For other countries, write to:

Registrar General
The General Registry
Judiciary Department
Court House Plaza
P.O. Box 87
Belize City
Belize, C.A.

Director General del Servicio
    de Registro Civil e Identificacion
Ministerio de Justice
Hurfanos 1570
Santiago
Chile

Director
Oficina de Registro del Estado Civil
    de las Personas
Ministerio de Justicia y Trabajo
Herrera 875
Asunción
Paraguay

Dirección General del Registro
    del Estado Civil
Ministerio de Educación y Cultura
Av. Uruguay 933
11.100 Montevideo
Uruguay

Dirección de Registro Civil y Notariado
Tribunal Supremo de Eleciones
AP 10218-1000
San Jose
Costa Rica

The *International Vital Records Handbook* includes copies of the forms for various countries

Census Records

Public, as well as church, censuses began at an early date in most Latin American countries. The FHL has census records of eight Latin American countries, taken prior to the arrival of any Germanic immigrants. Those for Chile are only for 1777-1816, i.e., they end before the Germans arrived. The microfilmed censuses for Argentina include those for 1869, i.e., prior to the period of the heaviest Germanic immigration, and 1895, by which time a majority of the Germans had arrived. Only the 1930 census is listed for Mexico, but this would be useful because the first large Germanic immigrant wave occurred in the 1920s. No microfilmed census records are listed for Brazil, Paraguay, or Uruguay.

Emigration and Immigration Records

Except for early German immigrants to Brazil, nearly all Germans went to Latin America during the period for which the Hamburg passenger lists are available (and most sailed from Hamburg). Since Hamburg had strong connections with Latin America, these are likely to be valuable in most cases.

Clifford Neal Smith has also published a few monographs that include passengers whose destination was Latin America.

The Hunsrück region in what is now the northern part of the state of Rhineland-Palatinate was one of the centers of pre-1845 emigration to Brazil. It was also the primary source for the 1845 emigrants who founded the city of Petropolis. Therefore, it would be worthwhile to check the huge emigrant file at the Institut für pfälzische Geschichte und Volkskunde in Kaiserslautern. Most parish registers for this area are in Koblenz (for Protestants) or in Trier (for Catholics). The addresses are listed in Chapter XV under **GERMANY**.

For the twentieth-century immigrants, passport records may be available. A large percentage of immigrants of Germanic stock went to Mexico, Belize, Costa Rica, Paraguay, and Bolivia during this period. The number of those who went to various other countries, especially in the temperate zones of South America, is substantial.

The post-1933 Jewish and political refugees from Austria also fit into this category, although what percentage remained in their country of refuge after 1945 is unknown. Ironically, the Dominican Republic, under the Trujillo dictatorship, was the most helpful, according to Franz Goldner, *Austrian Emigration, 1938 to 1945*. The English translation of this book was published by the Frederick Ungar Publishing Co., New York, in 1979.

Land Records

A variety of land records are available in Latin America. Since the overwhelming majority of Germanic immigrants were landowners (that desire being the main reason why many landless Germans migrated to Latin America), land grants are likely to be useful. Free land was often offered to induce immigration, especially to Brazil. Later immigrants had to pay a small price for farmland, often on a delayed basis. Land titles may be particularly valuable in such cases.

Probate and Notarial Records

These two types of records are lumped together inasmuch as they both include wills and probably guardianship records. Some wills may also appear in church death registers.

Notarial records also include mortgages and records of the sale and purchase of land or other property. These are especially likely to be helpful for urban dwellers. Some

Germans settled in the cities. Many more later moved to large cities, such as Buenos Aires, Sao Paulo, Santiago, or medium-sized ones like Curitiba (southern Brazil), Concepcion (central Chile), or Rosario (northeast Argentina).

Military Records

Records of active service personnel are likely to be significant only in Brazil, which entered World War I in 1917 and World War II in 1942. Although Mexico also declared war in 1942, the overwhelming majority of Mexican Germans were Mennonite conscientious objectors, who would not have served in the military. Argentina, Paraguay and Uruguay declared war in 1945, when the war was almost over, so military records in these countries are not likely to be helpful.

Although there were quite a few nineteenth-century wars among Latin American countries, these occurred before there were large numbers of Germans in the affected countries.

However, some military records included all males eligible for service or even all civilians protected by a military outpost. These records are often kept in town or municipal archives. It may be worth checking whether such records existed for the country or area in question.

Published Records

As elsewhere, there are numerous family histories, biographies, compilations of pedigree charts, and articles in genealogical periodicals in Latin America. Many of the family and local histories are in German, although this is less likely to be the case for recent publications. These can probably be found in local libraries or church archives. Biographies of prominent persons are likely to be found in state, university, or large city libraries.

Many published materials, often printed in small quantities largely for local use, may be hard to find. Multi-purpose Germanic societies may have copies of some of these.

It may also be worth checking the *Revista Genealógica Latina* [*Latin American Genealogical Journal*], published by the Federacao dos Institutos Genealogicos Latinos in Sao Paulo since 1949, because it contains articles in six languages, including German. Some issues are on microfilm.

Gazetteers, Maps and Atlases

The Family History Library has a good collection of gazetteers, maps and atlases, but few have been microfilmed. These would, of course, be available in many national, state, university, or possibly metropolitan libraries in the country in question. Researchers in other countries who are concerned with Latin America are most likely to find what they want at certain university libraries.

Language of Records

Records pertaining to Germans may be in German, Latin (mostly for Catholics), Spanish, Portuguese (Brazil), or English (Belize and some Caribbean countries).

Repositories

The Family History Library *Research Outline: Latin America* lists the addresses of nearly all the national archives and libraries in Latin America. The addresses for the national libraries of the six countries with the largest Germanic population are:

Biblioteca Nacional
México 564
1097 Buenos Aires
Argentina

Biblioteca Nacional
Av. Rio Branco 219-239
20042 Rio de Janeiro, RJ
Brazil

Biblioteca Nacional
Av. Bernardo O'Higgins 651
Santiago
Chile

Biblioteca Nacional de México
Instituto de Investigaciones
Bibliográficas
Universidad Nacional Autónoma
de México
Centro Cultural, Ciudad Universitaria
Delegación Coyoacán
Apdo. 29-124
64150 México
Mexico

Biblioteca y Archivo Nacionales
Mariscal Estigarribia 95
Asunción
Paraguay

Biblioteca Nacional del Uruguay
Centro Nacional de Documentación
Científica,
Técnica y Económica
18 de Julio 1790
Casilla 452
Montevideo
Uruguay

In Paraguay the archive is combined with the national library. The addresses of the other four archives important for Germanic genealogy are:

Archivo General de la Nación
Av. Leandro N. Alem 246
1003 Buenos Aires
Argentina

Arquivo Nacional
Rua Azeredo Coutinho 77
Centro
20230 Rio de Janeiro, RJ
Brazil

Archivo Nacional
Miraflores 50
Santiago
Chile

Archivo General de la Nación
Tacuba 8, 2o. piso
Palacio Nacional
Apdo. 1999
México 1
Mexico

Archivo General de la Nación
Calle Convención 1474
Montevideo
Uruguay

For other countries, see the Family History Library *Research Outline*. The FHL has an unfilmed book describing the contents of these archives, viz., Roscoe R. Hill, *Los Archivos Nacionales de la América Latina* [*National Archives of Latin America*], published by the Archivo Nacional de Cuba in Havana in 1948.

There are both English and German-language guides to all major archives in the world. The English one is *The World of Learning*, which should be available in any university library. The German one is *Internationales Bibliotheks-Handbuch* [*World Guide to Libraries*], published by K. G. Saur, Munich, in 1986. Various other repositories have been mentioned elsewhere.

Writing to Latin America

The Family History Library recommends that in writing to Latin America, you should:

- enclose an International Reply Coupon (this is a universal expectation for foreign requests and it is better to enclose two)

- enclose $5 per search when requesting photocopy or search services (you may be billed for more later if any extensive research is required)

- have your letter translated into the language of the country (unless you know that the addressee has a knowledge of German or English)

Useful Addresses

Asociacion Argentina de los Alemanes
del Volga
Crespo, Entre Rios
Argentina
(*The Volga German Society of Argentina*)

Centro Germano-Argentino de Entre Rios
Rivadava 1070
Crespo, Entre Rios
Argentina
(*German-Argentinian Center of Entre Rios*)

Sudetendeutsche Landsmannschaft
Argentinien
Warnes 95
1602 Florida - Buenos Aires
Argentina
(*Sudeten German homeland society*)

Prof. Ayrton Gonçalves Celestino
Associação Alema-Bucovina de Cultura
Rua Waldemar Kost, Vila Hauer
Curitiba, PR
Cep. 81.500-180 Brazil
(*Bukovina Germans in Brazil*)

Conselho de Curadores da Fundação
Cultural de Pomerode
c/o Prefeitura Municipal de Pomerode
Rua 15 de Novembro, 525
Caiza Postal, 36
89107 Pomerode, Santa Catarina
Brazil
(*genealogical-cultural organization in heavily Germanic area*)

Jason Epstein
c/o J. P. De Olivares
Rua Macedo Sobrinho No. 4/804
Humaita
22271 Rio de Janeiro
Brazil
(*English-speaking professional genealogist*)

Instituto Hans Staden
Rua Sete de Abril, 59
CEP 01043 - 000
Sao Paulo, SP
Brazil
(*institute for German family history research*)

Pr. Vilson Wutzke
Caixa Postal 07
85930-000 Nova Santa Rosa, PR
Brazil
(*Volhynian Germans in Brazil*)

Instituto Chileno de Investigaciones
Genealogicas
Casilla 1386
Santiago de Chile 1
Chile
(*Chilean institute for genealogical research*)

THE SOUTHWEST PACIFIC

AUSTRALIA

Although there is a tremendous amount of information in Nick Vine Hill, *Tracing Your Family History in Australia: A Guide to Sources*, 2nd ed. (Albert Park, Australia: Scriptorum Family History Centre, 1994), very little of it pertains specifically to Germanic genealogy. However, most of the sources would be applicable to all ethnic groups. He also lists a number of publications that concentrate more directly on the history and genealogy of German-speaking immigrants to Australia and their descendants. These include:

- Owen B. Mutzelburg, *How to Trace Your German Ancestors: A Guide for Australians and New Zealanders.* Sydney: Hale & Iremonger, 1989.

- M. J. Horst and J. McBride, *Austrians and Australians.* Blackburn, Australia: Australasian Educa Press Pty Ltd, 1987.

- Susanne Wegmann, *The Swiss in Australia.* Grusch, Switzerland: Verlag Ruegger, 1989.

- Ian Harmstorf and Michael Cigler, *The Germans in Australia.* Melbourne: AE Press, 1985.

- Jürgen Tampke and Colin Doxford, *Australia, Willkommen: A History of the Germans in Australia.* Kensington: New South Wales University Press, 1990.

- Josef Vondra, *German-Speaking Settlers in Australia.* Richmond, Australia: Cavalier Press Pty Ltd, 1981.

- Patricia Cloos and Jürgen Tampke, *Greetings from the Land Where Milk and Honey Flows: The German Immigration to New South Wales, 1838-1858.* Mawson, ACT, Australia: Southern Highland Publishers, 1993.

- Clifford Neal Smith, *Nineteenth Century Emigration of "Old Lutherans" from Eastern Germany (Mainly Pomerania and Lower Silesia) to Australia, Canada and the United States).* McNeal, AZ: Westland Publications, 1980.

- Colin Gordon Sheehan, "Germans in Australia: A Guide to Sources," in *Generation.* Stones Corner: Genealogical Society of Queensland, Vol. 6, No. 4, 1984.

- *200 Jahre Geschichte der deutschsprachigen Gemeinschaft in Australien, 1788-1988* [*200 Years of History of the German-Speaking Community in Australia, 1788-1988*]. Sydney: Europa Kurier Pty Ltd, 1988.

Unfortunately, the only one of these publications available to us on a timely basis was Smith's monograph, but we did have the following Australian materials to work with:

- Mary Mennicken-Cooley, *The Germans in Western Australia.* McLawley, WA, Australia: Edith Cowan University, 1993.

- Reg Butler, *A College in the Wattles: Hahndorf and Its Academy.* Hahndorf, SA: Hahndorf Academy, 1989.

- Carol Wardale and Margaret Jenner (comps.), *German Research Directory*, 7th ed. Stones Corner: German Research Group, Genealogical Society of Queensland, 1988.

- Jürgen Tampke, ed., *Wunderbar Country: Germans Look at Australia, 1850-1914.* Marrickville, NSW: Hale & Iremonger Pty Ltd, 1982.

- *Die Zeitung* [*The Newspaper*], the periodical of the German Research Group, Genealogical Society of Queensland

- A letter from Liz Twigden, Torrensville, SA (with enclosures) providing genealogical, historical and bibliographical information on Germans in South Australia

The "South Australiana Source Sheet No. 12" bibliography prepared by the State Library of South Australia lists numerous pertinent books, pamphlets, theses and newspaper articles. Those most valuable for genealogical research appear to be:

- Ian Harmstorf, *German Migration, with Particular Reference to Hamburg, to South Australia, 1851-1884.* Adelaide: M.A. thesis, University of Adelaide, 1971.

- David A. Schubert, *Kavel's People: Their Story of Migration from Prussia to South Australia for the Sake of Faith,...* (Adelaide: Lutheran Publishing House, 1985.

Die Zeitung [*The Newspaper*], published by the German Research Group in Queensland, also mentions a book by Alan Corkhill, *Queensland and Germany: Ethnic, Socio-Cultural, Political and Trade Relations 1838-1991* (Forest Hill, Vic, Australia: Academia Press, 1992). A second book by Dr. Corkhill on the cultural and social history of German immigration and settlement throughout Australia is in preparation.

Genealogical Societies

Australia's one specifically German-oriented genealogical organization is the:

> German Research Group
> Genealogical Society of Queensland, Inc.
> c/o Margaret Jenner
> 73 Plimsoll St.
> Greenslopes, Qld 4120
> Australia

It publishes a genealogical periodical, *Die Zeitung* [*The Newspaper*], edited by Valerie Dieckmann.

In Western Australia there is a European (i.e., continental, in contrast to British) Interest Group. This multi-ethnic group includes Germans and publishes the *Western Ancestor* quarterly. The address is:

> European Interest Group
> Western Australian Genealogical Society, Inc.
> Unit 5, 48 May St.
> Bayswater, WA 6053
> Australia

There is a lot of information on Germans (and not only in that state) available from the following society, which welcomes inquiries, according to Liz Twigden:

> South Australian Genealogy and Heraldry Society, Inc.
> GPO Box 592
> Adelaide, SA 5001
> Australia

New South Wales has at least 74 regional genealogical societies, with an umbrella group, the New South Wales Association of Family History Societies, which does not answer mail queries, according to Vine Hill. Regional societies that are readily identifiable as covering areas with a significant number of Germans (excluding those having a no-mail-queries policy) are:

> Albury Family History Group
> P.O. Box 822
> Albury, NSW
> Australia

> Broken Hill Family History Group
> P.O. Box 779
> Broken Hill, NSW 2880
> Australia

The two Victoria state genealogical societies, the Genealogical Society of Victoria and the Australian Institute of Genealogical Studies, Inc., do not respond to mail queries. However, the following regional societies in areas known to have Germans are believed to be willing to accept queries:

> Bendigo Regional Genealogical Society, Inc.
> P.O. Box 1049
> Bendigo, Vic 3550
> Australia

> Hamilton Family History Centre
> P.O. Box 179
> Hamilton, Vic 3300
> Australia

> Wimmera Association for Genealogy
> P.O. Box 880
> Horsham, Vic 3402
> Australia

The Genealogical Society of Tasmania has five branches, but the one in Hobart, where most of the few Germans live, does not answer queries. Neither does the Australian Jewish Genealogical Society (with an unknown number of Australians who had German-speaking immigrant ancestors). Nevertheless, there are quite a few publications that should provide clues about this number. The one appearing to have the greatest genealogical value is H. A. Cohen, *Resource Manual for Australian Jewish Genealogy* (Melbourne: Australian Jewish Historical Society, 1982). It is possible that the various state branches of the Australian Jewish Historical Society might answer queries.

Heather E. Garnsey and Martyn C. H. Killion have compiled two directories of genealogical societies, both published by the Australasian Federation of Family History Organisations in Sydney:

- *AFFHO Directory of Genealogical Organisations in Australasia* (1992)
- *AFFHO Directory of Member Organisations* (1993)

Civil Registers

Civil registers began early enough to include records on most of the Germanic immigrants, although they would not cover the earliest ones in New South Wales, Queensland and South Australia. The dates when civil registration went into effect in the various states and territories are as follows:

Australian Capital Territory	1911 (mandated 1930)	New South Wales	1856
Northern Territory	1876	Queensland	1856
South Australia	1842	Tasmania	1838
Victoria	1837 (mandated 1853)	Western Australia	1841

The registers for New South Wales, as well as those for 1911-1930 for the Australian Capital Territory and for 1855-59 for Queensland (then the Moreton Bay district of New South Wales) are at:

Registry of Births, Deaths and Marriages
191-199 Thomas St.
Haymarket, NSW 2000
Australia

The repositories for the other states and territories are:

Registry of Births, Deaths and Marriages
59 King William St.
Adelaide, SA 5000
Australia

The Registrar
Births, Deaths and Marriages
Department of Property and Services
295 Queen St.
Melbourne, Vic 3000
Australia

Queensland State Archives
435 Compton Road
Runcora, Qld 4113
Australia
  (*for 1860-1890*)

Registry of Births, Deaths and Marriages
33 Herschel St.
Brisbane, Qld 3000
Australia
  (*since 1891*)

Registry of Births, Deaths and Marriages
Westralia Square
141 St. George's Terrace
Perth, WA 6000
Australia

Archives of Tasmania
91 Murray St.
Hobart, Tas 7000
Australia
  (*19th century*)

Registry of Births, Deaths and Marriages
15 Murray St.
Hobart, Tas 7000
Australia
  (*20th century*)

Registry of Births, Deaths and Marriages
Building 3
ACT Administration Centre
London Circuit & Constitution Ave.
Civic, ACT 2600
Australia
  (*since 1930*)

Registry of Births, Deaths and Marriages
Cavanaugh & Bennett Sts.
Darwin, NT 0800
Australia

Parish Registers

Parish registers may be at:

- local churches
- church archives
- the offices for civil registers
- various other archives

Vine Hill lists an archive for only one of the two Lutheran synods, viz.:

> Lutheran Church of Australia
> 101 Archer St.
> North Adelaide, SA 5006
> Australia

The addresses of various Baptist and Catholic archives are listed on pp. 480 and 482, respectively, in Vine Hill's book. *Die Zeitung* [*The Newspaper*] indicates that there were German Baptists in the Fassifern district, Marburg/Tallagala area and at Albion in Brisbane. The pertinent address is:

> Baptist Union Archives
> 26 Hall St.
> Alderley, Qld 4051
> Australia

Two publications dealing with parish registers are:

- Nick Vine Hill, *Parish Registers in Australia*, 2nd ed. (Middle Park, Australia: author, 1990)

- Rev. H. F. W. Proeve, "Lutheran Records in Australia," in Andrew G. Peake, *Genealogical Papers—1990 Genealogy Congress (Supplement)* (Adelaide: South Australian Genealogy and Heraldry Society and Guild Books, 1981)

Marriage Records

When early parish registers cannot be found, marriage licenses (preceded by a marriage declaration) and marriage banns may prove especially helpful. They can sometimes be found in the same repositories as civil registers.

Banns were required to be read in the home parishes of both bride and groom, if different, which may provide clues for further research. Ministers were supposed to keep *Registers of Banns*, as well as marriage registers.

Passenger Lists

Since there was a strong Australian connection with Hamburg, the German passenger departures lists include many German-speaking immigrants. Bear in mind that many took the indirect route via Liverpool and Plymouth in England.

Eric and Rosemary Kopittke have published seven volumes of *Emigration from Hamburg to Australia for 1860-69*, one volume being the index. The series was published by the Queensland Family History Society, Inc., Indooroopilly, in 1991-93.

Many pre-1900 passenger arrival lists have been published and often filmed, or they are available in manuscript form. Newspapers also published such information. However, sometimes only the surnames are mentioned and even this is not always the case for passengers in steerage. Many Germans came to Australia as "assisted immigrants," i.e., they received free passage, in the early period. There are many publications and some indexes relating to these.

Monographs by Clifford Neal Smith and Charles M. Hall list the names of passengers on those fragments of the Bremen and Antwerp records that have been preserved, including quite a few who went to Australia. They are especially useful for the "Old Lutherans" who constituted the first significant group of immigrants to Australia.

Another source with exquisite detail about the early immigration and settlements of the "Old Lutherans" is A. Brauer, *Under the Southern Cross—History of the Evangelical Lutheran Church of Australia* (Adelaide: Lutheran Publishing House, 1956). This book begins with the voyages of the first group of Lutherans, led by Pastor A.L.C. Kavel, to emigrate to South Australia in 1838 and 1839 aboard the ships *Prairie George*, *Bengalee*, *Zebra* and *Catharina*. About 500 "Old Lutherans" emigrated from the district of Zuellichau in East Brandenburg (just north of Silesia) and a neighboring area of Posen, boarded barges to Hamburg and then boarded ships to Port Adelaide via Plymouth. They initially settled near Adelaide in towns such as Hahndorf, Klemzig, Lobethal, Bethany and Hoffnungstal. They were employed as farmers, shepherds and sheepshearers. Later chapters cover settlements of Lutherans in other areas of Australia. This book indicates that passenger lists of many of the ships carrying Lutheran immigrants are available from archives of the Evangelical Lutheran Church of Australia.

Naturalization Records

A very high percentage of male German immigrants became naturalized, since this carried with it the right to own land. The documents relating to this process include the name, place of birth or residence prior to emigration, length of residence in Australia, age and occupation. The problem is that these are scattered among many archives. However, a review of the pertinent information in Vine Hill's book should lead you to the right depository.

Other Records

Among the Australian records that are significant for genealogists, the following deserve particular mention: biographical and genealogical dictionaries, cemetery records (for on-site research), personal name changes (which were common because of the strong anti-German sentiment during and after World War II), various kinds of directories (especially those listing residents, similar to U.S. city directories and county atlases), electoral rolls (voting is mandatory in Australia), published genealogies and genealogical directories, the records of hospitals and asylums (which were essentially poorhouses in earlier times), land records, and the published and unpublished material of local historical societies.

Newspapers

There were numerous German-language newspapers, which often merged in order to survive. W. D. Borrie lists the *Südaustralische Zeitung* [*The South Australian Newspaper*] (Adelaide), the *Australische Zeitung* [*The Australian Newspaper*] (Melbourne and Tanunda), and the *Queenslander Herald* as of lasting significance. In view of the rapid assimilation of many Germans and the scattered nature of Germanic settlements in many areas, local English-language newspapers may be equally valuable. *Newspapers in Australia: A Union Catalog*, with the 4th edition published by the National Library of Australia, Canberra, in 1985, may help identify where the various newspapers are stored.

Gazetteers

A Geographical Dictionary or Gazetteer of the Australian Colonies, 1848 (facsimile edition by the Council of Libraries of New South Wales, Sydney, 1970; republished by the Library Council of Victoria, Melbourne, 1991, and available on microfiche) is valuable for the German settlements established during the first decade. Robert P. Whitoworth prepared a series, *Baillier's ... Gazetteer and Road Guide*, for each colony (Melbourne: F. F. Bailliere, 1865-77). *Gazetteer No. 40: Australia* (Washington: Department of the Interior, 1957) is a standard gazetteer of modern Australia. You will have to find the many place name changes elsewhere, for example, in the W. D. Borrie and J. Lyng books, which give quite a few examples, but are not comprehensive.

Record Repositories

The Australian Archives has its national headquarters in Canberra, but nineteenth-century materials will often be found in the branch archives in each state. Each state has its own state archives. There are also a large number of religious, local, university and specialized archives. Vine Hill has an extensive list of addresses. Published material (and possibly other records) can be found at the:

> National Library of Australia
> Parkes Place
> Canberra, ACT 2600
> Australia

A great deal of valuable material also exists in the various state libraries. The following library is of particular significance for German-Australians:

> Mortlock Library of South Australia
> State Library of South Australia
> Jervois Wing
> North Terrace
> Adelaide, SA 5000
> Australia

For further information on genealogical records and the addresses of repositories, check Nick Vine Hill's voluminous, detailed guide.

NEW ZEALAND

Several books listed under Australia, particularly the following, also include information about New Zealand:

- Owen B. Mutzelburg, *How to Trace Your German Ancestors: A Guide for Australians and New Zealanders* (Sydney: Hale & Iremonger, 1989)

- Heather E. Garnsey and Martyn C. H. Killion, comps., *AFFHO Directory of Genealogical Organisations in Australasia* (Sydney: Australasian Federation of Family History Organisations, 1992)

- Heather E. Garnsey and Martyn C. H. Killion, comps., *AFFHO Directory of Member Organisations* (Sydney: Australasian Federation of Family History Organisations, 1993)

Genealogical Societies

For information relating specifically to the genealogy of continental (as contrasted to British) ancestors, contact:

> Graham Clark, Secretary
> European Interest Group
> 1/2 Islington St.
> Ponsonby
> Auckland 1002
> New Zealand

The addresses of the national society and its Canterbury (South Island) Group are:

New Zealand Society of Genealogists P.O. Box 8795 Auckland New Zealand	New Zealand Society of Genealogists Canterbury Group c/o Miss M. Corsar 4/32 Elizabeth St. Christchurch New Zealand

Civil Registers

Birth and death records have been maintained since 1848 and marriage records since 1854. Information from civil registers can be obtained from:

Registrar-General
Births, Deaths and Marriages
P.O. Box 31115
Lower Hutt
New Zealand

Births, Deaths and Marriages Auckland
City Registry
Justice Departmental Building
Kingston St.
Auckland
New Zealand
(for the city of Auckland)

Passenger Lists

The Hamburg passenger lists are important, since many of the German-speaking emigrants embarked there. So, to some extent, are the Australian port arrival and departure records, considering the significant amount of migration between these countries, especially during the gold rushes of the mid-nineteenth century. New Zealand arrivals are covered under archival records.

Archives and Archival Records

The addresses of the National Archives and its regional offices are:

National Archives
10 Mulgrave St.
P.O. Box 12050
Wellington
New Zealand

Auckland Regional Office
B. J. Ball Building
Hardinge St.
P.O. Box 91220
Auckland 1
New Zealand

Christchurch Regional Office
90 Peterborough St.
P.O. Box 1308
Christchurch
New Zealand

Dunedin Regional Office
556 George St.
P.O. Box 6183
Dunedin
New Zealand

The National Archives has brochures on the *National Archives Record Groups* and on *Card Indexes at National Archives*. According to these, the records in Wellington include:

- shipping index (1840-ca. 1960s; incomplete after 1910), by ship
- assisted immigration index (ca. 1871-1888)—photocopies of lists of immigrants whose fare was paid by others
- records of the Immigration Department, 1870-1911
- notices of intention to marry, 1856-1956
- records of the Registrar-General of Births, Deaths and Marriages since 1856
- records of the Alien Registration Branch, 1915-77
- records of the Electoral Department since 1865
- records of the Social Security Department since 1883
- various archival records for Samoa that may be relevant for Germanic genealogical research in that former New Zealand mandate, 1879-1933
- private papers of a number of prominent New Zealanders bearing German names.

A booklet on *Genealogical Sources at National Archives, Auckland* lists:

- Auckland ship arrivals (not indexed), 1909, 1915-65
- Port of Wellington entry records, 1856-87
- records for Puhoi or the "German settlement," 1863-66
- various indexed probate and intestate records, 1842-1973
- some old age pension records (1896-1910)
- widow's pension records (1916-17)
- school class lists (1879-1953), including private schools since 1903

A Brief Guide to Family History Sources at National Archives Christchurch Office as of 1 September 1993 indicates the non-current official records of the Canterbury and Westland regions there include:

- probate files (1855-1979)
- maternity records (1876-1981)
- shipping papers, including passenger lists, for Canterbury (1850-84)
- Canterbury school records, including names and ages of students (also for schools that have closed)

The National Archives also has a three-page list of "Addresses for Genealogical Research in New Zealand," which may be helpful, especially with respect to specific areas or specific groups of people.

The records mentioned above may be incomplete, because in some cases they cover only certain areas and in others, there are gaps. Moreover, we have combined some of the listings for related records.

Family History at National Archives (Allen & Unwin, NZ Ltd., 1990) and its successor, "Beyond the Book," provide more comprehensive information about the archives' holdings and are available from the archives.

The National Archives offers written research services at various levels, but with some restrictions on the number of requests for basic research and a fee for all overseas research. Prepayment is not required for basic research (for example, a duplicated copy of a specific entry in a census, register, etc.), but is required for more extensive research.

Other Records and Sources

Land records are housed at:

> Lands & Deeds Registry
> Price Waterhouse Centre
> 41 Federal St.
> Auckland
> New Zealand

Church records for Catholics are at:

> Catholic Archives
> c/o Records Pompalier Centre
> Auckland Catholic Diocese
> Private Bag
> Auckland
> New Zealand

> Roman Catholic Diocese of Christchurch
> Archives
> c/o Rev. K. Clark
> 42 Douglas St.
> Timaru
> New Zealand

We do not have an address for Lutheran archives in New Zealand, but presumably the European Interest Group of the New Zealand Society of Genealogists can provide information as to the whereabouts of any Lutheran archives or registers.

Published books and other publications. Information about or from published books and other publications is available from:

> National Library of New Zealand
> Reference Service
> P.O. Box 1467
> Wellington
> New Zealand

Judith Williams of Puhoi provided information about a multi-purpose group, the Bohemian Association Originating in Puhoi-Ohaupo, which publishes the *Homeland News* (which is mostly of a local nature). The editor is:

Mrs. C. Krippner
Te Rore RD 6
Te Awamatu
New Zealand

A list of early German settlers on the west coast of South Island, including places and dates of birth, is available from:

Mrs. Jill Robinson
P.O. Box 48
Reefton 7853
New Zealand

FORMER GERMAN COLONIES AND PROTECTORATES

The only former German possession where a substantial number of German descendants can be found is Samoa, where registration began prior to the German occupation. For civil records, write to:

Registrar General
Justice Department
P.O. Box 49
Apia
Samoa

Prior to World War I, many Pacific islands, including (besides Samoa), the Solomon Islands, the Mariana Islands (except Guam), and the Marshall Islands, belonged to Germany. The German population was small. However, there was enough of a German settlement at one time to establish a German church in Pohnpei. It is not known whether any church records have survived. The Embassy of Micronesia might know of any archives or historical society that might have pertinent records. Alternatively, you could try writing to the office responsible for civil registration:

Clerk of Courts
State of Pohnpei, FSM
P.O. Box 1449
Kolonia, Pohnpei, ECI 96941
Micronesia

New Guinea was divided among the Dutch, British and Germans prior to World War I. There were quite a few missionaries and related staff in the German portion, but we know of no permanent German settlement.

The former German and British protectorates now form Papua New Guinea. The German portion became an Australian mandate after World War I. Nick Vine Hill's book (see **AUSTRALIA**) lists a number of addresses and resources for this region, in case you should want to explore whether any records pertaining to Germans have been preserved.

AFRICA

SOUTH AFRICA

Our information comes from the *Guide to Genealogical Research in the State Archives* and other information provided by the Transvaal Archives Depot, State Archives and Heraldic Services, Department of Arts, Culture, Science and Technology, Private Bag X236, Pretoria 0001, South Africa. This also included the table of contents of R. T. J. Lombard, *Handbook for Genealogical Research in South Africa*, 2nd ed. (Pretoria: Human Sciences Research Council, 1990), as well as some addresses listed in it. Lombard's book also covers Namibia and Zimbabwe. The Transvaal Archives Depot is, in fact, also the national government archives, not only the archives for that province.

Parish Registers

These are housed at the various church archives and State Archives Depots. Lutheran registers are at:

> The Secretary
> United Lutheran Church
> P.O. Box 873
> Edenvale
> 1610
> South Africa

Many of the early German settlers probably joined the Reformed church. There are Dutch Reformed Church (*Nederduitse Gereformeerde Kerk*) Archives Depots in Pretoria, Cape Town, Bloemfontein and Pietermaritzburg. The other branches of the Reformed church (which use no English name) have only one archive each. The addresses of the pertinent archives for the Cape Province are:

> The Archivist
> Nederduitse Gereformeerde Kerk
> P.O. Box 3171
> Cape Town
> 8000
> South Africa
> (*location: Church Centre, Gray's Pass*)

> The Archivist
> Nederduitse Hervormde Kerk
> P.O. Box 2368
> Pretoria
> 0001
> South Africa
> (*location: 224 Jacob Maré St.*)

> The Archivist
> Gereformeerde Kerk
> P.O. Box 20004
> Noordbrug
> Potschefstroom
> 2520
> South Africa

The address for the state archives for Cape Province is:

> The Chief
> Cape Archives Depot
> Private Bag X9025
> Cape Town
> 8000
> South Africa

For information from microfilmed copies of pre-1900 church registers for Cape Colony, write to:

> Section Genealogical Information
> Human Science Research Council Library
> Private Bag 41X
> Pretoria
> 0001
> South Africa

To view these in person, you have to make an advance appointment and pay a fee for the use of a microfilm reader.

The Transvaal Archives Depot also has the parish registers of the Dutch Reformed Church of the Cape Colony for 1665-1845.

Civil Registers

Birth registers (*Geboorteregisters*) are closed for a period of 100 years. Marriage registers (*Huweliksregisters*) are closed for 30 years. There is no restriction on access to death registers (*Sterfteregisters*). For information from civil registers, write to:

> Registrar of Births, Marriages, and Deaths
> Department of Home Affairs
> Private Bag X114
> Pretoria
> 0001
> South Africa

Other Records

Lombard, in his chapter on "Repositories of Genealogical Sources," lists the following kind of records at the Cape Archives Depot that might be of genealogical value for Germanic research: Master of the Supreme Court (1673-1928), British Kaffraria, Immigration Board of Port Elizabeth (1858-1862), Immigration Board of Cape Town (1858-1861), and Immigration Agent of Cape Town (1878-1885), with the dates supplied by the state archives in Pretoria.

He also lists the following records for the national government archives in Pretoria: Orphan Master (1873-1974), Chief Immigration Officer (1907-1912), and European and Indian Immigration (1857-1911).

Immigration and naturalization records are housed at the State Archives Depots and at the:

> Department of Home Affairs
> Private Bag X114
> Pretoria
> 0001
> South Africa

Wills, probate and orphan records are in the custody of the various Masters of the Supreme Court. For the western Cape Province, this would be the Orphan Master, Private Bag X9018, Cape Town 8000. For the eastern Cape Province, this would be the Orphan Master, Private Bag X1010, Grahamstown 6140. However, such records are regularly transferred to the State Archives Depots, so the Cape Archives Depot (or others, for the few Germans who lived elsewhere) would have the older ones, which are generally more useful for genealogy.

Microfilmed copies of the pre-1919 Cape estate files are at the Transvaal Archives Depot. Some estate documents are also in the various Magistrates Archives.

Land records are in the custody of the various Deeds Offices: for the western Cape, the Registrar of Deeds, P.O. Box 703, Cape Town 8000; for eastern Cape Province, the Registrar of Deeds, Private Bag X7402, King William's Town 5600. Tax records are not accessible to the public.

Military records for after 1912 can be accessed through:

> Director
> Directorate Documentation Service
> South African National Defence Force
> Private Bag X289
> Pretoria
> 0001
> South Africa

However, the Transvaal Archives Depot has Red Cross and casualty records for the Anglo-Boer War.

A particularly relevant book for Germanic genealogy is J. Hoge, *Personalia of the Germans at the Cape, 1652-1896*. The overwhelming majority of the Germans lived in Cape Province.

Genealogical Societies and Services

No specifically Germanic society in South Africa has been identified. The address for the national society that we received in the letter from the South African archives is:

> The National Secretary
> Genealogical Society of South Africa
> P.O. Box 2119
> Houghton
> 2041
> South Africa

Presumably the addresses of any state or regional genealogical societies could be obtained from this source.

Published books and records are available at:

> The State Library (legal deposit library)
> P.O. Box 397
> Pretoria
> 0001
> South Africa

> South African Library
> Queen Victoria St.
> Cape Town
> 8001
> South Africa

Non-genealogical institutions that might be able to provide helpful contacts for Germanic genealogy include:

> German Language and Cultural Institute
> 93 Lynburn Road
> Lynnwood Manor
> 0081
> South Africa

> Huguenot Memorial Museum
> P.O. Box 37
> Franschhoek
> 7690
> South Africa

> Kaffrarian Historical Society
> P.O. Box 1434
> King William's Town
> 5600
> South Africa

> South African-German Cultural
> Association
> P.O. Box 70944
> Die Wilgers, Pretoria
> 0041
> South Africa
> (*publishes journal titled Brucka*)

Ken V. André of the South African-German Cultural Association (who was our only non-archival source in South Africa) has written a 500-page genealogical study of about 250 Kaffrarian German families.

Key books for research in South Africa include:

An Alphabetical Guide to Gravestones in Smaller Cemeteries in South Africa, 28 vols. Pretoria. 1989-1993.

C. C. De Villiers and C. Pama. *Genealogies of Old South African Families*, 2 parts. Cape Town. 1981.

J. A. Heese and R. T. J. Lombard. *South African Genealogies*, 4 parts (1986-1992); continuing series.

J. Hoge. "Personalia of the Germans at the Cape, 1652-1806," in Coenraad Beyers et al (eds.), *Archives Year Book for South African History*, 9th year. Published by authority of the Minister of the Interior and printed by the Cape Times Ltd., Cape Town, for the Government Printer.

R. T. J. Lombard. *Handbook for Genealogical Research in South Africa*, 2nd ed. Pretoria: Human Sciences Research Council. 1990. 119 pp. + bibliography.

L. Zöllner. *The Descendants of Rhenish Missionaries to South Africa*. Pretoria. 1991.

L. Zöllner and J. A. Heese. *The Berlin Missionaries in South Africa*. Pretoria. 1984.

FORMER GERMAN COLONIES AND PROTECTORATES

For records pertaining to the former German South-West Africa, try writing to:

> Vital Registration Department
> Government House
> Windhoek
> Namibia

Lombard mentions that estate documents, newspapers, and military records are available in the Namibian archives.

For records pertaining to the former German East Africa, try writing to:

> Registrar General
> Ministry of Justice
> Office of the Administrator General
> P.O. Box 9183
> Dar-es-Salaam
> Tanzania

To get information about the location of any possible records in what became French mandates in West Africa after World War I, write to the Consular Section of the Embassy of the country in question. Alternatively, you could write to the offices in charge of civil registers (which did not exist at the time of German occupation, or began at the very end of it) in the hope that your letter would be forwarded to the appropriate archives or other offices. The addresses for these are:

> Ministre de l'Administration
>   Territoriale
> B.P. 7854
> Yaounde
> Cameroon

> Division des Affaires Politiques et
>   Administratives
> Ministre de l'Interieur
> Lome
> Togo

NORTH AFRICA

Algeria began civil registration for the northern areas, where almost all German settlers would have lived, in 1882. Civil registers were established in the south, where Germans might have served in the French Foreign Legion, in 1905, but it is more likely that any pertinent records would be in France than in Algeria.

Vital records can be requested from:

> Service d'État Civil des Communes
> Ministre de l'Interieur
> Alger
> Algeria

Births and deaths have been recorded in Egypt since 1839, but marriages were exclusively the province of ecclesiastical authorities. Civil records may be requested from:

> Department of Civil Registration
> Ministry of Interior
> Abassia, Cairo
> Egypt

Published and other documentary materials can be found at:

> National Library and Archives
> Corniche El-Nil Street
> Boulac, Cairo
> Egypt

Civil registration of Europeans in Morocco began in 1915. For records of births and deaths, contact:

> Chef
> Division d'État Civil
> Ministre de l'Interieur
> Rabat
> Morocco

Marriage records were kept exclusively by ecclesiastical authorities.

However, unless you can get your letters translated into Arabic or French (except Egypt), you are more likely to receive a reply from the Consular Section of the pertinent Embassy.

ASIA

Only two Asian countries had significant German settlement. China and Turkey had several thousand Germans each. This, of course, excludes the Asian portions of what was first the Russian Empire, then the Soviet Union and now the Commonwealth of Independent States. (See the section on **EAST AND SOUTH EUROPE** for the latter.)

CHINA

There are hundreds of pages of material on the Soviet German Lutheran refugees who fled via Siberia to Harbin (German: *Charbin*), Manchuria, dealing with arranging their resettlement in the Americas, at:

> Evangelical Lutheran Church of America Archives
> 5400 Milton Parkway
> Rosemont, IL 60018

These records include the names of many of the refugees, as well as letters and articles from the Nansen International Office for Refugees, functioning under the auspices of the League of Nations in Geneva.

Also included are records pertaining to food drafts sent to the Black Sea and Volga areas in 1921-23, including the names of the recipients and senders (who were relatives in many cases).

The archives is not in a position to answer queries, but researchers are welcome to use the archives.

The Northern Illinois Chapter of the American Historical Society of Germans from Russia has copied the following records:

- Group RG-2: Boxes 3, 4, 7, 8, 12, 17, 19, 20, 22, 23
- Group 3A: Boxes 14, 19, 23, 28, 33, 35, 36, 38, 41, 42, 43, 45, 46, 47, 49, 50, 51, 65

A copy of this material is now in the hands of the head office of AHSGR in Lincoln, which has a board member translating pertinent excerpts for publication.

A lot of research on the Mennonite refugees who were in Harbin is being done by:

> Dr. Wilmer Harms
> 2904-13 Ivy Drive
> North Newton, KS 67117

The Harbin refugees and their descendants (or at least those in North America) hold reunions every four years, so they constitute a tightly knit group. The contact person for the 1995 Harbin Reunion Committee is:

Nick Friesen
296 E. Curtis Ave.
Reedley, CA 93654

H. P. Isaak, *Our Life Story and Escape: From Russia to China to Japan to America* (Dinuba, CA: author, 1977), is a 181-page account of the flight of one group of Mennonite refugees, including the names.

Another book, *Immer weiter nach Osten: Südrussland-China-Kanada* [*Ever Farther Eastwards: South Russia-China-Canada*], by Abram J. Loewen chronicles the story of those refugees who ended up in Canada.

Records for Catholic refugees are at the Russian archives in Saratov and Engels.

The Summer 1994 issue of *Avotaynu* carried an article by Dr. Jonathan Goldstein on "Consular Records in Shanghai about Jewish Refugees," based on visits with Polish, Russian and American consular officials.

Copies of the Polish consular log book for citizens who passed through Shanghai or Nanjing between 1934 and 1941 (mentioned by Goldstein) are now in the Library of Congress and at the Sino-Judaic Archives of the Hoover Institution at Stanford. Dr. Ristaino of the Library of Congress is preparing an article on the book's usefulness.

The following institute is dedicated to the study of Jews in China, which presumably also includes some German Jews who were involved with commerce in Jiaozhou (*Kiautschou*) during the period when Germany had a lease on it (1898-99 to World War I):

Prof. Albert Dien, President
Sino-Judaic Institute
2316 Blueridge Ave.
Menlo, Park, CA 94025

Prof. Dien estimates that there are several thousand unindexed names in the Polish register mentioned by Goldstein, which sometimes includes such notes as "emigrant from Russia."

The Russian vice-consul indicated that all pertinent records had been sent to the Russian Central Archives in Moscow. He recommended the following two Russian-language books:

(1) V. D. Jiganoff, *Russians in Shanghai* (Shanghai, ca. 1930); and

(2) Natalya Ilyana, *Roads to Return* (Moscow, ca. 1952), which deals with the refugees in Harbin.

Any pertinent Chinese records are likely to be at the city level, especially in Harbin and Shanghai. Contact the Consular Section of the Chinese Embassy for further information.

TURKEY (ASIA MINOR)

Look under **TURKEY** in the section on **EAST AND SOUTH EUROPE** for any pertinent information concerning possible records pertaining to Germans.

SOUTH ASIA, MALAY PENINSULA, MALAY ARCHIPELAGO (EAST INDIES OR EAST INDIA)

The Portuguese, Dutch, English (later British), Danes, French and Swedes all formed East India (or East Indies) Companies to engage in what later become European (mostly British and Dutch) colonies and protectorates in Asia. This was generally accompanied by military and political dominion, although the home governments assumed this non-commercial role in time.

Of greatest interest for Germanic genealogy is the Dutch East India Co., which had many Germans in its service. It was established in 1598, joined with other companies to form a monopoly in 1602, and colonized the Cape of Good Hope (**SOUTH AFRICA**) in 1650-70.

In the seventeenth century it became dominant in what is now **INDONESIA**, although it did not conquer Java until 1750 and some outlying islands until the nineteenth century.

From 1658 to 1796 it was in control of present-day **SRI LANKA** (earlier called **CEYLON**). In a struggle following a 1654 incident, England temporarily lost control of all of its East Indies possessions to the Dutch. In 1663 the Netherlands won control of the Malabar coast of **INDIA** (roughly Kerala state) from the Portuguese. It even held **TAIWAN** briefly (1658-61).

Although few Germans are likely to have remained in these Asian areas permanently, it is possible that there may be some genealogical information on Germans in the archival records of the Dutch East India Co., now kept at:

Rijksarchiefdienst
Prins Willem Alexanderhof 20
2595 BE The Hague
Netherlands
(street location)

Rijksarchiefdienst
P.O. Box 90520
2509 LM The Hague
Netherlands
(mailing address)

The British East India Co. became dominant in what later became British India, the Malay Peninsula and part of the Malay Archipelago of islands (chiefly Borneo) in the last half of the seventeenth century, although it lost its political power to the British government a century later. Brunei and parts of India were ruled by local princes, but were really British protectorates.

This area constitutes **INDIA, PAKISTAN, BANGLADESH, MYANMAR** (formerly **BURMA**), **MALAYSIA, SINGAPORE**, and **BRUNEI** today.

Since many of the soldiers discharged from the (English) King's German Legion after the Crimean War chose to serve in **INDIA**, at least for a while, in preference to settling down as farmers in **SOUTH AFRICA**, there may be some pertinent information on them in the records of the British Colonial Office at:

Public Record Office
Kew
Richmond, Surrey
England TW9 4DU

It is considerably less likely that Germans served in the Portuguese, French, Danish or Swedish East India Companies (of which only the French company had a prolonged and major effect on the area), but it is conceivable that there could be rare instances of such service. Anyone inclined to pursue this remote possibility should contact the National Archives of the respective countries.

Chapter VII

PERSONAL NAMES

Once you have identified your immigrant ancestor using records in the country of immigration, you need to determine what his or her name was in Germany or elsewhere in Europe. Both the given name and the surname may have been changed during migration or later. For example, one factor was the change in language when migrating to another country; another was the anti-German hysteria that occurred in the United States and other Allied countries during World War I. This chapter will give you clues about the possible German spelling of the name. It also describes different types of German names.

Spelling variations are common in German surnames since German spelling wasn't standardized until the 1800s after surnames had already been established. The local German spoken dialect also had an impact on what surnames were used and how they were spelled. When researching older records, consider all possible spelling variations for a given surname. Usually the different spellings will have the same pronunciation.

Sometimes the name may have an ending added to it to indicate the possessive (genitive) case. This ending might be *-s*, *-n*, *-en* or *-ens*.

Common themes to look for in spelling variations are:

- *h* is a silent letter, unless it is the first letter of a syllable. It may be present in some names and missing in others. Standard spelling in the nineteenth century was *th* where only *t* would be used today.

- Some letters have the same sound and are interchangeable.

  i - y   *c - k*   *f - v*   *ei - ai*   *z - tz - ts*

- Other letters may have the same sound at the end of a word or syllable.

  d - t   *b - p*   *g - k*   *g - ch*

- Consonants may be single or double.

- Long vowels may be single or double, or they may be followed by an *h*.

- Short vowels may sound similar and may be interchanged.

  ä - e   *ü - i*   *ö - e*

GERMAN SURNAMES AND ANGLICIZED VERSIONS

German language surnames usually belong to one of four categories: patronymic, occupational, locational or descriptive. Surnames began to appear in parts of Switzerland in the 11th century. Their usage began around 1100 in Germany, first in the cities and then gradually spreading from southwestern German areas to the north and east. By 1600 surnames were in common usage throughout German speaking areas. However, many people continued to change their surnames from generation to generation, or even within their own lifetime. These surnames became permanent by decree between 1670 and the early 1800s depending on the German state. These decrees required surnames to be permanently attached to a family. The last regions to require permanent surnames were Schleswig-Holstein and Ostfriesland (East Frisia), where patronymic naming practices predominated, and Lippe.

PATRONYMIC AND MATRONYMIC NAMES

At one time patronymic naming practices were common in the northern and northwestern part of Germany. They continued in Schleswig-Holstein until the late 18th century and in the Ostfriesland (East Frisia) region until the early 19th century and in some cases as late as the middle part of that century.

Patronymic naming practices mean that the son or daughter derived his or her surname from the first name of the father, e.g.,

Father:	Friedrich Johannsen	Harm Simons	Fokke Hindriks
Son:	Karl Friedrichsen	Geerd Harms	Jan Fokken
Grandchild:	Hans Karlsen	Jeeljes Geerds	Udda Janssen

The most common surname endings are *s, es* and *(s)sen*. However, if the first name was Johan, the surname derived from that may be Johannsen or Janssen.

These patronymic names generally changed each generation. It became increasingly difficult for government agencies to fully identify individuals. This led to a decree outlawing the use of patronymics, first in Schleswig-Holstein (ca. 1770) and later in East Frisia (1811). However, many families delayed adopting a surname until well beyond these dates.

In some cases, the changes brought inconsistencies in the name that was used in the records. An example is Stientje Jeeljes Jacobs, the daughter of Jeeljes Geerds and Antje Abrams Janssen. At her birth in 1808, she was given the name of her maternal grandmother, Stientje Jacobs. Her marriage record in 1832 refers to her as Stientje Jacobs but later the same year she is called Stientje Jeeljes in the record for the birth of her first child. In subsequent records she is again called Stientje Jacobs. By her death in 1893 she was called Stientje Jeeljes Jacobs. The use of Jacobs is an example of the rare practice of matronymics.

In a few cases, to assure that a man's children were identified as his, all children (male or female) were given the father's first name as their middle name. As an example, between 1815 and 1850 Ede Reints Karsjens had 10 children. Nine of these children were given Eden as a middle name. The only exception was the first son who was named after the maternal grandfather and was called Ewe Mennen Karsjens. All ten of Ede's children were named after parents, grandparents and great grandparents. This can be important to keep in mind as you look for relationships and possible lineage in the patronymic system.

Searching for your ancestors with patronymic names does not have to be insurmountable. Valuable sources of information include microfilmed church records, *Ortssippenbücher* and *Deutsche Geschlechterbücher*. *Ortssippenbücher* are books that contain genealogies of families living in a specific village. Much of this information has been taken from church records. Over 20 *Ortssippenbücher* have been published for Ostfriesland. They are also available for some villages from other parts of Germany. New *Ortssippenbücher* continue to be published by German genealogists. The *Deutsche Geschlechterbücher* is a collection of over 200 volumes containing family genealogies for prominent German families and nobility. Further information about *Ortssippenbücher* and *Geschlechterbücher* may be found in Wolfgang Ribbe and Eckart Henning's *Taschenbuch für Familiengeschichtsforschung* [*Handbook for Family History Research*]. *Bibliographie der Ortssippenbücher in Deutschland* [*Bibliography of Village Histories in Germany*], by Franz Heinzmann, lists more than 6,000 of these books.

Although many surnames elsewhere in Germany had a patronymic derivation, it is unlikely that you will find generation-to-generation changes in other areas of Germany during the modern era.

SURNAMES DERIVED FROM OCCUPATIONS, LOCATIONS AND DESCRIPTIONS

Occupational surnames are very common in Germany. These evolved when people were named for the trade they performed. Later, when family members no longer performed these trades the surnames still remained. Examples of these can be found in the German vocabulary section of this book listing occupations (see Chapter XVII).

Many surnames are derived from locations. There are several different kinds of such names. Surnames from places might refer to a general area of origin, a specific village of origin, or some geographic aspect of the local place of residence.

Examples of those names referring to a general area of origin are:

Oesterreich	someone from Austria (Österreich)
Bayer	someone from from Bavaria (Bayern)
Weser	someone from the Weser river area
Schweitzer	someone from Switzerland
Hesse	someone from Hesse
Issel	someone from the Issel (lower Rhine) river area

Examples of a specific locality are:

Wiener	someone from Vienna (Wien)
Neukirch	someone from Neukirch
Bremer	someone from Bremen
Bessler, Bässler	someone from Basel
Kandel	someone from the village of Kandel
Frankfurter	someone from Frankfurt

Surnames from a small village usually meant that these people had originated in a nearby area, whereas those derived from a large city, state or region suggest the family may have come from relatively far away. For example, there were many Schweitzers in Alsace and the Palatinate, all usually stemming from one original migrant.

Examples based on local, non-place name features include:

Ambach, Bachmann	by the river
Bergmann, Amberg, Berger	on the mountain
Eichenhof, Eichhoff	oak farm

In a few areas, farms sometimes were, and still are, named after the man who initially established them. In earlier periods, when a son-in-law acquired a farm (or sometimes even when unrelated people bought them), the new owner might be referred to by either his surname at birth, or the name of the farm during his lifetime, or both. In some cases, the farm name became the permanent surname.

People moved for a variety of reasons. Residents of regions not greatly affected by the Thirty Years' War often moved to seriously devastated areas after 1648 to fill the vacant farms and repopulate the area. Journeymen often had to relocate if they wished to become masters of their trades, since the guilds strictly limited the number of master craftsmen in various localities (usually only one per village). Some people migrated for religious, personal or business reasons.

Such people were often known by the place from which they came. In fact, it is possible that their ancestors had moved several generations before the adoption of surnames, but oral history had preserved the place of origin.

Descriptive surnames are also prevalent in Germany. These may have originally described the person or may have been a nickname. Examples are:

short	Kurz	black	Schwarz, Schwartz
small	Klein	white	Weiss
tall	Lang, Lange	strong	Starke

Many such surnames reflected a temperamental or behavioral, rather than physical, characteristic. Examples: Wohlgemuth (good-natured), Esser (glutton), Schabbe (skinflint), Stolzmann (proud man). There are many names denoting drunkard or fighter.

Many surnames are in a particular dialect. This may help identify where the name originated. Germany has many dialects. The two major divisions are Low German, or *Plattdeutsch* (spoken in northern Germany where the altitude is low), and High German (actually a collection of dialects), spoken in the southern part of Germany and Austria. These dialects are very difficult for non-speakers of the dialect to understand, and contain many different pronunciations for the same words. Moreover, the Swiss dialect (*Schwyzerdütsch*) is quite different from dialects in Germany. The official German language is often referred to as High German (although it is actually based on Middle German), but Germans are more likely to refer to it as *Schuldeutsch* (school German) or *Schriftdeutsch* (written German). The standardization of the German language began with Martin Luther and continued through the nineteenth century.

Dialects use different words to describe the same thing and have different spellings and pronunciations of the same words. Ernest Thode's *Atlas for Germanic Genealogy* contains maps that show the approximate location where certain German names originated. Jürgen Eichhoff's research, summarized by Kevin Tvedt in the January/February 1990 issue of the *GGSA Bulletin*, provides further detail. For example, a butcher might be called the following, in different areas:

Fleischer	Fleischhacker	Fleischhauer
Knochenhauer	Metzger	Schlachter

For researchers literate in German, Adolf Bach in *Deutsche Namenkunde* gives a thorough discussion of the origin and meaning of many given names, surnames and place names in the German language territory. The index alone comprises 457 pages.

Common diminutive endings of both first names and surnames (often a permanent part of the latter) had an *l*-form in the South, including Switzerland, e.g., *-l*, *-el*, *-le* and *-li* (the last being Swiss). In the north, the endings were *-ke(n)*, *-che(n)* and *-tje(n)*, the last reflecting Dutch influence. However, many Southern Germans migrated to the Northeast to lands under Prussian and Russian control, so ancestors of Southern origin may have come to America from the North. Dutch-Flemish, Oldenburg and Hannover migrants have also left name traces far to the east.

An *-in* or *-en* at the end of a surname usually referred to a woman, e.g., Mrs. Schmidt became Schmidtin. But occasionally this ending became a permanent part of the surname for both sexes, e.g., Eiselin.

The prefix *von* originally denoted a noble, e.g., Heinrich *von* (from) a particular castle. It again has that connotation in Germany today, but that was not always the case. When commoners first assumed surnames, they sometimes took the name of the noble at whose court they worked, so *von* is not proof of aristocratic lineage.

The Dutch-Flemish *van* and *ten*, as well as the French *de*, are the equivalent of *von*. They denote ethnic origin, but not necessarily of high status. However, many Huguenot refugees were nobles.

Many people from east of the Elbe River (which was occupied by Slavs in the early Middle Ages) have Slavic names or surnames with Slavic endings, even though most of them have been "German" for many centuries. This was the result of German eastward expansion and inter-ethnic marriages.

Other non-German surnames are of two types: German names that have been translated into Latin or Greek to make them sound special, or surnames from a foreign emigrant. The most common foreign names are Polish, Czech, Lithuanian or Slavic (from border areas), French (from Huguenot emigrants) or Italian (from traveling artists or tradesmen). The original foreign name may have been preserved or Germanicized or it may have been translated. For example, the Latin name Faber may have been translated to Schmidt, the German equivalent, or vice versa.

Two surnames for one person can be a challenge. These may have come about when a change in status or location occurred. Some examples: a man acquires a farm and becomes known by both his original name and the farm name, or he marries into a wealthier family (perhaps nobility) and takes the surname of the wife, or he moves to a new town and is referred to by the place name he came from. Some of these double surnames have been passed on as hyphenated names. Other times, either one of the two names may have been used only for a few years or during a person's lifetime. The use of two surnames is very rare and occurs almost exclusively in the Westfalian region.

GERMAN NAME CHANGES IN ENGLISH-SPEAKING COUNTRIES

While some families kept the original spelling of their German names, many names underwent some change when or after emigrating. German surnames had spelling changes to maintain approximately the same pronunciation in English or they may have been translated into the English equivalent meaning. Some names that are compound words may have only one part of the name translated. Others chose to change their name later, e.g., during World War I to camouflage the fact that they were of German heritage. Examples are:

German	English	Translated as:
Alsbach	Alspaugh	
Apfelbaum		Applebaum
Eisenhauer	Isenhower, Eisenhower	
Fink		Finch
Jäger	Yeger, Yaeger	Hunter
Müller	Muller, Mueller	Miller
Rahmöller		Rahmiller
Schleppi	Sleppy	
Schmidt		Smith
Schneider	Snyder	Taylor, Tailor

When *ö*, *eh* and *e* (all approximating the same vowel sound in the English "they" to the English ear) became Anglicized, they were often replaced by a "long a," e.g., Römer became Ramer. Various things happened to *Umlauts* in foreign lands, e.g., Schröder might become Schroeder, Schroder, Schrader, etc.

For more information on this subject see Arta Johnson's book, *A Guide to the Spelling and Pronunciation of German Names*.

FINDING THE NAME AND LOCATION IN EUROPE

The best way to find out whether the name is or was found in Germany or another Germanic country is to check the International Genealogical Index (IGI) at Family History Centers. Check all possible spelling variations. Because this index was compiled manually, there are occasional incorrect spellings. While it does not contain every surname that ever existed in Germanic Europe, the chances are very good that you will find the surnames of your immigrant ancestors in this enormous index. You will also find the names of many, though far from all, localities where the name was found.

If you know your ancestors spoke German, but you cannot find the name in the IGI files for Germany (which cover the entire German Empire of 1871-1919), try the less extensive files for other European countries.

Many German and German-American genealogical organizations have large surname index files. The German Research Association, with headquarters in San Diego, has recently published a particularly extensive one. See chapter XIX for its address.

German names in Southeast Europe can be found in Wilhelm and Kallbrunner, *Quellen zur deutschen Siedlungsgeschichte in Südosteuropa* [*Sourcebook for Histories of German Settlements in Southeast Europe*]. The names in this work and numerous smaller books are indexed in Bruce Brandt and Edward Reimer Brandt, *Where To Look for Your Hard-to-find German-speaking Ancestors in Eastern Europe*.

For Swiss German names, see *Handy Guide to Swiss Genealogical Records* by Jared H. Suess.

Stumpp's book on the Germans in Russia, with comprehensive name lists, is also available in English translation for help in tracing Russian Germans.

MEANING OF NAMES

There are numerous German-language books that explain the meaning of surnames and where they were first recorded. The best known one is Hans Bahlow's *Deutsches Namen-Lexikon* [*Dictionary of German Names*].

There are also numerous specialized books of this nature. Some, including other books by Bahlow, deal more exhaustively with names in a given area, e.g., Silesia. Others deal with the names found in a given religious group, e.g., Mennonites or Jews.

If you are interested in what your surname means, see *German-American Names* by George F. Jones. This book also lists many Americanized German names, which are cross-referenced to the German originals. This may be valuable in connecting your name to those which appear in the other references mentioned above.

See Alexander Beider, *A Dictionary of Jewish Surnames from the Former Russian Empire*, and *A Dictionary of Jewish Surnames from the Kingdom of Poland*, and Rabbi Shmuel Gorr, *Jewish Personal Names: Their Origin, Derivation and Diminutive Forms*, for Jewish surnames.

GERMAN GIVEN NAMES

Once you know the German surname of your ancestor, given names are how you identify individuals. A brief discussion follows, which describes some of the different types of given names in use and some of the difficulties in making a positive identification of each individual.

German given names fall into one of the following categories: wish names, Christian names or heroes, and names of rulers. Wish names are some of the oldest Germanic names and describe a wish for strength of character, e.g., Bernhard (strong as a bear), Wolfgang (speedy as a wolf) or Conrad (wise counselor). Later the church's influence on names created new wish names, e.g., Gottlieb (love of God) and Gottlob (praise God).

With the increasing influence of the Christian church, Biblical names became prevalent: Adam, Josef, Maria, Johann, Margarethe. The strong rivalry between the Catholic church and the Protestants led both of them to encourage certain types of given names, e.g., the Catholic church encouraged the use of patron saint names.

Some names became extremely popular because they were German heroes or rulers: Friedrich or Wilhelm in Prussia, Heinrich in Saxony or Franz Josef in Austria.

A person might also be known by a nickname, e.g., Josef or Joseph may be called Peppi, Jupp, Sepp or Josel. There are also spelling variations of names: Anne or Anna; Johannes, Johann, Johan, Joann, Hannes or Hans. Other examples of common variations that might be baffling to Americans are: Dietrich, Diedrich, Dieter, Dirk and Richard (rare); Georg, Jörg, Jürgen and Gerhard; Heinrich, Henrich, Hendrich and Hendrick.

Abbreviations can also be puzzling, especially when they consist of only one letter. Common ones include: M. or Mar. for Maria; Marg. for Margaretha; A. for Anna; J. or Joh. for Johann; Jos. for Josef; Chr. or Christ. for Christian (in the north) or Christoph(er) (in the south). There may be some regional variations and exceptions. A rule of thumb is that when only one letter is used as an abbreviation and there are two names to which it could apply, it almost certainly refers to the one most common in the area in question. A straight line above the letter *m* or *n* meant that one should double the letter. For example, Aña means Anna. In Catholic records, an abbreviated form with a Latin ending may be used. For example, Jões, with a tilde (wavy line) above the *o* denoting omitted letters, means Jo(hann)es.

Diminutives were used more often for women than men, at least in the north. They frequently included dropping the first syllable, as well as adding an ending. Examples are Trienke (Katharina), Stienke (Justine) and Lenke (Helena), which reflects a Dutch influence.

For more examples of spelling variations and nicknames see the chapter on "Vornamen" (Given Names) in Ribbe and Henning's *Taschenbuch für Familiengeschichtsforschung* [*Handbook for Family History Research*].

Often there were two or three or more given names for each child. Frequently one of the names was selected to honor a godparent, grandparent or other relative. When there were two or more given names, the person might be referred to by different names even in official records. This might occur by leaving out one of the given names or by reversing their sequence or perhaps due to a spelling variation.

Some given names were extremely popular. Those selected varied from place to place. It was not unusual for 50% of the boys or girls in a village to have only four to six different given names. Consequently many people were referred to by one of their other given names, usually the second name. Within a single family, five children might be named Anna or Johann. There might even be ten or more cousins with the same first and last name. Because of this duplication, often two people would have completely identical names, e.g., Johann Friedrich Kleinschmidt. Where this occurs one must be extremely careful to identify and trace the correct person as one's ancestor. If one notes each person's occupation or status, residence, parents, spouse and age along with the complete name, much (but not all) of this confusion can be avoided.

If a child died as an infant, the parents often gave the same name to another child. Because of the high infant mortality rate and the desire to preserve the first names of the parents, grandparents or other relatives, it was common in some groups for three or four children to be given the same name before one survived.

Names were often listed in two (or three, counting Latin) languages in border areas. Examples from other languages are:

- French: Jean (German: Johann), Henri (German: Heinrich), Pierre (German: Peter)
- Polish: Jan (German: Johann)
- Latin: Henricus (German: Heinrich).

ANGLICIZATION OF GERMAN GIVEN NAMES

When a German immigrant emigrated to the United States he often changed his first name to the English equivalent. This is also true in other English-speaking countries. However, if he actually went by his second given name in Europe, that name would probably be the one he would translate and use here, e.g., "Johann Heinrich" becomes "Henry." In this case it becomes more difficult to identify him in German records.

Translation of common German surnames can be done by using a large German-English dictionary. Some more common names are:

Friedrich	Fred, Frederick	Anna	Ann
Jakob	Jacob, James, Jack	Gertraud	Gertrude
Johann	John	Johanne	Joan, Joanne
Karl	Carl, Charles	Justine	Justina, Jessie
Ludwig	Louis	Katharine	Catherine
Wilhelm	William	Maria	Mary

REFERENCES (See bibliography for full citations if not shown)

Adolf Bach. *Deutsche Namenbunde*. 3 vols. Heidelberg: Carl Winter. 1952-56.

Hans Bahlow. *Deutsches Namen-Lexikon*. Frankfurt am Main, Germany. 3rd edition, 1977. [*Dictionary of German Names*]

> A handbook about the origin of German names. (Bahlow also has books concentrating on Silesian, Low German, and Mecklenburger surnames.)

Alexander Beider. *A Dictionary of Jewish Surnames from the Former Russian Empire*.

Alexander Beider. *A Dictionary of Jewish Surnames from the Kingdom of Poland*.

Elizabeth Petty Bentley. *The Genealogist's Address Book*, 3rd ed. Baltimore: Genealogical Publishing Co. 1995. 653 pp.

> Sections on "Ethnic and Religious Organizations and Resource Centers" and numerous other valuable resources. Well-indexed. Has addresses of U.S. national and state archives.

Josef Karlmann Brechenmacher. *Deutsches Namenbuch*. [*Book of German Names*]. Stuttgart: Verlag von Adold Bonz & Comp. 1928. 388 pp.

> Describes first names and surnames based on the nature of their origin, e.g., pre-Christian German names, saints' names, foreign derivation, occupations, characteristics, etc. Difficult to use for those who do not know German, because of its extensive textual material.

Albert Heintze. *Die deutschen Familien-Namen*. [*German Family Names*]. Halle a.S., Germany: Verlag der Buchhandlung des Waisenhauses. 1882. 227 pp.

> Strong on names of foreign and North German origin. By a Pomeranian teacher.

William F. Hoffman. *Polish Surnames: Origins and Meanings* (Chicago: Polish Genealogical Society of America. 1993. 295 pp.

> Contains quite a few German names and often a Polonized form.

Shmuel Gorr. *Jewish Personal Names: Their Origin, Derivation and Diminutive Forms*. Teaneck, NJ: Avotaynu, Inc. 124 pp.

Max Gottschald. *Deutsche Namenkunde*, 3rd ed. [*The Study of German Names*]. Berlin: Verlag Walter de Gruyter & Co. 1954. 630 pp.

> Deals with origin or meaning of German surnames. Strong on names of the pre-Christian era.

Arta Johnson. *A Guide to the Spelling and Pronunciation of German Names*.

George F. Jones. *German-American Names*.

Wolfgang Ribbe and Eckart Henning. *Taschenbuch für Familiengeschichtsforschung* [*Handbook for Family History Research*].

> Has a chapter on "Namenkunde" (Study of Names) and "Ältere Vornamenformen" (Old given names) with a lengthy list of old German first name variations. Lists *Ortssippenbücher* (village genealogies) and *Deutsche Geschlechterbücher* (prominent family genealogies).

Kenneth L. Smith. *German Church Books: Beyond the Basics*. Has a chapter on names.

Dr. Karl Stumpp. *The Emigration from Germany to Russia in the Years 1763-1862*.

Ernest Thode. *Atlas for Germanic Genealogy*.

Kevin Tvedt. "Using Surnames to Trace German Origin," in *GGSA Bulletin*, January/February 1990.

Chapter VIII

PLACE NAMES

This chapter gives references for many gazetteers that will help you find even the smallest German place. Many of these places are no longer within the boundaries of Germany, Austria or Switzerland. Also included are tips on how to decipher possible misspellings of place names.

FINDING LOCALITIES: GAZETTEERS AND OTHER SOURCES

If your ancestors came from a locality that is not now in a German-speaking country, you will need to obtain the current name of that place before you are likely to obtain genealogical information from the country in question. Conversely, many microfilmed records at the Family History Library in Salt Lake City may be indexed under the old German name. There are numerous sources for determining the place name.

To check whether the village was part of the German Empire of 1871-1919, consult *Meyers Orts- und Verkehrs-Lexikon des Deutschen Reichs* [*Meyer's Directory of Places and Commerce in the German Empire*], edited by E. Uetrecht, which is available on microfilm at Family History Centers and in book form at some libraries with a good selection of meterials on Germanic genealogy. This will also enable you to identify where the village was located, in terms of pre-World War I jurisdictional units. If more than one locality had the same name, as was often the case, this source will provide you with the basic information needed to start finding the right one. *The German Researcher* by Fay and Douglas Dearden helps you to decipher the Gothic script and determine the meaning of many of the abbreviations in *Meyers Orts*. *Ritter's* gazetteer has less detailed information than *Meyers Orts*, but it is printed in the Roman script.

A more detailed gazetteer, with a separate volume for each Prussian province, is the *Gemeindelexikon für das Königreich Preussen* [*Gazetteer for the Kingdom of Prussia*], published by the Verlag des königlichen statistischen Landesamts in Berlin in 1907-1909.

An equally detailed gazetteer of the Austrian (but not Hungarian) provinces and crownlands, based on the 1900 census, is the 14-volume *Gemeindelexikon der im Reichsrate vertretenen Königreiche und Länder* [*Gazetteer of the Crownlands and States Represented in the Imperial Council*] (Vienna: K. u. k. Statistische Zentralkommission, 1903-1908).

These three gazetteers for the German Empire, the Prussian Empire (which encompassed most of North Germany before German unification, with those provinces still part of the kingdom of Prussia after unification), and the Austrian-ruled portion of the Austro-Hungarian Empire are all available on microfilm at Family History Centers.

If you wish to consult a gazetteer predating German unification as well as the establishment of the Austro-Hungarian Dual Monarchy, try H. Rudolf, *Vollständigstes geographisch-topographisch-statistisches Orts-Lexikon von Deutschland* [*Complete Geographical, Topographical and Statistical Place Name Gazetteer of Germany*], which also includes the non-German territories under the dominion of Austria and Prussia. It may well be the only gazetteer that provides information about all of the German-populated localities in Eastern Europe, except for those in Russia and under Turkish rule. While this gazetteer does not have as much detail about individual localities as *Meyers* does, it is ample for genealogical purposes. It was published by Karl Voigt, jun., Weimar, apparently in 1861 or 1862, although no date is shown. The Max Kade Institute at the University of Wisconsin has a copy of this rare gazetteer. Its address is shown in chapter XIX. Send a self-addressed, stamped envelope for a copy of the entry for the locality you are searching.

Swiss place names may be in German, French, Italian or Romansh. It is unlikely that their names would have changed since your ancestor's departure. However, if you seek further information in this respect, Jared H. Suess, in his *Handy Guide to Swiss*

Genealogical Records, lists the names of all the Swiss cantons in German, French and Italian and specifies the locally spoken language(s).

If the area was never under German rule, or ceased to be part of a German-speaking country in 1919, by far the most comprehensive reference work is *Deutsch-fremdsprachiges (fremdsprachig-deutsches) Ortsnamenverzeichnis [Gazetteer of Places, with German and Foreign Language Names]*, by Otto Kredel and Franz Thierfelder. This book lists the post-World War I names of former (and often then still existing) German settlements in 24 European countries. This should be considered to be an authoritative source.

A number of area-specific sources are also available.

John M. Michels, in *Introduction to the Hungarian-Germans of North Dakota* (February 1988), published by the Germans from Russia Heritage Society in Bismarck, has a 6-page list of "Banat Village Names in the Different Languages," which includes the German, Hungarian and Romanian or Serbian place names. This area was part of Hungary until 1919, hence the designation. It was subsequently divided between Romania and Yugoslavia after World War I, except for three villages that remained in Hungary.

Jared Suess's *Handy Guide to Hungarian Genealogical Research* lists county and personal names, as well as the Hungarian, German Gothic, Russian, Serbian (Cyrillic) and Croatian (Latin) alphabets.

The *Genealogical Gazetteer of Galicia*, compiled by Brian J. Lenius and published by the author in 1993, identifies all of the villages in which Germans lived and lists the Polish and Ukrainian names for the various localities. Galicia was part of Poland before 1772 and during the interwar period and an Austrian crownland during the disappearance of Poland from the map. It is now divided between Ukraine and Poland, with most of the former German settlements in areas that are now part of Ukraine.

A very useful book for finding Danube Swabian localities is Anton Scherer, *Donauschwäbische Bibliographie, 1935-1955: das Schrifttum über die Donauschwaben in Ungarn, Rumanien, Jugoslavien und Bulgarie sowie - nach 1945 - in Deutschland, Österreich, Frankreich, USA, Canada, Argentinien und Brasilien [Danube Swabian Bibliography, 1935-1955: Literature about the Danube Swabians in Hungary, Romania, Yugoslavia and Bulgaria, as well as - after 1945 - in Germany, Austria, France, USA, Canada, Argentina and Brazil]* (Munich: Verlag des Südostdeutschen Kulturwerks, 1966), which cross-references town names in German, Serbian and Romanian.

Henryk Batowski's *Slownik Nazw Miejscowych Europy Srodkowej i Wschnodniej XIX i XX [Dictionary of Place Names in Central and Eastern Europe in the 19th and 20th Centuries]* (Warsaw: Panstwowe Wydawnictwo Naukowe, 1964) lists selected place names in East and Central Europe in 24 languages.

The most thorough gazetteer of Hungary, which is on FHL microfilm, is the *Magyarország Helységnévtára [Gazetteer of Hungary]* compiled by János Dvorzág (Budapest: "Havi Fäzetek," 1877).

Sophie A. Welisch, in *Bukovina Villages/Towns/Cities and Their Germans*, lists the Romanian, and in some cases Ukrainian, names of former German settlements in the text, but not in list form.

There are several excellent gazetteers for Poland. The most comprehensive one is by Filipa Sulimierskiego, Bronislawa Chlebowskiego et al, *Slownik Geograficzny Królestwa Polskiego i innych krajów slowianskich [Geographical Dictionary of the Kingdom of Poland and Other Slavic Countries]*, 15 vols. (Warsaw: Sulimierski i Walewski, 1880-1902). This is on FHL microfiche. This gazetteer often gives more detailed entries of villages that were in Prussia (but are now in Poland) than does *Meyers Orts*. The entries are in Polish (with cross-reference citations of the German name of the village to the Polish name), but the introduction to this gazetteer gives a most helpful list of Polish terms and abbreviations with translations.

For those whose particular interest is the current Polish names of villages in Poland that had German names during the interwar period, there are two thorough German gazetteers: (1) M. Kaemmerer, *Ortsverzeichnis der Ortschaften jenseits von Oder und Neisse* [*List of Names for Localities East of the Oder and Neisse (Rivers)*] (Leer: Verlag Gerhard Rautenberg, 1988), which is a 3rd edition of what used to be *Müllers Verzeichnis der jenseits der Oder-Neisse gelegenen, unter fremder Verwaltung stehenden Ortschaften* [*Mueller's Gazetteer of Localities Lying East of the Oder-Neisse Line, Which Are under Foreign Administration*], and (2) *Amtliches Gemeinde- und Ortsnamenverzeichnis der deutschen Ostgebiete unter fremder Verwaltung* [*Official Gazetteer for the Localities in the (Former) German East under Foreign Administration*], published by the (German) Bundesanstalt für Landeskunde.

Both of these provide the old German and new Polish names for all localities. However, since many communities carried the same name, you may need to find out the name of the current Polish county in which the place is located in order to distinguish between two or more places that may now have different names. This information is listed in *Spis Miejscowosci Polskiej Rzeczypospolitej Ludowej* [*List of Place Names in the People's Republic of Poland*], published in 1967 by Wydawnictwa Komunikacji i Lacznosci in Warsaw.

If trying to use German- and Polish-language gazetteers seems too difficult, Larry O. Jensen has a very thorough and detailed description about how to use these sources in Chapter 9 ("Determining the Present Name of Localities") of *A Genealogical Handbook of German Research*, Vol. I.

Jensen's book also includes numerous other useful items. Appendix E of his book gives the Lithuanian place and county names of former German settlements, primarily in the Memel River area (which came under Lithuanian control in 1923). He provides comparable information for the northern tip of old East Prussia, which has belonged to Russia since World War II. Elsewhere he provides the names of the French departments, as well as the Belgian and Danish counties, of the German-named villages ceded to those countries after World War I.

Finding the current names of villages in the Soviet Union that used to have German names is still a matter wrought with confusion. Kredel and Thierfelder list new names for most of those villages, but these differ from later sources in many cases. One reason for this is that many villages were destroyed during wartime, with new villages built more or less on the same sites, but quite often with new names.

A second reason is that the names of some of these villages may have been changed several times, being named for the currently fashionable Marxist hero, depending on Stalin's moods and those of subsequent rulers. Moreover, the alternatives to the original name may have been either in Russian or in Ukrainian (at least in the Black Sea region) or both. Many German place names were changed to Russian names as early as 1893.

To further complicate things, some villages were known locally and unofficially by one name, which might have found its way into print, yet had a different official name. (Compare "Minneapolis" with "Mill City," a term favored by some St. Paulites!)

Finally, in some cases the original German name was either translated literally into Russian or Ukrainian, or simply Slavicized with the appropriate ending.

There are two major post-1945 American sources of information concerning the current names of former German villages. One is the gazetteer for the Soviet Union (No. 42) published by the U.S. government as part of the series, *Official Names Approved by the United States Board of Geographic Names*. The 1970 edition is not complete and is often inaccurate in its list of cross-referenced former German village names.

A more promising approach is to obtain maps showing the location of the various former German settlements in the Soviet Union. The late Dr. Karl Stumpp prepared comprehensive and detailed maps of these settlements, which can be purchased from the American

Historical Society of Germans from Russia (address in chapter XIX). These can then be compared with the U.S. Army maps of Eastern Europe, Series N501, which show comparable detail. While this can be a time-consuming process, it will pay off. Of course, there is a possibility that some of the villages shown on the maps may no longer exist, but it is unlikely that many of these localities ceased to exist after 1945.

For a very thorough discussion of maps and related materials that are useful in identifying ancestral locations in Eastern Europe, see Ron Neuman, "Maps and Your Family History," in *Journal of the American Historical Society of Germans from Russia*, Vol. 13, No. 4 (Winter 1990), pp. 31-38.

For detailed information comparing late nineteenth-century and contemporary political jurisdictions, see two articles by Dave Olinyk in the *East European Genealogist*: "Political Divisions of the Austro-Hungarian, German and Russian Empires: Eastern European Membership Interests" (March 1993) and "Modern East European Countries and Pre-World War I Regions" (June 1993).

If you are seeking a general orientation before searching for a specific village, Ernest Thode's maps in *Atlas for Germanic Genealogy* list the German and the Slavic (mostly Polish) names of some of the larger localities (apparently mostly former county seats) in Pomerania, Posen or Poznan, East and West Prussia, the former Kingdom of Saxony and Silesia. It also lists the French names of similar localities in Alsace-Lorraine.

MISSPELLED PLACE NAMES

In a great many instances, the notes left by an immigrant ancestor (and even more so, those recorded by descendants) concerning a place of birth or emigration cannot be found in any gazetteer or atlas because there is no place with a name spelled that way. If the village you are searching for cannot be found in *Meyers Orts* gazetteer, it is almost certain that the locality was outside the German Empire (dealt with above), the name of the locality changed, or the name is misspelled.

Many of our immigrant ancestors were barely literate, and some were completely illiterate. It should be no surprise that people with only a few winters of schooling had trouble spelling names. Moreover, many times these brief biographical notes were recorded in old age, decades after having left Germany, so what little had been learned could easily have been forgotten through lack of use. Even if the immigrants spoke German at home, they may have done very little writing in that language. In cases where a member of the second generation wrote down what he or she remembered of an oral communication with the parent, the problem was even greater. In many cases, members of a generation with no knowledge of the Gothic script incorrectly transcribed what was in the original, sometimes resulting in a distortion such as "Quiveriveide" for "Tiegerweide."

What can be done about this? If you have a reasonably precise idea of the region of origin, a thorough perusal of a detailed map for your misspelled town may solve the problem. If you have been able to identify the hometown of a spouse or relative, this should lead you to search the nearby area. If a couple was married in Germany, the odds are very good that they lived in nearby villages. Even if they were married in North America, such a search would be worthwhile, because it was very common for people from the same general area in Europe to settle in the same town in North America. Whether or not you have this kind of information, it is very helpful to know which letters in the town name were likely to be interchanged.

A great many spelling variations are possible for vowels, but the most likely to be interchanged, especially at the beginning of a name, would be *a* and *e*. Fortunately, a relatively small percentage of place names begin with vowels. The number of possibilities regarding erroneous use of vowels or double vowels in the middle of a word are so large that it is not practical to try to provide a complete list here.

Among consonants, *c* and *k* are identical sounds in German, as in English. You would be likely to find *ck* in the middle of a word or name, but never at the beginning. Other identically pronounced letters include *v*, *f*, *ff* and *ph*. *Pf* could also have been used interchangeably with these by people with little education. Other consonant combinations that were quite likely to be used interchangeably in the past include *b* and *p*, as well as *k* and *g*. The following can also have the same sound: *d*, *t*, *dt* and *tt*. The double letters would never be used at the beginning of a word. *I* and *J* were written the same way and could also be interchanged with the rarely used *y*. Other letters or combinations that could have been used mistakenly or interchanged in an earlier era include *s*, *ss*, *sz*, *z*, *ts* and *tz*.

The English "sh" sound is always spelled *sch* in German, but English speakers in America could have written *sh*. Also, East European Jews used "sh," e.g., "*shtetl*" for "*Städl*." Words beginning with *sp* or *st* have the *s* pronounced as "sh," but the pronunciation and spelling of *s* and *sch* were sometimes interchanged in olden days. The English "ch" sound is not found at the beginning of place names of German origin, but it is found in Slavic lands where Germans lived. The German spelling for this would be *tsch*, but the Slavic *cz* is quite likely to have been used instead in place names. However, when *cz* occurs at the end of a name, it has often become Germanicized as *tz*. The sound of a soft English *g* (as in "gem") is not found in German, but where this sound occurred as a result of foreign influences, it would be Germanicized as *dsch* (example: *Dobrudscha*).

In border areas, the spelling of a village name could easily follow the rules of the other language, e.g., French in Alsace-Lorraine. A particularly common linguistic alternative is *au* (German for "meadow") and *ow* in Eastern Europe at the end of a name.

The *j* in German is pronounced like the English *y*. Hence, the use of *y* instead of *j* could easily have occurred in writing among Germans in the United States, but not in Europe.

There is no English equivalent of either of the German "ch" sounds. These sounds could have been approximated by an *h* or *k* by a person writing in English. They could have been written as *g*, *k* or *ck* in Europe. A single *s* in German is pronounced like a *z* in English, except at the end of a word. Hence, an American-born descendant could easily have used a *z* in lieu of an *s*.

The German *Umlaut* letters (*ö*, *ä* and *ü*) are properly written as *oe*, *ae* and *ue*, when the *Umlaut* character is not practical, but in America the *e* as an equivalent was often dropped. German-Americans familiar with the spoken, but not the written, word might use *e* for *ö* or sometimes *ä*, and use *i* or *ie* for *ü*.

The German *h* is generally silent when used together with another consonant. The result is that *t* and *th*, *r* and *hr*, and *l* and *hl*, to cite a few of the more common examples, were often used interchangeably. Indeed, an old German dictionary often differs from a current one in this regard. Hence, wherever *h* appears together with another consonant, check for a spelling without an *h*. The other *h*-combinations are rare at the beginning of a word, but there are a few names that begin with *ch* and possibly *rh*. As for the other way around, a possibly silent *h* could occur after any vowel or vowel combination, but rarely when the same vowel is doubled. Herrmann Lange, in *German Composition* (Oxford: Varendon Press, 3rd ed., 1900) gives a most helpful synopsis of the changes in German spelling revised to meet the requirements of the government regulations of 1880.

If you need additional help identifying a misspelled locality, consult an expert.

LIST OF GAZETTEERS FOR EUROPE

See Bibliography for full citations if not shown.

Allgemeines geographisches statistisches Lexikon aller österreichischen Staaten [*General Gazetteer of All Austrian Lands*]. Vienna: Franz Raffelsperger. 1845-53.

Amtliches Gemeinde- und Ortsnamenverzeichnis der deutschen Ostgebiete unter fremder Verwaltung [*Official Gazetteer for the Localities in the (Former) German East under Foreign Administration*]. Remagen: Bundesanstalt für Landeskunde. 1955.

> Lists name changes resulting from World War II.

Henryk Batowski. *Slownik Nazw Miejscowych Europy Srodkowej i Wschnodniej XIX i XX.* [*Dictionary of Place Names in Central and Eastern Europe in the 19th and 20th Centuries*]. Warsaw: Pañstwowe Wydawnictwo Naukowe. 1964.

> Lists selected place names in East and Central Europe in 24 languages.

Chester G. Cohen. *Shtetl Finder: Jewish Communities in the 19th and Early 20th Centuries in the Pale of Settlement of Russia and Poland, and in Lithuania, Latvia, Galicia, and Bukovina, With Names of Residents.* Bowie, MD: Heritage Books, Inc. 1989. 145 pp.

> Lists former Jewish communities in the Pale of Settlement, Lithuania, Latvia, Galicia, Bukovina, and a few from other parts of East Europe. Gives names of some documented inhabitants.

Christian Crusius. *Topographisches Post-Lexikon aller Ortschaften der k.k. Erbländer,* [*Topographical Postal Directory of All Localities in the Hereditary (Hapsburg) Imperial and Royal Lands*] 4 parts in 13 vols., plus 3 supplemental volumes and an index of the original volumes. Vienna. 1798-1828.

> Early gazetteer of all localities in the Hapsburg Empire.

Randy Daitch. *The Shtetl Atlas.* Los Angeles: Self-published.

> Maps and 40,000 names of towns and villages in Poland, Lithuania, Belarus and Ukraine, i.e., the Pale of Jewish Settlement in the Russian Empire. Index for old Poland.

F. A. Doubek. *Verzeichnis der Ortschaften mit deutscher Bevölkerung auf dem Gebiete des polnischen Staates.* [*Directory of Places with German Residents within the Country of (Interwar) Poland*]. Berlin: Publikationsstelle. 1939.

> Gazetteer of localities in interwar Poland with German residents.

János Dvorzág, comp. *Magyarország Helységnévtára* [*Gazetteer of Hungary*]. 2 vols. Budapest: "Havi Füzetek." 1877.

> Most thorough gazetteer on pre-World War I Hungary. Can be used without knowledge of Hungarian.

Duncan B. Gardiner. *German Towns in Slovakia & Upper Hungary: A Genealogical Gazetteer,* 3rd ed. Lakewood, OH: The Family Historian, 1991; reprinted with addendum, 1993.

> Brief description of German towns in the Slovak Republic and Carpatho-Ukraine, with names in German, Hungarian and Slovak. Many detailed maps. Historical overview of German settlements in Eastern Europe. Addresses of Czech and Slovak archives, with instructions as to how to obtain data from them. Key terms in German, Latin, Hungarian, Slovak and Czech. Valuable bibliography.

Gemeindelexikon für den Freistaat Preussen [*Gazetteer for the Free State of Prussia,* i.e., all parts of the post-1919 German Empire that were Prussian provinces] Berlin: Verlag des preussischen statistischen Landesamts. 1931-32. 14 vols. (one for each province)

Gemeindelexikon für das Königreich Preussen [*Gazetteer for the Kingdom of Prussia,* i.e., all parts of the pre-1919 German Empire that were Prussian provinces] Berlin: Verlag des königlichen statistischen Landesamts. 1907-1909. 14 vols. (one for each province)

Gemeindelexikon der im Reichsrate vertretenen Königreiche und Länder [*Gazetteer of the Crownlands and States Represented in the (Austrian) Imperial Council*] Vienna: K. u. k. Statistische Zentralkommission, 1903-1908. 14 vols. (one for each crownland or state)

> Gazetteer based on the 1900 census. Arranged by district, with both German and non-German names listed.

Martin Gilbert. *The Atlas of Jewish History*. Revised edition. New York: William Morrow and Co. 1993. 123 pp. plus 4-page bibliography.

> Contains 120 outline maps of Jewish history. Many maps are related to Germany and Europe. Thorough guide of Jewish history and migrations.

Der grosse Shell Atlas. [*The Large Shell Atlas*] Ostfildern, Germany: Mairs Geographischer Verlag. Yearly editions. About 500 pp. In German.

> Detailed modern-day road atlas of Germany and Europe, including city maps and county boundaries, with index. Some explanations are in English.

Charles M. Hall. *The Atlantic Bridge to Germany*.

Larry O. Jensen. *A Genealogical Handbook of German Research*, Vol. 3. 1986.

> Includes brief history of each kingdom, province and duchy, with boundary and other changes. Excellent bibliography of German gazetteers and how to use them.

M. Kaemmerer. *Ortsverzeichnis der Ortschaften jenseits von Oder und Neisse* [*List of Names for Localities East of the Oder and Neisse (Rivers)*]. Leer: Verlag Gerhard Rautenberg. 1988.

> Third edition of what used to be *Müllers Verzeichnis der jenseits der Oder-Neisse gelegenen, unter fremder Verwaltung stehenden Ortschaften*. Lists German and Polish names of all places that were transferred from Germany to Poland after World War II.

Otto K. Kowallis and Vera N. Kowallis. *A Genealogical Guide and Atlas of Silesia*. Logan, UT: Everton Publishers, Inc. Presently out of print.

> Contains a cross reference of German place names in Silesia to their modern-day Polish names.

Wilfried Krallert, Walter Kuhn, and Ernst Schwarz. *Atlas zur Geschichte der deutschen Ostsiedlung*. [*Historical Atlas of the German East (European) Settlements*].

> Contains historical maps showing German settlements throughout East Europe. At Borchert Map Library at the University of Minnesota.

Otto Kredel and Franz Thierfelder. *Deutsch-fremdsprachiges Ortsnamenverzeichnis*. [*Gazetteer of Places, with German and Foreign Language Names*]. Prepared on behalf of the Praktischen Abteilung der Deutschen Akademie. Berlin: Deutsche Verlagsgesellschaft G.m.b.H. 1931. 1173 pp.

> Gives post-World War I place names of localities outside the Germanic countries that formerly had German names. Very comprehensive guide to Germanic settlements, including all European countries.

Wolodymyr Kubijovic. *Ethnic Groups of Southwest Ukraine (Halychyna-Galicia)*. 1983. Distribution rights: Wiesbaden: Otto Harrassowitz.

> Breakdown of each village in eastern Galicia by ethnic group, including Germans.

Heinrich Kuhn (comp. for Sudetendeutsches Archiv). *Ortsverzeichnis der Tschechoslowakei: Deutsch, Tschechisch, Slowakisch, Ungarish, Stand 1957*. [*Gazetteer of Czechoslovakia: German, Czech, Slovak, Hungarian, as of 1957*]. Munich: Sekretariat des Sudetendeutsches Archiv. 1957.

Brian J. Lenius, comp. *Genealogical Gazetteer of Galicia*. Anola, Manitoba: Self-published. 1993.

> Identifies all villages in which Germans lived and lists the Polish and Ukrainian names for the various localities.

Marilyn Lind. *Researching and Finding Your German Heritage*. Cloquet, MN: The Linden Tree. Updated 1991. 150 pp.

> Small maps showing where each pre-World War I German state, province or principality was located.

Erich Dieter Linder and Günter Olzog. *Die deutschen Landkreise: Wappen, Geschichte, Struktur*. [*The German Counties: Their Coats-of-Arms, History and Structure*]. Munich: Günter Olzog Verlag. 1986. 280 pp.

> Maps showing current boundaries of all 237 West German counties and brief history of changes.

Edward David Luft. "Map Resources for the Genealogist at the U.S. Library of Congress." (3-part series in *Nase Rodina*, 1992-93)

Paul Robert Magocsi. *A Historical Atlas of East Central Europe*. Seattle: University of Washington Press. 1993. 218 pp.

> More than 50 maps from ca. 400 to 1992 extending from Odessa to Bavaria and from Greece to Lithuania, with accompanying text, including ethnolinguistic, political and other maps.

Colin McEvedy. *The Penguin Atlas of Modern History (1483-1815)*. Baltimore, MD: Penguin Books. Copyright 1972. (n.d.) 95 pp.

> Small nondetailed maps show European political units, population, religion, towns, trade and revenues. Has excellent associated text. Available in some local bookstores and from Genealogy Unlimited.

Colin McEvedy. *The Penguin Atlas of Recent History: Europe Since 1815*. New York: Penguin. 1982. 95 pp.

John M. Michels. *Introduction to the Hungarian-Germans of North Dakota*. Bismarck: Germans from Russia Heritage Society. 1988.

> Map showing former German settlements in the Banat.

Gary Mokotoff and Sallyann Amdur Sack. *Where Once We Walked: A Guide to the Jewish Communities Destroyed in the Holocaust*. Teaneck, NJ: Avotaynu, Inc. 1991. 514 pp.

> Documents more than 21,000 towns in Central and Eastern Europe where Jews lived before the Holocaust, lists more than 15,000 Yiddish and other alternate names, gives exact location, and population figures.

Friedrich Müller. *Müllers grosses deutsches Ortsbuch*. [*Muellers Large German Gazetteer*]. Wuppertal-Barmen, Germany: Post- und Ortsbuchverlag Postmeister a.d. Friedrich Müller. 1958. 18th edition 1974.

> Lists 107,000 places in present-day Germany. Cross-references to the Shell atlas (see above). Useful for identifying present states of communities that belonged to different political entities before World War II.

Friedrich Müller. *Ortsbuch für Eupen-Malmedy, Elsass-Lothringen und Luxemburg* [*Gazetteer for Eupen-Malmedy (Belgium), Alsace-Lorraine and Luxembourg*]. 1942.

Dave Olinyk. "Political Divisions of the Austro-Hungarian, German and Russian Empires: Eastern European Membership Interests" and "Modern East European Countries and Pre-World War I Regions," in *East European Genealogist*, March and June 1993.

> Good cross-references between contemporary and pre-World War I jurisdictional units.

Österreichisches Statistisches Zentralamt. *Ortsverzeichnis von Österreich*. [*Directory of Austrian Place Names*]. Vienna: Verlag der Österreichischen Staatsdruckerei. 1965.

Ernst Pfohl. *Ortslexikon Sudetenland*. [*Sudetenland Gazetteer*] Nuremberg: Hermut Preussler Verlag. 1932. Reprinted 1987. 698 pp.

> Despite its more limited title, this gazetteer lists the German and Czech or Slovak names of all pertinent places in the Czech and Slovak Republics.

Das Postleitzahlbuch: Alphabetisch geordnet. [*The (German) Postal Code Book, Arranged Alphabetically*]. Marburg: Bundespost, Postdienst. 1993. 986 pp.

> Shows the postal code for every small community and every street address in big cities under the new postal code system adopted in Germany in 1993. There is a separate book for post office box addresses, which are not always the same as those of the street addresses. Accompanying map available.

Postleitzahlenverzeichnis—Abc-Folge [*Postal Code Directory, in ABC Order*].   Bonn: Bundesministerium für das Post- und Fernmeldewesen. 1986. 447 pp.
> Lists the pre-1993 postal codes for localities in East and West Germany.

Isabella Regényi and Anton Scherer. *Donauschwäbisches Ortsnamenbuch*. [*Book of Danube Swabian Place Names*]. Darmstadt: Arbeitskreis donauschwäbischer Familienforscher (AKdFF). 1980.
> Cross-references Danube Swabian town names in German, Serbo-Croatian and Romanian. Brief historical introduction, bibliography and 12 detailed maps.

Gerhard Reichling, ed. *Gemeindeverzeichnis für die Hauptwohngebiete der Deutschen ausserhalb der Bundesrepublik Deutschland*, 2nd ed. [*Directory of Places for the Major Areas Where Germans Are Living Outside the Federal Republic of Germany*]. Frankfurt a.M., Germany: Verlag für Standesamtswesen. 1982.
> Government gazetteer of settlements of German-speakers outside Germany.

H. Rudolf. *Vollständigstes geographisch-topographisch-statistisches Orts-Lexikon von Deutschland.* [*Most Complete Geographic, Topographic and Statistical Gazetteer of Germany*]. Weimar: Karl Voigt, Jr. ca. 1861-62.
> Lists all places that were under Germanic rule at the time, including the Austrian Empire.

Daniel Schlyter. *Gazetteer of German Colonies in Russia*. Davis, CA: John D. Movius for FEEFHS. Publication uncertain. Incomplete version on World Wide Web, 1995.

Robert Sobotik. *Westschlesien (Tschechoslowakei): Eine anthropogeographische Studie mit einem Atlas.* [*West Silesia (Czechoslovakia): An Anthropological-Geographical Study, with an Atlas*]. Prague: Geographisches Institut der Deutschen Universität in Prag. 1930.
> Deals with what was known as Austrian Silesia (now northern Moravia), which was actually south, rather than west of the Prussian province of Silesia.

Spis Miejscowosci polskiej Rzeczypospolitej ludowej. [*List of Place Names in the People's Republic of Poland*]. Warsaw: Wydawnictwa Komunicacji i Lacznosci. 1967. 2 vols.
> Provides current Polish names for former German counties, which may be needed because of duplicate village names.

Statistisches Staatsamt. *Administratives Gemeindelexikon für Mähren, Schlesien, die Slowakei und Karpatorussland.* [*Administrative Gazetteer for Moravia, Silesia, Slovakia and Carpatho-Russia*]. Brünn (Brno): Verlag von Rudolf M. Rohrer. 1928.

Dr. Karl Stumpp. Series of individual maps relating to the Russian Germans: both settlements in Russia and places of origin. Lincoln, NE: American Historical Society of Germans from Russia.

Filipa Sulimierskiego, Bronislawa Chlebowskiego, et. al. *Slownik Geograficzny Królestwa Polskiego i innych krajów slowianskich* [*Geographical Dictionary of the Kingdom of Poland and Other Slavic Countries*]. 15 vols. Warsaw: Sulimierski i Walewski. 1880-1902
> Most thorough gazetteer of localities in pre-partitioned Poland and associated areas.

Ernest J. Thode. *Address Book for Germanic Genealogy*, 5th ed. Baltimore: Genealogical Publishing Co. 1994. 174 pp.
> Lists German and Slavic or French names for larger localities in the former German Empire.

Ernest Thode. *Genealogical Gazetteer of Alsace-Lorraine.* Indianapolis, IN: Heritage House, 1986. 137 pp.
> Most of the book consists of German and French names of larger towns, as well as geographic features such as rivers.

Finn A. Thomsen. *Atlas of the Austro-Hungarian Empire, 1892.* 1990. 79 pp.
> Enlarged reproductions of map published by the Verlag des Bibliographischen Instituts, Leipzig and Vienna, 1892, with index.

Finn A. Thomsen. *Atlas of the German Empire, 1892.* 1989. 110 pp.

 Enlarged reproductions of map published by the Verlag des Bibliographischen Instituts, Leipzig and Vienna, 1892, with index.

Dr. E. Uetrecht, editor. *Meyers Orts- und Verkehrs-Lexikon des Deutschen Reichs.* [*Meyer's Directory of Places and Commerce in the German Empire*]. Leipzig, Germany: Bibliographisches Institut. 5th ed. Vol. 1 (A-K): 1912. 1092 pp. - Vol. 2 (L-Z): 1913. 1246 pp. plus 76 pp. appendices.

 Standard gazetteer for the pre-World War I German Empire, listing 210,000 localities. In Gothic print. Most of the German portion of the Family History Catalog at the Family History Library follows the organization presented in *Meyers Orts.*

U.S. Army. *Maps of Eastern Europe,* Series N501.

 Very thorough and detailed.

U.S. Board of Geographic Names. *Official Names Approved by the United States Board of Geographic Names.* Different volumes for various countries and dates.

 The one for the Soviet Union is very inferior for purposes of Germanic genealogy, since it is incomplete and inaccurate.

F. Vanderhalven. *Namensänderungen ehemals preussischer Gemeinden von 1850 bis 1942.* [*Name Changes of Former Prussian Communities from 1850 to 1942*]. Neustadt/Aisch, Germany: Verlag Degener. 1971.

 Quite a few places with Polish names were given German names during the late 1800s, changed back to Polish names (usually, but not always, the previous names) and changed again in a similar fashion during the Nazi occupation. This gazetteer is also helpful in locating villages or cities since the early years of the Industrial Revolution.

Max Vasmer. *Russisches geographisches Namenbuch.* [*Book of Russian Geographic Names*]. 12 vols. Wiesbaden: Otto Harrasowitz. 1964-89.

 Mostly Russian names, but some German and Polish ones, all arranged according to the Russian alphabet. Descriptive material in German.

Verzeichnis der Postleitzahlen. [*(Austrian) Postal Code Directory*]. Vienna, Austria. Published annually.

 Postal code directory for Austria.

Verzeichnis der Postleitzahlen. [*(Swiss) Postal Code Directory*]. Berne: Baubedarf AG. Published annually.

 Postal code directory for Switzerland and Liechtenstein.

Sophie A. Welisch. *Bukovina Villages/Towns/Cities and Their Germans.* Ellis, KS: Bukovina Society of the Americas. 1990. 78 pp.

 Includes maps of German settlements in the Bukovina and places of origin of the settlers in Germany, Bohemia and the Slovak Republic.

Peter Wörster. *Das nördliche Ostpreussen nach 1945: deutsch-russisch und russisch-deutsches Ortsnamenverzeichnis mit einer Dokumentation der Demarkationslinie.* [*Northern East Prussia After 1945: German-Russian and Russian-German Locality Name Gazetteer with Documentation of the (Russian-Polish) Line of Demarcation*]. Marburg/Lahn, Germany: J. G. Herder-Institut. 1980.

 Only gazetteer that lists Russian names of localities in what was formerly the northern part of East Prussia.

Suzan F. Wynne. *Galician Towns and Administrative Districts.* Washington, DC: Jewish Genealogical Society of Greater Washington. 1990. 2 microfiche forms.

CHAPTER IX

POLITICAL AND PHYSICAL GEOGRAPHY

Did your "German" ancestors *really* come from Germany? If so, which Germany: today's Germany, the much larger German Empire put together by Bismarck, or Germany when it was only a geographic concept, not a political one? Perhaps they never lived in Germany, but in Austria. But which Austria: today's small, solidly German-speaking country or the much larger polyglot Austrian Empire of former centuries? Maybe they came from one of the many German "colonies"—meaning settlements in non-Germanic areas, often not German-ruled territory—which were scattered throughout most of Russia, East Central Europe and the Balkans.

THE CHANGING POLITICAL GEOGRAPHY OF ANCESTRAL HOMELANDS

If you have a place of emigration listed on some old record or from an oral history by your ancestors, but can't find the place in any modern atlas or gazetteer, perhaps the outline presented later in this chapter will help you find it or at least give you a clue as to where to search. You may even be astonished to discover that your ancestors lived far from Berlin, Cologne, Munich, Vienna or Berne. Even if you know in which country or under which rulers your European ancestors lived, that information may be all wrong when applied to today's borders. The reason for this is that European boundaries were constantly changing. In fact, the birth or death of a country was not particularly unusual. However, the most significant changes which occurred, from the perspective of genealogical research on immigrant ancestors, were the following:

- the effect of the Napoleonic Wars and the settlement by the Congress of Vienna in 1815, which greatly reduced the number of sovereign territories on German soil (previously over 300), in spite of the fact that several dozen were left;

- the wars of German unification in 1864-71, which turned the previously independent states and Prussian provinces into sub-units of the German Empire;

- the redrawing of the map of Europe by the Treaty of Versailles with Germany (1919), the Treaty of St. Germain with Austria (1919) and the Treaty of Trianon with Hungary (1920), largely pursuant to President Wilson's principle of national self-determination, but with some exceptions at the expense of German-speaking countries; and

- the westward shift of Poland's location after World War II, as Russia took control of Eastern Poland, while Poland, in return, received the area west to the Oder-Neisse line, the current eastern border of Germany.

Many of the changes in the map of Germany are given in considerable detail in text and maps in the complete text of the Traité de Paix [Treaty of Peace] available from the federal government.

Since relatively few Germans emigrated to America before 1789, or even 1815, only those genealogists with colonial ancestors are likely to have to deal with the pre-Napoleonic hodge-podge of German mini-states at the outset of their research. Here, the German experts have problems too, and some of the German classics of genealogy are filled with errors as to places of origin as a result. If you don't know from which Germanic principality your colonial ancestor came, you are advised to seek the help of the best expert you can find, which often means the genealogist, historian or archivist living closest to the place in question.

Of course, if you know where the village is and you are searching parish registers, it may not matter whether you know to which principality the place belonged or how often this changed. But if you lose track of your lineage and wonder where to search for an earlier generation, it may matter.

However, sooner or later most German-American genealogists will encounter a problem with political jurisdictions. The reason is that if you can trace your ancestors back to Germany, you will almost certainly be able to trace them back to the pre-Napoleonic era, because Germans have earned their reputation of being meticulous record-keepers.

The units established in 1815 continued to describe the various parts of Germany reasonably accurately, despite some minor changes, until World War II, with the exceptions mentioned below. After 1815, Eastern and much of Central and Western Germany belonged to Prussia, while Southern, Northwestern and parts of Central Germany were independent.

The 11 Prussian provinces were:

Brandenburg	Posen	Westphalia
East Prussia	Rhineland	West Prussia
Hohenzollern (2 states)	Province of Saxony	
Pomerania	Silesia	

The independent states that belonged to the loose German Confederation included:

Anhalt	Hanover	Nassau
Baden	Hesse-Cassel	Oldenburg
Bavaria,	Hesse-Darmstadt	Kingdom of Saxony
including the Palatinate	Holstein	Thuringia
Brunswick	Lippe	(12 small states, later 8)[2]
Bremen[1]	Lübeck[1]	Waldeck
Frankfurt[1]	Luxembourg	Württemberg
Hamburg[1]	Mecklenburg (2 states)	

[1] Denotes city-states.
[2] Also known as the Saxon duchies and the Reuss and Schwarzburg principalities.

The states in the Confederation that belonged to the Austrian Empire were:

Austria proper (Upper, Lower)	Carinthia	Salzburg
Austrian Silesia	Carniola	Styria
Bohemia	Moravia	Tyrol

Switzerland was outside the Confederation, as were Hungary, Slavonia, Galicia, Lombardy and Venetia, all predominantly non-German parts of the Austrian Empire.

The three easternmost Prussian provinces (East Prussia, West Prussia and Posen) were also outside the Confederation, an anomaly harking back to the Holy Roman Empire, which had been abolished in 1806.

In 1866-67 Hanover, Hesse-Nassau (Hesse-Cassel plus Nassau) and Schleswig-Holstein (Schleswig having been taken from Denmark) became Prussian provinces.

Alsace and part of Lorraine were taken from France in 1871 and became a state of the empire (*Reichsland*).

The tinier states were frequently involved with splintering, consolidation, boundary changes and name changes. This applied particularly to Anhalt, Birkenfeld, Hesse, Lippe, Schaumburg, Thuringia and Waldeck. Prior to 1815, it applied to many other areas as well. If you want to make sense out of this fluctuating world of mini-states, try chapter 13 of Marilyn Lind, *Researching and Finding Your German Heritage*, for a fairly detailed treatment.

Meanwhile, the now small country of Luxembourg was once much bigger. In 1839 it lost the territory that is now the Belgian province of Luxembourg. The people of the two Luxembourgs represented the same German-French mixture. Their emigrants generally settled in the United States in or near communities of people from Germany, especially those from the adjacent Rhineland, part of which had also belonged to Luxembourg before 1815.

From 1871 to 1918 the following states, duchies and principalities comprised the German Empire:

Alsace-Lorraine
 (*Elsass-Lothringen*)
Anhalt
Baden
Bavaria (*Bayern*)
Brandenburg[1]
Bremen
Brunswick (*Braunschweig*)
East Prussia (*Ostpreussen*)[1]
Hamburg
Hanover (*Hannover*)[1]
Hesse (*Hessen*)
Hesse-Nassau
 (*Hessen-Nassau*)[1]
Hohenzollern[1]

Lippe
Lübeck
Mecklenburg-Schwerin
Mecklenburg-Strelitz
Oldenburg
Palatinate (*Pfalz*)[2]
Pomerania (*Pommern*)[1]
Posen[1]
Rhineland (*Rheinland*)[1]
Kingdom of Saxony
 (*Sachsen*)
Province of Saxony
 (*Sachsen*)[1]
Schaumburg-Lippe
Schleswig-Holstein[1]

Thuringia (*Thüringen*),
 comprising:
 Reuss-Gera[3]
 Reuss-Greiz[3]
 Saxony-Altenburg[3]
 Saxony-Coburg-Gotha[3]
 Saxony-Meiningen[3]
 Saxony-Weimar-Eisenach[3]
 Schwarzburg-Rudolstadt[3]
 Schwarzburg-Sondershausen[3]
Silesia[1]
Waldeck
Westphalia (*Westfalen*)[1]
West Prussia (*Westpreussen*)[1]
Württemberg

[1] Prussian province
[2] Bavarian province
[3] These 8 duchies and principalities of Saxony (*Sachsen*), except Coburg which joined Bavaria in 1920, became the state of Thuringia (*Thüringen*) in 1920.

It is important to make note of the provinces, because your "Prussian" or "Bavarian" ancestor may have come from west of the Rhine. A geographic outline of the European areas of Germanic settlement is in the next section.

In 1919-23 Germany lost the ethnically mixed territories to the recreated states of Poland and Lithuania, to a newly established Czechoslovakia, and to France, Denmark and Belgium.

In the case of Upper Silesia and East Prussia, plebiscites were held in the border regions to allow the populace to choose the national home. In both cases, smaller parts of the territory chose Poland, but the greater part of the areas in question chose to remain with Germany.

No plebiscite was held in West Prussia. The largest part went to Poland and constituted the Polish Corridor to the Baltic Sea, which meant the division of Germany into two non-contiguous territories. Parts of the province were attached to neighboring German provinces, while the overwhelmingly German-populated Vistula-Nogat delta area became the Free City of Danzig in order to safeguard Polish access to a major port on the Baltic Sea.

While the residents of the Free City had a locally chosen government, not a Polish one, the resentment caused by being severed involuntarily from Germany became fertile soil for Hitler's propaganda.

The changes in the Austro-Hungarian Empire were even greater. In 1914, the Austrian-ruled half consisted of Austria proper, Bohemia, Bosnia and Herzegovina, Bukovina, Carinthia, Carniola, Dalmatia, Galicia, Istria, Moravia, Salzburg, the Austrian part of Silesia, Styria, Trent, Tyrol and Vorarlberg. Hungary ruled Croatia, Slavonia and Transylvania, in addition to Hungary proper (then much larger than today). After World War I, Austria and Hungary each became a separate, small country. A part of the ethnically mixed Burgenland region, which hitherto had belonged to Hungary, became part of Austria pursuant to a plebiscite.

Changes of much greater consequence were:

- the creation of Czechoslovakia (Bohemia, Moravia, Austrian Silesia, Hungarian-ruled Slovakia) in the north;

- the establishment of Yugoslavia (meaning the land of the South Slavs), combining the previously independent nations of Serbia and Montenegro with parts of the old Austro-Hungarian Empire which became the republics of Slovenia, Croatia and Bosnia-Herzegovina, and the Vojvodina, now an autonomous Serbian province; and

- the expansion of Romania, so as to include the largest German settlements in historic Hungary, as well as Bessarabia, which it annexed when the Russian Empire collapsed.

A very small portion of the Banat was transferred from Romania to Yugoslavia a few years after the war.

These changes meant that most of the ethnic Germans living between the predominantly German-speaking areas in the west and Russian or Ukrainian-speaking areas in the east were now subjects of a different country than the one to which they had belonged before World War I.

Part 3 of the geographic outline identifies the country in which these islands of German settlement are now located, although in several cases, mostly along the Soviet borders, there were changes in boundaries as a result of World War II, modifying the post-World War I map so that this outline does not describe the jurisdictional boundaries between the two world wars.

The areas where the boundaries changed in 1945 are listed under part 2(a) of the geographic outline, viz., East and West Prussia (including Danzig), Eastern Pomerania, Eastern Brandenburg and Silesia, most of which became part of Poland and some of which became part of the Soviet Union. Also affected were some of the islands of settlement identified under part 3 of the outline, viz., the Baltic countries, Volhynia, East Galicia, Bessarabia, Northern Bukovina and Carpatho-Ukraine, all of which became part of the Soviet Union.

There were also many temporary boundary adjustments during the 1938-45 period, beginning with Hitler's annexation of Austria and the Sudetenland. For a description of these, see the *AGoFF Guide* (see **ANNOTATED BIBLIOGRAPHY** in Chapter XVIII). The 1940 Romanian-Bulgarian boundary change has been permanent.

It may be possible to trace some so-called "Germanic" ancestors back to other countries where they lived before becoming assimilated into the Germanic culture.

Of course, there were some inter-ethnic marriages in the border areas and islands of German settlements listed in parts 2 and 3 of the outline, although they were not nearly as numerous as they have been in the American "melting pot."

In addition, people of Flemish, Dutch and Frisians stock were quite numerous among the "Germans" who migrated to Eastern Europe during the late Middle Ages and the early centuries of the modern era, as the "Holländereien" testify. "Holendry," or "Oledry" in Polish, is still part of the name of some communities settled by people of Dutch origin, and later also sometimes by those of German descent. Sooner or later, these people became assimilated into the ethnically kindred Germans.

The trading relationships between England, Scotland, Scandinavia and the continent, dating back to the Hanseatic League, led some English and Scottish families to settle in northern German areas and the reverse was true of Germans who settled in London and these countries.

Religious refugees from France, Belgium and the Netherlands fled to Germany in the sixteenth and seventeenth centuries to avoid religious persecution.

Sweden controlled significant parts of the German Baltic coast, particularly Pomerania, during the 1600s and early 1700s, which obviously led to some Swedish-German marriages. Some Swedish soldiers are known to have remained in German-populated areas after 1648. The Swedish, Danish and Spanish soldiers who fought in Germany during the Thirty Years' War, and the French soldiers who did so in many wars, had progeny through unofficial liaisons, as well as through legal marriages.

The centuries of conflict between the Ottoman Turks and the European Christian powers led to the capture of some young attendants in the Turkish camp, who were taken home by officers and raised as Germans.

In other instances, Swiss, Palatine, Hessian, Hanoverian and other Germanic migrants went to England and Ireland, as well as to the New World. Some of the migrants stayed in Britain for an interim period and then continued on to North America.

PHYSICAL GEOGRAPHY AND HISTORIC DESIGNATIONS

In many cases people may find it hard to identify the location of their ancestors because they are identified as coming from a particular mountain, river or forest region. Ernest Thode, *Atlas for Germanic Genealogy*, has maps showing many of these physical features, especially the various rivers. You can also find many of them in the *National Geographic Society Atlas* or in German-language encyclopedias (e.g., *Brockhaus*) with some hunting. For your convenience, we have identified some of the commonly used references to geographic regions or to historical areas that may be hard for non-Europeans to identify.

We have also included references to historic regions whose names are no longer commonly used and which may or may not have been political entities. Of course, boundaries changed in earlier centuries, as well as in this century, so the identified area may not be accurate for all periods.

Alb: (Swabian and Franconian): hilly uplands running from the south end of the Black Forest (Baden-Württemberg) along the north side of the Danube to Bayreuth (Bavaria).

Alpen: (Alps): highest, largest European mountain range, extending from the French-Italian border near the Mediterranean through most of Switzerland and Austria and crossing the border into northern Italy and southwestern Slovenia; many different modifiers are used to describe certain portions of the Alps.

Altmark: area around and north of Magdeburg (Saxony-Anhalt); area of early eastward expansion of the Saxons.

Banat: area around Timisoara, Romania, including the area east of the Tisza river in the Vojvodina and a few Hungarian villages near Szeged.

Batschka (Backa, Bácska): area between the Tisza and Danube rivers (northeastern Vojvodina next to Croatia and Hungary; sometimes used to include the adjacent area in Hungary).

Bayerisches Oberland (Bavarian Uplands): foothills of the Alps in southern Bavaria.

Bayerischer Wald (Bavarian Forest): east of Regensburg; parallel to the Danube river.

Böhmerwald (Bohemian Forest): mountainous area along the border between southeast Bohemia (southwestern Czech Republic) and Bavaria.

Breisgau: region in southern Baden which includes the Rhine river plain and the western slopes of the Black Forest; Freiburg is the main city.

Cherson (Kherson): western Black Sea province of the former Russian Empire between Odessa and Kherson.

Dobrudscha (Dobruja, Dobrogea): eastern Romania between the Danube and the Black Sea, extending into the northeastern tip of Bulgaria.

Donauschwaben (Danube Swabians): Germans who settled near the Lower Danube in what was then southern Hungary (now western Romania, the Vojvodina and southern Hungary) after the territory was reclaimed from the Ottoman Turks; known as Hungarian Germans until the 1920s.

Dongebiet (Don River area): province of the former Russian Empire around and northeast of Rostov.

Eifel: mountains between the Rhine and Moselle rivers to the boundary with Luxembourg and Belgium, reaching north almost to Aachen; southwestern part of current state of Northrhine-Westphalia.

Ekaterinoslav/Jekaterinoslav: former province of the Russian Empire north of Taurida, around Dnepropetrovsk.

Ermland (Warmia): area southeast of Braunsberg (East Prussia), between Königsberg and Allenstein.

Erzgebirge (Ore Mountains): range along the border between northeast Bohemia (Czech Republic) and southwest Saxony.

Franken (Franconia): northern Bavaria; land of the Frankish tribe, from which the name France is also derived; the Ansbach-Bayreuth area is mostly Protestant.

Generalgouvernement: the part of Poland ruled but not annexed by Hitler, essentially the area around Warsaw, Cracow and Lwów (now Ukrainian: L'viv; Russian: L'vov; German: Lemberg).

Grosspolen (Great Poland): area around Posen (Poznan) and Gnesen (Gniezno), site of a prominent early Polish duchy.

Haardt: vineyard-rich uplands parallel to the Rhine from west of Worms into northeastern Alsace; mostly in Rhineland-Palatinate.

Harzgebirge: mountains where Lower Saxony, Saxony-Anhalt and Thuringia meet.

Hunsrück: hilly area between the Moselle and Nahe rivers, extending from northwest Saarland to west of Bingen; northern part of current state of Rhineland-Palatinate.

Ingermanland (Ingria): Russian area east of Estonia and northeastern Latvia from St. Petersburg to Lake Peipus.

Jura: low mountains from southeast of Geneva along the north side of the Danube through Württemberg to north of Nuremberg (*Nürnberg*) in northern Bavaria; subdivided into Swiss, Swabian and Franconian Jura.

Kleinpolen (Little Poland): south Poland; Galicia and the Cracow area; site of an early Polish duchy.

Kuban: former Russian province along the Kuban River, which flows into the Sea of Azov directly east of the Crimean peninsula (northwestern part of the North Caucasus).

Kujawien (Kuyavia): in the Thorn (Torun)-Plock area near the Vistula.

Kulmerland: between Kulm (Chelmno) and Thorn (Torun), extending eastward; southwest East Prussia.

Kur- (e.g., Kurhessen, Kurpfalz): *Kur* = Electorate; when duchies and principalities were subdivided (as happened frequently in some areas), the elder line had the right to vote for the Holy Roman Emperor.

Kurland (Courland): western and southern Latvia.

Ländl: Same as **Salzkammergut**; term commonly used by Protestant refugees from the archbishopric of Salzburg.

Lausitz (Lusatia): east Saxony and southeast Brandenburg, between the Elbe and Bober rivers; Slavic Sorbs (also called Wends), the largest native minority in Germany and still speaking their own language although becoming assimilated, live here.

Livland (Livonia): eastern Latvia and southern Estonia (east and northeast of Riga).

Lodomerien: seldom used part of the official name of the Austrian crownland of Galizien und Lodomerien, derived from a former Volhynian duchy.

Lüneburger Heide (Luneburg Heath): between the Elbe and Weser rivers, southeast of Lüneburg; northeastern Lower Saxony.

Masowien (Mazovia): central Poland, around Warsaw and Lodz.

Masurien (Mazuria): southern East Prussia and the adjoining part of interwar Poland.

Mittelmark: Brandenburg west of the Oder river.

Moldau (Moldavia): northeastern Romania and Moldova.

Narewgebiet (Narew River area): around Lomza, Poland, and Hrodna (Grodno), Belarus.

Neumark: Brandenburg east of the Oder river (now in Poland); often used to refer specifically to northeast Brandenburg along the Netze river.

Neu-Ostpreussen (New East Prussia): the area south and east of East Prussia, extending from Kaunas, Lithuania, to Warsaw, which was under Prussian rule in 1795-1806.

Neurussland (New Russia): term applied to Russian conquests from the Turks along the Black Sea; synonymous with Südrussland (South Russia).

Odenwald: forested area between the Main and Neckar rivers in south Hesse and north Baden-Württemberg.

Ostsee: Baltic Sea (literally East Sea to distinguish it from the North Sea).

Pannonien (Pannonia): an old Roman province in the vicinity of where the Danube Swabians later settled.

Podlachien (Podlachia): area around Brest Litovsk (western Belarus and east central Poland).

Podolien (Podolia): area east of Galicia around Khmel'nyts'kyi, Ukraine.

Pommerellen (Pomerelia): frequently translated as Pomerania (it was part of Pomerania 750 years ago), but roughly identical with the interwar Polish Corridor to the Baltic Sea.

Rheinhessen: area around Mainz on the west bank of the Rhine, which belonged to Hesse when the rest of the Palatinate belonged to Bavaria; still the name of a government district intermediate between a state and a county.

Salzkammergut: area east of Salzburg (Austria).

Samogitien (Samogitia/Zmudz): northwestern Lithuania.

Sauerland: area southeast of the Ruhr industrial complex, between the Ruhr river in the north and the Sieg and Fulda rivers in the south.

Schwaben: name derived from the Swabian, also known as the Alamanni, tribe; Württemberg and southeast Bavaria; often used as a synonym for Württemberg, which is surrounded by C-shaped Baden on the north, west and south; sometimes used as a generic term for Germans who settled in East Central Europe in the late 18th and early 19th centuries.

Seenplatte: coastal plains; differentiated by Mecklenburg, Pomeranian and Prussian plains.

Semgallen (Zemgalia, Semigalia): area south of the Western Daugava (Dvina) River in Latvia next to its border with Lithuania and Belarus.

Siebenbürgen (Transylvania): historically, the German area of settlement in what is now central Romania, north of Sibiu (*Hermannstadt*) and Brasov (*Kronstadt*); but Transylvania is now often used to describe the northwestern third of Romania.

Spessart: between the Kinzig river and Franconian fork of the Saale river in northwest Bavaria, crossing slightly into Hesse.

Steigerwald: forested area between the Main and Aisch rivers, west of Bamberg, Bavaria.

Strasse or **-strasse** with a prefix: refers to the area along one of many roads that are well-known in Germany, for example, the Weinstrasse is parallel to and west of the Rhine (roughly equal to Haardt), while the Romantische Strasse refers to a road, mostly in northeastern Württemberg, where many towns have retained their medieval features; such a term may occasionally be used to distinguish one village from another by the same name.

Sudetengebirge: mountains along the border of Silesia and the northeast Czech Republic.

Sudetenland: the C-shaped mountainous rim of the Czech Republic annexed by Hitler in 1938; not limited to the Sudeten mountain region; most of the area was populated chiefly by German-speakers, especially in the west and north.

Südpreussen (South Prussia): the area west of Warsaw that was under Prussian rule in 1795-1806; roughly equivalent to Great Poland or to the province of Posen without the Netze (Notec) river district in the north.

Südrussland (South Russia): the Black Sea areas won by Russia from the Turks under Catherine the Great; now roughly southern Ukraine.

Syrmien (Syrmia, Srem): area south of the Danube in the southeastern part of the Serbian Vojvodina (northwest of Belgrade).

Taunus: northeast of Wiesbaden in southwest Hesse.

Taurien (Taurida): eastern Black Sea province of the former Russian Empire (Crimea and northeast of it).

Terek: former Russian province along the Terek River, which flows into the Caspian Sea in southernmost European Russia (southeastern North Caucasus region); mostly in Dagestan, Chechnya and Ingushetia.

Thüringerwald (Thuringian Forest): from Eisenach (Thuringia) to northeast of Coburg on the Bavarian border; parallels the Werra river on the northeast.

Transnistrien (Transnistria): area northeast of Odessa between the Dniester and the southern Bug rivers (mostly southwestern Ukraine, but including the present breakaway portion of eastern Moldova).

U(e)ckermark: region of the U(e)cker river in the northeastern part of the present German state of Brandenburg and the eastern part of Mecklenburg-Vorpommern.

Vogesen (Vosges): mountains in western Alsace, parallel to the Rhine.

Vogtland: southwest Saxony in the vicinity of Plauen.

Warthegau: the Warta river region around Kolo and Konin, between Warsaw and the city of Posen, in the west central part of former Congress Poland or Russian Poland.

Walachei (Walachia): southern Romania.

Westerwald: forested area north of Koblenz, east of the Rhine, in the northeastern part of Rhineland-Palatinate, extending into Hesse.

Windisch Mark: roughly equivalent to Slovenia; southeastern corner of Charlemagne's empire; name derived from the Wends, one of several peoples who migrated to the area.

GEOGRAPHIC OUTLINE OF AREAS
OF GERMANIC SETTLEMENT IN EUROPE

OVERVIEW

1. The Germanic Heartland
2. Adjacent Ethnically Mixed Areas (the Rimland)
3. Scattered Settlements in Eastern Europe
4. Other Countries of Origin (or Transit) for Germanicized Ancestors

DETAILED OUTLINE

1. **The German Heartland.** Countries where German is now an official language.

   (a) **Germany**. The Federal Republic of Germany now includes the following *Länder*:

Baden-Württemberg	Hesse	Saarland
Bavaria	Lower Saxony	Saxony*
Berlin (unique status)	Mecklenburg-Vorpommern*	Saxony-Anhalt*
Brandenburg*	Northrhine-Westphalia	Schleswig-Holstein
Bremen	Rhineland-Palatinate	Thuringia*
Hamburg		

   The starred areas were part of the German Democratic Republic from 1949 to 1990. At that time they constituted the *Bezirke* (Districts) of:

Cottbus	Gera	Neubrandenburg
Dresden	Halle	Potsdam
East Berlin	Karl Marx-Stadt	Rostock
Erfurt	Leipzig	Schwerin
Frankfurt an der Oder	Magdeburg	Suhl

   The city of Berlin was divided between the two former German republics from 1949 to 1990.

   (b) **Austria**. Austria currently has the following states:

Burgenland	*Salzburg*	Upper Austria
Carinthia (*Kärnten*)	Styria (*Steiermark*)	(*Oberösterreich*)
Lower Austria	Tyrol (*Tirol*)	Vienna (*Wien*)
(*Niederösterreich*)		*Vorarlberg*

   (c) **Switzerland**. At least 94% of the people had German as their mother tongue in 1920 in the following Swiss cantons:

Aargau	Lucerne (*Luzern*)	*Solothurn*
Appenzell-Ausser-Rhoden	*Nidwalden*	*Thurgau*
Appenzell-Inner-Rhoden	*Obwalden*	*Unterwalden*
Basel-Land	St. Gall (*St. Gallen*)	*Uri*
Basel-Stadt (Basel City)	*Schaffhausen*	*Zug*
Glarus	*Schwyz*	*Zürich*

   Berne (*Bern*) canton was formerly 83% German. However, the French-speaking northwestern portion of this canton later became the canton of Jura, so the present Berne canton is also overwhelmingly German-speaking. *Graubünden* (Grisons), which was home to 91% of the Romansch-speakers in Switzerland, was nevertheless 51% German.

   About 31% of the people had German as their primary language in the French cantons of *Freiburg* (Fribourg) and *Wallis* (Valais). The German-speakers accounted for 10-12% of the people in the cantons of *Waadt* (Vaud), *Genf* (Geneva) and *Neuenburg* (Neuchâtel). Only 6% of the residents of overwhelmingly Italian *Tessin* (Ticino) canton were native German-speakers. The percentage of German-speakers in Jura canton is unknown but small.

For maps of the above present or recent jurisdictional units, see Ernest Thode, *Atlas for Germanic Genealogy*.

(d) **Luxembourg**. Luxembourg has the following cantons:

Capellen	Grevenmacher	Remich
Clervaux	Luxembourg-Campagne	Vianden
Diekirch	Luxembourg-Ville	Wiltz
Echtermach	Mersch	
Esch-sur-Alzette	Redange	

(e) **Liechtenstein**. Liechtenstein is too small to have any sub-units.

2. **The Germanic Rimlands.** Areas adjacent to the Germanic heartland that had a substantial German-speaking population during the nineteenth century.

(a) Formerly mostly German areas that were part of the Weimar Republic and the Free City of Danzig (now Gdansk in Poland), 1919-1945
   (i) East Prussia (now Poland and the Soviet Union)
   (ii) Free City of Danzig (formerly part of West Prussia, now Poland)
   (iii) Eastern Pomerania (Pomorze, now in Poland)
   (iv) Eastern Brandenburg (now Poland)
   (v) Nearly all of Silesia (Slask, now in Poland)

(b) Ethnically mixed areas that were part of the German Empire, 1871-1919
   (i) Transferred to Poland in 1919-21
       (1) Nearly all of *Posen* (Poznan)
       (2) The greater part of West Prussia (which ceased to exist as a province in 1919)
       (3) Eastern Upper Silesia (Slask)
       (4) The southern tip of East Prussia
   (ii) *Memelland* (now Lithuania)
   (iii) The *Hultschin* (Hlucín) region in Silesia (now the Czech Republic)
   (iv) Eupen-Malmedy (now Belgium)
   (v) Alsace-Lorraine (now France)
   (vi) North Schleswig (now Nord Slesvig in Denmark)

(c) Areas near interwar Austria and Germany that were part of the Austro-Hungarian Empire, 1867-1919
   (i) Sudetenland in Bohemia/Moravia/Austrian Silesia (now the Czech Republic)
   (ii) South Tyrol (now Alto Adige in Italy)
   (iii) Eastern *Burgenland* (Hungary)
   (iv) The *Teschen* (Cieszyn) part of Austrian Silesia (now in Poland)

(d) Adjacent to Luxembourg: the Belgian province of Luxembourg

3. **Major Islands of Germanic Settlements.** Major German settlements in non-Germanic lands.

(a) Contemporary Poland
   (i) Lodz area
   (ii) Lipno-Rypin-Gostynin area on both sides of the Vistula (*Weichsel*, Wisla) River, east and south of *Thorn* (Torun)
   (iii) On both sides of the Warta (*Warthe*) River, north and south of Konin and Kolo
   (iv) Western Galicia (*Westgalizien*, Galicja)
   (v) Eastern Poland (around Chelm)

(b) The Baltic countries (Estonia, Latvia, Lithuania)
(c) Russia
   (i) The Volga (*Wolga*) settlements
   (ii) Perm-Orenburg (near the foot of the Urals)

(iii) Siberia (along the Trans-Siberian Railway and along the border with Kazakhstan)

(iv) Northern Caucasus (southernmost European Russia)

(v) Near Rostov (northeast tip of Sea of Azov)

(d) Ukraine

(i) The Black Sea settlements (nearly all in Ukraine)

(ii) Volhynia (*Wolhynien*)

(iii) South Bessarabia (*Süd-Bessarabien*)

(iv) East Galicia (*Ostgalizien*, Halychyna)

(v) North Bukovina (*Buchenland*, Bukowina)

(vi) Carpatho-Ukraine (Subcarpathian Rus'; Karpato-Ukraine; *Karpatenland*; formerly eastern tip of Czechoslovakia)

(e) Moldova (Northern Bessarabia, *Glückstal* villages)

(f) Georgia and Azerbaijan

(i) South Caucasus (southern Georgia, northern Azerbaijan)

(ii) North Caucasus (northern Georgia)

(g) Kazakhstan and other Muslim republics belonging to the CIS
(now the main center of Germans; only a few pre-1914 settlements)

(h) Contemporary Romania

(i) Transylvania (*Siebenbürgen*)

(ii) Eastern Banat

(iii) Satu Mare (*Sathmar*)

(iv) Most of Dobruja (*Dobrudscha*, Dobrogea)

(v) Southern Bukovina (*Buchenland*)

(i) Yugoslavia (Serbia-Montenegro; almost all in the Vojvodina)

(i) Western Banat

(ii) Southern *Batschka* (Backa, Bácska)

(iii) Syrmia (*Syrmien*, Srem)

(j) Croatia

(i) Southern Baranya (*Baranja*)

(ii) Slavonia (*Slawonien*)

(k) Slovenia

(i) *Gottschee* (Kocevje)

(ii) Carniola (*Krain*, Krajnska): Maribor (*Marburg*), Ljubljana (*Laibach*), Cilli

(iii) Gorizia (*Görz*) and Gradisca (*Gradiska*)

(l) Contemporary Hungary

(i) Swabian Turkey (*Schwäbische Türkei*)

(ii) Northern Bácska (*Batschka*, Backa)

(iii) Central Highlands north of Lake Balaton (*Plattensee*), including Budapest

(m) Czech Republic

(i) Bohemia (*Böhmen*): outer rim, Jihlava (*Iglau*) and smaller enclaves

(ii) Moravia (*Mähren*): north and south, Hrebec (*Schönhengst*), Olomouc (*Olmütz*) and smaller enclaves

(iii) Former Austrian Silesia (*Österreichisch-Schlesien*), now part of Moravia

(n) Slovak Republic

(i) Bratislava (*Pressburg*) area

(ii) Spis (*Zips*)

(iii) Hauerland (*Kremnitz*/Kremnica, *Deutsch-Proben*/Nitrianske Pravno)

(o) Contemporary Bulgaria (Southern Dobruja/Dobrudza/*Dobrudscha*)

4. **Other Relevant Lands.** Other countries of origin (or transit) for Germanicized ancestors

(a) Netherlands
(b) Great Britain
(c) France
(d) Belgium
(e) Norway

(f) Sweden
(g) Spain
(h) Turkey
(i) Ireland

Chapter X

HISTORY OF GERMAN-SPEAKING PEOPLE IN EUROPE

Any classification of European political entities for purposes of tracing the history of the Germanic peoples is arbitrary to some extent, because the changes were so frequent and so drastic. In this instance, the material is presented on the basis of the boundaries between 1871 and 1919, when there was relatively little change. This was the period during which a large majority of German-speaking immigrants came to North America and some other New World countries, so this arrangement will simplify coordinating information regarding immigrant ancestors with the sovereign units that existed at that time.

If your ancestors ever lived under German-speaking rulers, they almost certainly did so during that period, when both the German Empire and the Austrian (Austro-Hungarian) Empire were at their largest. However, German-speakers were not a majority in all of the territory included in these empires. There was no independent Poland at the time and Germans were but one of many minorities in the Hapsburg Empire, which had no ethnic majority.

THE GERMAN EMPIRE OF 1871 TO 1919

THE EARLY AND MEDIEVAL ERAS

Although there were many Germanic tribes in northern Europe during the days of the Roman Empire (described by the Roman historian, Tacitus), they scattered throughout much of Europe and North Africa during the following *Völkerwanderung* (Great Barbarian Migrations).

The modern German identity can be traced back to 843, when Charlemagne's empire was divided among his grandsons, and Ludwig the German became king of the East Frankish Kingdom (roughly east of the Rhine), as contrasted with the West Frankish Kingdom, which became France, with the Middle Kingdom (Rhineland, Alsace-Lorraine, Low Countries, Burgundy, etc.) between them.

Early medieval "Germany" included only about half of the territory of the nineteenth century German Empire. Its eastern boundary approximated the Elbe River, along a line extending from just east of Hamburg to the northwest corner of the Czech Republic. Slavic tribes occupied the area east of the line during the early centuries of the medieval era after it had been vacated by the Goths and related tribes. Germans began to move into this area in the eleventh century as a result of overpopulation. In some instances they quietly settled in the uninhabited wooded or marshy areas between Slavic settlements. In other cases the eastward expansion was the result of military conflicts. The Teutonic Knights, the Hanseatic League, and the church were also driving forces, as concentrated Germanic settlement was extended to the Memel River.

Many of the people who became part of what German scholars refer to as the "new tribes" were actually Slavs who became Germanicized as a result of intermarriage, the policies of their rulers, the attractiveness of Western religions and technological influences, or sheerly because they were outnumbered by the incoming Germans. Thus in reality many of those easterners who identified themselves as Germans during the modern era had a mixed German-Slavic background. However, not all of the Slavs in Germanic territory became assimilated. The Slavs in Lusatia (Saxony) constitute an identifiable ethnic minority group in Germany to this day. Many Poles moved to the Rhine-Ruhr area to find jobs during the late decades of the Industrial Revolution. Some have retained a sense of their Polish heritage.

Nevertheless, by about 1350 the German-Polish linguistic border had come to approximate what it was until 1945, despite some relatively modest later changes along the entire line (but varying considerably in degree from one area to another). Bear in mind, that there was no clear-cut dividing line. There were substantial German minorities on the Polish side of the fuzzy border and, to a lesser extent, Poles on the German side.

In 962 Otto I, the Great, was crowned as emperor in Rome, reviving the empire established by Charlemagne (Karl der Grosse) in 800. The largest of the powerful duchies associated with this empire were those of Saxony, Bavaria, Franconia, Swabia and Lorraine.

This empire, established in 800 and re-established in 962, later came to be known as the "first" empire, and the one founded in 1870-71 as the "second" empire, hence Hitler's "Third Reich (Empire)."

The full name of this first empire came to be the Holy Roman Empire of the German Nation. Its territory was mostly Germanic. "Roman" signified the heritage it claimed and its religious connection with the pope in Rome, who crowned many of the early emperors.

After 1250, the emperor, who was chosen by 7 and later 9 electors, ceased to be a strong ruler except where he was the direct ruler and not just the overlord. After the Hapsburg dynasty took over the emperorship (initially in 1273, permanently from 1438 to 1806, with minor exceptions) the center of the empire shifted to Vienna, so it became more Austrian than German.

The Hapsburg Empire encompassed all of what is now Germany, Austria, Switzerland, the Czech and Slovak Republics, Hungary, the Netherlands, Belgium, Luxembourg, and Spain, as well as parts of Poland, Ukraine, Romania, the former Yugoslav federation, Italy and France, at some time during the sixteenth, seventeenth, or eighteenth centuries. Hence, even an emperor who was a weak overlord with respect to the many largely autonomous dukes and other local rulers was often a power to be reckoned with.

Other major developments of the Late Middle Ages included: the development of cities, beginning about 1070; the bubonic plague, known as the Black Death, which killed half the people in the mid-14th century and halted substantial Germanic eastward migration until the Protestant Reformation; the development of strong guilds and large-scale international trade and trade associations (*Hansas*) in the 14th and 15th centuries, with beginnings dating back to the 12th century; and the invention of movable type by Gutenberg in 1450, which rapidly changed the degree and significance of literacy.

THE REFORMATION ERA

The two primary initiators of the Protestant Reformation on the European continent were German-speakers: Luther and Zwingli. There were, however, many others who contributed to a proliferation of Protestant schools of thought, which developed into separate churches.

"Protestantism" actually predated Luther. Some Waldensians, originating with Peter Waldo in 1170, and the Moravian Brethren, stemming from the Hussite movement that gained strength after John Huss (Jan Hus) was burned for heresy in 1415, survived. Both groups later found refuge in Germany.

Protestantism (mostly Lutherans, but also Calvinistic with Anabaptist pockets in the south and west) became the dominant religion in German areas in the first few decades after the Reformation, but the Counter-Reformation regained Catholic predominance in Bavaria and the Rhineland, as well as portions of southwestern Germanic areas and Westphalia. The Peasants' War of 1524-25, which was directed against oppression by secular authorities and feudal lords but inspired by Luther's "revolt" against the church, was squashed and left the peasants in a miserable and lethargic condition for several more centuries, especially in southern Germany.

The Catholic Counter-Reformation led to the re-Catholicizing of Poland, Bohemia, Moravia, and Hungary. Thereafter, assimilation tended to follow religious lines, particularly in Poland. German Catholics, especially in the more isolated settlements, tended to become Polonized, whereas the reverse was true for what was left of Polish Protestantism after the Counter-Reformation. But by no means did all members of the two religious minorities become assimilated in terms of their cultural identity. For example, in the Czech Republic and in Hungary the Germans became more solidly Catholic than the Slavs or Magyars.

The Reformation caused a relatively substantial flight of Protestants, especially Dutch, Flemish and Frisian Mennonites, from the then Spanish-ruled Netherlands to what later became known as West Prussia. Calvinists from the Spanish-ruled area also fled eastward, with those speaking Dutch or Flemish going mostly to West Prussia, then under tolerant Polish rule, and the French-speaking ones, known as Walloons, going to German principalities with Reformed rulers, especially the Palatinate and Hesse. Calvinists from some Lutheran-ruled states, like Mecklenburg, also joined the stream of eastward-bound refugees.

The religious wars in the early Reformation period, interspersed with battles against the Turks on the Hungarian frontier, ended with the Peace of Augsburg in 1555. This required people to accept the religion of their ruler, but it applied only to Catholics and Lutherans. Not until 1648 did the Reformed (Calvinist) Church achieve parity.

The Thirty Years' War (1618-48) was the most devastating war ever fought on Germanic and Czech territory. It started as a war to suppress Protestantism in Bohemia, a goal quickly achieved, but continued, with a few truces, as a war that at one time or another involved most of the countries in Europe, with Sweden, Denmark, and France helping the Protestant princes break the power of the Holy Roman Emperor and the Spanish forces on the other side. After 1635, when Catholic France, rather than the Protestant duchies, became the main opponent of its imperial arch-rival, the war lost its religious significance.

Historians estimate that one third or more of the German and Czech people died, many from famine. Many villages were destroyed, survivors were forced to flee, farmland was left uncultivated and commerce virtually ceased. But the amount of devastation was much greater in some areas than in others. As part of the postwar reconstruction, there was a major migration of people from areas that had been spared, more or less, to those which suffered the most. This took nearly a century.

In particular, large numbers of people from the Alpine Swiss and Tyrolean area moved northward to Württemberg, Thuringia, the Palatinate, Alsace and neighboring areas. This helps explain why the Schweitzer surname occurs in so many villages in these regions. The west central and northwestern Germanic areas also suffered relatively little, so Flemings and Walloons (today's Belgians), as well as people from the Holstein area, were well represented among those who moved eastward and southeastward to repopulate almost empty villages.

Mecklenburg, Pomerania, Northern Brandenburg and Saxony-Anhalt were also areas that suffered heavily, but the northeasternmost German lands, including Prussia, escaped serious destruction. Mecklenburg and Western Pomerania never fully recovered from the deaths of two-thirds of their residents.

The Peace of Westphalia in 1648 recognized the independence of Switzerland and the Netherlands and gave the hundreds of German rulers almost complete independence from the emperor in Vienna, who technically remained their overlord until the empire was formally abolished in 1806.

The Hapsburgs continued to dominate the lands they ruled directly, i.e., what came to be the Austrian (after 1867, Austro-Hungarian) Empire, but they ceased to matter in the political affairs of Germany proper after 1648, except as an outside power seeking to influence events.

Most of Alsace became part of France in 1648, after the war, although it had previously belonged to the Holy Roman Empire. Lorraine had a distinct history, becoming a part of France in 1766. Alsace and the northeastern fifth of Lorraine (so-called "German Lorraine") were part of the German Empire from 1871 to 1919.

There were two significant post-1648 waves of religious migration into Germany. One was the flight of the French Huguenots into Calvinist-ruled German states in the Palatinate,

Franconia, Hesse, Saxony-Anhalt, Brandenburg and northwestern Germany after 1685. Around 1700 some 20-25% of Berliners had French Huguenot blood. The Huguenot impact on Magdeburg was comparable. The other wave was the sporadic exodus of Protestant exiles from Salzburg, Upper and Lower Austria, primarily to East Prussia, Brandenburg and Franconia, but also to Transylvania, mostly during the 1730s.

THE LATE MODERN ERA

Soon after the Thirty Years' War, a new German power began to arise in the northeast. In 1701 the Berlin-centered Mark of Brandenburg became the Kingdom of Prussia, taking its name from the Balto-Slavic tribe that the Teutonic Knights had largely annihilated. In 1740 it wrested almost all of Silesia from Austria. When Poland was partitioned in 1772-95, Prussia gained control over more than three-fourths of what constitutes Poland today, excluding only the southeastern area, roughly east of a line from Cracow to Warsaw. However, Central Poland, around Warsaw and Lodz, became the Duchy of Warsaw created by Napoleon and fell under Russian control after 1815. The eastern and western parts of Pomerelia (West Prussia) acquired by Prussia in the first two partitions were predominantly German-speaking, with a substantial German minority in Posen, central West Prussia, and the Netze River district, which belonged to Posen in the nineteenth century but constituted a distinct administrative entity during certain periods of history. Most of the Netze River area had a German majority in 1918. Prussian rule led to a heavy influx of Germans into Posen, and to a lesser but still quite significant degree, into Central Poland.

Meanwhile, Napoleon ruled many of the small independent German states much of the time from 1792 to 1815. There were many and frequent border changes, but the end result was the consolidation of over 300 existing principalities into 39 medium-sized ones. He also instituted civil registration of births, marriages and deaths. Such records have been maintained in Hanover, Hesse, Baden and the areas to the west of them since that time.

French nationalism led to German counter-nationalism, which led to the Wars of Liberation of 1813-15 and the liberal revolutions of 1830 and 1848 that sought a free and united Germany. After those events were suppressed, the German Empire was established under Otto von Bismarck's leadership as a result of the wars of 1864-71 against Denmark, Austria and France, respectively.

German nationalism, and especially Prussian policies seeking to Germanicize the Poles by coercion, in turn led to Polish nationalism. This produced the migration of many Germans in Central Poland to Eastern Poland, which had a substantial Ukrainian population and to a heavily Ukrainian Volhynia. The powerful wave of nationalism did not reach Russia and Ukraine until the 1870s, when it sparked German emigrations from there to the Americas.

Prussia controlled most of the northern half of Germany after 1815. Thus immigrants who renounced allegiance to the Prussian king upon naturalization as American citizens may have come from as far away from Prussia proper as the province of Rhineland.

The German Customs Union, established in 1833-36, and the building of a railroad system that bound the entire country together by the late 1850s, stimulated trade and facilitated travel. This made it much easier for a would-be emigrant from inland areas not close to navigable rivers to reach the ocean ports of Bremen, Antwerp, and especially Hamburg.

Karl Marx issued the *Communist Manifesto* in 1848. It was at about this time that the Industrial Revolution in Germany, begun in the 1840s, started to accelerate. Over the next several decades, mass production eliminated the cottage industries on which many small farmers depended for the supplemental income needed to survive.

The slums, which housed the early farm migrants turned factory workers, were probably one of the reasons why many villagers who were forced to relocate decided it might be better to go overseas (primarily to the United States) as farmers than to enter the industrial jungle. Bismarck instituted major social welfare programs in the 1880s in order to undercut the political appeal of the growing socialist party. The adoption of these measures was soon followed by the end of large-scale German emigration.

The wars of unification also contributed significantly to emigration, because many Germans did not care to serve in the armed forces of an empire dominated by Prussia, which had already long been regarded as a militaristic state. Those who fought in these wars often left in order to spare their sons that experience.

It is noteworthy, however, that many emigrants who had left Germany because of their antipathy to the authorities began to develop a sense of identification with German nationalism after Bismarck's many successes led to growing international respect for Germany as a major world power.

The end of World War I saw the reestablishment of an independent Poland, which included almost all of Posen, central West Prussia and eastern Silesia; and an independent Lithuania, which acquired the Memel territory, formerly belonging to East Prussia, in 1923. Germany also lost Alsace-Lorraine (which it had acquired in 1871) to France, the Eupen-Malmedy region to Belgium, and North Schleswig to Denmark. All of these, especially Alsace, were ethnically mixed areas from which a significant number of German-speaking emigrants went to both Eastern Europe and to the New World.

Bohemia and Moravia, which became part of Czechoslovakia, had belonged to the Austrian (not the German) Empire before 1918-19. But after World War I, these Germans began to identify more with a strong Germany than with a weak Austria. This area constituted the Sudetenland, which Hitler annexed in 1938.

In 1944-45 an estimated 5 million Germans fled westward from the areas east of the Oder-Neisse line in fear of the advancing Soviet armies. The Allies decided at the Potsdam Conference in 1945 to put this area under Polish administration, at least tacitly to compensate Poland for the loss of its eastern territories to the Soviet Union. Most of the Germans who had remained in the area (over 3 million) were expelled in or shortly after 1945. Most of those who were left (several hundred thousand, most of them married to Poles or otherwise largely assimilated into the Polish population) "resettled" in West Germany after both the Gorbachev "thaw" and the somewhat earlier and faster thaw in Poland made this possible. This area, eventually recognized *de jure* as part of Poland, included the former German states of East and West Prussia, most of Silesia, the eastern parts of Pomerania and Brandenburg, and a tiny corner of southeast Saxony.

The rest of Germany was divided into Soviet, American, British and French occupation zones, with four analogous sectors in Berlin. In 1949 the three Western zones were transformed into the Federal Republic of Germany, with a substantial rearrangement of the former states into what soon became 11 new states (*Länder*), including West Berlin, which had a special status, and the Saar, which remained under French control for a few years. The other states were Baden-Württemberg (3 states until 1952), Bavaria, Bremen, Hamburg, Hesse, Lower Saxony, Northrhine-Westphalia, Rhineland-Palatinate and Schleswig-Holstein. Lower Saxony, Northrhine-Westphalia and Rhineland-Palatinate were new political entities, not based on historic precedent. Hesse was a combination of several former states, as was Baden-Württemberg. Only Bavaria, Schleswig-Holstein and the city-states of Hamburg and Bremen represented continuity with the past.

The German Democratic Republic, a Communist state despite its name, was created by the Soviet Union as a response to an independent West Germany. Here the state boundaries were also changed, indeed twice, with the end result being 15 districts (*Bezirke*), which were deliberately drawn so as to represent a maximum break with the past.

In 1989-90, change overtook East Germany with lightning speed. Free elections were held when the Communist colossus collapsed very suddenly, following political liberalization in Poland, the Soviet Union, Hungary and Czechoslovakia and the mass flight of East Germans to the West through Hungary and Czechoslovakia. Within months Germany was reunited, and the "5 new states" of Saxony, Thuringia, Saxony-Anhalt, Brandenburg, and

Mecklenburg-Vorpommern (a 1990 reestablishment of states that existed for a brief period after World War II) were technically admitted into the Federal Republic of Germany.

Now, perhaps for the first time in history, there is no dispute by national governments as to what constitutes Germany. But a large number of New World residents have German-speaking ancestors who immigrated from areas outside contemporary Germany. Their common heritage is language and culture, not necessarily identification with any past or present political entity.

THE AUSTRO-HUNGARIAN EMPIRE OF 1867 TO 1919

During the last two decades of the nineteenth century, when the largest number of German-speaking immigrants came to America, the second largest population of ethnic Germans was in the Austro-Hungarian Empire.

Roughly the western half of this empire had belonged to the Holy Roman Empire of the German Nation prior to its abolition by Napoleon in 1806. This area could be divided into what had been the archduchy of Austria from 1359 to 1804 (and a duchy, or sometimes more than one duchy, since 1156) and what had been the kingdom of Bohemia since 1158.

The eastern half was the kingdom of Hungary (dating back to A.D. 1000), which had also elected the Hapsburg emperor to be king in 1526 when the Ottoman Turks defeated the Hungarians. It had remained under Hapsburg control thereafter, but never was a part of the Holy Roman Empire.

The German word for Austria, "Österreich," means "eastern kingdom or empire." This was the easternmost part of the empire of Karl der Grosse, better known to us as "Charlemagne," and came under his control about the time he was crowned "Emperor of the Romans" (A.D. 800). Known initially as the "Ostmark," or "Eastern March," it has had a continuous existence since the tenth century, when it began as a margravate of Bavaria.

In 843, Louis the German received the lands east of the Rhine in the tripartite division of Charlemagne's empire. This marks the beginning of the separate development of French and German ethnic or linguistic identities, both originating from the same Frank tribe (although other Germanic tribes lived in both areas). The area became increasingly disunited until 962, when Otto I (the Great), the Saxon king of what was then the northern Germanic area, established the Holy Roman Empire, or, in a sense, re-established the united empire of Charles the Great.

In 1273, Rudolph I of Hapsburg ("Rudolf von Habsburg" in German) was elected both king of Germany (a largely honorific title, since most power was in the hands of the legally subordinate dukes) and Holy Roman Emperor. Although the "Habsburg" (hawk's castle) was in Switzerland and the dynasty originated in Alsace, the Count of Hapsburg soon established control over Austria and Styria by defeating the local ruler. This remained the core of the Hapsburg dominions, and the area that they actually ruled directly (in contrast to the much larger imperial area over which they had only nominal control).

To their holdings, the Hapsburgs added Carinthia and Carniola (*Kärnten* and *Krain*) in 1335, Tyrol (*Tirol*) in 1363, Istria (*Istrien*) in 1374, what was to become Vorarlberg in and after 1375, Trieste in 1382, Gorizia in 1500 and other Friuli (*Friaul*) districts in 1511.

Hence, even though the emperorship itself was a weak office after 1250, the extensive holdings of the Hapsburgs made them a power to be reckoned with throughout Europe. Thus the fact that the Hapsburgs served almost continuously as Holy Roman Emperors from 1438 to 1806 has led quite properly to historical references to "the Hapsburg Empire" as a major factor in great power politics.

Since the Reformation and the Counter-Reformation are very significant events for the purpose of explaining subsequent migration within and from Europe, it is noteworthy that from 1519 to 1556 (i.e., during the infancy of Protestantism), the same Hapsburg dynasty, as a result of marriages, also ruled Spain, Burgundy, the Netherlands, much of Italy and the Spanish possessions in the Americas. In 1526, Hungary and Bohemia were added. Therefore, they had an extraordinary concentration of power in Europe at that time, despite the limits of imperial authority.

On the other hand, the Ottoman Turks reached the gates of Vienna in 1529 before being turned back. For nearly two centuries, they ruled most of the Balkans and forced the Austrian ruler to pay for the privilege of ruling the remaining sliver of Western Hungary and Northern or Upper Hungary, i.e., today's Slovak Republic and Carpatho-Ukraine. In 1683, the Turks again approached Vienna and were repelled. But this time their retreat led to the reconquest of nearly all of Old Hungary (which then included large parts of what later became Romania and Yugoslavia) by 1688 (officially recognized by treaty in 1699), and additional gains (the Banat) in 1718.

Meanwhile, however, Protestantism had made significant strides, especially in Bohemia. In fact, John Huss had preceded Luther as a "Protestant" by a century. The splintered Hussites were a significant (at times dominant) factor in Bohemia and Moravia for two centuries.

The Thirty Years' War (actually a series of wars, with brief truces) broke out in 1618 as a Catholic-Protestant conflict. The Protestant forces in Bohemia were squelched in 1620, but what had begun as a religious war gradually turned into a political war—fully so in 1635, when the Catholic French king intervened on the side of the Protestants in order to check his Hapsburg rival.

In 1648 an utterly exhausted Europe finally agreed to the Peace of Westphalia. Although it took more than another century before religious toleration became the policy in the Hapsburg lands, the days when dissident Christians were put to death for their beliefs were over. Swiss and Dutch independence, long a fact, was officially recognized.

For further information concerning the Hapsburg Empire, particularly as it relates to events of the Reformation era, see the previous section on **THE GERMAN EMPIRE**, since the Reformation had a greater impact on German history than on Austrian history.

The last 65 years of the Holy Roman Empire saw numerous changes in territorial control. In 1742, the Hapsburgs lost the greater part of tri-national Silesia (German, Czech, Polish) to Prussia and failed in the effort to gain it back in the Seven Years' War (1756-63). In the first partition of Poland in 1772, Austria gained the kingdoms of Galicia and Lodomeria. Adjacent territory to the north gained in 1795 was lost in 1809. The Bukovina (also known as "Buchenland") was obtained in 1775 from the Turkish-ruled principality of Moldavia in return for Austria's mediation in the Russo-Turkish Peace.

During the Napoleonic Wars (specifically in 1797, 1803-05 and 1809) numerous territorial changes took place, with most being Austrian losses. These included Tyrol and Salzburg. But when the wars were over in 1815, the Hapsburgs were left with full control over modern-day Austria, Czechoslovakia, Hungary, much of northern Italy, and significant portions of Yugoslavia, Romania and Poland, although they had lost Belgium and some Polish territory.

In 1859 and 1866, Austria lost most of its Italian territories in the Italian Wars of Unification. But the joint Austro-Hungarian government also expanded its territory by occupying Bosnia and Herzegovina and annexed this area in 1908.

Defeat by the Prussians in the Seven Weeks' War (1866) eliminated Austria as a political force in the lands that formed the German Empire in 1871. This weakening of the Hapsburg authorities also led to the Compromise of 1867, which produced the Austro-Hungarian Empire, a Dual Monarchy under the Hapsburgs, but with separate governments and separate policies in the Austrian-ruled and the Hungarian-ruled portions. The "Austrian" part of the empire was often referred to as Cis-Leithania, the Leitha being the small river separating Austria from Hungary.

The Slavs, unlike the Magyars (Hungarians), were not able to assert their authority. While there were more Slavs than Germans or Magyars in the empire, they were divided into numerous linguistic groups. In the north were the Czechs, Slovaks, Poles and Rusins (Ruthenians, closely related to the Ukrainians). In the south were the Slovenes, Serbs and Croats (the latter two with one language, but separate alphabets and different religions). In addition, there were the Romanians, Italians, Jews, Gypsies, and several small groups, which did not belong to any of the three big categories.

The arrangement from the Compromise of 1867 led to quite different language policies in the two halves. The Hungarians made strong efforts to "Magyarize" the non-Hungarians under their jurisdiction, resulting in a decline in those who spoke German, especially in the cities. Meanwhile, the Austrians sought to hold their monarchy together by de-emphasizing the importance of the German language. This led to Germans living in linguistic enclaves in predominantly non-German areas (Slovenia, for example) feeling pressure to adopt another language and it led to friction in Bohemia and Moravia, where there were large numbers of both Germans and Czechs. These policies may have been a factor in some emigration decisions. American and Hungarian statistics indicate that Germans accounted for 15-20% of the immigrants from Hungary in 1898-1913, a much higher emigration rate than that of the Magyars, although well below that of the Slovaks.

Incidentally, while the American "melting pot" never mirrored the pattern in Europe (where various ethnic groups lived side by side), there were probably more cases of assimilation than we may think. Germanicization, Polonization, Magyarization and absorption by other ethnic groups were a significant part of European history, although the process often took longer than it usually has in the New World.

Who absorbed whom? The answer can usually be found in one of two criteria: either the larger number swallowed the minority in its midst or those of higher status (be it authority or economic development) incorporated the others into their culture. Where these were at odds (e.g., a high-status minority within a low-status majority), separate identities sometimes continued to coexist for many centuries.

According to C. A. Macartney, in *The Habsburg Empire, 1790-1918*, there were about 2.8 million ethnic Germans in the Austrian hereditary and crown lands in 1780, about 1.6 million in the Bohemian crown lands and nearly 1 million in the Hungarian crown lands, accounting for about one quarter of the empire's total population. By 1900, these figures would have approximately doubled. Boundary changes would not have affected the figures greatly, for there were no large numbers of Germans living in the affected territories.

If we want to trace the distinct history of each major ethnic German group that belonged to the Austro-Hungarian Empire at the time of the major emigrations to North America, we can distinguish between the relatively solid Germanic core in and near Austria proper and the various islands of Germanic settlements elsewhere in the empire.

From 962 to 1438 (the chief era of Germanic eastward expansion), the emperors came mostly from present-day western Germany (or Luxembourg), with frequent conflicts for the imperial crown. From 1438 until the abolition of the empire in 1806, the Hapsburgs served as emperors (except for 3 years), thus effectively turning a German empire into an Austrian one (even though the Hapsburgs had roots in the west).

In the former Hapsburg Empire, the dividing line between areas where most people spoke German until the twentieth century and where they spoke other languages changed very little for 600 years or so. Besides what is now Austria, German-speakers predominated in a relatively large area in what is now the Czech Republic and a quite small area in what is now Italy. Of course, along both of these boundaries, as well as those with Hungary (Burgenland) and Slovenia (Styria), there were some ethnically mixed areas.

BOHEMIA AND MORAVIA

Since the Germans actually represented a majority of the population in those parts of the Czech Republic that bordered on Germany and Austria, and the Kingdom of Bohemia (which included this area) was a distinct entity for centuries, this sub-unit of the Austro-Hungarian Empire will be dealt with separately.

Relatively large-scale Germanic migration to the Czech Republic (Bohemia and Moravia, including the small part of Silesia that remained under Austrian control after the 1740s and was incorporated into Moravia in the 1920s) occurred during the twelfth and especially the thirteenth and fourteenth centuries, although there are traces of a German presence much earlier. The Hussite wars of the fifteenth century, which had ethnic overtones, resulted in a modest retreat in the area of German settlement.

Renewed Germanic immigration occurred during the modern era, especially as a result of the Thirty Years' War (1618-48), which devastated the Kingdom of Bohemia. Bob Ullman states that (mostly German) Catholics were awarded the estates of the (mostly Czech) Protestants during the 1624-37 period after the decisive Battle of White Mountain in 1620 (*German Genealogical Society of America Newsletter*, August 1994).

However, the Germans in the Czech Republic never were a cohesive group until after World War I, when the term, "Sudeten Germans" (which is geographically accurate only for those in northeastern Bohemia, northern Moravia and Austrian Silesia), came into being. The whole area became a part of the Hapsburg Empire in 1620, although members of the Hapsburg dynasty ruled Bohemia and Moravia most of the time after 1526.

Basically, the Germans settled along the mountainous outer rimland of Bohemia, Moravia and Austrian Silesia (now the Czech Republic), with each group coming mostly from the adjacent Germanic or Germanicized area. Counter-clockwise and starting from the northeastern tip of the C-shaped area, this meant they were a spillover from Silesia (comprised mostly of Germanicized Slavs), Saxony, Franconia (now Northern Bavaria, but with distinct tribal roots), Bavaria and Austria. Of course, there were ethnically mixed regions between the overwhelmingly German and the overwhelmingly Czech areas, especially in the south and in northern Moravia. There was a mixed Czech-Polish-German population in Eastern Austrian Silesia, with the area from Cieszyn (*Teschen*) east becoming part of Poland, and the area to the west now part of the Czech Republic. The mostly Germanic Czech rimland area became known as the Sudetenland and was annexed by Hitler, pursuant to the Munich Agreement of 1938.

As elsewhere in Eastern Europe, there were also many German urbanites, especially in Prague. Moreover, there were islands of German settlements in the interior or outside the Germanic core area. The largest one, which was not sharply separated from the German rimland, was the *Schönhengst* (Hrebec) area around *Mährisch-Trübau* (Moravská Trebová) and *Zwittau* (Svitavy). Others were at *Iglau* (Jihlava), *Brünn* (Brno), *Olmütz* (Olomouc), *Mährisch-Ostrau* (Ostrava), *Wischau* (Vysov) and *Budweis* (Cesky Budejovice).

Many Bohemian Germans moved farther eastward, especially between 1750 and 1850. They accounted for a large percentage of those who migrated to the Bukovina after 1775 and a small percentage of the so-called "Danube Swabians" in the last half of the eighteenth century. Bohemian weavers also were among those who settled along the southern and western borders of Posen, from where some of them migrated onward to Russian Poland.

Many migrated to the United States, Brazil, and New Zealand, beginning in the 1850s, but peaking in the 1880s and 1890s.

GERMAN ENCLAVES IN NON-GERMANIC PARTS OF THE HAPSBURG EMPIRE

After World War I, the eastern parts of the Hapsburg Empire, from which most German emigrants came except during the Nazi era, were fragmented into countries whose borders were roughly along ethnic lines, but with sizable German and other minorities in all of them.

South Tyrol: On the Italian boundary, even after the unification of Italy, Austria continued to rule over an Italian-speaking area around Trent (Trient/Trento). In 1910 what was then the Austrian province of Tyrol had a ratio of about 4:3 in German and Italian speakers, respectively. After World War I, this was remedied by giving South Tyrol to Italy. But there was a small overcorrection, putting German-speaking Bozen (Bolzano) and Meran(o) in Italy, so that the boundary would be at the strategic Brenner Pass. This led to a German revanchist movement, which seems to have quieted down in the last two decades, after the Italian government liberalized its policies toward identification with a Germanic heritage.

With respect to the German islands in the non-German areas, these can be divided into those dating back to the Middle Ages and those resulting from colonization efforts during the modern era, mostly in the eighteenth century.

Transylvanian Saxons: The Transylvanian Saxons are probably the most well known of the medieval settlers. They were invited to settle in the eastern border area of Hungary by its king in the twelfth century. In reality, they were mostly Franks, not Saxons, but since the Saxons lived next to the Hungarians, the latter may have thought of all Germans as Saxons. They seem to have come from a broad belt, reaching from Flanders (northern Belgium) on the Atlantic to easternmost Franconia (now northeastern Bavaria) on the Czech border. However, language patterns indicate that the largest number came from the Rhine-Moselle area in what is now Luxembourg and close to the present boundary between Northrhine-Westphalia and Rhineland-Palatinate.

These settlers in the *Siebenbürgen* (Erdély) area were under Turkish rule for about a century and a half, but they retained some local autonomy as a vassal state and suffered much less than those areas closer to the battlefront. There are several remarkable things about this group. Firstly, they lived as free and relatively equal people, never experiencing the feudal system. Secondly, they maintained their German identity very strongly a long time. Thirdly, they all became Lutherans while under Turkish rule, which in effect protected them from any pressures by Catholic secular or church authorities.

German-speakers from Saxony, the Rhineland, Flanders, Bavaria and Austria settled in Slovakia (especially in the *Zips* region), beginning in the early 1100s, more or less simultaneously with the Transylvanian Saxons and for the same defensive purposes. Some of these *Zips* residents migrated to northern Transylvania, where they became known as the *Nösner Zipser*. They lived in the area around Bistrita (*Bistritz*).

In 1241 the Mongols destroyed many of these settlements, but they were again rebuilt by Germans, especially during the period up to 1270, with significant immigration continuing until 1346, when the bubonic plague (Black Death) largely halted Germanic eastward migration. By then, there were several hundreds of thousands of Germans in what was known as Upper Hungary at the time. They dominated the political and commercial life of the towns. Compared with other Germanic settlements, an unusually high percentage of these Germans earned their living from non-agricultural pursuits, such as mining, commerce and various crafts.

Slovakia: The Turkish conquest of much of Hungary in the sixteenth and seventeenth centuries resulted in a large influx of Hungarians from the south. As a result, the influence of Magyars and Slovaks increased, with German-majority areas reduced to several enclaves.

These included the *Hauerland* in central Slovakia, Bratislava (*Pressburg*) and the surrounding area on the Austrian border, and the Spis (*Zips*) region in eastern Slovakia, as well as areas in Subcarpathian Rus', which was ceded to the Soviet Union in 1945. Each of the three enclaves (each one actually consisting of proximate, but not adjoining, clusters of villages) in Slovakia had about 40,000-50,000 Germans in 1930.

The *Hauerland* (the term derives from "hauen," i.e., clearing the land of woods, in this case mostly for mining purposes) actually consists of two twin enclaves centered around *Deutsch-Proben* (Nitrianske Pravno) and *Kremnitz* (Kremnica).

The *Zips* towns are somewhat farther apart, but also divided into two major enclaves, mostly in or near the Poprad and Hornad-Hnilec river valleys. The Upper *Zips* settlement, somewhat 8-shaped, is around Kezmarok (*Käsmark*) and Levoca (*Leutschau*). These towns formed the *Zipser Bund* (Zips League), which served to foster their commerce, and obtained local autonomy at an early date.

The Lower *Zips* area, west of Kosice (*Kaschau*), had a flourishing metalworking industry until the 1860s, when it was severely hurt by the Industrial Revolution. As a result, many of these Germans emigrated to larger industrial centers in Europe or to the United States.

The best treatment of this group is in Duncan B. Gardiner, *German Towns in Slovakia and Upper Hungary*.

Subcarpathian Rus': For information on the Germans in this area (also known as Carpatho-Ukraine), who were transferred from Czechoslovakia to the Soviet Union as a result of World War II, see Victoria Nied, "My Heritage in the Sub-Carpathian Ukraine," in the summer 1993 issue of *Nase Rodina* (the newsletter of the Czechoslovak Genealogical Society International). She refers to a book, *Deutsch Mokrá-Königsfeld: Eine deutsche Siedlung in den Waldkarpaten*. Some 200 people from Upper Austria moved here in 1775, with others following for at least four decades.

Slovenia: Germans also lived in various localities in northern Slovenia, particularly around Ljubljana (*Laibach*) and Maribor (*Marburg*) as early as the twelfth century and began settling around *Gottschee* (now Kocevje) in the south, beginning about 1310. The first wave of settlers apparently came from Carniola. Later waves of settlers are believed to have come mostly from eastern Tyrol. The more cohesive *Gottschee* group is of special interest to American genealogists because of massive emigration to the United States. Their story is told by L. Edward Skender in *A Short History of the Duchy of Carniola and Gottschee County*.

Danube Swabians: By far the most numerous among the modern German settlers are the Danube Swabians, formerly known as Hungarian Germans. However, the largest number came from Lorraine, with only a minority of them coming from Swabia (Württemberg). But they were called Swabians because they embarked at Ulm in Swabia and sailed down the Danube River to the many settlements in what was then Hungary. These areas had been won back from the Turks in 1699 and 1718. Most of the migrants arrived in 1765-72 and 1784-88, after an earlier wave of settlers in 1722-29 had been virtually annihilated in the 1737-39 Turkish War.

The largest of these settlements was in the Banat, the area around Timisoara (*Temeschwar* or *Temeschburg*) and southwest to Belgrade. The eastern Banat is now in Romania and the western part in Serbian Vojvodina, with the northwestern tip reaching toward Szeged in Hungary. A second major colony was in the Bácska (*Batschka*), northwest of Belgrade and overlapping Serbian Vojvodina and present-day Hungary, with a smaller settlement in Syrmia (*Syrmien*) squeezed between Belgrade and the Bácska.

Still farther west was the Baranya (*Baranja*) settlement, along with other villages in Eastern Croatia (Slavonia) and the adjacent parts of Bosnia. The Germans in Bosnia were mostly government officials and entrepreneurs, who arrived after Austria took over this area in 1878, or people from the Banat, the Bácska and Syrmia migrating one step farther southwestward in the second half of the 1880s.

Some German Catholics, especially from the Rhineland, settled in the Banja Luka area in north central Bosnia as a result of Bismarck's anti-Catholic *Kulturkampf* in the 1870s, which left many parishes without priests.

Swabian Turkey is in today's Hungary, in the area near Pécs (*Fünfkirchen*). There were also German settlements in the Central Highlands near Budapest. In fact, three-fourths of the residents of Budapest 1848 were German-speakers. This percentage, however, included such a substantial number of Jews that the city was sometimes referred to colloquially as "Judapest." But Budapest rapidly became Magyarized after that date, so that by 1905, 85% of the residents were Hungarians (which category now included the 23% who were Jewish), with only 9% Germans.

Satu Mare: Germans in the Satu Mare (*Sathmar*) region, in what is now the northwesternmost corner of Romania, arrived from "Swabia" between 1712 and 1815, so they are kin to the Danube Swabians in terms of origin and period of immigration, although far away from the Danube. The most thorough account of this group can be found in Jacob Steigerwald, *Tracing Romania's Heterogeneous German Minority from Its Origins to the Diaspora*.

Galicia: Large numbers of Germans were settled in Galicia, primarily in East Galicia, in 1782-85, after this fell into Austrian hands. There had been Germans in Western Galicia in the Middle Ages, but they had been thoroughly Polonized by the time the new stream arrived.

These German immigrants came mostly from the southwest Germanic area, with the largest number coming from what is now the state of Rhineland-Palatinate.

The Bukovina: It is estimated that 1,750-2,000 German-speakers immigrated to the Bukovina: 350-400 from Swabia; 1,100-1,300 from Bohemia; and an additional 3,000-4,000 from other parts of the Austrian Empire. See Sophie A. Welisch, "The Bukovina-Germans during the Habsburg Period: Settlement, Interaction, Contributions," in *Immigrants and Minorities*, Vol. 5, No. 1 (March 1986).

The first Danube Swabians migrated from the Banat to the Bukovina in 1782 without government sponsorship. Most of their ancestors had come from the Mannheim-Mainz areas.

In 1787, after the Bukovina had been annexed to Galicia, Galician authorities settled 74 mostly Protestant families in eight existing communities on a line between *Czernowitz* (Cernauti, now Chernivtsi, Ukraine) and *Sutschawa* (Suceava). Over two-thirds of these families had their roots in Württemberg, the Rhine Palatinate, Baden, and Nassau (Hesse-Nassau). About the same time, Germanic families came from the *Zips* district to work in a mine at Jakobeny on the Bistritz River, with other Zipsers arriving in 1797, and went to work at a new silver mine in Kirlibaba. A third group of Germans were Catholics of Bohemian origin who settled in the Bukovina in 1793. Beginning in 1843, farm families began arriving from the *Pilsen* (Plzen) and Prachatitz districts in Bohemia.

The Hungarians made distinctions among the "Saxons" in Transylvania; the "Swabians" along the Danube or its tributaries; and the "Germans," a term they applied only to the residents of cities (merchants, officials, etc.).

Religion: One important event should be borne in mind in researching German immigration to the eastern parts of the Hapsburg Empire. In 1781, the *Toleranzpatent* guaranteeing religious liberty was issued. This means that the modern immigrants prior to 1781 were exclusively Catholic, whereas the later immigrants represented a religious mix, with the Protestants (who were a combination of Lutheran and Reformed, with a tiny Mennonite minority) dominant at least in Galicia. Austrian Protestant refugees fled eastward, mostly to Transylvania, where they were given a haven by its German Lutherans, prior to 1781. Jews far outnumbered other German-speakers in Galicia and the Bukovina.

Population in Germanic Enclaves: Relying on *The Ethnic German Refugee in Austria, 1945 to 1954*, by Tony Radspieler, and other sources, the number of Germans in each group outside present-day Austria must have been approximately as follows prior to 1938: Sudeten Germans, 3-4 million; Danube Swabians, over 1 million; Transylvanian Saxons, 250,000; the Bukovina, Galicia and Satu Mare, each 50,000-100,000; Slovenia, Bosnia-Herzegovina and South Tyrol, each 15,000-25,000. Galicia and the Bukovina had about 100,000 Jews each, many of whom later moved to Vienna. Since they were sometimes classified as Germans in the censuses and sometimes not, this explains widely differing figures from different sources.

Repatriation, Expulsion and Emigration: Under the Hitler-Stalin Pact of 1939 and similar agreements with Romania (1940), Italy (1941) and Croatia (1942), ethnic Germans were given the opportunity for repatriation to a *Reich* that their ancestors had left more than five generations earlier. Actually they were sent mostly to the *Warthegau*, or Warta River region in Poland. Over 400,000 Germans, including many from former Austro-Hungarian areas (the Bukovina, the Dobruja and Yugoslavia) made that "choice." The first two groups came from what had been designated as Stalin's "sphere of influence" (but not from within the then existing Soviet borders).

In 1945-48, after the Hitler era, most Germans were expelled from the non-Austrian countries formerly part of the Hapsburg Empire. This was true to the greatest extent in Yugoslavia and Czechoslovakia, and least likely in Romania. While they went to Germany and Austria initially, many of these expellees were soon scattered throughout the Americas, Australasia and other areas. Many Romanian Germans followed them overseas in the 1980s, when the conditions for emigration were eased.

THE RUSSIAN EMPIRE of 1815 TO 1917

The third great continental European empire that included many German-speaking residents during the years of peak immigration to North America was the Russian Empire. This will be dealt with in three sub-sections: the Baltic countries, Central Poland and the rest of what was then Russia.

THE BALTIC COUNTRIES (ESTONIA, LATVIA AND LITHUANIA)

The oldest German settlements in the Russian Empire were those in the Baltic countries, especially Latvia and Estonia. Latvia and Southern Estonia were known for centuries as Livonia (eastern part) and Courland (western part). These settlements date back to the late twelfth century, when Germans and Danes sought to Christianize the local tribes. Germans founded the city of Riga ca. 1200.

In 1226, the Polish Duke of Masovia invited the Teutonic Knights to come to the Baltic to convert the neighboring peoples. This Order, originally founded to provide a hospital for the Crusaders in Palestine, soon absorbed the earlier knights, and by 1280 its sword had finished the task of "Christianizing" Livonia (*Livland*), Courland (*Kurland*) and Estonia (*Estland*), as well as (East) Prussia (*Preussen*). The original Prussians (*Borussians*) were a non-Germanic tribe that vanished as a result of decimation, with the survivors assimilating into the conquerors who now took over their name.

In 1385, the grand duke of Lithuania (*Litauen*) married the queen of Poland (*Polen*) to form a personal union of the two countries. Since this act was accompanied by the acceptance of Christianity by the Lithuanians, the original mission of the Teutonic Knights had now been fulfilled. However, the Knights had been authorized by the pope to rule the previously heathen lands they conquered. They continued to govern the entire Prussian-Baltic area, and rather harshly.

In 1410, the Knights suffered a crushing defeat by the Poles at the Battle of Tannenberg (German) or Grunwald (Polish). By 1466, the combined forces of the German cities near the Baltic Sea, who chafed under the rigid rule of the Knights, and Poland had ended the days of the Knights as a major power. The cities were now under the Polish crown, but had a great deal of local autonomy, unlike their status under the Knights. The Knights moved their headquarters from *Marienburg* (now Malbork) to *Königsberg* (now Kaliningrad) and had to accept Polish overlordship with respect to the territory they still ruled. In 1525, the Order of Teutonic Knights accepted Lutheranism, possibly stimulated by the lack of imperial and papal support for their interests.

Livonia and Courland fell under Polish rule in 1561, while Estonia became Swedish. That was the end of the Order of Teutonic Knights in the Baltic East, although it retained scattered possessions in western Germany until it was finally abolished in 1809.

Poland and Lithuania were officially united as one country, rather than two countries with the same monarch, in 1569. For a time, this large empire was the major power in the

Baltic. However, Sweden expanded its holdings in the Baltic, step by step, and dominated the coastal regions throughout much of the seventeenth century.

The Great Nordic War of 1700-21 ended Swedish hegemony and substituted that of Peter the Great of Russia. The third, final partition of Poland in 1795 completed Russian acquisition of the Baltic area, except for a Lithuanian-Polish area, which belonged to Prussia from 1795 to 1806 and was known as New East Prussia at the time.

The Baltic German barons became one of the principal sources of administrative, military and diplomatic leaders for the Russian Czars for nearly two centuries. Since Germans owned most of the large estates in the Baltic and constituted the core of the urban mercantile and educational elite, they were in a dominant economic position until after World War I, when the newly independent countries nationalized their estates.

In 1897, there were somewhat more than 200,000 Germans in the Baltic lands, about half of them in Livonia, where they constituted about 8% of the population. In the key city of Riga, however, Germans represented 18% of the residents.

CENTRAL POLAND

The top expert on the Germans in Central Poland is Dr. Oskar Kossmann. His book, *Die Deutschen in Polen seit der Reformation*, is the most detailed history of this group and lists well over 1,000 communities in which Germans lived.

The strongly Polish-populated area under Russian control after 1815 was known as "Congress Poland" from 1815 to 1830, when the First Polish Revolt caused the Czar to terminate the relatively liberal and autonomous constitutional monarchy and place Poland directly under his autocratic personal control. This area continued to be called "Mittelpolen" (Central Poland) by Germans. In 1795, this area had been divided between Prussia (north and west of Warsaw) and Austria (southeast). In 1807, it formed the Grand Duchy of Warsaw, created by Napoleon. At the Congress of Vienna in 1815, it was given to Russia.

The most significant German immigration into this area in the early modern period took the form of "Holländereien." The term originally applied to the farms of the Dutch Mennonite religious refugees in the Danzig-Elbing area. In time, it came to mean their kind of agriculture, i.e., farming based on draining marshy lowlands and emphasizing dairy cattle. Though the very first *Holländereien* in Central Poland probably were the creation of these Dutch people, a heavy majority of those to whom this term later applied were German immigrants. These lowland farms initially were found along the Vistula, but a mixture of lowlands and uplands farms (the latter "Hauländereien," based on Pomeranian experience) developed in the areas east of *Thorn* (Torun) and north of *Kalisch* (Kalisz).

The large number of German settlements along the Vistula River consisted mostly of people who came up the river from West Prussia, although there were some South Germans there.

There were also a few Silesian weavers who came to the Lodz area in the sixteenth and seventeenth centuries. There they served as a magnet for the tremendous influx of both tradesmen and peasants into Poland in general, and the Lodz area in particular, beginning in the 1780s. The religious toleration decreed by the Polish Diet in 1768, and the increasing land rents in German areas as they developed, probably contributed to this wave of immigration.

Most of the immigrants were peasants from the Netze River region and neighboring parts of Pomerania, West Prussia, and the Neumark, with a second major influx from Swabia and other areas in southwest Germany in 1795-1806, when Prussia ruled the area. There was a huge class distinction between the two, with the terms "Kashubs" and "Schwabs" used in a highly pejorative sense. The term "Schwabs" was an abbreviation of "Swabians." The Kashubians are actually a tribe closely related to the Poles, but the Germans from the northwest came from the general vicinity of the medieval Duchy of Cassubia (bounded approximately by the Oder, Netze and Vistula rivers).

The Lodz area was the primary beneficiary of German immigration in the 1819-34 period, when the Lutheran population of Central Poland, an approximation of the German population, increased 50%. This was even more the case thereafter, when Lodz grew at what Kossmann calls an "American tempo," and was the only part of Central Poland with a strong inflow of German immigrants. Tradesmen, particularly weavers, moved to Lodz in huge numbers after 1815, especially from Posen and Silesia. The reason was access to the Eastern markets for cloth and clothing, since this location put them within the Russian customs zone instead of having to pay heavy duties to export their products. In its heyday, Lodz was one of the foremost textile centers in the world.

Notwithstanding that, a large majority of the Germans lived in rural areas and pursued farming. The crowded conditions that developed in the areas west and north of Warsaw led many to move farther east, where there had been few Germans previously. The Second Polish Revolt in 1863 and the freeing of the Polish serfs in 1864, which changed both the political and the economic climate, led many Germans to migrate to Volhynia. A smaller number settled in the Chelm area west of the Bug River, thus remaining within Central Poland.

The principal concentrations of Germans in Central Poland prior to 1944-45 could be found along the Vistula River, from Thorn to slightly south of Warsaw, in the area between the Vistula and Drewenz Rivers east of Thorn; along both sides of the Netze and Warta Rivers, as well as between them and south of the latter almost to Kalisz; and in the area around Lodz. In 1865, 80% of the people in Lodz, including many Jews, spoke German. By 1905, after an influx of Polish factory workers, 40% of the residents were identified as Germans and 25% as Jews.

There were over 400,000 Germans in Central Poland in 1897. Although this number declined somewhat over the next 40 years, the main exodus occurred in 1944-45, when the Germans either fled before the advancing Soviet armies or were expelled pursuant to the Potsdam Agreement. Most of those who were left (who tended to be Polonized) emigrated to West Germany after liberalized Polish policies and the advent of *glasnost* in 1987 made this possible.

RUSSIA, UKRAINE, THE CAUCASUS AND ASIA

If we look at German immigration to what our ancestors considered to be "Russia" at the time, it all began with Catherine the Great's Manifesto of 1763.

To be sure, there was a prologue. A "German Suburb" of Moscow, which had isolated foreigners since the sixteenth century, stimulated Peter the Great's "Westernization" in the first quarter of the 1700s. He had won Russia's window on the Baltic and built St. Petersburg there.

But it was the German-born Catherine II (1762-96) who best recognized Russia's backwardness and immediately set out to do something about it. Her first manifesto in 1762 was a dud, but the famous second one was spectacularly successful in attracting foreign settlers. By far the majority of these were Germans, but there were also a few from elsewhere.

A primary reason for the effectiveness of this invitation is that it was accompanied by a propaganda and recruitment campaign of Madison Avenue proportions. Another reason why it was so effective is that German peasants had suffered severely from the just ended Seven Years' War (1756-63). This, in addition to their heavy feudal obligations and religious persecution, put them in a mood to listen.

What they heard must have sounded as appealing as the "gold-paved streets" of America did to later generations. They were promised an impressive array of freedoms: free land and freedom to settle where they wanted to (with no feudal overlord), freedom from military service, freedom of religion, freedom to practice any trade, free transportation, interest-free loans for ten years, freedom from taxation for a period of years, freedom to choose their own local government, an assurance of these freedoms to their descendants in perpetuity, and freedom to leave Russia if they did not like it. Small wonder that the Germans in Russia saw this as their "Magna Carta!"

Reality turned out to be less attractive when they found out how undeveloped Russia was. But except for the freedom to locate where they wanted, which was not granted to the first group, these freedoms were honored — for over a hundred years.

The first huge wave of settlers came in 1764-67 before being stopped by German rulers alarmed at the population loss. Most of these newcomers were directed to the hinterlands near the Volga River, where they suffered from robbers, Cossack rebels and Kirghiz nomads who sold their captives into slavery. But the pioneers turned their ill fate around in 20 years and by 1800 they had indeed achieved remarkable prosperity.

A very small percentage of the first immigrants were allowed to settle in scattered locations in the west, particularly near St. Petersburg and Riga.

The Russo-Turkish Wars of 1768-74 and 1787-91 resulted in Russia acquiring approximately the southern half of Ukraine. Since this area had nomads, but few permanent residents, developing what was first known as New Russia, and then as South Russia, became the next colonization objective.

Immigration of Germans to the Black Sea area began with a few Lutherans and a larger group of Mennonites in 1787-89, the first large colony being Chortitza, near Alexandrovsk (now Zaporozhye). A second, still larger migration to the Black Sea area occurred in 1803-10. Prussian Lutherans and Mennonites settled in Eastern Ukraine, primarily in the Molotschna and Prischib colonies near Molochansk, northwest of the Sea of Azov.

During the same period there was a large migration from southwestern Germanic regions, particularly Württemberg, Baden, Bavaria, Hesse, Alsace and the Palatinate, to the area north of Odessa. These settlers included a much higher percentage of Catholics than found in Eastern Ukraine. The Liebental, Kutschurgan, Glückstal and Beresan colonies were the largest early settlements in this area. Some of these Swiss and Württemberger immigrants also founded the first colonies on the Crimean peninsula in 1804-05. There was a larger minority of Reformed church members (Calvinists) in this group than in most others.

In 1806-12, there was another Russo-Turkish War, which led to Russian acquisition of Bessarabia, west of Odessa. Napoleon's crushing of Prussia in 1806-07, his establishment of the Grand Duchy of Warsaw in 1807 and his ultimately disastrous march on Moscow in 1812 created conditions that served as a strong incentive for Germans from Poland and Prussia to move on. This was especially true of the South Germans, known as Swabians, who had been settled in predominantly Polish-speaking areas by the Prussian government in 1795-1806, when Prussia ruled the greater part of Central Poland, as well as the Polish-majority areas in most of Posen and central West Prussia that remained under Prussian, later German, rule until 1918. Many went to Bessarabia in 1814-16.

Another important motivation for eastward migration was the large number of Württembergers forced to serve in armed forces allied with Napoleon and the very tiny percentage who survived and returned at the end of these wars.

This was followed by the emigration of religious dissidents from Württemberg in 1816-20. While some went to America, a larger group went eastward and dispersed themselves in settlements from Hungary in the west, to Bessarabia in the middle, and the Caucasus region between the Black and Caspian Seas in the east. They founded the Hoffnungstal colony in Western Ukraine and the Berdyansk colony in Eastern Ukraine, as well as the first settlements in the Southern Caucasus region near Tiflis (Tbilisi).

The post-Napoleonic depression and the 1816 crop failure, which produced famine in Western Europe, induced further immigration to Western Ukraine until about 1822. Bessarabia continued to draw immigrants until 1842. There was also another stream of migrants to Eastern Ukraine, chiefly in the 1818-24 period, but periodic wavelets continued until about 1848. Some of these came from West Prussia and farther south along the Vistula, while others came from southwestern Germanic areas, including Alsace. The largest group of new colonies was the one northwest of Mariupol (Zhdanov). There are also scattered references to Hungarian Germans, especially from the Batschka, migrating to the Russian Empire in the early nineteenth century.

The last group immigration of Prussian German settlers went to the Samara (Kuybyshev) region on the Volga River, north of the early settlements near Saratov. This occurred in the third quarter of the nineteenth century. With this one exception, nearly all of the new colonies founded by Germans after 1848 (and a few before then) represented daughter colonies for the surplus population in the original settlement areas. How striking this was is indicated by the fact that by the mid-1860s the number of landless Germans outnumbered the landowners in every colony, often by a substantial margin. Between the end of the Crimean War (1856) and 1890, a huge number of daughter colonies were established, wherever possible in areas near the older colonies, as well as in the Northern Caucasus (between Krasnodar and the Caspian Sea) and in the Don River region north and west of Rostov.

After 1890, large quantities of land could be obtained only in the areas near the Ural Mountains, such as Orenburg and Ufa, or in Asia. Many of the new colonies were along the Trans-Siberian Railway and on both sides of the border between Siberia and Kazakhstan, with a few farther south. How vast Russia's equivalent of the American "Wild West" was is indicated by the fact that these colonies extended from Orenburg, just west of the Urals, to Semipalatinsk in the east, a distance that is greater than that between Orenburg and St. Petersburg (i.e., the entire width of European Russia).

German immigration to Volhynia, which is now the northwestern part of Ukraine, was an entirely different phenomenon. It consisted chiefly of individual families moving to Volhynia upon invitation from private landowners, in contrast to group immigrations, often with governmental sponsorship or support, which characterized the German migrants to other areas. This has made genealogical research for descendants of the Volhynian Germans more difficult.

Although there were a few Germans in Volhynia before 1800, there was little immigration prior to 1830-31, when the First Polish Uprising against Russia stimulated some Germans in Poland to move farther east and others to return to Prussian-ruled areas. The bulk of the immigration, however, occurred between 1863-64, when the Second Polish Uprising against Russia was accompanied by strong anti-German sentiment as a result of Prussia's policy of coerced Germanicization of Poles, and 1900, by which time German immigration to other parts of Russia had virtually ceased. A lesser flow of German immigration continued for another decade.

The Germans in this region also had different experiences in other ways. Volhynia was the only Russian area where there was a significant amount of emigration (to North America and to the Baltic lands) and immigration (mostly from Poland) at the same time. These Germans also were deported to the east in 1915, an experience not widely shared by other Germans until World War II.

Meanwhile, the end of the promised "forever" came in 1871, when the colonists' special privileges were ended. Growing nationalism led to the Russification programs of 1881-1905, which sought to turn people who spoke little Russian into people who spoke primarily Russian.

This led to large-scale emigration to North and South America, beginning in 1873-74, but in growing numbers after 1883. The American Great Plains and the Canadian Prairie Provinces, as the last frontiers of settlement, absorbed large numbers of these people. In western Canada, North Dakota and certain counties in all the intervening states as far south as Oklahoma, including Colorado, Germans from Russia outnumbered Germans from Germany. A large number also went to Argentina.

For those who remained in Russia, the Bolshevik Revolution and the following Civil War induced many to leave in the 1920s, most of them going to Canada or Latin America rather than the United States. But the New Economic Policy (1921-28), which reversed agricultural collectivization, as well as catering to non-Russian nationalities, exemplified by the creation of the Volga German Republic in 1924, persuaded many that things would not be so bad after all.

Then came the decade of disaster. In 1928-30 the more prosperous farmers ("kulaks") were liquidated and their families deported, as collectivization was re-instituted with a vengeance. Ruthless government requisitioning of farm products after the crop failures of 1932 and 1933 led to a "man-made" famine in the heart of what had been the "granary of Europe." In 1929-37 all pastors were arrested and religious services suppressed. Next came the Great Purge of 1936-38, which sent millions to their deaths, and millions more to slave labor camps. The rise of Hitler fanned anti-German sentiment in the mid-1930s. Because the Germans tended to be relatively well-to-do, they suffered disproportionately from some of these tragedies.

Under the 1939 Hitler-Stalin Pact, 400,000 Germans, most of them from the Baltic countries, Western Volhynia, East Central Poland and Bessarabia (all of which had been ruled by the Russian Czar), were returned to the *Reich* (really to West Central Poland), since their home areas had been designated as Stalin's "sphere of influence."

But Hitler's invasion of the Soviet Union produced a dramatic change for the worse, as could be expected. Perhaps two-thirds of a million Germans, mostly from the Volga and Ukrainian areas east of the Dnieper River were deported. When the smoke had cleared after 1955, the new "German heartland" turned out to be Kazakhstan, rimmed by other Islamic republics to the south and Siberia on the north. Many Germans had been in slave labor camps in the northeasternmost corner of European Russia.

However, several hundred thousand Germans, mostly from west of the Dnieper River, managed to escape deportation because the German armies advanced so rapidly that these plans could not be carried out. When the tide of battle turned at Stalingrad in 1943, most of them moved west. Many settled in the Warta River region in Poland, in homes expropriated from their Polish owners. In January 1945 the Soviet armies advanced toward this area so rapidly that these people had to flee on extremely short notice, in the worst of winter weather. Many made it to West Germany; many did not.

The Soviet government insisted that these were Soviet citizens who had to be returned to the Soviet Union. In the early months after the war, when Westerners still thought of the Soviet Union principally as an ally, the Western powers cooperated in returning many of these people. Others "at large" did what they could to hide their identity.

In the Soviet Union itself, conditions for Germans did not improve until after German Chancellor Adenauer's 1955 visit, which led to the restoration of personal freedom for the Germans in the Soviet Union, but still banned them from returning to their old homes.

After *glasnost* began in 1987, large numbers of German *"Aussiedler"* (resettlers) emigrated to Germany. The fear that anti-Russian nationalism in the Central Asian republics may not distinguish between the two European ethnic groups is an unsettling factor for those Germans who might otherwise choose to remain in what they consider to be their homeland.

In late 1991, after the failed coup, the Soviet Union broke apart, as many component republics declared their independence. Except for the Baltic countries, most of these soon joined the Commonwealth of Independent States, a very loose federation.

Many people of German origin continued to emigrate to Germany. However, the German government has provided extensive aid to German communities in Siberia and the Muslim republics in order to dissuade people from leaving, because the growing resentment against foreigners during the German recession has also created hostile attitudes toward these people of Germanic origin.

SWITZERLAND

The Germanic population of Switzerland originated with the Alamanni and Burgundian tribes invading what had been Roman territory. The Burgundians have become assimilated French since then. The Almannis, strongly opposed to central rule, have had a dominant influence on the political, economic and social development of Switzerland, with its emphasis on cantonal rather than national government.

The Swiss Confederation dates back to 1291, when three very mountainous cantons (including Schwyz, from which the country's name comes) asserted their independence from the Holy Roman Empire. By 1499, when the Confederation had quintupled in size but was still less than half the size of Switzerland today, the country had won its complete independence. However, its independence was not officially recognized until 1648.

By 1513, the confederation had expanded to 13 cantons. Soon thereafter, it adopted a policy of permanent neutrality, which was violated by Napoleon. The Congress of Vienna expanded the country to its present size, adding three cantons previously ruled by France. However, most of the German-speaking population already belonged to Switzerland before that. Today German is the primary language of 70% of the people, with other languages dominant in the southern and western areas, although many people are bilingual. See Swiss map in **Appendix B** for details on the growth of Switzerland.

Switzerland was the cradle of the Reformed religion, begun by Zwingli, and given its form by Calvin in Geneva. This branch of Protestantism was strong in various parts of Germany, especially the Palatinate, Hesse and Brandenburg, prior to the Lutheran-Reformed merger. It was dominant among the French Huguenots, many of whom fled to Germany. The Netherlands and Scotland also favored this form of Protestantism, known as Presbyterianism in Scotland and among the descendants of the Scots.

However, Switzerland was split right down the middle into the Reformed Protestant and the Roman Catholic camps. Four religious wars, the last in 1712, changed little. Today the Protestants have a 5:4 majority, with the most Catholics in central and southern Switzerland, but also in a few northern and eastern cantons.

One wing of the Anabaptist movement, out of which the Mennonite church developed, also had its birth in Switzerland. But its adherents were persecuted and had to flee for their lives, just as they had in their other birthplace, the then Spanish-ruled Netherlands. Mennonite refugees, long known as "Brethren," went down the Rhine, settling on both the French and German sides of the border, as far north as the Palatinate, after being expelled, primarily from the canton of Berne.

Despite its religious strife, Switzerland managed to stay out of the Thirty Years' War. As a result, it was the source of many post-1648 immigrants to areas that had been badly devastated, particularly the Palatinate and Alsace.

Switzerland also experienced the revolutionary turmoil of 1830 and 1848, which affected much of the rest of Europe. A struggle between pro- and anti-reform forces led to a brief civil war in 1847. The end result, however, was the triumph of democracy, contrary to what happened in Germany. Switzerland was the only European country with a federal system similar to that in the United States until Germany adopted such a model in 1949. Industrialization in Switzerland, unlike the rest of continental Europe, preceded that in England.

Swiss immigration to North America seems to have been heaviest during three periods: 1816-17, when Europe suffered crop failures similar to the more severe ones of 1846-47; the 1840s; and the 1880s. However, a significant number of German-speaking colonial immigrants came from Switzerland. Swiss have also migrated to many other countries (South America, New Zealand, Australia, South Africa) in noticeable numbers.

GRAND DUCHY OF LUXEMBOURG

Luxembourg is both a very old and a very new country. It established a separate identity in 963 when a castle was built on the site of the present-day Luxembourg City. Its ruling dynasty provided several Holy Roman Emperors in the Middle Ages, prior to the Hapsburg era. However, it was ruled by Burgundy, Spain, Austria, France or the Netherlands throughout most of modern history.

In 1815, Luxembourg became a grand duchy of the Netherlands. It became largely self-governing in 1839, although its independence was not recognized internationally until 1867 and it was ruled by the Dutch king until 1890. It was also part of the German Confederation from 1815 to 1866.

However, while the country was gaining greater autonomy, it was also losing territory. It had already lost some of its southern territory to France in 1659. In 1815 it lost the territory east of the Moselle and Oure Rivers to the Prussian province of Rhineland. In 1839 it ceded its western half to Belgium. Today this is the Belgian province of Luxembourg.

These changes left a definite impact on the migration patterns and the family ties of the Luxembourgers. Many American families can trace their ties back to ancestors living in close proximity on both sides of the rivers now forming the eastern border of the country. But until 1815, or about a generation before large-scale emigration to America, these people had been countrymen. Immigration from Luxembourg to the United States was truly "large-scale," if measured as a percentage of the country's population.

The same ties of culture and kinship exist between the people of the two Luxembourgs, i.e., the grand duchy and the Belgian province. Again, one finds overlapping patterns of emigration and settlement in this country.

The Luxembourgian language, or *Letzeburgesch*, is a German dialect. German and French are both official languages. At the time of immigration to the United States, which coincided pretty well with that from Germany, the affinity of Luxembourgers was mostly for Germans, as indicated by demographic patterns and parish allegiances in this country. However, the country's occupation by German forces in both World Wars has brought about a reorientation.

Luxembourgers are overwhelmingly Catholic, as is the case with the border residents in all the adjacent countries.

PRINCIPALITY OF LIECHTENSTEIN

Unlike other European mini-states, independent Liechtenstein is only a modern creation, although its identity goes back to the Middle Ages and its boundaries have remained constant for longer than nearly all other countries on the continent. It became a principality in 1719, but like so many other German-speaking areas, it belonged to the Holy Roman Empire and later to the German Confederation. In 1866 it became independent. Its external affairs are handled by Switzerland, which lies just across the Rhine River to the west.

THE OTTOMAN TURKISH EMPIRE

Hardly any ethnic Germans ever emigrated to North America from the Ottoman Turkish Empire, yet there were immigrants from territories that were formerly Turkish-ruled.

Historically, the most significant experience was that of the Transylvanian Saxons in the *Siebenbürgen* region of what is now Romania. These settlements, which date back to the Middle Ages, had been under Ottoman control for about a century and a half before they were "liberated" in 1688. But they retained some autonomy as a vassal state. Under Islamic overlordship, these Germans opted for Protestantism without any of the religious troubles that brewed in "Christian Europe."

A more recent experience with Turkish rule was that of the Germans in the Dobruja. Most of this Black Sea coastland is now part of Romania, but the southern portion belongs to Bulgaria. Germans from the Odessa region and Bessarabia settled in this territory in the 1840s and 1850s, when it was still under Turkish rule. Following the Russo-Turkish War the Dobruja became part of Romania in 1878, when that country achieved complete independence. However, the southern tip of the Dobruja, which had only a few Germans, went to the new country of Bulgaria. The new Christian rulers turned out to be less accommodating than the Moslems, leading to emigration to Western Canada and North Dakota within a few years.

Not all German settlers fared well in the hands of the Turks. Those who were settled on the Austrian Military Border in 1718-37, on land recently won from the Turks, were largely wiped out in later Turkish raids on the area. However, the conflict was military, not religious.

One other intriguing "Turkish connection" should be mentioned. Michael Palmer's article, "Moorish and Turkish Blood in German Families" (*GGSA Bulletin*, September 1987), has a 14-item bibliography of documented cases of Germanicized Turks, mostly captured during the 1683-99 war with Turkey, or Moors. The latter term was used to describe people from both North Africa and sub-Saharan Africa, including blacks in the Americas.

Genealogical research has revealed that there were young boys in the Turkish army, whose job was similar to what we would have called "stable boys" in the pre-auto era. A few of these boys were captured by German nobles/officers and taken home, where they were raised and assimilated as Germans. If you can go back several centuries in your research, there could be a Turkish ancestor in your past.

REFERENCES (See bibliography for full citations if not shown)

Wilhelm Baum. *Deutsche und Slowenen in Krain: Eine historische Betrachtung.* Klagenfurt, Austria: Carinthia Verlag, 1981. [*A Historical View of Germans and Slovenians in Carniola*]

Eugen Bellon. *Scattered to All the Winds, 1685-1720: Migrations of the Dauphine French Huguenots into Italy, Switzerland and Germany.* West Lafayette, IN: Belle Publications, 1983. Translation.

Edgar Bonjour. *A Short History of Switzerland.* Westport, CT: Greenwood Press, 1985 reprint of 1952 book.

Irma Bornemann. *The Bukovina Germans.* Sophie A Welisch, trans. English translation of 1986 German original, 1990. Ellis, KS: Bukovina Society of the Americas. 21 pp.
>   History, geography, politics, culture and 1940 repatriation of Germans, including places of origin (southern Germany, Bohemia, Slovakia).

Hans Fehlinger. *Deutsche in der Fremde: Eine Übersicht nach Abschluss des Weltkrieges.* Leipzig: Dieterich'sche Verlagsbuchhandlung, 1920. [*Germans in Foreign Lands: An Overview after the Conclusion of World War I*]

John Foisel. *Saxons Through Seventeen Centuries: A History of the Transylvanian Saxons.* Cleveland: Central Alliance of Transylvanian Saxons. 1936.
>   History of the Germans who migrated to Eastern Hungary (now Romania) in the twelfth century, with an introductory chapter on the earlier history of the Saxons.

Adam Giesinger. *From Catherine to Khrushchev: The Story of Russia's Germans.*

Peter Grassl. *Geschichte der deutsch-böhmischen Ansiedlungen Banat.* [*History of the German-Bohemian Settlements in the Banat*]. 1904.
>   Early account of the Bohemian Germans who settled in what was then southern Hungary in the late 1700s.

Hugo Grothe. *Grothes Kleines Handwörterbuch des Grenz- und Ausland-Deutschtums,* multiple volumes. [*Grothe's Small Encyclopedia of Germans in Border Areas and Abroad*]. 1932.

> The most complete book on the Germans in border areas and in foreign lands.

Otto Heike. *Schwabensiedlungen in Polen, 1795-1945.* [*Swabian Settlements in Poland, 1795-1945*]. Leverkusen, Germany. 1979.

> Account of the settlement of Swabians and other South Germans in Polish territory.

Larry O. Jensen. *A Genealogical Handbook of German Research,* Vol. III.

Robert A. Kann. *The Multinational Empire: Nationalism and Reform in the Habsburg Monarchy, 1848-1918.* New York: Octagon Books, Vol. II, 1964.

A. Karasek and K. Lück. *Die deutschen Siedlungen in Wolhynien* [*The German Settlements in Volhynia*]. 1931.

> Brief but good book on the Germans who migrated to Volhynia (now northwest Ukraine), mostly between 1860 and 1910.

Viktor Kauder. *Das Deutschtum in Ostpolen* [*The Germans in East Poland*]. 1939.

> Deals with Germans who settled in the Cholm-Lublin area, mostly after 1860.

W. Kessler. *Ost- und südostdeutsche Heimatbücher und Ortsmonographien nach 1945: Eine Bibliographie zur historischen Landeskunde der Vertreibungsgebiete.* [*East and Southeast Local History Books and Locality Monographs Since 1945: A Bibliography of Local Histories for the Regions Where Germans Were Expelled*]. Munich. 1979.

> Bibliography of local histories of German villages in east and southeast Europe.

Manfred Klaube. *Deutschböhmische Siedlungen im Karpatenraum* [*German Bohemian Settlements in the Carpathian Area*]. 1984.

> Bohemian German settlements in the area transferred from Czechoslovakia to the Soviet Union as a result of World War II.

Rolf Kosiek. *Jenseits der Grenzen: 1000 Jahre Volks- und Auslandsdeutschen.* [*Beyond the (German) Borders: 1000 Years of Ethnic Germans in Foreign Lands*]. Tübingen: Grabert-Verlag, 1987.

Oskar Kossmann. *Die Deutschen in Polen seit der Reformation: historisch-geographische Skizzen.* [*Germans in Poland Since the Reformation: Historical and Geographical Sketches*] Marburg/Lahn: J. G. Herder-Institut: 1978.

C. A. Macartney. *The Habsburg Empire, 1790-1918.* London: Weidenfeld and Nicolson, 1968.

William O. McCagg, Jr. *A History of the Habsburg Jews, 1670-1918.* Bloomington, IN: Indiana University Press. 1989, 1992. 289 pp.

> Deals mostly with the 1800-1918 period. Specific chapters or sections on Vienna, Bohemia, Hungary, Galicia, Bukovina and Trieste.

Richard Memel. *Das Memelland.* [*The Memel Territory*]. 1957.

> Deals with the former East Prussian border area transferred from German to Lithuanian control in the early 1920s.

John M. Michels. *Introduction to the Hungarian-Germans of North Dakota.* Bismarck, ND: Germans from Russia Heritage Society, February 1988.

Sepp Müller. *Von der Ansiedlung bis zur Umsiedlung: Das Deutschtum Galiziens, insbesondere Lembergs, 1772-1940.* [*Ethnic Germans in Galicia and Especially Lemberg, 1772-1940: From Early Settlement to Emigration (Repatriation back to Germany)*]. Marburg/Lahn: J. G. Herder-Institut, 1961.

Géza C. Paikert. *The Danube Swabians: German Populations in Hungary, Rumania and Yugoslavia and Hitler's Impact on Their Patterns.* The Hague: Martinus Nijhoff, 1967.

Edward A. Peckwas. *A Historical Bibliography of Polish Towns, Villages, and Regions (except Warsaw and Krakow).* Chicago: Polish Genealogical Society of America. 1990 reprint of 1971 bibliography compiled by Wiktor Kazmierczak.

> Lists almost 1,000 local histories, nearly half of them German.

Carl Petersen and Otto Scheel, *Handwörterbuch des Grenz- und Auslanddeutschtums.* [*Encyclopedia of Germans in Border Areas and Abroad*]. Breslau: Ferdinand Hirt. 1933.

> This book is one of the two comprehensive multi-volume works on German-speakers in non-Germanic areas of Europe.

Tony Radspieler. *The Ethnic German Refugee in Austria, 1945 to 1954.* The Hague: Martinus Nijhoff, 1955.

Wilhelm Rohmeder. *Das Deutschtum in Südtirol.* [*Ethnic Germans (Austrians) in South Tyrol*] Berlin: Verein für das Deutschtum im Ausland, 1919.

Georg Wilhelm Sante, ed. *Geschichte der deutschen Länder: "Territorien-Ploetz."* [*History of German Countries, or "Ploetz-Territories"*]. 2 vols. Würzburg: A. G. Ploetz Verlag. The second title is the publisher's abbreviated title.

Hermann Schreiber. *Teuton and Slav: The Struggle for Central Europe.* London: Constable, 1965. English translation by James Cleugh.

Ernst Schwarz. *Handbuch der Sudetendeutschen Kulturgeschichte* [*Handbook of Sudeten German Cultural History*], 4 volumes. 1961-1966.

> Authoritative work on the Germans in Bohemia and Moravia.

L. Edward Skender. *A Short History of the Duchy of Carniola and Gottschee County.* Sonora, CA: Gottscheer Research and Genealogy Association. 1994. 29 pp.

> History of this Slovenian area since Celtic times, with emphasis on the German connection. Many detailed maps, including one on Germans in northeastern Italy.

Jacob Steigerwald. *Tracing Romania's Heterogeneous German Minority from Its Origins to the Diaspora.*

Karl Stumpp. *The Emigration from Germany to Russia in the Years 1763-1862.*

Anton Tafferner, Josef Schmidt and Josef Volkmar Senz. *Danube Swabians in the Pannonia Basin: A New German Ethnic Group.* Milwaukee. 1982.

> Historical overview and maps of Danube Swabian settlements.

Mario Toscano. *Alto Adige, South Tyrol: Italy's Frontier with the German World.* Baltimore: Johns Hopkins University Press, 1975; translation.

Paul Traeger. *The Germans in the Dobrudscha (Dobrogea).* English translation serialized in the *Heritage Review.* Bismarck: Germans from Russia Heritage Society. 1985-88.

> Authoritative account of the German settlements near the Black Sea coast of Romania, extending slightly into Bulgaria.

Edward von der Porten. "The Hanseatic League: Europe's First Common Market," in *National Geographic,* Oct. 1994.

Ernst Wagner, et. al. *The Transylvanian Saxons: Historical Highlights.* Cleveland: Alliance of Transylvanian Saxons. 1982.

> History and maps pertaining to the Transylvanian Saxons in Europe and North America.

Johann Weidlein. *Die Deutschen in der Schwäbischen Türkei.* [*Germans in Swabian Turkey (South Hungary)*].

> One of the few books about the Germans in the southern part of contemporary Hungary.

Sophie A. Welisch. *Bukovina Villages / Towns / Cities and Their Germans.*

Franz Wilhelm and Josef Kallbrunner. *Quellen zur deutschen Siedlungsgeschichte in Südosteuropa.* [*Sourcebook for Histories of German Settlements in Southeast Europe*].

Chapter XI

RELIGION

Religion is probably a more complicated subject for the study of the migration and genealogy of German-speaking ancestors than is true for any other European group. This chapter provides a cohesive treatment of the topic, even though some of the material is also covered in other chapters.

DESCRIPTION AND NATURE OF GERMANIC CHURCHES

Although there were many dissident groups within the Christian church before and during the Middle Ages, only two of these had any significant impact on the Germanic peoples, if we exclude the Arianism of early Germanic tribes who migrated to other areas during the *Völkerwanderung* (known in English as the Great Barbarian Migrations) and totally lost their Germanic identity.

The first was the reform movement begun by Peter Waldo (Waldus) of Lyons in southern France around 1170. However, the Waldensians have no impact on Germanic history until much later.

The reform movement initiated by John Huss, who was executed in 1415, had a profound effect in Bohemia and Moravia, which were subject to the Hapsburgs, until 1620, when the Hussites were finally crushed. See the history of the AUSTRO-HUNGARIAN EMPIRE in Chapter X for further details.

The Moravian Church (also known as Moravian Brethren, Czech Brethren, or *Herrnhuter*) began as the Unity of Brethren (*Brüder-Unität*, Unitas Fratrum), established by Hussites in 1457. A decade later it established its own ministry and formally separated itself from the Catholic church.

However, only a tiny percentage of people who spoke (or adopted) the German language during the modern era belonged to either of these groups. The big change began with Martin Luther of Saxony.

The early years of the Reformation gave birth to three wings of Protestantism on Germanic soil. The first and largest one developed into the Lutheran church.

The second most significant group was begun by Ulrich Zwingli, a Swiss German. But he was killed in battle within a few years, so it was French-born John Calvin of Geneva who molded it to a large extent. Hence, this stream of religious thought is usually referred to as Calvinism, although it was called the Reformed church in continental Europe. It soon became and remained the dominant Protestant church in Switzerland, as well as in France, the Netherlands and Scotland.

The third, most diverse and least known was the Anabaptist movement initiated by Conrad Grebel, originally a Swiss follower of Zwingli. The name means "re-baptizers" and comes from its belief in adult baptism, which meant that its earliest members, who had been baptized as infants in the Catholic church, were baptized again as adults. It soon spread to the Netherlands, Flanders and adjoining parts of Germany, especially along the Lower Rhine.

At first it was an amorphous movement with many individual leaders preaching very different ideas. One group captured the city of Münster in 1534, where it established a dictatorship, with a society based on bigamy and communal sharing. The city was recaptured in 1535, but the Münsterites frightened the authorities and gave the movement a reputation totally inconsistent with its later development.

The Calvin of Anabaptism was Menno Simons, a former Frisian priest, and consequently the members of this non-violent church soon became known as Mennonists, later Mennonites, although the Swiss-South German wing referred to itself as Brethren for a long time.

The Amish splintered off from the Mennonites, just as the Mennonites themselves split into many different denominations: The Hutterites, who believe in community of property, the Schwenkfelders, the German Baptist Brethren (also known as *Tunkers* or Dunkards), and the various Brethren churches are also part of the Anabaptist wing.

The Anglican (in the U.S., Episcopalian) church was the dominant church in England. From this sprang the reformist Methodist church, which established its first congregations in Germany and Switzerland in the early nineteenth century as a reaction against the moral laxity of the state church. Many German immigrants are reported to have joined the church in the United States because it reached out to them as a kind of "Welcome Wagon."

Various Baptist and Adventist churches were also exported from Anglo-Saxon countries to Germany, Switzerland or German-speaking enclaves. They were not numerous among German emigrants, although the Baptist church is fairly significant among ethnic Germans in the member states of the Commonwealth of Independent States today and there are passing references to Adventist missionaries in books on the Germans in several New World countries.

For an informative chart on the "Genealogy of Churches, with an Emphasis of German-American Churches" by Dr. David H. Koss of Illinois College, see Arta F. Johnson's *Bibliography and Source Materials for German-American Research*, Volume I: USA (updated 1984).

The Prussian king ordered the Lutheran and Reformed churches to merge into the Evangelical church in 1817. Those Lutherans who rejected this merger became known as "Old Lutherans." The merger took place in other parts of Germany at about the same time or a little later. A significant minority of the Reformed churches did not become part of the Evangelical church.

The Catholic church, too, had its dissidents. The Old Catholics, found in Germany and Austria, rejected the principle of papal infallibility.

THE EARLY REFORMATION/COUNTER-REFORMATION ERA, 1517-1648

Religious persecution and coerced conversion among Christians was the rule, rather than the exception, in Germanic areas until the end of the Thirty Years' War (1618-48). Even expulsion, execution and torture were fairly common. Mainstream Protestants were often just as intolerant of smaller sects as the Catholics were of Protestantism. The worst pre-Holocaust persecution of the Jews had already occurred prior to the Reformation.

The Peace of Augsburg in 1555 provided that Catholic and Lutheran rulers could require their subjects to be of the same religion. However, the truce was by no means always honored. Not until 1648 were Reformed rulers granted equal status. In a place like the Palatinate, where rulers of the three different denominations succeeded each other, this meant frequent changes in the religion imposed upon subjects.

The sheer exhaustiveness of the Thirty Years' War, which is estimated to have killed one-third or more of the German and Czech people, led to an alleviation of the harsh treatment of religious minorities, but discrimination continued to exist until the latter half of the nineteenth century.

Protestantism had made great inroads in Poland, Hungary and Southern Germany after the Reformation, but the Catholic Counter-Reformation resulted in the re-Catholicization of these areas a half-century later. Many of the Polish and Hungarian Protestants belonged to the Reformed faith, with some of the Unitarian persuasion (earlier known as Socinianism). Poland, and later Bohemia, Moravia, Hungary and Walachia (Romania), provided a haven of refuge for dissidents. The Commonwealth of Poland and Lithuania was the one North European country that welcomed adherents of all faiths, both in the late Middle Ages (Jews) and in the early decades of the modern era (various sorts of Protestants).

Although Inquisitions were instituted in most Catholic countries after the Reformation, the Spanish Inquisition was the most cruel one. As background, Spain had driven the last Muslim rulers out of Southern Spain in 1492 and promptly proceeded to homogenize the country by forcibly converting the Jews and Muslims who had helped make Spain such a glorious civilization in the late Middle Ages.

At the time of the Reformation, the Spanish Hapsburgs ruled the Low Countries, where the Reformed and Mennonite denominations spread rapidly. They were largely successful in stamping out Protestantism in Belgium, which existed mostly around the provincial capital of Brussels.

The Walloons (French-speaking Calvinists from southern and eastern Belgium) fled mostly to Germanic principalities with Reformed rulers, including the Palatinate, Hesse and Franconia (now northeastern Bavaria).

The Anabaptists, who believe in separation of church and state, had no rulers of their own faith to protect them. Flemish Anabaptists initially fled mostly to Friesland, a second major center of Anabaptism and one where the arm of the law was not quite as effective, although numerous executions were carried out there, too. Before long, the majority of the Mennonites had fled eastward, mostly to West Prussia, a predominantly German-speaking area that was under Polish rule, but with local autonomy until 1569. Some originally found refuge in Emden (Ostfriesland) and others went to Schleswig-Holstein (especially Altona, now northwestern Hamburg).

The northern provinces, however, rebelled against Spain's autocratic rule. By the 1580s, the Netherlands had achieved de facto independence, although Spain did not recognize it as such until 1648, when an independent Switzerland also gained international recognition.

POST-1648 RELIGIOUS FLIGHT AND MIGRATION TO AND WITHIN GERMANIC EUROPE (INCLUDING EAST EUROPEAN ENCLAVES)

Persecution and expulsion did not end with the Thirty Years' War. For example, while the Dutch Mennonites found security in the independent Netherlands, their counterparts in Switzerland were hunted down and expelled. Most of them went down the Rhine, settling on both the German (Baden-Württemberg, the Palatinate, southern Hesse) and French (Alsace, Montbéliard) sides of the river, where some can still be found today. However, the fact that this new refuge left something to be desired is indicated by the fact that some of them later moved to Galicia, Volhynia and Poland, whereas the Hutterites followed an even more difficult migration trail through Eastern Europe, finally ending up in eastern Ukraine, when they were on the verge of extinction.

Furthermore, France, which had seen the Thirty Years' War more as a struggle against the Austrian Empire for hegemony than as a religious war (as indicated by its choice of allies), had enunciated the Edict of Nantes, which guaranteed religious tolerance in 1598, after the same kind of internal religious strife as had existed in Germany. However, after the revocation of this edict in 1685, most of the Huguenots (French Reformed) scattered throughout the world, with quite a few fleeing to Switzerland, Brandenburg, Saxony-Anhalt, and the areas around Bremen and Frankfurt. Some had already fled after the St. Bartholomew's Day Massacre of 1572.

Some of the Waldensians, who had survived extinction for centuries in the almost inaccessible Alps along the Franco-Italian border, joined the Huguenot emigration. The two groups established close ties.

Both the French and Belgian Protestants were relatively well-educated middle class people and the Huguenots included quite a few nobles. As a result, they had a major impact on the development of Berlin and Magdeburg. They kept the French language for a considerable period of time, often had separate French churches and have retained a strong sense of a special identity, somewhat like the Sons and Daughters of the American Revolution or the United Empire Loyalists in Canada.

In 1772 the Moravian Brethren were given refuge on the estate of a nobleman in Herrnhut in southeastern Saxony, whence they derived the name *Herrnhuter*, and soon became Germanicized.

The Austrian Empire and the Archbishopric of Salzburg also banned Protestantism for a long time. The Transylvanian Saxons had become Lutherans while under Ottoman Turkish rule. The Hapsburg emperors were pragmatic enough not to attempt to forcibly re-Catholicize them after the area was regained from the Turks. Transylvania thus also became a place of refuge for some Austrian Protestants, since Protestantism was generally not tolerated elsewhere by the Hapsburgs until 1781.

The Archbishop of Salzburg expelled some 20,000 Protestants, mostly from the *Salzkammergut* or *Ländl* east of Salzburg, in the 1730s. Salzburger refugees (German: *Exulanten*) found homes in many places, especially in East Prussia (where there was an active program to colonize sparsely populated areas), but also in Franconia (now northern Bavaria), and Brandenburg.

Bismarck's anti-Catholic *Kulturkampf* (1871-78) caused some Catholic emigration, especially from the Rhineland, with some ending up in Bosnia.

Mennonites from West Prussia migrated to the Russian Empire (Eastern Ukraine), mostly in 1789-1806 but with the last small wave (which went to the Upper Volga area) in the 1850s. This was due primarily to restrictions on landownership imposed by the Prussian king after Poland lost the area in 1772 and 1793, since the Mennonites, as conscientious objectors, did not provide the soldiers that the land was supposed to produce.

Conservative Württemberg Separatists, many of them millennialists, who were dissatisfied with the Lutheran state church at home, migrated to the Odessa and Berdyansk areas and to Bessarabia (all near the Black Sea), as well as to the southern Caucasus region around Tiflis (now Tbilisi, the capital of Georgia), in 1816-19, with later daughter settlements in the Crimea. Many of them later migrated to North and South Dakota.

The East European countries that had become the homeland of most Jews established anti-Jewish policies after the dismemberment of Poland, which also caused migration.

The Russian government forced all Jews living elsewhere (some 700,000) to relocate in the Pale of Settlement, essentially the former Polish-Lithuanian territory, which included Belarus and Ukraine, by 1891. By 1882, it had already forced half a million Jews living in rural areas in the Pale to give up their homes and settle in *shtetls* (literally, small towns). This made them easy targets for the pogroms (anti-Jewish riots) that destroyed much of their property, killed quite a few of them and endangered many more, forcing them to flee. Not until 1917 were the Russian Jews emancipated, a step that all West European countries, except Spain and Portugal, had taken by 1874.

POST-1648 RELIGIOUS FLIGHT AND MIGRATION FROM EUROPE

Krefeld Mennonites and Palatine Quakers represented the first German group migration to America in 1683-85, attracted by the religious tolerance of William Penn's colony. This colony soon became a haven for others seeking freedom of religion.

Some Huguenots who had lived in Germany for some time later migrated overseas, especially to South Africa.

Some of the Protestant refugees expelled from Salzburg emigrated to the American state of Georgia in the 1730s. Silesian Schwenkfelders settled in Pennsylvania about the same time, while Moravians went to both Pennsylvania (1740) and North Carolina (1753).

Compulsory military service, without exceptions for conscientious objectors, became the law shortly after German unification. By then, the vast majority of Prussian Mennonites had become so acculturated that they accepted this, but a small minority left for North America because of this.

In 1785 Father George Rapp established a group dedicated to total community of property, excluding even marital ties. In 1804 this group came from Germany and settled in Harmony, Pennsylvania. Ten years later they founded New Harmony, Indiana, but after another decade they returned to Pennsylvania, specifically to Old Economy. In 1905, when membership had already dwindled greatly, the Harmonists were dissolved. John Duss then took the belongings to Florida, but the Harmonists do not consider this to be a valid continuation of the group.

Old Lutherans who rejected the Lutheran-Reformed merger imposed by the king of Prussia in 1817 migrated to Australia, Canada and the United States in 1837-54 because of attempts to suppress them. In *Nineteenth-Century Emigration of "Old Lutherans" from Eastern Germany (Mainly Pomerania and Lower Silesia)*, Clifford Neal Smith lists a large number of the emigrants who emigrated to Australia, Canada and the United States.

Despite the fact that most Germanic emigration to overseas countries occurred after this merger, it had little effect in the immigrant countries, where there were many Lutheran churches of German origin, with the Reformed minority often joining one of the various Calvinist churches.

The Methodists in western Germany and Switzerland encountered harsh social intimidation and lack of protection, about the same time as the "Old Lutherans," so a disproportionate number emigrated to the United States.

Another small group of dissidents who migrated across the Atlantic in the nineteenth century were the Labadists, a mystic and pietistic splinter within the Reformed church.

Many of the Germans who migrated to the Americas from the Russian Empire in the last generation of the nineteenth century and again after each of the two world wars also left at least partly for religious reasons. This was especially true of the Mennonites and the refugees from Communism. Those who left during the interwar period settled mostly in Canada and Latin America, because the United States adopted restrictive immigration laws in the early 1920s.

But quite a few post-World War II displaced persons (including East European Germans who had become "stateless") were allowed to enter the United States, although more apparently went to Canada and other New World countries.

Most of the post-*glasnost* Germans from the Soviet Union and Poland went to, and stayed in, Germany. But many of those from the Balkans crossed the ocean.

There was extremely heavy Jewish emigration from the Russian Empire to the United States, Canada, Latin America, Australia and Western Europe in 1880-1914, often as a result of the pogroms that coincided with the period of severe Russification policies toward ethnic minorities. Even after the Bolshevik Revolution, they suffered from considerable discrimination, as indicated by the substantial emigration in the 1920s and by the much more massive exodus to Israel, the United States and Western Europe in recent years.

Anti-Jewish actions in the Austro-Hungarian Empire, combined with severe starvation in Galicia and the Bukovina, led to the emigration of over a million Jews from these areas to the United States alone during the late 1800s and early 1900s. Others went to Western Canada, Argentina, etc.

The most recent German-speaking religious refugees to America and elsewhere were the Jews who left Germany and Austria during the pre-Holocaust era of growing anti-Semitism.

For further information on religious migration, see Chapter X on **HISTORY**.

CHRISTIAN-JEWISH RELATIONS IN GERMANIC AREAS

The history of German-speaking Jews and their relationship to Germanic Christians is a very complex one. Jews were expelled from most of Western Europe, including the Germanic areas, during the 1100-1400 period, primarily as a result of the indiscriminate hatred spawned by the crusades and because they were made scapegoats considered responsible for the Bubonic Plague of 1348-50, which decimated most of Western Europe, although Poland escaped relatively unscathed.

In some cases, they were readmitted, often selectively, and then forced to leave again. The practice of isolating Jews in ghettos began in Italy as early as 1215. Officially decreed ghettos existed in Frankfurt, Mainz and Vienna, as well as in major cities in most other continental European countries. Expulsion directives resulted in the almost complete obliteration of Jewish communities in Spain, as well as a sharp reduction in England and France. Most of these expellees, however, had no connection with Germanic Europe.

Because Germany was so fragmented, the cyclical pattern of expulsion (sometimes to a nearby area) and readmission left a relatively large number of West European Jews there. But the majority of German Jews fled to Poland (later the Commonwealth of Poland and Lithuania). Poland was a haven of religious tolerance in northern Europe during the late medieval and early modern centuries, although this changed to some degree after the Catholic Counter-Reformation. Nearly all Russian Jews lived in what had earlier been Polish-Lithuanian territory.

But while the Jews were always a separate group, they often identified with Germans in Eastern Europe. Indeed, Yiddish is derived mostly from the Old High German language, the name itself stemming from *jüdisch*, meaning Jewish. Germans, Flemings and Jews were the main forces in developing commerce and the cities in much of Eastern Europe.

For cartographic data regarding Jewish expulsions, ghettos, persecution, the Holocaust, etc., see Martin Gilbert, *The Atlas of Jewish History*.

Hitler's policies were in marked contrast to the relatively good relations between German Christians and Jews, especially in the East, which had existed since the abatement of the fury of the Middle Ages.

Between Hitler's ascent to power in 1933 and U.S. entrance into World War II in 1941, approximately a quarter of a million Jews fled to the United States and half that many went to other parts of the Western Hemisphere. Another quarter of a million Jews took refuge in the Soviet Union, while others went to various European countries or to Palestine.

An estimated six million Jews (half from Poland) perished in concentration camps (in the gas chambers or from starvation or illness) during World War II. Less than 5% came from Germany; many Jews had already fled from there before the war. Jewish losses in the Holocaust were proportionately much lower in Hungary and especially in Italy, even though these countries were German allies (until Italy switched sides in 1943).

GEOGRAPHIC DISTRIBUTION OF RELIGIOUS GROUPS

THE CHRISTIAN POPULATION

The religious demography of the major churches in the German-speaking countries has remained relatively constant since the population was stabilized by the rather substantial migration to repopulate areas devastated by the Thirty Years' War.

Internal migrations since the beginning of the Industrial Revolution have modified the patterns somewhat, although even these changes were relatively minor, except perhaps in the bigger cities. The mass flight and expulsion of Germans from Eastern Europe, beginning in late 1944, changed the demographic map more drastically. Today all-Catholic or all-Protestant villages are rarities. At the time most of our ancestors emigrated, they were not uncommon.

To begin the sketch, Luxembourg, largely unaffected by recent migrations, remains 97% Catholic.

Austria is still 85% Catholic, despite an influx of refugees, and little Liechtenstein has about the same proportion of Catholics. The largest number of Austrian Protestants are in the Burgenland, formerly part of Hungary.

There are slightly more Protestants than Catholics among the German-speakers in Switzerland. The Alpine core of Switzerland is staunchly Catholic, while most northern and eastern cantons are predominantly Protestant.

What used to be West Germany has about an equal number of Catholics and Protestants. Bavaria (except for central and eastern Franconia), Saarland and the Rhineland are heavily Catholic. The northern Länder are heavily Protestant. Westphalia, as well as the central and southeastern areas of West Germany have a more mixed religious composition. Catholics constitute only a very small minority in the new eastern states, formerly under Communist rule.

Before the Evangelical merger, Reformed Church members were concentrated in Brandenburg, Hesse, Franconia, the Palatinate and some northwest German areas. The considerably more numerous Lutherans were a significant part of the population in these areas and a large majority of the Protestants elsewhere.

In what is now France, Germans in Lorraine were heavily Catholic, while Alsace had a significantly larger Protestant minority that produced many emigrants. The Reformed influence was strong in Alsace.

The parts of interwar Germany that now belong to Poland and what was the Soviet Union were heavily Lutheran, with the Catholic minority greatest in Warmia (part of East Prussia) and near the prewar German-Polish border.

The territory ceded to Poland after World War I was mostly Catholic, but split largely along ethnic lines with respect to religion.

The Germans from the Sudetenland (in the Czech Republic) were nearly all Catholics, with the few Protestants mostly along the border with Saxony and Silesia.

For those who are looking for American sources of information concerning Germans of the Roman Catholic, Lutheran, or Reformed faiths, Arta Johnson also has some bibliographical material on them. The various American church archives that may have material on German-Americans are also listed in the *Yearbook of American and Canadian Churches*. A comprehensive list of church archives in Europe can be found in Thode's *Address Book*.

THE JEWISH POPULATION

In 1905, Jews constituted about 1% of the population of the German Empire. Nearly 100,000 of the 600,000 Jews lived in Berlin, with about 55,000 each in the Rhineland and Bavaria.

When we look at the Jews as a percentage of the regional population, an entirely different picture emerges. In Hamburg, Hesse and Hesse-Nassau, at least 2% of the inhabitants were Jewish. Other states or provinces with an above average percentage of Jews included Alsace-Lorraine, Posen and Baden. The percentage was especially high in Lower (northern) Alsace and in the Mannheim district (northern Baden). The Jewish population was above the national average in northeastern Bavaria, but much lower in historic Bavaria.

A map in *Meyers Kleines Konversations-Lexikon* [*Meyer's Small Conversational Encyclopedia*] shows that in 1900, German Jews were concentrated near medieval or modern trading centers. Except for parts of Hesse, the Jews lived mostly near the Rhine, Main and Moselle Rivers, in addition to the modern cities of Berlin and Hamburg. In the eastern Prussian provinces, they were mostly in or near Posen.

There were over 2 million Jews in the Austro-Hungarian Empire in 1900, i.e., more than three times the number in the German Empire. However, less than 2% of them lived in Austria proper, where the only concentration was in Lower Austria, with most of these in Vienna.

About two-thirds of the Jews lived in Galicia, which had been part of Poland before 1772. More than 10% of the people in the Bukovina and Galicia were Jewish. More modest concentrations of Jews in the Austrian part of the Dual Monarchy existed in the Trieste area and what is now the Czech Republic.

No comparable geographic breakdown for the Hungarian portion of the empire is provided by the *Meyers* encyclopedia. However, 23% of the nearly 800,000 inhabitants of Budapest were Jewish, according to Meyer. Paul Robert Magocsi, *Historical Atlas of East Central Europe*, shows Jewish concentrations in northeastern and south central Hungary, but even more so in Slovakia and northwestern Romania, which were part of Hungary in 1900. There were a modest number of Jews in some areas of Danube Swabian settlement.

Prior to the establishment of the Austro-Hungarian Empire, Jews throughout the Hapsburg empire were sometimes counted as Germans. In Galicia and the Bukovina, the Jews far outnumbered the German Christians.

It is unclear how many of the Jews in the former Russian Empire should be considered Germanic in terms of the language of commerce and secular culture. But the large number of Jews in the Lodz area in westernmost Russian Poland, where there were also many German Christians, definitely belonged in this category.

In *The Jewish History Atlas*, Martin Gilbert shows Jewish settlements in Berne, St. Gall(en), Winterthur, Schaffhausen and Lucerne in the thirteenth century. Refugees from Alsace and Swabia fled to Neuchâtel and Basel in 1330. No date is given for the settlements in Aargau and Solothurn cantons. No other part of Central Europe had as many Jewish settlements within such a small geographic area. The Swiss Jews were emancipated in 1874 (later than in other countries between Spain and Russia).

There are many archives in North America, Israel and Europe that contain records relating to Jewish genealogy. By far the most comprehensive data for American Jews tracing ancestors from the German and Austro-Hungarian empires is the:

Leo Baeck Institute
129 E. 73rd St.
New York, NY 10021

The following institute deals with East European Jewish genealogical research:

YIVO Institute for Jewish Research
555 W. 57th St., Ste. 1100
New York, NY 10019-2925

Thode's *Address Book* lists numerous others. Hebrew Union College and the Jewish Theological Seminary Library, both in New York, would appear to be especially useful.

For records on Jewish immigrants to Canada, see chapter V.

There are several Jewish genealogical periodicals. The address of one is shown below. Others are listed in Thode's *Address Book*.

Avotaynu: The International Review of Jewish Genealogy
155 N. Washington Ave.
Teaneck, NJ 07621

Three books on Jewish genealogy are:

- Arthur Kurzweil, *From Generation to Generation: How to Trace Your Jewish Genealogy and Personal History*.

- Dan Rottenberg, *Finding Our Fathers: A Guide to Jewish Genealogy*. This book has recently been reprinted.

- Miriam Weiner, comp., *Bridging the Generations: Researching Your Jewish Roots*.

Weiner's book has an up-to-date bibliography of other relevant books and also lists Jewish genealogical societies in the United States, Canada, Israel and Europe. Thode's *Address Book* also has an extensive list of North American Jewish genealogical societies. For those researching Jewish ancestors in the Russian Pale of Settlement, Chester G. Cohen's *Shtetl Finder Gazetteer* may be helpful.

According to Angus Baxter's *In Search of Your Roots: A Guide for Canadians Seeking Their Ancestors*, Jewish records of over 900 communities in Poland, Hungary and Germany have been microfilmed by the FHL. These records are listed by county and by town in *Toledot: The Journal of Jewish Genealogy* (address in Chapter XIX).

RESEARCHING ANCESTORS FROM SMALL DENOMINATIONS AND DISTINCT GROUPS

Most of this book deals with the denominations to which a large majority of the Germanic emigrants belonged (Lutheran, Reformed, Catholic, including dissident groups within these churches).

The following material is designed to help genealogists with a different religious ancestral background. Key works for researching both small and large denominations are: (1) Dr. Arta F. Johnson, *Bibliography and Source Materials for German-American Research*, Vol. 1, (2) Clifford Neal Smith and Anna Piszczan-Czaja Smith, *Encyclopedia of German-American Genealogical Research*, and (3) the annual *Yearbook of American and Canadian Churches*.

Knowing the religion of your German ancestor is very helpful because church records are the primary source of genealogical information in Germany prior to the keeping of civil records. Although some areas began keeping civil records around 1800 it was not mandatory until 1876. In contrast, church records can often be traced back to 1650 or even earlier. In other countries, parish registers began earlier (Switzerland, Austria) or later (Russia).

Both Catholics and Evangelical (earlier as Lutheran and Reformed) Churches maintained these records. The smaller Christian denominations and the Jews did not maintain many records during the time when they were still subjected to persecutions. However, their members were sometimes recorded in the Catholic or Evangelical records. Five main types of records were kept: birth and/or baptism, confirmation, marriage, and death and/or burial registers, as well as funeral sermons. See Chapters XIV and XV for more details about church records.

Although each church generally kept its own parish registers, there were some exceptions. Particularly if you get back to very early records, you may find that the official church in the area was required to keep a record of all births, deaths and marriages, regardless of the religion of the individual or family. This was true in Austria until 1781. This was sometimes even true of Jewish entries, at least in some eastern areas. For members of small sects, like the Mennonites, this practice continued sporadically into the eighteenth century.

In areas where only a small handful of individuals belonged to a particular church, the records might be kept by the majority church, either because there was no pastor ministering to the minority or because he lived so far away from the areas where their records were kept. Combined registers for Lutherans and Reformed Church members were quite common even before the Evangelical Union. With these exceptions in mind, certain key sources of information have been identified for genealogists whose German ancestors belonged to one of the less widespread religious groups.

FRENCH-SPEAKING PROTESTANT REFUGEES: Huguenots, Waldensians, Walloons

The *Geschichtsblätter des deutschen Hugenottenvereins* [*Historical Papers of the German Huguenot Society*], published in the 1890s and microfilmed by the Family History Library, provide a comprehensive history of virtually all identifiable Huguenot congregations that once existed in Germany. This information is not only valuable for tracing ancestors in a known community, but it can also be very helpful in tracing people who have disappeared from the locality being researched.

Huguenots who left their homes to find work elsewhere, to marry or to flee from the devastation of war usually migrated to other Huguenot communities, sometimes including those relatively far away. This pattern, incidentally, is generally characteristic of all small religious minority groups. Thus having a historical overview of such settlements is the genealogist's clue to finding that needle in the haystack.

Many publications of the German Huguenot Society (including coverage of the Waldensians) are in the library of the National Huguenot Society in Minneapolis, which is open only by appointment with the librarian, Arthur Finnell.

There is a Museum of Waldensian Heritage in Valdese, North Carolina.

Walloon records are mostly in the German Reformed parish registers.

ANABAPTISTS: Mennonites, Brethren, Amish, Hutterites, Baptists, Baptist Brethren (Dunkards), Schwenkfelders

The bibliography in Arta F. Johnson, *Bibliography and Source Materials for German-American Research*, Vol. 1, lists many works relevant for Anabaptist research.

Mennonites

Most of the Mennonites who originated in the Dutch-Flemish-Frisian-Lower Rhenish area migrated to the Danzig-Elbing area (Gdansk-Elblag in current Poland), though some remained in the Netherlands and others settled around Hamburg. A sizable percentage of these moved in 1789 and 1804-05 to Chortitz, Molochna and other settlements in what is now Eastern Ukraine (then known as South Russia), with smaller numbers later. A large number of the Mennonites in Russia moved to Manitoba, Nebraska and Kansas in and shortly after 1874. There is a huge card index file of this group of Mennonites at:

> Mennonite Genealogy, Inc.
> P. O. Box 393
> Winnipeg, Manitoba R3C 2H6
> Canada

The Mennonites who originated in Switzerland fled to the Palatinate, Alsace, Montbéliard, Württemberg and other areas. Most of them came from the Berne and Zurich areas. Some moved on to the Vistula valley in Poland, Volhynia, Galicia and Russia. A small number of Galician Mennonites migrated to the Midwest and to Western Canada in the late 1800s.

Of particular interest to genealogists is that a substantial number of early immigrants to the United States (primarily to Pennsylvania) came directly from the southern German-speaking areas of Europe, although the first group of German immigrants in 1683 were Mennonites from Krefeld on the lower Rhine. Most of the Mennonites living east of the Mississippi or in the province of Ontario stem from this group, many of whom arrived during the colonial period.

Published and unpublished family histories are very common in Mennonite circles. A large number of them can be found at:

Mennonite Historical Library
Goshen College
1700 South Main St.
Goshen, IN 46526-4724

Mennonite Heritage Centre
600 Shaftesbury Blvd.
Winnipeg, MB R3P 0M4
Canada
(*has many Mexican church books*)

Center for Mennonite Brethren Studies
Tabor College
Hillsboro, KS 67063-1799

Mennonite Library and Archives
Bethel College
300 East 27th
North Newton, KS 46526-9989

Centre for Mennonite Brethren Studies
1-169 Riverton Ave.
Winnipeg, MB R2L 2E5
Canada

Fresno Pacific College Archive
4824 E. Butler Ave.
Fresno, CA 93727-5097

The California Mennonite Historical Society at the same Fresno address publishes a *Bulletin* which carried genealogical articles, at least until 1995, when its genealogical project committee started its own newsletter, *Mennonite Genealogist*. The Manitoba Mennonite Historical Society's *Mennonite Historian*, published jointly by the two Winnipeg institutions, also carries genealogical articles and book reviews.

Archival material can be found at all of the previous locations, as well as at:

Mennonite Historical Library and
    Archives of Eastern Pennsylvania
1000 Forty Foot Rd.
Lansdale, PA 19446

Mennonite Archives of Ontario
Conrad Grebel College
Waterloo, ON N2L 3G6
Canada

Other pertinent historical/genealogical societies include:

Lancaster Mennonite Historical
    Society
2215 Millstream Rd.
Lancaster, PA 17602

Illinois Mennonite Historical and
    Genealogical Society
P.O. Box 819
Metamora, IL 61548

There are two specifically Mennonite genealogical periodicals:

Mennonite Family History
P.O. Box 171
Elverson, PA 19520-0171
(includes Amish and Brethren)

Mennonite Genealogist
Fresno Pacific College Archives
4824 E. Butler Ave.
Fresno, CA 93727

For a more complete list of resources pertinent for Mennonite genealogy, see Lawrence Klippenstein and Jim Suderman, eds., *Directory of Mennonite Archives and Libraries*, English-German-French 3rd ed. (Winnipeg: Mennonite Heritage Centre, 1990). It lists resource centers in Australia, Brazil, Canada, France, Germany, the Netherlands, Paraguay, Switzerland, the United Kingdom, the United States, and Uruguay, as well as for three Asian countries whose Mennonites are not of Germanic origin.

Amish

The Amish are often included in materials dealing with the Mennonites, particularly in periodicals or archives in Pennsylvania and Indiana. There are Amish settlements in many American states and Canadian provinces. The outstanding scholarly expert on the Amish is John A. Hostetter, who published an *Annotated Bibliography on the Amish* (Scottdale, PA: Herald Press, 1951). Arta Johnson also reports that a list of all available printed Amish genealogies was published in the Autumn 1969 issue of *Pennsylvania Folklife*.

Betty Miller, *The Amish in Switzerland and Other European Countries* (Berlin, OH: Author, 1984) and J. Virgil Miller, "The Swiss Family Origins of the Amish-Mennonite Migration to America" (*Mennonite Family History*, 1993), deal with the group's roots in Switzerland and their flight down the Rhine in the seventeenth and eighteenth centuries.

Hutterites

The FHL published Delbert Gratz's presentation on "Records Relating the Mennonite Story" at the 1969 World Conference on Records, which also briefly discusses the Hutterites. The most comprehensive history of the Hutterites is John Horsch's *Hutterite Brethren, 1528-1931* (Goshen, IN: Mennonite Historical Society, 1931).

Brethren and Baptist Brethren

The German Baptist Brethren, now known as the Church of the Brethren, founded the famous Ephrata Cloister.

Dr. Arta Johnson's *Bibliography* lists publications concerning the history of German Baptist Brethren, including obituaries and family history data. The Fellowship of Brethren Genealogists publishes a newsletter.

Dr. Emmett Bettinger, R. # 3, Box 116, Bridgewater, VA 22812, is a retired church historian. *Mennonite Family History* has published a number of his articles on the Brethren.

For more information, write to:

> Fellowship of Brethren Genealogists
> 1451 Dundee Ave.
> Elgin, IL 60120-1694

Baptists

Many German-speaking Baptists in the Americas have a background that is quite distinct from the Baptist Brethren. This is true, for example, of those who came from the Russian Empire. A significant number of Germans from other denominations became Baptists in Eastern Europe and in Latin America. There were also German Baptist immigrants from Ostfriesland, some of whom settled in Iowa and the Dakotas.

Pertinent information may be available from the:

> North American Baptist College Archives
> 11525 - 23 Ave.
> Edmonton, AB T6J 4T3
> Canada

Schwenkfelders

The Schwenkfelders settled in Pennsylvania in colonial times, after the same kind of religious flight within Europe, which was characteristic of most of the smaller dissident sects. The following publication, listed by Arta Johnson, is particularly pertinent for genealogists: Samuel Kriebel Brecht, *The Genealogical Record of the Schwenkfelder Families, Seekers of Religious Liberty Who Fled from Silesia to Saxony and Then to Pennsylvania in the Years 1731 to 1737* (New York: Rand, McNally, 1923). There is a Schwenkfelder Exile Society in Pennsburg, PA.

OTHER DENOMINATIONS

The Church of Jesus Christ of Latter-day Saints (Mormons)

This church was established in Germanic Europe by missionaries from America, but its members in Germanic Europe are mostly native Germans. The best source of pertinent information is the Family History Library.

Harmonists (Rappists)

The key source for this communitarian group is Karl J. R. Arndt, *George Rapp's Disciples, Pioneers and Heirs.*

An organization dealing with the German communal Harmonists of 1785-1905 is:

> Harmonie Associates
> Old Economy Village
> 14th & Church Sts.
> Ambridge, PA 15003

The following museum published a newsletter devoted to the Harmony Society, which had its first home there in 1804-1814, and the Mennonites who populated the area later in the nineteenth century:

> Historic Harmony/Harmony Museum
> 218 Mercer St.
> P.O. Box 524
> Harmony, PA 16037

Methodists

Kenneth E. Rose edited the multi-volume *Methodist Union Catalog: Pre-1976 Imprints,* which details the contents of major Methodist research collections in the United States and Europe. See Arta Johnson's *Bibliography* for a list of books and articles that deal more directly with German-American Methodists.

Moravians

Arta F. Johnson's *Bibliography and Source Materials for German-American Research,* Vol. 1, lists the following sources of information in the U.S., among others:

- There are Moravian Church archives in the group's two principal settlements in the United States: Bethlehem, Pennsylvania, and Winston-Salem, North Carolina.

- The *Transactions of the Moravian Historical Society,* published in Bethlehem in the nineteenth century, contain genealogical information.

- *The Palatine Immigrant,* published by Palatines to America, also has carried a number of articles pertinent to Moravian genealogy.

Ernest Thode's *Address Book* lists archives in Basel, Switzerland, and in Herrnhut in the eastern part of Germany, which contain biographical and other genealogically relevant materials, including some regarding the Moravian settlements in the Volga River region of Russia. Moravians (or Moravian Brethren) were also known as the *Herrnhuter.*

Although the archives in Winston-Salem, North Carolina, also has a periodical, most of the material mentioned by Arta F. Johnson is published by the:

> Moravian Historical Society
> Whitefield House
> 214 E. Center St.
> Nazareth, PA 18064

Moravian history and genealogy are also emphasized by the:

> Tuscarawas County Genealogical Society, Inc.
> P.O. Box 141
> New Philadelphia, OH 44663-0141

Information about the Moravians in Canada may be accessible through the:

> Canadian Moravian Historical Society, Edmonton Chapter
> 4204 - 116 St.
> Edmonton, AB T5N 0M6
> Canada

Salzburgers

The genealogy of the 1734 Protestant refugees from Salzburg is the focus of the following society, which publishes a newsletter:

> The Georgia Salzburger Society
> P.O. Box 478-B
> Rincon, GA 31326

Seventh-Day Adventists, Adventists

These are several Adventist denominations, with common theological roots. This church sent many missionaries to a large number of countries, so that traces of them can be found in various immigrant countries, despite the small number of German Adventist emigrants. The German Adventists in Bohemia and Transylvania eventually converted to Judaism. For further information, consult the reference works already mentioned.

REFERENCES (See bibliography for full citations if not shown)

For books relating to more than one religious group, see the **ANNOTATED BIBLIOGRAPHY** in Chapter XVIII.

Karl J. R. Arndt. *George Rapp's Disciples, Pioneers and Heirs: A Register of the Harmonists in America.* Edited by Donald E. Pitzer and Leigh Ann Chamness. Available from Michael Goelzhauser, University of Southern Indiana Bookstore, 8600 University Blvd., Evansville, IN 47712.

Martin G. Brumbaugh. *A History of the Brethren.* Mount Morris, IL: Brethren Publishing Co., 1899.

John M. Byler. *Amish Immigrants of Waldeck and Hesse.* Bowie, MD: Heritage Books. 1993. 231 pp.
> Specific genealogical records of Amish immigrants and their descendants up to 1865.

Irmgard Hein Ellingson. *The Bukovina Germans in Kansas: A 200 Year History of the Lutheran Swabians.* Fort Hays, KS: Fort State University. 1987.
> Deals with one of the largest Bukovina Lutheran groups who emigrated to North America.

H. Frank Eshleman. *Historic Background and Annals of the Swiss and German Pioneer Settlers of Southeastern Pennsylvania.* 1917. Baltimore: Genealogical Publishing Co. reprinted 1991. 386 pp.
> Focuses on Mennonite families and Lancaster County, with historic background in Germany, Switzerland and the Netherlands. Lists of early settlers and biographical sketches.

Charles M. Franklin. *Huguenot Genealogical Research.* Indianapolis, IN: Self-published. 1985. 58 pp.
> Lists specific records in Germany and Switzerland for Huguenots who fled from France between 1520 and 1787. Also lists some church records for Walloons (French-speaking Belgians) who fled from what was then the Spanish Netherlands, mostly in 1568.

Hugh F. Gingerich and Rachel W. Kreider. *Amish and Amish Mennonite Genealogies.* Pequea Publishers. 1986. 858 pp.
> Comprehensive encyclopedia of Amish families up to 1850, including all known early settlements.

Constant H. Jacquet, Jr. *Yearbook of American and Canadian Churches.* Nashville: Abingdon Press. 1977. Published annually. A later edition may be available and may have a different author for later editions.
> Lists the main depositories for church historical materials for nearly all denominations in the U.S. and Canada.

Arta F. Johnson. *Bibliography and Source Materials for German-American Research.* Volume 1.

George F. Jones. *The Salzburger Saga: Religious Exiles and Other Germans Along the Savannah.* Athens, GA: University of Georgia Press. 1984. 209 pp.
> Key work on the Germans in the American state of Georgia.

J. Kaps. *Handbuch über die katholischen Kirchenbücher in der ostdeutschen Kirchenprovinz östlich der Oder und Neisse und dem Bistum Danzig.* [*Handbook of Catholic Parish Registers in the East German Archbishopric East of the Oder and Neisse (Rivers) and the Bishopric of Danzig*]. Munich. 1962.
> Deals with Catholic parish registers of the former German eastern provinces.

Eduard Kneifel. *Die evangelisch-augsburgischen Gemeinde Polen, 1555-1939.* [*The Evangelical Church (Augsburg Creed) in Poland, 1555-1939*]. Vierkirchen, Germany. 1972.
> History of the Lutheran congregations in Poland. "Augsburger" refers to the Religious Peace of Augsburg in 1555, which allowed each ruler to determine the religion in his own land. This resulted in many people fleeing to Poland and other places to seek religious freedom.

David H. Koss, Kenneth Smith and Arta F. Johnson. *Pages from the Past.* No. 6 in "Publications Plus" series. Columbus, OH: Palatines to America. 1994.
> Articles on German-American churches and German church records by three leading authorities: Dr. David H. Koss, Kenneth Smith and Dr. Arta F. Johnson.

Margrit B. Krewson, *The German-Speaking Countries of Europe: A Selective Bibliography*.
Has information about more books dealing with religion among German-speaking peoples.

Rev. Reuben Kriebel. *Genealogical Record of the Descendants of the Schwenkfelders Who Arrived in Pennsylvania in 1733, 1734, 1736, 1737 (from the German of Rev. Balthasar Heebner and from Other Sources)*. 1879. Baltimore: Clearfield Co. Reprinted 1993. 371 pp.
Vital records of about 10,000 individuals descended from 140 families who fled from Silesia. Descendants today number hundreds of thousands.

Carl Mauelshausen. *The Salzburg Lutheran Expulsion and Its Impact*. Bowie, MD: Heritage Books. Reprinted 1962. 167 pp.
Background of Salzburgers who migrated eastward to Georgia.

Edward A. Peckwas. *Register of Vital Records: Roman Catholic Parishes from the Region Beyond the Bug River*. Chicago: Polish Genealogical Society of America. 1984.
Coverage includes German Catholic parish registers from East Galicia and West Volhynia.

G. Elmore Reaman. *The Trail of the Huguenots in Europe, the United States, South Africa and Canada*. Baltimore: Genealogical Publishing Co. 1963; reprinted 1993. 318 pp.
Indexed record of Huguenots who left France after 1685, many of them going to Germany, from where many of their descendants migrated to North America.

Clifford Neal Smith. *Nineteenth-Century Emigration of "Old Lutherans" from Eastern Germany (Mainly Pomerania and Lower Silesia) to Australia, Canada and the United States*. McNeal, AZ: Westland Publications. 1980.
Translation of 1943 German book by Wilhelm Iwan.

Clifford Neal Smith and Anna Piszczan-Czaja Smith. *Encyclopedia of German-American Genealogical Research*.
An especially helpful chapter, "German Ethnic Religious Bodies in America," discusses each religious denomination and shows the location of German-speaking congregations in the United States. Another helpful chapter is "Jews in Southwestern Germany."

Christa Stache. *Verzeichnis der Kirchenbücher im Evangelischen Zentral Archiv in Berlin* [*Inventory of Parish Registers in the Evangelical Central Archive in Berlin*]; Part I, *Die östlichen Kirchenprovinzen der evangelischen Kirche in der altpreussischen Union* [*The Eastern Church Provinces of the Evangelical Church in the Old Prussian Union*], 2nd ed., 297 pp.; 1987); Part II, *Berlin*. Berlin: Evangelisches Zentralarchiv.
Lists and dates of Protestant records for particular parishes in the former German eastern provinces in Vol. I. Vol. II includes Old Lutherans, French and other Reformed, and Moravian Brethren, with a few entries for Jews. A few records from the 1600s, most from 1700s or 1800s. Easy to use without knowledge of German.

Ernest J. Thode, Jr. *Address Book for Germanic Genealogy*.

Benjamin Heinrich Unruh. *Die niederländisch-niederdeutschen Hintergründe der mennonitischen Ostwanderungen im 16., 18. und 19. Jahrhundert.* [*The Netherlandish-Low German Background of the Mennonite Eastward Migrations in the 16th, 18th and 19th Centuries*]. Karlsruhe: Author. 1955.
The most comprehensive listing of Mennonite migrants from Prussia to the Russian Empire (Ukraine), with historical information on the Mennonite flight from the Spanish Netherlands to Polish Prussia during the Reformation era.

Oren Windholz. *Bohemian Germans in Kansas: A Catholic Community from Bukovina*. 1993. Hays, KS: author. 50 pp.
History of the Bohemian Germans who moved to the Bukovina and later to Kansas.

Ewald Wuschke. *Protestant Church Records on Microfilm for the Former Congress Poland (1815-1915) and Volhynia*. Vancouver: self-published. 1992.
Covers Lutheran, Reformed, Mennonite and Baptist church records and includes references to some parish registers that either have not been microfilmed or are not known to have survived World War II.

Chapter XII

GENEALOGICAL RESOURCES FOR GERMAN JEWISH ANCESTRY

By George Arnstein, Ph. D.

Jews have lived in German lands since Roman times. In terms of genealogy the research offers many of the same challenges as it does for all Germans, but in other ways — related to the Jewish religion and minority status — there are major differences.

The common elements are the scattered and shifting jurisdictions among bishoprics, duchies, and empires. Instead of today's Austria, the Austrian empire included seaports on the Adriatic, annexed parts of Poland (Galicia), included Bohemia and Moravia, and also claimed Hither Austria (*Vorderösterreich*) with tentacles deep into today's Baden-Württemberg and Bavaria. Jews were especially affected by these shifts in rulers who usually taxed them, sometimes expelled them, and often recruited them as a source of economic development. The result was instability as well as links and trading patterns that differed from those of the Christian majority. Regarding genealogy, at least some records typically were kept separately.

Here is an example: An 18th century *Landrabbiner* (regional rabbi) had his seat in Günzburg in the Margravate (*Markgraftum*) of Burgau. His jurisdiction included Hohenems in today's Vorarlberg. In Hohenems there are visible ties northward into Swabia and Bavaria. For that matter, from 1806 to 1813 Hohenems was Bavarian, including the year of mandated family names, a pivotal event for genealogy.

That Bavarian interlude over parts of today's Austria is a reflection of the rise of Napoleon, which in turn is a reminder that common to all genealogy is the need to know history and the historical context. Napoleon not only extended his sway over many German principalities but also brought with him ideas and innovations derived from the French Revolution of 1789. He enlisted the rulers of Bavaria, Württemberg and others as his allies, and he promoted these rulers to kings. He also promoted a major consolidation so that the new Kingdoms of Bavaria and Württemberg, as well as the Grand Duchy of Baden, were larger than their non-royal predecessors. There are startling changes in borders as a result of the so-called *Reichsdeputationshauptschluss* of 1803 — the decision to compensate German princes for territories lost to France. This represented the end of the Holy Roman Empire (of which Voltaire said that it was neither Holy nor Roman nor an Empire).

The rise and decline of Napoleon merely illustrate the importance of the historical context. There had been earlier events, like the Thirty Years' War (1618-48), which depopulated entire villages. The significance for Jews is that some rulers actively sought those Jews expelled from one jurisdiction as a means of repopulating and revivifying their domains.

Another pre-Napoleonic impact on history and geography was the dismemberment of Poland, which had a large Jewish population. Here the three partitions of Poland come into play. In 1772 West Prussia (Pomerelia) went to Prussia, while Galicia went to Austria, including Lwów which the Austrians called Lemberg (and today is Ukrainian L'viv). In 1793 the city of Danzig and the province of Poznan went to Prussia, which called it Posen. In 1795 there was a third partition between Russia, Prussia and Austria, leaving a Polish balance of zero.

By 1787 the Austrians passed a law providing for family names, as described by Suzan Wynne in "Demographic Records of Galicia 1772-1919" in *Avotaynu* 8:2. In 1919, of course, Poland was reconstituted and included Galicia. Today Galicia is divided between Poland and Ukraine. By recalling these historic events, the researcher has a better notion of where to look for records. For example, the Paul Diamant collection of family histories is primarily Austrian but includes Czechoslovakia, Hungary and Poland. The collection is part of the Central Archives for the History of the Jewish People, Sprinzak Building, Hebrew University (Givat Ram Campus), P.O. Box 1149, Jerusalem, Israel.

Given the extent of the Austrian empire, here are some citations for the former Czechoslovak Republic, which included Bohemia, Moravia, Austrian Silesia, and Slovakia: *The Jews of Czechoslovakia*, 2 vols. Philadelphia: Jewish Publication Society of America, 1968.

More recent is Jiri Fiedler, *Guide Book: Jewish Sights* [sic] *of Bohemia and Moravia*, (Prague: Sefer, 1991), available from U.S. Commission for the Preservation of America's Heritage Abroad, 1101 15th St. NW, Suite 503, Washington, DC 20005.

German Jewish records sharply increased around 1800. The beginning of Jewish emancipation was marked by a series of laws that typically required family names and better records, as shown in the following table.

Table 4: Laws Mandating Jewish Family Names

Austria	23 Jul. 1787
South Prussia and New East Prussia (formerly Polish)	17 Apr. 1797
City of Frankfurt (Main)	30 Nov. 1807
French possessions on the Rhine and in NW Germany	20 Jul. 1808 12 Jan. 1813
Kingdom of Westphalia	31 Mar. 1808 04 Jul. 1811
Oberhessen-Starkenburg	15 Dec. 1808
Baden	13 Jan. 1809
Lippe	16 Dec. 1809
Sachsen-Altenburg	20 Jun. 1811
Prussia proper (East of Elbe)	11 Mar. 1811
Mecklenburg-Schwerin	22 Feb. 1813
Bavaria, Voralberg, Tyrol, & Salzburg	16 Jun. 1813
Schleswig-Holstein (Danish)	29 Mar. 1814
Mecklenburg-Strelitz	01 Jun. 1814
Anhalt-Dessau	1822
Sachsen-Weimar	1823
Kingdom of Württemberg	1828
Grand Duchy of Posen (Prussian)	1833
Sachsen (Saxonia)	1834
Oldenburg	1852

The records continued even though the trend toward equality suffered some serious setbacks as well as later advances to the point where there was a veritable flowering, a transformation of rural peddlers, traders and craftsmen into a German Jewish bourgeoisie, in the period up to World War I.

For genealogy the Jewish custom of patronymics (first name followed by the father's first name) is important. This changed around 1800 when various jurisdictions enacted laws that mandated last names for Jews. The laws were quite similar but not identical; typically they also called for improved communal records, related in turn to the need of governments to achieve better control of their jurisdictions. (See table above.)

Representative of these records is a *Familienregister, Israeliten Gemeinde Buchau* [*Family Register of the Jewish Congregation in Buchau*] — today Bad Buchau in Baden-Württemberg. It begins on 1 January 1809 and ends in December 1853, prepared by Max I. Mändle, *Gemeindepfleger*, i.e., secretary of the Buchau Jewish Community. The original of this *Familienregister* is now at the Leo Baeck Institute in New York City (see address later in this chapter). Many of the early entries were prepared almost certainly by the local Roman Catholic priest, with a focus on families. Since this includes the date of birth of husband and wife, plus the names of their parents, some entries allow research back to as early as about 1740. The format is almost exactly the same as a modern family group sheet; the same form was used for Christian and Jewish congregations.

Many of these *Familienregister* still exist, largely because of Nazi efforts to establish racial purity for its own purposes. The Nazis were microfilming the Württemberg records as late as April 1945, when French and American troops were already well across the Rhine and the end of the Third Reich clearly was in sight. The few surviving originals and the many microfilmed records are in the Landesarchiv Baden-Württemberg in Stuttgart, or care of the Israelitische Gemeinde in Stuttgart.

Because Germany was unified only in 1871, researchers will have uneven success in various jurisdictions. And because different jurisdictions vary in their efforts to recall or remember the Jews who used to live among them — just a bit less than one percent of the German population before World War II — there are uneven results. Today there are very few Jews in Germany, the majority being descendants of the so-called Displaced Persons (DPs), survivors of Nazi persecution and displacement, who did not go back to the places where they had been kidnapped or impressed or from which they had fled, often behind the Iron Curtain. A file on more than 11,000 DP's dating from 1945-47 is now stored at Heidelberg (see below).

Given the slow tightening of the Nazi noose, the majority of the 600,000 German Jews managed to flee and survive. Some were overtaken when Germany invaded places like France and Holland; others and their descendants are citizens of Israel and especially the United States. Between the German tradition of research and scholarship, and the Jewish interest in history and tradition, there has resulted a veritable flood of published and unpublished material.

A *Gedenkbuch* [*Memorial Book*], in two volumes, has been published by the German archives, an admittedly incomplete listing of all Germans who perished at the hands of the Nazi regime. It supersedes an earlier, localized compilation by Paul Sauer, *Die Opfer der NS Judenverfolgung in Baden-Württemberg 1933-45: Ein Gedenkbuch* [*The Victims of the National Socialist (Nazi) Persecution in Baden-Württemberg. 1933-45: A Memorial Book*] (Appendix to Volume 20 of the Archival series. Stuttgart: Kohlhammer, 1969).

Earlier there had been allegations that Jews had not done their share during World War I. To counter this, the Reichsbund jüdischer Frontsoldaten [Imperial Federation of Front-line Soldiers] in 1932 counted some 100,000 who served and 10,275 names, with additional data for those who died: *Die jüdischen Gefallenen ... Ein Gedenkbuch* [*The Jews Who Fell in Action ... A Memorial Book*]. In addition there were specialized rosters like "Jüdische Frontsoldaten aus Württemberg und Hohenzollern" ["Jewish Front-line Soldiers from Württemberg and Hohenzollern"] published in Stuttgart in 1926 by the Centralverein deutscher Staatsbürger jüdischen Glaubens [Central Society of German Citizens of the Jewish Faith]. There even is a specialized roster, compiled by Felix Theilhaber, "Jüdische Flieger im Weltkrieg" ["Jewish Airmen in World War I"] (Berlin: Der Schild, 1924).

A major center, devoted to the preservation of Jewish culture and history, is affiliated with Heidelberg University: Zentralarchiv zur Erforschung der Geschichte der Juden in Deutschland, Bienenstr. 5, D-69117 Heidelberg. One of its major activities is a project to capture data on German Jewish cemeteries; it has not yet been completed and inquiries are discouraged until the material is published.

Similarly there is the Hamburg Staatsarchiv, which has a separate department devoted to genealogy and biography, including religious minorities. See for example the article by Jürgen Sielemann on "Lesser Known Records of Emigrants in the Hamburg State Archives" (*Avotaynu*, 7:3).

There is much less interest in the former German Democratic Republic, although this is beginning to change. The Deutsche Zentralstelle für Genealogie in Leipzig has German domestic records that cover Danzig/Gdansk, Posen, and also data collected by the *Reichssippenamt* under Nazi auspices, for regions like Bessarabia, Bukovina, the Baltics,

Sudetenland, Slovenia and South Tyrol. The inventory of the archives is listed in the **Annotated Bibliography**.

This is not the only legacy of former German conquests and hegemony. A list of some 1300 Polish and ex-Soviet places with records now located in Berlin was published by Verlag für Standeamtswesen in Frankfurt. It is *Standesregister und Personenstandsbücher der Ostgebiete in Standesamt I in Berlin* [*Civil Registry and Civil Registration Books of the (German) Eastern Regions in the Civil Registration Office I in Berlin*]. Coverage and contents are uneven.

There are Jewish museums in some communities while others avoid memories of a difficult period. Here is a small sampling of exhibits and memorials:

Nordstetten, in the Black Forest, commemorates Berthold Auerbach, a native son who became a celebrated secular German author, especially with his Black Forest Stories. He is the subject of a special issue of *Marbacher Magazin* 36/1985, to accompany the permanent exhibit at the Auerbach Museum in Horb-Nordstetten. Relevant, as to lifestyle, are autobiographical "Childhood Memories from Nordstetten," translated into English by George Arnstein, in *Mishpocha* (1991), publication of the Jewish Genealogy Society of Greater Washington. Auerbach was born on 28 February 1812 as Moses Baruch Auerbacher; he earned his doctorate at Tübingen. He also illustrates the then common secularization of names: "I was born on Haman's feast, the night of Purim ..."

Austria. Of general interest is the Institute for Historic Family Research (IHFF), which relocated in early 1994: IHFF Genealogie Gesellschaft mbH, Pantzergasse 30/8, A-1190 Vienna. Phone/Fax 011/43/1/317-8806.

There are two Jewish museums in Austria:

- Jewish Museum of the City of Vienna, Dorotheergasse 11, A-1010 Vienna, Austria. Phone: 011/43/1/535-0431. For Fax, the final four digits are -0424.

- Jewish Museum Hohenems, Villa Heimann-Rosenthal, Schweizer Strasse 5, A-6845 Hohenems, Vorarlberg, Austria. Phone: (0043) 05576/3989.

The Hohenems Jewish community began about 1631, suffered expulsion, returned, thrived and then declined after about 1900. The most famous local offspring was Salomon Sulzer, cantor, who became an honorary citizen of Vienna. Much genealogical information was compiled by Dr. Tänzer, the rabbi at the turn of the century, since updated by others.

Tänzer, Aron, *Geschichte der Juden in Tirol und Vorarlberg*. Teil 1 + 2: *Die Geschichte der Juden in Hohenems und im übrigen Vorarlberg* [*History of the Jews in Tyrol and Vorarlberg*. Parts 1 & 2: *History of the Jews in Hohenems and the Rest of Vorarlberg*]. Meran, 1905. He completed only the Hohenems portion of this book, reprinted in Bregenz 1982 with additional material. Copies of first edition are at Leo Baeck Institute (LBI) and Library of Congress (LOC).

Göppingen/Jebenhausen. The same Dr. Tänzer became rabbi and wrote a comparable history for the Jewish community of Jebenhausen, which merged with adjacent Göppingen. More recently, Naftali Bar-Giori Bamberger published a monograph on the Jewish cemetery with many photographs.

Tänzer, A. *Geschichte der Juden in Jebenhausen und Göppingen* [*History of the Jews in Jebenhausen and Göppingen*]. Kohlhammer 1927. He was rabbi in Göppingen. Reprint 1988, with two additional chapters by Karl-Heinz Ruess, Göppingen: Stadtarchiv, Band 23.

Bar-Giori Bamberger, Naftali. *Memorbuch: die jüdischen Friedhofe Jebenhausen und Göppingen* [*Memorial book: the Jewish Cemeteries at Jebenhausen and Göppingen*].

Sulzbach-Rosenberg plans to convert the former synagogue into a city museum and documentation center for Jewish history in the Oberpfalz (Upper Palatinate, a government district in Bavaria).

Haigerloch, formerly in Hohenzollern, has a memorial, has published three books dealing with their former Jewish citizens, and has inventoried them in a computerized database. All are available from the Stadtverwaltung, D-72394 Haigerloch, Germany.

While the memorial and collections are uneven, there is a pre-war, pre-Holocaust tradition of genealogy and history. The sources are still plentiful and much of the material has survived the war, especially because of the success of the **Leo Baeck Institute**, 129 East 73rd Street, New York, NY 10021 (212-744-6400). Explicitly organized to preserve the legacy of the German Jewish community, broadly defined to include German-speaking areas like Bohemia, this archival and historical collection has filled a Manhattan townhouse to overflowing. It is the single best place for Germanic Jewish research and has generated a series of yearbooks and bulletins that are of pivotal importance. The *Yearbooks*, published jointly with the LBI in London and Jerusalem, are in English; the *Bulletin* is primarily in German.

Genealogy may well be the most popular or fastest growing hobby in America; among Jews it is increasingly established, a kind of *deja vu* among bourgeois German Jews who often compiled their ancestry, sometimes in handwritten documents or in books, often privately published. Many of these have been microfilmed with the largest collection at the Hebrew Union College library in Cincinnati. Some of these are available through the Family History Centers.

For an illustration of the wealth of available material, there is the work of Monika Richarz, a historian who skillfully mined the archives of the Leo Baeck Institute and produced three volumes, later condensed into one:

- Richarz, Monika, ed. *Jüdisches Leben in Deutschland: Selbstzeugnisse zur Sozialgeschichte* [*Jewish Life in Germany: Personal Accounts About Social History*] (Stuttgart: DVA 1976-82) Three volumes of 126 autobiographical excerpts from LBI Archives.

- Richarz, Monika, ed. *Bürger auf Widerruf 1785-1945* [*Citizenship Retracted, 1785-1945*], (Munich: C.H. Beck 1989), 51 essays from the three volumes. English version *Jewish Lives in Germany; Memoirs from Three Generations*. Indiana Univ. Press, 1991.

Switzerland, too, has a Jewish tradition going back at least to the 17th century, especially in two historic villages on the Rhine between Basel and Lake Constance. A local association concerns itself with the cemeteries and in 1993 issued *Der Judenfriedhof Endingen-Lengnau* [*The Jewish Cemetery in Endingen-Lengnau*], some 400 pages in two volumes: Menes Verlag, CH 5405 Baden, Postfach 5070. To keep informed about current research, the quarterly *Majaan, Die Quelle* [*Majaan, The Source*], is a German language quarterly published by the Swiss Society for Jewish Genealogy, P.O. Box 876, CH 8021 Zürich. It focuses on German-speaking Switzerland, with frequent ties to Alsace, southern Germany, but also to Posen and Austria.

For another look at Jewish life, there are monographs prepared in a variety of academic settings. Bernhard Purin, for example, received his master's degree at the university in Tübingen, based on a study of the short-lived Vorarlberg community in Sulz. This is the town where many of the Jews expelled from Hohenems sought refuge. Purin's study, which offers a marvelous slice of Jewish small town life, has been published:

- Purin, Bernhard. *Die Juden von Sulz: eine jüdische Landgemeinde in Vorarlberg, 1676-1744* [*The Jews of Sulz: A Jewish Rural Community in Vorarlberg, 1676-1744*]. Bregenz: Vorarlberg. Autoren Gesellschaft 1991.

The trick, of course, is to find some of these studies, including unpublished ones, complicated by the fact that Germany has nothing comparable to the American "Dissertation Abstracts." There are, however, valuable compilations like the massive bibliography by Angelika G. Ellman-Krueger, *Auswahlbibliographie zur jüdischen Familienforschung vom Anfang des 19. Jahrhunderts bis zur Gegenwart* [*Selected*

Bibliography of Jewish Family Research From the Beginning of the 19th Century to the Present], D-65183 Wiesbaden, Postfach 2929: Otto Harrassowitz, 1992. It contains more than 2500 well-organized citations, with a name and separate place index.

Other compilations seek to capture and list all residual Jewish evidences. Here are two of these:

- Schwierz, Israel. *Steinerne Zeugnisse Jüdischen Lebens in Bayern: eine Dokumentation* [*Harsh Testimonies of Jewish Life in Bavaria: A Compilation of Documents*]. Munich: Bayerische Landeszentrale für politische Bildungsarbeit, 1988.

- Hahn, Joachim. *Erinnerungen und Zeugnisse Jüdischer Geschichte in Baden-Württemberg* [*Memories and Testimonies of Jewish History in Baden-Württemberg*]. Stuttgart: Theiss, 1988. Detailed list, town by village, of whatever traces remain of Jewish life in southwestern Germany.

The Rev. Dr. Hahn's book cited some unpublished and published theses and *Zulassungsarbeiten* (a kind of senior thesis), like these, cited here mostly to indicate the variety and obscurity of some of the resources.

- **Archshofen, Creglingen**: Bauer, E. *Die Geschichte der jüdischen Minderheit in Archshofen* [*History of the Jewish Minority in Archshofen*]. Zulassungsarbeit zur Fachgruppenprüfung in Geschichte 1964. (Apparently published in 1985 — no details).

- **Aufhausen (Bopfingen)**: Laurentzsch, U. *Zur Geschichte der Judengemeinde Aufhausen bei Bopfingen* [*History of the Jewish Community in Aufhausen near Bopfingen*]. Pädagogisch Hochschule Schwäbisch Gmünd 1978. Typescript thesis.

- **Buchau**: Adler, Reinhold. *Beiträge zu einer Geschichte der israelitischen Gemeinde Buchaus von den Anfängen bis zu Beginn des Hitlerreiches* [*Contributions to the History of the Jewish Community of Buchau from Its Early Beginnings to the Start of the Hitler Regime*]. (Kreisarchiv Biberach Nr. 961). Pädagogisch Hochschule Weingarten, 1973 (Typescript thesis; copy at LBI, NYC, filed under G=Gemeinden, then B=Buchau). Also note: Mohn, J., *Der Leidensweg unter dem Hakenkreuz*, Buchau 1970. Lists all who suffered, ranging from Jews to Wehrmacht soldiers who died.

- **Bühl (Baden)**: Pieges, H. *Schicksale jüdischer Familien Bühls* [*Fate of the Jewish Family Bühl*]. Pädagogisch Hochschule Freiburg 1962/63. Thesis.

- **Freiburg im Breisgau**: Blad, G. *Die Entstehung der israelitischen Gemeinde Freiburgs 1849-1941* [*The Origin of the Jewish Community of Freiburg, 1849-1941*], Freiburg University, Thesis, 1985.

- **Göppingen, Jebenhausen**: Kühner, J. *Der Rabbiner Dr. Aron Tänzer und die jüdischen Gemeinde in Göppingen* [*Rabbi Dr. Aron Tänzer and the Jewish Community of Göppingen*]. Pädagogisch Hochschule Schwäbisch Gmünd, Thesis, 1981

- **Görwihl, Oberwihl, nr. Waldshut**: Fichtner R. and Wegemer, B. *Kindern eine Zukunft; von zwei Kinderheimen in der Weimarer Zeit* [*Children a Future; from Two Children's Homes During the Time of the Weimar Republic*]. Tübingen University, Erziehungswissenschaft, Thesis 1986. (One of the children's homes was Jewish).

- **Haigerloch**: Schäfer, W. *Geschichte und Schicksal der Juden in Haigerloch* [*History and Fate of the Jews in Haigerloch*]. Pädagogisch Hochschule Reutlingen. Thesis 1971.

- **Hechingen**: Breimesser, H. *Ursprung, Entwicklung & Schicksal der jüdischen Gemeinde Hechingen* [*Origin, Development and Fate of the Jewish Community of Hechingen*]. Pädagogisch Hochschule Schwäbisch Gmünd. Thesis 1968.

- **Heilbronn-Sontheim**: Gräf, H., in charge of the project of students of the Helene-Lang Real Schule and others: *Der Jüdische Friedhof Heilbronn-Sontheim, eine Dokumentation* [*The Jewish Cemetery Heilbronn-Sontheim, A Documentation*]. Typescript, processed, 1987.

- **Hemsbach**: Hössler, H. *Juden in Hemsbach von 1660-1933* [*Jews in Hemsbach from 1660 to 1933*]. Pädagogisch Hochschule Heidelberg 1984. Thesis. Also a 1984 compendium by students of the Friedrich-Schiller Hauptschule Hemsbach: Documentation "Traces and Recollections" in *Our Neighbors of the Jewish Faith*. 1984.

- **Jebenhausen, Göppingen**: Munz, G. *Die Geschichte der Juden in Jebenhausen.* [*History of the Jews in Jebenhausen*]. Pädagogisch Hochschule Schwäbisch Gmünd, Thesis, 1963.

- **Laupheim**: Indlekofer, Sybille. *Jüdisches Gemeindeschicksal aufgezeigt am Beispiel der Stadt Laupheim* [*Fate of the Jewish Community As Shown in the Example of the City of Laupheim*]. Pädagogisch Hochschule Lörrach/Baden, 1970. (Kreisarchiv Biberach 431). Copy at LBI, NYC. No mention of Kohl thesis in bibliography; contents heavily overlap.

- **Laupheim**: Kohl, Waltraut. *Die Geschichte der Jüdischen Gemeinde in Laupheim* [*History of the Jewish Community in Laupheim*]. Pädagogisch Hochschule Weingarten, 1965. (Kreisarchiv Biberach Nr.365) Typescript thesis, copy at LBI, NYC (donated or arranged by John Bergman, Media, PA).

- **Ludwigsburg**: Gut, B. *Die Judenverfolgungen im Dritten Reich und deren Darstellung in der Ludwigsburger Zeitung* [*Persecution of Jews During the Third Reich and Its Portrayal in the Ludwigsburg Newspaper*]. Pädagogisch Hochschule Schwäbisch Gmünd. Thesis 1971.

- **Oberdorf (am Ipf, Bopfingen)**: Kucher, W. *Die Geschichte der Oberdorfer Judengemeinde von der Gründung bis zur Emanzipation* [*History of the Jewish Community of Oberdorf From Its Origin to Its Emancipation*]. Pädagogisch Hochschule Schwäbisch Gmünd, 1976. Thesis.

- **Offenburg**: Möschle, S. *Das Schicksal der jüdischen Bevölkerung Offenburgs in der Zeit des Nationalsozialismus* [*The Fate of the Jewish Population of Offenburg during Nazi Times*]. Freiburg University, Thesis 1977.

- **Schwäbisch Gmünd**: Grimm, J. A. *Zur Geschichte der Juden in Schwäbisch Gmünd* [*History of the Jews in Schwäbish Gemünd*]. Pädagogisch Hochschule Schwäbish Gmünd, 1962. Thesis.

- **Ulm**: Engel, A. *Juden in Ulm im 19. Jahrhundert. Anfänge & Entwicklung der jüdischen Gemeinde von 1803-1873* [*Jews in Ulm in the 19th Century. Beginning and Development of the Jewish Community from 1803 to 1873*]. Tübingen University, 1982. Master's thesis.

The following appear to be obscure publications or typescripts:

- **Nordstetten**: Wagenpfeil, H. "Manuskripte zur Geschichte der Juden in Nordstetten" ["Manuscripts of the History of Jews in Nordstetten"]. Typescript, before 1988.

- **Rastatt**: Stiefvater, O. "Geschichte und Schicksal der Juden im Landkreis Rastatt" ["History and Fate of the Jews in the County of Rastatt"] in *Um Rhein und Murg* 5 (1965), pp. 42-83.

- **Reutlingen**: Schön, Th. "Geschichte der Juden in Reutlingen" ["History of the Jews in Reutlingen"] in *Reutlinger Geschichtsblätter* V (1894), pp. 36ff, 59-62; VI (1895) p. 64.

- **Schwetzingen and Ketsch**: Lohrbächer, A. and Rittmann, M. "Sie gehörten zu uns. Geschichte und Schicksale der Schwetzinger Juden" ["They Belonged to Us. History and Fate of the Schwetzingen Jews"]. *Schriften der Stadt A. Schwetzingen* 7, 1978. (City archive).

Similarly there is much valuable material in obscure publications, accessible only through diligent searches. The LBI yearbooks annually have massive lists, organized by major topics, of books and articles touching on German Jewish history. Here are some entries culled because they are of potential interest for the southwest corner of Germany:

- **Baisingen**: Geppert, Karlheinz. "Vom Schutzjuden zum Bürger" ["From Protected Jew to Citizen"] in *Der Sülchgau* Vol. 23:145-168. Sülchgauer Altertumsverein, Rottenburg am Neckar, 1988. Copy at Harvard Library.

- **Baisingen**: Becker, Franziska. "Die nationalsozialistische Judenverfolgung in Baisingen" ["Nazi Persecution of Jews in Baisingen"] in *Der Sülchgau* Vol. 23:169 ff. Copy at Harvard Library.

- **Hechingen**: Kuhn-Rehfus, Maren. "Das Verhältnis von Mehrheit zu Minderheit am Beispiel der Juden von Hohenzollern" ["The Relationship of the Majority to the Minority by Example of the Jews of Hohenzollern"] in *Zeitschrift für Hohenzollern Geschichte* 14 (1978), pp. 9-54.

- **Hechingen**: Werner, Manuel. "Die Juden in Hechingen" ["The Jews in Hechingen"] in *Zeitschrift für Hohenzollern Geschichte* 20 (1984), pp. 103-213; and 21 (1985), pp. 199-215.

- **Hechingen**: Werner, Otto. "Die Jüdische Gemeinde in Hechingen bis 1933" ["The Jewish Community in Hechingen through 1933"] in *1200 Jahre Hechingen*, pp. 177-97. Hechingen: 1987.

- **Hohenems (Austria)**: Welte, Thomas. "Die Hohenemser Judengemeinde im 20. Jahrhundert" ["The Hohenem Jewish Community in the 20th Century"]. Diplom-arbeit Innsbruck 1990.

German Jewish genealogical research is like all others: it relies on passenger lists and their indices, census records, telephone directories and communal records. It tends to be easier because Jews are strong on tradition, thus tend to be more historically oriented than most others, a generalization that is open to challenge although at least partly valid. It also is one area where past discrimination has some benefits: German Jewish data and records tend to be segregated, thus easier to find, consult and use.

Yizkor (memorial) books are published histories of individual Eastern European Jewish communities, which memorialize the town and its Holocaust victims. Many deal with localities that were part of the Austrian empire. There is usually a narrative section on the town's history, culture, institutions and rabbis, and sometimes a list of Holocaust victims, survivors, or emigrants. Most memorial books are entirely in Hebrew and/or Yiddish, though some do have sections in English or other languages. Yizkor books have been published for over 700 towns. The most complete list is *Bibliography of Eastern European Memorial (Yizkor) Books*, compiled by Zachary M. Baker (51 pages, July 1992), available from the JGS of New York. This list also contains call numbers at six libraries in New York. A previous version of this list appears in Estelle Guzik's *Genealogical Resources in the New York Metropolitan Area*, pages 323-372.

Most yizkor books were published in the 1950s and 60s in very limited quantities, and are therefore usually difficult to find and expensive to purchase. Most books currently sell for $40 to $100. The following establishments sell yizkor books:

- J. Robinson & Co., 31 Nachlat Benjamin St., P.O. Box 4308, Tel Aviv 65162, Israel

- Moshe Schreiber, Mea Sharim St. 16, Jerusalem, Israel

- Pinat Ha-Sefer, P.O. Box 46646, Haifa 31464, Israel

- Central Yiddish Culture Organization, 25 East 21st St., 3rd floor, New York NY 10010
- National Yiddish Book Center, P.O. Box 969, Amherst, MA 01004

Many immigrants belonged to *landsmanshaftn*, organizations of people from the same ancestral town. Synagogues were often comprised of members from the same area of origin. Check where your immigrant ancestor is buried. Many used congregational or *landsmanshaft* plots. Tombstones might also yield clues. Hebrew names are patronymic, giving the father's name also. Be sure you copy all of the Hebrew from the headstones.

PUBLICATIONS AND RESOURCES

Warren Blatt must be credited for this material, which he updates frequently. He organizes it as Frequently Asked Questions (FAQ in computer jargon), then makes it available electronically via the Jewish Genealogy Echo. The file name is JEWGFAQ.ZIP.

Avotaynu: The International Review of Jewish Genealogy is a quarterly publication, founded in 1985, devoted to Jewish genealogical issues: new record sources, tips on research, travel experiences, book reviews, "Ask the Experts" column, summaries of articles in other sources, and more. It is the premier publication documenting the field today. Avotaynu subscriptions are currently $29 per year ($37 overseas), and back issues ($7 each) are available from the publisher. See Chapter XIX for the address of *Avotaynu*.

The *Jewish Genealogical Family Finder* (JGFF) is a computer-indexed compilation of surnames and towns currently being researched by over 2,000 Jewish genealogists worldwide. It contains over 28,000 entries: 10,000 ancestral surnames and 7,000 town names, and is indexed and cross-referenced by both surname and town name. The JGFF is maintained by Gary Mokotoff of the Jewish Genealogical Society (New York).

Researchers should search the JGFF for genealogists with similar research interests, and can then contact them for exchange of information. The JGFF is a great networking tool, which is updated quarterly. All Jewish Genealogical Societies (JGSs) have a print-out copy of the JGFF. The JGFF is also available on over a dozen on-line bulletin boards (BBSs). See the Jewish Genealogy Echo for information on how to obtain a listing of these BBSs. It is also available for purchase from Avotaynu, Inc.

The Jewish Genealogical Person Finder (JGPF) is a database of individuals on family trees submitted by Jewish genealogists, somewhat like the LDS Ancestral File. While the Jewish Genealogical Family Finder (JGFF, see above) contains only surnames and town names, the JGPF contains data on individual people: birth date and place, death date and place, parents' names and spouse's name.

Family trees in GEDCOM format can be submitted for inclusion in the JGPF without charge. All Jewish genealogists are encouraged to participate. Send your diskettes to Avotaynu, Inc. (see above). Copies of the JGPF (on 15 microfiche) are available at all JGSs and may be purchased from Avotaynu, Inc. The JGPF was first released in July 1992. The 2nd edition contains over 230,000 individuals submitted by over 200 Jewish genealogists. It is NOT available on-line.

There are over 50 Jewish Genealogical Societies (JGSs) world-wide, in 40 U.S. cities, plus Australia, Brazil, Canada, France, Germany, Great Britain, Israel, Netherlands, Romania, Russia and Switzerland. For the address of the JGS nearest you, send an SASE to the Association of Jewish Genealogical Societies (AJGS), 1485 Teaneck Road, Teaneck, NJ 07666. The addresses of all JGSs are published annually in the Spring issue of *Avotaynu*. Many Jewish Genealogical Societies also publish a journal or newsletter.

In addition to local JGSs, there are also several "Special Interest Groups" (SIGs), whose interest is a geographic region of origin; several include parts of the former Austrian empire.

Currently formed SIGs and their publications are:

- Germany: *Stammbaum*, $20/year, c/o Harry Katzman, 1601 Cougar Court, Winter Springs, FL 32708.

- Romania: *ROM-SIG News*, $15/year, c/o Sam & Joy Elprin, 27 Hawthorne Street, Greenwich, CT 06831.

- Suwalk & Lomza gubernias (today southern Lithuania and northeast Poland): *Landsmen*, $22/year, c/o Marlene Silverman, 3701 Connecticut Avenue NW, Apt. 228, Washington DC 20008.

- Galicia (today southern Poland and western Ukraine): *The Galitzianer*, $15/year, c/o Suzan Wynne, 3128 Brooklawn Terrace, Chevy Chase, MD 20815.

- Hungary (and Hungarian-speaking regions): *H-SIG*, $7/year, c/o Louis Schonfeld, P.O. Box 34152, Cleveland, OH 44134-0852.

- Czech/Slovak: c/o Mindy Gottesgen, 733 Juniper Walk, Apt. B, Goleta, CA 93317.

Since 1981, an annual "Summer Seminar on Jewish Genealogy" has been held, in a different city each year. Details appear in *Avotaynu*. For more information, write to Avotaynu, 155 N. Washington Ave., Bergenfield, NJ 07621.

The German Historical Institute (GHI) in Washington, DC (and another one in London) has a fair selection of materials dealing with Jewish interests. It subscribes to *Ashkenas*, an annual magazine in German, now in its fourth year. GHI holdings, by way of illustration, include such standard works as:

- Hundsnurscher, Franz, and Taddey, Gerhard. *Die jüdischen Gemeinden in Baden* [*Jewish Communities in Baden*]. Stuttgart: Kohlhammer 1968.

- Sauer, Paul. *Die jüdischen Gemeinden in Württemberg & Hohenzollern* [*Jewish Communities in Württemberg and Hohenzollern*]. Stuttgart Kohlhammer 1966.

- Zelzer, Maria. *Weg und Schicksal der Stuttgarter Juden* [*The Direction and Fate of the Jews from Stuttgart*]. Stuttgart: Stadtarchiv, 1964. Contains long lists that are not quite reliable, partly because it was compiled relatively soon after World War II.

ELECTRONIC RESEARCH

A resource of increasing importance for all of genealogy is the computer and its capability for outreach. With a modem researchers can tap into the so-called FIDOnet, a network of local electronic bulletin boards (BBS). Several dozen of these carry a national "conversation" known as the Jewish Genealogy Conference (JGC) or Echo. There are questions and answers, exchanges of data including entire branches of family trees, and listings of citations and bibliographies. The list of theses and unpublished materials shown above, for example, was available on the JGC and later was published in *Stammbaum*.

To be sure, there is the very large "haystack" known as the National Genealogy Conference, the smaller JGC of which items of German interest are merely a small subset. With software, however, it is easy to "capture" all of this daily information, then quickly search it in order to select only those items of possible interest.

Analogous to FIDOnet, there are genealogical conferences — newsgroups — on the Internet, including at least one with specific Jewish, not necessarily German Jewish, focus.

Both of these networks — FIDOnet and Internet — have German participants who are Jewish or have Jewish interests. Tentacles reach to Israel, Netherlands, Australia and other places, with obvious research possibilities.

A third electronic tool or method deals with CD-ROM. The LDS Church through its Family History Centers now makes available the Social Security Death Index as well as the International Genealogical Index (IGI). Researchers with computers need only bring an empty diskette to a Family History Center, reserve some time on the computer, search for missing ancestors or dates, then "capture" the data for transfer to their own computers for inspection and possible preservation.

CD-ROM is a growing medium, a means for easy compilation of U.S. Census data, national telephone files, and other reference materials, especially those amenable to search by keyword.

A modem also makes it increasingly possible to search library catalogs from a distance. The Library of Congress (LOC) catalog is now on line, via Internet. As an example of how LOC can be used, Peter Lande in the Summer 1993 *Stammbaum* published a generous sampling of what he found simply by extracting all items under the call letter DS 135.

The JEWISHGEN echo is a FIDOnet computer conference devoted to Jewish Genealogy, carried by over 150 Bulletin Board Systems (BBSs) around the world. Users can request help with problems, post new sources of information, and network globally. For a list of BBSs that carry the echo, either: 1) download the file JBBSyymm.zip or GBBSyymm.zip (where "yy" and "mm" are the most recent year and month respectively, e.g., GBBS9311); or 2) Send a SASE to Bruce Kahn, 265 Viennawood Dr., Rochester NY 14618, for a list of BBSs in your area. The JEWISHGEN echo is moderated by Bruce Kahn and Susan King.

The JEWISHGEN echo is now also available via Internet, using a gateway set up by Susan King in September 1993. To subscribe to the conference, send an e-mail message to: "listproc@israel.nysernet.org", containing the message "SUBSCRIBE JEWISHGEN *your-real-name*". Your message will be handled by an automated list processor. This will result in 20-50 messages a day delivered to your e-mail inbox. To receive only one message per day, a "digest" of all of today's genealogy messages concatenated, send the message "SET JEWISHGEN Mail Digest" to the list processor after subscribing. This will greatly reduce your e-mail traffic.

All messages sent from either FIDOnet or Internet will eventually appear in both networks, thanks to the gateway. To submit a message to the network, address it to: "JEWISHGEN@israel.nysernet.org". To stop subscribing to the Internet list, send the message: "UNSUBSCRIBE JEWISHGEN" to get more information about the list processor commands, send the message "HELP" to the list processor (listproc@israel.nysernet.org).

REFERENCES (See bibliography for full citations if not shown)

Alexander Beider. *A Dictionary of Jewish Surnames from the Russian Empire*. Teaneck, NJ: Avotaynu Press. 784 pp.
> Contains 50,000 Jewish surnames from the Russian Pale of Settlement, excluding the Kingdom of Poland.

Alexander Beider. *Jewish Surnames from Prague (15th-18th Centuries)*. Teaneck, NJ: Avotaynu Press.
> Identifies 700 surnames from the ancient city of Prague. Provides etymology of each name.

Chester G. Cohen. *Shtetl Finder Gazetteer*. Bowie, MD: Heritage Books. 1989.

Ruth Gay. *The Jews of Germany: Historical Portrait*. New London, CT: Yale University Press. 1992. 297 pp.

Martin Gilbert. *The Atlas of Jewish History*, rev. ed. New York: William Morrow and Co., Inc. 1993. 123 pp. + bibliography.

Estelle M. Guzik. *Genealogical Resources in the New York Metropolitan Area*. New York: Jewish Genealogical Society. 1989. 404 pp.
> Describes the collection of major research facilities, Jewish and others, in the New York City area.

Joram Kagan. *Poland's Jewish Heritage*. New York: Hippocrene Books. 1992. 208 pp.

Arthur Kurzweil. *From Generation to Generation: How to Trace Your Jewish Genealogy and Personal History*. New York: Harper Collins. 2nd ed. 1994. 388 pp.

> Updated version of standard guidebook for tracing Jewish ancestry.

Arthur Kurzweil and Miriam Weiner, eds. *The Encyclopedia of Jewish Genealogy*. Vol. I: *Sources in the United States and Canada*. Northvale, NJ: Jason Aronson, Inc. 1991. 226 pp.

> A summary of North American record repositories and their holdings, with some useful appendices.

Daniel N. Lesson. *Index to the 1754 Census of the Jews of Alsace*.

> Documents about 20,000 Jews, with given names and surnames, including the maiden names of married women.

William O. McCagg, Jr. *A History of the Habsburg Jews, 1670-1918*. Bloomington/ Indianapolis: Indiana University Press. 1989. 289 pp.

Gary Mokotoff and Sallyann Amdur Sack. *Where Once We Walked: A Guide to the Jewish Communities Destroyed in the Holocaust*. Teaneck, NJ: Avotaynu Press. 1991. 544 pages.

> A gazetteer of over 21,000 Central and Eastern European localities, arranged alphabetically and phonetically, with references for each locality. See also Chapter VIII.

Gary Mokotoff. *WOWW Companion: A Guide to the Communities Surrounding Centran and Eastern European Towns*. Teaneck, NJ: Avotaynu Press.

> Identifies towns in the vicinity of any town listed in *Where Once We Walked*. Easy-to-use tables. See above and also Chapter VIII.

Dan Rottenberg. *Finding Our Fathers: A Guide to Jewish Genealogy*.

Sallyann Amdur Sack. *A Guide to Jewish Genealogical Research in Israel*. Baltimore: Genealogical Publishing Co. 1987. 110 pp.

Clifford Neal Smith and Anna Piszczan-Czaja Smith. *Encyclopedia of German-American Genealogical Research*.

Christa Stache. *Verzeichnis der Kirchenbücher im Evangelischen Zentral Archiv in Berlin* [*Inventory of Parish Registers in the Evangelical Central Archive in Berlin*]; Part I, *Die östlichen Kirchenprovinzen der evangelischen Kirche in der altpreussischen Union* [*The Eastern Bishoprics of the Evangelical Church in the Old Prussian Empire*], 2nd ed., 297 pp.; 1987); Part II, *Berlin*. Berlin: Evangelisches Zentralarchiv.

> This inventory also includes a small number of Jewish records.

Malcolm H. Stern. *First American Jewish Families, 1654-1988*, 3rd ed. Baltimore: Genealogical Publishing Co. 1991. 464 pp.

> Family trees of all Jews known to have come to America before 1840. Index to 50,000 persons.

Peter Strauss. *Familienforschung bei jüdischen Vorfahren aus Baden-Württemberg: Schwerpunkt Landkreis Hohenlohe*. [*Family Research for Jewish Ancestors from Baden-Wuerttemberg: Primarily Focused in Hohenlohe County*]. PO Box 0204, D-20307, Stuttgart, Germany: Privately published.

> About 540 localities that had Jewish communities.

Lawrence Tapper. *Biographical Dictionary of Canadian Jewry*, 1909-1914. 256 pp.

> Births, bar mitzvahs, marriages and deaths from *The Canadian Jewish Times*.

Miriam Weiner. *Bridging the Generations: Researching Your Jewish Roots*.

David S. Zubatsky and Irwin M. Berent. *Jewish Genealogy: A Sourcebook of Family Histories and Genealogies*. New York: Garland Publishing Co. 1984. Rev. ed. 1991. Two volumes: 422 pages, 452 pages.

> A guide to published and manuscript genealogies in archives and libraries, arranged by surname.

Chapter XIII

GERMANIC MIGRATION TO NON-EUROPEAN COUNTRIES

This chapter describes the migration patterns of Germans outside the European continent. First comes a description of the German migration to the United States; it includes when and why Germans came and where they settled. German migration to Canada is then described. Numerous Germans also went to South America, the Far East and Africa; these are described in Chapter VI.

Wilhelm Winkler, *Statistisches Handbuch des gesamten Deutschtums* [*Statistical Handbook of All German Regions*] (Berlin: Verlag Deutsche Rundschau G.m.b.H., 1927) estimates (pp. 22-23) that there were 5,000 or more Germans in each of the following countries outside Europe and the Soviet Union:

Table 5: Germans Outside Europe and the Soviet Union, 1927

Country	Population	Country	Population
United States	10,000,000	New Zealand	18,000
Brazil	600,000	Egypt	11,000
Canada	300,000	Namibia (Southwest Africa)	10,000
Australia	141,000	Algeria	7,500
Argentina	130,000	Morocco	6,800
South Africa	57,000	Asian Turkey	5,500
French Foreign Legion	31,000	Mexico	5,000
Chile	30,000		

These figures almost certainly refer only to people who were born in Germany (or possibly other Germanic countries) or who had at least one German-born parent, since this is the kind of data usually available from censuses.

These data greatly understate the number of people of Germanic descent. For example, the 1990 census records 60 million Americans (certainly an undercount because of people who no longer know of their ancestry) who have German-speaking ancestors, considerably more than have ancestors from any other country, including England. They are almost as numerous as the current population of Germany.

To cite other examples, Argentina is estimated to have had a million residents in 1978 who had Volga German ancestors and James N. Bade estimates that several hundred thousand New Zealanders have Germanic ancestors, even though relatively few Germans emigrated to that country.

Moreover, large-scale Germanic immigration (including many displaced persons from Eastern Europe who crossed the seas after 1945) has occurred since 1925. Since the United States had comparatively restrictive immigration laws, a disproportionately large number went to Canada and to various Latin American countries. There has also been substantial migration within the western hemisphere, so that Mexico and Paraguay are estimated to each have at least 50,000 residents of Germanic origin (most of whom came from Canada and still speak German).

REASONS FOR GERMANIC EMIGRATION

Among the more important reasons for Germans to emigrate to the United States were:

Escape from economic hardship. The Thirty Years' War (1618-1648) devastated Germany. With the setbacks caused by several further wars, it took Germany 100 years to recover. The Seven Years' War (1756-1763) again created harsh conditions. The Palatinate, in particular, suffered from being the front-line battleground between French and German forces.

Religious freedom. This was particularly important for some of the earliest immigrants. It remained significant for non-mainstream groups, like the Mennonites, the Old Lutherans and dissident Catholics. Persecution was also a major factor for the Jews, but more so for those from Eastern Europe (who often spoke German or its derivative, Yiddish) than for those from Germany — until the 1930s, of course.

Abundant free or cheap farmland. The vast majority of immigrants came from rural villages, where there was insufficient farmland for all. German inheritance laws were of great importance in explaining emigration. Where one son inherited the entire farm, the others were effectively excluded from making a living off agriculture. Where the land was divided among all, the plots soon became too small for sustenance, which is why many peasants also practiced a trade. In areas east of the Elbe River there was often very little opportunity for land ownership, because much of the land was in the hands of a comparatively small number of owners of large estates. This was true especially in Mecklenburg and Pomerania, which had the highest rates of emigration in the 1870s, according to Mack Walker, *Germany and the Emigration, 1816-1885*. Hence, the opportunity for land ownership in America was very appealing. Most of the German immigrants, however, did not homestead on free land. Instead, for about $1.25 per acre they purchased land that others had already broken, whereupon the original pioneers moved one step farther west.

Freedom from compulsory military service. The frequency of wars and the expectation of more wars led many to emigrate. This was particularly true of those who lived under the militaristic Prussian Empire, which already ruled most of northern Germany before 1871, and which thereafter had the dominant voice in the new German Empire. Some emigrated to avoid the draft. In other cases, fathers who had served in the military left so that their sons would not have to do the same. Most of this emigration occurred during and after the German Wars of Unification. Many Germans also left Russia after 1873, when their previous exemption from military service was threatened and then abrogated. The Hessians who deserted from the British forces during the American Revolution also showed their distaste for the fighting that had been thrust upon them.

Political freedom. This was especially important for the refugees from the unsuccessful liberal democratic revolutions of 1830 and 1848, mostly the latter. These immigrants, though relatively few in number, had a strong impact upon the German-American community and American society in general, because these "Latin farmers" (so-called because of their education and lack of farming skills) included many intellectual and political leaders, like Carl Schurz. However, the ethnic Germans who came from the Soviet Union after the Bolshevik Revolution and after World War II also fled from severe political oppression, although they had never lived under an elected democratic government before then.

Hope for economic betterment in American cities. While most of the German immigrants (except perhaps the late ones) sought farms, a significant number also settled in the cities, where the streets were reputedly "paved with gold." When they discovered how misleading this was, some returned to Germany, but the vast majority stayed, either because they found opportunity anyway, or because they could not afford to return.

Nationalism and national policies. With respect to Germany itself, this factor applied only to the post-Napoleonic emigration to the Black Sea. However, this was an important factor in other areas. Most of the emigration from the Russian Empire was due to the removal of "eternal" special privileges of the Germans, and "Russification" policies soon thereafter as a result of the development of nationalistic attitudes. This was also a factor in areas ruled by Hungary after 1867, since its government also sought to force linguistic assimilation. In the areas ruled by Austria, nationalism affected Germans in a somewhat different way. Austria, unlike Prussia/Germany, Russia and Hungary, had very liberal policies in this respect, since the Hapsburgs realized that the only hope for saving their empire lay in an emphasis on its multilingual and multi-cultural nature. However, the result of this was that Germans living in predominantly Slavic areas experienced local pressures and felt that they had no government to protect them.

Personal and family reasons. Many came to join relatives or former neighbors who were already here. It was quite common for large numbers of German emigrants from the same village or neighboring villages to settle in the same American community. Of course, this would not have been an adequate reason unless some of the other reasons also applied.

Illegal emigration. A considerable number of people left Germanic lands without legal permission. This occurred most often for the sake of avoiding compulsory military service, but there were also other reasons: refusal of the lords of the feudal area to grant permission, government restrictions on emigration, or inability to meet the requirements for getting permission. Six professional German genealogists have now developed the "German Emigrants Register" for 1820-1918, which covers the entire former German Empire. It currently includes over a quarter of a million names of "missing people," culled from military, probate and other records. It is expected to include 800,000 persons eventually. You can obtain a form to request information from the register from the Immigrant Genealogical Society.

By and large, one or more of these reasons also applied to those who emigrated to other New World countries. Of course, some Germans (those poor enough to need public assistance, petty criminals, single mothers) were shipped off involuntarily by state and local authorities in the mid-nineteenth century, although criminals were deported even earlier.

German Jews who came to this country in the 1930s were much like the "Forty-Eighters," in that a relatively small number of professional people made a rather substantial contribution to education and science.

GERMANIC MIGRATION TO THE UNITED STATES

Individual Germans were on the first voyage of Columbus in 1492 and individual German soldiers were in St. Augustine about 1585. There is good evidence that some of the first colonists in Jamestown in 1607 were Germans. Other individual German immigrants were included in the Dutch settlement in New Netherlands (now New York), between 1624 and 1664.

The first group immigration of Germans to the New World was in 1683, when Mennonites from Krefeld emigrated to Germantown near Philadelphia. An estimated 65,000 to 70,000 Germans came to the American colonies, primarily to Pennsylvania, during the following half-century or so.

The next large wave came in 1709-11 via England. They were generally known as Palatines. Indeed, a large number came from the Palatinate, but others came from elsewhere close to the Rhine River, extending from Switzerland to the Netherlands, especially from the Middle and Upper Rhine regions. Many, but by no means all, of them settled in New York state. This group is well documented by numerous books, especially those by Hank Z. Jones, Jr. Another colonial wave appears to have crested in the 1750s. However, in sheer numbers, these colonial immigrants were dwarfed by nineteenth century immigration. Nevertheless, because their descendants have been on this side of the Atlantic for many generations, they constitute a significant percentage of German-Americans.

There are many publications on the colonial immigrants. The organization, Palatines to America, which has many state chapters in the eastern half of the country, focuses on them.

Those who came here during the colonial period settled mostly near what was then the frontier in New York, Maryland and Virginia, and especially in Pennsylvania, which had about half of the 225,000 Germans in America in 1776. About 10% settled in the Carolinas and Georgia. Those in Pennsylvania became known as the Pennsylvania Dutch — from the German word for German: *Deutsch*. A large percentage of them came from the southwestern parts of German-speaking Europe, particularly from the Palatinate, Württemberg, Baden, Alsace and Switzerland. Some of those of Swiss origin had migrated down the Rhine, especially after the Thirty Years' War, before their descendants went overseas.

Nearly 30,000 German soldiers, about two-thirds of them from Hesse, fought for the British in the American Revolution pursuant to contracts between their rulers and Britain. They were often referred to as mercenaries, troops paid to fight for foreign governments, but their rulers were the primary financial beneficiaries of this arrangement. Five thousand or more of these defected during the Revolutionary War and chose to stay in their new country.

There was very little German immigration to the United States prior to about 1830, as the bulk of German emigration was to Eastern Europe, but a modest flow began about 1818. A total of over seven million Germans immigrants have come to this country, most of them in three great waves between 1845 and 1895. If we add the German-speaking people from other countries (where the official immigration statistics do not show a breakdown by ethnicity) and those who went to Canada, the total is probably about 9 million.

The first big wave of Germans crossing the Atlantic lasted from 1846 to 1858. It began as a result of famine produced by the crop failures of 1846 and 1847, which affected most of Europe. Those who fled as a result of the unsuccessful liberal revolts of 1848, which occurred in nearly all of the many Germanic states, added to the flow. This wave peaked in 1854. Many Luxembourgers came in this wave.

The second wave occurred immediately after the American Civil War, lasting about a decade. Three factors were important in generating this stream: free or cheap land in the United States as a result of the homesteading provisions of the Morrill Act of 1862; the desire to escape from military service in the Prussian (after 1871, the German) army; and economic conditions, particularly the dislocations caused by the Industrial Revolution in Germany as the new factories squeezed the small peasants out of their supplemental earning opportunities as artisans.

The third and largest wave of German and Luxembourger immigrants occurred from 1879 to the early 1890s. Immigration from Germany reached an all-time peak in 1882. The closing of the American frontier in 1890 and the Panic (today we would say Depression) of 1893 halted this flow.

It is important, however, to remember that much of the "German" immigration was not from "Germany." For one thing, Germany did not exist until 1871. Before and after this, there was a second large "German" state, namely the Austrian Empire, which became the Austro-Hungarian Empire in 1867.

Moreover, a disproportionately large percentage of German-speaking immigrants came from Luxembourg and possibly also from Switzerland, which were independent countries throughout the period of German immigration.

Many also came from the Russian Empire and these continued to come to North America in relatively large numbers even after immigration from Germany itself had almost stopped. Furthermore, German-speaking Jews came to North America not only from Germany, but also from Eastern Europe, most of the latter immigrants coming in 1903-14, with an afterflow in 1921-24.

A major portion of the third wave of German immigrants came from the northeastern provinces of East and West Prussia, Pomerania, Posen and Russian Poland. Almost all of Posen and, half of West Prussia and the eastern end of Silesia became part of the new Poland when that country was re-established in 1919. The Germans living in German-

Polish linguistic border areas, as well as in German settlements in heavily Polish areas, constituted a significant portion of the German immigrants to America.

The same is true of the Germans living in Bohemia and Moravia, in what later came to be known as the Sudetenland, which was part of the Hapsburg Empire and became a part of the newly established state of Czechoslovakia in 1919. According to Josef Reiter's "Ein Kirchspiel im südlichen Egerland" ["A Church Parish in Southern Egerland"], in the 1992 book, *Heimat auf den Laurenziberg* [*The Homeland at Laurenziberg*], edited by Hertha Herzog, the first significant wave of emigration from this western Bohemian region occurred in the 1850s and 1860s, with a much larger wave in the 1890s. This is based on a translated excerpt on "Emigrants" by Kari Fangel in the June 1994 issue of the *German-Bohemian Heritage Society Newsletter*.

Another ethnically mixed area, which was part of "Germany" for less than half a century, but contributed large numbers of German-speaking immigrants to the United States, was Alsace-Lorraine in France.

Finally, even those areas east of the Oder-Neisse line (the boundary of contemporary Germany) that were overwhelmingly German in language and culture during the modern period of history, are now a part of Poland. While huge numbers of immigrants from this region came to America from "Germany," their ancestral lands are no longer part of any German nation.

Crossing the Atlantic by sailboat before 1840 was an arduous journey, which took 30-90 days, costing many lives and weakening others. The coming of the steamship in the 1840s reduced this to 2-3 weeks. This same decade saw the establishment of a large network of railways, which reduced emigrant dependence on river transportation. The chief ports of departure switched from Le Havre and Rotterdam, first to Bremen and Antwerp, and finally to Hamburg. This was, at least in part, a reflection of the changing origins of immigrants from southwestern to northwestern and then northeastern Germany, since most of those who emigrated chose the most accessible ports. Small numbers, however, came from various lesser ports. Many ships sailed directly to North American ports, but many immigrants took the indirect route via British ports. In particular, many went from Hamburg to Hull, crossed England by train and then sailed from Liverpool. This was a less expensive route, strange as it may seem to us today.

After 1840 the vast majority of immigrants landed at New York, being processed by the authorities first at Castle Garden and then, beginning in 1892, at Ellis Island. But there were some passenger arrivals at about 60 other ports, including about 15 of some significance. New Orleans was relatively popular for Germans coming to the Midwest, because boat fares up the Mississippi River were very inexpensive.

Quite a few ships went to the Canadian ports of Halifax, Quebec and Montreal. While most of their passengers stayed in Canada, a significant number also went to the United States, especially prior to the Civil War.

Many German-speaking immigrants came to North America and other New World countries from the Austro-Hungarian Empire, but few of them (at least prior to 1933) came from present-day Austria. Those who did came mostly from the Burgenland, which belonged to Hungary until after World War II and had a significantly larger Protestant minority than the rest of Austria.

The vast majority came from regions where they constituted ethnic minorities: *Gottschee* (Slovenia), the Lower Danube (so-called Swabians), Transylvania (so-called Saxons), Galicia, the Bukovina, Slovakia, and enclaves in modern-day Hungary. This pattern explains why there was a much larger percentage of Protestants among the immigrants than one would expect on the basis of the religious makeup of Austria.

The Germans from Bohemia and Moravia were a special case. These staunch Catholics came mostly from overwhelmingly German communities, but they represented a national minority, albeit a very large one, in what is now the Czech Republic and was historically a distinct political entity, although under Austrian rule for most of the modern era.

The immigrants from the Austrian heartland differ from other German-speaking immigrants in that a relatively large number came from Vienna. By contrast, German-speaking immigrants from elsewhere came overwhelmingly from rural areas.

CONCENTRATIONS OF GERMANIC SETTLEMENTS IN THE UNITED STATES

At the time of the American Revolution, Pennsylvania was "the German state." Today Wisconsin has that reputation. The belt stretching from one to the other with a small balloon in the east to encompass the other mid-Atlantic states and a larger balloon in the west to include the entire Midwest, remains the heart of German-America today.

In the case of the settlements west of the Alleghenies, a significant percentage of Germans came from Pennsylvania and other seaboard states, rather than directly from Europe. Many families continued to hop-scotch westward to the Great Plains. The Great Plains states, including eastern Colorado, are also noteworthy for having a much larger percentage of Germans from the Russian Empire, as well as the eastern parts of the German and Austro-Hungarian Empires. Many Danube Swabians, Transylvanian Saxons and Gottschee Germans, however, settled in Cleveland and other eastern cities. The hop-scotching to the frontier of the nineteenth century has continued into the current era, so that there are now large numbers of Germans in the Pacific states.

The South is known as a region with limited German immigration, but there are some significant pockets of German settlements, especially in Texas, with smaller ones in Virginia, the Carolinas, Georgia and Louisiana.

Howard B. Furer, in *The Germans in America, 1607-1970*, provides the following population estimates of Germans in America in 1776.

Pennsylvania	110,000	Maryland-Delaware	20,500	North Carolina	8,000
New York	25,000	New Jersey	15,000	Georgia	5,000
Virginia	25,000	South Carolina	15,000	New England	1,500

Ernest Thode, in his *Atlas for Germanic Genealogy*, shows concentrations of German settlements in the following areas in 1880:

Philadelphia, Pennsylvania	Saginaw, Michigan	Saint Louis, Missouri
Buffalo, New York	Chicago, Illinois	Brenham, Texas
Cleveland, Ohio	Milwaukee, Wisconsin	San Antonio, Texas
Cincinnati, Ohio	Madison, Wisconsin	

Thode's map shows the number of German-born residents in 1930. It also shows counties with over 1,000 such residents in the following states in addition to those listed above. There was only one such county or cluster of adjacent counties in the states indicated by stars.

California	Indiana	Minnesota	Utah*
Connecticut	Iowa	Nebraska	Washington
Delaware	Maryland	New Jersey	
Florida*	Massachusetts	Oregon*	

A similar map by Thode for 1900 also lists significant concentrations of German-born residents in North Dakota, Kansas, Colorado and New Hampshire. Since these maps are based on numbers, not percentages, they do not fully reflect the importance of the German-American element in the more sparsely populated states, especially the Great Plains. Furthermore, these maps show only the German-born population.

Allen and Turner's *We the People: An Atlas of America's Ethnic Diversity* shows that counties with the highest percentage of residents of German ancestry were clustered in the Great Plains states, Minnesota, Wisconsin and Iowa in 1980, with a geographically smaller cluster in Pennsylvania. German-Americans comprised at least 10% of the population of most counties north of a shallow "V" from eastern Washington to northwestern Oklahoma to New York, but excluding New England.

Emigration from Switzerland to America began as early as 1710 when certain "undesirables" (people following minority religions, the poor and non-landowners) were encouraged to leave. These folk settled mainly in North Carolina, Pennsylvania and Virginia. By 1732 more came to South Carolina and Mississippi. The 18th century immigrants mostly arrived from Bern, Basel, Zürich, Schaffhausen, Aargau, Solothurn, Luzern and Graubünden cantons. By 1920, over 300,000 Swiss immigrants had entered the United States, many settling in the Midwest and California. In 1980 the largest number of Swiss-Americans were in Wisconsin, Indiana and Ohio, with lesser concentrations in southern New England, New York, Pennsylvania, New Jersey, Michigan, Illinois, Iowa, Kansas, and along the Pacific coast.

Luxembourgers tended to settle in Illinois, Wisconsin, Iowa and Minnesota. Many Bohemian Germans came to Wisconsin, Minnesota and Michigan's Upper Peninsula. Bukovina Germans went to Kansas and other midwestern states.

German-speaking Austrians, mostly Burgenlanders, are concentrated in Chicago, Detroit, the Cleveland-Washington-Boston triangle, and in the Sunbelt states of Florida and California.

German Jews settled mostly in the big cities from St. Louis and Chicago to Washington, DC, and Boston, but 20% went to the South.

Today more Americans have Germanic forebears than any other ancestry, including the English.

A map in Adam Giesinger's *From Catherine to Khruschev: The Story of Russia's Germans* shows that large settlements of Russian-born Germans were founded in North and South Dakota, Nebraska, Kansas and Colorado. Significant numbers moved on to Oklahoma, as well as to the Pacific Coast.

In 1980, German-born residents constituted 5-10% of the population of Philadelphia, Phoenix, Detroit, Washington, Chicago, San Antonio and Dallas. Those born in Austria constituted at least 1% of the population in Philadelphia, New York, Detroit and Chicago. The combined Germanic element was strongest (in terms of percentages) in Philadelphia, Phoenix, Detroit, Chicago, Washington, San Antonio, New York and Dallas, in that order, among the biggest metropolitan areas.

Almost all of these would have arrived here after the end of heavy emigration from Germany in 1893. The Sun Belt cities probably include a large number of retirees who may have come here during the following half-century. The figures for the northern cities probably reflect post-World War II and some Nazi-era immigration.

GERMANIC MIGRATION TO CANADA

Germans who settled in Canada were small in numbers compared to those who settled in the United States. Early settlements of Germans were almost exclusively in two provinces: Nova Scotia and Ontario. The first German immigrants to Nova Scotia came to Lunenburg and Halifax in 1750-52.

The first twenty-five or so German families in Ontario moved from Pennsylvania about 1786 to the Kitchener (Berlin) area of Waterloo County in Ontario (then called Upper Canada). Because land was costly in Pennsylvania, more families had come to settle the inexpensive Canadian lands by 1807. These first Germans were predominantly Mennonites. In the early days, virtually all Germans in Canada were related to families in the United States. Waterloo became the chief center of German settlement in Eastern Canada, with a secondary concentration on the Niagara peninsula. After the American Revolution, about 2500 German soldiers stayed in Canada (about one-third as many as stayed in the U.S.). Nearly all of them settled in Ontario. See *The German Canadians, 1750-1937*, by Heinz Lehmann, for a detailed account of the settlement of Germans in Canada.

The mid-1830s brought a new surge of German immigrants from Europe. They came from Alsace-Lorraine, Baden, Bavaria, Hesse-Darmstadt, Holstein, Mecklenburg, Württemberg and the German settlements in the Baltic areas of Estonia, Latvia and Lithuania. Many religious denominations were represented: Lutherans, Moravians, Baptists, Swedenborgians, and by the 1850s, Catholics.

Many Germans immigrating through the port of Quebec were very poor. Upon arrival they boarded the Grand Trunk Railroad that went directly to the Berlin area. In 1916 during World War I, the name of Berlin was changed to Kitchener. Researchers of this area should consult the many family histories and resources in the Grace Schmidt Room of the Kitchener Public Library and the large collection of Mennonite records at the Conrad Grebel College, University of Waterloo. Other Mennonite sects have deposited their records in various areas. See Angus Baxter, *In Search of Your German Roots*, for these repositories.

Germans who came to Nova Scotia were almost exclusively directly from Europe, mostly emigrating through the port of Rotterdam in the Netherlands and going directly to Halifax, Nova Scotia. The British government encouraged the immigration of Protestants. These Germans came from Baden, Hesse, Württemberg and Rhineland-Palatinate, as well as a few from Switzerland. Ten of the twelve ship's passenger lists are published by Terrence Punch in *Genealogical Research in Nova Scotia* (Halifax, 1978). See also the bibliography in Angus Baxter's *In Search of Your German Roots* and Eric Jonasson's *The Canadian Genealogical Handbook*.

Western Canada has more ethnic Germans than Eastern Canada. This immigration began in 1874 and continued until 1914, with peaks in 1874-76, 1901-03 and 1911-14. The Germans who came to Western Canada came primarily from Europe. Lehmann estimates that 44% of the German immigrants who came to Western Canada before 1914 came from Russia, 18% from the Austro-Hungarian Empire, and 6% from the Dobruja, with some 18% from the U.S. (many of them originally from Eastern Europe) and only 12% directly from Germany.

There was a relatively large stream of German immigrants to Canada between the World Wars, namely Mennonite refugees from the Russian Revolution who arrived mostly in 1923-26 to join their co-religionists who had come in the 1870s, and a later, more diverse stream of immigrants in 1927-31, roughly one-half of whom were from Eastern Europe, and a fourth directly from Germany.

Among the German-Canadians, Lutherans were the largest group in Ontario and Alberta, with Catholics being the largest group in Saskatchewan, and Mennonites in Manitoba. Many of the Jewish immigrants to Canada came from the Austro-Hungarian Empire, specifically Galicia, then an Austrian crownland.

In terms of numbers, the 1931 Canadian census reported the largest number of Germans living in Ontario (174,000), followed by Saskatchewan (129,000), Alberta (74,000), Manitoba (38,000) and Nova Scotia (27,000). However, in Manitoba, Saskatchewan and Alberta, the number of residents who reported German as their mother tongue was greater than the number who identified themselves as being of German origin. This discrepancy reflects the confusion regarding national origin in the case of Germans from Eastern Europe. For example, Mennonites might list their origin as Dutch (historically correct, if one goes back to the sixteenth century), German (their mother tongue since the 1700s) or Russian (their citizenship at the time of immigration). On the other hand, the number of German residents who reported German as their mother tongue in Nova Scotia was almost negligible, while in Ontario only one-half of German residents made this claim, reflecting the longer time span since immigration.

The largest concentrations of German-speakers in Western Canada were found in a belt in northern Saskatchewan, near Saskatoon, reaching from the Alberta border to east of

Humboldt; in and south of Edmonton; and in and south of Winnipeg. But there were also many other scattered settlements, especially in Saskatchewan and Alberta, as well as in Regina and other cities.

One complication in tracing a German-Canadian connection is that virtually all of the pre-1846 German emigrants to Canada initially arrived in New York before heading north. Conversely, over half of those who arrived in Quebec, at least prior to 1870, appear to have gone to the United States. Furthermore, there has been extensive two-way migration of Germans between Canada and the United States in the post-immigration period.

The Danube Swabians and Gottschee Germans (most of whom came after Lehmann's publications) seem to have settled mostly in Ontario. Urbanization has attracted many German-Canadians of East European origin to Toronto and Vancouver, as well as to the cities in the Prairie Provinces.

GERMANIC MIGRATION TO LATIN AMERICA

Among the Latin American countries with a large number of German-speaking immigrants, those from the German Empire represent a majority only in Brazil and Chile.

ARGENTINA

The first wave of Germanic immigration began in 1878 when most of the Volga Germans who had begun arriving in Brazil in 1877 moved on to Argentina to find more favorable farming conditions. They settled in Buenos Aires province (south of the capital) and in Entre Rios province (directly west of Uruguay). These remained their chief centers.

Substantial immigration both directly from the Volga and indirectly via a brief stay in Brazil was heavy during the 1878-89 period. There seems to have been a lull in direct immigration from Europe in 1883-85. Onward migration from Brazil peaked in 1881-82, but continued throughout the 1880s.

From Buenos Aires province, some moved westward into La Pampa province. The Entre Rios Germans spread out even more: to Santa Fe and Cordoba to the west, as well as to Chaco and Formosa to the north. By the centennial year of 1978, Argentina had an estimated one million residents of Volga German descent.

Those in the southern provinces seem to have been mostly Catholics. In and around Entre Rios, both Catholics and Lutherans were numerous, although they rarely settled in the same village. There were also a few Baptists, Moravian Brethren, Reformed and Mennonites in Argentina. Other churches were established after immigration, usually due to North American missionary activity.

The small number of Mennonites are concentrated mostly in the Buenos Aires metropolitan area today. Volhynian Germans settled mostly in Misiones province and neighboring parts of Brazil and Paraguay. Germans from Romania settled in Entre Rios province in the 1980s.

Among the many English-language sources for the Volga Germans in southern South America, we relied most heavily on Adam Giesinger, *From Catherine to Khrushchev: The Story of Russia's Germans* and the *Journal of the American Historical Society of Germans from Russia* (especially the Winter 1978 issue, which was devoted largely to a tour of Argentina, Brazil and Paraguay in connection with the Volga German centennial celebration in Argentina). Ewald Wuschke provided information on the Volhynian Germans. The information on the Romanian Germans comes from Jacob Steigerwald's book.

Georg Hiller, *Einwanderung und Kolonisation in Argentinien* [*Immigration and Colonization in Argentina*], Vol. 1: *Einwanderung und Einwanderungspolitik* [*Immigration and Immigration Policies*] (Berlin: Dietrich Reimer/Ernst Vohsen, 1912, 155 pp.), indicates that the heaviest period of Germanic immigration occurred in 1867-1911. The countries of origin were as follows:

Table 6: Germanic migration to Argentina

Russia	115,827
Austria-Hungary	73,750
Germany	49,943
Switzerland	29,621

Unfortunately, this does not coincide with ethnicity. Those from Russia were almost exclusively German Christians and Jews. An unknown number of immigrants appear to have come from the western Black Sea area, according to Joseph S. Height, *Paradise on the Steppe: The Odyssey of a Pioneering*, and other sources. Those from Austria-Hungary, on the other hand, appear to have included few German-speakers. The percentage of Swiss who were German speakers is also unknown, but they were numerous. The peak year for Swiss immigration was 1873, but the largest sustained wave occurred in 1883-89.

The peak years of immigration from the German Empire were 1882-90, 1895-96 and 1902-1911. The last period, which occurred after immigration to the United States had largely ceased, was by far the largest. The number of German-speaking immigrants was probably 2-3 times the number of immigrants from Germany, although no reliable statistics exist. Those from the German Empire settled mostly in Buenos Aires and other cities, but they included farmers in the provinces of Santa Fe, Entre Rios and Buenos Aires.

The total number of foreign-born in Argentina approximately doubled between 1895 and 1910. For Swiss, it went up less than that; for Germans, it tripled; for those directly from the Russian Empire, it increased more than fourfold.

BELIZE AND JAMAICA

Mack Walker, *Germany and the Emigration, 1816-1885*, mentions that after the emancipation of the slaves in the British possessions in the West Indies and Central America in 1833, planters sought German bond servants to provide labor. He estimates that thousands arrived at the Jamaica plantations and in the jungles of Central America (Belize, formerly British Honduras, and possibly British-dominated east Nicaragua).

In 1958 several thousand Mexican Mennonites began settling in Belize. They were subsequently joined by Mennonites from Alberta, as well as some Amish and Old Order Mennonites from the United States. Their biggest settlements are at Shipyard, Orange Walk and Spanish Lookout, but there are quite a few other settlements. For further information, see Gerhard S. Koop's "Mennonite Families in Belize" in the January 1995 issue of *Mennonite Family History*.

BOLIVIA

Virtually all of the known German-speakers in Bolivia are Mennonites who began moving to the Santa Cruz area from the Paraguayan Gran Chaco in 1954. Later they were joined by immigrants from Canada, Mexico and Belize. Their ancestors were among the Russian German Mennonites who came to North America, mostly Canada.

BRAZIL

The story of German immigration to Brazil is very complex, despite the fact that the Germans are overwhelming concentrated in the southernmost states of Rio Grande do Sul, Santa Catarina, Parana and Sao Paulo, decreasing significantly in number as one goes north from the Uruguayan border.

The first settlers were convicts deported from Mecklenburg-Schwerin in the early 1800s or possibly already beginning in the late 1700s, according to *Hundert Jahre Deutschtum in Rio Grande do Sulm 1824-1924* [*One Hundred Years of German Culture in Rio Grande do Sul, 1824-1924*] (Porto Alegre: Verband deutscher Vereine, 1924; 568 pp.). Quite a few Mecklenburgers followed later. Four German parishes were already established in this state in 1809.

Pre-1824 colonization efforts also included two German villages established in Bahia in 1818 and a Swiss settlement in the Rio de Janeiro area in 1818-20. Both floundered. Furthermore, there were German mercenaries in the Brazilian army before this. After they had revolted, they were settled in the interior of Santa Catarina state in the 1820s. But they soon fled to the coastal city of Florianopolis because of the hostility of the natives.

Heavy German immigration occurred in 1823-29, when Brazil was the favored destination of those who left Germany. Mack Walker estimates that 7-10 thousand Germans took advantage of the opportunity of free passage in return for military service. This immigration came to an abrupt halt in 1830, because of the bad reputation that the German recruiting agent in the service of the Brazilian government got and because the Brazilian emperor instituted a policy of requiring immigrants to prove that they were self-sufficient.

The city of Sao Leopoldo in Rio Grande do Sul was founded in 1824. The first settlers were mostly Protestants from the Hamburg area. Nearly 5,000 came to this state in the 1820s. Eventually the Germans in this area came to be closely balanced between Lutherans (including some from the separate Missouri Synod) and Catholics, with a few Baptists, Seventh-Day Adventists and Jews.

The majority of the immigrants appear to have come from the Hunsrück-Eifel uplands in the northern part of what is now Rhineland-Palatinate, with a significant number from the various Hessian duchies.

The Rio Grande do Sul centennial book indicates that nine colonies were founded in 1830-36, but these may have been daughter colonies.

In 1837 German immigrants bound for Australia (probably Old Lutherans) forced their continuously drunk captain to land in Brazil. There they founded Petropolis. For an account of this, see Hanzheinz Keller, *Neuer Beitrag zur Auswanderungsgeschichte unter besonderer Berücksichtigung der Gründung von Petropolis bei Rio de Janeiro* [*New Contribution to Emigration History with Particular Regard to the Establishment of Petropolis near Rio de Janeiro*] (1963).

Beginning in the mid-1840s Brazil again actively recruited German colonists, offering free passage or other assistance to many. This recruitment was aided by numerous "push" factors in Germany. Many government officials, the press and the elite had come to favor emigration as the answer to poverty. Some states and villages thought providing assistance for emigration would cost the public treasury less in the long run than paying for poorhouses. Thus the poor, single mothers and petty criminals were strongly encouraged, and sometimes virtually forced, to emigrate.

German colonization societies were also founded and very active in 1846-54. They were established partly for the purpose of preventing immigrants in foreign countries from being ripped off. But they also actively encouraged emigration — sometimes, but not always, with the ideal of creating a "New Germany" abroad.

Emigration was also stimulated by the failure of the 1848 Revolution for freedom and German unity, which stemmed from the impact of the French Revolution. Although the number of political refugees was not large, the environment they created undoubtedly influenced others to leave.

Moreover, the early years of the Industrial Revolution had the effect of depriving many rural residents of their livelihood. An example was the destruction of iron mining as a "cottage industry" in the Hunsrück area. Working conditions of industrial laborers in those years were as bad as Marx depicted them. Besides, Germans were always hungry for a piece of their own land. In Hesse, feudal obligations (although not serfdom) still imposed a heavy burden on the peasants. Therefore, overseas emigration often seemed more attractive than internal migration. Thus again the center of emigration was a broad belt that stretched approximately from Trier to Giessen, including the Hunsrück, Hesse and adjacent areas.

These push and pull factors contributed to large-scale emigration to Brazil in 1845-59. In 1858, the peak year, Brazil was the destination of 8% of German emigrants, a higher percentage than at any other time except the 1820s, when there was little emigration to the United States.

This wave seems to have started when the provincial government of Rio de Janeiro asked a French agent to recruit 600 laborers. He overfilled his quota by sending 2,500, but when the promise of free passage was withdrawn, many poor people were stranded in Dunkirk. Santa Izabel, in the state of Espirito Santo northwest of Rio de Janeiro, was founded in 1847. Preston E. James, *Brazil* (New York: Odyssey Press, 1942; 262 pp.), estimates that 35,000 Germans and Austrians settled in eastern Espirito Santo in 1840-50. A private landowner brought 400 Germans to the state of Sao Paulo in 1847.

But most of the Germans went to the three southernmost states. James reports that over 20,000 Germans settled on small farms in Rio Grande do Sul with government aid during the 1824-59 period. The Rio Grande do Sul centennial book shows that 50 colonies were established by the government, 27 by societies, and 187 privately, so the total influx was several times 20,000.

One of the most important German centers, Blumenau in eastern Santa Catarina state, was established in 1850 and named for its founder. The initial settlers were Pomeranians and they always remained the largest group. But by 1870 more than 6,000 immigrants had arrived from many parts of Germany. They were joined by Swiss and Austrians.

A number of very small Swiss settlements were founded in Sao Paulo in 1854-57, with the largest number from the canton of Glarus and the others primarily from Berne and Freiburg. Presumably the Zürich canton police chief, Dr. J. Christian Heusser, was sent out to investigate complaints that these colonists were being exploited in that their debts (for passage or land) increased, because the yearly interest exceeded the value of their crops. His account, *Die Schweizer auf den Kolonien in St. Paulo in Brasilien* [*The Swiss in the Colonies in Sao Paulo, Brazil*], was a graphically critical evaluation.

Similar complaints (or maybe even this specific one) caused the Prussian government to ban emigration to Brazil in 1859. This sharply reduced the number of immigrants, although its effectiveness seems to have declined over the years. For example, Mack Walker reports that during the heaviest period of German emigration (1871-85, by his classification), when 3.5% of the total German population emigrated, 95% went to the United States, but Brazil was still the second most popular destination, even though the ban was not lifted until the 1890s, by which time German emigration had dropped sharply.

Twentieth-century German authors acknowledge that there were a few cases in Sao Paulo of immigrants forced into virtual peonage, but they argue that this never happened in the three southern states where a large majority of the Germans lived. Their claims that the reports of abuse that led to the Prussian ban were greatly exaggerated are credible, since Dr. Heusser reported on only a few dozen families in small, isolated clusters.

Meanwhile, various groups of East European Germans began to come to Brazil. Volga Germans settled there in 1877-79. A majority of them soon left for Argentina, but some remained in Brazil, mostly in the Ponta Grossa in Parana. Dr. Mathias Hagin (*Journal of the AHSGR*, Fall 1984) mentions that at that time an estimated 17,000-18,000 Brazilians had Volga German ancestors.

Prof. Ayrton Gonçalves Celestino's manuscript, "Die Bukowiner von Rio Negro und Mafra, in Brasilien" ["The Bukoviners of Rio Negro and Mafra, in Brazil"], reports on a particular, but significant, group of Bukovina Germans, as well as Bohemian Germans, settling in Brazil. This group had its roots in the Bavarian Woods from whence it migrated to the Bohemian Forest. He lists Bavarian towns of origin, but has no information as to when they moved, except that it was long ago. He also gives a reason: lack of land for all sons because of inheritance laws.

Many Bohemian Germans had already moved to the Bukovina (under Austrian rule after 1775) in the late 1700s. The ancestors of the Brazilians, however, arrived in the predominantly Romanian southern Bukovina in 1835-40. Some immediately sold their land and migrated to the United States, Canada and Brazil. Bohemian Germans had already migrated to Brazil before that. Bohemians founded the city of Sao Bento do Sul in the Brazilian state of Santa Catarina.

Those who went to the Americas from the Bukovina and from Bohemia, the former home, settled in the same countries, often even in the same areas. Some Bukovina Germans arrived in 1877 and settled in Rio Negro, Parana, and Mafra, Santa Catarina (across the Parana River). Among their neighbors were Germans who had gone to the area in 1829. But some of the immigrants returned home because of a poor crop, massive flooding that year, a major epidemic, and complaints about the soil, the climate, the lack of wood and the Indians.

Gonçalves found the names of the 1887-88 immigrants from the Bukovina in the National Archives of Brazil and lists them, including all family members, identifying the returnees. He lists others mentioned by Ignatz Schelbauer in "Manuskripte eines der Pioniere" ["Manuscript of One of the Pioneers"], but at least one of these families had already come in 1877.

All of these Bohemian and Bukovina Germans were, of course, staunch Catholics. There were also Catholics from Germany in the area.

The Bukovina Germans immediately established new colonies, or moved to individual farms, in the two states as the population grew. According to Schelbauer's research, there were 3,687 persons of Bukovina German descent in 1837, when this group celebrated its 50th anniversary.

There are numerous brief references to a new wave of Brazilian immigration beginning in the late 1890s. Although Germans clearly represented a minority of the post-1890 immigrants, the closing of the American frontier in 1890 may have led to an increased percentage of the smaller number of German emigrants going to Brazil. Among the immigrants of this period are the Volhynian Germans who settled in the Santa Rosa area in northwestern Rio Grande do Sul.

According to the *Encyclopedia Americana*, German immigration to Brazil peaked in the 1920s, since American immigration laws had become so restrictive.

Later Germanic immigrants include thousands who left the Soviet Union legally or illegally. German Lutherans and Catholics settled mostly in Rio Grande do Sul in 1928-33, while Mennonites who fled from the Soviet Union via China settled in the interior jungle around 1930, but soon moved to Curitiba. Next came the political and racial refugees from Hitler-dominated areas who settled in Brazil, as in most other countries in the Americas, but how many of them became permanent Brazilian residents is another question. Finally, a significant number of Danube Swabian displaced persons must have settled at Entre Rios in Parana in 1951, since Jacob Steigerwald cites three books about them. (Note that place names like Entre Rios and Parana occur in both Brazil and Argentina. The latter, derived from the Parana River, is also relevant in Uruguay and Paraguay.) This group was only one among the numerous displaced, stateless East European Germans who migrated to many overseas countries after World War II.

Migration of Mennonite refugees to Brazil is chronicled in Peter Pauls, Jr., *Urwaldpioniere: persönliche Erlebnisse mennonitischer Siedler aus den ersten Jahren am Krauel und von Stolzplateau, S.C. [Jungle Pioneers: Personal Experiences of Mennonite Settlers in the Early Years on the Krauel and from the Stolzplateau, Santa Catarina]*, published on behalf of the Festkommission der Jubiläumsfeier (Witmarsum, 1980).

In any case, the founding of new colonies in Brazil after 1859 is primarily the story of internal expansion, not immigration. The German colonies in the eastern portions of both Rio Grande do Sul and Santa Catarina expanded westward and northward, overflowing into Parana state, as the population increased. For example, the Rio Grande do Sul centennial book lists 15 new colonies founded in 1846-64 (nearly all by 1858, i.e., toward the end of the period of heavy immigration), but a peak of 19 in 1872-78 before the number began declining, presumably due to urbanization, which led Blumenau to become a sizable Germanic city. Those who went to the metropolises later in the twentieth century went mostly to Sao Paulo, which has been gaining both internal migrants and immigrants from abroad. The Hitler-era refugees who contributed to this were mostly urbanites.

A map in James's 1942 book shows the whole area from northwest of Sao Paulo to the Uruguayan border, except for western Parana, was populated largely by post-1824 European immigrants and their descendants. Of course, these were by no means all Germans, but the farther south you go, the more Germanic the population becomes.

The Blumenau-Curitiba area is a primary example of Germanic influence because of its cohesiveness. As late as 1927, the census showed that 63% of the people in Blumenau, and 75% in the surrounding rural area, claimed German as their mother tongue. German was the language of instruction until 1938. Since then the Brazilian government has allowed it to be taught only as a foreign language, beginning in the fifth grade. Thus linguistic assimilation is undoubtedly occurring. Nevertheless, given the Germanic nature of the area and the introduction of German-language classes at the elementary school level, a substantial residue of the ancestral mother tongue remains.

Although German-speaking immigrants came from all parts of Germany, as well as from Austria, Switzerland and non-Germanic countries, the literature suggests that the majority came from:

- a broad belt extending roughly from Trier in the southwestern Rhineland to Giessen in Hesse (often referred to as the Hunsrück which is, however, only the major part of this region, not all of it)

- Pomerania and probably also the area to the west to around Hamburg, chiefly Mecklenburg-Schwerin

James estimates the number of Brazilians of German descent in the most Germanic states in 1942 as:

Rio Grande do Sul	520,000
Santa Catarina	275,000
Parana	126,000

Sparse earlier data suggest that 40-50% of the Germans lived in Rio Grande do Sul. If this was reasonably accurate, there would have been at least 1 million Brazilians with German ancestors at that time. That was more than 50 years ago. Thus it is safe to assume that there are at least several million German-Brazilians today. If inter-ethnic marriages have increased even almost as much as in North America, the actual figure could be in the 5-10 million range.

CENTRAL AMERICA AND THE CARIBBEAN (HISPANIC COUNTRIES)

There is abundant literature on an ill-fated colony at Santo Tomas in **Guatemala**. The Belgian Colonization Company recruited an estimated 1,000 Europeans, including Germans, to settle on the land it had bought in 1843 and 1845. Hundreds died in the jungle, while others became dispersed throughout the land.

Karl Sapper, in "Ansiedlung von Europäern in Mittelamerika" ["European Settlement in Central America"] in the volume published by the Verein für Sozialpolitik, reported that there were quite a few Guatemalans with German names and that this was the only Central American country where Germans were the most significant non-Hispanic, non-native element. This suggests that a significant number of Germans must nevertheless have survived and multiplied, since there is no report of any later colonization.

In 1846-48 some German princes sought emigrants to settle on the Mosquito Coast of **Nicaragua**. Clifford Neal Smith, in *Passenger Lists (and Fragments Thereof) from*

Hamburg and Bremen to Australia and the United States, 1846-49 (McNeal, AZ: Westland Publications, 1988; German-American Research Monograph Number 23), mentions both Nicaragua and **Honduras**.

Because of strongly adverse commentaries, generated at least partly by the Santo Tomas disaster, the project was aborted. But some East Prussians sailed there, unaware of the cancellation, according to Mack Walker. Since the British had established a *de facto* protectorate in the area, the British consul was left with the problem of what to do about the stranded Germans.

There are some brief references to immigrants going to **Cuba**. Gonçalves mentions this as one of the places to which Bukovina and Bohemian Germans went. Refugees from Hitler also went there.

Goldner writes that the **Dominican Republic** was especially helpful toward the refugees from Nazi-ruled countries. It seems doubtful, however, that many of these refugees regarded the country as more than a temporary haven.

Sapper reports that there were 137 Germans in **Panama** and about 20 German small landowners in **Honduras** at the time of the 1908 census. But Winkler estimates the total number of Germans in Central America and the West Indies in 1925 at only 2,000 (which appears to include only first- and second-generation immigrants), so this was not a significant area of settlement, especially considering that his designation apparently also includes the British and Dutch possessions.

In recent years, a few Dutch-Prussian-Russian-Canadian-Mexican-Belizean Mennonites have found yet another country: **Costa Rica**.

CHILE

This is the only Latin American country with a substantial number of residents of Germanic origin that has no documented German immigrants from Eastern Europe. It is also one of the few where Germans have been able to maintain their mother tongue as the language of instruction in the schools.

This account on the Chilean Germans is based on George F. W. Young, *Germans in Chile: Immigration and colonization, 1849-1914* (New York: Center for Migration Studies, 1974). Because of inadequate data, the information is not always consistent.

Hamburg already had strong trade ties with Chile during the pre-immigration decades. It appears that almost all the German emigrants for Chile left from that port. Although there were comparatively few Germans, they were nevertheless the largest group of non-Mediterranean origin. Moreover, a disproportionately large number came from the Austro-Hungarian Empire and Switzerland. Of the Hapsburg subjects, about half came from Austria proper and half from the Czech Republic. What percentage of the immigrants from Bohemia, Moravia, and Switzerland were German-speakers is unknown.

Despite the small number of Germans in Chile, both in absolute numbers and relative to the United States, Canada, Brazil and Argentina, Young says that, with the possible exception of Paraguay, only in Chile did the concept of a "national colony" or "New Germany" succeed and survive. He finds this ironic in that the idea originated with the liberal democrats of the 1848 Revolution and yet the pro-German sentiment was obvious even during World War II, when the German government was the exact opposite of what the liberal democrats had envisioned.

The first German settlements were established in south central Chile, around Valdivia and, to a lesser extent, near Lake Llanquique in 1846-66, peaking in 1852 and 1856-57, with a smaller afterflow in 1872-75. These were agriculturalists and craftsmen with some means who sought economic independence. It was chiefly in this area that a sense of German identity was preserved. One reason for this may be that this area was effectively isolated from populous central Chile because it was occupied largely by the Araucanian

Indians. Only after the 1880-82 uprising of the latter was defeated did this situation change.

This area, bordering Valdivia on the north, then became the province of La Frontera. A small number of Germans who had gone to this area in 1858-59 had quickly become assimilated. However, the Chilean government settled a substantial number of Germans here in 1882-89, with a small afterflow in 1900-02. These were poorer than the earlier immigrants so that the Chilean government had to pay for their passage against future repayment.

The poorest ones of all, including Swiss as well as Germans, were sent to Chiloé province, south of Valdivia, in 1895-97, but many later left this poor area with its unfavorable climate.

The province of Valdivia-Llanquique accounted for half the Germans in Chile in 1917. Together with neighboring La Frontera, they amounted to two-thirds. The overwhelming majority of the others lived in the cities of Santiago, Valparaiso, and Concepcion. These consisted mostly of industrial workers, professionals, and businessmen. However, the support of the more well-to-do urban element, and especially the German-language newspapers in Santiago and Valparaiso (1870-1943), did a lot to nurture the preservation of a German identity in south central Chile.

Young attributes most of the German immigration (especially the early immigration) to Chile to individual recruiting agents, especially Bernhard-Eunom Philippi, and to colonization promotion societies established in the 1840s. However, the first Germans arrived in 1846-47 primarily as a result of famine (caused by potato rot and poor harvests) and the industrial depression of those years, while recruited immigration did not begin until 1848 and did not pick up speed until the 1850s.

At first the Chilean government instructed Philippi to recruit only German Catholics. However, because Catholic bishops were disinclined to work with the Protestant Philippi, the Chilean government guaranteed freedom of religion in 1850. As a result, a considerable majority of the German immigrants were Protestants. Moreover, the German Catholics, who shared the religious beliefs of the native Chileans, were therefore more likely to become assimilated, as has been documented for La Frontera for example. Nevertheless, Catholics from Westphalia, Prussian and Austrian Silesia, and a few impoverished ones from Württemberg were among the immigrants. The Llanquique region had about an equal number of German Catholics and Protestants. In 1910, there were 9 Protestant schools, 2 Catholic schools and 21 non-denominational schools in Chile.

MEXICO

Almost all of the Germans in Mexico are Russian German Mennonites. Though mostly of Dutch-Flemish origin, they stress the importance of the German "mother tongue" their ancestors finally adopted after centuries in West Prussia.

In 1922-27 some 6,000 very traditional Mennonites left Saskatchewan and Manitoba (with a few from Kansas and Oklahoma) to settle in remote parts of Mexico, primarily because of fears about "worldly" influences and increased government regulation of their schools. Most of them settled in the state of Chihuahua, with a smaller number in Durango. In 1929-30 a small group of Soviet Mennonite refugees joined them.

In 1948 another 1,700 Manitoba Mennonites went to Chihuahua for the same reason as the earlier group. Since then, they have spread out, some returning to Canada or the United States, with others going on to new frontiers in Belize, Costa Rica, Paraguay and Bolivia.

The best accounts of the Mexican Mennonites can be found in:

- Harry Leonard Sawatzky, *They Chose a Country* (which also has a chapter on Belize)

- Walter Schmiedehaus, *Die Altkolonier-Mennoniten in Mexico* [*The Old Colonial Mennonites in Mexico*]

- William Schroeder and Helmut T. Huebert, *Mennonite Historical Atlas* (which is all-encompassing and has a text accompanying the maps)

PARAGUAY

George Young estimates that there were 30,000 Germans in Paraguay in 1914, although Winkler's 1925 estimate is only 4,000. Some are known to have come from Bohemia, the Bukovina and Volhynia. By the time Young published his book in 1974, a lot of Mennonites had migrated to Paraguay. However, when he parenthetically refers to Paraguay as possibly having become a "New Germany," this could only be true in a cultural-linguistic — not a political — sense, for the Mennonite immigrants were totally apolitical, in sharp contrast to the Chilean Germans as he saw them.

The first group of over 2,000 Mennonites came in 1926-27 at the same time as, for the same reasons as, and from the same area of emigration as the Mexican Mennonites. They settled in the Gran Chaco in western Paraguay. A fifth found the rigors too great and returned to Canada. There is a brief account of this by Irene Enns Kroeker in "Immigration (Paraguay)," found in *Preservings*, the newsletter of the Hanover/Steinbach (Manitoba) Historical Society (No. 4, July 1994).

Nearly 5,000 Soviet Mennonite refugees founded settlements in both eastern and western Paraguay in 1947-50. In 1948 another 2,000 Canadian Mennonites migrated to eastern Paraguay, with a larger percentage returning home (probably because they were better able to afford it than the immigrants of the 1920s). Beginning in 1969, some Mexican Mennonites, as well as some Old Order Mennonites from the United States, relocated in Mexico.

By 1954 the Paraguayan Mennonites had begun to migrate onward again, this time to Bolivia.

PERU

Mack Walker makes brief mention of "scandalous stories" from Peru, resulting from the activity of Peruvian agents in Austrian Tyrol in or about 1859. Whether the number of immigrants was as small as the few dozen Swiss in Brazil on whose condition Heusser made such an unfavorable report is not specified, but the lack of further information on the subject suggests that this may have been the case.

Winkler's estimate of 1,800 Peruvian Germans may have been a reference to missionaries or businessmen, since any descendants of survivors of the Austrians who apparently went there in 1859 would be likely to have been of the third generation already (i.e., not included in census data as Germans).

URUGUAY

According to Winkler's estimate, there were only about 1,500 Germans in Uruguay in 1925. If this is interpreted as "German-speaking" or "of German descent," the Russian Germans, who settled mostly in western Uruguay, may have accounted for the total number. However, Winkler's low estimates on the other non-European countries suggest that he may have meant 1,500 "German-born" residents.

VENEZUELA, SURINAM, CURACAO, COLOMBIA AND EQUADOR

Winkler estimated that there were 2,600 Germans in Venezuela in 1925. George Young refers to an 1846 article about Germans in Tovar, Venezuela. Gonçalves states that some Bohemian and Bukovina Germans went there. Steigerwald mentions post-World War II Danube Swabian refugees going there. But documentation is sparse.

On the other hand, attempts to settle Germans in Dutch Guiana (now Surinam), have been thoroughly chronicled by D. von Blom, in "Niederländisch-West-Indien" in *Die Ansiedlung von Europäern in den Tropen* [*European Settlement in the Tropics*] (Verein für Sozialpolitik, Vol. 147) even though all these efforts seem to have been a flop. The record: immigrants from the Palatinate and the Basel area, 1749; some arrivals in the 1840s, after the governments of Saxony and Prussia had inquired about sending criminals and poor people there; Württemberg immigrants, 1853-55; and a final colonization effort in 1896. Nearly all of these died, returned to Germany, or forsook farming and went to the capital, Paramaribo.

Von Blom makes only a passing reference to Europeans of many nationalities on the island of Curacao.

Winkler estimates that there were 1,400 Germans in Colombia and 1,100 in Ecuador in 1925. These may have been missionaries or businessmen, since we have seen no reference to actual immigrants.

GERMANIC MIGRATION TO THE SOUTHWEST PACIFIC

AUSTRALIA

Among the non-European countries, only the United States, Brazil, Canada and Argentina received more German-speaking immigrants than Australia.

A large majority of the Germans settled in South Australia, Victoria, New South Wales and Queensland. The number who went to Western Australia was much smaller and includes a disproportionately large percentage of post-1945 immigrants. There were a few thousand German immigrants scattered in various parts of Tasmania, especially around Hobart. The sparsely populated Northern Territory had only a few dozen.

Our coverage is based mostly on the following books, although we included some useful contemporary information received from Liz Twigden of South Australia:

- J. Lyng, *Non-Britishers in Australia: Influence on Population and Progress* (Melbourne: Macmillan & Co. with Melbourne University Press, 1927; 242 pp.); and

- W. D. Borrie, assisted by D. R. G. Packer, *Italians and Germans in Australia: A Study of Assimilation* (Melbourne: F. W. Cheshire for The Australian National University, 1954; 236 pp.)

Both Lyng and Borrie have valuable maps of German settlements, and both also list the names of specific German communities, including some name changes.

South Australia had the first significant number of immigrants, whereas the bulk of the German immigrants to Queensland (which consistently had the largest percentage of German-born from 1881 until at least 1921) arrived later than in the other three states.

The names listed by Clifford Neal Smith in *German-American Genealogical Research Monograph*, Number 7, suggest that nearly one third of the "Old Lutherans" who emigrated in 1838-1854 because they objected to the forced merger of the Lutheran and Reformed Churches into the Evangelical Church went to Australia. They constituted the first large group of Germanic immigrants in South Australia.

While Queensland and South Australia clearly have the largest number of Australians concerned with researching German ancestry, there may be more residents of New South Wales and Victoria with at least one German ancestor. This is because of greater intermarriage among ethnic groups, related to the scattering of the Germans, the transitory presence of gold miners (especially in Victoria, but also in New South Wales) in the early decades of the second half of the nineteenth century, and the twentieth-century phenomenon of urbanization.

There can be a big difference between the place of immigration and the later residence of the immigrants and especially their descendants. Australia is a classic case of this. Victoria benefited the most from this internal migration of German-Australians during much of the nineteenth century, whereas New South Wales seems to have received the largest number of internal migrants since the late nineteenth century, based on inferences from the census statistics.

In 1921 there were over 36,000 German-born residents in Australia, with over 61,000 of the second generation. But the total number of Germanic descendants was much larger, because the Germanic population multiplied so rapidly, as documented by the fact that German-born wives had considerably more children (averaging 5.81) than those of other nationalities, based on Lyng's data.

The overwhelming majority of Germans were Lutherans. On the other hand, the overwhelming majority of Lutherans were Germans, although there was a significant Scandinavian minority in some areas.

The Lutheran Church, initially that of the "Old Lutherans," soon split into many synods, but by 1927 they had been combined into two. The number of pastors in each state, including both synods, for that year was: South Australia, 166; Queensland, 101; Victoria, 64; New South Wales, 39.

In 1914, when the two largest Lutheran groups had 99 parishes, these included 4 in Western Australia, 4 in New Zealand and 1 in Tasmania.

If we look at the proportion of all-German families, we find a clear distinction between South Australia and Queensland, on the one hand, and Victoria and New South Wales, on the other. In the former, the ratio of German-born males to females remained constant at about 1.5:1 during the censuses from 1881 through 1921. But in Victoria and New South Wales, the ratio was constantly higher than 2:1 from 1871 through 1933, wavering around 2.5:1 most of the time.

In 1861 the number of German-born residents in the more populous states was: Victoria, 10,400; South Australia, 8,900; New South Wales, 5,500; Queensland, 2,100.

The large in-migration to Victoria, especially of miners, explains the high German figures for that state. The number of South Australian Germans is reduced both by out-migration and the fact that there were a large number of Australian-born Germans in that state by that time. The percentage of Germans in Queensland, compared to other states, climbed constantly and sharply, at least during the half-century from 1871 to 1921.

In 1891 the number of German-born residents was:

Table 7: German-born Residents in Australia, 1891

Queensland	14,910
Victoria	10,772
New South Wales	9,565
South Australia	8,553
Western Australia	290
Tasmania	918
Northern Territory	3

In addition to those counted in the foregoing as Germans, there were other groups that included German-speakers. From 1871 to 1911 the censuses counted about 5% as many Swiss-born as German-born. In 1921 the figure was considerably higher, but many of the Swiss who went to Australia were not Germanic.

There is also a separate category for Jews. Jewish immigration was about 20-25% of that of Germans during the last 30 years of the nineteenth century, over 50% in 1911, and almost equal in 1921. How many of them were German-speakers is unknown.

With respect to the urban population, Borrie's maps show more Germans in the Greater Melbourne area than any place else in 1891, with the Greater Sydney area second. However, if we lump together the six centers in the general vicinity of Brisbane, southeast Queensland would have had the largest urban population.

According to Jacob Steigerwald, *Tracing Romania's Heterogeneous German Minority from Its Origins to the Diaspora*, many Romanian Germans, especially Danube Swabians, who left for Germany after World War II soon went on to numerous other countries, with some settling in South Australia.

Cornelius J. Dyck, *An Introduction to Mennonite History*, states that some 2,000 Templer Mennonites, who went to Palestine in the 1870s, were deported to Victoria and New South Wales during World War II. He also indicates that a few thousand Dutch Mennonites emigrated to Australia in the 1960s and 1970s. They now live mostly in Sydney, Melbourne and Brisbane. However, while they have the same religious and ethnic roots as the Prussian and Russian Mennonites, they never underwent the process of "Germanicization" because they stayed in the Netherlands.

New South Wales

According to J. Lyng, the German element was stronger in New South Wales than in any other state, except Queensland. This appears to be based on the number of German-born residents, rather than the number of those of German descent. The overwhelming majority of Germans migrated to New South Wales from other states (or New Zealand), rather than directly from Europe, so this was the second or third, not the initial, home of most of the immigrants. However, most of them arrived at a rather late date, with the first sizable group coming from South Australia in the late 1860s. Thus they had had only two generations to multiply, not three as in South Australia. A small group of vine dressers had already arrived in 1838, at the same time that a larger group of Germans went to South Australia. But there was no connection between the two, since they came from different areas and for different reasons.

There was a steady stream of immigrant rural laborers from Germany to New South Wales from the 1840s until 1879, with some interruptions, according to Jenner in Carol Wardale and Margaret Jenner, *German Genealogy Directory*. But these immigrants appear to have been few in number for most of this period, compared to those who settled in South Australia. In any event, there was nothing resembling a concentrated German settlement until the 1860s. Even today, the Germans in New South Wales are more widely scattered than in South Australia, Queensland or even Victoria. Those who came directly from Germany (with no further specification of origin) settled northwest of the Newcastle area, according to Lyng. Those from Queensland established widely scattered settlements, mostly in the northeastern part of the state.

The first substantial internal migration (and probably the largest one), however, came from South Australia. Many of them trekked to the area north of Albury in the 1860s and farther north, around and beyond Temora, in the 1870s. In the 1880s many went up the Murray River and settled in the western part of the state, around and south of Broken Hill. Most were wheat farmers. Some of these were ex-miners (from Victoria as well as New South Wales). The largest number probably came from the Woomera district in western Victoria, where they had already pioneered in low-rainfall farming. Many of both groups had originally come from South Australia.

Lyng's map of the 1920s shows German settlements mostly northwest of Albury, two-thirds of the way to Queensland. Borrie's map of the 1950s shows more in the coastal area, primarily near Sydney and Newcastle, with more scattered settlements farther northeast. He also shows Broken Hill in the west as one of two urban centers. Although Sydney had the most Germans, Germans constituted a much larger percent of the population in the west around Broken Hill.

Queensland

A substantially larger number of Germans immigrated to Queensland than to any other state, but most came at a relatively late time. Between 1861 and 1891 the German-born population of South Australia and Victoria remained fairly constant. In New South Wales it went up by 70%, but in Queensland it jumped 700%.

Thus the recency of immigration is a big help in determining the origin of the Queensland Germans. A large majority of the early settlers came from Pomerania, West Prussia and

Silesia, with quite a few from Württemberg. However, the Ueckermark, which is in eastern Mecklenburg-Vorpommern and northeastern Brandenburg, is mentioned most frequently as a place of origin by Queensland German genealogists. Later immigration came from all parts of Germany, but with the eastern areas apparently still dominant.

Apart from missionaries, the first Germans arrived in 1838-44. These were the only ones who had religious reasons for leaving Germany. By the time the Moreton Bay district of New South Wales became Queensland in 1861, there were already 2,000 Germans there, a significant percentage of the population. However, as a result of very active recruitment by the government of Queensland (offering free passage, i.e., to the so-called assisted settlers), the number of Germans had doubled by 1864 and increased to more than 12,000 in 1881.

Many of the early Germans went to the Toowoomba area (in the mountains west of Brisbane) to work on railroad construction. But a large majority went into farming. Borrie shows an overwhelming concentration to the south, west and north of Brisbane. Lyng also shows a concentration in the Darling Downs area farther west, on the other side of the Great Dividing Range, which hugs the east coast.

There is a much smaller, but still significant, number of Germans in the Maryborough-Bundaberg area, a good 100 miles north of Brisbane, with scattered settlements farther north along the coast (e.g., near Mackay), as well as in the interior.

South Australia

The first sizable group of German immigrants to Australia were "Old Lutherans," who arrived in 1838-39. Although a few seem to have gone to other parts of Australia, most of them settled just north (Klemzig) and east (Hahndorf) of Adelaide. In 1842 an important village was established at Robethal (near Hahndorf). This migration continued through 1854, with the emigrants favoring the United States some years and Australia (mostly South Australia) in others, in a see-saw fashion. Clifford Neal Smith's lists indicate that Australia was favored in 1841-42, 1844-45, 1847-51, and 1854. Most of the immigrants came from the general vicinity of the Oder River and especially from the east of it (Silesia, Brandenburg and Posen, with fewer from Saxony and Pomerania).

Twigden states that according to the 1861 census, about 7% of South Australians were of German extraction. By 1891 this figure had risen to 9%, according to Lyng, despite the substantial out-migration from the colony.

In the late 1840s, a large number of immigrants came from the Harz mountains when the lead and silver mines there experienced economic difficulty. Furthermore, Sorbs from Lusatia began coming to South Australia in 1845 with steadily increasing numbers until 1860. They constitute the largest distinct ethnic minority group in modern Germany. But in South Australia they soon became integrated into the German Lutheran community. Moreover, Rhinelanders settled in the Barossa valley north of Adelaide, where they developed viticulture.

A larger percentage of Germans than any other immigrant group settled in rural areas, mostly east of Adelaide and in the Tanunda region north of Adelaide.

South Australia represented the mother colony for many German settlements in other states. Thousands of Germans went to the gold fields in Victoria after 1851. Some returned, whereas other stayed there or moved on to New South Wales. The small number of early German settlers in Western Australia also came mostly from South Australia.

After 1881, deaths and departures exceeded the number of new immigrants, according to Lyng. But by that time the German settlements were so well established that this became irrelevant. By 1900 over half of the German immigrants went to the city of Adelaide, but they were easily outnumbered by the descendants of the early immigrants, most of whom remained in the rural areas.

There were far more communities that had enough Germans to establish a Lutheran church than in any other colony. In part, this may have been due to the influence of the first immigrants who came for reasons of religious freedom. The Lutherans were all Germans, except for a Scandinavian minority that was distinctly smaller than in Queensland. Many of the later immigrants, especially those who went to Adelaide, either did not join or left the Lutheran church.

During World War I about 70 German place names were changed to English or aboriginal names, although some were changed back again later. This means that the problem of identifying the current name of a locality that originally bore a German name is greater than in most other countries.

The name lists in Borrie's book show that 39% of the Germans naturalized in this colony from 1836 to 1900 came from northeast Germany, 27% from central Germany, 24% from northeast Germany, and the rest from western and southern Germany.

Victoria

In the late 1840s and early 1850s immigrants who came directly from Germany settled in a semicircle around Melbourne, with the first group arriving in the Port Philip district. By 1849 there were Germans in Geelong and soon thereafter in Germantown (now Grovedale). The first large group apparently consisted of Moravian Brethren recruited by a Bremen agent in 1849.

Immigrants from Mecklenburg, Saxony and Silesia settled around Thomastown in 1850. In 1853, Germans (mostly Silesians) settled in the Duncaster and Berwick areas. But in the 1851-1861 decade, large numbers migrated from South Australia to central and western Victoria. Many came to dig for gold. Miners from South Island in New Zealand joined them. The gold fields were mainly around Ballarat, Bendigo and Castlemaine. In the 1857 and 1861 censuses a majority of German-born Australians were in the mining area.

Between 1861 and 1881 the Germanic population decreased significantly, primarily because many miners returned home after the gold rush petered out. However, ex-miners and other migrants from South Australia became wheat farmers, mostly in the Wimmera area around Horsham. Some of the Wimmera Germans moved to the Mallee district. The Wimmera region became the stronghold of Lutheranism in Victoria. Viticulture was introduced into Victoria by a few Swiss in Geelong, but it did not become significant until 1847 when Rhinelanders developed vineyards in the Barrabool Hills.

Many of the miners and later immigrants also went to Melbourne. By 1933 a slight majority of the Victorian Germans were urbanites.

Victoria never had the dense concentrations of Germans found in South Australia. But Borrie estimates that there were 20,000 first- and second-generation Germans in the colony by 1891. About half of that number had been born in Germany, but not all of these migrated directly from Germany to Victoria. The 1921 census counted nearly 100,000 first- and second-generation Germans. By then there must have been quite a few of the third generation already.

Western Australia

In 1947 the percentage of Western Australians who were German-born was only 0.7%, compared to 2% for the whole country. Due to post-World War II immigration, the respective figures for 1971 were 2.5% and 4.3%, respectively. Since immigration from Germany to Western Australia peaked in 1982-83, the percentage may have increased somewhat.

Furthermore, Swiss immigration has increased, so that in 1990-91 it was two-thirds of immigration from Germany. Moreover, the ratio of Austrian to German immigrants has been relatively high. In 1986 there were one-seventh as many Austrian-born as German-born in the five metropolitan local government areas with the largest number of residents from Germanic countries (Stirling, Wanneroo, Perth, Melville, and Gosnells).

In the 1986 census, fewer than 30,000 Western Australians claimed German ancestry. Of these, nearly 7,000 had been born in Germany and over 500 each in the United States and in England.

Nevertheless, this small number has been well documented by Mary Mennicken-Cooley in *The Germans in Western Australia: Innovators, Immigrants, Internees* (Mt. Lawley, Western Australia: Edith Cowan University, 1993), the sole source of our information on this Australian state. Because of the small numbers, however, it is possible only to list the places of origin of specific immigrants or small groups, rather than to offer broad generalization as to the chief places of origin. Among the places of origin that are listed are Bremen, Hamburg, Saxony, Lower Silesia, Baden, Hanover, East Friesland, Schleswig-Holstein, Pomerania, Magdeburg, and Bavaria, as well as Austria and Switzerland. Of the 1841-1903 naturalizations, Prussia is named as the previous place of residence for well over half of those for whom this information is listed (only a minority). But most of northern Germany belonged to Prussia at the time.

Despite the small numbers, there were more Germans naturalized in Western Australia in 1841-1903 than immigrants from any other country. Those who came from Britain were British subjects, so no naturalization was involved. The list of names published in Mennicken-Cooley's book shows that the overwhelming majority were naturalized between 1894 and 1903, with only a few before 1887.

The first few permanent German settlers arrived in the state in 1836 from England. The introduction of regular steamship service from Germany to Fremantle in the 1880s and especially the gold rush of 1884-92 led to a more significant number of immigrants of Germanic origin. However, many of the Germans (especially the miners and to some extent the "Old Lutherans") first settled in the eastern states and moved to Western Australia in the late 1800s and 1900s, while others came from England.

The early German pioneers were mostly farmers and tradesmen who settled throughout the state, especially in the Swan River district just northwest of Perth. When gold was discovered, the wheatbelt town of Katanning in the southwestern part of the state attracted Germans (many of them farmers) from South Australia. The turn-of-the-century immigrants from both the eastern states and Germany settled especially in the Fremantle-Perth area, the southern wheatbelt and around the gold fields (Coolgardie, Kalgoorlie, Kenawa) in the interior of the south central part of the state, with a small number in the northwest in the vicinity of Broome.

Very few immigrants came from Germany during the interwar period, due to the lingering anti-German sentiment, which caused not only German nationals, but also Australians of German descent, to be interned during both World Wars. There is an interesting reference to World War II internees receiving charitable packages from Brazil and Argentina, an indication that relatives and neighbors from Germany had settled on both continents and maintained contact. However, the post-World War II period produced by far the largest wave of German and Swiss immigrants.

The overwhelming majority of Germans were Lutherans, although Scandinavians, Estonians, and Latvians also belonged to this church. But there are isolated references to German Catholics, Baptists, and Moravian Brethren.

NEW ZEALAND

The total number of German-speakers who immigrated to New Zealand, which has a current population of less than 3.5 million, was small. This was even true in terms of percentages. Nevertheless, James N. Bade, ed., *The German Connection: New Zealand and German-speaking Europe in the Nineteenth Century*, states that they were the second largest group of immigrants. He estimates that several hundred thousand New Zealanders have Germanic ancestors.

Nearly all of the information in this section comes from this source. Particularly helpful are the articles by Marian Minson on "Trends in German Immigration to New Zealand," by

Gertraut Maria Stoffel on "The Austrian Connection with New Zealand in the Nineteenth Century," and by Hans-Peter Stoffel on "Swiss Settlers in New Zealand."

For more details, see the articles by James N. Bade on the province of Nelson (the northernmost part of South Island), by Rolf E. Panny on the Lower (i.e., southern) North Island, by Judith Williams on the Bohemian Germans in Puhoi (in the northern part of the North Island) and by Pauline J. Morris on the settlements in the southernmost part of South Island.

The book is a model because of its careful distinction between "German" and "German-speaking." It is also a classic illustration of the importance of a multi-ethnic approach to Germanic genealogy in that it deals carefully with the immigrants from German Poland, Bohemia and Dalmatia (the Adriatic coast of southern Croatia).

The mixture of Germanic and Slavic names in the case of those from Poland and Bohemia show that neighbors belonging to different ethnic groups moved together and that many people with a Germanic (or Slavic) identity were the product of mixed marriages and/or assimilation, even though these events might have occurred centuries ago.

Minson states that the three major waves of Germanic immigration were in 1842-1845, 1861-67 and 1872-86. The first two waves were primarily the product of maritime traders from the Hanseatic League (Hamburg, Bremen), but also from the Austrian Adriatic ports.

These came mostly from Hamburg, Bremen, Hanover, Hesse, Saxony, Holstein and Prussia. The number from southern Germany, Austria and Switzerland was always comparatively small, although they were more important in certain particular areas.

It is interesting to compare these with the major waves in the United States. The first New Zealand wave occurred just before the first major American wave began in 1846. The other two New Zealand waves began about the time when the American Civil War and the Panic (Depression) of 1873 interrupted large-scale immigration to the United States.

The German-speaking migrants to New Zealand were overwhelmingly Lutheran, with two exceptions: the Bohemians in the extreme north and the Poles in the southern part of the South Island.

The first German group settlement was in the Nelson area, one contingent arriving from North Germany (Hamburg, Hanover, Holstein and the Rhineland) in 1843 and the second group from Mecklenburg in 1844. Additional shiploads arrived from 1850 to 1869.

The opening of gold fields in the northern part of Westland province on the west coast of South Island led to an influx of north Germans and Austrians in the 1860s and 1870s. Pomeranians settled in Jackson's Bay Special Settlement in southern Westland province between 1865 and 1880. All of the latter and many of the former group left before long.

More permanent settlements were established in Canterbury province on the east coast, particularly in the Christchurch area, but also in the southeasternmost part of the province. Many Germans arrived in the late 1860s and 1870s under the Assisted Immigration Scheme. The early immigrants came particularly from Hanover, Austria and East Prussia. Others came from Bavaria, Saxony, Moravia and German Poland.

German-speaking immigrants were first attracted to the Otago-Southland region in the 1860s to seek gold. But the first substantial number came in 1872 from German Poland. The overwhelming majority of them were identified as German Poles.

Many of them soon went to the Dunedin area to build the Southern Trunk Railway. By 1873 many had become farmers around Allanton (Greytown until 1895). Waibola Township, somewhat farther south, included a proportionately larger number of German names. The Otago-Southland German-speaking immigrants consisted mostly of nuclear and extended family groups.

German names were also common among immigrants who came to Otago in 1874 from the vicinity of Lunow near the Oder River and to Southland (where a Germantown was founded) in 1875. Settlers from Hanover and Austria were also significant in Canterbury.

While all of the above settlements are on South Island, most of the German-speakers eventually ended up on North Island, which has 2½ times as many residents. The first immigrants to North Island seem to have been Pomeranians, Brandenburgers and Rhinelanders who settled in the province of Hawkes Bay in the southeastern part of the island. Little trace of them has been left.

A more significant concentration was established in Taranaki province (on the west side) by immigrants from Switzerland, Pomerania, Prussia and German Poland. These early settlements have largely disappeared. Toward the end of the nineteenth century, Germans settled farther south in the same province.

The Rangitikei River region (around Marten) on the west coast of Wellington province attracted a large group of Germans. Many German Lutherans from the Neisse River region, who had settled in the Adelaide region in South Australia in 1838, arrived in 1860. Others arrived from Otago province.

The Bohemian Germans (many bearing Czech names) came to Puhoi, north of Auckland, in 1863. They were staunch Catholics from Mies county in the Pilsen district, who spoke the Egerland dialect. Three more groups of immigrants followed in 1866, 1872, and 1876.

Apart from the Bohemians, North Island settlers from the Austro-Hungarian Empire included male Moravians and Austrians who participated in the 1860s gold rush in the southern provinces, as well as families who settled in Canterbury province in the 1870s. However, the largest number of Austrians have always lived in populous Auckland province. But immigrants from the Austro-Hungarian Empire also included Dalmatian Croats, who did not identify themselves as German-speakers.

Most of the Swiss immigrants were German-speakers from southwestern Graubünden canton, close to its border with Ticino, but immigrants also included people who spoke French, Italian, or Romansch. The early arrivals came between 1850 and 1880. There was a very high ratio of males to females (which was also true of non-Swiss miners), which gradually decreased. There was a parallel migration of Swiss to the Australian state of Victoria in 1855-58 to work in the gold fields. Most of them spoke Italian or French. Some migrated onward to the gold fields in New Zealand's South Island. Others came directly from Europe. About half of the first naturalized Swiss in New Zealand seem to have been French or Italian.

The first permanent Swiss settlers, as contrasted with gold-seekers, came to the province of Taranaki (North Island). Those in the 1870s and 1880s were mostly German-speakers from Graubünden. Later ones came from Central Switzerland. In 1874 nearly 25% of the New Zealand Swiss lived in this province. In 1886 only 54% of the Swiss lived on North Island, but by 1916 this had increased to 89%. The decline on South Island must have been largely mining-related. On the other hand, almost 43% of the New Zealand Swiss lived in Taranaki province in 1916, with another 33% in Auckland and Wellington provinces, which contain the two largest cities (of the same name) in the country.

There was significant migration between New Zealand and Australia: mostly with Victoria in the case of miners, and mostly with South Australia in the case of farmers (especially from the Nelson area).

By the mid-1880s quite a few people of German ancestry lived in the major cities of Auckland (especially north Germans, but also Bavarians, Swiss, Saxons, and Austrians), Wellington (Swiss, north and northeast Germans), Christchurch (Bavarians, Moravians, Swiss, Austrians, "Poles," and north Germans) and Dunedin ("Poles" and northeast Germans). People from Hanover constituted a particularly significant component of the North Germans in most areas.

The largest percentage of urban residents who were of Germanic origin was found in the medium-sized city of Palmerston North in northern Wellington province.

FORMER GERMAN COLONIES AND PROTECTORATES IN THE PACIFIC

Samoa

According to Bade, this was the only island where permanent German immigrants were numerous enough to have left a significant number of descendants, as evidenced by German names in the telephone books, even though the number of Germans was only 248 in 1908. Germany, Britain and the United States acquired contractual rights to ports in 1878-79, but not until 1899 did Germany finally obtain Western Samoa.

Papua New Guinea and the Western Pacific Islands

The German government established a protectorate over northeast New Guinea in the 1880s. The protectorate included the Bismarck Archipelago, Kaiser-Wilhelms-Land, the German Solomon Islands, the Mariana Islands (exclusive of Guam), the Caroline Islands and the Marshall Islands. This protectorate actually included the largest number of Germans in the South Seas, but there is little evidence of permanent immigration. Nevertheless, the hopes were reflected in such place names as Neu-Pommern and Neu-Mecklenburg.

However, there was a large enough settlement in Pohnpei (*Ponape*) to have a German church at one time.

The Solomon Islands are now independent, as is Belau (Palau), but most of the islands, excluding New Guinea, now belong to the Federation of Micronesia. Papua New Guinea is a combination of the former German and British possessions in the eastern half of this large island.

GERMANIC MIGRATION TO AFRICA

OVERVIEW

The overwhelming majority of German immigrants went to South Africa. The next largest number settled in Namibia, which was German South-West Africa for a generation before World War I. A modest number went to other former German colonies, primarily to German East Africa, now mainland Tanzania.

The Germans in Cameroon and Togo, which were pre-World War I West African German colonies, numbered only in the hundreds. Included were some plantation owners and livestock farmers in Cameroon. The northwestern part of former German Cameroon became a part of Nigeria in 1961.

A tiny handful of job-seekers or adventurers went from South Africa to Rhodesia (now Zimbabwe and Zambia) or British East Africa (now Kenya).

There is a record of some German immigrants to Algeria, which had an estimated 7,500 Germans in 1925. These may have been augmented by some German members of the French Foreign Legion who may have chosen to stay there after completion of their service. The number of Germans who served in Africa with the French Foreign Legion in the 1920s exceeded the total number of Germans in Africa who lived north of Namibia, according to data on pages 18-23 of Winkler's *Statistisches Handbuch des gesamten Deutschtums* [*Statistical Handbook of All German Regions*]. The fact that there were also an estimated 6,800 Germans in Morocco at the time strengthens the supposition. However, we have no explanation for the estimated 11,000 Germans in Egypt, nor do we have any knowledge of any permanent immigration to that country.

Most of the Germans in North Africa were probably there for business reasons and, in the case of Egypt, perhaps scholarly reasons. Such people may have lived in the country in question for a long period, so that pertinent vital records may exist. But it seems likely that only a small percentage stayed there permanently.

SOUTH AFRICA

Werner Schmidt-Pretoria, in his book, *Der Kulturalanteil des Deutschtums am Aufbau des Burenvolke* [*The Cultural Contributions of Germans to the Development of the Boer People*], argues that some 55-65% of the original Boer forefathers were Germans, almost all of them soldiers in the service of the Dutch East Indies Co. He acknowledges, however, that the male-female ratio among Germans who settled in South Africa in the early centuries was 20:1. Hence, there were few German foremothers. Those German veterans who got married almost always had wives of Dutch, or later Dutch-German mixed, descent. However, a few married Huguenots who had fled to Germany and lived there for several generations before going to South Africa.

But J. Hoge, in "Personalia of the Germans at the Cape, 1652-1806" in *Yearbook for South African History*, 1946, argues that the percentage of Germans in the service of the Dutch East Indies Co. was not as high as estimated (24% in 1716, 64% in 1767), because Schmidt-Pretoria's well-documented work was based on the incomplete and inaccurate data gathered by H. T. Colenbringer.

However, E. L. Schnell, in a recent book, *For Men and Women Must Work; An account of German immigration to the Cape with special reference to the German Military Settlers of 1857 and the German immigrants of 1858*, cites statistics and estimates from various sources that suggest that slightly over a quarter of the Cape residents in 1807 were of German origin.

One problem is that because of inter-ethnic intermarriage in all immigrant countries (and especially so in pre-1857 South Africa), all figures that total 100% are misleading. The number of Caucasian Cape residents with at least one German ancestor clearly exceeds 50%. On the other hand, the number of those of predominantly German background is much smaller and the number of those who have retained a sense of Germanic identity still smaller.

Almost all the Lutherans in South Africa were Germans, although there was a Scandinavian minority. However, because of intermarriage and lack of permission to build a Lutheran church until 1779 according to Schnell, many Germans (or at least their mixed-descent children) joined the Reformed Church.

German immigration was heaviest in 1750-1800. A large majority came from the North German plains (from the Dutch-German borderland to East Prussia), where the Low German dialect (a cross between German and Dutch) is spoken, facilitating communication and assimilation. But there was also a Württemberg regiment (1786-1808) and there are some references to origins in Bavaria, Alsace, Bohemia, the Palatinate, Breslau and Leipzig.

Schmidt-Pretoria also cites H. T. Colenbringer's article (translated from the Dutch into German by Franz Thierfelder as "Die Herkunft der Buren" ["The Origins of the Boer People"]) as stating that 24% of the burghers in 1657-62 were Germans, according to the *Freibücher* [books of free men, who were property owners]. Incomplete records for 1718-91 show that about half were Germans.

According to Schnell's recent book, 63% of the deeds of burghership between 1817 and 1851 (thus spanning the bridge between the early assimilated Germans and the later ones who retained their sense of a German identity) were granted to Germans. Moreover, nearly 60% of the private teachers in South Africa in the nineteenth century were Germans. The data show that nearly all of them came from predominantly Protestant areas, but scattered from Latvia to Alsace to Switzerland. Another group he mentions are the *Herrnhuter*, or Moravian Brethren, missionaries (1737), a Germanicized denomination of Czech origin.

Colenbringer (Dutch original, "De Afkomst der Boeren," published by Het Nederlandsche Verbond) and George McCall Theal seem to be the leading authorities on the origins of South Africans. Theal's work was first published in two volumes in Cape Town in 1896 and later in three English volumes as *History and Ethnography of Africa South of the*

Zambesi, from the Settlement of the Portuguese at Sofala in September 1505 to the Conquest of Cape Colony by the British in September 1795.

Schmidt-Pretoria also lists the following article on German Jews in South Africa in a footnote: S. A. Rochlin, "Die ersten deutschen Juden in Südafrika" ["The First German Jews in South Africa"], in *Jahrbuch der jüdisch-literarischen Gesellschaft* [*Yearbook of the Jewish Literary Society*], Vol. 21.

However, these early German settlers, whatever the percentage, have long since been totally assimilated, so that dealing with their family history would be tantamount to covering all of South African genealogy, which is far beyond our scope. The extent of assimilation is illustrated by the fact that not a single surname on the 1780 Lutheran congregation roll could be found in the 1860 list, as noted by Schnell.

The history of those South Africans who have retained a distinct ethnic identity begins in the 1850s. The most detailed treatment is Johannes Spanuth's "Britisch Kaffraria und seine deutsche Siedlungen" ["British Kaffraria and Its German Settlements"] in *Schriften des Vereins für Sozialpolitik* [*Publications of the Society for Social Betterment*], Vol. 147, Part 4. Briefer accounts are in English-language histories by T. R. H. Davenport and by Donald Denoon et al. Our information is based mostly on Spanuth. The more extensive work by Schnell was not available to us, except for short excerpts dealing mostly with the pre-1857 period.

The first settlers were soldiers of the (English) King's German Legion, which was dissolved before going into action, since the Crimean War ended. They were given the choice of being mustered out and transported to any place in the world.

Some 8,000 men were willing to settle in British Kaffraria (now the southeastern part of Cape Province) as military settlers. They agreed to bring their families or to get married. Despite mass marriages before departure, only 2,400 Legionnaires arrived in 1857. They brought only 330 wives and daughters with them, according to T. R. H. Davenport, *South Africa: A History*.

However, they were not farmers at heart. Most asked to go to India for military service and nearly half of them did. About one third of those sent to India later returned to the Cape Colony, but they scattered to the four winds. Thus this scheme had to be regarded as a failure and the military settlement in Ciskei, i.e., the area on this (west) side of the Kei River, was dissolved. Quite a few of their village names indicate origins from Brandenburg or northwest Germany, and there were also some from Hesse.

The government soon made arrangements to recruit German civilian settlers, providing them with free passage, to be repaid later. Some 2,700 arrived in 1858-59. Ken André reports that most of the 444 families who sailed from Hamburg to East London (South Africa) in 1858-59 came from Pomerania. Other sources indicate that 60-80 of them are believed to have moved to other parts of South Africa. Schnell also indicates an afterflow of German immigrants through 1862.

The largest percentage came because of the desire to own their own farms. This was impossible for most of them in Germany, especially in the areas where most of the land belonged to large estates. This was especially true of Mecklenburg and the Prussian provinces to the east of it. Smaller numbers came from such places as Hanover, Bavaria, Baden, and Silesia.

The census of December 31, 1859, listed 1,494 German civilians and 1,165 Legionnaires. According to Spanuth, those figures understate the total number of Germans, because they did not include those who resided east of the Keiskama River (Transkei), an area that was not part of Kaffraria at the time, nor those who went elsewhere to find work.

Few of the Legionnaires were farmers, but some were in middle-class urban occupations and others moved to other parts of South Africa.

After a rough start, the villages prospered, due to the discovery of gold in the 1860s (when Kaffraria also became a part of Cape Colony), which led to more demand for foodstuffs and other goods. Some farm villages remained entirely or largely German, while others (primarily administrative centers) soon had a mixed population. There was a significant German minority in the towns in eastern Cape Province.

After the Transkei region, between the original Kaffraria and Natal, was annexed, more Germans moved to trading stations or even native villages in that area.

By around 1880, isolated individual farms began to replace the European-style villages, a change that was still in progress in 1914, although the vast majority of farmers appear to have moved away from villages by then.

A few of the Kaffrarian Germans bought farms in the Orange Free State. An even smaller number migrated to German South-West Africa, Rhodesia or British East Africa.

In 1878-79 there was another wave of German settlers. Schnell identifies the later waves as occurring in 1877 and 1883. Many settled on the sandy plains near Cape Town, while others went to the vicinity of King William's Town in Kaffraria. There was a small afterflow in the immediately following years, but virtually no German immigration during the two decades before World War I.

The most concentrated Germanic settlement continues to be in a semi-circular area around East London, but especially to the northwest toward Stutterheim (ca. 50 miles away).

There may be an even larger number of residents of German descent in the Cape Town area. However, because they represent a more scattered minority in a more densely populated region, they are less likely to have retained a Germanic identity.

Ken V. André has written a 400-page work, *10 Generations, 1720-1990: Some Aspects of German Immigration to the Eastern Cape*. He has incidentally also done smaller studies based on visits to Australia, Chile and Wisconsin.

With respect to the much smaller number in other provinces, Maurice C. Evans (in an article on Natal, translated into German by G. von Poellnitz and published in 1913 in Part 3 of the *Schriften* already mentioned) refers to diverse missionary activity in Natal, including Trappist Catholics, Moravian Brethren, and Lutherans.

NAMIBIA

Most of our information about what was German South-West Africa from 1884 to World War I comes from two sources: (1) Donald Denoon with Balan Nyeko and the advice of J. B. Webster, *Southern Africa Since 1900*, and (2) Jan H. Hofmayr (with the 2nd rev. ed. prepared by J. P. Cope), *South Africa*.

South-West Africa became a German protectorate in 1884, although German missionaries had been active there since 1814.

The Herrero and Nama tribes resisted the Germans, especially in 1890-94. After a significant number of German settlers had started arriving, there was a more serious uprising in 1903-05, which was ruthlessly crushed by the Germans. Small-scale local resistance began as early as 1896 and did not end until 1908.

The result was that South-West Africa was largely depopulated, except for the Ovambo territory in the north, which was unaffected by the Germans.

Apart from the civilian immigrants, many German soldiers decided to remain in the country. By 1914 there were about 15,000 Germans in the country, attracted mainly by the discovery of gold.

Many Germans left or were deported after World War I. Nevertheless, Winkler estimates that there were still 10,000 Germans in the country in 1925. Furthermore, German remained a language of instruction and one of the country's three official languages even in the 1920s, after the area had become a South African mandate.

TANZANIA

There is an abundance of literature on the former German East Africa, despite its small European population. There were 4,107 Germans among 5,356 Europeans in the colony in 1913. Winkler estimates the number of Germans in 1925, when it had become a British mandate, at 2,000.

This colony represents a classic example of the conflict between commercial interests concerned with trade and those who sought colonies for the sake of settlement. Bismarck, who was not favorably inclined toward colonies, especially settler colonies, nevertheless declared what was known as Tanganyika until its union with Zanzibar in 1964 to be a German protectorate in 1884, when the domestic electoral advantage of doing so became apparent.

The pressure for the establishment of colonies came from the middle class, which desired colonies for settlers. Despite his contempt for this group, Bismarck immediately granted a charter to the Deutsche Ostafrika Gesellschaft [German East Africa Co.], or DOAG, to rule the area, as if to get the matter off his hands. The company proceeded with settlement forthwith, but in 1891 the German government reluctantly assumed responsibility for governing the area because of the DOAG's ruthless behavior and near-insolvency.

Settlement occurred first along the coastal area, then in the temperate northern highlands bordering Kenya, and thereafter in central and, to a lesser extent, southern German East Africa.

The propaganda arm of the DOAG had its strongest support in the kingdom of Saxony, according to Fritz Ferdinand Müller, *Deutschland-Zanzibar-Ostafrika: Geschichte einer Kolonialeroberung* [*Germany-Zanzibar-East Africa: History of a Colonial Conquest*]. It also had strong support in Bavaria, Brandenburg, Silesia, and Baden. It seems logical to suppose that most of the settlers would have come from the areas where the colonization scheme was promoted most actively.

The major conflict with the Hehe and Fiti tribes in 1891-98, due to German land-grabbing, may have stunted the growth of German population in central German East Africa. However, this area was also much less conducive to European settlement than the north, due to its climate.

The large-scale Maji Maji rebellion of 1905-07 against the hut tax, which resulted in forced labor as a practical matter, also occurred in this area and may have had an even greater effect on settlement potential.

The scorched earth policy of the German army in this war resulted in the appointment of the first civilian governor. He immediately instituted reforms greatly benefiting the Africans. These were opposed by the settlers, who eventually forced his resignation but could not reverse the reforms.

The revolt and the reaction to it also re-ignited the conflict between the settlers and the international traders, who favored an African small-holder peasant economy. The German government supported the latter.

Actually, one cannot accurately describe the German population in Tanzania accurately in these terms. There were two groups of settlers with differing interests: the plantation owners and those with more modest-sized farms.

Albert F. Calvert, in *German East Africa*, describes three plantation areas:

- the Usambara highlands in the north,
- along the central rail line leading to Lake Tanganyika and the Rufiji River somewhat to the south, and
- along the southern coast near the port of Lindi.

He mentions isolated plantations in other areas.

Although there were initially cotton, coffee, rubber, kapok and sisal plantations, H. H. Y. Kaniki, editor for the Historical Society of Tanzania, in *Tanzania under Colonial Rule*, states that by 1914 European agriculture consisted chiefly of sisal plantations and coffee grown by the smaller European landholders.

According to the German population map (plate 219 in Calvert's book), there were only seven districts with at least 100 Europeans: four along the Kenyan border, where 1,222 whites lived (the largest number in the Moshi district), two in the central area (with 803 Europeans, 618 of them in the Dar-es-Salaam district and the others in the Morogoro district immediately to the west); and one in the southeast near Lake Nyasa (with 118).

Only in the Moshi district and the coastal Dar-es-Salaam districts did Europeans constitute 5% of the population.

In terms of occupation, we find that only 25% were planters and farmers. The others were engineers, mechanics and laborers (20%), merchants and traders (15%), government officials (16%), missionaries, including Lutherans, Catholics and Moravian Brethren (14%), and military and civilian support personnel (5%). The engineers, mechanics and laborers worked on railroad construction and possibly also in mining.

This breakdown offers clues concerning the makeup of the German population in the various other German colonies, protectorates and even the North African countries that had never been under German domination, despite obvious and substantial differences among them.

During World War I, when there was prolonged military action in German East Africa, many settlers and missionaries abandoned the farms and plantations that had been destroyed. This reduced the European population by half during World War I.

Nevertheless, many Germans returned after the war. They were the dominant group of Europeans until World War II in what had become a British mandate. Even today, there are still a noticeable number of Germans in Dar-es-Salaam and the northern plantations.

CAMEROON

There were a small number of German cacao and rubber plantation owners, as well as some cattle farmers, in Cameroon. Germans are known to have lived in Douala (*Duala*), Buea (*Buëa*), and Victoria. The stock farmers were mostly in the Adamowa (*Adamáua*) region straddling the current border between Cameroon and Nigeria. However, the total German population never quite rose to 1,000.

ALGERIA

In 1845 French agents were hired to recruit German immigrants for Brazil. However, the Germans kept arriving at Dunkirk long after the quota had been overfilled. In 1846 the French government provided free transportation to Algeria for 900 of the stranded, destitute Germans. Since many of those who went to Brazil came from the Hunsrück and Trier districts of the southern Rhineland, it is possible that some of those who ended up in Algeria may have also originated there.

GERMANIC MIGRATION TO ASIA

No country in Asia ever had a substantial number of German residents, but the largest number lived in Asian Turkey (Asia Minor) and China. Wilhelm Winkler estimates that in 1925, Palestine, Indonesia and the "British East Indies" (which included what are now India, Pakistan, Sri Lanka, Myanmar and possibly Hong Kong) each had about 2,000 Germans, with about 1,000 in Japan. At least some of those in Palestine were Templer Mennonites. Those in the other countries were probably mostly people involved with commerce.

CHINA

In 1898-99 Germany obtained a 99-year lease over Jiaozhou (*Kiautschou*) in the southern part of the Shandong peninsula (eastern part of the state by that name). It asserted a sphere of influence over a larger area.

According to *Meyers Kleines Konversations-Lexikon* [*Meyer's Small Conversational Encyclopedia*], there were 3,298 Germans in this briefly held "German Hong Kong" in 1905. This territory had a Protestant and a Catholic church. Most of the Germans were engaged in commerce.

A second Chinese city that has indirect German connections is Harbin (*Charbin*) in Manchuria (now in Heilongjiang province). Thousands of Russian Germans fled across the Soviet-Chinese border in the late 1920s and stayed in Harbin for a while, until they could find a new homeland (mostly in Canada and Latin America).

TURKEY (ASIA MINOR)

Some Russian Germans, particularly Templar Mennonites who were later deported to Australia, established temporary colonies in Asia Minor, with Palestine as their ultimate goal. However, the Germans who were there in the twentieth century were probably mostly commercial and professional personnel.

REFERENCES (See bibliography for full citations if not shown)

Willi Paul Adams. *Die deutschsprachige Auswanderung in die Vereinigten Staaten: Berichte über Forschungsstand und Quellenbestände.* [*Emigration of German-Speakers to the United States: Report on Research and Sources*]. Berlin: John F. Kennedy Institut für Nordamerikastudien, Freie Universität Berlin. 1980.

Ken V. André. *1720-1990: Some Aspects of German Immigration to the Eastern Cape.*

James N. Bade, ed. *The German Connection: New Zealand and German-speaking Europe in the Nineteenth Century.* Auckland/Melbourne/New York/Toronto: Oxford University Press. 1993.

Annette K. Burgert, "Are Your Pennsylvania Dutch Ancestors Really Swiss?" and "Selected Bibliography for Swiss Research in German and French Territories," in *The German Connection* (1st quarter 1995).

Albert F. Calvert. *German East Africa.* Originally, London: T. Werner Laurie, Ltd., 1917. Reprinted, New York: Negro Universities Press. 1970. 122 pp. + photos, diagrams and maps.

Liga Chileno-Alemana, comp. *Los Alemanes en Chile en su primer centenario: resumen histórior de la colonización alemana de las provincias del sur Chile.* [*The Germans in Chile on Their First Centennial: Historical Summary of the German Colonization of the Southern Provinces of Chile*]. Santiago, comp., 1950.

A. H. Chote. *German Community in Western Australia.* Typescript in Battye Library, Perth. 1973.

Armin Clasen. "Deutsche Auswanderung nach Chile: 1850-52; 1853-56; 1857-1875" ["German Emigration to Chile: 1850-52; 1853-56; 1857-1875"], in *Niedersäschsische Familienkunde.* Mar. 1957-Jan. 1959.

Patricia Cloos and Jürgen Tampke. *Greetings from the Land Where Milk and Honey Flow: The German Immigration to New South Wales, 1838-1858.*

T. R. H. Davenport, *South Africa: A History.* London: Macmillan. 1977.

Donald Denoon with Balan Nyeko and the advice of J. B. Webster. *Southern Africa Since 1900.* New York: Praeger Publishers. 1973. 242 pp.

Cornelius J. Dyck, ed. *An Introduction to Mennonite History*, 2nd ed. Scottdale, PA/ Kitchener/ON: Herald Press. 1981. 452 pp. + maps and diagram.

Europa Kurier Printing, Ltd. (ed.) *200 Jahre Geschichte der deutschsprachigen Gemeinschaft in Australien, 1788-1988.* [*200-Year History of the German-speaking Community in Australia, 1788-1988*]. Sydney: Europa Kurier. 1988.

Lester Firth and Murton Ptg, Ltd. *Barossa Valley Heritage Study.* Adelaide: Lutheran Publishing House. 1981.

Eckhart G. Franz, compiler. *Hessische Truppen im amerikanischen Unabhängigkeitskrieg (HETRINA).* [*Hessian Troops in the American Revolution (HETRINA project)*]

Alfred Funke. *Die Besiedlung des östlichen Südamerika mit besonderer Berücksichtigung des Deutschtums.* [*The Colonization of Eastern South America with Particular Attention to the Germans*]. Inaugural doctoral dissertation at Friedrich-Wilhelms Universität Halle-Wittenburg. Printed by Gebauer Schwetschke, Druckerei und Verlag m.b.H., Halle a.S., 1902. 48 pp.

Howard B. Furer. *The Germans in America, 1607-1970.* Dobbs Ferry, NY: Oceana Publications. 1973.

Goethe Institut. *The German Network in Australia.* Melbourne: Contemporary Press. 1992.

Franz Goldner. *Austrian Emigration, 1938 to 1945* (New York. Frederick Ungar Publishing Co. 1979. 212 pp.

Ian Harmstorf and Michael Cigler. *The Germans in Australia.* Melbourne: AE Press. 1985.

Georg Hiller. *Einwanderung und Kolonisation in Argentinien* [*Immigration and Colonization in Argentina*], Vol. 1: *Einwanderung und Einwanderungspolitik.* [*Immigration and Immigration Policy*]. Berlin: Dietrich Reimer (Ernst Vohsen) Verlagsbuchhandlung. 1912. 155 pp.

Jan H. Hofmayr (2nd rev. ed. prepared by J. P. Cope). *South Africa.* New York/Toronto: McGraw-Hill Book Co., Inc. 1952. 253 pp.

Preston E. James. *Brazil.* New York: Odyssey Press. 1942, 1946. 262 pp.

Norbert Jansen. *Nach Amerika! Geschichte der liechtensteinischen Auswanderung nach den Vereinigten Staaten von Amerika.* [*To America! History of Emigration from Liechtenstein to the United States of America*]. Vaduz: Verlag des Historischen Vereins für das Fürstentum Liechtenstein. 1976.

K. Kaerger. *Landwirtschaft und Kolonisation im Spanischen Amerika* [*Agriculture and Colonization in Spanish America*], Vol. 1: *Die La Plata Staaten.* [*The States of La Plata*]. Leipzig. 1907.

H. H. Y. Kaniki, ed. *Tanzania under Colonial Rule.* London: Longman Group, Ltd., for the Historical Society of Tanzania. 1980.

Gerhard S. Koop. *Pioneer Years in Belize.* Translation by author of *Pionier Jahre in Britisch Honduras.* Belize City: author, 1991. 133 pp.

Irene Enns Kroeker. "Immigration (Paraguay)," in *Preservings.* No. 4, July 1994. Steinbach, Manitoba, Canada: Hanover/Steinbach Historical Society, Inc. Steinbach, MB, Canada K0A 2A0.

Hugo Kung. *Chile und die deutschen Colonien.* [*Chile and the German Colonies*]. Leipzig: Klinkhardt. 1891.

Henry Lange. *Süd-Brasilien.* [*South Brazil*]. Leipzig. 1886.

Augustin Lodewyckx. *Die Deutschen in Australien.* [*Germans in Australia*]. Stuttgart. 1932.

R. Lubetzky, "Sectoral Development and Stratification in Tanganyika, 1890-1914," mimeographed for the 1972 Universities Social Science Conference in Nairobi and frequently cited as a source on population matters.

Wilhelm Lütge, Werner Hoffmann and Karl Wilhelm Körner. *Geschichte des Deutschtums in Argentinien.* [*History of the Germans in Argentina*]. Buenos Aires. 1955.

Peter Marschalck. *Inventar der Quellen zur Geschichte der Wanderungen, besonders der Auswanderung, in Bremer Archiven.* Bremen: Self-published. 1986. Part of series *Veröffentlichungen aus dem Staatsarchiv der Freien Hansestadt Bremen.* [*Inventory of the Sources Related to the History of Migration and Especially Emigration Found in the Bremen Archives*]

Mary Mennicken-Cooley. *The Germans in Western Australia: Innovators, Immigrants, Internees.* Mt. Lawley, Western Australia: Edith Cowan University. 1993. 156 pp.
> Extensive research based on the national and state Australian Archives, reports of the Australian Bureau of Statistics, the Censuses of the Commonwealth of Australia for various years, publications of the Australian Department of Immigration, Local Government and Ethnic Affairs, newspapers, libraries, church records, and books.

Meyers Kleines Konversations-Lexikon, 7th ed. [*Meyer's Small Conversational Encyclopedia*]. 6 vols. Leipzig/Vienna: Bibliographisches Institut. 1908-09. (8th ed. 3 vols. 1931)

Olga K. Miller. *Migration, Emigration, Immigration: Principally to the United States and in the United States.*

Eduard Moritz. *Die Deutschen am Kap unter der holländischen Herrschaft, 1652-1806.* Weimar. [*The Germans at the Cape Under the Dutch Government*]. 1938.

Michael George Mulhall. *Rio Grande do Sul and its German colonies.* London. 1873.

Fritz Ferdinand Müller. *Deutschland-Zanzibar-Ostafrika: Geschichte einer Kolonialeroberung.* [*Germany-Zanzibar-East Africa: History of a Colonial Conquest*]. Berlin: Rutten & Loening. 1959.

Pomerode: sua história, sua cultura, suas tradições [*Pomerode: Its History, Its Culture, Its Traditions*], Historical Series, Volume 5. Pomerode, SC, Brazil: Prefeitura Municipal de Pomerode/Fundação Cultural de Pomerode. 1991. 60 pp.

C. A. Price. *German Settlers in South Australia.* Melbourne. 1945.

George Rath. *The Black Sea Germans in the Dakotas.* Freeman, SD: Pine Hill Press. 1977. 435 pp.

La Vern J. Rippley. *The German-Americans* Boston: Twayne Publishers. 1976.

Richard Sallet. *Russian-German Settlements in the United States.* tr. La Vern J. Rippley and Armand Bauer. Fargo: North Dakota Institute for Regional Studies. 1974. 207 pp. plus map.

Harry Leonard Sawatzky. *They Sought a Country: Mennonite Colonization in Mexico.* Berkeley: University of California Press. 1971. Includes a chapter on migration to Belize.

D. Schäfer. *Kolonialgeschichte.* [*Colonial History*]. Leipzig. 1906.

Leo Schelbert. *Swiss Migration to America: the Swiss Mennonites.* New York: Arno Press. 1980.

Walter Schmiedehaus. *Die Altkolonier-Mennoniten in Mexico.* [*The Old Colonial Mennonites in Mexico*]. Winnipeg: CMBC Publications. 1982. 216 pp.

Werner Schmidt-Pretoria. *Der Kulturanteil des Deutschums am Aufbau des Burenvolkes.* [*The Cultural Contributions of Germans to the Development of the Boer People*]. Hanover: Hahnsche Verlagsbuchhandlung. 1938. 303 pp. + map.

E. L. Schnell. *For Men and Women Must Work; An account of German immigration to the Cape with special reference to the German Military Settlers of 1857 and the German immigrants of 1858.* Cape Town: Maskew Miller Ltd.

Ferdinand Schröder. *Die deutsche Einwanderung nach Süd-Brasilien bis zum Jahr 1859.* [*German Immigration to South Brazil up to the Year 1859*]. Berlin. 1831.

William Schroeder and Helmut T. Huebert. *Mennonite Historical Atlas.* Winnipeg: Springfield Publishers. 1990. 133 pp.

John M. Spalek. *Guide to the Archival Materials of the German-Speaking Emigration to the United States After 1933.* Charlottesville, VA: University Press for the Bibliographical Society of the University of Virginia. 1978.

Fritz Sudhaus. *Deutschland und die Auswanderung nach Brazilien im 19. Jahrhundert.* [*Germany and the Emigration to Brazil in the 19th Century*]. Hamburg. 1940.

Jürgen Tampke and Colin Doxford. *Australia Willkommen: A History of the Germans in Australia.* New South Wales University Press. 1990.

George McCall Theal. *History and Ethnography of Africa South of the Zambesi, from the Settlement of the Portuguese at Sofala in September 1505 to the Conquest of Cape Colony by the British in September 1795.* London: George Allen & Unwin, Ltd. 1923. 3 English vols.

Berend von Tiesenhausen. *Deutsche in Australien.* [*Germans in Australia*]. Leipzig, Lahe & Co. 1938.

Liz Twigden. *Letter of July 16, 1994.* Torrensville, SA.

Verein für Sozialpolitik. *Schriftenreihe des Vereins für Sozialpolitik* [*Publications of the Society for Social Betterment*], Vol. 147; Part 1: *Deutsch-Ostafrika als Siedlungsgebiet für Europäer unter Berücksichtigung Britisch-Ostafrikas und Nyassalands* [*German East Africa as a Settlement Region Regarding British East Africa and Nyasaland*], 1912, 114 pp. + map; Part 2: *Die Ansiedlung von Europäern in den Tropen* [*European Settlement in the Tropics*], 1912, 171 pp.; Part 3: *Die Ansiedlung von Europäern in den Tropen* [*European Settlement in the Tropics*], 1913, 162 pp.; Part 4: *Britisch-Kaffraria und seine deutschen Siedlungen* [*British Kaffraria and its German Settlements*], 1914, 82 pp. + map; Part 5: *Die deutschen Kolonisten im brasilianischen Staate Espirito Santo* [*The German Colonists in the Brazilian State of Espirito Santo*], 1915, 149 pp. + photos and maps. Munich/Leipzig: Verlag von Duncker & Humblot.

> Part 2 covers settlement in Central America, Lesser Antilles, Dutch West Indies, Dutch East Indies. Part 3 covers settlement in Natal, Rhodesia, British East Africa and Uganda. Part 4 covers British Kaffraria, a region of the Cape Province of South Africa.

Mack Walker. *Germany and the Emigration, 1816-1885.* Cambridge, MA: Harvard University Press. 1964. 284 pp.

Johann Wappäus. *Handbuch der Geographie und Statistik des Kaiserreichs Brasilien.* [*Handbook of Geography and Statistics of the Brazilian Empire*]. Leipzig. 1871.

J. B. Webster. *Southern Africa Since 1900.* New York: Praeger Publishers. 1973. 242 pp.

Maralyn A. Wellauer. *German Immigration to America in the Nineteenth Century: A Genealogist's Guide.* Milwaukee: Roots International. 1985.

Wilhelm Winkler. *Statistisches Handbuch des gesamten Deutschtums.* [*Statistical Handbook of All German Regions*]. Berlin: Verlag Deutsche Rundschau G.m.b.H. 1927.

George F. W. Young. *Germans in Chile: Immigration and Colonization, 1849-1914.* New York: Center for Migration Studies. 1974. 234 pp.

Gordon Young. *Early Barossa Settlements.* 1978.

Chapter XIV

GENEALOGICAL RECORDS RELATING TO GERMAN-SPEAKING ANCESTORS IN EUROPE

This chapter presents a brief introduction to the kinds of records available for genealogical research in German-speaking areas of Europe. Once you understand the kinds of records that are available, you can better utilize the next chapter, which contains more detailed information about the kinds of records and their location for each country of Europe. See Chapters II, III and IV regarding records available in the United States, and Chapters IV, V and VI for other immigrant countries.

How to Find My German Ancestors and Relatives by Dr. Heinz F. Friedrichs, one of the leading German authorities, presents a brief overview of the subject presented here. Although the records listed below refer particularly to Germany, similar records (sometimes using different terms) can be found in German-speaking countries and sometimes for the German-speaking enclaves in other countries.

KINDS OF RECORDS AVAILABLE

Many types of records helpful for your genealogical research can be found in Germany. Although some records were destroyed during various wars or by fires, the vast majority of records are intact and can be found mainly in the local and state archives or at the local parishes. Since Germany has no central index to its records, you must refer to the state archive that contains regional records of interest to you, as well as checking local and church archives. Church records are nearly always the most useful resource, at least for information prior to the 1870s. Civil registration and wills can also be very useful. These and other kinds of records are described in the following checklist. Some records are only found in a few regions. Larry Jensen mentions a few other, less common kinds of records in his handbooks.

Many of the records have been microfilmed by the Family History Library (FHL). Contact a local Family History Center to see what is available for localities where your German-speaking ancestors lived.

1. **Relatives of ancestors** who remained in Germany. You may learn of them from German genealogical societies, from the local parish church, from a local German phone book (available at FHL, Immigrant Genealogical Society, etc.) or *Glenzdorfs*. They may be able to provide you with a great deal of information.

2. **Church records** (*Kirchenbücher* or *Kirchenregister*). Earliest church records for a parish may date back to 1650, and as early as 1480 for a few churches. Catholic Church records were written in Latin, while Evangelical (Reformed, Lutheran) records were written in German. Gothic script was used until about 1920. The Evangelical Church was established by the formal union of the Reformed (Calvinist) and Lutheran Churches in 1817 in Prussia by a royal edict. The merger took place in the rest of Germany soon thereafter, mostly voluntarily. Some Lutherans protested and continue to worship as Old Lutherans (*Altlutheraner*).

   Members of other German religions included Jews (*Juden*), Mennonites (*Mennoniten*), Baptists, Brethren (*Brüdergemeinden*), Dunkards, Schwenkfelders and Moravians (*Herrnhuter*), Seventh-Day Adventists (*Adventisten*), and Methodists. There are some cases where the records of one church (apart from the Lutheran-Reformed combination) included entries of members of other churches. This was most likely to happen in the early years when there were still strong restrictions on the privileges of the dissenting churches, or in cases where the religious minority was so small that it did not have its own church in the village or nearby.

Regional church archives now have many of the original parish registers or microfilms of them; but most of the originals can still be found at the parish church. The most valuable church records include:

- **Baptism register** (*Taufregister*) or sometimes birth register (*Geburtsregister*), that contains date of baptism and/or birth, name and legitimacy of the child, and names of the parents and godparents. Also usually included are the residence and occupation or status of the parents and godparents, the maiden name of the mother, the name of the clergyman, and notes.

- **Confirmation register** (*Konfirmationregister*), which contains the name and age of the confirmand, the date and place of confirmation. Also sometimes included are the name and occupation of the father and name of the mother.

- **Marriage register** (*Trauregister*), which contains name, age, residence and occupation of the bride and groom, marriage date and place, and often the names of their parents and the fathers' occupations. Information regarding consent to the marriage, place and time of the proclamation of banns, the name of the pastor, and remarks are also sometimes included.

- **Death register** (*Sterberegister*), which includes name, age, occupation, date and place of death and sometimes includes cause of death, date and place of burial and names of spouse and children.

- **Funeral sermon** (*Leichenpredigt*), which may list birth and death date and other information. These are not available in many areas.

Very helpful records that are sometimes available include family registers, lists of communicants, and church council records.

Many terms that are used in these records may be found in the **German Vocabulary** section of Chapter XVII. One of the best books describing how to get the most out of German church books is *German Church Books: Beyond the Basics* by Kenneth L. Smith.

3. **Civil registration** (*Zivilregister*) of births, deaths, and marriages was required after 1876. Baden and some regions west of the Rhine have records from the early 1800s when they were introduced by French occupation authorities. National civil registration was adopted for Switzerland in 1848. These records are kept at the town civil registry (*Standesamt*).

4. **Passenger lists** (*Passagierlisten*) give names, ages and occupations for all family members, and often the place of origin. Passenger lists are covered in Chapter IV.

5. **Tax lists** (*Steuerlisten*) beginning in the 14th and 15th century list taxpayer's name and address.

6. **Land records** are among the oldest records, some dating prior to the 8th century, but records of land deeds did not begin until the 1300s or 1400s for most regions. The number of landowners was greatly restricted during feudal times, which continued until the 1700s or 1800s. These records are found in the local courthouse (*Amtsgericht*).

7. **Emigration records** (*Auswandererlisten*) may be found in some state archives (*Staatsarchiv*) from the early 1800s. However, many people left without recording their intent to emigrate.

8. **Wills** (*Testamente*) may be found in Germany dating from about 1200. They list the heirs and their relationships to the deceased. They are found in local courthouses (*Amtsgerichte*).

9. **Court records** may also provide family relationships of those involved, and will be located at the court house (*Amtsgericht*).

10. **Census records** (*Volkszählungslisten, Bauernverzeichnisse, Einwohnerlisten*, etc.) exist in only a few cases, except for the regions listed below, because censuses were not conducted regularly, nor were they national in scope before 1871. The census records that do exist may be found in local and state archives (*Staatsarchiv*).

> Mecklenburg (tax and tithing records of the 16th through 19th century)
> Schleswig-Holstein (19th century)
> Württemberg (family registers of the 16th through 19th centuries)

There are also several censuses of Mennonite (and possibly other) farm households in Prussia, the most extensive one being the special "Consignation" of 1776, after the Vistula-Nogat delta area had been transferred from Polish to Prussian rule in 1772. These have been published in various books, including *Die ost- und westpreussischen Mennoniten*, Volume I (Weierhof, Germany: Mennonitischer Geschichtsverein, 1978), by Horst Penner.

11. **Family registers** (*Familienregister*) of Württemberg and other regions may be helpful.

12. **Burgher rolls** or **citizen records** (*Bürgerbücher*) were kept until about 1850 for prominent residents. They contain name, occupation, father's name and hometown. Many have been published. Others may be found in the city archives (*Stadtarchiv*).

13. **Police registers** (*Polizeiregister*) replaced the *Bürgerbücher* and kept track of name and address of every permanent resident. These registers are kept at the town office of registration (*Einwohnermeldeamt*).

14. **City directories** or **address books** (*Adressbücher*) date from the early 1800s, depending on the town. Ribbe and Henning's *Taschenbuch für Familiengeschichtsforschung* lists the years each town printed address books. The address books may be found in local archives.

15. **Apprentice** and **guild books** (*Gilderbücher*) from 1500-1900 list name, parents, occupation, residence and employer. They are scattered. Write to the local archive to see whether they have been preserved (since there are many gaps) and, if so, where.

16. **Military records** (*Kriegslisten* or *Militärakten*) are scattered throughout the country in local and state archives near where soldiers were stationed.

17. **University student lists** that are available are shown in Ribbe and Henning's *Taschenbuch für Familiengeschichtsforschung*.

18. **Printed family histories** (*Sippenbücher* or *Familiengeschichten*) may be available from German genealogical societies. Those published in genealogical journals have been indexed in *Der Schlüssel* [*The Key*], a multi-volume series. The first volumes of *Der Schlüssel* were originally published by the now defunct Hans Reise Verlag; the volumes have been reprinted and the series continued by Verlag Degener & Co.

19. **Local histories** show the genealogy of a village (*Dorfsippenbücher* or *Ortssippenbücher*). Thousands are listed in Franz Heinzmann's bibliography of such books. They are extremely helpful when they are available for a particular place.

20. **Pedigree charts** (*Ahnenpässe*) for each individual were required during the Nazi era. Despite some false data to hide Jewish ancestors, these are very valuable, but hard to find.

The August 1983 issue of *The German Connection*, published by the German Research Association (address in chapter XIX) carried a table showing what kind of records were available in Germany, Austria and Switzerland, and where they could be found. The data came from Robert Ward's *German-American Genealogical Workshop Bulletin*.

Chapter XV

RESEARCHING EUROPEAN RECORDS BY COUNTRY

This chapter gives you specific helps for researching in each European country where your Germanic ancestors may have lived. Included for each country are key addresses and the most important kinds of records. Unique record sources for each country are also highlighted.

Prior to the publication of our predecessor book, *Research Guide to German-American Genealogy*, there was no English-language genealogical or even historical book that dealt comprehensively with ethnic Germans in all European non-Germanic countries. Ribbe and Henning, in their *Taschenbuch für Familiengeschichtsforschung* [*Handbook for Family History Research*], list several pertinent German-language bibliographies.

For more addresses, see particularly Ernest Thode's *Address Book for Germanic Genealogy*. For more detailed information about kinds of records available, see the two books by Angus Baxter, *In Search of Your German Roots* and *In Search of Your European Roots*, as well as *Research Outlines* and *Research Papers* on various countries by the Family History Library.

There are several books that are useful for German-related genealogical research in every country. One is the German-language classic by Wolfgang Ribbe and Eckart Henning, *Taschenbuch für Familiengeschichtsforschung* [*Handbook for Family History Research*].

Also check "German-American Genealogical Sources in the Library of Congress Division of Manuscripts" by Michael Palmer in the April and May 1989 issues of the *GGSA Bulletin*, which deals with American copies of foreign manuscripts, if you are interested in doing archival research in Washington, DC. He cites a *Guide to the Manuscript Materials Relating to American History in the German States Archives* by Marion Dexter Learned, (New York: Kraus, 1912, reprinted 1965), as well as later supplements.

Don Ligett, P.O. Box 120, Toulon, IL 61483, has a large number of audio tapes of presentations on Germany, Eastern and Northern Europe, maps and gazetteers, and miscellaneous other topics available for sale.

THE GERMAN-SPEAKING COUNTRIES

A useful starting point for an overview of the literature concerning Germany, Austria, Switzerland and Liechtenstein is *The German-Speaking Countries of Europe: A Selective Bibliography* by Margrit B. Krewson. It lists a number of other bibliographies, most of which are in German, but including John M. Spalek's *Guide to the Archival Materials of the German-Speaking Emigration to the United States After 1933*.

GERMANY
(Deutschland)

In 1994 the Family History Library published a 52-page *Research Outline: Germany*. It provides comprehensive coverage of topics relating to research on the pre-World War I German Empire, with some limited information about East European Germans and individual German states. This booklet is an absolute must for beginners and includes information of value to more experienced genealogists as well. For more detailed information on various aspects of Germanic genealogy than is provided in this guide, see the books listed in the bibliographies, as well as Larry O. Jensen, *A Genealogical Handbook of German Research*, and George K. Schweitzer, *German Genealogical Research*.

POSTAL CODES AND FORMS OF ADDRESS

The postal code (*Postleitzahl*) for all locations in the recently reunited Germany was changed in 1993 to D- followed by a five digit number. The city is no longer underlined in German mailing addresses, as was the case until recently. Instead, it is now customary to leave a blank line between the street or post office box and the city in typed or pre-printed addresses. We have not done so in this guide in order to conserve space.

CHURCH RECORDS IN GERMANY

Local Churches. You can write to the local church pastor using the following address format:

Roman Catholic:	**Evangelical (Lutheran):**
Das katholische Pfarramt	Das evangelische Pfarramt
D-*(postal code)* *(name of town)*	D-*(postal code)* *(name of town)*
Germany	Germany

If you write to the local church, you may have only limited success. Many young ministers are not able to read the old Gothic script. Most pastors in the new eastern states, as well as older pastors in the western states, have little or no knowledge of English, so you should write in German.

Church Archives. Duplicate copies of some church records can be found in regional church archives. Expect to pay a research fee when writing to an archive. Check the Family History Library microfilms before writing to Germany, since many parish registers have been microfilmed. If the records you want are not on film, you can find the addresses of all the major church archives in Thode's *Address Book*.

The Family History Library has been unable to microfilm some German parish registers, including the Catholic and Lutheran registers in Bavaria and the Lutheran registers in Saxony, Thuringia and Hanover. "Microfilming in Germany, Poland, Bulgaria and Armenia" by John D. Movius (*FEEFHS Newsletter*, December 1994) provides an up-to-date report on alternative records being microfilmed. The current filming in Poland also includes areas where there were many Germans (Breslau, Posen, Danzig).

PUBLIC RECORDS IN GERMANY

Civil Registration was required in Prussia by 1874 and in all of Germany by 1876. But Hanover, Hesse, Baden and areas to the west of them have records predating 1815. Birth, marriage and death records are kept at the local civil registry office (*Standesamt*). Write to the *Standesamt* of the town in question. Check the *Postleitzahlenbuch* (postal code directory of Germany) for German postal code information. Write to:

> Standesamt
> *(street address if known, but not needed for small villages)*
> D-*(postal code)* *(name of town)*
> Germany

Military Records of the German government were thought to have been destroyed during World War II, but the Family History Library now has films of some of those in Prussian State Privy Archives in Berlin. The *Ostdeutsche Familienkunde* published a list of 4,087 military church registers, most of which are in the Privy Archives or the Evangelical Central Archives in Berlin, in its April-June 1994 issue. *German Military Records as Genealogical Sources*, by Horst A. Reschke, very thoroughly covers the records of various German states that were not under Prussian rule.

Guild Records can be very useful to genealogists with artisan ancestors. But such records are widely scattered and have many gaps. For the most comprehensive article on which of such records have been microfilmed by the Family History Library and the German state and city archives know to have some, see "Guild Records in Germany," an adaptation of a lecture given by Gerhard Jeske in the Winter 1994 issue of the *German Genealogical Digest*.

Local Court House (*Amtsgericht*) has records, deeds and other land records as early as the 7th century, municipal records and tax lists. Write to the *Amtsgericht* of the city in question using the *Postleitzahlenbuch*. Write to:

> Amtsgericht
> (*street address if known*)
> D-(*postal code*) (*town name*)
> Germany

City Archives (*Stadtarchiv*) contain documents such as births, marriages and deaths since 1876, as well as city directories, some funeral sermons, apprentice and guild records, school and university records, house books, some census records and burgher rolls. Some date back to the Middle Ages. Lists of city archives are too numerous to mention here; please refer to the *Address Book for Germanic Genealogy* by Ernest Thode. Write to the *Stadtarchiv* of the city in question using the *Postleitzahlenbuch* [*German postal code directory*]. Write to:

> Stadtarchiv
> (*street address if known*)
> D-(*postal code*) (*town name*)
> Germany

National Archives. Because of the fragmentation of Germany until 1871, the national archives are not at all comparable to those of most Western countries with respect to their significance for genealogical research. However, they do contain a few genealogical treasures, particularly with respect to the ethnic Germans in Eastern Europe who were "repatriated" during the Hitler era. There are extensive genealogical materials for the repatriates, since each one had to complete a genealogical questionnaire and there are lists of all the Germans who were residents in each of the affected villages. The address is:

> Bundesarchiv
> Potsdamer Strasse 1
> Postfach 320
> D-56075 Koblenz
> Germany

The voluminous records of the Berlin Document Center, which pertain to the Nazi period, will be transferred to the national archives, but not before being microfilmed by the United States government.

State Archives (*Staatsarchiv*). Each state or regional archive has different holdings; if you cannot locate the information needed, write to archives in the following list, asking the whereabouts of the information you need. They will refer you to the right source.

The following central state archive is the main archive of the former German Democratic Republic. It has official records of the former German Empire and the former German Democratic Republic. All materials formerly at the central archive in Merseburg have now been transferred to Potsdam.

Zentrales Staatsarchiv
Historische Abteilung I
Berliner Strasse 98-101
Postfach 42
D-14467 Potsdam
Germany

BADEN-WÜRTTEMBERG STATE ARCHIVES:

Generallandesarchiv
Nördliche Hildapromenade 2
D-76133 Karlsruhe
Germany

Baden

Staatsarchiv
Colombistrasse 4
Postfach 323
D-79098 Freiburg
Germany

Württemberg

Hauptstaatsarchiv
Konrad-Adenauer-Strasse 4
D-70173 Stuttgart
Germany

Württemberg

Staatsarchiv
Schloss Ludwigsburg
Schloss-Strasse 30
D-71634 Ludwigsburg
Germany

Hohenzollern

Staatsarchiv
Karlstrasse 3
Postfach 526
D-72488 Sigmaringen
Germany

BAYERN (BAVARIA) STATE ARCHIVES:

Bayerisches Hauptstaatsarchiv I
Arcisstrasse 12
Postfach 200507
D-80005 München
Germany

Coburg

Staatsarchiv
Schloss Ehrenburg
D-96450 Coburg
Germany

Mittelfranken

Staatsarchiv
Archivstrasse 17
D-90408 Nürnberg
Germany

Niederbayern

Staatsarchiv
Burg Trausnitz
D-84036 Landshut
Germany

Oberbayern

Staatsarchiv
Schönfeldstrasse 3
D-80539 München
Germany

Oberfranken

Staatsarchiv
Hainstrasse 39
Postfach 2668
D-96047 Bamberg
Germany

Oberpfalz

Staatsarchiv
Archivstrasse 3
D-92224 Amberg
Germany

Schwaben

Staatsarchiv
Salomon-Idler-Strasse 2
D-86159 Augsburg
Germany

Unterfranken

Staatsarchiv
Residenzplatz 2
D-97070 Würzburg
Germany

BRANDENBURG STATE ARCHIVES:

Brandenburgisches
    Landeshauptarchiv
Sanssouci-Orangerie
Postfach 48
D-14469 Potsdam
Germany

BREMEN STATE ARCHIVES:

Staatsarchiv
Am Staatsarchiv 1
D-28203 Bremen
Germany

HAMBURG STATE ARCHIVES:

Staatsarchiv
ABC-Strasse 19A
D-20354 Hamburg
Germany

HESSEN (HESSE) STATE ARCHIVES:

Nassau

Hauptstaatsarchiv
Mosbacher Strasse 55
D-65187 Wiesbaden
Germany

Hessen-Darmstadt

Staatsarchiv
Schloss
D-64283 Darmstadt
Germany

Hessen-Kassel

Staatsarchiv
Friedrichsplatz 15
Postfach 540
D-35037 Marburg
Germany

MECKLENBURG-VORPOMMERN STATE ARCHIVES:

Mecklenburg

Staatsarchiv
Graf-Schack-Allee 2
D-19053 Schwerin
Germany

Vorpommern

Staatsarchiv
Martin-Andersen-Nexö-Platz 1
D-17489 Greifswald
Germany

NIEDERSACHSEN (LOWER SAXONY) STATE ARCHIVES:

Hauptstaatsarchiv
Am Archiv 1
D-30169 Hannover
Germany

Braunschweig

Staatsarchiv
Forstweg 2
D-38302 Wolfenbüttel
Germany

Bückeburg

Staatsarchiv
Schloss
Postfach 1350
D-31675 Bückeburg
Germany

Oldenburg

Staatsarchiv
Damm 43
D-26135 Oldenburg
Germany

Osnabrück

Staatsarchiv
Schloss-Strasse 29
D-49074 Osnabrück
Germany

Ostfriesland

Staatsarchiv
Oldersumer Strasse 50
D-26603 Aurich
Germany

Stade

Staatsarchiv
Am Sande 4c
D-21682 Stade
Germany

NORDRHEIN-WESTFALEN (NORTHRHINE-WESTPHALIA) STATE ARCHIVES:

Hauptstaatsarchiv
Mauerstrasse 55
D-40476 Düsseldorf
Germany

Lippe

Staatsarchiv
Willi-Hofmann-Strasse 2
D-32756 Detmold
Germany

Rheinland

Nordrhein-Westfälisches
Personenstandsarchiv Rheinland
Schloss-Str. 12
D-50321 Brühl
Germany
(devoted to the preservation of civil and parish registers, especially for the Rhineland; has a publication listing the Rhenish civil registers; contains the library of the Westdeutsche Gesellschaft für Familienkunde)

Westfalen

Staatsarchiv
Bohlweg 2
D-48147 Münster
Germany

RHEINLAND-PFALZ (RHINELAND-PALATINATE) STATE ARCHIVES:

Rheinland

Landeshauptarchiv
Karmeliterstrasse 1-3
D-56068 Koblenz
Germany

Pfalz

Staatsarchiv
Otto-Meyer-Strasse 9
Postfach 1608
D-67346 Speyer
Germany

SAAR (SAARLAND) STATE ARCHIVES:

Landesarchiv
Scheidter Strasse 114
Postfach 101010
D-66010 Saarbrücken
Germany

SACHSEN (SAXONY) STATE ARCHIVES:

Sächsisches Hauptstaatsarchiv
    Dresden
Archivstrasse 14
D-01097 Dresden
Germany

Aussenstelle Bautzen des Sächsischen
    Hauptstaatsarchivs
Schloss Ortenburg
D-02625 Bautzen
Germany

Aussenstelle Freiberg des Sächsischen
    Hauptstaatsarchivs Dresden
    (Bergarchiv)
Kirchgasse 11
D-09599 Freiberg
Germany

Sächsisches Staatsarchiv Leipzig
Georgi-Dimitroff-Platz 1
D-04107 Leipzig
Germany

SACHSEN-ANHALT (SAXONY-ANHALT) STATE ARCHIVES:

Landeshauptarchiv Sachsen-Anhalt
Hegelstrasse 25
Postfach 92
D-39104 Magdeburg
Germany

Aussenstelle Wernigerode
    des Landeshauptarchivs
    Sachsen-Anhalt
Orangerie
Leninalle
D-38855 Wernigerode
Germany

Aussenstelle Oranienbaum
    des Landeshauptarchivs
    Sachsen-Anhalt
Schloss
D-06785 Oranienbaum
Germany

SCHLESWIG-HOLSTEIN STATE ARCHIVES:

Landesarchiv
Schloss Gottorf
D-24837 Schleswig
Germany

THÜRINGEN (THURINGIA) STATE ARCHIVES:

Thüringisches Hauptstaatsarchiv
    Weimar
Marstallstrasse 2
D-99423 Weimar
Germany

Reuss-Greiz:

Aussenstelle Greiz des
    Thüringischen Hauptstaatsarchivs
Oberes Schloss
D-07973 Greiz
Germany

Sachsen-Altenburg:

Aussenstelle Altenburg des
    Thüringischen Hauptstaatsarchivs
Schloss 2a
D-06429 Altenburg
Germany

Sachsen-Coburg-Gotha:

Aussenstelle Gotha des
    Thüringischen Hauptstaatsarchivs
Schloss Friedenstein
D-99867 Gotha
Germany

Sachsen-Meiningen:

Thüringisches Staatsarchiv
    Meiningen
Schloss Bibrabau
D-98617 Meiningen
Germany

Schwarzburg-Rudolstadt:

Thüringisches Staatsarchiv
    Rudolstadt
Schloss Heidecksburg
D-07407 Rudolstadt
Germany

GENEALOGICAL SOCIETIES FOR RESEARCH IN GERMANY

Religious archives are not listed here because many parish registers are still in the local parsonages and because the archives are so numerous. Addresses can be found in Thode's *Address Book* and the Immigrant Genealogical Society's *1993 Updated Addresses to German Repositories*, with less complete coverage in many other books.

NATIONAL GENEALOGICAL SOCIETIES

The Deutsche Arbeitsgemeinschaft genealogischer Verbände (DAGV) is an umbrella organization for 56 German genealogical associations representing 19,000 genealogical researchers, with its office at Schloss-Strasse 12, D-50321 Brühl, Germany. Its list of member organizations (*Mitgliederverzeichnis*) provides details concerning services and addresses. It is published by the Verlag Degener & Co., Postfach 1360, D-91403 Neustadt/Aisch, Germany, as part of the series, *Aktuelle Themen zur Genealogie* [*Current Topics in Genealogy*].

The Zentralstelle für Personen- und Familiengeschichte, Birkenweg 13, D-61381 Friedrichsdorf, Germany, is a genealogical institute that was founded in Leipzig in 1904, not a genealogical society in the strict sense of the word. It is specifically concerned with providing information and research tips to genealogists throughout the world, in addition to registering *Ortssippenbücher* or *Dorfsippenbücher* (village genealogies) and publishing a genealogical yearbook.

The Verein zur Förderung der Zentralstelle für Personen- und Familiengeschichte e.V., Archivstrasse 12-14, D-14195 Berlin-Dahlem, Germany, is a membership organization devoted to the promotion of the above-mentioned genealogical institute. The HEROLD at the same address is a related society that emphasizes publications specifically about heraldry and diverse disciplines that have some relevance to heraldry and genealogy.

Another organization that is devoted to the dissemination of information about genealogical research is the Akademie für Genealogie, Heraldik und verwandte Wissenschaften e.V., Gutenbergstr. 12 B, D-38118 Braunschweig, Germany.

STATE AND REGIONAL SOCIETIES

Baden-Württemberg
Verein für Familien- und Wappenkunde
   in Württemberg und Baden e.V.
Konrad-Adenauer-Strasse 8
Postfach 105441
D-70047 Stuttgart
Germany

Baden-Württemberg (Baden)
Landesverein Badische Heimat
Ausschuss für Familienforschung
Heilbronner Strasse 3
D-75015 Bretten
Germany

Bayern (Bavaria)
Bayerischer Landesverein
   für Familienkunde e.V.
Hauptstaatsarchiv
Ludwigstrasse 14/I
D-80539 München
Germany

Bayern (Franken area)
Gesellschaft für Familienforschung
   in Franken e.V.
Staatsarchiv
Archivstrasse 17
D-90408 Nürnberg
Germany

Bayern (Oberpfalz area)
Gesellschaft für Familienforschung
   in der Oberpfalz e.V.
Pustetstr. 13
D-93155 Hemau
Germany

Berlin
Interessengemeinschaft Genealogie
   Berlin
Heinrich-Heine-Str. 11
D-10179 Berlin
Germany

Bremen

"Die Maus"
Gesellschaft für Familienforschung e.V.
Staatsarchiv
Am Staatsarchiv 1/Fedelhören
D-28203 Bremen
Germany

Hamburg

Genealogische Gesellschaft e.V.
Alsterchaussee 11
Postfach 302042
D-20307 Hamburg
Germany

Hessen (Hessen-Darmstadt area)

Hessische Familiengeschichtliche
Vereinigung e.V.
Karolinenplatz 3 (Staatsarchiv)
D-64283 Darmstadt
Germany

Hessen (Kurhessen & Waldeck area)

Gesellschaft für Familienkunde
in Kurhessen und Waldeck e.V.
Postfach 101346
D-34013 Kassel
Germany

Hessen (Nassau & Frankfurt area)

Familienkundliche Gesellschaft
für Nassau und Frankfurt e.V.
Hessisches Hauptstaatsarchiv
Mosbacher Strasse 55
D-65187 Wiesbaden
Germany

Hessen (Fulda area)

Vereinigung für Familien- und
Wappenkunde zu Fulda
Taunusstrasse 4
D-36043 Fulda
Germany

Mecklenburg-Vorpommern

Arbeitsgemeinschaft Genealogie
und Heraldik
Zum Netzboden 14
D-23966 Wismar
Germany

Niedersachsen

Niedersächsischer Landesverein
für Familienkunde e.V.
Am Bokemahle 14-16 (Stadtarchiv)
D-39171 Hannover
Germany

Niedersachsen (Göttingen area)

Genealogisch-Heraldische Gesellschaft
Untere Karspüle 10
Postfach 2062
D-37010 Göttingen
Germany

Niedersachsen (Oldenburg area)

Oldenburgische Gesellschaft
für Familienkunde
Lerigauweg 14
D-26131 Oldenburg
Germany

Niedersachsen (Ostfriesland area)

Upstalsboom-Gesellschaft für
historische Personenforschung und
Bevölkerungsgeschichte in
Ostfriesland e.V.
Flotowweg 4
D-26386 Wilhelmshaven
Germany

Nordrhein-Westfalen (Aachen area)

Genealogie ohne Grenzen
Postbus 10
NL-6343 ZG Klimmen
The Netherlands
(regional society for the tri-national area
around Aachen)

Nordrhein-Westfalen (Berg area)

Bergischer Verein für Familienkunde e.V.
Zanellastr. 5
D-42287 Wuppertal
Germany

Nordrhein-Westfalen (Dortmund area)

Roland zu Dortmund e.V.
Hansastrasse 61
Postfach 103326
D-44033 Dortmund
Germany

Nordrhein-Westfalen (Kleve area)

Mosaik: Familienkundliche
Vereinigung für das Klever
Land e.V.
Mosaik-Archiv
"Christus-Königschule"
Lindenallee 54
D-47533 Kleve
Germany
(half-German, half-Dutch society for this
area where political and linguistic
borders shifted)

Nordrhein-Westfalen (Lippe area)
Lippischer Heimatsbund
Bismarckstrasse 8
D-32756 Detmold
Germany

Nordrhein-Westfalen
(Mark & Sauerland area)
Arbeitskreis für Familienforschung
im Hagener Heimatbund e.V.
Hochstr. 74
D-58095 Hagen
Germany

Nordrhein-Westfalen
(former Rhein province area)
Westdeutsche Gesellschaft für
Familienkunde e.V.
Postfach 100822
D-51608 Gummersbach
Germany
*(branches in Aachen, Bonn, Düsseldorf,
Essen, Gummersbach, Kleve, Koblenz,
Köln, Krefeld, Mönchengladbach, Trier
and Wuppertal)*

Nordrhein-Westfalen (Westfalen area)
Westfälische Gesellschaft für
Genealogie und Familienforschung
Warendorfer Strasse 25
Postfach 6125
D-48133 Münster
Germany

Rheinland-Pfalz
Arbeitsgemeinschaft für
Pfälzisch-Rheinische
Familienkunde e.V.
Staatsarchiv
Rottstrasse 17
D-67061 Ludwigshafen
Germany

Saarland
Arbeitsgemeinschaft für Saarländische
Familienkunde e.V.
Hebbelstrasse 3
D-66346 Püttlingen
Germany

Sachsen (Annaberg-Buchholz area)
Arbeitsgemeinschaft Genealogie
Hauptstr. 118
D-09477 Arnsfeld
Germany

Sachsen (Auerbach area)
Arbeitsgemeinschaft Genealogie
Poststr. 4
D-08233 Treuen
Germany

Sachsen (Chemnitz area)
Arbeitsgemeinschaft Genealogie
Str. Usti nad Labem 23
D-09119 Chemnitz
Germany

Sachsen (Dresden area)
Arbeitsgemeinschaft Genealogie
Krenkelstr. 9
D-01309 Dresden
Germany

Sachsen (Leipzig area)
Leipziger Genealogische Gesellschaft e.V.
c/o Deutsche Zentralstelle für Genealogie
Postfach 274
D-04002 Leipzig
Germany

Sachsen (Plauen area)
Arbeitsgemeinschaft Genealogie
Weststr. 73
D-08523 Plauen
Germany

Sachsen-Anhalt (Halle area)
Genealogischer Abend "Ekkehard"
Halle e.V.
Otto-Hahn-Str. 2
D-06126 Halle-Neustadt
Germany

Sachsen-Anhalt (Magdeburg area)
Arbeitsgemeinschaft Genealogie
Magdeburg
Thiemstr. 7
D-39104 Magdeburg
Germany

Schleswig-Holstein
Schleswig-Holsteinische Gesellschaft
für Familienforschung
und Wappenkunde e.V.
Postfach 3809
D-24307 Kiel
Germany

Schleswig-Holstein (Lübeck area)
Arbeitskreis für Familienforschung e.V.
Mühlentorturm
Mühlentorplatz 2
D-23552 Lübeck
Germany

Thüringen
Arbeitsgemeinschaft Genealogie
Thüringen e.V.

Martin-Andersen-Nexö-Str. 62
D-99096 Erfurt
Germany

GENEALOGICAL RESOURCE CENTERS FOR EASTERN EUROPE

The former Zentralstelle für Genealogie in der Deutschen Demokratischen Republik, established in 1967, which served as the main archives for researching genealogy in former East Germany, will accept letters written in English requesting genealogical information. Its archives are open to visiting American genealogists without any restrictions or prior application procedures. It is now addressed as:

> Deutsche Zentralstelle für Genealogie
> Postfach 274
> D-04002 Leipzig
> Germany
> (*located at: Käthe-Kollwitz-Strasse 82*)

Literally, the name means "German Central Office for Genealogy." But its actual nature is more complicated. It has records for all of the former German Empire that were gathered by various other institutions dating back to 1904, but it is not a repository where all German genealogical information is centralized. It served as the key genealogical contact with the current German eastern states during the Communist era. It has a large number of microfilms for the former German eastern territories, with a significant, but lesser, number of parish registers and other records for German linguistic enclaves in East European territory that was never under German rule.

It is now more likely that letters sent directly to local parish offices in the "five new states" of Germany (the current preferred terminology for the territory of the former East German state) will be answered, but writing in English may be a barrier in some cases.

The Zentralstelle, however, continues to have resources which are unique in their comprehensiveness regarding ancestors who lived in these eastern states, namely:

- a special library collection of about 20,000 items including all important genealogical periodicals, reference works, collections of material and monographs as well as several thousand diverse manuscripts and materials relating to seals, coats-of-arms, pictures, etc.

- the 5 million lineage cards (*Ahnenstammkartei*) that grew out of the former "Deutschenahnengemeinschaft," housed in Dresden until 1967. This integrates various lineages connected by marriage. Most of the data are for the 1650-1800 period. Members may send in lineages traced back at least until the middle of the eighteenth century (or otherwise, if all readily accessible sources have been exhausted). This information is periodically updated and circulated to members. This enormous collection of genealogical data on a large number of German families has been microfilmed by the Family History Library. John D. Movius of the Federation of East European Family History Societies (FEEFHS) is now seeking volunteers to extract records for particular groups, e.g., Jews and Mennonites. See his article in the July 1994 *FEEFHS Newsletter* for more details.

- an alphabetized catalog of writings relating to particular individuals (*Personalschriftenkatalog*) begun by the "Roland" Society in Dresden in 1919 and constantly expanded since then. About 150,000 index cards identify the location of over 100,000 documents (funeral sermons and other written materials relating to prominent persons) that can be found in public archives, libraries and collections, including three collections from Sweden.

- various parish registers (some originals, some microfilms) from the former German eastern territories, but also some from non-Germanic countries. A two-volume inventory of indexed parish registers has now been published. However, the archive is reported to have many additional boxed, unindexed registers of Germans in foreign countries. These registers were acquired in World War II but are not currently accessible.

There is a fee for any research that is done and an annual subscription of DM 25 for participation in the circulating *Ahnenstammkartei* network.

Register to the Ahnenstammkartei des deutschen Volkes [*Lineage Cards of the German People*], by Thomas Kent Edlund, to be published by the Germanic Genealogy Society in 1995, will greatly facilitate access to the information in the *Ahnenstammkartei*. It is an alphabetized list to the 2,700,000 names in the microfilmed lineage cards at the Zentralstelle.

There are also copies or microfilms of many Protestant parish registers in the former German eastern territories at the:

> Evangelisches Zentralarchiv
> Jebensstr. 3
> D-10623 Berlin
> Germany

Both the Leipzig and Berlin records have been microfilmed by the Family History Library. Each archive has published an easy-to-use inventory of its church records. Records for eastern Pomerania are widely scattered. A large number of East Pomeranian Lutheran registers are in various archives in Greifswald, including the Landesarchiv and the:

> Pommersche Evangelische Kirche
> Landeskirchliches Archiv
> Bahnhofstr. 35/36
> Postfach 187
> D-17489 Greifswald
> Germany

For a list of those in and near Naugard County, see the summer 1994 issue (Vol. 16) of *Die Pommerschen Leute*.

The following archive has many East European Catholic registers, especially for ex-German territories, but also for some other areas (including the 1780-1820 duplicate registers for the Egerland, i.e., the western tip of the Czech Republic, which belonged to the diocese of Regensburg at the time):

> Bischöfliches Zentralarchiv
> St. Peters-Weg 11-14
> D-93047 Regensburg
> Germany

If you are unable to find out whether the parish registers for which you are looking have been preserved or, if so, where, you can obtain the best available information for $30 from the former executive director of AGoFF, who is fluent in English:

> Heike Brachwitz
> Genealogischer Computerdienst
> Am Mühlenhof 5
> D-26180 Rastede
> Germany

Many civil registers remained at the local civil registry offices in Poland. Those that were taken to Germany are at:

> Standesamt I in Berlin
> Rheinstr. 54
> D-12161 Berlin
> Germany

Some of the Transylvanian German Lutheran parish registers are believed to be at the:

Archiv des Landeskirchenamts der Evangelischen Kirche von Westfalen
Altstädter Kirchplatz 3
Postfach 2740
D-33603 Bielefeld
Germany

In the 3rd edition of *In Search of Your German Roots*, Angus Baxter indicates that a large number of microfilmed parish registers and other records pertaining to Germans in Estonia and Latvia are at the:

Johann-Gottfried-Herder-Institut
Gisonenweg 5-7
D-35037 Marburg/Lahn
Germany

The institute also has some records for the former eastern parts of Germany and the Sudetenland. The Herder-Institut has a very large library and will copy any books, parts of books, articles and other materials in its collection that are no longer in print. Its archives includes a substantial map collection. In addition, it is a publisher.

There are a great many government records for the former German eastern territories at the Prussian State Privy Archives (which are not secret, despite the title):

Geheimes Staatsarchiv Preussischer Kulturbesitz
Archivstr. 12-14
D-14195 Berlin
Germany

A two-volume inventory, *Übersicht über die Bestände des Geheimen Staatsarchivs in Berlin-Dahlem* [*Overview of the Contents of the Privy State Archives in Berlin-Dahlem*], was published in 1965-67, but many of the records are reportedly not indexed, which impedes access.

The Prussian State Privy Archives also has a library at Potsdamer Str. 33, D-10785 Berlin, which participates in the international inter-library loan program.

The principal German society for researching German ancestors from Eastern Europe, including both former German and non-German areas, which is widely known by its acronym (**AGoFF**), is:

Arbeitsgemeinschaft ostdeutscher Familienforscher (AGoFF)
Detlef Kühn, Vorsitzender
Zum Block 1A
D-01561 Medessen
Germany

It has numerous regionalized research centers and subcenters, with the main ones listed below. The addresses are based primarily on the 1994 membership roster of the German genealogical umbrella group (*Mitgliederverzeichnis 1994 der DAGV*, compiled by Dieter Zwinger and published by the Verlag Degener & Co., Neustadt/Aisch). Many of these centers are staffed by older people who left Eastern Europe in 1945, so relatively frequent changes can be expected. They are all run by volunteers, often consisting of only one person, and vary greatly in the kind of information they can provide.

Some of the researchers know English, but many don't, so writing in German is advisable. They charge no fees for their services, beyond reimbursement of costs, but they welcome contributions to promote further research. It is appropriate to enclose 3 International Reply Coupons with your request and to make a donation.

Bukovina: Dipl.-Ing. Kurt Neumann, Platanenstrasse 13, D-58644 Iserlohn

Central Poland and Volhynia: Heinz Ulbrich, Sperberweg 6, Postfach 1039, D-92661 Altenstadt

Danube Swabians: Dr. Martin Armgart, Graitengraben 41, D-45326 Essen

East Brandenburg-Neumark: Rita Sydow, Veilchenweg 12, D-26203 Hundsmühlen

Galicia: Manfred Daum, Hafrekamp 25, D-29525 Ülzen

Pomerania: Elmar Bruhn, Lohkamp 13, D-22117 Hamburg (also publishes *SEDINA-Archiv*). Knows English.

Posen: Hilde Möller, Oppenheimer Str. 50, D-60594 Frankfurt am Main; for **East Netze district (i.e., the Bromberg area)**: Otto Firchau, Nachtigallenweg 6, D-32105 Salzuflen

Russia, Ukraine and Bessarabia: Dr. Paul Edel, Ziegelstr. 11, Postfach 1232, Aalen

Silesia: Neithard von Stein, Talstr. 3, D-31707 Bad Eilsen

Southeast Europe: Dr. phil. Martin Armgart, Graitengraben 31, D-45326 Essen; with subcenters for the successor states to **Yugoslavia**, pre-World War I **Hungary**, including **Slovak Republic/Carpatho-Ukraine**, **Burgenland/West Hungary**, **Transylvania (Siebenbürgen)**, and pre-1914 **Romania**

Sudetenland/Bohemia, **Moravia** and former **Austrian Silesia** (now the Czech Republic): Adolf Fischer, Juttastr. 20, D-90480 Nürnberg

Genealogical researchers for the various sub-centers (not all listed above) are included in the *AGoFF-Wegweiser*. The second German edition was published in 1994 by the Verlag Degener & Co. and the second edition, under the title, *Genealogical Guide to German Ancestors from East Germany and Eastern Europe*, in 1995. (East Germany means the former eastern German territories that are now a part of Poland or Russia.)

Other societies devoted to Eastern Europe include:

Baltics:

> Deutsch-Baltische Gesellschaft
> Herdweg 79
> Haus der Deutsch-Balten
> D-64285 Darmstadt
> Germany

East and West Prussia:

> Verein für Ost- und Westpreussen e.V.
> Wilhelm Kranz
> Wiedauweg 13B
> D-21147 Hamburg
> Germany

Sudeten Germans:

> Sudetendeutsches Genealogisches Archiv
> Erikaweg 58
> D-93053 Regensburg
> Germany
> *(also a library at this address)*

Danube Swabians:

> Arbeitskreis donauschwäbischer Familienforscher
> Hohlweg 5
> D-75181 Pforzheim
> Germany

> *U.S. contact:*
> Michael Stoeckl
> 1420 W. Farragut
> Chicago, IL 60640

Other Sources:

There is another multi-purpose organization concerned with East Central Europe that includes five genealogically-oriented study groups for Posen and Poland, Silesia, Central Poland and Volhynia, West Prussia and Pomerania, and Estonia. It consists of nominees, rather than general members. Contact:

> Gesellschaft für ostmitteleuropäische Landeskunde und Kultur
> Zum Nordhang 5
> D-58313 Herdecke
> Germany

There is an extremely large card index file of emigrants from the Palatinate to various countries, including the United States, as well as Ernst Hexel's voluminous Galician German data, at:

> Institut für pfälzische Geschichte und Volkskunde
> Benzinoring 6
> D-67657 Kaiserslautern
> Germany

Other important libraries and research centers devoted to the study of Germans in foreign countries are:

> Institut für Auslandsbeziehungen
> Charlottenplatz 17
> D-70173 Stuttgart
> Germany
> (*specializes in Southeast Europe, and the Volga and Black Sea Germans*)

> Heimatarchiv der Deutschen aus Mittelpolen und Wolhynien
> Platz der Republik
> D-41065 Mönchengladbach
> Germany
> (*archive for Germans from Central Poland and Volhynia*)

> Landesarchiv
> Scheidter Strasse 114
> Postfach 101010
> D-66010 Saarbrücken
> Germany
> (*has substantial records relating to Danube Swabians*)

> Studienstelle ostdeutsche Genealogie der Dorschungsstelle Ostmitteleuropa
> Universität Dortmund
> Emil-Figge-Strasse 50
> D-44227 Dortmund
> Germany
> (*has large genealogical name index file for West Prussia, which can be accessed through Dieter God, Schorlemmerskamp 20, D-44536 Lünen, Germany*)

There is also a *Heimatortskartei* (a card file of German refugees and expellees) for every non-German country that was under Communist rule. The addresses for the various areas (not always coinciding with national borders) are listed in the *AGoFF Guide*. The information in these files is more likely to be helpful for finding relatives than ancestors, but it may provide useful genealogical contacts.

OTHER SPECIALIZED GENEALOGICAL RESOURCE CENTERS

Huguenots, Waldensians and Walloons

The German Huguenot Society has published a periodical devoted to history for over a century. The current title is *Der Deutsche Hugenott* [*The German Huguenot*]. Its publications are valuable for tracing Huguenot and other originally French-speaking ancestors. At least some of them have been microfilmed by the Family History Library. The society's address is:

Deutsche-Hugenotten-Gesellschaft
Deutsches Hugenottenzentrum
Hafenplatz 9a
D-34385 Bad Karlshofen
Germany

The society's genealogical expert is:

Frau Ute Bilshausen-Lasalle
Fuhrberg
An der Schale 14
D-30938 Burgwedel
Germany

The one for the Waldensians is:

Dr. Theo Kiefner
Lehengasse 5
D-75365 Calw
Germany

Records of assistance given to Huguenot refugees, which contain specific genealogical data, are in Frankfurt, which was a central location for many nearby Huguenot settlements in Hesse, the Palatinate and Franconia. Contact:

Stadtarchiv
Stadtverwaltung (Amt 41A)
Postfach 3882
Karmeliterkloster
Karmelitergasse 5
D-60311 Frankfurt am Main
Germany

American and Canadian Military Forces in Germany

This organization was founded to help defense personnel with their genealogical research. However, it also includes English-speaking German members and may thus be able to provide information concerning German genealogists who know English. It can be contacted at either of the following addresses:

Genealogical Association of English-Speaking Researchers in Europe
USAREUR Headquarters Library and Resource Center
Mark Twain Village/Heidelberg
APO New York, NY 09099

Genealogical Association of English-Speaking Researchers in Europe
USAREUR Library and Resource Center
Zengerstr. 1 (Mark Twain Village)
D-69126 Heidelberg
Germany

Salzburger Protestant Emigrés

The organization listed below is devoted primarily to research relating to the Protestant refugees who left the archbishopric of Salzburg, mostly in the 1730s, and settled in East Prussia. It may, however, be a useful contact for the descendants of those Salzburgers who migrated to other areas, including the American state of Georgia.

Salzburger Verein e.V.
Memeler Str. 35 (Wohnstift Salzburg)
D-33605 Bielefeld
Germany

Germans of Dutch Descent

This Dutch society is devoted to promoting the research of amateur German genealogists with Dutch roots:

Werkgroep Genealogisch Onderzoek Duitsland
P. C. Hooftlaan 9
NL-3818 HG Amersfoort
The Netherlands

Lineage Societies

The following federation includes about 200 societies devoted to genealogy involving specific families:

Bund der Familienverbände e.V.
Kirchgasse 18
D-98693 Ilmenau
Germany

Nobility and Historic Upper (Governing) Class

The nobles of all Germanic countries are the concern of the following institution:

Deutsches Adelsarchiv
Schwanallee 21
D-35037 Marburg
Germany

The following institute is concerned with the historic elite, including prominent burghers or laypersons:

Friedrich-Wilhelm-Euler-Gesellschaft für personengeschichtliche Forschung e.V.
Ernst-Ludwigstr. 21
D-64625 Bensheim
Germany

The New Eastern States of the Federal Republic (ex-GDR)

The following association has been involved with research in this area (including Berlin) for over 30 years:

Arbeitsgemeinschaft für mitteldeutsche Familienforschung e.V.
Strasse der Freundschaft 2
D-99706 Sondershausen
Germany
(*archives in Hessisches Staatsarchiv, Marburg*)

AUSTRIA
(Österreich)

The Austro-Hungarian Empire existed from 1867 to 1918. Prior to 1867 it was the Austrian Empire. Vienna (Wien) was the imperial capital, but there was a Hungarian government headquarters in Budapest. The sub-units of this empire, not all of an identical nature in a jurisdictional sense, are listed in the table on the next page. All of these areas had a significant number of German-speaking people, with the possible exception of the areas along the Adriatic coast.

If your ancestors are supposed to have come from Austria, it is highly likely they came from some part of the empire that is not part of Austria today, unless you have specific information to the contrary. Those people whose ancestors had already migrated once were more likely to emigrate than those who had stayed in the original homeland. Also, those who came from present-day Austria are most likely to have come from the Burgenland, which was part of Hungary until after World War I. Some records concerning all of the areas that were once under Austrian rule are still in the Austrian archives, but check the sections on the various countries that now exist for further information regarding relevant records. Keep these facts in mind when researching ancestors from "Austria," since relatively few pre-1945 immigrants came from within the present borders of Austria.

Austria today is a much smaller country than when it was the Austro-Hungarian Empire prior to 1919. Austria is made up of the following nine provinces:

Burgenland	Oberösterreich (Upper Austria)	Tirol (Tyrol)
Kärnten (Carinthia)	Salzburg	Vorarlberg
Niederösterreich (Lower Austria)	Steiermark (Styria)	Wien (Vienna)

GAZETTEERS

See Chapter VIII, section (c), for information on Austrian gazetteers.

CHURCH AND SYNAGOGUE RECORDS

The vast majority of people living in what is now Austria have always been Catholic. However, about 15% of the people in the Burgenland were Protestants. Moreover, there were a lot of Protestants in some eastern parts of the former Austro-Hungarian Empire, especially in Transylvania, Galicia and Slovakia. The Transylvanian Saxons converted to Lutheranism while under Turkish rule. German-speakers settled in Galicia shortly after religious toleration was decreed in 1781. Prior to that date, Catholic priests kept the records for everyone, including Protestants and Jews. Some of these records for Austria proper go back to 1648. Archives of Catholic archbishoprics are located at:

Erzbistum Wien	Erzbischöfliches Konsistorialarchiv
Diözesanarchiv	Kapitelplatz 2
Wollzeile 2	A-5010 Salzburg
A-1010 Wien	Austria
Austria	

There are diocesan archives, whose addresses can be found in Thode's *Address Book*, at Eisenstadt (for Burgenland), Feldkirch (for Vorarlberg), Graz (for Styria), Klagenfurt (for Carinthia) and Linz (for Upper Austria).

Table 8: Present Location of Former Austro-Hungarian Territories

German name	English name	Today located in:[8]
Banat	Banat	Romania, Serbia[7] & Hungary
Baranja	Baranya	Croatia & Hungary
Batschka	Backa, Bácska	Serbia[7] & Hungary
Böhmen	Bohemia	Czech Republic
Bosnien[1]	Bosnia	Bosnia-Herzegovina
Bukowina	Bukovina	Romania & Ukraine
Burgenland	Burgenland	Austria & Hungary
Dalmatien	Dalmatia	Croatia
Dobrudscha	Dobruja	Romania & Bulgaria
Fiume	Rijeka	Croatia
Galizien	Galicia	Ukraine & Poland
Görz & Gradiska	Gorizia & Gradisca	Slovenia & Italy
Herzegowina[1]	Herzegovina	Bosnia-Herzegovina
Istrien	Istria	Croatia
Kärnten	Carinthia	Austria
Karpato-Ukraine	Carpatho-Ukraine	Ukraine
Krain	Carniola	Slovenia
Kroatien	Croatia[5]	Croatia
Mähren	Moravia	Czech Republic
Österreich	Austria	Austria
Österreichisch-Schlesien	Austrian Silesia	Czech Republic
Salzburg	Salzburg	Austria
Sathmar	Satu Mare	Romania & Hungary
Schwäbische Türkei	Swabian Turkey	Hungary
Siebenbürgen[4]	Transylvania[5]	Romania
Slawonien[3]	Slavonia[5]	Croatia & Serbia[7]
Steiermark	Styria	Austria & Slovenia
Syrmien	Syrmia, Srem	Serbia[7]
Tirol	Tyrol	Austria & Italy
Trient	Trent	Italy
Triest[2]	Trieste	Italy
Ungarn[6]	Hungary	Hungary
Vorarlberg	Vorarlberg	Austria

[1] Bosnia and Herzegovina were one unit, not two.

[2] Trieste was part of Istria.

[3] Slovenia, which exists today, should not be confused with Slavonia, which used to exist. Slovenia was the northwesternmost republic of the former Yugoslav federation. The former Slavonia was east and southeast of present-day Slovenia and belongs to the present republic of Croatia and to the Vojvodina (Serbia).

[4] While Germans generally use "Siebenbürgen" as the equivalent of "Transylvania," the latter designation has sometimes been applied to a larger area than the old Siebenbürgen "Saxon" settlement.

[5] Hungary also ruled Transylvania, Croatia and Slavonia, although these were separate, semi-autonomous political entities.

[6] Parts of what was pre-1914 Hungary now belong to Austria, Croatia, Slovenia, Slovakia, Romania, Serbia and Ukraine.

[7] Virtually all of the German settlements in Serbia were in the formerly autonomous province of Vojvodina.

[8] Where more than one present-day country is listed, the first-named one has the largest portion of the area in question.

The headquarters of the "Old Catholics," a conservative minority group, are at:

> Alt-Katholische Kirche Österreichs
> Schottenring 17
> A-1010 Wien
> Austria

The Protestant archive, which has parish registers for the whole Austro-Hungarian Empire after 1878 and some records (not parish registers) back to 1758, is at:

> Archiv des evangelischen Oberkirchenrats
> Severin-Schreiber-Gasse 3
> A-1180 Wien
> Austria

The Jewish archive is at:

> Israelitische Kulturgemeinde
> Schottenring 25
> A-1010 Wien
> Austria

CIVIL RECORDS

The first census was taken in 1754 and civil registration began in 1784, but few of the early records appear to have survived. The modern records are available at the local civil registry office (*Standesamt*). There is a special civil registry for members of various religious minorities at the *Standesamt* in Vienna, but it dates back only to 1870.

The information listed for Galicia under **CIVIL RECORDS** in the section on **POLAND** with respect to land cadasters (land survey and ownership records for tax purposes) and accompanying maps is also applicable to other parts of the Hapsburg Empire.

MILITARY RECORDS

After 1869, men had a lifelong obligation for military service in the Austro-Hungarian Empire, with exemptions for Catholic clergy, nobles and some government officials. There were separate military parish registers, as in Germany. The Family History Library has microfilmed many records of the Austrian War Archives. The military archive, one of four branches of the Austrian national archives, has records for the whole empire going back to 1740. Its address is:

> Österreichisches Staatsarchiv
> Kriegsarchiv
> Nottendorfergasse 2
> A-1030 Wien
> Austria

MISCELLANEOUS RECORDS

Other records, some going back to the sixteenth century, which are available for at least some places and time periods, include: city directories, emigration records, police registers, census lists, school and university records, house books, citizen registers, probate records, apprenticeship and guild records, land records, records pertaining to the nobility, tax records, orphan records, poorhouse records and court records. Of particular significance are the city archives of Vienna:

> Wiener Stadt- und Landesarchiv
> Neues Rathaus
> Felderstrasse 1
> A-1082 Wien
> Austria

Of the four branches of the Austrian national archives, the one with more information of genealogical value for ancestors from Austria (it has emigration records from 1861-1919) is:

> Österreichisches Staatsarchiv
> Haus-, Hof- und Staatsarchiv
> Minoritenplatz 1
> A-1010 Wien
> Austria

However, records pertaining to the German settlers in the Banat, Galicia and Transylvania can be found at:

> Österreichisches Staatsarchiv
> Hofkammerarchiv
> Johannesgasse 6
> A-1010 Wien
> Austria

Since the Bozen-Südtirol area was under Austrian rule until 1919, documents concerning Germanic emigrants from there are more likely to be available from the archive listed below. This archive indicates, however, that no centralized emigration records were kept, so the prospects of locating ancestors without knowing the village from which they came are slim.

> Tiroler Landesarchiv
> Herrengasse 1
> A-6010 Innsbruck
> Austria

But check Edward Reimer Brandt, "Consular Records on Austrian Emigration and Immigration at the Austrian State (National) Archives," in the *Heritage Review*, vol. 23, no. 2, 1993.

For further details about Austrian records, see *Ward's German-American Genealogical Workshop Bulletin*, which contains a table that is reproduced in *The German Connection*, August 1983.

GENEALOGICAL SOCIETIES

The principal Austrian genealogical societies are:

Heraldisch-genealogische
  Gesellschaft "Adler"
Haarhof 4a
A-1014 Wien
Austria

Arbeitsbund für österreichische
  Familienkunde
Bürgergasse 2A/1
A-1040 Wien
Austria

Also check at the address for the Institute for Historic Family Research in Vienna listed in Chapter XII under **AUSTRIA**.

Thode lists the genealogical societies or branches for specific provinces, as well as the central archives for the Teutonic Knights (whose chief impact, interestingly, was in areas never part of the Holy Roman Empire). See under **GERMANY** for the address of a genealogical society for the Salzburger Protestants (*Exulanten*) expelled in the 1730s.

SWITZERLAND
(die Schweiz)

SEARCHING THE RECORDS

The most important factor in researching Swiss ancestry is to determine the place of origin or the community in which the person possessed rights of citizenship. All vital statistic information is recorded at the place of origin of the Swiss citizen. Most communities have records for three or four generations and some records data back to the 1600s.

Before undertaking research in the records of Switzerland, keep in mind the following facts:

1. Of the four national languages, French is spoken in the west, Italian in the south, Romansh in the southeast, and German in the rest of the country, as well as being interspersed with Romansh in the southeast.

2. Although the cantons are united to form one Confederation of Switzerland, each canton is politically independent with its own government and record keeping system. Access to the records differs from canton to canton. If you write to Swiss record offices, be sure to state that you are researching your own family line.

3. A Swiss person becomes a **citizen of the community of origin** and this automatically makes the person a citizen of that canton and of Switzerland (in contrast to the United States, where national citizenship makes a person a citizen of all states and local areas of the United States). Records of the citizen remain at the community of citizenship, even if the person moves from town to town (or goes to America). Movements are often noted in these records. When women marry, they forfeit their native rights of citizenship and assume the rights of citizenship in the husband's community.

4. Most people are members of the Catholic or Reformed Church, but there are also members of smaller churches, especially Mennonites and Baptists. Many Huguenots passed through Switzerland on their flight from persecution.

CHURCH RECORDS

These records are extensive and are among the best kept in Europe. Some date as far back as 1490. Church or parish records include records of baptisms, confirmations, marriages and deaths. Confirmation books contain records of 15-year-old boys and girls preparing themselves for this event. Catholic records are kept in the local churches, while Protestant registers are either in the city or town archives, the state archives, or the civil registrar's office. Many have been microfilmed by the Family History Library in Salt Lake City. Always check these records before writing to Switzerland.

CIVIL AND MISCELLANEOUS RECORDS

Civil records for all of Switzerland began in 1848 at the church level and in 1876 at the federal level. Each municipality or community keeps all records for its citizens. Included in these papers are vital records, ecclesiastical records and family records (*Familienscheine*). **Family records** show names of parents (and often grandparents), their children and their marriages (naming the spouse). They give details regarding births, marriages, deaths, and mention religions and occupation. These cover 1820 to the present day (some go back to the 1600s), and are kept at the local registrar's office.

Other civil records include **wills**, often dating back to the 1600s, and **census records** starting in 1836-38 and continuing. These records are housed at the state and city archives. **Military records** dating from 1800 and **emigration records** from the early 17th century to 1848 are found in the state archives of the canton; after 1848 the records were kept by the Schweizer Bundesregierung, Bundeshaus, CH-3000 Bern. Sometimes the local registrar has **burgher rolls** (*Bevölkerungsverzeichnisse*) dating back to the 11th century. For additional details concerning the nature and location of various records, see *Ward's German-American Genealogical Workshop Bulletin*, referenced under Austria.

A unique reference source for locating a Swiss family's origin is the set of books called *Familiennamenbuch der Schweiz* (*Swiss Surname Book*), published by Polygraphischer Verlag in Zürich. This collection lists every Swiss surname, in which town it is found, and the time period when the name first appeared in the records. The lists are compiled from the citizenship records in each town.

Another resource to locate a Swiss surname and family information is the data compiled between 1896 and 1950 by Swiss genealogist, Julius Billeter, who traced many Swiss lines. The information was obtained from parish and civil registers. It is arranged in family groups with entries dating from 1500-1900. Billeter's surname work and data on family groups has been microfilmed by the FHL. See *Handy Guide to Swiss Genealogical Records* by Jared H. Suess for alphabetical listings with film numbers. Also check *The Swiss Emigration Index* by Cornelia Schrader-Muggenthaler.

You can get a brief pamphlet, *A Genealogical How-To for Americans of Swiss Descent*, free from the Swiss National Tourist Office, 608 Fifth Ave., New York, NY 10020. This pamphlet describes the services and fees of the Central Office for Genealogical Information in Zürich, which is maintained by the Swiss Genealogical Society, or SGFF. The pamphlet also lists researchers for specific cantons, as well as several private Swiss and American services providing genealogical research assistance.

GENEALOGICAL SOCIETIES

For general genealogical information, you may write in English to:

> Manuel Aicher, Manager
> Central Office for Genealogical Information
> Vogelaustrasse 34
> CH-8953 Datikon
> Switzerland

You must enclose a $20 fee with the inquiry for any name or place of interest. In your letter you should include available details on your family, especially its place of origin. Otherwise, more extensive research will need to be done, involving a higher fee. This office will send you information as to what kinds of archival, published and unpublished material are available. But you will have to hire a professional researcher to do specific research on your family.

The following is the Jewish Genealogical Society of Switzerland:

> Schweizerische Vereinigung für jüdische Genealogie
> c/o Rene Loeb
> P.O. Box 876
> CH-8021 Zürich
> Switzerland

LUXEMBOURG
(Luxemburg)

CHURCH RECORDS

The chief religion in Luxembourg is Roman Catholic. Church registers have been kept since the 1600s, with the majority written in Latin. Most of the records are still kept in the parish office, although the records of larger cities have been incorporated in the commune archives. The commune is a political division roughly similar to our township. The FHL has filmed many of these church records. You will have to know the name of the canton (county) in which the town is located before being able to use these films.

CIVIL REGISTRATION

The French occupied Luxembourg and introduced the system of civil registration in 1795. These vital statistics are referred to as *état civil*. By 1802, all communes were recording births, marriages, and deaths. Every ten years an index (*Tables Decennales*) was prepared for each commune. These name indexes are located at the Luxembourg State Archives and have also been microfilmed by the FHL. Individual registers for 1802 to 1875 have also been filmed by the FHL. Records after that time are considered private, although specific privilege can be obtained to research an individual record.

CENSUS RECORDS

The first census was taken in 1843 and one has been taken at various times since then. They have not been microfilmed, but are available for consultation in the Luxembourg archives as long as the record is older than 100 years. There is no general index, so you will have to know the name of the town in order to use them.

Luxembourg National Archives:

Archives de l'État
Plateau-du-St. Esprit
Bôite Postale 6
L-2010 Luxembourg Ville
Grand Duchy of Luxembourg

Luxembourg Genealogical Society:

Association Luxembourgeoise de
    Généalogie et d'Héraldique
Kuebenek 1
L-5404 Bech/Kleinmacher
Grand Duchy of Luxembourg

LIECHTENSTEIN

CHURCH RECORDS

Roman Catholicism is the chief religion. Church records for the period before 1878 remain in the local churches and often go back to 1640. For more information about birth, marriage and death records, write to the Catholic parish (*katholisches Pfarramt*) of the town in question.

CIVIL RECORDS

All records from 1878 forward are now kept in the Civil Registry Bureau in Vaduz, the capital of Liechtenstein. Wills are in the custody of the local courts in each district, with the earliest dated 1690. The Civil Registry Bureau will look up records for a fee (or sometimes free if staff is available and the records are easily located). Send inquiries to:

Kanzlei der Regierung des Fürstentums Liechtenstein
FL-9490 Vaduz
Liechtenstein

You may also want to write to the archives if you need help with your Liechtenstein family:

Liechtensteiner Landesarchiv
Regierungsgebäude
FL-9490 Vaduz
Liechtenstein .

INTRODUCTION TO NON-GERMANIC COUNTRIES

Few Americans realize how many German-speaking immigrants came to North and South America from non-Germanic countries, in addition to those from areas that were once Germanic. Two factors account for most of this:

- There was a large eastward migration of German-speakers in Europe over a period of a thousand years. Some of the medieval pioneers became assimilated Slavs. More Slavs became Germanicized. However, some of the medieval and nearly all of the modern migrants to German-speaking enclaves in Eastern Europe (many of them far from the Germanic core of Central Europe) retained their Germanic identity. In terms of the size of the population of those days, this eastward migration was of a magnitude almost comparable to the later, but overlapping, period of trans-oceanic migration.

- People whose ancestors or relatives had already migrated once were much more likely to migrate again than the descendants of those who stayed at home. Therefore, while a substantial majority of German-Americans have ancestors who emigrated from within the boundaries of the 1871-1918 German Empire (but with a rather large number from the former eastern provinces), several million North Americans are descended from East European Germans.

It is impossible to get very accurate figures on the number of German-speakers, or ethnic Germans, who lived in non-Germanic countries. However, Wilhelm Winkler has made a valiant effort in his *Statistisches Handbuch des gesamten Deutschtums* [*Statistical Handbook of All German Regions*]. So long as we keep in mind that there is a large possible margin of error, as he himself acknowledges, the following table will nevertheless give us some idea of the size of the Germanic population in non-Germanic Europe, based on data in the early 1920s, within the boundaries then existing:

Table 9: Germanic Population in Non-Germanic Europe, 1920s

Country	Population	Country	Population
Czechoslovakia	3,500,000	Belgium	150,000
France	1,700,000	Lithuania	131,000
Poland	1,350,000	Netherlands	80,000
Soviet Union	1,180,000	Latvia	75,000
Romania	800,000	Denmark	60,000
Yugoslavia	700,000	Great Britain	50,000
Hungary	600,000	Estonia	35,000
Italy	300,000	Turkey	25,500

Nearly all of those in Eastern Europe had previously been under German, Austro-Hungarian or Russian rule, but 3-4 million were nowhere close to a Germanic "homeland." On the other hand, the overwhelming majority of Germans in non-Germanic countries on the west, south and north lived in a border territory that had previously been under German or Austrian rule.

Clearly Winkler's figures require some modification. The number for France is much too high, unless one counts all of the mixed German-French families in Alsace-Lorraine as German (and even then the figure is too high). On the other hand, the actual 1897 census figures for the Russian Empire listed about 1,790,000 Germans and even the 1926 Soviet census (which excluded about 750,000 Germans in territory no longer under Soviet Russian rule, as well as the large number who emigrated in 1874-1914) was higher than Winkler's figure. Thus we can see that the German-speaking population in non-Germanic European countries was in the vicinity of 10 million, or in excess of the combined German-speaking population of Austria, Switzerland, Luxembourg and Liechtenstein.

The best source for the new non-Germanic names of villages that had German names before World War I is the FHL-microfilmed gazetteer by Kredel and Thierfelder. See Chapter VIII.

The number of North and South Americans descended from these East European German immigrants is even harder to calculate, but estimates for those of Russian German descent alone range up to as high as 5 million in the U.S., with probably half as many in Canada and several million in Latin America, particularly in Argentina.

EAST AND SOUTH EUROPEAN COUNTRIES

A key resource for researching German-speaking ancestors from Eastern Europe is the *Genealogical Guide to German Ancestors from East Germany and Eastern Europe*, prepared by the Arbeitsgemeinschaft ostdeutscher Familienforscher (AGoFF), i.e., the Working Group of Genealogists Concerned with Germans in the East (which is more accurate than a literal translation of the words). The second edition of this book, which contains maps showing all the German settlements in Eastern Europe, has been translated into English by Joachim O. R. Nuthack and Dr. Adalbert Goertz. It will be referred to in some places as the *AGoFF Guide*. Significant portions of the information in this book stem from that source. There is now a fourth German edition (which has not been translated into English). The fourth German edition will be referred to as the *AGoFF-Wegweiser*. (For further information on resources pertinent to East Europe, look under **GERMANY** and **AUSTRIA** earlier in this chapter.)

Many of the parish registers and other archival documents for Germanic areas in Eastern and Southern Europe are at the Deutsche Zentralstelle für Genealogie in Leipzig. Others are at Evangelisches Zentralarchiv in Berlin. See **GERMANY** for the addresses. The Leipzig records have been microfilmed by the Family History Library and are inventoried in an easy-to-use list form in Martina Wermes, Renate Jude, Marion Bahr, and Hans-Jürgen Voigt, *Bestandsverzeichnis der Deutschen Zentralstelle für Genealogie*, Vol. II: *Die archivalischen und Kirchenbuchunterlagen deutscher Siedlungsgebiete im Ausland: Bessarabien, Bukowina, Estland, Lettland und Litauen, Siebenbürgen, Sudetenland, Slowenien und Südtirol* (see bibliography).

The *Ratgeber '92: Familienforschung GUS/Baltikum* [Advisor '92: Family History Research in the CIS and Baltic Countries] lists the names of a large number of individual researchers throughout the former Soviet Union (mostly in Russia, Belarus and the Baltics) who are willing to undertake private research. This article mentions the foreign language competence of the various researchers. Most of them know English, while all of the others know German, which simplifies the translation problem. The use of private researchers is complicated by the factors listed under **RUSSIA**, as well as by the slowness of mail service to the Commonwealth of Independent States (CIS). Irina and Rainer Zielke have compiled the *Ratgeber '93-'94*, which is supposed to be published by the Verlag Degener & Co., Neustadt/Aisch.

For a good geographical sampling of CIS and Baltic researchers, see "Genealogical Spring in the Former Soviet Union" by Edward R. Brandt and David F. Schmidt, in the June 1993 issue of the *East European Genealogist*, published by the East European Branch of the Manitoba Genealogical Society.

For information on German-speaking Jews from Eastern Europe and elsewhere, see *Avotaynu* and *Dorot*, two of the leading Jewish genealogical periodicals, as well as the books listed in the bibliography.

There is also a lot of information pertaining to immigrants from East Europe, including the papers of the Jewish Archives Center, at:

The Balch Institute of Ethnic Studies
Temple University
18 S. 7th St.
Philadelphia, PA 19106

The following institute also deals with East European Jewish genealogical research:

YIVO Institute for Jewish Research
555 W. 57th St., Ste. 1100
New York, NY 10019-2925

Robert Ward, 21010 Mastick Rd., Fairview Park, OH 44126, is the leading American historical and genealogical expert on Germans who immigrated from Southeast Europe.

The rapid increase in information about genealogical resources and researchers in Eastern Europe after the collapse of the Iron Curtain, and the fact that so many parts of Eastern Europe had ethnically mixed populations or significant minorities, led to the formation of the multi-ethnic Federation of East European Family History Societies (FEEFHS) in 1992. The first newsletter of that society was published in December 1992, in order to facilitate the rapid spread of such information. Both organizations and individuals may become members. Most East European-oriented ethnic genealogical societies are members, but currently only a few Jewish ones. Most major German-American genealogical societies also belong to FEEFHS. The permanent address of FEEFHS is P.O. Box 21346, Salt Lake City, UT 84121, from where mail will be forwarded to officers, board members and others, as necessary. The area of interest of FEEFHS includes all of Germany and Austria, because of their historic links to Eastern Europe, but the focus is on the ex-Communist areas.

FEEFHS has now published a *Resource Guide to East European Genealogy*, which will be updated semi-annually. It includes information about all member societies and also provides information about professional genealogists and translators specializing in Eastern Europe (including the Germanic countries in Central Europe). To order a copy or subscribe to the updates, write John D. Movius, P.O. Box 4327, Davis, CA 95616-4327.

Following American practice, the term "Eastern Europe" is used in this book to include what Europeans and historians refer to as East Central Europe and Southeast Europe.

THE SOVIET UNION: SUCCESSOR STATES

The migration of Germans to the Russian Empire is dealt with in Chapter X on **HISTORY**. The most authoritative history of the German settlements in the Russian Empire is Dr. Adam Giesinger, *From Catherine to Khrushchev: The Story of Russia's Germans*. The most comprehensive source of information as to the places of origin of these immigrants is Dr. Karl Stumpp, *The Emigration from Germany to Russia in the Years 1763 to 1862*. Robert and Margaret (Zimmerman) Freeman of the Glückstal Colony Research Association, prepared a place name index to Adam Giesinger's *From Catherine to Khrushchev* in 1986.

RECORDS OF THE FORMER RUSSIAN EMPIRE

The availability of genealogical records from the successor states to the former Soviet Union changes frequently and unpredictably. Therefore, some of the information provided here is likely to be out of date by the time this reaches the printer.

For example, there are many as yet unfilmed religious and civil records for the Volga and Black Sea Catholics, as well as for a few Black Sea German villages, in the archives at Engels (formerly Pokrovsk) and in Saratov. Many records in the Russian State Historical Archive (RGIA) in St. Petersburg (the former capital) and the Russian State Archive of Ancient Acts (RGADA) in Moscow have not been filmed. The same is true of the numerous archives in Ukraine and other countries that were part of the Soviet Union.

There are undoubtedly many records that have not even been found yet, in view of the secrecy of the Soviet era, the absence of adequate archival finding aids, and the shortage of researchers with a significant amount of genealogical experience.

A Handbook for Archival Research in the U.S.S.R. (1989) by Patricia Grimsted Kennedy, the leading American expert on Soviet archives, is the best introduction to this subject, dealing with archival organization, research strategies and general reference tools. Appendices list the major repositories in the former Soviet archives. The book is available from IREX (International Research & Exchanges Board), attn. Ann Robertson, 1616 H St. N.W., Washington, DC 20006. But it is of very limited value unless you know Russian and can read the cyrillic script.

Vladislav Soshnikov of the former Archives of Russia Society, Ltd. (AROS) told the 1994 convention of the Federation of East European Family History Societies (FEEFHS) that while a few former Soviet archives suffered considerable damage in World War II, the archival holdings are relatively complete on the whole, since many of the records had been evacuated to the east after the German invasion, while those taken to Germany during the war had since been returned.

The archives in Saratov, and especially Engels, are particularly useful for the records of the provinces of Saratov and of the *Wiesenseite*, which was separated from it in 1852 and included the Samara villages founded later farther north along the Volga River. (The *Wiesenseite* or "meadow side" referred to the flat land on the east side of the Volga, as contrasted with the *Bergseite* or "hilly side" on the west.) These records include incomplete revisions of 1834, 1850 and 1857, as well as parish registers and early settlement lists resembling revisions, and other post-1857 records. Soshnikov has a list of the Saratov records, and Igor R. Pleve has done extensive research in both archives. A revision was somewhat similar to a census.

The territorial administrative structure during the Soviet and post-Soviet eras is quite different from that of the Czarist days. The Russian Empire was divided into *guberni(y)as* or *gubernii* (provinces), with roughly analogous regions known as *oblasts* or *oblasty* in Asia and the Caucasus. *Guberniyas* were divided into districts, each known as an *u(y)ezd*. (These terms are sometimes spelled with, and sometimes without, the *y*. We will use the *y* form, because it reflects the pronunciation and may therefore be less confusing to English-speakers.)

The number, boundaries and size of *guberniyas* changed frequently, beginning with 8 in 1709 and increasing to 11 in 1719. During the 1775-1914 period that is most relevant for Germanic research, the number of *guberniyas* increased from 40 (each comprised of about 10 *uyezds* or *uyezdy*) to 78 (plus about 20 *oblasts*). In 1974 there were more than 125 Soviet *oblasts*. (Since English-speakers are accustomed to *s* as a plural, we will follow this practice, although it is contrary to Russian usage.)

Nineteenth-century imperial provinces in current Ukrainian or Moldovan territory included Kherson, Ekaterinoslav, Taurida, Bessarabia, Volhynia (*Zhitomir*), Podolia, Kiev and Kharkiv (Kharkov). Those in the Caucasus area included Kuban, Terek, and one for the trans-Caucasian province south of Terek.

Today an *oblast* serves roughly the same jurisdictional purpose as the former *guberniya* (a term no longer in use), with *uyezd* being the term still used for the sub-unit.

RESEARCH DIFFICULTIES

One difficulty is that some pre-revolutionary letters of the Russian alphabet no longer exist, so people with a knowledge of modern Russian (even native speakers) may have difficulty in deciphering the records.

Also, the members of the Commonwealth of Independent States, like other countries, generally have privacy laws that may permit access to records relating to your ancestors, but may impede access for the purpose of commercial publication. But the significant number of articles that have been published show that at least the nature of various records can be printed, even though the publication of information on specific unrelated individuals may be a different matter. Moreover, the archives charge access fees for researchers who search the records for other people for pay.

In order to find the records that you would like to have researched, it is necessary to explain the organization of the archival collections. According to Schmidt, co-author of "Genealogical Spring in the Former Soviet Union" (*East European Genealogist*, June 1993), the largest unit in a Russian archive is a *fond*. Each *fond* (record group) is further subdivided into a collection known as an *opis* (series). A *delo* is a still smaller unit, a file or storage unit. (Different terms are used in some of the other countries.)

For example, the 1798 Volga lists are in the Russian State Historical Archive (RGIA) in St. Petersburg in *fond* 393, *opis* 19, with the *delo* varying according to the village, according to Schmidt.

Since archival finding aids are rare, although they are now being developed, it may take a researcher many hours to find the records for which you are searching, if you do not have the identification number at all three levels.

Other difficulties include the shortage of archivists in Russia (and even more so in other CIS states) who are familiar with genealogy as we know it, the scattered records that are sometimes incomplete or in poor condition, and the field travel that is often required, complicated by weather, road conditions and various restrictions that may apply when researchers have to travel to other republics.

Pleve's article provides excellent insight into the many problems facing the genealogical researcher.

Another difficulty is that there is no secure way of sending money to CIS countries, except to Moscow. This makes it advisable to work through non-profit or commercial agencies, which provide courier services.

LUTHERAN, REFORMED, SEPARATIST AND MORAVIAN BRETHREN RECORDS

Slightly over three-fourths of the Germans in the Russian Empire at the time of the 1897 census were Lutherans, according to Giesinger. It is not clear whether this percentage includes the other non-Anabaptist Protestants, since Reformed and Lutherans alike prefixed their name with "Evangelical," the name of the merged church in Germany. Many of the Reformed churches (which had always constituted a minority) had become part of the Lutheran church organization by then, as had the smaller number of Separatists and Moravian Brethren.

The Family History Library has now microfilmed a collection of Lutheran parish registers of the Consistory of St. Petersburg. A total of 276 volumes of church books for over 199 parishes have been found in record group (*fond*) 828, series (*opis*) 14, at the Russian State Historical Archive in St. Petersburg. These records begin in 1833, when such vital registration became mandatory in the Russian Empire, and end in 1885. They are the duplicate copies that were sent yearly to the consistory office.

This consistory included the Black Sea region and Volhynia (i.e., all nineteenth-century settlements in Ukraine, except for those areas that belonged to the Austro-Hungarian Empire), as well as Belarus, western Russia and Moldova.

These records are mostly in the German language, are all in good shape, and are easy to read, but they have one drawback that makes them very difficult to use. Since they are the duplicate records that were sent yearly to the consistory office, they were filmed just that way, i.e., by year of receipt of the records in St. Petersburg (not always the year to which the records actually pertained), and without any geographic distinction. One roll of film can contain records from hundreds of different parishes. This means that a lot of time can be wasted in accessing these records.

Fortunately, Thomas Kent Edlund and a staff of volunteers at the Family History Library have spent over a year indexing these registers. The indexes contain the parish names, years covered, type of records, volume and page numbers, film numbers and item numbers on the film. In addition, Mr. Edlund details the historical background of German settlements in the Imperial Russian Empire. He also describes the history of the Lutheran Church and its jurisdictions.

The Germanic Genealogy Society thinks this parish index to be so valuable for researchers that we are publishing it under the title *The Lutherans of Russia*, Vol. 1: *Parish Index to the Church Books of the Evangelical Lutheran Consistory of St. Petersburg, 1833-1885*, (ISBN 0-9644-337-1-0) during the summer of 1995. This is just the first step, we hope, in locating and microfilming other church records of the former Russian Empire.

Lists of a few of these film numbers, indicating which areas and dates are included, were published recently in an article on "German-Russian Church Records & Registers (27 Oct. 93)," based on a compilation by Margaret Johnson and others, in the *Newsletter of the Puget Sound Chapter of GRHS* (reprinted by all other major American publications that focus on Russian Germans). "St. Petersburg Consistory Microfilms: 19th Century Lutheran Church Records" by Jerry Frank with the assistance of Howard Krushel (*Wandering Volhynians*, December 1994) lists the numbers for all Volhynian records.

Ewald Wuschke, publisher of *Wandering Volhynians*, is putting the film numbers for Volhynia on a computer database, a project expected to take several years.

The location of most records for churches that did not belong to parishes is unknown, but 24 registers for such churches are in the records of the Religious Council of the Evangelical Lutheran Church of St. Mary in *fond* 849 in the Saratov archive, according to Kahlile Mehr, "German-Russian Genealogical Records," in Vol. I, No. 22 (1994), of the *Genealogical*

Journal published by the Utah Genealogical Association. The staff of the American Historical Society of Germans from Russia reports (in the Winter 1994 issue of its *Newsletter*) that *fond* 852 contains records for six Black Sea parishes. In the same issue, Russian archivist O. K. Pudovochkina, "Information About the Black Sea Records in Saratov," states that 80% of the records in this *fond* are in German.

Sparse samplings have also been found in the St. Petersburg City Archive (18 churches for 1712-1926), Minsk (Belarus) Central Historical Archive (record group 1952), Grodno (Belarus) Central Historical Archive (record group 649 and others), and L'viv (Ukraine) Central Historical Archive (records group 427), as well as in local civil registry offices. Most of them, however, are believed to have been destroyed or lost. A few records from the Upper Volga area around Nizhny Novgorod, which became part of the St. Petersburg Consistory, have been microfilmed, but they include little, if any, information about Germans.

Gwen Pritzkau and Miriam Hall Hansen, Family History Library volunteers working with these records, have also compiled data for certain parishes. But there are gaps in the records for certain years and perhaps also certain parishes. Not all churches belonged to parishes because of the scattered German settlements in some areas.

The original parish registers for Ingria (*Ingermanland*, i.e., the St. Petersburg area) are known to be in Finland, which was also Lutheran and adjacent to St. Petersburg. This relatively small German settlement was older than the Volga colonies, but it is unknown whether these registers predate those of the other Germans.

A Lutheran consistory was opened in Saratov in 1819 and moved to Moscow in 1834, according to Pudovochkina. Some records for the Lutheran Consistory of Moscow have also been found in the Moscow City (formerly Regional) Archive, according to Mehr, who states that a 1961 description of this record group lists 62 items for 1803-1917.

Besides the consistories of St. Petersburg and Moscow, there were also six in the Baltics, viz., in Courland, Livonia, Estonia, Ösel (now Saarema), Riga and Reval (now Tallinn). There were 415 parishes in the Baltics, with a heavy concentration in Latvia, as contrasted with 87 in the St. Petersburg and 65 in the Volga river areas, in 1832. Lithuanian records are not included in this account, since most of the Lithuanian German parishes were in what was then East Prussia.

We are not aware of any published references to parish registers of the Reformed Church. However, Giesinger (on whose book we have relied for information about the Reformed, Separatist Lutherans, and Moravian Brethren) states that there were originally 3 Reformed parishes in the Volga area and that these were eventually absorbed into the Lutheran Church organization (apparently between 1810 and about 1840), although retaining their distinctive practices. In the early years, Catholic priests occasionally served the Reformed who were not close to one of the parish centers because of the antipathy between the major Protestant denominations. Somewhat less than one quarter of the Volga Protestants belonged to the Reformed Church in 1861.

In the Black Sea region, the pattern was somewhat different. Lutheran pastors served some of the Reformed living in scattered areas in the early years. Many of these became Lutherans. However, the remaining Reformed parishes never joined the Lutheran consistory.

Because of these complicated developments, the Lutheran parish registers may include data on members of the Reformed Church. For the early Volga years, Catholic records may also be include data on Reformed Church members.

There were also fervent Separatists (dissident Lutherans from Württemberg) in the Black Sea region and the Caucasus. They were served by their own lay preachers, and later trained preachers, for decades, but they eventually returned to the Lutheran Church.

The missionary-minded Moravian Brethren established a Volga village in 1765. They became part of the Lutheran Church in 1894.

ROMAN CATHOLIC RECORDS

About two-thirds of the Roman Catholics in the Russian Empire in the mid-nineteenth century were Germans, with Poles accounting for most of the rest (Giesinger). Presumably Russian Poland is excluded from this calculation.

The Tiraspol Consistory, established in 1847-50 (Giesinger), actually had its first seat in Kherson (Ukraine), then moved to Tiraspol (Ukraine) in 1852-53 (implied by Pudovochkina) and finally to Saratov (Volga area of Russia) in 1856-58 (Pudovochkina; Richard Rye of AHSGR). But it was generally known as the Tiraspol Consistory. There had been six Roman Catholic dioceses in the western *guberniyas* of the Russian Empire prior to this, but there were very few German Catholics in those areas.

According to Mehr, 647 Catholic parish register transcripts for the consistory located at Mogilev (Belarus) in 1783, and the Tiraspol Consistory, which assumed jurisdiction over the Black Sea and Volga Catholics, are in Saratov, specifically in *fond* 1166 ("Mogilev Roman Catholic Consistory") for 1801-1852 and in *fond* 365 ("Tiraspol Roman Catholic Consistory") for 1853-1918. The *fond* titles come from Pudovochkina, who also identifies the location more specifically as the State Archive of Saratov Oblast and specifies 513 files in *fond* 1166, *opis* 1, and 36 in an addendum thereto. About 500 of these files are registers, with the remainder devoted to other kinds of church business.

Fond 1267 ("Kherson Roman Catholic Consistory") in Saratov also includes copies of church books for 1850-53 that were sent from Kherson to Tiraspol, per Pudovochkina.

One set of volumes includes the provinces of Saratov, Samara and Astrakhan, while the other part covers the Black Sea region (provinces of Kherson, Taurida, and Bessarabia), and the Caucasus, according to Mehr and Pudovochkina.

The address Mehr lists is:

> Russia
> 410710 Saratov
> Kutyakova St., Building 15
> Regional Government Archive

The Family History Library has not yet received permission to film these records. You can write to the archives for information, but no one in the reference section speaks English, so it would be best to write in Russian. It may be more practical to go through the Russian-American Genealogical Archival Service (RAGAS, Box 236, Glen Echo, MD 20812), which will provide a bilingual form. RAGAS can be reached by phone at 202-501-5205 and via e-mail on Internet at "ragas@sovusa.com".

An alternative is to work through private researchers, such as Dr. Igor R. Pleve, who has found some German Catholic parish registers for the Volga area, as well as some Lutheran registers, since the Volga area was not within the ecclesiastical jurisdiction of St. Petersburg.

According to a statement by Mehr at the May 1994 FEEFHS convention (confirmed by Pudovochkina), a Roman Catholic diocese also existed in Zhitomir, but very few of the Volhynian Germans were Catholics.

Catholic registers were mandated in the Russian Empire in 1826. Three copies were required: one for the church, one for the diaconate, and one for the consistory.

MENNONITE AND BAPTIST RECORDS

There are two major sources of genealogical information about the Mennonites in the Russian Empire, nearly all of whom originally settled in Eastern Ukraine (with a small number on the Upper Volga, near Samara).

One is Benjamin Heinrich Unruh, *Die niederländisch-niederdeutschen Hintergründe der mennonitischen Ostwanderungen im 16., 18. und 19. Jahrhundert* [*The Netherlands and Northern German Background of Mennonite Migration to the East in the 16th, 18th and*

19th Centuries], which includes the revision lists for 1795 and 1808, in addition to various other archival records listing the emigrants from Prussia to South Russia, usually including the village of origin and the village of residence in Russia.

The other one is the 140,000-page Peter J. Braun Collection of records pertaining to the Molochna (*Molotschna*) colonies assembled during the Russian Civil War, which includes the 1835 revision (in Russian) and incomplete 1854-62 village pupil lists (in German). These records were discovered a few years ago in Odessa and are now available in Canada at the Mennonite Historical Centre, Winnipeg; Conrad Grebel College, Waterloo, Ontario; and at the University of Toronto.

Ingrid Epp, *The Peter J. Braun Russian Mennonite Archive, 1803-1920* (Toronto: Conrad Grebel College/University of Toronto Research Program in Russian Mennonite Studies, 1993), is designed to help users of the collection. Henry N. Fast, 497 Ash Ave., Steinbach, MB R0A 2A0, Canada, has made a rough translation of the 1835 revision.

Dr. Harvey Dyck is working on a major book on this collection. It will be published by the University of Totonto Press sometime in the summer of 1995.

Ewald Wuschke, *Protestant Parish Records on Microfilm for the Former Congress Poland (1815-1915) and Poland*, lists two Baptist registers for the 1870s in Central Poland. He also lists the records of four Mennonite parishes in Volhynia (1780-1940) and two in the Warsaw (1832-1876) and Gostynin (1863-64) areas of Poland.

A pioneering article by Charles Weisser, "The Baptist Movement Among the Germans in Russia," in the March 1992 issue of the *Heritage Review,* indicates that the Baptist movement began to gain ground in Russia between 1840 and 1860, and that by 1886 it had 12,000 members. It particularly attracted those who were affected by the Pietist movement, which influenced Lutherans, Mennonites, and even a few Catholics. By and large, the Baptist church, which also gained some Orthodox converts, was not the church of the immigrants, but rather a church to which Germans later flocked, although a few late immigrants to Volhynia were Baptists.

Several historical articles on German Baptists in or from the Russian Empire have been published in the *Journal of the American Historical Society of Germans from Russia.*

JEWISH RECORDS

Jewish registers were mandated in 1835, but are more complete after 1885. Duplicate copies were required, one for the government. Many of these records are in the rabbinates. There are 19 registers in Kiev. Records for some 70 localities in Galicia, which was formerly an Austrian crown province, are in L'viv (German: *Lemberg*). Some of these records are also in Warsaw. "What May be Learned from 19th-Century Czarist Jewish Birth Records and Revision Lists" by Harold Rhode is the latest (Fall 1994) of several detailed articles published in *Avotaynu* on Jewish records in the Russian Empire.

Those with Jewish ancestors from Ukraine (as well as Moldova and Poland) are in good luck. The following Jewish researcher spends half her time in these countries and has purchased an apartment in Ukraine to facilitate research:

> Miriam Weiner, C. G.
> 136 Sandpiper Key
> Secaucus, NJ 07904

A small number of Russian German immigrants, or their descendants, converted to Judaism, in addition to the Yiddish-speaking Jews who had been there for centuries in most cases.

CIVIL REGISTRATION

Civil registration was mandated in 1879, with duplicate copies required, one going to the government. Members of smaller religious groups, like the Baptists, are included in these. Civil registration was mandated by Austria in Galicia (now partly in Ukraine) in 1874.

Civil records for the period after the Russian Revolution are in the *ZAGS* (Russian) or *ZAHS* (Ukrainian) offices, archival units of the ministries of justice. Many parish registers can also be found here.

REVISION LISTS

Besides the parish registers, the most valuable sources of genealogical information appear to be the Russian revision lists, i.e., poll tax lists (also referred to as censuses), for every head of household had to pay a tax. Although there are some differences in the details provided by various revisions, they all include the names and ages of all members of the household. Some of them list the Russian patronymic form as the middle name, so that when you find a record of a male property owner, you automatically know the first name of his father. Unfortunately, the maiden names of the wives are often not recorded.

These revisions generally show what happened to the owners since the previous revision, i.e., the date of death or the place to which the family had moved and when. Property was only infrequently listed as belonging to widows. Mothers, the families of unpropertied siblings or children, and others residing in the same household are recorded. Some of the early revisions record the village from which the immigrant came.

There is some confusion concerning the dates, and even the numbers, of the various revisions. Using the numbers provided by Mehr, but expanding the range of years to include all of those mentioned by various sources, revisions made after the settlement of the Volga and Black Sea Germans include 1761-69 (3rd), 1775-88 (4th), 1794-1809 (5th), 1811-12 (6th; interrupted by the Napoleonic War and thus incomplete), 1815-25 (7th), 1833-35 (8th), 1849-52 (9th) and 1857-59 (10th).

However, David F. Schmidt has received entries from the 1798 Volga revision that clearly show the documents as part of the 6th revision. The most logical explanation for the discrepancy is that there may have been two revisions during the 1775-88 period. This is because Volga records for both 1775 and 1788 have been found, and the 1815-25 revision was a continuation of the one begun in 1811-12. No cases have been discovered where a revision was conducted in the same village during both of these periods.

Mehr states that lists for the last six (5th-10th) revisions (presumably only for the Volga area) can be found in the Saratov archive. But Richard Scheuermann's table, received from the American Historical Society of Germans from Russia, indicates that the 5th revision for the Volga region is at the St. Petersburg Historical Archive.

There could have been two copies of each revision, since there are other discrepancies in reports as to whether various revisions were left in the central or provincial archives. In fact, in one known case, the revision, or a later transcription of it, was found in an entirely different location. For example, some revisions prior to 1850 are said to have been kept in local archives, i.e., in the *guberniya* capital, while later ones are supposed to be in the central archives, but this conflicts with information about the known contents of the local archives in the Volga area.

According to the *Ratgeber '92: Familienforschung GUS/Baltikum*, the 3rd, part of the 4th and the 5th revisions are at the Russian Central State Archive of Ancient Acts (RGADA) in Moscow. But David F. Schmidt believes that the records of the 4th revision for the Volga Germans have been destroyed. Soshnikov reported that the 8th, 9th and 10th revisions that have been found are incomplete, at least for the Volga area. The first three revisions are reported to be in the archives in Moscow. The 3rd revision was the first one to list females (but not maiden names), but the mass migrations to the Volga River, the Black Sea region and Volhynia did not occur prior to this.

The American Historical Society of Germans from Russia now has a complete set of the 1798 Volga German revision lists.

The years when these revisions took place are usually not identical for the Volga and Black Sea areas. Therefore, it may be easier to find the records by specifying the revision list number than the year, once this is clearly established.

The 1st (1719-28), 2nd (1743) and 3rd (1761-69) revisions, as well as prior unnumbered revisions in 1646-48, 1676-78, 1710 and 1717, might be useful for the small number of Germans who were in St. Petersburg or Moscow by that time. Russia acquired the St. Petersburg area (Ingria) and the northern Baltics in 1721, adding Courland (southern and western Latvia) in 1795. Thus these early revisions could also be helpful for some Baltic Germans. However, the nobility and high-ranking public or church officials (to which class many of these Germans belonged) were exempt from taxation and thus are not listed.

Soshnikov reported that supplementary revisions were also made, but these are hard to find, since they are not indexed. A RAGAS flyer mentions local censuses, which may refer to the same kind of record. Scheuermann suggests that there may have been a partial 1880 Volga revision. The Unruh book includes the entries for the Chortitza Mennonites in both 1795 and 1808 (which fall within the same revision period), suggesting that the first one may have been a special census for the recent (1789-1794) arrivals.

THE 1897 CENSUS

The only comprehensive census in the Russian Empire, which included everyone, was conducted in 1897.

According to Giesinger, the 1,790,489 Germans were broken down by area as follows:

Table 10: Germanic Population in the Russian Empire, 1897

Area	Germanic Population
Russian Poland	407,274
Volga region	390,864
Black Sea region	377,798
Volhynia	171,331
Baltics	165,627
St. Petersburg district	50,780
Caucasus and trans-Ural areas	71,027
Elsewhere in European Russia	155,788

By 1926 the number of Germans shrank to 1,238,549. This was due to relatively large-scale emigration after 1873, the severance of the Baltics, Russian Poland and half of Volhynia from the Soviet Union after World War I (areas that had about 750,000 Germans, per Giesinger), and the short-term consequences of the Russian Civil War. Despite flight from harsh Stalinist measures, famine, and the terroristic Stalinist purges, the total had climbed to 1,424,000 in 1939. The first post-Stalinist census in 1959 showed 1,619,000 and the 1970 census 1,846,000, despite the fact that German had been suppressed after Hitler's invasion of the Soviet Union (so that most young Russian Germans know little or no German) and talking about one's ancestors was a dangerous subject.

According to more recent published official figures, there are over 2 million Germans in the former Soviet Union, but a large number (known as *Aussiedler*) have since "resettled" in Germany.

The archives in Dnepropetrovsk (Ukraine) are known to have the complete 1897 census for that area. Some archives have only statistical reports.

NOBILITY AND BURGHER RECORDS

Genealogy is much more closely associated with heraldry in Europe, and especially Eastern Europe, than in the New World, which is one reason why it was suppressed by the Communists. Nobility records (many of which have been published, often in Germany for Russian German aristocrats) may be the best source of information for many Baltic Germans. Similar lists and published works exist for prominent burghers who did not belong to the aristocracy. According to Giesinger, there were about 25,000 German hereditary nobles and 17,000 non-hereditary nobles or officials in the Russian Empire in 1897, i.e., about 2% of the Germanic population.

Most of the Russian records pertaining to the Baltic German nobles are at the Russian State Historical Archive (RGIA) in St. Petersburg.

The *Ratgeber '92* lists researchers who have more research experience involving the nobility than in the tracing of non-aristocrats, with many of them in St. Petersburg or the Baltics. Even the archivists who work most closely with North American genealogical societies have often concentrated on this group in their graduate theses.

OTHER RECORDS

Other records that may be particularly helpful for Volga German research include:

(1) the Ivan Kuhlberg lists of German settlers arriving in Oranienbaum, near St. Petersburg, in the 1760s; these are in Russian and at Saratov, with a second, less detailed copy in Moscow; the birthplace of the head of household is included in the Saratov lists (David F. Schmidt)

(2) the list of 9,000 colonists transported to the Volga region (a small number were settled elsewhere); these are in German (David F. Schmidt)

(3) the 1767-68 list of settlers in the Saratov area (i.e., the original 1763-67 Volga settlement) compiled by the Saratov Office of Immigrant Affairs; a few villages are missing (David F. Schmidt)

(4) Volga family lists for 1798 (David F. Schmidt); similar lists were prepared for some early Black Sea settlements (Unruh)

Some of these records are described by Pleve in "Specific Genealogical Research Materials of Volga Germans" in the Fall 1993 issue of the *Journal of the American Historical Society of Germans from Russia*.

Dr. Alfred Eisfeld of Göttingen, Germany, plans to publish the original Volga settler lists and the American Historical Society of Germans from Russia has offered to assist him in marketing the book. He also intends to publish an inventory of the Odessa archives (Michael Miller).

Records mentioned in a RAGAS flyer that may be applicable to all Russian Germans include: (1) records of permission to emigrate (some of these are in Saratov, according to Jo Ann Kuhr of AHSGR); (2) military lists; (3) land and property records.

Those who are researching relatives, rather than ancestors, may be interested in knowing that the former KGB (secret police) records are now available for inspection, according to Prof. Borys Klein of the University of Hrodna (Russian: *Grodno*) in Belarus.

NORTH AMERICAN RESOURCES

The American Historical Society of Germans from Russia has extensive files, especially obituaries, as well as a library, relating to the Germans from throughout the former Russian Empire, except for the Baltics.

The Germans from Russia Heritage Society concentrates on Germans from the western Black Sea region, including Bessarabia and the Dobruja (which includes areas now part of Moldova, Romania and Bulgaria). GRHS has a large number of family, church or local histories, which may have useful background information on the German ancestors in the former Russian Empire, in its library.

The periodical, *Wandering Volhynians*, which publishes a surname index (as do the above), is the best source of information on Volhynia. Jerry Frank of Calgary has published this surname index in book form (*Research Helper for Germans from Poland and Volhynia*).

Various individuals, including Leona Janke of AHSGR and Tom Hoffman of GRHS, have accumulated a large amount of unpublished material.

Records pertaining to North Americans who went back to the Russian Empire for a visit, applied for visas to do so, or had other contacts with Russian consulates were rediscovered following a lengthy disappearance after the Russian Civil War. The authoritative work on this is Dr. Sallyann Amdur Sack and Suzan Wynne, *Russian Consular Records Index and Catalog*. Angus Baxter has a succinct treatment of this subject in the 1994 edition of *In Search of Your German Roots*.

THE BALTIC COUNTRIES (ESTONIA, LATVIA, LITHUANIA)
(das Baltikum: Estland, Lettland, Litauen)

The history of the Germans in Estonia and Latvia is covered by Chapter X on **HISTORY**.

Germans in Lithuania are distinct from those in Estonia and Latvia in that the largest number of them lived in the Memel region, which belonged to East Prussia until after World War I and was thus contiguous to other Germanic territory. Much smaller numbers of Germans later moved to other parts of Lithuania, mostly to the area east of Memel, but with scattered later settlements in other areas. The Lithuanian Germans, for the most part, were not members of the nobility, but peasants, along with some burghers.

Lithuania also differed in that most of it was never conquered by the Teutonic Knights. It was part of the Commonwealth of Poland and Lithuania for several centuries and remained a Catholic country, except for the Germans.

Some German parish registers for the Baltic countries have been copied by the Family History Library (FHL) from the microfilms at the Deutsche Zentralstelle für Genealogie in Leipzig, Germany.

There are numerous German genealogical publications pertaining to the Baltic Germans, many of whom left after World War I, when they were deprived of their privileged status and most of their land.

See earlier under **GERMANY** for additional pertinent genealogical information.

Since the Baltic countries were part of the Russian Empire for more than two centuries, you should also check the information on the **RECORDS OF THE FORMER RUSSIAN EMPIRE** and under **RUSSIA**.

ESTONIA (Estland)

There are microfilms of a few German parish registers at Leipzig, especially from the area of Dorpat (now Tartu), the site of the major university and seminary for the Germans in the Russian Empire. These have been copied by the FHL.

The other major German cities in Estonia were Tallinn (*Reval*) and Pärnu (*Pernau*).

Estonia became Lutheran in the early sixteenth century.

In addition to the few Estonian records in Leipzig, FHL crews are making rapid progress in filming the parish registers in Estonia. Some of these date back to the 1600s and continue through the 1940s.

The Estonian archives also cooperate with RAGAS. (See under **RUSSIA** for address.) Similarly, commercial firms with ties to the Russian State Historical Archive (RGIA) in St. Petersburg have also been successful in obtaining Estonian records.

The Estonian national archives are at:

> Eesti Ajaloo Arhiiv
> Tartu
> Estonia

LATVIA (Lettland)

A large number of Latvian German parish registers are on microfilm in Leipzig, as well at as the Family History Library.

There was a considerably larger urban element among the Germans in Latvia than in the other Baltic countries. Riga, Jelgava (*Mitau*), Liepäja (*Libau*) and Ventspils (*Windau*) were the major German urban settlements.

Latvia does not work with RAGAS. The Latvian State Historical Archive, which contains many records of births, marriages and deaths for the second half of the nineteenth and early twentieth centuries, is at:

> Latvijas Valsts Vestures Arhives
> 16 Slokaskiela
> Riga
> Latvia

However, most vital statistics records for the 1906-1940 period are stored at the Archive of Vital Records:

> Dzimtsaraktu Arhives
> 24 Kalku St.
> Riga
> Latvia

The latter archive is not open to private researchers, but written requests to the archives sometimes result in the receipt of documents.

Incidentally, many records for Jews, as well as German Christians, were kept in German, despite a Russian law to the contrary.

A useful article for all, although it focuses on Jewish research, is "Jewish Vital Statistic Records in the Latvian Archives," by Dr. Aleksandrs Feigmanis of the Museum and Documents Center of the Jews of Latvia in the Spring 1994 issue of *Avotaynu*. Some of the above information comes from this source.

The Family History Library has begun filming records in Riga.

LITHUANIA (Litauen)

The Lutheran records for the Memel area at the Evangelisches Zentralarchiv in Berlin are on microfilm at the Family History Library.

For the Memel (Klaipeda) area, where most of the Germans lived, try some of the books and addresses for East Prussia under **GERMANY**. For those parts of Lithuania that were part of interwar Poland, where there were a few scattered German settlements, see the information under **POLAND**.

The FHL has had little success in microfilming Lithuanian records to date. Lithuania has its own arrangements for genealogical research and does not participate in RAGAS.

The national archives of Lithuania are at:

> Lietuvos Valstybinis Istorijos Archyvas
> Gerosios Vilties 10
> 2015 Vilnius
> Lithuania

You can write to LVIA in English, but you must provide the town and the religion of the ancestors you are researching, according to Jessie L. Daraska, Department Chairperson, Immigration History & Genealogy Department, Balzekas Museum of Lithuanian Culture, 6500 Pulaski Road, Chicago, IL 60629-5136. The museum can assist people in finding the right religious (Catholic, Jewish, Lutheran) records and especially in determining the correct town. This institution recently established the Lithuanian American Genealogy Society, which uses the above address.

Do not send money with your initial inquiry to LVIA. You will be informed of the cost, based on the available information. The archives will accept money orders or bank transfers from American Express, Bankers Trust Co., Citibank North America, and

Midland plc (London), according to Bruce Kahn (*Avotaynu*, Fall 1994). Kahn reports that it costs $50 per family to initiate a search, $10 for extracts, and $20 for photocopies, including translation.

COMMONWEALTH OF INDEPENDENT STATES (CIS)
(Gemeinschaft unabhängiger Staaten/GUS)

Some of the addresses of former Soviet archives (listed above and below) are taken from "Archive Addresses: Lithuania, Belarus, Ukraine" in the Winter 1992 issue of *Pathways & Passages*, published by the Polish Genealogical Society of the Northeast. The addresses are also given in the Cyrillic alphabet to facilitate mail delivery.

RUSSIA (Russland)

More progress has been made in getting records from the archives of Russia than from any of the other countries belonging to the Commonwealth.

The Soviet-American Genealogical Archival Service (SAGAS) originally developed as a partnership between the then still Soviet archives, later the Archives of Russia, Ltd. (AROS), and the National Archives Volunteer Association (NAVA). It has now become the Russian-American Genealogical Archival Service, with the Genealogy and Family History Society (GFHS) founded by Soshnikov (formerly of AROS, which no longer exists) as the Russian partner.

For bilingual request forms for research through this channel, write to:

> RAGAS
> 1929 - 18th St. N.W., Suite 1112
> Washington, DC 20009

An initial non-refundable fee of $50 for a preliminary search of sources must be enclosed with each completed request. If the search is successful, there is an additional charge of $6 per hour for research, with a minimum deposit for 20 hours if you want a full genealogical profile, as contrasted with a request for a specific document. This deposit is refundable if the work takes less than 20 hours. (Prices are, of course, subject to change.)

A form is included for you to authorize expenditures up to a specified sum in addition to the minimum fee. Estimates, including all costs (record searches, copying and other archival fees, translation and compilation of reports, and travel expenses), will be provided for any research exceeding this amount. The $50 fee will be deducted from the total cost of the work.

Questions may also be sent directly to:

> Russia
> 127349 Moscow
> P. O. Box 459
> Genealogy and Family History Society

or via Internet at "vladrag@glas.apc.org".

Note that the customary form of address in the CIS is in the opposite order from ours.

GFHS has cooperative relationships with archives in many other CIS member states, as well as in Estonia. Moreover, this service is very valuable for other countries, because many of the records pertaining to all parts of the former Russian Empire (including the Russian-ruled part of Poland) are in the Russian State Archive of Ancient Acts (RGADA) in Moscow or the Russian State Historical Archive (RGIA) in St. Petersburg.

RAGAS has achieved excellent results, although the service is rather slow, due to the factors already mentioned. GFHS has now become independent of American support. However, Patricia A. Eames is now editing an enormously informative periodical with news of the most recent CIS developments. The address is: RAGAS Newsletter, Box 236, Glen Echo, MD 20812.

With respect to the Volga region, very thorough reports (including all of the descendants of the Volga settlers, insofar as they are listed in the various records that have been preserved) have been received from the dean of the history faculty at Saratov State University, who has made several presentations in the United States and who receives substantial research assistance from his wife. Contact:

> Russia
> 410 005 Saratov
> B. Gornaja st. 272, kv. 2
> Pleve, Dr. Igor R.

Pleve can also be reached by faxing 011-7-095-975-3273, with the notation, "for Pleve at Saratov" or through Internet e-mail at "igor@pleve.saratov.su".

He has consulted many sources, not only in the Volga region, and has prepared a complete chart of all descendants of an ancestor who immigrated to the Volga, and who remained there for $450-$750. Sources include the Kuhlberg lists, revision lists and parish registers, when available. Not all parish registers have been preserved or found.

Numerous commercial channels for obtaining data from the Russian archives in Moscow and St. Petersburg also exist. Results vary from excellent to nil. The best service has been rendered by Urbana Technologies, according to David F. Schmidt. This firm was sold in 1993, but the cooperative arrangement with MITEK Information Services in Moscow continues, through the following agent:

> Julia Petrakis
> United States Agent
> Facts OnLine
> 812 Vista Drive
> Camano Island, WA 98292

This company has also established contacts with researchers in other countries (Poland, Czech and Slovak Republics) and has access to TASS (government newspaper) files.

UKRAINE (Ukraine/Ukraina)

There were German settlements scattered throughout Ukraine, but none represented such a cohesive concentration as those in the Volga River region. Most of the Germans fell into one of two groups: the Black Sea Germans and the Volhynian Germans (in what is now northwestern Ukraine).

In addition, Ukraine includes three areas of German settlement in eastern parts of the former Austro-Hungarian Empire: East Galicia, North Bukovina, and Carpatho-Ukraine (which belonged to Czechoslovakia during the interwar period between World War I and World War II).

Most of the Bessarabian parish registers were microfilmed by the Family History Library in 1948, as a result of German access to this area when it still belonged to Romania.

For those parts of Ukraine that belonged to interwar Poland (i.e., western Volhynia and eastern Galicia), see the information under **POLAND**. For areas that belonged to **AUSTRIA**, **HUNGARY** or **ROMANIA** (i.e., the Bukovina, Bessarabia, Galicia and Carpatho-Ukraine (also known as Subcarpathian Rus'), check those countries, as well as **GERMANY** and **RUSSIA** for possible additional information. Records for Carpatho-Ukraine may also be in the **SLOVAK REPUBLIC** or possibly even in the **CZECH REPUBLIC**.

Soshnikov reported that some Ukrainian archives (Poltava and Kharkiv) were largely destroyed in World War II. However, relatively complete German records exist in Odessa, Kiev (both central and regional historical archives), L'viv (*Lemberg*), Dnepropetrovsk, and

Podolski. The Dnepropetrovsk archives has an index of German records, as does Zhitomir for the early (1795-1858) revision lists of Germans in the Zhitomir *guberniya* (Volhynia). However, only a few Germans migrated there before 1861, so this will not help many genealogists. Unfortunately, the other archives have no genealogically-oriented finding aids. However, there are revision lists in most of these archives.

Some of the revision lists for Germans have been published or microfilmed. These include various Black Sea German revision lists published (often only in part) in Karl Stumpp, *The Emigration from Germany to Russia in the Years 1763 to 1862*, and the Mennonite lists in Unruh's book.

The Kiev Central Historical Archive has Jewish rabbinical lists, including those for Volhynia.

The Russian archivists working with RAGAS have generally good relations with most of these archives, but Moscow-based field travel is sometimes necessary. The Odessa and Dnepropetrovsk archives are said to be very cooperative.

The two central state historical archives are:

Ukraine
290 006 L'viv - 4
Tsentralnyi derzhavnyi arkhiv Ukrainy
pl. Vozziednannia 3A

Ukraine
252 601 Kiev - 1000
Tsentralnyi derzhavnyi arkhiv Ukrainy
u m. Kyievni
vul. Solomianska 24

Incidentally, there are both central and *oblast* archives with genealogically significant records in both cities.

"Report on a Recent Trip to Ukrainian Archives" by Dr. George Bolotenko of the National Archives of Canada in the Spring 1994 issue of *Avotaynu* provides an extremely detailed description of the genealogically valuable contents of several archives in Western Ukraine, as well as the extremely difficult conditions under which these archivists are working. Topics covered by the article include the very complete 1785-88 Josephinian and the somewhat less accurate 1819-20 Franciscan revision lists (or land cadasters) for Galicia, as well as court records from 1372 to the end of the nineteenth century, found in the L'viv Central State Historical Archives. The Josephinian records are in German; the other records are mostly in Latin.

There are also metrical records (vital statistics books, including parish and synagogue registers), as well as various kinds of civil records, in L'viv.

The 37 *oblast* archives under the supervision of the Main Archival Directorate of Ukraine (MADU) also have valuable records.

Bolotenko reported that the procedure for written requests for information from these archives did not work very well in 1993, despite the willingness of local archivists to do research, because foreign requests had to be cleared by two national ministries, which rarely got around to dealing with these requests because of other priorities. However, *Avotaynu* editor, Dr. Sallyann Amdur Sack, says that top officials of the Archival Ministry of Ukraine stated, during a January 1994 visit to the National Archives of Canada, that the archives are now freely open to all foreigners on the same basis as they are to Ukrainians. This shows how rapidly policies can change. Other sources confirm this, but indicate that policy changes in CIS member countries are not necessarily irreversible.

In addition to the Bolotenko article, Brian J. Lenius has reported on the transfer of some East Galician Jewish and German Catholic records, respectively, from Ukraine to archives in Poland, viz., to Warsaw, Przemysl, and Lubaczów, in several articles in the *East European Genealogist*. The East European Branch of the Manitoba Genealogical Society also has the addresses of several North American researchers who accept genealogical assignments in Western Ukraine.

According to Paul Polansky of the Bukovina Society of the Americas (per letter from Roland Wagner), the last mayor of Rastadt (in the Odessa area) took the village archives with him when he left Ukraine, but he was detained in Poland, the material was confiscated and it somehow ended up in the archive in Poznan (Posen).

See Krushel, "Genealogical Research in Volhynia" (*Wandering Volhynians*, September 1994), for the most comprehensive treatment of that area. He is a representative of the MIR Corporation (USA and Ukraine), which works with the Ukrainian state archives to obtain ancestral information. Contact:

> Howard Krushel
> 136 Silver Springs Dr. N.W.
> Calgary, AB T3B 3G4
> Canada

The FHL has been less successful in gaining access to archival records in Ukraine than in Russia, but at least four film crews are now at work in that country. However, the records being filmed in L'viv and Kiev are not pertinent for Germanic research.

The archive in Uzhhorod has many records for Carpatho-Ukraine (historically part of Slovakia). However, it does not have any parish registers. There were Germanic enclaves around Mukachevo (*Munkatsch*) and in the *Theresienthal* (Theresa valley) around Deutsch-Mokra. This area is known variously as Carpatho-Ukraine, Sub-Carpathian Ukraine and Subcarpathian Rus'.

BELARUS (Weissrussland/Bjelorussland)

Except for the many Jews (who may or may not have had a close Germanic connection), there were comparatively few German settlers in Belarus, although there were German traders and business establishments there.

However, there were a few German Protestant villages on both sides of the Bug River, along the Belorussian-Polish border, according to a Polish article received from Henryk Skrzypinski of Bydgoszcz, Poland. Some of these are known to have been of Mennonite origin.

Almost complete records for the Bialystok area in Northeastern Poland, which was briefly under Prussian rule in 1795-1806 and where there were a few German settlements, can be found in the following archive:

> Belarus
> Tsentralny dziarzhauny histarychny arkhiu Belarusi
> u h. Hrodne
> 230 023 Hrodna
> vul. Kozlova 26

The other major Belorussian archive is:

> Belarus
> 220 038 Minsk
> Tsentralny dziarzhauny histarychny arkiu Belarusi
> u h. Minsku
> pl. Lenina 2

Some Belorussian records can be found in local archives.

Soshnikov, "Belorussian Archives Revisited" (*Avotaynu*, Fall 1994), provides a thorough report on records found there.

MOLDOVA (Moldau)

The northern part of the Bessarabian colonies and most of the Glückstal villages in the Odessa region are now in Moldova. Obtaining records from there has been difficult to date.

The problem is complicated by the fact that the area east of the Dniester River (not part of Bessarabia) is not under the control of the Moldovan government.

However, Weiner has succeeded in getting Jewish records by going to the Moldovan archives in person.

THE CAUCASUS (Der Kaukasus)
(GEORGIA, AZERBAIJAN, ARMENIA, SOUTH RUSSIA)

Germans settled in the South Caucasus (southern Georgia and northern Azerbaijan, extending slightly into Armenia) in the early nineteenth century. Later, the Black Sea (and, to a lesser extent, the Volga) Germans established daughter colonies in the northern Caucasus. Most of this area is actually the southernmost part of European Russia, along the Georgian border, but it is partly in the autonomous regions of Ossetia, Chechnya, Ingushetia, Dagestan, Kabardino-Bulkaria, Adygea and Abkhazia (Abkhazia and the southern part of Ossetia being in northwestern Georgia), inhabited by distinct ethnic groups that have a degree of autonomy.

Although relatively few Germans appear to have emigrated from the Caucasus before World War I, they constituted an important share of the political refugees of the 1920s, partly because they were close to the Turkish and Iranian borders. At least one group escaped to Iran via the Caspian Sea, thus eluding border patrols. But most made their way to Harbin, Manchuria, using the Trans-Siberian Railway and then crossing the Amur River at night, with a large majority ending up in Western Canada or Latin America (especially Brazil and Paraguay). The Northern Illinois Chapter of the American Historical Society of Germans from Russia has copies of some records pertaining to the Harbin refugees.

Records from Azerbaijani archives have been obtained through RAGAS.

SIBERIA AND THE ASIAN MUSLIM REPUBLICS
(KAZAKHSTAN, TURKMENISTAN, KYRGYZSTAN, TAJIKISTAN)

Although only a small number of Russian German emigrants came from Asia, any surviving relatives of immigrants are likely to be found there. Many of these people have become *Aussiedler* (resettlers who returned to Germany). The American Historical Society of Germans from Russia has an active program interviewing these "returnees." It has helped unite both *Aussiedler* and Germans remaining in CIS member states with relatives in North America.

Michael M. Miller, Bibliographer of the Germans from Russia Heritage Collection at the North Dakota Institute for Regional Studies (North Dakota State University) in Fargo, has also been very active in seeking to re-establish ties between the descendants of Germans from Russia in North America and the Germans remaining in the ex-Soviet Union, primarily in the Muslim republics and Siberia.

He is also the compiler of *Researching Germans from Russia*, an annotated bibliography of the Germans from Russia Heritage Collection (the largest of its kind in North America, although oriented more toward history than genealogy), as well as the holdings of the Germans from Russia Heritage Society library in Bismarck, which contains many family and village histories.

BULGARIA
(Bulgarien)

Only a very small number of ethnic Germans ever lived in what is now Bulgaria. Significant group migration of Russian Germans to the Dobruja began in 1842, with a second wave starting in 1873 or 1874. Paul Traeger, in *Die Deutschen der Dobrudscha* [*The Germans in the Dobruja*], mentions five older settlements in the interior of Bulgaria, but there is hardly any literature on these settlements.

The southern part of the Dobruja (*Dobrudza* in Bulgarian) region, known as Cadrilater, has fluctuated between Romanian and Bulgarian control since the Ottoman Turkish Empire lost it in 1878, but most of the time it has been under Bulgarian control. About 15,000 Dobruja Germans were resettled in German-ruled territory in 1940, but few lived in Bulgaria.

The *AGoFF Guide* and Thode's *Address Book* list the following village directory of those relocating as a source of information:

> Heimatortskartei Südosteuropa-Umsiedler
> Abteilung Deutsche aus Russland, Bessarabien, Bulgarien und Dobrudscha
> Rosenbergstrasse 50
> D-70176 Stuttgart
> Germany

Check under **TURKEY** later in this chapter for potential governmental records.

CZECHOSLOVAKIA: SUCCESSOR STATES
(die Tschechoslowakei)

Czechoslovakia was formed as an independent state in 1918 from the Czech crownlands (Bohemia and Moravia), Austrian Silesia, Slovakia, and Subcarpathian Rus' (also known today as Carpatho-Ukraine). As a result of World War II, the Soviet Union assumed control over the last-mentioned area, formerly the eastern tip of the country. In 1993 Czechoslovakia split peacefully into the Czech and Slovak Republics.

The following publications and information apply to both the Czech and Slovak republics.

"Ethnic German Research in Czechoslovakia" by Michael Palmer (*German Genealogical Society of America Bulletin*, November 1989) represents the most thorough English-language genealogical article on this subject.

See "Jewish Genealogical Research in Czechoslovakia," by Edward David Luft, in *Avotaynu*, Vol. IV, No. 3 (Winter 1988), for details on Jewish records in both successor states. He also deals with civil records.

According to the *AGoFF-Wegweiser*, the Military Historical Institute in Prague (see Ernest Thode's *Address Book*), has all the military records of Czech and Slovak soldiers who served in the Austro-Hungarian army, including those who still had military obligations when Czechoslovakia was established. These records include the place of origin. However, you need to be able to identify the regiment.

There are also less detailed military registers at the Military Archives (*Kriegsarchiv*) in Vienna (listed earlier under **AUSTRIA**).

A *Handbook of Czechoslovak Genealogical Research* by Daniel M. Schlyter may also be helpful, although it may be hard to find since it is currently out of print.

You no longer have to get advance permission to use the Czech or Slovak archives in person. But the records may be in Latin, as well as in German or Czech (in the Czech Republic) or Hungarian or Slovak (in the Slovak Republic), so some knowledge of these languages is important if you want to do any substantial amount of research. Some archives are closed on Mondays and Fridays.

An American genealogical researcher who makes regular research visits to Czech and Slovak archives and who is very familiar with records pertaining to Germans in these archives, since he knows German, Czech, Slovak, Russian and some Polish, is:

> Dr. Duncan B. Gardiner, C.G.
> 12961 Lake Ave.
> Lakewood, OH 44107-1533

His gazetteer, *German Towns in Slovakia & Upper Hungary*, is the only major English-language book on this subject. He has also contributed significant information on the Czech Republic.

Since the Czech Republic was part of **AUSTRIA** and the Slovak Republic part of **HUNGARY**, check the information for those countries as well. In addition, look under **GERMANY**, since most of the Germans went there after World War II. Thus there are pertinent genealogical societies, archives, periodicals, etc., in Germany and, to a lesser extent, also in Austria.

THE CZECH REPUBLIC
(die Tschechische Republik)

Germans comprised 37% of the population of Bohemia (the western Czech area), 28% of the population of Moravia (in the southeast) and 45% of the population of Austrian Silesia (in the northeast) around 1900. There were more Poles than Czechs in Austrian Silesia at that time; the eastern part of this territory now belongs to Poland.

The Jewish population (included among the German-speakers) was 1.5% in Bohemia and 1.8% in the other two territories. Almost all of the German Christians in Bohemia and Moravia were Catholics in 1900, with only 2-3% of the total population being Protestant. Some 13-14% of the people in Austrian Silesia were Protestant, but the percentage among Germans was much lower.

However, Prague was the birthplace of the pre-Luther Hussite movement that crossed ethnic lines, although John Huss seems to have had the strongest appeal to Czechs. The flight of Protestants began with the Austrian victory at White Mountain in 1620 and the subsequent coerced re-Catholicization of the area. The refugees included the Moravian Brethren, who are also known as the Czech Brethren, *Unitas Fratrum* in Latin, or *Herrnhuter*, after the place of refuge they found in southeastern Saxony in 1722, which led to their Germanicization, although some of the earliest records in Germany are in Czech. Others, especially Bohemian weavers, fled to the German-Polish linguistic border area and later migrated to Russian Poland.

PARISH RECORDS

The Deutsche Zentralstelle für Genealogie in Leipzig has microfilms of registers for about 70 of these parishes; these microfilms are also available from the Family History Library. Palmer lists many German publications containing a description or inventory of the registers for specific areas.

Records can, however, be accessed through the Czech archives, or through private Czech, German or North American genealogical researchers.

You can write in English to the Archive Administration of the Czech Archives (specifying a monetary limit for the research you want to have done):

> Archivní spravá MV
> Třída Milady Horákové 133
> 16 621 Praha 6
> Czech Republic

The state archives in Prague have the pre-1900 parish registrations of births, marriages and deaths. Later parish registers are in the local civil registry offices. Czech law permits civil records offices to allow access to records that are 50 years old or more, which would include nearly all records of Germans.

The Archive Administration can inform you as to the whereabouts of duplicate parish registers, which were begun about 1800.

Birth records since about 1830 give the following information: child's name; parents' names, occupations, and address; all four grandparents' names, occupations, and addresses; names of the godparents; name of the midwife; and name of the baptizing priest. Before 1830, the data are less detailed.

Marriage records include the complete names of the spouses and sometimes those of the parents. Death records indicate the name of the person, the date and place of death, and sometimes the cause of death.

The 1780-1820 duplicate registers for those western Bohemian parishes that used to belong to the Catholic diocese of Regensburg are at the Catholic central archives there. See **GERMANY**.

JEWISH RECORDS

Jewish communal records are at:

> Státní ústredni archiv
> Karmelitská 2
> 118 01 Praha 1 (Malá Strana)
> Czech Republic

CIVIL RECORDS

Mandatory civil registration was not introduced until the interwar period. These records are in the regional archives listed below.

Besides the two state archives for Bohemia and Moravia, respectively, which are in Praha (German: *Prague*), there are regional archives in Trebon (southern Bohemia), Plzen (*Pilsen* in western Bohemia), Litomerice (*Leitmeritz* in northern Bohemia), Zámrsk (eastern Bohemia), Prague (*Prag* in central Bohemia), Opava (*Troppau*) and its branch at Olomouc (*Olmütz*, which has most of the parish registers of northern Moravia, including former Austrian Silesia), and Brno (*Brünn* in southern Moravia). For current addresses, see the 3rd edition of Duncan B. Gardiner, *German Towns in Slovakia & Upper Hungary*.

Vladimír Bystricky and Václav Hruby, *Prehled archivu CSR* (Prague: Tisková, 1985), is a comprehensive guide that briefly describes the contents of every Czech regional, district and city archive (as well as special archives). It is available from the Archive Administration.

Dr. Milan Coupek of Brno wrote an article on "Old Cadastral Maps" for Bohemia, Moravia and Silesia, published in *Nase Rodina* (Winter 1992). It deals with surveys of land ownership, the oldest one dating to 1653-56.

Sudeten German genealogical societies, archives and libraries are listed earlier under **GERMANY**. Sudeten German researchers in immigrant countries include:

Gary N. Deckant
27955 Hoover Red., Apt. 2
Warren, MI 48903
U.S.A.
(*address may be obsolete*)

Joachim Nuthack
11418 70th St.
Edmonton, AB T5B 1T4
Canada

Judith Williams
Puhoi, P.O.
New Zealand

Sudetendeutsche Landsmannschaft
    Argentinien
Warnes 95
1602 Florida-Buenos Aires
Argentina

You may also be able to get genealogical information from the following society:

> German-Bohemian Heritage Society
> P.O. Box 822
> New Ulm, MN 56073

Border People: The Böhmisch (German-Bohemians) in America by Ken Meter and Robert Paulson contains many surnames of those who immigrated to Minnesota, Wisconsin and Michigan's Upper Peninsula.

THE SLOVAK REPUBLIC
(die Slowakische Republik)

The Slovak Republic was historically part of Hungary and was also known as Upper Hungary.

PARISH RECORDS

Parish registers in Slovak archives have been, or are being, microfilmed by the FHL, pursuant to an agreement with the Slovak government. Of particular interest to Americans with German-speaking ancestors is the filming that has been done, or is underway, at Levoca (*Leutschau*), Kosice (*Kaschau*) and Banská Bystrica (*Neusohl*), the latter in the *Hauerland* region.

Most of the Germans in the *Zips* area, with its historical connection to Transylvania, became Lutherans. Germans in the other Slovak settlements remained overwhelmingly Catholic.

The book by Jana Sarmányá, *Cirkevne matriky na Slovensku zo 16. - 19. storocia* [*Church Registers in Slovakia from the 16th to the 19th Centuries*], published in Bratislava in 1991, lists all the parish registers held in the Slovak regional archives. The former Czechoslovak embassy was willing to check the guide that had been published earlier, if you specified the geographic location, the type of records and the dates of the events you are researching. The Slovak embassy may be willing to continue this practice with the new book. Its temporary address is:

> Embassy of the Slovak Republic
> 2201 Wisconsin Ave. N.W.
> Washington, DC 20007

ARCHIVAL RECORDS

For various genealogical records in the Slovak Republic, you can write to the National Archives:

> Archívná správa
> Krizkova 7
> 811 04 Bratislava
> Slovak Republic

JEWISH RECORDS

Jewish records in the Slovak Republic (as well as parish registers of the various churches) are held in the regional archives at Bratislava (German: *Pressburg*), Banská Bystrica (*Neusohl*), Bytca, Kosice (*Kaschau*), Levoca (*Leutschau*), Nitra (*Neutra*) and Presov (*Preschau*). Special Jewish registers were kept beginning in the 1830s, though actual records are very sparse before the 1860s.

LAND RECORDS

The land records (*urbariums*), which also have considerable genealogical value, are not being microfilmed.

HUNGARY
(Ungarn)

In discussing Hungarian German genealogical records, we need to keep two important facts in mind.

The first one, which also applies to other countries in Southeast Europe, is that records concerning Germans in modern-day Hungary can be found in three European countries: Hungary, Austria and Germany. What became the Austro-Hungarian Empire in 1867 was the Austrian Empire before that. Consequently, some of the relevant public records are in the Austrian state archives, whose addresses are listed in the *AGoFF Guide*. See the preceding section on **AUSTRIA** for information about the Austrian national archives; especially valuable are the Haus-, Hof- und Staatsarchiv (the chief archives for governmental records), and the Kriegsarchiv (which has extensive military records for the whole empire, beginning in 1740). Thode's *Address Book* also lists Austrian regional and special archives that may have pertinent information (especially the Burgenländisches Landesarchiv).

It is probable that some of the Catholic, Protestant and Jewish religious archives in Austria (*AGoFF Guide* and Thode's *Address Book*) also have records pertaining to Hungary. Prior to 1781, Catholic priests kept records for everyone, including Protestants and Jews. The voluntary or involuntary departure of most Germans from all Eastern European countries, including Hungary, in 1945 and the difficulty of obtaining records from there during the period of Communist rule, led to the assembling and reconstructing of a great deal of genealogical data by the refugees in Germany and Austria. The *AGoFF Guide* has a lengthy section on Southeast Europe, including the addresses of many organizations and institutions with a greater or lesser interest in genealogy. It also lists such resources as gazetteers and bibliographies. The major portion of this information is potentially relevant to Hungary.

The second important fact to keep in mind is that Hungarian records may also relate to Germans in the Slovak Republic, Croatia, the Serbian Vojvodina, Carpatho-Ukraine and Northwestern Romania. This is because Hungary historically included all or most of the territory surrounded by Austria, the Ottoman Turkish Empire, Poland-Lithuania and Russia. This area shrank and expanded substantially over the millennium of Hungary's existence, particularly with respect to the waxing and waning of Turkish fortunes in the Balkans.

The Transylvanian (*Siebenbürgen*) Saxons were invited by the king of Hungary to settle on his eastern frontier in the twelfth century for defensive reasons. They survived a long period of Turkish rule before becoming part of Hungary again in the late seventeenth century. The Germans in Slovakia were invited at the same time to defend the northern frontier. But this area was never under Turkish rule.

Virtually all of the other German colonies in the Balkans, except those near the Black Sea or close to Austria proper, were part of the large group usually referred to as the Danube Swabians, for they embarked in Swabia and sailed down the Danube River to Lower Hungary. They were known as Hungarian-Germans until 1922, because the area in which they settled was on the Southern Hungarian frontier, where the Turkish forces had been pushed back. But Hungary lost most of this territory after World War I.

Thus these settlements were part of Hungary even before Hungary achieved co-equal imperial status with Austria in 1867, so that pertinent records for all of these groups may be found in the archives in Budapest (and possibly local Hungarian archives) for the period prior to 1919, when the map of Europe was drastically redrawn.

The address of the Hungarian national archives, which has a substantial amount of relevant information, is:

> Magyar Országos Levéltár
> Bécsikapu tér 4, Postafiók 3
> H-1250 Budapest 1
> Hungary

The archives provided the following information in December 1990 concerning German-American genealogical research:

(1) Archival contents include: church and synagogue registers (births, baptisms, marriages, deaths) that were created in the present territory of Hungary prior to October 1, 1895, when civil registration started; conscription records pertaining to nobles, serfs, etc.; socage contracts (*urbariums*); judicial archives; and military

conscription records (for 1820-1910, according to Eva Liptak). About 95% of the parish registers are in good condition. There are some insufficiencies in the Jewish registers.

(2) The original church registers are kept by the parish. Copies of the registers (1828-95) are kept by the county archives. Civil registers have been kept by local administrative authorities since October 1, 1895. Requests for information may be sent to any of the three. The Family History Library has microfilms of the pre-1895 parish registers.

(3) Some of the above records date back to as early as the thirteenth century.

(4) The administrative language of Hungary historically was Latin, except for a short period toward the end of the eighteenth century, when German was used. However, local records in areas of German settlement were in German. This was also true for Jewish records, which began about 1830, according to Eva Liptak. She indicated that early Protestant records were in Latin.

(5) Dr. Ivan Bertenyi is the secretary of the Heraldic and Genealogical Society in Budapest, V. Pesti Barnabas u. 1., which is interested in all ethnic groups in Hungary, including Germans. He is primarily a heraldic specialist and speaks German, but not English.

(6) The national and regional or local archives do not undertake genealogical research assignments, but will provide information. However, their letter implies that some archivists may be willing to do private research, so a query may be worthwhile.

(7) For a response to a preliminary inquiry to the national archives of Hungary, enclose $20 (US) or the equivalent in any convertible currency by international money order or cash transfer to the archives' bank account.

(8) The national archives will respond to letters written in English and to queries specifying a locality if only limited research is required.

(9) Foreign genealogists have access to the archives in Hungary on the same basis as Hungarian researchers.

The *AGoFF Guide* states that an inventory catalog of the microfilm copies of pre-1895 ecclesiastical records was compiled by Margit Judak in 1977 as Volume 72 of the inventory of all the archives records.

Thode reports that the synagogue registers in the Hungarian national archives also include those for the part of the Burgenland region that went to Austria in the boundary changes of 1919.

Martha Remer Connor is transcribing the microfilmed 1828 land records, with 5 volumes plus an index published to date. Eva Liptak reported that the Family History Library has filmed some tax records. Both kinds of records include counties that are no longer, or only partly, in Hungary.

ITALY
(Italien)

By far the largest concentration of Germans in present-day Italy is in the area around Bolzano (Bozen) and Merano (Meran), known to Germans as Südtirol (South Tyrol) and now called the Alto Adige region in Italy. (Adige is the Italian name for what Germans call the Etsch River, which flows through this Alpine region just south of the Brenner Pass.) The area around these two cities had a predominantly German-speaking population until recently. There were other pockets of German settlement farther south in the Trent (Trento/Trient) area. These areas were part of the same jurisdiction under both Austrian and Italian rule. This region was once part of Lombardy.

The following office, which includes the Staatsarchiv Bozen and the Südtiroler Landesarchiv, indicates that it has some relevant documents and welcomes visiting genealogists, but is not in a position to fulfill research requests:

Abteilung III: Öffentlicher Unterricht und Kultur für die deutsche
    und ladinische Volksgruppe
Amt für Archivwesen, historische Bibliotheken und Volkskunde
Autonome Provinz Bozen Südtirol
Ansitz Rothenpuech
Armando-Diaz-Strasse 8
I-39100 Bozen
Italy

There were also small islands of German settlement in the Aosta River region bordering Switzerland and France and in Friuli (Friaul) on the Slovenian border. The latter once belonged to the province of Venetia.

The Trent State Archives (Archivio di Stato di Trento) has civil, land, and property tax records for various localities in the Trent area (south of Bolzano) where there were islands of German settlement. Parish registers may be found at the local parishes.

Anyone who succeeds in tracing ancestors back to the period of severe religious persecutions may find that the French Huguenots who fled to Germany included, or were closely related to, Waldensians from the Piedmont region in northwestern Italy. The FHL has microfilmed some rather old Waldensian parish registers from the Aosta region.

Also check under **AUSTRIA** for pertinent information.

POLAND
(Polen)

From the perspective of genealogical research, Poland's history is even more complex than that of Germany. For this reason and for the sake of cohesiveness (since Poland was divided among Prussia/Germany, Russia and Austria during the nineteenth century), we are including some historical material here, despite our efforts to incorporate historical information into Chapter X wherever feasible.

At the end of the Middle Ages, the union of Poland and Lithuania created the largest country in Europe, including most of what is now Belarus, Ukraine and Moldova. Poland offered a greater degree of religious freedom than any other European country, except for the Ottoman empire. Already in the Middle Ages, large numbers of Jews had fled to Poland, primarily from Germany, as Poland became the haven of the world's largest Jewish community. In the sixteenth century, Mennonites, Socinians (Unitarians), Calvinists and various other religious dissidents found a refuge there. Many of these settled in the Danzig (Gdansk) area, whose residents were primarily Germans who had shaken off the rule of the autocratic Teutonic Knights.

However, a Poland weakened by internal dissension began to lose territory and power in 1648. Russia, Prussia and Austria took advantage of its weakness and divided the country among themselves in the three partitions of 1772, 1793 and 1795. Although Russia got over half of Poland's territory, the German residents lived primarily in the area of Poland that became part of Prussia. But an influx of Germans to previously Polish-populated areas, as well as to Austrian-ruled Galicia, followed.

Napoleon created the Grand Duchy of Warsaw in 1807. After he was defeated in 1815, Posen was given to Prussia, but the rest of the duchy, including the Polish core around Warsaw and Lublin, which had been controlled by Prussia and Austria, respectively, after 1795, became an autonomous Polish kingdom (Congress Poland) under the Russian czar. After the Polish Revolt of 1830-31, Russia assumed total control.

Poland was reestablished as an independent nation after World War I, with its western border approximating the dividing line between Polish and German residential majorities, but German-populated Danzig was made into a Free City in order to assure Poland access to the Baltic Sea. However, the Netze River region at the base of the Polish Corridor to the sea was incorporated into Poland, even though much of it had a German majority, since the Corridor would have had a very narrow bottleneck otherwise.

Germany attacked Poland on September 1, 1939, and Russia followed suit on September 17. When the war was over, Russia kept a large portion of Eastern Poland, which contained many Ukrainians and Belorussians. As compensation, the Polish border was pushed west to the Oder-Neisse.

Records pertaining to Germans in areas that belonged to Germany or the Free City of Danzig during the interwar period, but are now part of Poland, are scattered. Some (especially civil records) remained in Poland. In many cases (especially for Pomerania), it is unknown whether the records survived. For those that were taken west, see under **GERMANY**.

The best Polish-American genealogical guide (and the only one that is multi-ethnic) is Rosemary A. Chorzempa, *Korzenie Polskie: Polish Roots* (Baltimore: Genealogical Publishing Co., 1993. The Family History Library plans to publish a *Polish Research Guide* in 1995.

CHURCH RECORDS

Although church records had already begun in some Polish areas in the 1400s, existing German parish records only date back to the 1700s, or occasionally to the 1600s. About 80% of the records in the Polish archives have reportedly been filmed by the Family History Library.

Of course, a substantial number of the parish registers from the pre-World War II German areas were taken to Germany. Many registers (or microfilms of them) are in Berlin, Leipzig and Greifswald, but others are scattered in various places.

As examples of what can be found on a trip to Poland, read the three articles under the overall title, "Research in German Areas Now in Poland," especially the one by Clarence Bittner on "Church Records in Niederschlesien," in the *German Genealogical Digest*, Vol. VI, No. 4 (4th quarter 1990). Names and addresses of several archivists and genealogists are listed.

A good example of a German-oriented article in a Polish-American periodical is "Expeditions to Several Catholic and Lutheran Parishes of Breslau (Wroclaw)" by Werner Freiherr von Zurek-Eichenau in the November 1993 issue of *Rodziny: The Journal of the Polish Genealogical Society of America*.

Virtually complete Roman Catholic registers for the 350 parishes, including German Catholic parishes, in the West Galician dioceses of Przemysl and Cracow have been preserved for the period after 1826. For Przemysl, they date back to 1786 and include some parishes in East (Ukrainian) Galicia. For information, write to:

Archiwum Diecezjalne
pl. Katedralny 4A
PL 37-700 Przemysl
Poland

For further information, see Brian J. Lenius, "German Catholics from Galizien [Galicia], Austria," in the September 1991 issue of the *East European Genealogist* and Edward A. Peckwas, *Register of Vital Records: Roman Catholic Parishes from the Region Beyond the Bug River* (Chicago: Polish Genealogical Society of America, 1984). In the meantime, Lenius has visited this archive and made copies of a large amount of material.

For the parts of Ukraine (mostly East Galicia and West Volhynia), Belarus and Lithuania that were part of Poland during the interwar period, vital records of many German parishes and churches for 1890-1945 can be found in the following archive, which is a part of the civil registry system, rather than the Polish state archival system:

> Urzad Stanu Cywilnego
> Warszawa Sródmiescie
> Archiwum Akt Zabuzanskich
> ul. Jezuicka 1-3
> PL 00-281 Warszawa
> Poland

Although there have been some difficulties and delays in getting records from this source, some genealogists have had success. These records have not been microfilmed by the FHL because of privacy laws and the recency of most of the records.

Pre-1890 records can be found at the following archive, which belongs to the Polish state archival system and can thus be accessed by writing to the National Directorate of State Archives (first address listed under **POLISH SOURCES** later in this section):

> Archiwum Glówne Akt Dawnych w Warszawie
> ul. Dluga 7
> PL 00-950 Warszawa
> Poland

For more details, see "The Zabuzanski Collection: New Information on Jewish, Lutheran, Mennonite and Catholic Genealogical Resources for Galicia and Volhynia" by Brian J. Lenius in the December 1992 issue of the *East European Genealogist*.

The Roman Catholic archdiocese of L'viv in what is now Ukraine (formerly Polish: *Lwów*; earlier Austrian, bearing the German name, *Lemberg*; Russian *L'vov*) was moved to Lubaczów, Poland, as result of Soviet control over East Galicia due to World War II. Records can now be found at:

> Kuria Arcybiskupia w Lubaczowie
> ul. Mickiewicza 85
> PL 37-600 Lubaczów
> Poland

There is a list of current addresses of "Lutheran Churches Within Pre-1939 Borders of Poland" in the June 1991 issue of *Wandering Volhynians*. In addition, Ewald Wuschke, editor and publisher of *Wandering Volhynians*, has published a booklet, *Protestant Church Records on Microfilm for the Former Congress Poland (1815-1915) and Volhynia*, which covers Lutheran, Reformed, Mennonite and Baptist church records and includes references to a few parish registers that either have not been microfilmed or are not known to have survived World War II.

CIVIL RECORDS

Military and guild records began in the 1400s, but an inventory of what is available in the various archives is lacking. Civil registration in the Prussian-ruled area was instituted in 1874, but there may be some records in Central Poland dating back to the Napoleonic era.

The most complete book on German genealogy in Poland is Alfred Lattermann's *Einführung in die deutsche Sippenforschung in Polen und dem preussischen Osten [Introduction to German Genealogy in Poland and the Prussian East]*, originally published in 1938 and 1941 but reprinted in 1985 by Wilfried Melchior of Vaihingen, Germany. The *AGoFF Guide* provides relatively up-to-date information concerning available records and where they are located.

The Winter 1992 issue of *Pathways & Passages*, published by the Polish Genealogical Society of the Northeast, has an article on "The Keeping of Vital Statistics Records in the Austrian Partition" (of Poland, referring to Galicia). Also of great value for the Austrian land cadasters (land survey and maps) is the article by John D. Pihach, "Galician Land Cadastre Maps: Land Surveys of 1849 and 1874" in the *East European Genealogist* (June

1994). He found the records and very detailed maps (1:2,800) for the 1849 and 1874 land surveys, as well as a large book of records for the surveys of the 1780s and 1820, in the Central State Historical Archives in L'viv. He did not find the military maps accompanying the earlier land surveys, and suspects that they may be in Vienna. The East European Branch of the Manitoba Genealogical Society has the call numbers for the records in L'viv that pertain to each village.

Land records, developed for tax purposes, are also dealt with in some detail by Dr. John-Paul Himka in "A Neglected Source for Family History in Western Ukraine: The Josephinian and Franciscan Land Cadastres" (*East European Genealogist*, December 1992).

The early civil records (1780s, 1812, 1820) were used as source material by Ludwig Schneider in his classic work on Galicia, *Das Kolonisationswerk Josefs II. in Galizien: Darstellung und Namenliste* [*The Colonization Activities of (Hapsburg Emperor) Jsoeph II in Galicia: Description and Lists of Names (of Settlers)*]. Schneider's book is based partly on the extensive research in the Austrian State Archives pertaining to the migration of the original German settlers to Galicia in the 1780s (as well as the Danube Swabians going to what was then southern Hungary in the second half of the 1700s and the early 1800s) done by Franz Wilhelm and Josef Kallbrunner and published by them in *Quellen zur deutschen Siedlungsgeschichte in Südosteuropa* [*Sourcebook for Histories of German Settlements in Southeast Europe*].

Both of these classics were recently reprinted by the Helmut Scherer Verlag in Berlin. The names are indexed in Bruce Brandt and Edward Reimer Brandt, *Where to Look For Hard-to-Find German-Speaking Ancestors in Eastern Europe*, 2nd ed.

JEWISH RECORDS

For information concerning Family History Library microfilms of Jewish records in various towns, see the Family History Library catalog. Other information may be available in *Avotaynu*.

NORTH AMERICAN SOURCES

Wandering Volhynians: A Magazine for the Descendants of Germans from Volhynia and Poland is compiling a rapidly expanding "Surname & Village Research List." The focus is on Volhynia, but there is also a fair amount of material on Germans from Russian Poland (i.e., Central and Eastern Poland), since most of the Volhynians came from there.

There are 11 Polish-American genealogical societies that devote a varying amount of attention to the Germans in Poland. (An 11-page list of "Some Resources for Research on Polish-American Genealogy," including addresses and publications, is available from Edward R. Brandt.) The following ones are known to have substantial periodicals:

Polish Genealogical Society of America
984 N. Milwaukee Ave.
Chicago, IL 60622-4199

Polish Genealogical Society of the
Northeast
8 Lyle Rd.
New Britain, CT 06053-2104

Polish Genealogical Society of Michigan
c/o Burton Historical Collection
Detroit Public Library
5201 Woodward Ave.
Detroit, MI 48202-4007

Polish Genealogical Society of Texas
15917 Juneau Dr.
Houston, TX 77040-2155

There are also societies in California, Ohio, Maryland, Massachusetts, Minnesota, New York, and Wisconsin.

POLISH SOURCES

The best chance of obtaining genealogical information from Poland is to write to the Directorate of the Polish National Archives:

Naczelna Dyrekcja Archiwów Panstwowych
ul. Dluga 6 — skrytka pocztowa Nr. 1005
PL 00-950 Warszawa
Poland

You should enclose a payment of $20 (US) for the initial fee to ensure a response. The fee is $10 per hour of research and $20 per page for copies of material. You should be aware that this can add up to quite a sum of money if the search is successful and numerous documents are found in the archives.

It is now becoming acceptable to write to Polish regional and local archives. However, the National Archives in Warsaw will respond to English-language letters, whereas this may be a problem elsewhere. The National Archives will query the pertinent archives for the area you are researching.

The addresses of the numerous regional Polish archives in former German territory can be found in the 5th edition of Ernest Thode's *Address Book for Germanic Genealogy* and in George K. Schweitzer's *German Genealogical Research*.

One problem is that most archival inventories in Poland are incomplete, out-of-date and used only as in-house documents. The most comprehensive guide for all of Poland is the *Katalog Inwentarzy Archiwalnych* [*Catalog of the Inventory of the Archives*] by M. Pestkowska and H. Stebelska (Warsaw: Naczelna Dyrekcja Archiwów Panstwowych, 1971). Most regional archives are planning to publish an updated inventory and those in Szczecin (*Stettin*), Warsaw and Gdansk (*Danzig*) have already done so.

The recently established genealogical society in Poznan (*Posen*) is compiling inventories of archival sources and bibliographies, indexing vital registers, building up a genealogical library collection, and starting or coordinating other such research projects, but it does not offer research services at the present time. However, members will receive a *Genealogical Data Bank*, listing surnames being researched and updated semi-annually, as well as information sheets every 2-3 months about current events, new publications, etc. These will also be issued in English, as soon as the number of foreign members is sufficient. The society also publishes a quarterly, *GENS*, in Polish, with short summaries in English. Annual membership is $15 and subscription to *GENS* is $10, payable by postal money order or bank draft. Write to:

Towarzystwo Genealogiczno-Heraldyczne
Societas Genealogica AC Heraldica
ul. Wodna 27 (Palac Górków)
PL 61-781 Poznan
Poland

An organized cluster of three genealogical and surname societies (specifically including German families from Galicia who stayed in Silesia), under the same leadership, was established in 1994. Its quarterly *Chronicle* is available in English, German, Polish or Esperanto for $25 per year (plus $7 fee for cashing U.S. money orders or bank drafts) from:

Silesian Genealogical Society
P.O. Box 312
PL 50-950 Wroclaw
Poland

Genealogical research services for all of Poland are provided by:

Osradan Badan Genealogicznych
(Piast Genealogical Research Centre)
P.O. Box 9
PL 00-957 Warszawa 36
Poland

The center describes its services as: "The Center offers genealogical advice and information on the descent of the family name and the family itself. It works out the history of the family, genealogical tree and copies of the coats-of-arms. The Center collects and elaborates documentation concerning the history of Polish families since the earliest times to the present day. The materials cover families living in the historical territories of Poland, regardless of nationality, religion and social class. The Center has also established a Bank of Polish families which, being fully computerized, can admit all the data about Polish families."

Bear in mind that genealogy focused on the nobility. About 10% of the Polish people belonged to the *szlachta* (nobility), even though many of them were about as poor as the peasants. So don't expect too much in the way of results for families of German peasants.

The following multilingual historian, genealogical consultant and tour guide has been recommended for American genealogists visiting Poland to search for German ancestors:

> Henryk Skrzypinski
> ul. Grunwaldzka 10a/68
> PL 85-236 Bydgoszcz
> Poland

Also check the earlier section on **UKRAINE** in this chapter for information about Galicia.

ROMANIA
(Rumänien)

More Germans settled in Romania than in any other Balkan country. However, according to Hans Fehlinger, in 1911 there were only 32,000 Germans in Romania, half in the capital city of Bucharest, compared to about 900,000 after World War I. The explanation for this is that most of these Germans lived in Transylvania and the eastern Banat, which were transferred from Hungary to Romania after the war. The others lived chiefly in Bessarabia, the Bukovina and the Dobruja, which had been under Russian or Austrian rule.

Nearly all of the Germans in Romania settled there when the territory in question belonged to Hungary, Austria, Russia, or Turkey. The ancestors of Germans who migrated to America from this region, with rare exceptions, never lived under Romanian rule or did so only briefly.

However, Paul Traeger indicates that a significant number of Russian Germans migrated to Moldavia and Walachia in the 1840s and 1870s. But these apparently were not concentrated settlements, since little has been published on them. These two areas joined to form Romania in 1861, although its independence did not receive international recognition until 1878. An English translation of Traeger's German-language book, *Die Deutschen in der Dobrudscha* [*The Germans in the Dobruja*] was printed in serial installments in the *Heritage Review* (December 1985-December 1988).

Germans were granted considerable cultural freedom even under Communist rule and relations between German and Romanian ethnic groups have been relatively friendly.

The Romanian national archive contains both civil and parish registers of births, deaths and marriages. Also included are court records, land records, census records and guild records. Civil records are available 100 years after their creation and all other documents after 30 years. Access to documents is the same throughout the country. Contact the General Directorate to arrange a personal visit to the archive. Requests for genealogical information may be written in English and should be addressed to the General Directorate of the state archive:

> Directia Generala A Archivelor Statului
> B-dul M. Kogalniceanu 29
> R-70602 Bucuresti
> Romania

Thode's *Address Book* states that the archive has passport records for 1885 and 1890-1918 for several Transylvanian districts, as well as civil registers for Walachia and Moldavia since 1831-32. There are numerous sources of potentially helpful genealogical information in Germany listed in the *AGoFF Guide* and the Thode's *Address Book*.

Many Bukovina records have been filmed by the FHL. Paul J. Polansky has made several research trips to the Bukovina and photocopied civil records kept there. His address is:

Paul J. Polansky
104 Church St.
Spillville, IA 52168-0183

The Bukovina Society of the Americas also shares information with the following institute, which recently initiated shared historical research with the Czernowitz (Cernauti) University (now in Ukraine, but the administrative headquarters for the Bukovina, even though most of the Germans lived on the Romanian side of the current border):

Bukowina-Institut
Landsmannschaft der Buchenlanddeutschen e.V.
Alter Postweg 97a
D-86159 Augsburg
Germany

It was also through the Bukovina Society of the Americas that we learned of the Bukovina German Cultural Association in Brazil (address in chapter VI). The leading American Danube Swabian genealogist is Michael Stoeckl (address in earlier section on **GERMANY: Genealogical Resource Centers for Eastern Europe**).

The name of an English-speaking Romanian genealogist who is interested in founding a Romanian genealogical society follows. He would like to establish North American connections and may be able to provide helpful advice, although he says there are no professional genealogists in the country.

Ing. George Musat
Bucarest - 1, Str. B-dul 1 Mai
Nr. 111, Bloc 12 A, Sc. 1, Ap. 1
Romania

Check under **TURKEY** for census records that may be applicable to the Dobruja.

TURKEY
(die Türkei)

The modest number of Germans in modern Turkey were mostly business or professional people resident in cosmopolitan Istanbul, where a church served the international community from Christian Europe.

There may be some records in Turkey for the Transylvanian Saxons and Dobruja Germans who lived in vassal states of the Ottoman Empire at one time.

There are about 150 million documents, beginning in the fifteenth century and ending with the dissolution of the Ottoman Turkish Empire in 1922, in the Ottoman Archives. However, only about 15% of these records have been classified to date and are thus accessible to researchers. Population records (censuses), taxes, military records and land registers constitute an important part of this vast collection.

Kahlile Mehr has confirmed that the 1876 Ottoman Nufüs census records include Bulgaria. It seems reasonable to believe that they include all of the Dobruja (including the much larger portion in Romania), since the whole area was under Ottoman rule until 1878. However, the 1884, 1905, 1911 and 1915 Nufüs records could be valuable for Germans in those areas that remained under Ottoman rule at the time.

The archive does not undertake research and knows of no private genealogists. However, you can request a copy of a specific document by filling out two Turkish forms, *Arastirma Talebinde Bulunanlar İçin Müracaat Formu* [*Application Form for People Who Want to Search for Information*] and *Taahhütname* [*Agreement Form for Those Undertaking Research*], and enclosing two photographs. The forms are only in Turkish, so you will have to get a translator, unless you know the language. The first one is an application form for searching the files and the second one requests personal information, including your passport number. It may be that this applies only to census records. There is no charge, except for the cost of photocopies. Requests should be mailed to the Head of the Department of Ottoman Archives of the Prime Ministry's General Directorate of State Archives in Istanbul:

> Basbakanlik
> Devlet Arsivleri Genel Müdürlügü
> Osmanli Arsivi Daire Baskanligi
> Ticarethane Sokak
> Cagaloglu-Istanbul
> Turkey

Researchers may use the archives in person. Any published materials (which may include books or articles that are not in the Turkish language) are likely to be available at the Turkish State Library:

> Beyazit Devlet Kütüphanesi
> Imaret Sok. 18, Beyazit
> Istanbul
> Turkey

YUGOSLAVIA: SUCCESSOR STATES
(Jugoslawien)

Overview

Roughly the northwestern half of the former Yugoslavia was under Austro-Hungarian rule before World War I, although part of it was under Austria, part of it under Hungary, and Bosnia-Herzegovina was under the rule of the joint imperial government with its seat in Vienna. Practically all of the Germans in ex-Yugoslavia lived in the former Austro-Hungarian area, but mostly in the northeastern part of the country, where the Danube Swabians lived.

While the ultimate boundaries of the various states that formerly belonged to the Yugoslav Federation are still in doubt, it is clear that there are five successor states. The only one of these new states that had a negligible number of Germans is Macedonia, which thus is not covered below. The archival addresses listed below stem from the period when Yugoslavia was still united. It is possible that the postal code prefixes may change.

The *Arbeitsgemeinschaft ostdeutscher Familienforscher (AGoFF)*, listed under **GERMANY**, has a research center for the former Yugoslavia, with a sub-center for Slovenia. In addition, some of the pertinent records may be in various Austrian or Hungarian archives.

BOSNIA-HERZEGOVINA

The Danube Swabian settlements in the Romania-Hungary-Vojvodina area eventually spilled over into northeastern Bosnia. Some refugees from Bismarck's 1871-78 anti-Catholic *Kulturkampf* also went to north central Bosnia.

There has never been a permanent German settlement in Herzegovina, which is a small part of the hyphenated state in the south, along the border with Montenegro.

The address for the national archive is:

> The Archives of Bosnia and Herzegovina
> Save Kovacivica 6
> 71001 Sarajevo
> Bosnia-Herzegovina

CROATIA

There were quite a few Danube Swabian settlements in Eastern Croatia (essentially the territory occupied by the Serbs, as of early 1995), specifically a major part of the Baranya (German: *Baranja*) and East Slavonian villages.

A few Germans (primarily merchants, artisans and other middle-class non-peasant groups) lived in:

(1) Istria, which now forms the northwesternmost part of Croatia, but was ruled by Austria, instead of being part of pre-World War I Croatia, which was an autonomous part of Hungary;

(2) Dalmatia, the southern part of present-day Croatia, which also was under Austrian rule; and

(3) Zagreb, the capital city (*Agram* in German)

The first two areas are along the Adriatic coast. Any Germans who emigrated from there probably left from the port of Trieste (which may also have been the case for some of those leaving from other southern parts of the Austro-Hungarian Empire).

The Family History Library is making good progress in microfilming Croatian records and reportedly filmed some in eastern Croatia (where most of the Germans lived) prior to the Serbo-Croat fighting that destroyed the most significant archive.

The address of the national archive is:

> The Archive of Croatia
> Marulicevtrg 21
> 41000 Zagreb
> Croatia

SLOVENIA

There were various German settlements in Carniola (German: *Krain*), south of the present-day Austrian border. Urbanites lived in the cities of Kranj (*Krainburg*), Ljubljana (*Laibach*) and Maribor (*Marburg/Drau*). Quite a few German Catholic parishes in Minnesota (and maybe elsewhere) were originally served by German-speaking Slovenian priests, whose ethnic origin is not always clear.

There were also some Germans in Gorizia and Gradisca, which is now divided between western Slovenia and northeastern Italy.

However, the agriculturists farther to the south, in the Kocevje (*Gottschee*) area, dating back to about 1330, retained their Germanic identity to a much greater degree. Large numbers of them were already in the United States by the 1920s. Another major wave of immigration occurred after World War II. They came from Germany, since the Gottscheers had already been forced to leave their home during the war as a result of a Hitler-Mussolini agreement about "spheres of influence," and thus they were considered "stateless persons." Others came after World War II. This group accounted for a disproportionately large number of emigrants, both to the United States and to Germany.

The Gottscheer Connection is published by:

> Gottscheer Research & Genealogy Association
> Elizabeth Nick, President
> 174 South Hoover Ave.
> Louisville, CO 80027

Elizabeth Nick (Liz Information Services) also publishes *The Gottschee Tree*.

Most of the key vital records for Slovenia have been microfilmed by the FHL recently. However, microfilms of Slovenian German parish registers and other archival records, chiefly for the *Gottschee* area, have already been in Leipzig for half a century. The FHL made copies of these before the current filming in Slovenia began.

The address of the national archives is:

> The Archive of Slovenia
> Zvezdarska 1
> 61000 Ljubljana
> Slovenia

YUGOSLAVIA (SERBIA-MONTENEGRO)

The "Yugoslav" rump state includes Serbia, with its formerly autonomous provinces of the Vojvodina and Kosovo, and Montenegro.

There were a very large number of Germans in the Vojvodina, which included Syrmia or Srem (*Syrmien* in German), most of the Backa (*Batschka*) and a significant portion of the Banat. This region, north of Belgrade, was ruled by Hungary before World War I and also has many Hungarian residents. Novi Sad (*Neusatz*) was the "Danube Swabian capital" of interwar Yugoslavia.

The Family History Library is now filming records in:

> The Archive of Vojvodina
> Dunavska 35
> 21000 Novi Sad
> Serbia

As an alternative, it may be possible to obtain birth, marriage or death records through the Bureau of East European Affairs, U.S. Department of State, Washington, DC 20520, which will contact the American embassy in Belgrade, according to a communication received from the embassy of Yugoslavia before the country was dissolved.

There were very few Germans in Serbia proper, Kosovo or Montenegro.

WEST AND NORTH EUROPEAN COUNTRIES

BELGIUM
(Belgien)

Like the Netherlands, Belgium experienced several rulers throughout its history. In 1815, after the fall of Napoleon, Belgium and Holland were merged into the Kingdom of the Netherlands. The area around Eupen and Malmedy became part of the Prussian province of Rhineland, only to be returned to Belgium one hundred years later. This area is now in the province of Liège. Church and civil records for the Eupen, Malmedy and Moresnet areas are at the Provincial Archives:

> Archives de l'État a Liège
> Rue Pouplin 8
> B-4000 Liège
> Belgium

Meyers Kleines Konversations-Lexikon [*Meyer's (Small) Conversational Encyclopedia*], a 6-volume "mini-encyclopedia," states that there were 11,000 Germans in the Belgian province of Luxembourg in 1900. This is not to be mistaken with the country by that name, although it belonged to Luxembourg until 1839.

Flanders was a highly developed and densely populated area in the late Middle Ages, so many people migrated eastward from it during that time. In the 16th century many Protestant refugees, both Flemings and Walloons, fled today's Belgium, which was under Spanish rule. Thus many Germans have historic roots in Belgium, but it is doubtful whether many families can be traced back directly to specific communities, where there might be some pertinent records.

There are two main languages in Belgium: French, spoken in the south, and Flemish, spoken in the north. These regions are known as Wallonia and Flanders. In addition, a small eastern area of Belgium has German-speaking people, because of the border changes with Prussia mentioned above.

CHURCH RECORDS

Belgium is predominantly Catholic, with church records beginning about 1600 written in Latin. Protestant Church records also begin about 1600 and are written in French or Flemish. Older records are found in the municipal archives and have been filmed by the FHL. From 1800 to present, church records can be found in the church office.

CIVIL RECORDS

The French occupation of 1795 brought about detailed civil registration. These population registers are cataloged by town name and have been filmed by the FHL. If you know the town of origin, you can also write directly to the town hall for information.

MISCELLANEOUS RECORDS

The FHL has filmed many of the military, notarial, and court records that are kept in the archives of Belgium. These records should be consulted first before writing to Belgium.

National Archives of Belgium:

Archives Generales du Royaume
Rue de Ruysbroeck 2-6
B-1000 Bruxelles/Brussels
Belgium

Genealogical Society of Belgium:

Vlaamse Vereniging voor Familienkunde
Van Heybeeckstrat 3
B-2060 Antwerpen-Merksem
Belgium

DENMARK
(Dänemark)

The country of Denmark first appeared as an independent kingdom during the Middle Ages. At one time, the southern part of this country was part of Germany. The duchies of Schleswig and Holstein had long been the object of disagreement, and in 1864 Austria and Prussia forced Denmark to cede the two duchies. They remained German until after World War I, when the northern part of Schleswig was returned to Denmark while the southern part remained in Germany.

The Danes are a Scandinavian people and the majority of Danish records reflect this heritage. In the 1500s the Lutheran Church was established as a state church, and the populace has remained Protestant to this day. Beginning in 1646 the government required births, marriages and deaths to be recorded in the parishes. Among the oldest church books are those for the cities of Lauenburg and Ratzeburg. Duplicate copies were kept after 1812. The church records have not been filmed. The address of the Evangelical (Lutheran) Church archives and headquarters is:

Evangelisch-lutherische Landeskirche Schleswig-Holsteins
Dänische Strasse 27-35
D-24103 Kiel
Germany

The first Danish census was taken in 1787, and others have been taken at varying intervals since then. Those of Schleswig-Holstein for 1803-1860 are on microfilm, and are listed according to district (*Herred*). Also filmed are public, notarial, land and probate records as well as tax and military documents.

The Danish state archives contains records of the northern part of Schleswig that returned to Denmark in 1920. Its address is:

Landesarckivet for der sonderjyske Landesdele
45 Haderslevvej
DK-6200 Åbenrå
Denmark

FINLAND
(Finnland)

Finland has been influenced primarily by its two powerful neighbors: Sweden and Russia. For a time, Finland and a significant portion of the German coastal area were both under Swedish rule. Finland was part of the Swedish kingdom until 1809 when it was taken over by Russia. The Czar of Russia allowed Finland to have its own government as an autonomous grand duchy. Finland officially became an independent country in 1917.

German influence in Finland has not been great. Very few Germans immigrated to Finland. The Finnish language belongs to the Finno-Ugric linguistic family, but many records were kept in Swedish. Many of these records have been microfilmed.

There was some contact by German Teutonic Knights and the Hanseatic League. Finland was allied with Germany in World War I and World War II. German troops fought in Finland against Russia in World War II. Finnish emigration has been primarily to the United States and Sweden.

Genealogical data on quite a few German individuals or families, dating back as far as 1486, are listed by Martha Müller in *Mecklenburger in Osteuropa* [*Mecklenburgers in East Europe*].

It seems reasonable to believe that Germans also went to Finland from other areas along the Baltic coast, perhaps especially from West Pomerania which, like Finland, was ruled by Sweden for a considerable period of time.

The address of the Finnish national archives is:

Genealogiska Samfundet i Finland
Snellmaningatan 9-11
SF-00170 Helsingfors 17
Finland

FRANCE
(Frankreich)

Nearly all of the German-speaking immigrants who came to the United States from what is now France came from Alsace-Lorraine. This area also provided a large number of German-speaking emigrants to Eastern Europe, mostly in the late eighteenth and early nineteenth centuries. A goodly number of their descendants emigrated to North America about a century later.

In the early years of the French Revolution (1789-94), all the French provinces were reorganized into a much larger number of departments. Alsace was divided into the departments of Haut-Rhin (Upper Rhine) and Bas-Rhin (Lower Rhine), while (German) Lorraine became the department of Moselle.

Old records in this area may be in French, German, or Latin. While some villages retained a clear-cut German ethnic identity until recent times, and others a French one, French-German marriages were not unusual.

Quite a few German-Americans may be able to trace their ancestry back to French-speaking Huguenots, who found refuge particularly in the Palatinate, Hesse, Franconia, Brandenburg, and Northwestern Germany, which had Reformed (Calvinist) rulers, in the sixteenth and seventeenth centuries. The largest number fled after the revocation of the Edict of Nantes (which had guaranteed religious tolerance) in 1685. Look under **GERMANY** for the address of the German Huguenot Society.

There are also some settlements of Mennonites of German-speaking Swiss origin in Montbéliard. For information, see articles in *Mennonite Family History*.

CHURCH RECORDS

The church records of German parishes in Alsace-Lorraine are listed in the *Mitteilungen der Zentralstelle für Deutsche Personen- und Familien-Geschichte* [*News from the Center for German Personal and Family History*], published by the H. A. Ludwig Degener Verlag shortly after World War I, when Alsace-Lorraine was part of the German Empire. Volume 9, titled *Die Kirchenbücher von Elsass-Lothringen* [*Church books of Alsace-Lorraine*], lists the Lutheran parishes, while Volume 10, with a slightly different title, *Die Kirchenbücher des Reichslandes Elsass-Lothringen* [*Church books of the Imperial Province of Alsace-Lorraine*], lists the Reformed and Catholic parishes. These publications may be hard to find, but the Family History Library has them. For further detail, see Larry O. Jensen, *A Genealogical Handbook of German Research*, Volume II.

Some Catholic records go back to the Middle Ages, with the Lutheran records beginning in 1525 and the Reformed Church records in 1559. The pre-1792 records can be found in the regional archives listed below. Later ones are probably still in the local parish office. Duplicate registers were required to be deposited with the town clerk and may still be available in the town hall.

CIVIL RECORDS

It was the French Revolution that started the whole business of civil registration in Europe. These records, beginning in 1792, are kept in the town hall, since the mayor or his designated representative serves as the registrar. The regional archives listed below have copies of these records up to 1870.

The French Revolutionary calendar was used for the most part between 1792 and 1805. To convert these dates to the Gregorian calendar that we use, see chapter XVII and Larry O. Jensen, *A Genealogical Handbook of German Research*, Volume I.

EMIGRANT RECORDS

The 2-volume *Alsace Emigration Book* compiled by Cornelia Schrader-Muggenthaler provides detailed information, alphabetized for convenience, concerning 13,500 French and German emigrants who left Alsace during the 1817-69 period.

There are records of German emigrants in transit through Strasbourg to the French port of Le Havre, which have been microfilmed by the FHL. If your immigrant ancestor came from Southern Germany in the 1817-66 time period (and particularly if there is supposedly some Alsatian connection that you can't verify), try this. The earlier that people emigrated, the greater is the likelihood that they left via Le Havre or Rotterdam.

MISCELLANEOUS RECORDS

Other records include census, guild, notarial, and various public records. For information about these records or the Le Havre passenger records, write:

> Archives nationale de France
> 60 rue des Frances-Bourgeois
> F-75141 Paris
> France

For a more comprehensive list of relevant French records, see *In Search of Your European Roots*, by Angus Baxter.

REGIONAL ARCHIVES

The most extensive public and church records for the formerly German Alsace-Lorraine area can be found in the following regional archives (the records have been microfilmed by the FHL):

For Alsace:

> Archives départementales du Haut-Rhin
> rue Fleischauer
> F-68000 Colmar
> France

> Archives départementales du Bas-Rhin
> 5-9 rue Fischart
> F-67000 Strasbourg
> France

For Lorraine:

> Préfecture de la Moselle
> 9 place Préfecture
> F-57000 Metz
> France

> Archives départementales de Meurthe-et-Moselle
> 3 rue de la Monnaie
> F-54000 Nancy
> France

For further information, see:

(1) The Church of Jesus Christ of Latter-day Saints, *French Records Extraction*.

(2) Francois J. Himly, "Genealogical Sources in Alsace-Lorraine (France)," a 12-page paper presented to the World Conference on Records and Genealogical Seminar.

(3) Hugh T. Law, "Locating the Ancestral Home in Elsass-Lothringen (Alsace-Lorraine)," an article in the *German Genealogical Digest*, 3rd quarter, 1990.

GENEALOGICAL SOCIETIES

There are genealogical societies concerned particularly with the Alsace and Lorraine areas. They can be reached by writing to the Cercle Genealogique de Alsace at the Strasbourg archives address above, or the Cercle Genealogique de Lorraine in care of the Nancy address above.

IRELAND
(Irland)

About 850 Palatine religious refugees landed in Dublin in 1709. Many of this same group of emigrants continued on to the mid-Atlantic states. However, some settled in Limerick and Kerry counties in Ireland, where surnames of German origin are still found.

Those searching for ancestors or collateral lines here should check *The Palatine Families of Ireland* by Henry Z. Jones for further information. This is a study of Palatine immigrants who came to Ireland about 1710, and lists 170 surnames of families with German ancestry, including some names that may have been modified or corrupted. Angus Baxter's book, *In Search of Your British & Irish Roots*, identifies the kinds of records that are available, but has no specific reference to the Palatine immigrants. The section on the **UNITED KINGDOM** later in this chapter contains additional references to German immigrants.

An Irish Palatine Association, which offers a genealogical research service regarding this group, has been recently established. It can be reached at:

> The Irish Palatine Information Office
> Rathkeale, Co. Limerick
> Ireland

This information comes from an article on "The Palatines of County Limerick" by Austin Bovenizer in the Winter 1990-91 issue of *The Palatine Immigrant*. The author details relevant historical and contemporary developments in Ireland and mentions a new book, *People Make Places: The Story of the Irish Palatines*, by Patrick O'Connor.

THE NETHERLANDS
(die Niederlande)

The Netherlands is often referred to as Holland, although the latter is properly only the name of the two most populous provinces in the northwest. Dutch and the Flemish spoken in Northern Belgium are essentially the same language. However, Frisian, still spoken in the province of Friesland, is a different language. At one time a Triple Frisia extended from Antwerp in the west to German Ostfriesland, on the Dutch border, and the islands and coastal areas of Schleswig-Holstein. Similarities in naming are still recognizable. Furthermore, Dutch linguistic and cultural influence extended up the Rhine beyond the current German-Dutch border until the Napoleonic Wars.

At the time of the Reformation, the Low Countries were under the control of the Spanish Hapsburg emperors, who were the harshest persecutors of the Protestants, the terror peaking under the Duke of Alva in 1568. This led to the declaration of a Dutch Republic in 1581. Although Spain did not recognize Dutch independence until 1648, the new nation soon prospered and became the world's greatest maritime power in the first half of the 1600s. Among other exploits, it established New Netherlands in the present-day Greater New York area in 1624. Although the English captured New Netherlands in 1664, the area attracted German immigrants who felt an affinity for the closely related Dutch.

Meanwhile, many Dutch, Frisians and Flemings fled eastward by land and by sea, following earlier routes of traders and marshland-draining pioneers, before religious freedom had been won at home. Thus many Germans in Prussia, Pomerania, Brandenburg, Posen and Mecklenburg have historic roots in the Atlantic Lowlands.

The Mennonite migration from the Netherlands to West Prussia is thoroughly chronicled by Benjamin Heinrich Unruh in *Die niederländisch-niederdeutschen Hintergründe der mennonitischen Ostwanderungen im 16., 18. und 19. Jahrhundert* [*Background of the Mennonite Eastward Migration in the 16th, 18th and 19th Centuries from the Netherlands and Northern Germany*] (Karlsruhe: self-published, 1955). An article on "Hollanders in Germany" in the December 1988 issue of the *GGSA Bulletin* details information concerning the Dutch religious refugees in Mecklenburg.

Although many German emigrants, especially during the colonial period, embarked at Dutch ports, only fragments of these lists have been preserved. However, information about 17th century emigrants may be available in the chamber records and contracts of the Dutch East and West India Companies.

According to *Meyers Kleines Konversations-Lexikon* [*Meyer's (Small) Conversational Encyclopedia*], there were 32,000 Germans in the Netherlands in 1907. Also look under **Other Specialized Resource Centers** under the previous section on **GERMANY** in this chapter for a Dutch-German genealogical society.

CHURCH RECORDS

The majority of the Dutch people are Protestant and church records have been kept since 1600. Most of the Protestants belong to the Dutch Reformed Church, but there are also some Mennonites, Lutherans, and members of other denominations. Over one third of the Dutch are Catholics, but these would be likely to have emigrated to Germany only in the Rhine area. The country had a larger percentage of Jews than Germany, but these are more likely to have come *from* Germany than vice versa. Early records are in the city and state archives. Later records are in church archives and many have been filmed by the Family History Library (FHL). The FHL has also filmed Mennonite parish registers, the oldest dating back to 1632, about half a century after mass migration to Prussia ended.

CIVIL REGISTRATION

Registration of births, marriages, and deaths began in the south in 1796, coinciding with the French occupation. In the north, registration began in 1811 and included population registers. Records are in the municipality and duplicates are in the state provincial archives. Registers after 1892 are not available to the public, but information can be obtained by writing to the city registry office.

CENSUS AND GUILD RECORDS

The first federal census was taken in 1829 and then every 10 years after that. Before that time, enumerations were taken locally for taxation purposes. Guild records have been kept since the 1500s and are generally found in the city archives. Some have been microfilmed by the FHL.

MILITARY RECORDS

Recruiting lists, service records, and national militia records began about 1700. These include the census of able-bodied men and those who died in the French service (1809-14). They are available at the state archives and some have been filmed by the FHL.

There are eleven provinces in the Netherlands, each with its own archive. The Central State Archive in the Netherlands is:

> Algemeen Rijksarchief
> Bleijenburg 7
> NL-2500 's Gravenhage
> Netherlands

Genealogical societies located in the Netherlands are:

> Zentraal Bureau voor Genealogie
> Prins Willem-Alexanderhof 22
> Postbus 11755
> NL-2595 BE 's Gravenhage
> Netherlands

> Nederlandse Genealogische Vereniging
> Postbus 976
> NL-1000 AZ Amsterdam
> Netherlands

NORWAY
(Norwegen)

The Christian religion became important in Norway during the 10th century, with a national church being formed about 1070. Olaf II, called St. Olaf, was responsible for the forceful introduction of the Christian religion. The Reformation came to Norway at Bergen through the Hanseatic merchants from Germany. By 1536, Lutheranism had replaced the Catholic religion.

In 1250, Haakon IV granted trading privileges to the Hanseatic League, which controlled European trade during the 1300s and 1400s. By the late 1300s several German nobles had married into Norwegian royal families and the Norwegian crown had a strong German element. By the 1600s, many royal officials were imported from other countries, some being Germans from Holstein. Other German elements were refugees from war torn areas, especially South Jutland. Many German burghers with business experience and money moved into the towns of Norway about the same time. The German influence was stronger in the eastern part of Norway, with many of the wealthy in Christiania (Oslo) coming from South Jutland. There were also many German merchant families at Trondheim. Hanseatic League trade resulted in the settlement of a significant number of Germans in Norwegian ports, especially Bergen, as early as the fourteenth century. There were Hanseatic trading offices in Bergen, Oslo and Tønsberg. For more information about the see Hanseatic League, see Chapter X, or a book on the Hanseatic League. Examples are Helen Zimmern, *The Hansa Towns*, 3rd ed. (1881. Reprinted New York: G. P. Putnam's Sons; 1891; 389 pp. plus illus. and map) and John Allyne Gade, *The Hanseatic Control of Norwegian Commerce During the Late Middle Ages* (Leiden: E. J. Brill; 1951; 139 pp. plus 7-page bibliography).

In the 1600s a renewed interest in mining occurred throughout Europe, and in the 1620s King Christian IV of Norway formed several ironworks, with many of the miners being German. The Kongsberg silver mine opened in 1624 in the mountains west of Oslo. The copper mine at Kvikne opened in 1633, followed by several others, the most important being at Røros in 1644. Most of the miners in these mines were also German. *Beiträge zur Geschichte des Deutschtums in Norwegen: Die Deutsche Einwanderung in Kongsberg* [*Contributions to the History of the Germans in Norway: German Immigration to Kongsberg*], Dr. Alfred Hunhäuser, ed. (Oslo: Verlag Deutsche Zeitung in Norwegen A.S., 1944), details the history of silver mining by Germans in Kongsberg in the 1500s and 1600s.

Norway was controlled by the Danish monarchy from 1030 until 1814 when Sweden forced Denmark to cede Norway. After Norwegians refused to accept the Treaty of Kiel, the National Assembly convened and adopted its own Constitution on May 17. A Danish prince was elected King of Norway. But before the year ended, the King resigned and the National Assembly agreed to a union with Sweden. Norway became independent in 1905 when that union was dissolved.

LANGUAGE

There are two things you must know about the Norwegian language. First, there are three unique vowels (æ, ø and å) that are alphabetized after *z* in Norwegian publications but as *ae*, *oe*, and *aa* in American publications. Second, there is a considerable variation in spelling since there are two official languages and dozens of dialects. The Norwegian language is part of the Germanic family of languages. In the mid-1800s, *nynorske* (new Norse) originated to create a distinctly Norwegian language that is based on many rural dialects. The old language, which is still used, is called *bokmål* (book language). *Bokmål* is closely related to Danish.

GEOGRAPHY

The basic geographical unit is the parish (*sogn* or *sokn*). This is often identical with the township or *herred*, although many townships contain several parishes. The townships are grouped into districts, the districts into counties (*fylke*). The simplest way to follow these subdivisions is in volumes 2 and 3 of *Norge* (Oslo: Cappelen, 1963. 4 vol.). In 1919, a major reorganization was made and the *amts* (counties) were changed to *fylke*. Norwegian reference sources are arranged by *fylke* in geographical order (southeast, central, south, west coast, north) rather than alphabetically.

NAMES

A Norwegian name generally consists of a first name, a patronymic, and a farm name. A person's farm name changed whenever that person moved to a different farm. Sharing a farm name does not mean that people were related. The first name was usually chosen according to a set pattern. The first son was named after the father's father, the second after the mother's father. The girls were named after their grandmothers. If a child died, the name was generally reused. Also children were often named after a deceased spouse of one of their parents.

To trace the farm name, you need to know the parish in which it is located since there are many common names for farms, e.g., *Dalen* - Dale; *Nygaard* - New farm, etc. There are two main resources for determining the possible location. The first is Oluf Rygh's *Norske gaardnavne* [*Norwegian Farm Names*] (Oslo, Fabritius, 1897-1936, 20 vols.) and the second is the postal guide, *Norsk stedfortegnelse* [*Norwegian Place-Lists*] (Oslo, Postdirektorastet).

CHURCH RECORDS

The Lutheran Church is the state church in Norway, with records beginning in the 1600s. The early records are in Gothic script. Samples of church records with their translations can be found in *Genealogical Guidebook & Atlas of Norway* by Frank Smith and Finn A. Thomsen (Logan, UT; Everton Publishers, Inc. 1979. 56 pp.). This source also contains sectional maps of Norway with an index to towns, a calendar of church feast days, a list of Norwegian counties and parishes and when records began in each parish, Gothic alphabet examples, a short Norwegian word list, and a short introduction to Norwegian records. The records of many Norwegian parishes have been microfilmed and are available through Family History Centers.

COMMUNITY HISTORY BOOKS (BYGDEBØKER)

Another important source for family information is the *bygdebok*. *Bygdebøker* are historical-genealogical books for a particular community in Norway. They will usually include a general history of the area with one or more volumes detailing the history of farm sites within the area. Stories will often include the genealogical heritage of the families residing on the farm sites. They are still being written for many parts of Norway. Also many communities are writing supplementary volumes to bring old volumes up to date. Excellent collections of *bygdebøker* can be found in the libraries at St. Olaf College (Northfield, MN), University of Wisconsin (Madison, WI), University of Minnesota (Minneapolis, MN), Concordia College (Moorhead, MN), Luther College (Decorah, IA), and the University of North Dakota (Grand Forks, ND).

CIVIL REGISTRATION

The 1664-66 tax list of Norway includes all men and boys who were over 12 years of age. In 1701, another list of males was made. In 1769, a census was taken that was mainly statistical, but some parishes listed complete families by name. The first national census was taken in 1801. It gives every person in each household and includes relationships, ages, occupations and status of marriage. The 1865 census includes the same information as the 1801 census plus the addition of the place of birth. The 1875 census includes the same information as the 1865 census except the year of birth is given in place of the age. The 1890 and 1900 census returns have similar information. Most of the tax and census information is available through the Family History Centers and the Vesterheim Museum (Decorah, IA).

Probate records began around 1660 and were more universal after the passage of a probate law in 1685. Each county was divided into probate districts with some of the larger towns having their own probate jurisdiction. The probate matters of clergy and school teachers were handled through the ecclesiastical courts of the archdeaconries.

GENEALOGICAL SOCIETIES

Vesterheim Genealogical Center is a division of Vesterheim ("Western home"), The Norwegian-American Museum, Decorah, Iowa, and is designed to help and encourage genealogists with Norwegian and Norwegian-American research problems. A quarterly newsletter, *Norwegian Tracks*, is included with membership. An extensive collection of microfilmed church records owned by the Genealogical Center may be borrowed by members. Genealogical research in libraries, archives, and other resources is available at a reduced cost to members. Its address is:

Vesterheim Genealogical Center and Naeseth Library
415 W. Main Street
Madison, WI 53703

The documentation center of *Utvandrermuseet* (Norwegian Emigrant Museum) in Hamar includes a research library, a collection of letters written by Norwegian emigrants to their relatives at home, several private archives, a collection of photographs, microfilms of parish registers of 2,000 Norwegian Lutheran congregations in the United States, and lists of emigrants from various districts of Norway. The museum's Genealogical Society (NUSU) accepts genealogical inquiries concerning roots in Norway. The address is:

Utvandrermuseet
Strandveien 100
Postboks 1053
N-2301 Hamar
Norway

The Norwegian Emigration Center was established in 1986 as a research and information center with the stated objective to develop contact between Norwegians around the world. It includes an extensive library of genealogical books and records, as well as providing a genealogical service. It has an excellent collection of *bygdebøker*, microfilmed Norwegian church records, national censuses of 1801 and 1865, and emigrant indexes. The minimum fee is $25 (in 1994) for answering written requests. Their yearbook, *Norse Heritage*, contains articles about Norse culture around the world. The address is:

Norwegian Emigration Center
Bergjelandsgate 30
N-4012 Stavanger
Norway

NATIONAL AND REGIONAL ARCHIVES

The Norwegian National Archives preserve the non-current records of government departments and other central offices. The Norwegian Regional Archives preserve documents from the regional and local branches of the state administration. As a rule, expect that records dating from before 1900 have been transferred to these central repositories. The archives are not obliged to make extensive searches, but you will receive some help. They will supply copies of baptismal, marriage, and death certificates, at fixed rates, and also photocopies, if accurate information is supplied. For extensive research they will help you find someone to hire. They have an informational booklet, *How to Trace Your Ancestors In Norway*, available through Norwegian consulates. The address of the consulate in Minnesota is:

Norwegian Consulate General
Foshay Tower
821 Marquette Ave.
Minneapolis, MN 55402

The addresses of the Norwegian national and regional archives are:

The National Archives:	***Østfold, Akershus, Oslo:***
Riksarkivet	Statsarkivet i Oslo
Folke Bernadottesvei 21	Folke Bernadottesvei 21
Postboks 10 Kringsjå	Postboks 8 Kringsjå
N-0807 Oslo	N-0807 Oslo
Norway	Norway

Buskerud, Vestfold, Telemark:
Statsarkivet i Kongsberg
Froggsveien 44
Postboks 384
N-3601 Kongsberg
Norway

Hedmark, Oppland:
Statsarkivet i Hamar
Strandgaten 71
N-2300 Hamar
Norway

Aust-Agder, Vest-Agder:
Statsarkivet i Kristiansand
Vesterveien 4
N-4600 Kristiansand
Norway

Rogaland:
Statsarkivet i Stavanger
Bergjelandsgate 30
N-4012 Stavanger
Norway

Hordaland, Bergen, Sogn og Fjordane:
Statsarkivet i Bergen
Årstadveien 22
N-5009 Bergen
Norway

Møre og Romsdal, Sør-Trøndelag,
Nord-Trøndelag, Nordland:
Statsarkivet i Trondheim
Høgskoleveien 12
Postboks 2825 Elgesæter
N-7001 Trondheim
Norway

Troms and Finnmark:
Statsarkivet i Tromsø
Skippergaten 1C
N-9000 Tromsø
Norway

SPAIN
(Spanien)

Spain controlled the Netherlands and Belgium at the time of the Protestant Reformation and thus was primarily responsible for driving many religious dissidents out of this area into Germany. It ruled Belgium until 1830. Spanish soldiers fought on German soil during the Thirty Years' War. A small number of Spanish-German liaisons must have resulted. Whether anything of significance could be found in Spanish archives is unlikely.

SWEDEN
(Schweden)

Sweden as well as Norway was settled by Germanic tribes. Swedish sailors, along with their Norwegian and Danish counterparts, explored Europe to plunder, trade, and settle during the Viking era from 800 to 1050. By 1250 Sweden controlled part of Finland and had established the city of Visby as a military and trading base on the island of Gotland where many foreign merchants settled, especially those of the Hanseatic League. Having been attracted by Sweden's minerals, forests, and dairy products, the Hanseatic League was in control of Swedish trade by the 1300s.

Germans at first migrated into southern Sweden, especially to Kalmar, giving it a German character. Later German migration from the middle of the 13th century onwards went more to central Sweden, with Germans apparently playing an important part in the founding of Stockholm about 1251. The Stockholm-Lübeck route was the vital artery of trade, being mostly controlled by Lübeck merchants and more by Stockholm merchants of German origin. The Hanseatic League developed the copper resources at Falun in the latter part of the 13th century, and miners from the Harz region of Germany settled around Falun. There were Hanseatic ports at Stockholm, Visby, Kalmar, and Falsterbo.

In the latter 1300s, the bubonic plague killed about one-third of the Swedish population and Sweden entered an economic decline through the 1400s. By the late 1300s, a German, Albrecht of Mecklenburg, succeeded to the throne of Sweden and there was a strong reaction against his efforts to decrease the power of the Swedish nobles. The Swedish ruling council turned to Norway's Queen Margareta to rule Sweden and by 1397 she had united Sweden, Norway and Denmark in the Union of Kalmar. Her successor and nephew, Erik of Pomerania, who taxed Swedish peasants heavily to fund Denmark's wars and forced the Hanseatic merchants to pay a toll, quickly lost popularity and was soon overthrown.

In the early 1500s, the Danes forcibly took over rule of Sweden, and Sweden's opposition to Danish rule increased until Gustav Vasa organized a peasant uprising and drove the Danes from Sweden. Gustav was elected king of Sweden in 1523. He stimulated mining, agriculture and commerce, and also allowed the government to seize the property of the Roman Catholic Church (which owned one-fifth of the country's land). Gustav encouraged Protestantism, to undermine the authority of the Catholic Church, and the Lutheran Church became Sweden's official religion. Gustav's grandson, Gustavus Adolphus, came to the throne in 1611.

About 1619, the Hapsburg Emperor, Ferdinand II, a militant supporter of the Counter-Reformation, and his Catholic allies in Germany fought their way north to Jutland and the Baltic coast. They forced the Danes to abandon their Protestant German allies with the Treaty of Lübeck of May 1629 and threatened annihilation of German Protestantism. King Gustavus Adolphus of Sweden did not want to see his country's domination of the Baltic challenged by the Catholic empire. Under his leadership the Swedes defeated the Hapsburgs at the Battle of Lützen in 1632, and after the end of the Thirty Years' War Sweden had extensive holdings in northern Germany, including most of the duchies of Bremen and Western Pomerania. In 1640, Sweden also occupied much of Brandenburg. However, Sweden's presence began declining after the mid 1600s and it lost much of its control of the Baltic to Russia.

Prussia gained part of Western Pomerania in 1720. Sweden lost all of its German territories by 1815. Sweden took control of Norway from Denmark as compensation for its loss of Pomerania and Finland. This control lasted until early in the twentieth century.

CHURCH RECORDS

The Lutheran Church became the state church in Sweden, and the church law in 1686 made it mandatory for the minister in each parish to keep a record of every person living within the parish, as well as a record of all religious ordinances he performed. Records of marriages (*vigsellängd*) including residences and parents' names were also required to be kept, as well as births (*födelselängd*) and baptisms (*doplängd*) of all children, including names of parents, sponsors, birth date, christening date and place of birth. Also required were records of deaths (*dödslängd*) and burials (*begravningslängd*) and records of those people moving into (*inflyttningslängd*) or out of (*utflyttningslängd*) the parish. Records of confirmations (*konfirmationslängd*) and marriage banns (*lysningslängd*) were also kept, and later other secular records such as smallpox vaccinations were also kept.

As in Norway, the patronymic method of naming was prevalent in Sweden. Surnames were rarely kept, except for foreign surnames and those surnames taken by men who entered the Swedish military. Note also that the Swedish alphabet contains three additional letters (*å, ä* and *ö*) at the end of the alphabet after the letter *z*.

A unique record kept by Swedish churches is the Clerical Survey, or House Examination Roll (*Husförhörslängd*). It is a record of a clerical religious examination of all members of the parish. Many parishes kept these records as early as 1700, although a few did not begin until about 1820. This record is a genealogical gold mine since it organizes people by place of residence and shows entire households together. In effect, it constitutes a running continuous census, with each particular record book covering a period of about five to ten years. Cross-outs and additions are indicated, and intermediate events are recorded, such as people moving within, into and out of the parish, where they came from and where they went. A person can usually be traced continuously from birth to death in this record. Do not miss using this record when doing genealogical research in Sweden.

Records of all Swedish parishes are available at Swedish archives and on microfilm through the Family History Centers. Other available records include emigration records from about 1865 (among the world's best), census and land records from about 1630, court records from the 1700s and military records from the 1600s. For those interested in genealogical research in Swedish records, *Cradled in Sweden: A Practical Help to Genealogical Research in Swedish Records*, by Carl-Erik Johansson, is an excellent and comprehensive guide. The following are two outstanding associations interested in Swedish genealogical research. The first is primarily interested in genealogical facts of a person or family, while the second is more interested in the history of an individual person or family. Their addresses are:

Genealogiska Föreningen
Arkivgatan 3
S-111 28 Stockholm
Sweden

Personhistoriska Samfundet
Arkivgatan 3
S-111 28 Stockholm
Sweden

There is extensive material on Swedish Pomerania (part of which remained under Swedish rule until 1815) available at the following archives. (For further information regarding the relevant contents, see the *AGoFF Guide*.)

Riksarkivet
Fack
S-100 26 Stockholm 34
Sweden

Krigsarkivet
Fack
S-104 50 Stockholm 80
Sweden

THE UNITED KINGDOM OF GREAT BRITAIN AND NORTHERN IRELAND
(Grossbritannien/Nordirland)

The Angles and Saxons who settled in England in the fifth century were actually North German tribes. Even before that, Germanic soldiers served in the Roman army that occupied England for several centuries. Some must have had children and stayed there after being mustered out.

Early German immigration to England, after distinct German and English identities developed, was the product of trade relationships. The Hanseatic League's major non-German establishment was the Stahlhof (Stapelhof) in London, dating back to the league's origin in the thirteenth century (or perhaps even before the Hanseatic cities joined together). The Hansa dominated trade with England, pursuant to the Privilege of 1377. The Stahlhof was not actually liquidated until 1853. However, the Hanseatic League reached its peak of power in the fifteenth century and existed only in name after 1669.

These connections resulted in two-way migration between England/Scotland and northern German areas. The Hanseatic League comprised not only port cities on the North and Baltic Seas, but also cities extending inland as far as Cologne (Köln), Göttingen and Breslau.

Traders from England and Scotland settled in Mecklenburg, Pomerania and Prussia, as well as in western Germany. In most cases, their names became Germanicized (e.g., Piper became Pfeiffer), but in other cases the British spelling persisted (e.g., Howe is quite common in Westphalia). Danzig and Elbing had a number of Scottish and English council members.

Tens of thousands of Scottish mercenaries fought on the continent, since it was hard to sustain many people in the highlands. How many may have remained on German soil is unknown.

German businessmen and craftsmen helped rebuild London after the Great Fire of 1666. Tin miners were another early group of German immigrants.

England was often a temporary home for those who sailed onward. The Palatines of 1709, most of whom went on to the American colonies, are the best known example, but others followed this pattern, going to North America or Australasia. However, some who set out for the New World stayed in England, possibly due to lack of funds.

Royal connections also were conducive to an interchange of Germans and Britons. The British royal lineage has been of German origin since 1714, when the son of the Elector of Hanover became king of Great Britain. Queen Victoria married Prince Albert of Saxe-Coburg-Gotha, thus establishing that as the British royal house in 1901, although the name was changed to Windsor in 1917. The next king will begin the house of Mountbatten, which was originally Battenberg.

The Hanoverian kings brought many of their German subjects to England. Very informative records relating to the soldiers in the various regiments of the King's German Legion survive. Quite a few became Chelsea pensioners.

Britain fought numerous wars in alliance with various German states in the eighteenth and nineteenth centuries. This served as a backdrop for such events as the British hiring of Hessian soldiers to fight in the American Revolution.

However, the largest number of immigrants came to Britain (as well as to the New World) between the 1840s and World War I. Of course, a huge number merely traveled across England (from London, or more often Hull, to Liverpool) before embarking for their transoceanic destinations.

Most German peasants and craftsmen went to Britain for economic reasons. There was a large exodus in 1870-72 in order to avoid military service during or immediately after the Franco-Prussian War. There seem to have been at least a few at the time of Napoleon, although their objection may have been to Napoleon, rather than to military service *per se*.

The late nineteenth century immigrants already found a thriving German community in London, where German bakers, especially sugar bakers in the East End, had established a dominant position by the early nineteenth century. London had ten German churches (nine Protestant), a very large German hospital, German schools and German welfare institutions around 1880. At least ten German newspapers were published in London before 1914 (although not simultaneously). While the vast majority of Germans resided in London, there were German communities in many cities.

There seem to have been few Germans in Scotland, Wales or Northern Ireland. But there must have been some in the major Scottish cities. A small number of Germans of Huguenot origin settled in (mostly Northern) Ireland during the Plantations Era (1600s, early 1700s), according to Bill and Mary Durning, *The Scotch Irish*.

Immigrants came from all parts of Germany, but most seem to have come from the southwest, according to hospital records. Many apparently sailed on wine-laden small boats down the Rhine and all the way to London.

There is a Moravian Church, known as the Church of United Brethren, in England, but very few of its members are of Germanic origin.

The Anglo-German Family History Society publishes a periodical, the *Mitteilungsblatt* [*Communications Sheet*, i.e., *Newsletter*], and numerous booklets on specialized topics. Despite the absence of passenger arrival lists, it has compiled a master index listing more than 70,000 Germans who lived or worked in Britain, based on surviving parish registers, shipping lists and internment lists. There were about 100,000 Germans, including many seasonal workers, in England when World War I began. Nearly half that number were interned. For information, contact:

> Anglo-German Family History Society
> 14 River Reach
> Teddington, Middx.
> England TW11 9OL

If you have ancestors among the Palatine immigrants of the early eighteenth century (or others who came to the New World via England), the following archive has unindexed Colonial Office records relating to them:

> Public Record Office
> Kew
> Richmond, Surrey
> England TW9 4DU

MISCELLANEOUS OTHER COUNTRIES

A few Greek architects and artisans are known to have served at German royal courts, e.g., in Munich. Nothing is known of any German family ties to Albania, Cyprus, Portugal, Malta, Iceland, or the mini-states of Monaco, Andorra and San Marino. Vatican City is a special case, since only high-ranking church officials, or their assistants and clerks, would have had any residential connection there.

Chapter XVI

CORRESPONDING WITH EUROPEAN SOURCES

Some things to consider when corresponding with sources in Europe include determining the official language, how to send payment or money and where to find foreign language translators. This chapter discusses those items and also provides samples of genealogical letters written in the German language.

LANGUAGE OF CORRESPONDENCE

It is best to write in the current official language of the country involved. However, it is usually acceptable to write in English if you are writing to an archive with a paid professional staff that will charge you for its services. This applies to most Eastern European countries today because they are eager to get dollars.

If you are writing to a pastor or to some other person who is not engaged in making a living as a professional researcher, you should write in German or whatever the appropriate language for that country may be. You should expect that the chances of a reply will be reduced if you do not. Even if your letter is answered, there may be a long delay. If you must write in English, keep the letter short, simple and direct.

The following table lists the official languages of selected European countries.

Table 11: Official Languages of Selected European Countries

Country	Language(s)	Comments
Austria	German	
Belgium	French, Flemish	Includes Eupen, Malmedy
Czech Republic	Czech	Includes Bohemia, Moravia
Denmark	Danish	Includes North Schleswig
France	French	Includes Alsace, Lorraine
Germany	German	
Hungary	Hungarian	
Italy	Italian	Includes South Tyrol
Liechtenstein	German	
Luxembourg	French, German	
The Netherlands	Dutch	
Norway	Norwegian	
Poland	Polish	Includes Posen, East Pomerania, Silesia, East and West Prussia, East Brandenburg
Romania	Romanian	
Russia	Russian	
Slovak Republic	Slovak	
Switzerland	German, French, Italian, Romansh	Depends on the canton
Former Yugoslavia	Serbian, Croatian, Slovenian, Macedonian	Depends on the republic

SENDING MONEY ABROAD

You may want to send money to other countries to pay for research, order records or books, etc. Bear in mind that nearly all Western institutions, organizations and individuals want to be paid in their own currencies because of the bank charges they have to pay to cash checks made out in dollars.

By far the best, simplest and most economical way to get checks in German marks or other Western currencies is to obtain them from Ruesch International, 700 Eleventh St. N.W., Washington, DC 20001-4507. Call 1-800-424-2923 to order checks. This is a new address, but the telephone number remains unchanged. The service charge is $2 per check. You will be given a confirmation number. The requested check will be mailed to you upon receipt of your payment. If you use this service frequently, you can get an account number and speed up the process a few days as the checks cross in the mail. Ruesch has branch offices in larger metropolitan areas like New York, Los Angeles and Chicago. If using these is more expedient for you, check the telephone directory.

On the other hand, almost everybody in East Europe wants to be paid in dollars or other hard currencies, primarily because of the high inflation rates. However, the bank charges for dollars, checks or money orders are even higher (currently about $7 per check in Poland). International Reply Coupons are not very useful since they cost about double their value and post offices in smaller localities may be unfamiliar with them. So be sure to add $7 (or whatever other sum may be requested as policies change) to the amount you owe. It may be cheaper to get a money order in dollars from the post office than to get a bank draft.

WRITING LETTERS TO GERMANY

Toward the end of World War II, some German records and church registers from places in East Brandenburg, East and West Prussia, Pomerania, Posen and Silesia were moved to archives in present-day Germany. At least a few remained in Poland. There are published inventories of the eastern holdings of major archives in Leipzig and Berlin. However, their records are far from complete. Although some records were destroyed in World War II in areas where there was heavy fighting, many were not. In some cases (especially East Pomerania), the problem is that the records are widely scattered. This makes it more difficult to find the records, but the situation is not hopeless.

Local church parishes will have baptism, marriage and death records. If writing to a church pastor, you can offer to pay for the research and copying expenses. Whether or not payment is requested, it is courteous to enclose a donation to the church. Many church records are being transferred to regional church archives. These regional archives will be able to check multiple church parishes at the same time, but they may be more expensive and may not give you as much detailed attention as you would receive at the local level.

If you are writing to the local civil registry office (*Standesamt*), the local city archives (*Stadtarchiv*) or the state archives (*Staatsarchiv*), expect to be billed for any research they perform. Rates will probably be higher at the state archives. Send no money at first. In your letter include an ancestor chart, family group sheet or brief narrative of the facts related to your ancestor. German language charts and group sheets are available. If the person or place you write to cannot help, ask for a recommendation of someone who can.

Print or type your letters and write them as clearly and concisely as you can. Do not include too many requests in your letter. Write in German if possible. Include two International Reply Coupons for postage (available at any U.S. post office) and offer to pay for documents or research. Include more coupons if you expect to receive back more than a relatively simple letter. It may take quite a while, but you will get an answer from the archives. If a given archive cannot locate the information for you, write to another one nearby.

SAMPLE LETTERS

Four sample German letters and their translations follow. They are letters to a church pastor, a possible relative, a genealogical or historical society, and a mayor in charge of city archives.

These letters may be useful starting points. You probably will wish to add to them or interchange sentences between them. If you make modifications or additions to the letters, however, they should be proofread by a German speaker before sending them overseas.

Print or type your letter, since United States handwriting can be difficult for Germans to read. Remember to keep the letter short and to the point. You may wish to begin your letter with your name, address and date, then the name and address of whom you are writing to, as in the first sample. German nouns are always capitalized. It is a good idea to consult a German (or other) postal code book (*Postleitzahlenbuch*) in order to find the current postal code. Postal code directories for Germany, Austria, Switzerland and Liechtenstein are shown in the bibliography.

When requesting information from anyone in your own country, you should always enclosed a self-addressed, stamped envelope (SASE), unless you expect to pay for the services and information. Experts may get hundreds of requests for information.

When you are requesting information from any foreign country, you should always include one or more International (Postal) Reply Coupons (IRCs or IPRCs). Unless you expect only a brief letter in return, you should enclose two. If you are expecting actual documents as well, you should enclose three. These are available from any post office, although in small post offices where there is little demand for them, only the most senior employee may know where they are.

Of course, you should always offer to pay any expenses and fees in connection with research. Professional genealogists and archives will usually charge you, but many pastors and volunteer genealogists (who may be extremely knowledgeable) do not charge for their services. In such cases, enclose a donation to the church or for the promotion of further research.

Letter to a church pastor:

Your name
Street
City, State   ZIP Code
Date (day.month.year)

Herr Pfarrer _____
Street number
Postal-Code City
Country

Sehr verehrter Herr Pfarrer!

Anlässlich meiner Familienforschung ergab sich, dass mein Vorfahr _____(name)_____ aus _____(city)_____ stammte. Die Namen dieser Linie sind aus der hier beiliegenden Ahnentafel ersichtlich. Ich möchte die Linie gern weiter verfolgen und Sie bitten, mir Fotokopien über diesbezügliche Eintragungen zu machen und mir zuzusenden.

Für Ihre Bemühungen danke ich Ihnen im voraus und lege hier eine Teilzahlung von _____ DM bei.

Ihrer Antwort sehe ich mit Interesse entgegen.

Hochachtungsvoll

_____

Anliegend:
  1 Ahnentafel
  2 Antwortscheine
  __ DM Anzahlung

- -

Your name
Street
City, State   ZIP Code
Date (day.month.year)

Dear Reverend,

According to my research my ancestor _____(name)_____ came from _____(city)_____. I am enclosing an ancestor chart to show the names of those in that line. I would like to trace the line further and request that you send me copies of the relevant church records.

I thank you for your effort in advance and enclose a partial payment of ___ Marks.

I look forward to your answer.

Respectfully,

_____

Enclosed:
  1 ancestor chart
  2 reply coupons
  __ German marks (advance payment)

Letter to a possible relative:

Your name
Street
City, State   ZIP Code
Date (day.month.year)

Herrn _____ Frau _____
Street number
Postal-Code City
Country

Sehr geehrter Herr _____! Sehr geehrte Frau _____!

Ihren Namen habe ich aus dem Telefonbuch entnommen. Mein Grossvater hatte den gleichen Familiennamen _____(name)_____ (wie auch ich). Meine Vorfahren stammten aus _____(city)_____ in _____(state)_____. Mein Urgrossvater kam im Jahre _____(year)_____ nach Amerika.

Könnte es sein, dass wir miteinander verwandt sind? Zu Ihrer Kenntnisnahme lege ich hier eine Ahnentafel bei, der Sie die Namen meiner Vorfahren entnehmen können. Stammt Ihre Familie eventuell aus der gleichen Gegend? Haben auch Sie Ihre Familie erforscht?

Ich würde mich freuen, von Ihnen eine Antwort zu bekommen. Zwei Antwortscheine, die gegen Rückporto beim Postamt eingelöst werden können, sind beigefügt.

Mit besten Grüssen

Anliegend:

_____

  1 Ahnentafel
  2 Antwortscheine

- -

Your name
Street
City, State   ZIP Code
Date (day.month.year)

Mr. _____ Mrs. _____
Recipient's name
Address

Dear Mr. _____, Dear Mrs. _____,

I found your name in a telephone book. My grandfather's surname was also _____(name)_____ (it is also my name). My ancestors came from _____(city)_____ in _____(state)_____. My great grandfather arrived in America in _____(year)_____.

Perhaps we're related? I am enclosing an ancestor chart to show who my ancestors were. Do you have any ancestors from the region? Have you traced your family?

I am looking forward to hearing from you. I have enclosed two international reply coupons that you can exchange for return postage at the post office.

Best Wishes,

Enclosed:

_____

  1 ancestor chart
  2 reply coupons

Letter to genealogical or historical society:

Your name
Street
City, State   ZIP Code
Date (day.month.year)

Sehr geehrte Damen und Herren!

Wie ich bei verschiedenen Nachforschungen festgestellt habe, stammten meine Vorfahren aus _____ *(city)* _____.

Ich lege einen Auszug meiner Ahnentafel hier bei, aus der Sie Einzelheiten ersehen können.

Würden Sie gewillt sein für mich weitere Sucharbeit durchzuführen? Wenn ja, bitte teilen Sie mir mit, welche Kosten für mich damit verbunden sind. Falls Sie selbst keine Forschungsarbeiten tun, wäre ich Ihnen dankbar, wenn Sie mir einen Ahnenforscher empfehlen könnten, der Zugang zu den Archiven und Bibliotheken hat.

Für Ihre Bemühungen danke ich im voraus.

Mit besten Grüssen

_____

Anliegend:
  1 Ahnentafel
  2 Antwortscheine

- -

Your name
Street
City, State   ZIP Code
Date (day.month.year)

Dear ladies and gentlemen,

Using various sources I have found that my ancestors came from _____ *(city)* _____.

I am enclosing an ancestor chart to show who they were.

Would you be willing to conduct further research for me? Please tell me in advance what the expenses might be. If you don't do such research, could you suggest a researcher with access to the archives and libraries who might?

Thank you in advance for your effort.

Best wishes,

_____

Enclosed:
  1 ancestor chart
  2 reply coupons

Letter to a small town or local archive:

Your name
Street
City, State   ZIP Code
Date (day.month.year)

Sehr geehrter Herr Bürgermeister!

Auf der Suche nach meiner Herkunft entdeckte ich, dass mein Vorfahr _____ (name) _____
aus _____ (city) _____ stammte. Ich möchte die Familie weiter zurück verfolgen und brauche
dazu Ihre Hilfe. Würden Sie die Sucharbeit für mich durchführen?

Bitte geben Sie mir die entstehenden Kosten bekannt, oder nennen Sie mir eine Person,
die gewillt wäre, Nachforschungen für mich durchzuführen.

Ich lege eine Ahnentafel und zwei Antwortscheine bei.

Ich danke Ihnen im voraus.

Mit besten Grüssen

_____

Anliegend:
  1 Ahnentafel
  2 Antwortscheine

- -

Your name
Street
City, State   ZIP Code
Date (day.month.year)

Dear Mr. Mayor,

According to my research my ancestor _____ (name) _____ came from _____ (city) _____. I
want to trace the family further and need your help to do so. Would you conduct this
research for me?

Please tell me in advance what the expenses might be or give me the name of someone who
would be willing to do research for me.

I am enclosing an ancestor chart and two reply coupons.

Thank you in advance.

Best wishes,

_____ _____

Enclosure:
  1 ancestor chart
  2 reply coupons

TRANSLATIONS

Sooner or later, you must deal with records and documents in another language. We all try to struggle through basic terms ourselves, but to learn the exact meaning in its context we may need to hire a translator.

The Germanic Genealogy Society has a list of people in Minnesota who will do professional translations for most European languages. So do some other German-oriented societies. The *Resource Guide to East European Genealogy*, published by FEEFHS, lists translators for nearly every European language. Always contact the translator and ask about fees. Also ask how well they know the language and how much experience they have translating it to and from English. Also ask the translators about their experience in doing Germanic genealogical research. Competent hands-on experience in translating genealogy-related documents is very helpful, and often necessary to get an accurate and thorough translation.

Request an estimate of possible costs if the project is a lengthy one; provide the details of your project and enclose a self-addressed stamped envelope (SASE). Language teachers in your local schools or at a university may also be willing to do translations. Many other genealogical organizations provide translation services or refer people to translators. Translation services found in the Yellow Pages are likely to be expensive since they concentrate on commercial work.

If your material is in the Gothic script, you need to check the experience of the translator in deciphering this script, since many translators cannot. Be aware that most Catholic church records are in Latin, not German. Written records vary greatly in clarity, so deciphering the script may take much longer than the translation itself. For this reason, the cost of translating the same number of pages or words may vary tremendously from document to document.

Part-time and full-time translators may differ considerably with respect to how long they take to complete an assignment. If you have a deadline or are willing to wait only a certain length of time, be sure you inform the translator of this.

Always send the translator a good copy of the material you have, unless the copy is so poor as to make deciphering it difficult. In that case, send the original to the translator and keep a copy for yourself, but be sure that there are always two copies as insurance against any possible loss or damage.

If the handwriting is hard to read, it may help to make an enlarged copy. In this case, you should send a copy of the whole page along with the enlarged copy of the key material.

In the case of parish registers, it may be helpful to send the translator a whole page or several pages, rather than just the entry you want translated. Then if the translator cannot decipher a personal or family name in which you are interested, seeing a larger sample of the handwriting may make deciphering possible.

FAMILY AND ANCESTOR CHARTS

The following Ancestor Charts and Family Group Sheets are helpful when corresponding with someone who reads the German, Polish or French language. These charts have a universal identity in format and are a great help in organizing the family information at a glance. In doing research on Germanic ancestry, any one of these may be useful since records are found in each of these languages.

Ahnentafel

Namen des Einsenders _____

Straße _____

Stadt _____ Staat _____

Datum _____

8
Geburtsdatum
Geburtsort
Heiratsdatum
Heiratsort
Sterbedatum
Sterbeort

4
Geburtsdatum
Geburtsort
Heiratsdatum
Heiratsort
Sterbedatum
Sterbeort

9
Geburtsdatum
Geburtsort
Sterbedatum
Sterbeort

2
Geburtsdatum
Geburtsort
Heiratsdatum
Heiratsort
Sterbedatum
Sterbeort

10
Geburtsdatum
Geburtsort
Heiratsdatum
Heiratsort
Sterbedatum
Sterbeort

5
Geburtsdatum
Geburtsort
Sterbedatum
Sterbeort

11
Geburtsdatum
Geburtsort
Sterbedatum
Sterbeort

1
Geburtsdatum
Geburtsort
Heiratsdatum
Heiratsort
Sterbedatum
Sterbeort

Namen des Ehemannes oder der Ehefrau

12
Geburtsdatum
Geburtsort
Heiratsdatum
Heiratsort
Sterbedatum
Sterbeort

6
Geburtsdatum
Geburtsort
Heiratsdatum
Heiratsort
Sterbedatum
Sterbeort

13
Geburtsdatum
Geburtsort
Sterbedatum
Sterbeort

3
Geburtsdatum
Geburtsort
Sterbedatum
Sterbeort

14
Geburtsdatum
Geburtsort
Heiratsdatum
Heiratsort
Sterbedatum
Sterbeort

7
Geburtsdatum
Geburtsort
Sterbedatum
Sterbeort

15
Geburtsdatum
Geburtsort
Sterbedatum
Sterbeort

Ehemann

	Tag	Monat	Jahr		Stadt	Kreis	Staat oder Land
Geburt				Ort			
Sterbe				Ort			
Beerdigung				Ort			
Heirat				Ort			

Vater

Mutter

Ehefrau

	Tag	Monat	Jahr		Stadt	Kreis	Staat oder Land
Geburt				Ort			
Sterbe				Ort			
Beerdigung				Ort			
Heirat			Religion				

Vater

Mutter

Kinder	Geburtsdatum			Geburtsort			Heirat (datum / ort)	Sterbedatum			Beerdigungsort		
	Tag	Monat	Jahr	Stadt	Kreis	Staat oder Land		Tag	Monat	Jahr	Stadt	Kreis	Staat oder Land
1													
Ehe.													
2													
Ehe.													
3													
Ehe.													
4													
Ehe.													
5													
Ehe.													
6													
Ehe.													
7													
Ehe.													
8													
Ehe.													
9													
Ehe.													
10													
Ehe.													

Name und Addresse des Einsenders des Bogens

Zakres Przodkow

8
Data urodzenia
Miejsce
Data sluba
Miejsce
Data smierci
Miejsce

4
Data urodzenia
Miejsce
Data sluba
Miejsce
Data smierci
Miejsce

9
Data urodzenia
Miejsce
Data smierci
Miejsce

2
Data urodzenia
Miejsce
Data sluba
Miejsce
Data smierci
Miejsce

10
Data urodzenia
Miejsce
Data sluba
Miejsce
Data smierci
Miejsce

5
Data urodzenia
Miejsce
Data smierci
Miejsce

11
Data urodzenia
Miejsce
Data smierci
Miejsce

1
Data urodzenia
Miejsce
Data sluba
Miejsce
Data smierci
Miejsce

Maz lub zona

12
Data urodzenia
Miejsce
Data sluba
Miejsce
Data smierci
Miejsce

6
Data urodzenia
Miejsce
Data sluba
Miejsce
Data smierci
Miejsce

13
Data urodzenia
Miejsce
Data smierci
Miejsce

3
Data urodzenia
Miejsce
Data smierci
Miejsce

14
Data urodzenia
Miejsce
Data sluba
Miejsce
Data smierci
Miejsce

7
Data urodzenia
Miejsce
Data smierci
Miejsce

15
Data urodzenia
Miejsce
Data smierci
Miejsce

maz

	dzien	miesiac	rok		miasto	hrabstwo	stan lub kraj
urodzenie				miejsce			
smierci				miejsce			
pogrzeb				miejsce			
sluba				miejsce			

Ojciec

Matka

zona

	dzien	miesiac	rok		miasto	hrabstwo	stan lub kraj
urodzenie				miejsce			
smierci				miejsce			
pogrzeb				miejsce			
sluba			religja				

Ojciec

Matka

dzieci

	data urodzenie			miejsce urodzenie				data smierci			miejsce pogrzeb			
	dzien	miesiac	rok	miasto	hrabstwo	stan lub kraj		dzien	miesiac	rok	miasto	hrabstwo	stan lub kraj	
1														
malzonka														
2														
malzonka														
3														
malzonka														
4														
malzonka														
5														
malzonka														
6														
malzonka														
7														
malzonka														
8														
malzonka														
9														
malzonka														
10														
malzonka														

sluba: data, miejsce

nom _____

rue _____

ville _____ état _____

date _____

tableau
généalogique

2

date de naissance

lieu

date de mariage

lieu

date du mort

lieu

1

date de naissance

lieu

date de mariage

lieu

date du mort

lieu

époux / épouse

3

date de naissance

lieu

date du mort

lieu

4

date de naissance

lieu

date de mariage

lieu

date du mort

lieu

5

date de naissance

lieu

date du mort

lieu

6

date de naissance

lieu

date de mariage

lieu

date du mort

lieu

7

date de naissance

lieu

date du mort

lieu

8

date de naissance

lieu

date de mariage

lieu

date du mort

lieu

9

date de naissance

lieu

date du mort

lieu

10

date de naissance

lieu

date de mariage

lieu

date du mort

lieu

11

date de naissance

lieu

date du mort

lieu

12

date de naissance

lieu

date de mariage

lieu

date du mort

lieu

13

date de naissance

lieu

date du mort

lieu

14

date de naissance

lieu

date de mariage

lieu

date du mort

lieu

15

date de naissance

lieu

date du mort

lieu

mari

	jour	mois	an	ville	comté	état ou pays	lieu
naissance							lieu
mort							lieu
enterrement							lieu
mariage							lieu

père

mère

femme

	jour	mois	an	ville	comté	état ou pays	lieu
naissance							lieu
mort							lieu
enterrement							lieu
	religion						

père

mère

enfants

	date de naissance			lieu de naissance			mariage	date du mort			lieu d'enterrement		
	jour	mois	an	ville	comté	état ou pays		jour	mois	an	ville	comté	état ou pays
1							date						
époux / épouse							lieu						
2													
époux / épouse													
3													
époux / épouse													
4													
époux / épouse													
5													
époux / épouse													
6													
époux / épouse													
7													
époux / épouse													
8													
époux / épouse													
9													
époux / épouse													
10													
époux / épouse													

Chapter XVII

READING THE RECORDS

There are many obstacles that must be overcome in order to read the records of your Germanic ancestors. The records will most likely be written in German or some other non-English language, and will probably be written in Gothic script. This chapter provides both a brief introduction to the Gothic script and some German language notes, including lists of terms you will encounter in genealogically pertinent records. It also gives information regarding other languages you may encounter when reading the records.

THE GOTHIC SCRIPT

Gothic script, sometimes also known as German script, came into existence over a thousand years ago. It was used in many Germanic areas of Europe until the early 1800s, and persisted in Germany (as well as the United States) until World War II. It has been replaced with the script we use today, which is called Roman or Latin script. Whereas Latin letters are based on rounded shapes, lowercase Gothic letters follow more of a straight line, giving the script an angular appearance.

A knowledge of the language in which the document is written is essential in trying to decipher it. The first step here is learning what words to expect in certain documents. Look for them first and then fill in the other words.

Reading Gothic script can be a complex task, since everyone has different handwriting and the handwriting of each individual also varies from time to time. However, you can use this variation to your advantage, since you may be able to read a letter, word or phrase in another portion of a document and then use that information to help read a difficult area.

Pick difficult words apart by letters or groups of letters. It helps a great deal to know common German words, and also which letter groups do and don't occur together in the German language. First, pick out the parts you can clearly read, and then work on the other parts. Ultimately with practice you can start to pick out whole words at a time.

When a given handwriting is particularly difficult to read, prepare a list of capital and small letters as you can make them out. Trace them if possible. You can use this list to help decipher other areas.

A mixture of both Gothic and Latin scripts is very common in church records. Names tend to be written in Latin script with the rest being in Gothic. Of course, exceptions are common.

A bar over a consonant indicates that it is doubled. The bar over the letter *n* is easy to confuse with the mark over the letter *u*.

There are two forms of the letter *s*. The first form (similar in appearance to *f*) is used in the middle of words (e.g., *deutsch*). The second form, known as the *Schluss-s* (final *s*), is used at the end of words (e.g., *das*), and within compound words (e.g., *Geburtstag*) when the component root ends in *s* (*Geburts* in this case).

The s-tset *ß* (*sz*) looks similar to the English *B*. This is equivalent to *ss* at the end of a word or root of a compound word, and it is often written *ss* today.

Some words are occasionally abbreviated with an ending squiggle that looks like the Gothic letter *x*.

Common German word contractions are: *am = an dem, vom = von dem, zum = zu dem, ans = an das*. Apostrophes are not used in contractions.

Common abbreviations are: *ehel. = ehelich, u. = und, d. = den, M. = Mutter, V. = Vater, S. = Sohn, T. = Tochter, Taufz. = Taufzeugen, Fr. = Frau, Jgfr. = Jungfrau, ev. = evangelisch, kath. = katholisch.* An *X* is sometimes used to abbreviate certain names as in *Xan =*

Christian. Latin abbreviations sometimes also occur, such as: *ej. = ejusdem*. See the German vocabulary list later in this chapter for more examples.

German spelling has changed over the years. For example, *h* after *t* has been dropped, e.g., *verheirathet* is now *verheiratet*. About the only exceptions to this are in place names and surnames, although even these may have changed (especially place names). A synopsis of those changes in German spelling brought about through the government regulations of 1880 is given in *German Composition* by Hermann Lange (3rd. edition, Oxford: Clarendon Press, 1900).

European dates are generally given with day ahead of month, e.g., *den 17. Juni 1843* is June 17, 1843. A period after the day indicates the ordinal number, e.g., *17.* = "17th," so *den 17. Juni* literally means "the 17th of June."

Following is a chart of printed and written Gothic letters. Practice writing words from the genealogical word list using the written Gothic letters so you will have an idea what they should look like in Gothic before you get involved in trying to decipher a document.

ROMAN TYPE	GERMAN TYPE	GERMAN SCRIPT	ROMAN TYPE	GERMAN TYPE	GERMAN SCRIPT
A a	𝔄 a		N n	𝔑 n	
B b	𝔅 b		O o	𝔒 o	
C c	ℭ c		P p	𝔓 p	
D d	𝔇 d		Q q	𝔔 q	
E e	ℭ e		R r	𝔑 r	
F f	𝔉 f		S s	𝔖 ſ s	
G g	𝔊 g		T t	𝔗 t	
H h	ℌ h		U u	𝔘 u	
I i	𝔍 i		V v	𝔙 v	
J j	𝔍 j		W w	𝔚 w	
K k	𝔎 k		X x	𝔛 x	
L l	𝔏 l		Y y	𝔜 y	
M m	𝔐 m		Z z	𝔷 z	

Adapted from Beginning German by
Schinnerer, Otto P., 1935

GERMAN LANGUAGE NOTES

The German language uses three genders for its nouns. The gender for each German word must be learned.

(masculine)	*der Mann*	the man
(feminine)	*die Frau*	the woman; also wife
(neuter)	*das Kind*	the child

There are four different cases: nominative (subject), genitive (possessive), dative (to whom) and accusative (object). These cases are used to indicate the relationship of words within a sentence. Here is an example with the English translation:

Das Mädchen gab mir das Buch ihrer Mutter.
The girl gave me her mother's book.

(nominative case)	*das Mädchen*	the girl	(subject)
(genitive case)	*ihrer Mutter*	her mother's	(possession)
(dative case)	*mir*	(to) me	(to whom)
(accusative case)	*das Buch*	the book	(object)

This example illustrates some patterns in German. All German nouns are capitalized, although some writers may not always have been too careful about it. The gender and case of the noun changes the endings or forms of associated articles (a, the) and adjectives. Sometimes the noun itself will have a different ending. Prepositions belong to either dative, accusative or sometimes the genitive case.

Article changes:

(nominative case)	*der Mann*	*die Frau*	*das Kind*
(genitive case)	*des Mannes*	*der Frau*	*des Kindes*
(dative case)	*dem Mann*	*der Frau*	*dem Kind*
(accusative case)	*den Mann*	*die Frau*	*das Kind*

Article with adjective:

	(the old man)	(the young woman)	(the small child)
(nominative case)	*der alte Mann*	*die junge Frau*	*das kleine Kind*
(genitive case)	*des alten Mannes*	*der jungen Frau*	*des kleinen Kindes*
(dative case)	*dem alten Mann*	*der jungen Frau*	*dem kleinen Kind*
(accusative case)	*den alten Mann*	*die junge Frau*	*das kleine Kind*

The endings used when the article *ein* is present (*ein* is German for *a* or *an*):

	(an old man)	(a young woman)	(a small child)
(nominative case)	*ein alter Mann*	*eine junge Frau*	*ein kleines Kind*
(genitive case)	*eines alten Mannes*	*einer jungen Frau*	*eines kleinen Kindes*
(dative case)	*einem alten Mann*	*einer jungen Frau*	*einem kleinen Kind*
(accusative case)	*einen alten Mann*	*eine junge Frau*	*ein kleines Kind*

German plurals have a different article and the noun may have one of the following endings:

ending	singular	plural	English
-	*der Schüler*	*die Schüler*	pupil
-e (may add Umlaut)	*der Tisch*	*die Tische*	table

-er (may add Umlaut)	*das Buch*	*die Bücher*	book
-n	*die Lampe*	*die Lampen*	lamp
-en	*der Student*	*die Studenten*	student
-s	*das Auto*	*die Autos*	car

German verbs are often put at the end of sentences, e.g.,

> *Er ist am 17. Mai 1793 geboren.* He was born on May 17, 1793.

German has many compound words built from simpler words.

> Examples: *der Geburtstag* - birthday; *der Taufschein* - baptismal certificate.

German words are almost always spelled phonetically, i.e., the way they are pronounced. Spelling is much more consistent in German than in English, and without as many silent letters.

The sounds of the German vowels *a*, *o* and *u* are modified by putting an Umlaut over the vowel (i.e., *ä*, *ö* and *ü*). This changes the pronunciation and meaning of the word. Some German dictionaries alphabetize Umlauted vowels as if the vowel were followed by the letter *e*.

See Chapters VII and VIII, as well as the German vocabulary list in the next section, for more information regarding the spelling of German names and other German words.

For more information about the German language please refer to a German language textbook or a book on German grammar.

GERMAN VOCABULARY RELATED TO GENEALOGY

KINSHIP, JURISDICTIONAL AND OTHER TERMS

German	English	German	English
A.C. (Augsburger Confession)	Lutheran (creed)	ebenda	the same place
		Ehe, die	marriage
Ahn(e), der	male ancestor	Ehefrau, die	wife
Ahne, die	female ancestor	Ehegatte, der	husband
Ahnfrau, die	female ancestor	Ehegattin, die	wife
Ahnherr, der	male ancestor	ehelich (ehel.)	legitimate
Akte, die	public record, file	Ehemann, der	husband
Alter, das	age	einbürgern	naturalize
Ältere, der/die (d.Ä.)	senior	einwandern	immigrate
Amt, das (A.)	office	Einwilligung, die	consent
Amtsbezirk, der	lowest court	Einwohnermeldeamt, das	civil registration office
Amtsgericht, das (AG.)	local court house		
Amtsgerichtsbezirk, der	district court jurisdiction	ejusdem (ej.) (Latin)	the same
		Enkel, der	grandson/child
Amtshauptmannschaft, die	government district	Enkelin, die	granddaughter
		Enkelkind, das	grandchild
Anwohner, der	resident	Eltern, die	parents
Anzeige, die	notice	Erbe, das	inheritance
Aufgebot, das	publication/banns	Erbe, der	heir
ausgestorben	(line is) extinct	Erbschaft, die	inheritance
auswandern	emigrate	evangelisch (ev.)	Evangelical, Protestant (Lutheran-Reformed)
Band, der	volume		
Base, die	female cousin		
Base, die	aunt (in Switzerland)		
Beerdigung, die	burial	Familienforschung, die	genealogy
Begräbnis, das	burial		
Bemerkungen, die	remarks, notes	Familienname, der	surname
Berg, der	mountain, hill	Familienregister, das	family register
Beschneidung, die	circumcision	Filiale, die	branch church
beziehungsweise (bzw.)	respectively, or	Fluss, der	river, stream
Bezirk, der	district	Frau, die (Fr.)	woman, wife
Bezirksamt, das	district office	Fräulein, das	unmarried woman, miss
Bezirksgericht, das	district court		
Bezirkskommando, das (BKdo.)	district military office	Fürstentum, das	principality
		Gatte, der	husband
Braut, die	bride	Gattin, die	wife
Bräutigam, der	bridegroom	geboren (geb.)	born
Brief, der	letter, document	Geborene, die	the one who was born
Bruder, der	brother	Geburt, die	birth
Burg, die	fortress, castle	Geburtsort, der	birthplace
Confirmation, die	confirmation	Geburtstag, der	birthday
confirmiert	confirmed	Geburtsschein, der	birth certificate
Copulation, die	marriage	Gemeinde, die (Gem.)	community, parish, congregation
copuliert	married		
Cousin, der	male cousin	Gericht, das	court
Cousine, die	female cousin	Gerichtstag, der	day that court is in session
Departement, das	department (French unit of government)	geschieden	divorced
Diaspora, die	diaspora, dispersion (in foreign countries)	gestorben (gest.)	died
		Gestorbene, die	the decedent
Dorf, das (D.)	village	getauft (get.)	baptized
Drilling, der	triplet	getraut (getr.)	wed

German	English	German	English
getrennt	separated	Knabe, der	boy
Gevatter, der	godfather	Kreis, der (Kr.)	county
Gevatterin, die	godmother	Kusine, die	female cousin
Grafschaft, die	earldom	Land, das	land, country, state, province, rural area
Grosseltern, die	grandparents		
Grosskind, das	grandchild (Swiss/Mennonite)	Landgemeinde, die	rural parish, town(ship)
Grossmutter, die	grandmother	Landgericht, das	county court
Grosssohn, der	grandson	Landkreis, der (LKr.)	rural county
Grosstochter, die	granddaughter	Landratsamt, das	district office
Grossvater, der	grandfather	ledig	single, unmarried
Gut, das	estate, property	Leibeigene, der/die	serf (male/female)
H.C. (Helvetier Confession)	Reformed (creed) - Calvinist	lutherisch (luth.)	Lutheran
		Mädchen, das	girl
Halb(bruder)	half-(brother)	majorenn	of legal age
Hausmutter, die	mother	Mann, der	man, husband
Hausvater, der	father	männlich	masculine
hebräisch	Hebrew, Jewish	Matrikel, die	register
Heirat, die	marriage	Meer, das	sea, ocean
heiraten	to marry	mennonitisch	Mennonite
Herrschaft, die	domain, rule	minderjährig	underage
Herzogtum, das	duchy	minorenn	underage
hiesig	local	Mutter, die	mother
Hinterlassenen, die	survivors, heirs	nachgelassen	surviving
Hochzeit, die	wedding ceremony	Nachlass, der	legacy
Hof, der	farmstead	Name, der	name
hugenottisch	Huguenot	noch lebende	still living
israelitisch	Jewish, Hebrew	nota bene (NB) (Latin)	note well
Jahre, die (J.)	years	Obergericht, das	supreme court (Swiss)
jüdisch	Jewish		
Junge, der	boy	Oberlandesgericht, das	highest provincial court
Jüngere, der/die (d.J.)	junior		
Jungfer, die (Jgfr.)	unmarried woman	öffentlich	public(ly)
Jungfrau, die (Jgfr.)	unmarried woman	Onkel, der	uncle (also figurative)
Junggeselle, der	bachelor		
Jüngling, der	youth	Ort, der	place
Kaiserreich, das	empire	Ortschaft, die	locality
Kanton/Canton, der	canton	Pass, der	identification paper, passport
katholisch (kath.)	Catholic		
Kind, das	child	Pate/Pathe, der	godfather, or sometimes godson
Kinder, die	children		
Kirche, die	church	Paten/Pathen, die	godparents
Kirchenbuch, das	parish register	Patenkind/ Pathenkind, das	godchild
Kirchengemeinde, die	parish		
Kirchsprengel, der	diocese	Patensohn/ Pathensohn, der	godson
Knabe, der	boy		
Kolonie, die (Kol.)	colony	Patin/Pathin, die	godmother, or sometimes goddaughter
Kommunion, die	Communion		
Konfirmand, der	male confirmand		
Konfirmandin, die	female confirmand	Pfarramt, das	church office
Konfirmation, die	confirmation	Pfarrkirche, die (Pfk.)	parish church
konfirmiert (konf.)	confirmed	Pflege(kind)	foster-(child)
Königliche und kaiserliche (k.u.k.)	royal and imperial	Predigt, die	sermon
		Protokoll, das	official record
Königreich, das	kingdom	reformiert	Reformed
Kopulation, die	marriage	Regierungsbezirk, der (RB.)	administrative area
kopuliert	married		

German	English	German	English
Reich, das	empire	Trauschein, der	marriage certificate
Reichsgericht, das	supreme court	Trauung, die	marriage (ceremony)
Rittergut, das (Rg.)	Nobleman's, knight's or Junker's estate	unehelich (unehel.)	illegitimate
		Untertan, der	subject, vassal
Schein, der	certificate	unverheiratet	single, unwed
Schwester, die	sister	Urkunde, die	document
Schwieger(mutter)	(mother-)in-law	Ursache, die	cause
Schwurgericht, das	juried court	Vater, der	father
See, der	lake	verehelichen	to marry, to give one's daughter in marriage
See, die	sea, ocean		
Seite, die	page	Verehelichung, die	marriage
Selbe, der/die (usually one word)	same (male or female)	verheirat(h)en	to marry, to be given in marriage
siehe (s.)	see	verheirat(h)et	married
Sohn, der (S.)	son	Verheirat(h)ung, die	marriage
Staat, der	state or province	verlobt	engaged
Staatsarchiv, das	regional archive	verstorben	deceased
Stadt, die	city	Verstorbene, der	(the) deceased
Stadtarchiv, das	city archive	Verwaltungsbezirk, der	administrative area
Stadtgemeinde, die	urban parish, urban community	verwandt	related
		verwitwet	widowed
Stadtkreis, der	urban county	Verzeichnis, das	register, index
Stand, der	position or occupation	Vetter, der	cousin, relative
		vide (Latin)	see
Standesamt, das (StdA.)	registry of vital statistics	volljährig	of legal age
		Vorname, der	given name
Sterbefall, der	case of death	Wahlkreis, der	voting ward
Stief(vater), der	step(father)	Waise, die	orphan
Synagoge, die	synagogue	Waisenkind, das	orphan
Tante, die	aunt (also figurative)	Weib, das	wife, woman
		weiblich	feminine
		weiland	deceased
Taufe, die	baptism	Weiler, der	hamlet
Taufpate, der	godfather	wie oben	as above, ditto
Taufpatin, die	godmother	wie vorher	as before, ditto
Taufschein, der	baptismal certificate	Wiedertäufer, der	Anabaptist
Taufzeuge, der	godfather	Witwe, die	widow
Taufzeugin, die	godmother	Witwer, der	widower
Tod, der	death	Wohnort, der	place of residence
Todesursache, die	cause of death	Zeuge, der	witness
totgeboren	stillborn	Zwilling, der	twin

GERMAN PREPOSITIONS

auf	on
an	on, to
aus	from, out of
bei	by, near
mit	with
nach	to, after
seit	since
um	about, in order to
über	over, above
unter	under, below
von	from, of
vor	before, in front of
zu	to, at

GERMAN GENEALOGICAL SYMBOLS

*	born
†*	stillborn
≈	christened
o	engaged
∞	married
†	died
☐	buried
††	line is extinct
o│o	divorced
✕	died in battle

Germanic Genealogy Society

OCCUPATIONS AND RELATED TERMS

German	English	German	English
Ackerer, der	farmer	Grützmüller, der	grain miller
Ackermann, der	farmer	Gutsbesitzer, der	estate owner
Ackerwirt(h), der	farmer	Häcker, der	vine grower
Älteste(r), der	elder	Hafner, der	potter
Altflicker, der	jobbing cobbler	Hakenbüdner, der	hook seller
Apotheker, der	pharmacist	Handarbeiter, der	manual laborer
Arbeiter, der	male worker	Handelsmann, der	merchant, trader
Arbeiterin, die	female worker	Handwerker, der	artisan, worker
Arbeitsfrau, die	female worker	Hausgenosse, der	household member
Arbeitsmann, der	male worker	Hebamme, die	midwife
Arzt, der	physician	Hirt, der	shepherd, cowherd
Bauer, der	farmer	Hofmann, der	courtier
Bäcker, der	baker	Holzflösser, der	raftsman
Beruf, der	occupation	Holzhändler, der	lumber dealer
Bierbrauer, der	beer brewer	Holzhauer, der	lumberjack
Bortenmacher, der	lacemaker	Honighändler, der	honey dealer
Brandweinbrenner, der	distiller	Hospitaler, der	nursing home resident
Brandweinschenker, der	liquor retailer	Hufschmied, der	farrier, blacksmith
Brauer, der	brewer	Kantor, der	choir leader, organist, lead singer
Brettschneider, der	sawyer	Kantorlehrer, der	lay minister, teacher
Briefträger, der	mailman	Kaufmann, der	shopkeeper
Büdner, der	stallkeeper	Kirschner, der	cherry brandy maker
Bürger, der	citizen		
Bürgermeister, der	mayor	Knecht, der	farmhand
Canonier, der	cannon gunner	Kolonist, der (Kol.)	settler, pioneer
Dienstbote, der	domestic servant	Kornmüller, der	grain miller
Dienstmädchen, das	maid	Krämer, der	shopkeeper
Distillateur, der	distiller	Krankenschwester, die	nurse
Dragoner, der	dragoon, soldier		
Eigengärtner, der	independent gardener	Krüger, der	innkeeper
		Künstler, der	artist
Eigenkätner, der	independent cottager	Küster, der	sexton
		Küsterlehrer, der	lay minister, teacher
Eigentümer, der	property owner	Kutscher, der	coachman
Einlieger, der	lodger, tenant farmer	Landfrau, die	female farmer
		Landmann, der	male farmer
Einwohner, der (E.)	inhabitant	Landwirt, der	farmer
Erbpächter, der	hereditary tenant	Lederhändler, der	leather dealer
Essigbrauer, der	vinegar maker	Lehrer, der	teacher
Färber, der	dyer	Leinenweber, der	linen-weaver
Fischer, der	fisherman	Magd, die	domestic servent, maid
Fleischer, der	butcher		
Fleischhacker, der	butcher	Mälzer, der	maltster
Förster, der	forester	Matrose, der	sailor
Füselier, der	light infantryman	Maurer, der	mason
Fusssoldat, der	foot soldier	Meister, der	master
Gärtner, der	gardener	Messner, der	sexton
Gastwirt, der	innkeeper	Metzger, der	butcher
Geselle, der	journeyman	Mietsfrau, die	female tenant
Gewerbe, das	occupation	Mietsgärtner, der	tenant gardener
Gewürzkrämer, der	spice trader	Mietsmann, der	male tenant
Grützer, der	grain miller	Milchträger, der	milkman

German	English	German	English
Mosquetier/ Musketier, der	musketeer	Soldat, der	soldier
		Spinner(mann), der	spinner
Müller, der	miller	Steinmetz, der	stone mason
Pfarrer, der	clergyman	Stellmacher, der	wheelwright
Posamentierer, der	haberdasher	Tagelöhner, der	day laborer
Postbeamte, der	postal worker	Tischler, der	cabinetmaker, carpenter
Posteleve, der	postal apprentice		
Posthalter, der	post-horse keeper	Töpfer, der	potter
Postillion, der	coachman	Tuchmacher, der	fabric maker
Tabbiner/Rabbi, der	rabbi	Uhrmacher, der	clockmaker
Rademacher, der	wheelwright	Unvermögende, der	pauper
Richter, der	judge, justice	Vormund, der	legal guardian
Rotgerber, der	tanner	Vorsänger(in), der (die)	choir leader, precentor, officiating minister
Schäfer, der	shepherd		
Schiffer, der	sailor		
Schmid/Schmied, der	blacksmith	Wagenmeister, der	wagonmaster
Schneider, der	tailor	Wagner, der	cartwright
Schuhflicker, der	cobbler	Wassermüller, der	watermill operator
Schuhmacher, der	shoemaker	Weber, der	weaver
Schulhalter, der	teacher	Weingärtner, der	vine-dresser
Schullehrer, der	male teacher	Weinschenker, der	waiter
Schullehrerin, die	female teacher	Winzer, der	vine-dresser
Schulmeister, der	schoolmaster (teacher)	Wirt, der	innkeeper
		Zeugkrämer, der	cloth merchant
Schulze, der	village mayor	Zeugmacher, der	fabric maker
Schuster, der	cobbler, shoe repairman	Ziegelbrenner, der	brickmaker
		Zimmermann, der	carpenter
Seifensieder, der	soapmaker	Zwirnmacher, der	thread or twine maker
Seidenkrämer, der	silk merchant		
Seiler, der	rope maker		

TIME

Abend, der	evening	tags	during the day
abends	p.m.	Uhr, die	hour
ejusdem anni (ej:a.) (Latin)	of the same year	Vormittag, der	forenoon
		vormittags	in the forenoon
ejusdem mensis (ej:m.) (Latin)	of the same month	weniger	less
		Woche, die	week
früh	early (a.m.)		
Jahr, das	year	7ber, 7bris	September
Jahrhundert, das	century	8ber, 8bris	October
Jahrzehnt, das	decade	9ber, 9bris	November
Mittag, der	noon	10ber, 10bris	December
mittags	at noon		
Monat, der	month	halb sechs	5:30 (half of six)
morgen	tomorrow	viertel vor sechs	5:45 (quarter to six)
Morgen, der	morning, tomorrow		
morgens	in the morning (a.m.)	viertel nach sechs	6:15 (quarter past six)
Nachmittag, der	afternoon	drei viertel sechs	5:45 (three quarters of six)
nachmittags	in the afternoon		
Nacht, die	night		
nachts	at night		
spät	late (p.m.)		
Stunde, die	hour		
Tag, der	day		

NUMBERS

eins, erste	1, first	zwölf, zwölfte	12, twelfth
zwei, zweite	2, second	dreizehn, dreizehnte	13, thirteenth
drei, dritte	3, third	vierzehn, vierzehnte	14, fourteenth
vier, vierte	4, fourth	fünfzehn, fünfzehnte	15, fifteenth
fünf, fünfte	5, fifth	sechzehn, sechzehnte	16, sixteenth
sechs, sechste	6, sixth	siebzehn, siebzehnte	17, seventeenth
sieben, sieb(en)te	7, seventh	achtzehn, achtzehnte	18, eighteenth
acht, achte	8, eighth	neunzehn, neunzehnte	19, nineteenth
neun, neunte	9, ninth	zwanzig, zwanzigste	20, twentieth
zehn, zehnte	10, tenth	ein und zwanzig,	21, twenty-one,
elf, elfte	11, eleventh	ein und zwanzigste	twenty-first

ILLNESSES, DISEASE, CAUSES OF DEATH

German	English	German	English
Abzehrung, die	consumption, emaciation	Krupp, der	croup
		Lungenentzündung, die	pneumonia
Alterentkräftung, die	debility of old age		
Altersschwäche, die	debility of old age	Mandelbräune, die	tonsillitis
Anfall, der	stroke	Mandelentzündung, die	tonsillitis
Angina, die	angina		
Auszehrung, die	consumption	Masern, die (plural)	measles
Blattern, die	smallpox	Mumps, der	mumps
Blutvergiftung, die	blood poisoning, toxemia	Pest, die	plague
		Pocken, die (plural)	smallpox
Bräune, die	angina	Rachenbräune, die	diphtheria
Cholera, die	cholera	rote Ruhr, die	dysentery
Diarrhöe, die	diarrhoea	Röteln, die (plural)	German measles
Diphtherie, die	diphtheria	Ruhr, die	dysentery
Durchfall, der	diarrhoea	ruhrartig	dysenteric
Ertränkung, die	drowning	ruhrkrank	suffering from dysentery
Fieber, das	fever		
Geschwulst, die	swelling, tumor	Scharlach, der	scarlet fever
Gift, das	poison	Scharlachfieber, das	scarlet fever
Halsentzündung, die	throat inflammation	Schlag(anfall), der	stroke
häutige Bräune, die	croup	Schwäche, die	debility, infirmity
Herzschlag, der	heart attack	Schwindsucht, die	consumption
Keuchhusten, der	whooping cough	Selbstmord, der	suicide
im Kinderbett gestorben	died while giving birth	Sumpfieber, das	swamp fever
		Tuberkulose, die	tuberculosis
Kindbettfieber, das	puerperal fever	Typhus, der	typhus
Kinderlähmung, die	infantile paralysis	unbekannt	unknown
Krampf, der	cramps, convulsions	Unfall, der	accident
in Krämpfen bewusstlos	convulsions while unconscious	Unterleibstyphus, der	typhoid fever
		Vergiftung, die	poisoning
krank	sick, ill	Wassersucht, die	dropsy
Krankheit, die	illness	weisse Ruhr, die	diarrhoea
Krebs, der	cancer	Ziegenpeter, der	mumps
Krebsgeschwür, das	cancer	Zuckung, die	cramps, convulsions

Ernest Thode's *German-English Genealogical Dictionary* is by far the most comprehensive book of its kind. It also includes many abbreviations and Latin terms.

If you cannot find the words you want in Thode or in a good modern German-English dictionary, look for an old one in a university library. A good one is the *Thieme-Preusser Wörterbuch der englischen und deutschen Sprache* [*Thieme-Preusser's Dictionary of the English and German Languages*], one edition of which was published in 1904. For specialized terms, consult the following:

Germanic Genealogy: A Guide to Worldwide Sources and Migration Patterns

- Larry O. Jensen, "Legal Terms Used in German Court Records," in *German Genealogical Digest*, Vol. V, No. 1 (1989), pp. 7-14.
- Maralyn A. Wellauer, *Tracing Your German Roots*, includes several lists of abbreviations (which may puzzle even Americans with a good knowledge of German), including one relating to maps, one relating to military terms and one that includes bibliographic citations.

RECORDS IN OTHER LANGUAGES

When searching for your German ancestors in Europe, records written in languages other than German may be encountered. This can happen with respect to records in what is now German-speaking Europe, as well as in border areas that may have changed hands and, of course, where there were larger or smaller islands of German settlement.

Latin was frequently used for Catholic Church records in all countries. During the Napoleonic period (1796-1815), records were sometimes kept in French in western Germany. Religious refugees who fled to Germany often kept their records in French or Dutch-Flemish for several generations.

The table at the top of the next page lists the languages that may have been used on documents and records (in addition to German or Latin) in various countries.

The Family History Centers have modest-sized Genealogical Word Lists for many languages, with more expected. Other sources that include genealogical terms in other languages, in addition to English and/or German, are listed at the end of the chapter.

CALENDARS AND DATE PROBLEMS

From the Roman Kalends came our methods of dividing time into hours, days, weeks, months and years. The solar day is based on daily rotation of the earth around the sun, the solar year on the cycle of seasons, the month on the phases of the moon: all natural divisions of time. The hour, week and civil month are conventional divisions.

Several calendars have been used over the centuries but the following two are of greatest importance to genealogists. The civil calendar of all European countries has been based on that of the Romans and the early church calendar. At the time of Julius Caesar, the year was fixed at 365¼ days. It was decreed that every fourth year have 366 days, otherwise 365 days. This calendar year was longer than the solar year by 11 minutes and 14 seconds, or one day in 128 years. By 1580 there were ten days too many. To correct this, a new calendar was proposed. The Gregorian calendar, named after Pope Gregory XIII, directed ten days to be excluded from the Julian calendar, retaining each fourth year as a leap year. Century years were also to be leap years only when divisible by 400, e.g., 2000 will be a leap year, but 1700, 1800 and 1900 were not. Accumulation of extra days was greatly reduced with this method. The Gregorian calendar is regulated partly by the solar and partly by the lunar cycles. It determines the dates of Easter and other church feast days.

The old Julian calendar was abolished in most Catholic countries of Europe in March 1582, with the new Gregorian calendar being adopted in 1582-85. The change was made in most European Protestant states in 1699-1701. Most German states fit the above pattern, each according to its religion. Prussia adopted the new calendar in 1612, Alsace and several small states in the 1600s, Lorraine in 1760, a few Swiss cantons between 1597 and 1812, and the Russian Empire/Soviet Union in 1918-20.

Table 12: Languages Used on Documents and Records

Country	Region(s)	Possible language(s)
Austria	Burgenland	Hungarian
Belgium	Eupen, Malmedy, Luxembourg province	French
Commonwealth of Independent States (CIS) (former U.S.S.R.)	European part	Russian, Ukrainian, Polish, Romanian, Belorussian
	Asian part	Russian, Kazakh, Uzbek, Tajiki, Turkmen
Czech Republic	Bohemia, Moravia	Czech
Denmark/Germany	Schleswig	Danish
Estonia		Estonian, Russian
France	Alsace, Lorraine	French
Hungary		Hungarian
Italy	South Tyrol	Italian
Latvia		Latvian, Russian
Lithuania	Memel region	Lithuanian
Luxembourg		French
Netherlands		Dutch
Norway		Norwegian
Poland		Polish, Russian
Poland/Germany	Pomerania	Swedish
Romania	Transylvania, Dobruja	Romanian, Hungarian, also Turkish
	Eastern areas	Russian, Ukrainian
Slovak Republic		Slovak, Hungarian
Switzerland	Western cantons	French
	Ticino canton	Italian
Former Yugoslavia		Serbian, Croatian, Slovenian, Hungarian

Table 13: Comparison of Julian and Gregorian Calendars

Julian (Old Style) (Replaced betweeen 1582 and 1920)	Month in Year	Gregorian (New Style)
March (25th, beginning of year)	1st month	January
April	2nd month	February
May	3rd month	March
June	4th month	April
July	5th month	May
August	6th month	June
September	7th month	July
October	8th month	August
November	9th month	September
December	10th month	October
January	11th month	November
February	12th month	December

References to "Old Style" and "New Style" were common during the 1583-1700 transition period to identify the calendar being used. Britain and its American colonies used double dating for the January 1-March 25 period, e.g., 1740/41, until 1782, because March 25 was the first day of the year.

In continental European countries, dates are written as day-month-year, e.g., 10.5.1860 means 10 May 1860.

The bottom table on the previous page shows a comparison of the Julian and Gregorian calendars and how to determine the month if only numbers were used.

Occasionally you may find other month names written in records. The following table shows old German names with variations, and Dutch month names, along with their modern German month name counterparts.

Table 14: Modern German, Old German and Dutch Month Names

Modern German Month Names	Old German Month Names	German Name Variations	Dutch Month Names
Januar, Jänner[1]	Hartung	Eismond	Louwmaand
Februar, Feber[1]	Hornung		Sprokkelmaand
März	Lenzing	Lenzmond	Lentemaand
April	Ostermond		Grasmaand
Mai	Wonnemond	Maien	Bloeimannd
Juni	Brachet	Brachmond	Zomermaand
Juli	Heuert	Heumond	Hooimaand
August	Ernting	Erntemond	Oogstmaand
September	Scheiding	Herbstmond	Herfstmaand
Oktober	Gilbhard	Weinmond	Wijnmaand
November	Nebelung, Nebelmond	Wintermond	Slachtmaand
Dezember	Christmond, Heilmond	Julmond	Wintermaand

[1] in Austria

The French Revolutionary calendar was used for civil records in western Germany during Napoleon's occupation of that region. In Ostfriesland, Dutch calendar months were used during this period. The French Revolutionary calendar for 1792-1805 had the following months, with the corresponding day of the Gregorian calendar for the first of each French month (varying slightly from year to year). Each month had 30 days. The additional 5 or 6 days each year were named complementary days and were added between the months of Fructidor and Vendémiaire. For exact dates each year, see Jensen's book.

Table 15: French Revolutionary Calendar

French Month	Gregorian Calendar	French Month	Gregorian Calendar
Vendémiaire	September 22-24	Germinal	March 21-22
Brumaire	October 22-24	Floréal	April 20-21
Frimaire	November 21-23	Prairial	May 20-21
Nivôse	December 21-23	Messidor	June 19-20
Pluviôse	January 20-22	Thermidor	July 19-20
Ventôse	February 19-21	Fructidor	August 18-19

REFERENCES (See bibliography for full citations if not shown)

Edna M. Bentz. *If I Can, You Can Decipher Germanic Records.*

Inger M. Bukke, Peter K. Kristensen and Finn A. Thomsen. *The Comprehensive Feast Day Calendar.* Bountiful, UT: Thomsen's Genealogical Center. 1983. 119 pp.
> Lists both fixed and movable feast days for both the Julian and the Gregorian calendar (1437-1837), as well as dates of calendar change in various countries, principalities and provinces. Also shows the 1792-1805 French revolutionary calendar.

Larry O. Jensen. *A Genealogical Handbook of German Research.*
> Lists specific dates when various German political entities adopted the Gregorian calendar.

Karl H. Lampe, ed. *Latein II für den Sippenforscher*, 2nd ed. [*Latin II for Genealogists*].
> Latin to German (mostly names and occupations).

Frank Parise, ed. *The Book of Calendars.* New York: Facts on File. 1982. 350 pp.

Wolfgang Ribbe and Eckart Henning. *Taschenbuch für Familiengeschichtsforschung* [*Handbook for Family History Research*].
> See its section entitled "Zeitrechnung (Chronologie)" for computing dates.

Jonathan D. Shea and William F. Hoffman. *Following the Paper Trail: A Multilingual Translation Guide.* New Milford, CT: Language & Lineage Press. 1991. 240 pp.
> Provides genealogical terms, sample documents, written and cursive script, and diacritical marks in German, Swedish, French, Italian, Latin, Portuguese, Romanian, Spanish, Czech, Polish, Russian, Hungarian and Lithuanian.

Kenneth Smith. *German Church Books: Beyond the Basics.*

Jared H. Suess, *Central European Genealogical Terminology*: German, French, Hungarian, Latin, Italian.

Jared H. Suess, *Handy Guide to Swiss Genealogical Records*: German and Swiss-German, French, Italian, Latin.

Ernest Thode. *German-English Genealogical Dictionary.*

Fritz Verdenhalven, *Familienkundliches Wörterbuch*. [*Genealogical Dictionary*].
> Latin and German, including abbreviations and archaic terms.

Chapter XVIII

ANNOTATED BIBLIOGRAPHY

Items shown here are included because of their broad applicability to German genealogical research. Gazetteers are listed in Chapter VIII, except for books that have a substantial amount of other information. References at the end of various chapters include books more specialized or less directly related to genealogy, as well as those that deal with non-European immigrant countries outside North America; many of those are not repeated here. Complete addresses of publishers are given in chapter XIX. Some of these books have been published in more than one country. Most of the following books are located in the Germanic Genealogy Society collection in the Buenger Memorial Library, Concordia College, Hamline Avenue & Marshall Street, St. Paul, MN 55104.

BOOKS

James Paul Allen and Eugene James Turner. *We the People: An Atlas of America's Ethnic Diversity*. New York: Macmillan Publishing Co. 1988. 315 pp., maps, indexes, 11-pg. bibl.
> Huge atlas. Could be considered geographic counterpart to the history in the *Harvard Encyclopedia of America's Ethnic Groups*.

Almar Associates. *Bukowina Families: 200 Years*. Ellis, KS: authors. 1993.
> Contains the genealogy of many Catholic Bohemian families who emigrated to the Bukovina in 1799-1842 and later to the United States, Brazil and Germany, with references to emigrés to Canada.

Arbeitsgemeinschaft ostdeutscher Familienforscher e.V. *Genealogical Guide to German Ancestors from East Germany and Eastern Europe*. 4th German ed. Herne, Germany (AGoFF). Neustadt/ Aisch, Germany: Verlag Degener & Co. 1994. 2nd English ed. 1995.
> Most comprehensive list of sources of genealogical information for ethnic Germans in Eastern Europe. Gives information about former areas of Germany not in present-day Germany. These areas include East & West Prussia, Pomerania, Brandenburg (East), Silesia, Posen, Poland, Russia, Czechoslovakia, Hungary, Romania, Yugoslavia and Bulgaria. This major work includes maps, addresses of archives, bibliographies, etc. Referred to in this book as the *AGoFF Guide* (English edition) or *AGoFF-Wegweiser* (German edition).

Karl R. Arndt and May Olson. *German-American Newspapers and Periodicals, 1732-1955*. Heidelberg, Germany: Quelle & Mayer. 1955. Revised and expanded 1961.
> German-American newspapers are listed by state and county. Shows where existing copies may be found.

Ayer Directory of Publications. Philadelphia: Ayer Press. Published annually from 1869 until the 1980s. ca. 1200 pp. (varies by year). Replaced by *IMS Directory of Publications: The Professionals's Reference of Print Media Published in the United States, Canada and Puerto Rico*. (See following.)
> Directory of print media (newspapers) published in the U.S. and Canada. Gives name of newspaper, place of publication and other information. Includes atlas of U.S. and Canada.

Fredrick H. Barth and Kenneth F. Thomsen, comps. *The Beginner's Guide to German Genealogical Research*. Bountiful, UT: Thomsen's Genealogical Center. 1988. 34 pp.
> Good short, simple starter for genealogical newcomers.

Angus Baxter. *In Search of Your European Roots: A Complete Guide to Tracing Your Ancestors in Every Country in Europe*, 2nd ed. Baltimore, MD: Genealogical Publishing Co., Inc. 1994. 304 pp.
> Specifies the kinds of records available in every European country, which is useful because ethnic Germans lived throughout almost all of Europe.

Angus Baxter. *In Search of Your German Roots: A Complete Guide to Tracing Your Ancestors in the Germanic Areas of Europe*, 3rd ed. Baltimore, MD: Genealogical Publishing Co., Inc. 1994. 118 pp. map.

> Expansion of material on Germany in the author's book on European roots, but with added material on Germans who lived outside Germany.

Angus Baxter. *In Search of Your Roots: A Guide for Canadians Seeking Their Ancestors*, 2nd ed. Toronto, Canada: Macmillan of Canada. 1994. 368 pp.

> An overview of researching the Canadian records for your emigrant ancestor from other parts of the world. Includes sections on European countries as well as other major countries of the world.

Alexander Beider. *A Dictionary of Jewish Surnames from the Former Russian Empire*. Teaneck, NJ: Avotaynu. 1993. 782 pp.

> Compilation of 50,000 surnames from the Pale of Settlement, including Ukraine, Moldova, Belarus, Lithuania, and Latvia, including a liberal sprinkling of Germanic names from the Kingdom of Poland.

Alexander Beider. *A Dictionary of Jewish Surnames from the Kingdom of Poland*. Teaneck, NJ: Avotaynu. 1995.

Elizabeth Petty Bentley. *The Genealogist's Address Book*, 3rd ed. Baltimore: Genealogical Publishing Co. 1995. 653 pp.

> Sections on "Ethnic and Religious Organizations and Resource Centers" and numerous other valuable resources. Well-indexed. Has addresses of U.S. national and state archives.

Edna M. Bentz. *If I Can, You Can Decipher Germanic Records*. San Diego, CA: Self-published. 1982. Revised and corrected, 1987. 85 pp.

> A handbook of Germanic script, including English, German, Latin and Danish terminologies. Lists many feast days.

Scharlott Goettsch Blevins. *Guide to Genealogical Research in Schleswig-Holstein, Germany*. Davenport, IA: self-published. 1994.

> Most comprehensive book for the Schleswig-Holstein area.

Bruce Brandt and Edward Reimer Brandt, compilers. *Where to Look For Hard-To-Find German-Speaking Ancestors in Eastern Europe: Index to 19,720 Surnames in 13 Books, with Historical Background on Each Settlement*, 2nd ed. Baltimore: Clearfield Co. 1993. 122 pp.

> Indexes nearly all major books on Germans in the eastern part of the Austro-Hungarian Empire and the Mennonite migrants to Ukraine, plus a few other books.

Edward Reimer Brandt. *Contents and Addresses of Hungarian Archives, with Supplementary Material for Research on German Ancestors from Hungary*, 2nd ed. Baltimore: Clearfield Co. 1993. Slightly revised 2nd printing 1995. 85 pp.

> Besides description of archival material, includes key historical dates, statistical tables relating to Germans, maps, bibliography, and names of selected localities in pre-1914 Hungary in Hungarian, German and other current languages.

Inger M. Bukke, Peter K. Kristensen, and Finn A. Thomsen. *The Comprehensive Feast Day Calendar*. Bountiful, UT: Thomsen's Genealogical Center. 1983. 119 pp.

> Lists both fixed and movable feast days for both the Julian and the Gregorian calendar (1437-1837), as well as dates of calendar change in various countries, principalities and provinces. Also shows the 1792-1805 French revolutionary calendar.

Annette Kunselman Burgert. *18th Century Emigrants from German-Speaking Lands to North America*. Camden, ME: Picton Press.

Vol. I: *The Northern Kraichgau* [area south of Heidelberg]. 1983. 485 pp.
Vol. II: *The Western Palatinate*. 1985. 421 pp.
Vol. III: *The Northern Alsace*. 1992. 714 pp.
One of the classics on Pennsylvania German research by a leading expert on colonial-era immigration. Originally published by the Pennsylvania German Society in its *Proceedings*.

Annette Kunselman Burgert and Henry Z. Jones, Jr. *Westerwald to America: Some 18th Century German Immigrants*. Camden, ME: Picton Press. 1989. 284 pp.

The most extensive work on immigrants from the area north of the Lahn River on both sides of the current boundary between western Hesse and northeastern Rhineland-Palatinate.

Bruce E. Burgoyne. *Waldeck (Germany) Soldiers of the American Revolutionary War*. Bowie, MD: Heritage Books. 1991. 182 pp.

Contains brief biographies of every man who served in the 3rd British Waldeck Regiment, including date and place of birth, and who remained in America.

Eugene Camann. *Uprooted from Prussia—Transplanted in America*. Niagara Falls, NY: Self-published. 1992. 140 pp.

Lists names and details about 800 "Old Lutherans" from the Uckermark who settled in Wheatfield, New York, in 1843.

The Church of Jesus Christ of Latter-day Saints. *French Records Extraction*. Salt Lake City: The Church of Jesus Christ of Latter-day Saints. No date but apparently early to mid-1970s. 171 pp.

Shows examples of the form and content of French civil and parish registers. Includes terminology, symbols, old scripts, and dates.

Sanford Hoadley Cobb. *The Story of the Palatines: An Episode in Colonial History*. New York & London: G. P. Putnam's Sons. 1897. 319 pp. maps. Reprinted Bowie, MD: Heritage Books. 1988. 319 pp. maps.

Covers Palatine communities along the Rhine River and migration in the early 1700s to the Carolinas, Virginia, New Jersey, Pennsylvania, and New York, with emphasis on New York.

Martha Remer Connor. *Germans & Hungarians — 1828 Hungarian Land Census*. Las Vegas: Author. Ongoing series. 5 vols. plus index to date.

Extracts from the census now available for Bacs Bodrog, Baranya, Torontal and Tolna counties (parts of which are in Romania and the Serbian Vojvodina today), where there were many Danube Swabians. First four volumes include over 150,000 names.

Fay and Douglas Dearden. *The German Researcher: How to Get the Most Out of an LDS Family History Center*. Minneapolis, MN: Family Tree Press. 1983. 4th edition, revised and expanded 1990. 72 pp.

The author takes you step-by-step in finding and using the Family History Library's German microfilms. Sections include using the Hamburg passenger lists (with microfilm numbers and illustrations), library catalog, handwriting found in the German records (with illustrations), words and phrases found in German records (typed, in German script, and translation), terms and letter writing, translation of terms and abbreviations found in *Meyers Orts- und Verkehrs-Lexikon* (see chapter III).

Deutsche Bundespost, Postdienst. *Das Postleitzahlenbuch*. [*The (German) Postal Code Book*] 1993. Distributed by Postamt Marburg, Dienststelle 113-21, Postfach 1100, D-35035 Marburg, Germany. 986 pp.

Alphabetical postal code book shows codes for each town and for each street address in cities. Versions are also available in numerical postal code order, for post office boxes (no longer always the same as for street addresses), CD-ROM, BTZ, diskettes, and microfiche. Accompanying map of postal code discricts (*Übersichtskarte der Postleiteinheiten*) also available.

Johann Christian Dressler. *Illischtie, a Rural Parish in Bukovina: Primary Source Records for Family History* [tr. by Irmgard Hein Ellingson]. Ossian, IA: translator. 1994. 517 pp.

> This compilation presents church, cemetery and school records; immigration lists; census and tax rolls; family letters; and personal interviews for 440 Bukovina families, covering the 1549-1949 period.

Thomas Kent Edlund. *Register to the Ahnenstammkartei des deutschen Volkes* [*Lineage Cards of the German People*]. St. Paul, MN: Germanic Genealogy Society. 1995. 133 pp.

> Shows how and where to find ancestral surnames in the collection of 2,700,000 lineage charts at the Deutsche Zentralstelle für Genealogie (German Central Office for Genealogy) in Leipzig, collected from 1922-1991, and now contained on Family History Library microfilms. Organized phonetically by surname, somewhat similar to, but not the same as, the U.S. census Soundex system (details of the system used are given at beginning of the book). Allows you to readily determine which microfilms may contain information about the surnames that interest you.

Thomas Kent Edlund. *The Lutherans of Russia.* Vol. 1: *Parish Index to the Church Books of the Evangelical Lutheran Consistory of St. Petersburg, 1833-1885.* St. Paul, MN: Germanic Genealogy Society. 1995. (ISBN 0-9644-337-1-0)

> This consistory included western Russia, Volhynia and the Black Sea settlements.

Irmgard Hein Ellingson. *The Bukovina Germans in Kansas: A 200-Year History of the Lutheran Swabians.* Hays, KS: Fort Hays State University Ethnic Heritage Studies. 1987; reprinted 1993. 107 pp.

> Summarizes the history of German Lutheran settlement in the Bukovina and immigration to Kansas.

Familiennamenbuch der Schweiz. [*Book of Family Names of Switzerland*] Polygraphischer Verlag. 1858-71. 6 vols.

> Contains an alphabetical list of surnames, showing the Swiss towns and villages where those names occur. This collection is available on microfilm from the Family History Library.

Family History Library. *Research Outline: Germany.* Salt Lake City: Family History Library. 1994. 52 pp.

> Very thorough coverage of pre-World War I German Empire, with some information on ethnic Germans elsewhere.

Albert B. Faust and Gaius M. Brumbaugh. *List of Swiss Emigrants in the Eighteenth Century to the American Colonies.* 2 vols. in 1; reprint of 1920-25 work with corrections from the *National Genealogical Society Quarterly* (March 1972). Baltimore: Genealogical Publishing Co. 1991. 429 pp.

> Indexed, authoritative work on immigrants from the canton of Zürich (1734-1744) in Vol. I, and of Berne (1706-1795) and Basel (1734-1794) in Vol. II.

P. William Filby and Mary K. Meyer, eds. *Passenger and Immigration Lists Bibliography, 1538-1900.* Detroit, MI: Gale Research Co. 1981. 5 volumes, ongoing.

> A guide to published arrival records of about 500,000 passengers who came to the United States and Canada in the 17th, 18th and 19th centuries.

John Foisel. *Saxons Through Seven Centuries: A History of the Transylvanian Saxons.* Cleveland: Central Alliance of Transylvanian Saxons. 1936.

> History of the Germans who migrated to Eastern Hungary (now Romania) in the twelfth century, with background information on earlier Saxon history.

Eckhart G. Franz, compiler. *Hessische Truppen im amerikanischen Unabhängigkeitskrieg (HETRINA).* [*Hessian Troops in the American Revolution (HETRINA project)*] Marburg, Germany: Archivshule. 1972. 3 vols.

> This series gives the full names, birth years, towns of origin, military units and other facts about 15,000 Hessian troops who fought in the American Revolutionary War 1776-1784. Volume 1 has a surname index of four Grenadier battalions. Most of these came from Hessen-Cassel but some were from the city of Frankfurt and other places to the south.

Dr. Heinz F. Friederichs. *How to Find My German Ancestors and Relatives.* (Send 5 International Reply Coupons to: Verlag Degener & Co., Postfach 1360, D-91403 Neustadt/Aisch, Germany.) 2nd ed. 1985. 16 pp.

> Brief overview of German research opportunities and problems by a leading German genealogical authority.

Adam Giesinger. *From Catherine to Khrushchev: The Story of Russia's Germans.* Battleford, Saskatchewan, Canada: Marian Press. 1974. 443 pp. Reprinted 1993 by the American Historical Society of Germans from Russia.

> The most authoritative and comprehensive account of the German settlements in Russia.

Hugh F. Gingerich and Rachel W. Kreider. *Amish and Amish Mennonite Genealogies.* Pequea Publishers. 1986. 858 pp.

> Comprehensive encyclopedia of Amish families up to 1850, including all known early settlements.

Montague S. Giuseppi. *Naturalization of Foreign Protestants in the American and West Indies Colonies.* Published by Huguenot Society of London, 1921; reprinted Baltimore: Genealogical Publishing Co., 1979. 196 pp.

> Records of 6,500 naturalizations (mostly of Germans), 1740-1722. Indexed.

Ira A. Glazier and P. William Filby. *Germans to America: Lists of Passengers Arriving at United States Ports.* Wilmington, DE: Scholarly Resources, Inc. 48 vol. covering January 1850 - April 1884 published to date. Series is to continue through 1893.

> Information taken from the original ship manifests kept at Temple-Balch Institute for Immigration Research. Gives name, age, sex, occupation, date of arrival, and many times the former residence of each passenger. 1850-55 lists all passengers, but only on ships where at least 80% of the passengers were "German." 1856 and on includes all ships, but only passengers who called themselves Germans, including some from Switzerland, Luxembourg, and France. Includes some ships from Latin America and the Caribbean.

Johann Glenzdorf. *Glenzdorfs Internationales Genealogen-Lexikon.* [*Glenzdorf's International Directory of Genealogists*] Germany: Wilhelm Rost Verlag, D-31848 Bad Münder/Deister. Vol. 1 - 1977, Vol. 2 - 1979, Vol. 3 - 1984. In German.

> Each volume contains an alphabetical list of genealogists submitting German genealogical information together with an individual biography, an index including surnames being researched and submitters, and an index to places the surnames are from. Volume 2 also includes genealogists who will do research by region. Volume 3 contains an alphabetical list of genealogists in all three volumes.

Nicholas Gonner. *Luxembourgers in the New World.* Edited and translated into English by Jean Ensch, Jean-Claude Muller and Robert E. Owen. Esch-sur-Alzette, Luxembourg: Editions-Reliures Schortgen, 1889. New edition, 1987.

> Volume I contains Luxembourger emigration information between 1840-1890, Luxembourger settlements in the U.S. and aspects of the Luxembourger presence in the U.S. Volume II contains a personal and place-name index to the *Luxemburger Gazette* newspapers (1871-1918).

Charles M. Hall. *The Atlantic Bridge to Germany*. Vol. 1-7: Logan, UT: Everton Publishers, Inc. 1978 through 1995. Vol. 8-9: Monda Genealoga Ligo. 9 volumes, others in progress.

>Each volume concentrates on a particular area or areas in Germany. Lists resources unique to the area, detailed maps showing small communities not included on other maps, and German records available at the Family History Library in Salt Lake City for each town.
>Vol. 1 - Baden-Württemberg
>Vol. 2 - Hessen, Rheinland-Pfalz (The Palatinate)
>Vol. 3 - Bavaria
>Vol. 4 - Alsace-Lorraine, Saarland and Switzerland
>Vol. 5 - Bremer., Hamburg and Schleswig-Holstein
>Vol. 6 - Mecklenburg (consisting of former East German districts of Neubrandenburg, Rostock and Schwerin)
>Vol. 7 - Nordrhein-Westfalen (includes the Ruhr valley, Minden, Bielefeld, Lippe-Detmold, Cologne and Bonn)
>Vol. 8 - Prussia (Brandenburg, East Prussia, West Prussia, Pomerania, Posen)
>Vol. 9 - Saxony

Charles R. Haller. *Across the Atlantic and Beyond: The Migration of German and Swiss Immigrants to America*. Bowie, MD: Heritage Books. 1993. 324 pp.

>Deals with changes of personal and place names, reasons for emigration, number and period (mostly 1727-1775) of colonial immigrants, the postwar whereabouts of Revolutionary War German conscripts, the rise of Protestantism, and quadripartite dialectic divisions, with maps of the Rhine valley, from where most early immigrants came.

Joseph S. Height. *Homesteaders on the Steppe: The Odyssey of a Pioneering People*. Bismarck, ND: North Dakota Historical Society of Germans from Russia. 1975. 431 pp.

>Deals with the cultural history of Lutheran colonies near Odessa, 1804-1945.

Joseph S. Height. *Paradise on the Steppe: The Odyssey of a Pioneering People*. Bismarck, ND: North Dakota Historical Society of Germans from Russia. 1973. 411 pp.

>Deals with the cultural history of three clusters of Catholic villages near Odessa, 1804-1972.

Franz Heinzmann. *Bibliographie der Ortssippenbücher in Deutschland* [*Bibliography of Village Lineage Books in Germany*]. 1991. 400 pp.

>Lists 6,486 books, including quite a few for villages outside Germany.

Richard Hordern, ed./tr. *St. John's Evangelical Lutheran Church, 1890-1990*. Balgonie, SK: St. John's Lutheran Church, c/o Barbara Siebert. 1990. 138 pp.

>Translates the the parish registers of 1890-1927, as well as records of the work of early pastors in the districts of Assiniboia and Saskatchewan (Northwest Territories), later the province of Saskatchewan.

Immigrant Genealogical Society. *1993 Updated Addresses to German Repositories*. Burbank, CA: Immigrant Genealogical Society. 1994. 44 pp.

>Lists 1,224 German archives and 333 genealogical and historical societies, alphabetized by locality.

IMS Directory of Publications: The Professionals's Reference of Print Media Published in the United States, Canada and Puerto Rico. Fort Washington, PA: IMS Press. ca. 1500 pp. (varies by year).

>Replacement for *Ayer Directory of Publications*. (See previous.)

Larry O. Jensen. *A Genealogical Handbook of German Research*. Pleasant Grove, UT: Jensen Publications. Vol. 1: 1980 (209 pp.), Vol. 2: 1983 (210 pp.), Vol. 3: 1986.

>Guide to locating origins of German ancestors, maps and vital records. Includes information on naming practices of the Germans, Jewish genealogy, terminology and handwriting analysis of old records. Vol. 3 consists of maps and short histories for each area within the German Empire. Contains a listing of gazetteers for areas in Germany that were not Prussian provinces.

Arta F. Johnson, ed. *Bibliography and Source Materials for German-American Research.* Vol. 1. Columbus, OH: privately printed. 1982. 112 pp. Updated 1984.
> Comprehensive list of German genealogical books, materials and sources printed in the United States.

Arta F. Johnson. *A Guide to the Spelling and Pronunciation of German Names.* Columbus, OH: privately printed. 1981.
> Helps determine possible spelling variations of a German name.

Keith A. Johnson and Malcolm R. Sainty, eds. *Genealogical Research Directory (GRD).* Published annually since 1984. 1990 edition, 936 pp.
> Lists genealogists researching particular German surnames on a worldwide basis. The U.S. representative is Mrs. Netti Schreiner-Yantis, 6818 Lois Dr., Springfield, VA 22150.

George F. Jones. *German-American Names.* Baltimore, MD: Genealogical Publishing Co. 1990. 268 pp.
> Lists spellings and meanings of over 12,000 German-American names. Includes spelling variations.

Henry Z. Jones, Jr. *The Palatine Families of Ireland*, 2nd ed. Camden, ME: Picton Press. 1990. 166 pp.
> Lists Palatine families who went to Ireland in 1710. Shows Irish and German spellings of 172 surnames. Establishes German ancestry of 33 families.

Henry Z. Jones, Jr. *The Palatine Families of New York.* Camden, ME: Picton Press. 2 vols. 1985. 1298 pp.
> Lists original Palatine families who came to New York state about 1710.

Henry Z. Jones, Jr. *More Palatine Families: Some Immigrants to the Middle Colonies, 1777-1776.* Universal City, CA: privately published. 1991. 592 pp.
> Majority of names listed are those who went to New Jersey. Every-name index.

Marion J. Kaminkow, ed. *Bibliography of Genealogies in the Library of Congress and Various Complements Thereto.* Baltimore: Genealogical Publishing Co.
> Series lists tens of thousands of genealogies in the Library of Congress through 1985. Continued by: Library of Congress, *Genealogies Cataloged by the Library of Congress*, since 1986.

Thomas Jay Kemp. *International Records Handbook.* 3rd ed. Baltimore: Genealogical Publishing Co. 1994. 417 pp.
> Consists chiefly of forms that can be photocopied for use in applying for information from various agencies.

Walter A. Knittle. *Early Eighteenth Century Palatine Emigration.* 1937. Reprinted Baltimore: Genealogical Publishing Co. 1989. 320 pp.
> Indexed list of about 12,000 Palatine immigrants to Pennsylvania, North Carolina and New York.

Margrit B. Krewson. *The German-Speaking Countries of Europe: A Selective Bibliography*, 2nd ed. Washington, DC: Library of Congress. 1989. 318 pp.
> A highly diverse sampling of books in the Library of Congress, including many dealing with genealogy and migration history. For sale by Supt. of Docs., U.S. Govt. Printing Office.

Margrit B. Krewson. *Hidden Research Resource in the German Collections of the Library of Congress.* Washington, DC: Library of Congress. 1992. 170 pp.
> A selective bibliography of reference works in the German collection at the Library of Congress. For sale by Supt. of Docs., U.S. Govt. Printing Office.

Arthur Kurzweil. *From Generation to Generation.* 1980. 388 pp. Revised and updated 1994.

Heinz Lehmann. *The German Canadians, 1750-1937: Immigration, Settlement and Culture.* Translated by Gerhard P. Bassler. St. John's, Newfoundland: Jesperson Press. 1986. 541 pp.

> Incredibly detailed account of all German settlements in Canada, including place of emigration; maps; has few names of individuals.

Kate Everest Levi. *Geographical Origin of German Immigration to Wisconsin.* Originally published in *Collections of the State Historical Society of Wisconsin*, 1898. Reprinted Minneapolis: Edward R. Brandt. 1992. 28 pp.

> Detailed account of areas of origin of Germans who settled in various counties of Wisconsin.

Library of Congress. *Genealogies Cataloged by the Library of Congress Since 1986.* Washington, DC: Cataloging Distribution Service, Library of Congress. 1992. 1349 pp.

> With a list of established forms of family names and a list of genealogies converted to microform since 1983. Continuation of series by Marion J. Kaminkow, which ended in 1985.

Glen E. Lich. *The German Texans.* San Antonio: University of Texas Institute of Texan Cultures at San Antonio. 1981. 240 pp.

Marilyn Lind. *Researching and Finding Your German Heritage.* Cloquet, MN: The Linden Tree. 1984. 132 pp. Updated 1988.

> A major strength of this book is its brief historical description of a large number of German states and provinces, with small maps showing their locations.

Erich Dieter Linder and Günter Olzog. *Die deutschen Landkreise: Wappen, Geschichte, Struktur.* [*The German Counties: Their Coats-of-Arms, History and Structure*] Munich: Günter Olzog Verlag. 1986. 280 pp

> Description of all 237 West German rural counties, including municipalities within each, state maps (showing intermediate district and county boundaries), historical development, tourist attractions and coats-of-arms. Excludes larger cities, each of which forms its own urban county (depicted on maps), and areas under Communist rule in 1986.

Erwin Massier, et al. *Fratautz and the Fratautzers: The Rise and Fall of a German Village Community in Bukovina* [tr. by Sophie A. Welisch]. Regina: Saskatchewan Genealogical Society. 1992. 231 pp.

> The book traces the history of Fratautz and discusses local customs, daily experience and the dialect spoken by the villagers.

Brenda Dougall Merriman. *Genealogy in Ontario, Searching the Records.* Toronto, Ontario: Ontario Genealogical Society. 1988. 168 pp.

Ken Meter and Robert Paulson. *The Böhmisch (German-Bohemians) in America.* Minneapolis: Crossroads Resource Center, with the German-Bohemian Heritage Society, New Ulm. 1993. 32 pp.

> Packed with surnames of German immigrants from southwestern Bohemia to Wisconsin, Minnesota and Michigan's Upper peninsula.

Mary K. Meyer, ed. *Meyer's Directory of Genealogical Societies in the U.S.A. and Canada*, 9th ed. Mt. Airy, MD: Mary Keysor Meyer. 1992. 123 pp.

> Also lists special interest organizations (ethnic, religious, geographic, adoptees).

Michael M. Miller. *Researching Germans from Russia.* Fargo: North Dakota State University, Institute for Regional Studies. 1987. 224 pp.

> Annotated bibliography of the Germans from Russia Heritage Collection at the North Dakota Institute for Regional Studies, North Dakota State University Library (mostly historical) and the library collection of the Germans from Russia Heritage Society in Bismarck, which includes family, local and church histories.

Olga K. Miller. *Migration, Emigration, Immigration: Principally to the United States and in the United States.* Logan, UT: Everton Publishers, Inc. 1974. 278 pp. 2 vols. 2nd ed. revised 1981.

> Shows many routes and timetables of our emigrating ancestors. Has a large bibliography.

MINERVA-Handbücher: Archive im deutschsprachigen Raum. [MINERVA Handbooks: Archives in German-speaking Regions]. Berlin, Germany: de Gruyter. 2nd edition 1974. 2 volumes. 1418 pp.

> This valuable German work describes each German archive and what historical material may be found there.

Mario von Moos. *Bibliography of Swiss Genealogies.* Camden, ME: Picton Press. 1993. 848 pp.

> Includes registers of towns and names.

John D. Movius, comp. *Resource Guide to East European Genealogy.* Davis, CA: FEEFHS. 1994; updated twice a year.

> Lists names, addresses and periodicals of member societies of the Federation of East European Family History Societies, including member societies in North America, Europe and Australia. Also lists professional genealogists and translators specializing in Eastern Europe, including Germanic countries.

Martha Müller. *Mecklenburger in Osteuropa: Ein Beitrag zu ihrer Auswanderung im 16. bis 19. Jahrhundert. [Mecklenburgers in East Europe: A Contribution to Their Emigration in the 16th to 19th Centuries].* Marburg/Lahn, Germany: Johann Gottfried Herder Institut. 1972. 471 pp.

> Vital records on Mecklenburgers who migrated eastward, both within and outside the pre-World War I German Empire.

Margaret Krug Palen. *German Settlers of Iowa, Their Descendants, and European Ancestors.* Bowie, MD: Heritage Books. 1994. 361 pp.

> Includes nearly 2,000 surnames. Alphabetical listing of entries, plus index of surnames buried in the text. Traces some families back to the 1600s.

Michael P. Palmer. *Genealogical Resources in Eastern Germany (Poland).* Claremont, CA: privately published. 1993. 12 pp.

> Lists historical bibliography, gazetteers, maps, genealogical societies and their publications, archives, and information about church registers (known information about survival, location, inventories and other relevant publications), with Family History Library film and book numbers, for the former German eastern provinces.

Edward A. Peckwas. *Register of Vital Records of Roman Catholic Parishes from the Region Beyond the Bug River.* Reprinted with an introduction by Edward A. Peckwas. Chicago: Polish Genealogical Society of America. 1984. 44 pp.

> Coverage includes German Catholic parish registers of East Galicia and West Volhynia.

Pennsylvania Archives. Series 1-9. 138 volumes. Phildephia: J. Severns & Co. 1852-56. Harrisburg. 1874-1935.

> An excellent genealogical source for early Pennsylvania and related areas. Has many lists of early Pennsylvania Germans, especially from the 18th century. (See *Genealogical Research in the Published Pennsylvania Archives* by Sally Weikel for a guide to the series.)

Pennsylvania German Church Records: Births, Baptisms, Marriages, Burials, Etc., with an introduction by Don Yoder, 3 vols. Baltimore: Genealogical Publishing Co. 1983. 2,371 pp.

> Some 125,000 persons are listed in the index. Includes all church records ever published in the *Proceedings and Addresses of the Pennsylvania German Society.*

Brian A. Podoll. *Prussian Netzelanders and Other German Immigrants in Green Lake, Marquette & Waushara Counties, Wisconsin.* Bowie, MD: Heritage Books. 1994. 241 pp.

> Primarily marriage, naturalization and death records of Germans in these counties. Brief history of the Netze River area. Maps of various counties in Posen, Pomerania, West Prussia and the Neumark (Northeast Brandenburg), as well as in Wisconsin (and Minnesota, to which the Netzelanders went).

Ratgeber '92: Familienforschung GUS / Baltikum. [*Adviser '92: Family History Research in the CIS and Baltic States*]. Münster, Germany: Zielke-Verlag. 1992.

> Articles deal with new sources of information, including addresses of private researchers, in the former U.S.S.R. A 1993-94 edition with a slightly different title was due to be published in 1994.

Horst A Reschke. *German Military Records as Genealogical Sources.* Salt Lake City: Author. 1990. 12 pp.

> Not all German military records were destroyed. This is a gold mine of information for those records that have been preserved (basically those of non-Prussian areas).

Wolfgang Ribbe and Eckart Henning. *Taschenbuch für Familiengeschichtsforschung.* [*Handbook for Family History Research*] Neustadt/Aisch, Germany: Verlag Degener & Co. 10th edition, 1990. 479 pp.

> Standard research guidebook for Germans. The six sections include:
> 1) German ancestor and family group sheets
> 2) social, biological and legal aspects of genealogy
> 3) source indexes for German research materials including: church registers, records of religious sects, funeral sermons, civil records, city directories, university student lists, entire village genealogies (200 plus), address books and bibliographies by region
> 4) handwriting, calendars, heraldry, meaning of names, using computers
> 5) genealogical terms, meaning of German first names, occupations, diseases, nobility titles
> 6) addresses for German city and state archives, libraries, genealogical and historical societies. Also contains information about and addresses for *Heimatortskarteien* (HOK), which is a special search service to locate people displaced by World War II. Combined catalogs list over 17 million people.

La Vern J. Rippley and Robert J. Paulson. *The German-Bohemians: The Quiet Immigrants.* New Ulm, MN: German-Bohemian Society. 1995. 246 pp.

> History of German-Bohemian immigration to southern Minnesota in the 1800s.

Dan Rottenberg. *Finding Our Fathers: A Guidebook to Jewish Genealogy.* New York: Random House. 1977. Reprinted Baltimore, MD: Genealogical Publishing Co. 1986, 1995. Ca. 400 pp.

> Guide showing how to trace Jewish families back many generations. Includes a guide to over 8,000 Jewish family names, giving their origins and a country-by-country guide to tracing Jewish ancestors abroad.

Israel Daniel Rupp. *A Collection of Upwards of 30,000 Names of German, Swiss, Dutch, French and Other Immigrants into Pennsylvania, 1727-1776.* Leipzig, 3rd ed., 1931. 2nd (English) rev. ed., with an index by Ernst Wecken from the Third Edition (1931) and added index to ships. Baltimore, MD: Genealogical Publishing Co. 1994. 583 pp.

> Passenger lists from 319 ships, giving name of ship and its origin arranged by date of arrival. Also included is a list of over 1,000 settlers who came to Pennsylvania from other states. Index to ships and surname index. Separately published index by Marvin Vastine Koger: *Index to the names of 30,000 Immigrants — German, Swiss, Dutch and French — into Pennsylvania, 1727-1776, Supplementing the I. Daniel Rupp, Ship Load Volume*, Pennington Gap, VA, 1935, 232 pp.

G. Rusam. Österreichische Exulanten in Franken und Schwaben. [Austrian Exiles in *Franconia and Swabia*]. Verlag Degener & Co., Neustadt/Aisch, Germany.

> Protestant Austrian refugees in Franconia and Swabia.

Sallyann Amdur Sack and Suzan Fishl Wynne. *The Russian Consular Records Index and Catalog.* New York: Garland Publishing Co. 1987. 897 pp.

> Indexes records of Czarist Russia's consulates in the U.S. and Canada, e.g., visa applications.

Trudy Schenk, Ruth Froelke and Inge Bork. *The Wuerttemberg Emigration Index.* Salt Lake City, UT: Ancestry, Inc. 1986. 5 volumes, ongoing.

> Each volume extracts a small area of Württemberg from German emigration records. Gives name, place and date of birth and often the destination of each emigrant.

Daniel M. Schlyter. *A Handbook of Czechoslovak Genealogical Research.* Buffalo Grove, IL: Genun Publishers. 1985. 131 pp.

> Written by the Eastern European specialist at the Family History Library in Salt Lake City. Currently out of print.

Josef Schmidt. *Die Banater Kirchenbücher.* [*The Parish Registers of the Banat*] Stuttgart: Institut für Auslandsbeziehungen. 1979.

> List of Banat parish registers (mostly pre-1860) in Stuttgart that were microfilmed in Romania and Yugoslavia during World War II (all of which are available from Salt Lake City). This book and a supplementary list of German parish registers in the Romanian archives in Timisoara and Arad are available from the Arbeitskreis donauschwäbischer Familienforscher.

Ludwig Schneider. *Das Kolonisationswerk Josefs II. in Galizien: Darstellung und Namenlisten.* [*The Colonization Activities of (Hapsburg Emperor) Joseph II in Galicia: Description and Lists of Names (of Settlers)*] Leipzig: Verlag von S. Hirzel for the Historische Gesellschaft für Posen, Poznan. 1939. Recently reprinted by the Helmut Scherer Verlag, Berlin.

> The authoritative book on Galicia, including genealogical data from the 1780s, 1812 and 1820.

Cornelia Schrader-Muggenthaler. *The Alsace Emigration Book.* Vol. 1, 277 pp.; Vol. 2, 203 pp. Apollo, PA: Closson Press. 1989-1991.

> Vol. 1 provides detailed information, in alphabetized form, on 13,500 German and French emigrants who left Alsace in 1817-69. Vol. 2 adds over 8,000 18th and 19th century emigrants and includes a list of all villages in Upper and Lower Alsace.

Cornelia Schrader-Muggenthaler. *The Baden Emigration Book.* Apollo, PA: Closson Press. 1992. 193 pp.

> Lists emigants, including some from Alsace, found in Karlsruhe archives.

Cornelia Schrader-Muggenthaler, comp. *The Swiss Emigration Book*, Vol. 1. Apollo, PA: Closson Press. 1993. 216 pp.

> Lists 18th and 19th century emigrants who migrated from or through Switzerland to America. Vol. 1 lists ca. 7,000 emigrants, with origins in Switzerland, Germany, Italy and France, recorded in the cantons of Solothurn, Basel and Aargau.

Karin Schulz, ed. *Hoffnung Amerika: Europäische Auswanderung in die Neu Welt.* [*The Hope of America: European Emigration to the New World*] Bremerhaven Nordwestdeutsche Verlaggesellschaft. 1944. 293 pp.

> Deals with emigration from Germany and Eastern Europe through German ports. Heavy emphasis on Jewish migration to the United States.

George K. Schweitzer. *German Genealogical Research.* Knoxville, TN: privately printed. 1992. 253 pp.

> German-American genealogical guide containing valuable information on geography, history, language, original and secondary records, location of records in Germany, and research procedures in the United States and Europe. Unindexed.

Dagmar Senekovic. *Handy Guide to Austrian Genealogical Records.* Logan, UT: Everton Publishers, Inc. 1979. 97 pp.

> Includes maps, addresses of Austrian archives and genealogical societies, lists of Jewish registers, Austrian Catholic and Lutheran parish names and dates of records.

Jonathan D. Shea and William F. Hoffman. *Following the Paper Trail: A Multilingual Translation Guide.* Teaneck, NJ: Avotaynu Press. 256 pp.

> A guide to translating vital statistic records in 13 European languages. Shows alphabets, word lists and sample vital statistic records for each language.

Ronald Smelser, editor. *Preliminary Survey of the German Collection: Finding Aids to the Microfilmed Records of the Genealogical Society of Utah.* Salt Lake City, UT: University of Utah Press. 1979. 580 pp.

> A comprehensive guide to the Family History Library's microfilm collection as of 1979. Listed by German state and province.

Clifford Neal Smith and Anna Piszczan-Czaja Smith. *American Genealogical Resources in German Archives (AGRIGA): A Handbook.* New York, NY: R. R. Bowker Co. 1977. 336 pp.

> Has lists arranged alphabetically by village and individuals; also court records, emigration records, and other documents. Includes a bibliography of published emigration lists in German with English titles in brackets.

Clifford Neal Smith and Anna Piszczan-Czaja Smith. *Encyclopedia of German-American Genealogical Research.* New York, NY: R. R. Bowker Co. 1976. 273 pp.

> Contains in-depth study of German naming patterns and information on German churches in the United States, cites German history, describes German records, contains information about Jews in southwestern Germany, and lists manuscripts and source materials in the United States and Germany.

Kenneth L. Smith. *Confirming a Place of Origin.* Columbus, OH: privately printed. 1985. 28 pp.

> Gives many examples of how to find and confirm the place of origin, mostly for German ancestors.

Kenneth L. Smith. *German Church Books: Beyond the Basics.* Camden, ME: Picton Press. 1989. 224 pp.

> This excellent book for advanced genealogists provides detailed information about German church records: baptism, confirmation, marriage and death records. Other topics include German names, spelling, miscellaneous records and Gothic script handwriting examples.

Christa Stache. *Verzeichnis der Kirchenbücher im Evangelischen Zentral Archiv in Berlin* [*Inventory of Parish Registers in the Evangelical Central Archive in Berlin*]; Part I, *Die östlichen Kirchenprovinzen der evangelischen Kirche in der altpreussischen Union* [*The Eastern Bishoprics of the Evangelical Church in the Old Prussian Empire*], 2nd ed., 297 pp.; 1987); Part II, *Berlin.* Berlin: Evangelisches Zentralarchiv.

> Lists and dates of Protestant records for particular parishes in the former German eastern provinces in Vol. I. Vol. II includes Old Lutherans, French and other Reformed, and Moravian Brethren, with a few entries for Jews. A few records from the 1600s, most from 1700s or 1800s. Easy to use without knowledge of German.

Standesregister und Personenstandsbücher der Ostgebiete im Standesamt I in Berlin: Gesamtverzeichnis für die ehemaligen deutschen Ostgebiete, die besetzten Gebiete und das Generalgouvernement. Frankfurt a.M., Germany: Verlag für Standesamtswesen. 1992.

Jacob Steigerwald. *Tracing Romania's Heterogeneous German Minority from Its Origins to the Diaspora.* Winona, MN: Translation and Interpretation Service. 1985. 61 pp.

> Detailed history of the many German settlements in Romania, but excluding those in the eastern part of that country. Includes 7-page bibliography.

Ralph B. Strassburger and William J. Hinke. *Pennsylvania German Pioneers, 1727-1808.* Pennsylvania German Society, Norristown, PA. Baltimore, MD: Genealogical Publishing Co., Inc. 3 volumes, 1934. map. Reprinted in 2 volumes, 1966 and 1980.

> Has all of the original lists of early Germans coming to the port of Philadelphia from 1727-1808. Includes 29,837 names in the index.

Karl Stumpp. *The Emigration from Germany to Russia in the Years 1763 to 1862.* Translation by Prof. Joseph S. Height and others. Lincoln, NE: American Historical Society of Germans from Russia. 1982. Reprinted 1993.

> Most exhaustive lists of Germans who migrated to Russia, including places of emigration and immigration.

Jared H. Suess. *Central European Genealogical Terminology.* Logan, UT: Everton Publishers, Inc. 1978. 168 pp.

> Contains German, French, Hungarian, Latin and Italian genealogical terminology.

Jared H. Suess. *Handy Guide to Hungarian Genealogical Records.* Logan, UT: Everton Publishers, Inc. 1980. 100 pp. maps.

> Includes Hungarian, German and Latin genealogical terms, Hungarian history, gazetteers, guide to genealogical records, sample parish records, and more.

Jared H. Suess. *Handy Guide to Swiss Genealogical Records.* Logan, UT: The Everton Publishers, Inc. 1978. 92 pp.

> This guide includes a brief history of Switzerland, guides to Swiss parish and civil records, terms in Swiss records given in four languages, religions, addresses and letter writing, maps and examples.

Anton Tafferner, Josef Schmidt and Josef Volkmar Senz. *Danube Swabians in the Pannonia Basin: A New German Ethnic Group.* Milwaukee. 1982.

> Historical overview and maps of Danube Swabian settlements.

Stephan Thernstrom, ed. *Harvard Encyclopedia of American Ethnic Groups.* Cambridge: MA: Belknap Press. 1980. 1076 pp.

> Broad coverage. One of the few books dealing explicitly with Austrian immigration.

Ernest J. Thode, Jr. *Address Book for Germanic Genealogy*, 5th ed. Baltimore: Genealogical Publishing Co. 1994. 174 pp.

> Lists addresses of archives, genealogical societies (including religious societies), genealogists, publishers, libraries, *Heimatortskarteien*, German-language newspapers in North America, and other sources of information for German-American genealogical research in both Europe and North America. Latest edition includes the new German postal codes and quite a few additional East European addresses.

Ernest Thode. *German-English Genealogical Dictionary.* Baltimore, MD: Genealogical Publishing Co. 1992. 286 pp., plus 29 pp. introduction. map.

> Dictionary with genealogical emphasis. Contains at least 30,000 entries including historic place names, abbreviations, some Latin and French terms, and terms from bordering languages found in German research materials.

Don Heinrich Tolzmann, ed. *Americana Germanica: Paul Ben Baginsky's Bibliography of German Works Relating to America, 1493-1800.* 1942. Reprinted; Bowie, MD: Heritage Books, Inc. 1995. 219 pp.

> Especially useful for those with colonial ancestors.

Don Heinrich Tolzmann. *German-Americana: A Bibliography.* Metuchen, NJ: Scarecrow Press. 1975. Reprinted Bowie, MD: Heritage Books, Inc. 1994. 384 pp.

> About one third of the 5,300 listed sources relate to history. A survey of libraries, archives, and other institutions is also included.

Don Heinrich Tolzmann, ed. *German-Americans in the American Revolution: Henry Melchior Muhlenberg Richards' History.* 1908. Reprinted by Heritage Books, Bowie, MD, 1992. 552 pp.

> Definitive history of the involvement of Germans in Pennsylvania and neighboring colonies in the Revolutionary War. Extensive biographical information.

Don Heinrich Tolzmann, ed. *The German Element in Virginia: Herrmann Schuricht's History*. Original published in 1898; edited, expanded reprint: Bowie, MD: Heritage Books. 1992. 426 pp.

> Documents the history of Germans in Virginia, 1607-1898.

Don Heinrich Tolzmann. *German Immigration in America: The First Wave*. Bowie, MD: Heritage Books. 1993. 352 pp.

> Focuses on reasons for the first German wave of emigration to North America, beginning in 1708. Uses *The German Exodus to England in 1709* by Frank Reid Diffendorfer and *The German Emigration to America, 1709-1740* by Henry E. Jacobs.

Don Heinrich Tolzmann, ed. *John Andrew Russell's History of the German Influence in the Making of Michigan*. 1927. Reprinted: Bowie, MD: Heritage Books, Inc. 1995. 415 pp.

> The key book for researching Germanic ancestors in Michigan, where 29% of the population was Germanic in 1927.

Don Heinrich Tolzmann. *Ohio Valley Biographical Index*. Bowie, MD: Heritage Books. 1992. 78 pp.

> Alphabetical index of 3,754 names of German settlers in the tri-state Greater Cincinnati area, including some who migrated onward to other states, e.g., Iowa and Minnesota.

Don Heinrich Tolzmann. *Upper Midwest German Biographical Index*. Bowie, MD: Heritage Books. 1993. 125 pp.

John Tribbeko and George Ruperti. *Lists of Germans from the Palatinate Who Came to England in 1709*. Baltimore: Clearfield Co. 1965; reprinted 1994. 44 pp.

> Detailed information on nearly 2,000 families, most of whom continued on to America, found in the British Museum and the *New York Genealogical and Biographical Record*.

United States Department of State. *Foreign Consular Offices in The United States*. Washington: U.S. Department of State, issued periodically. ca. 100 pp.

> Lists addresses of foreign chanceries (embassies, missions) and consular establishments in the U.S. Cultural affairs attaches may be helpful in directing you to the proper archival and other genealogical sources in their countries. Especially helpful for countries that have split apart in recent years.

Benjamin Heinrich Unruh. *Die niederländisch-niederdeutschen Hintergründe der mennonitischen Ostwanderungen im 16., 18. und 19. Jahrhundert.* [*The Netherlands and Northern Germany Background of Mennonite Migration to Eastern Europe in the 16th, 18th and 19th Centuries*] Karlsruhe: Ruppur. 1955. 432 pp.

> The most comprehensive listing of Mennonite migrants from Prussia to the Russian Empire (Ukraine), with historical information on the Mennonite flight from the Spanish Netherlands to Polish Prussia during the Reformation era.

Verzeichnis der Postleitzahlen. [*(Austrian) Postal Code Directory*] Vienna, Austria. Published annually.

> Postal code directory for Austria. Can be ordered through Genealogy Unlimited.

Verzeichnis der Postleitzahlen. [*(Swiss) Postal Code Directory*] Baubedarf AG, Thunstrasse 5, Postfach, S-3000 Bern 22, Switzerland. Published annually.

> Postal code directory for Switzerland and Liechtenstein. Can be ordered through Genealogy Unlimited.

Ernst Wagner, et. al. *The Transylvanian Saxons: Historical Highlights*. Cleveland: Alliance of Transylvanian Saxons. 1982.

> History and maps pertaining to the Transylvanian Saxons in Europe and North America.

Diane J. Wandler and Prairie Heritage Chapter members, eds. *Handbook for Researching Family Roots, With Emphasis on German-Russian Heritage, Featuring a Step-By-Step Guide to Researching Family History*. Mandan, ND: Prairie Heritage Chapter (of Germans from Russia Heritage Society). 1992. 286 pp.

> Three books in one: good manual for beginners, regional directory for North Dakota and nearby areas, and several chapters on Russian (mostly Black Sea) Germans. Includes 4-page bibliography and index.

Sally A. Weikel. *Genealogical Research in the Published Pennsylvania Archives*. Harrisburg, PA: Pennsylvania Department of Education. 1978.

> This is a guide to the *Pennsylvania Archives* (see above).

Miriam Weiner. *Bridging the Generations: Researching Your Jewish Roots*. Secaucus, NJ: Self-published. 1987. 57 pp.

> A collection of genealogical columns, lists of resources and how-to information by a leading American Jewish genealogist.

Sophie A. Welisch. *Bukovina Villages/Towns/Cities and Their Germans*. Ellis, KS: Bukovina Society of the Americas. 1990. 78 pp.

> Detailed history of 22 German villages in the Bukovina, with surnames of settlers, maps, places of origin and village names in all relevant languages.

Maralyn A. Wellauer. *Family History Research in the German Democratic Republic*. Milwaukee, WI: Roots International. 1987. 49 pp.

> A guide for doing research in the former German Democratic Republic. Somewhat dated, but still useful.

Maralyn A. Wellauer. *Tracing Your Polish Roots*. Milwaukee, WI: Private printing. 1990-91.

> Contains Polish history, sketches of former German territories, addresses in Poland and information about Polish genealogical sources in the United States.

Maralyn A. Wellauer. *Tracing Your Swiss Roots*. Milwaukee, WI: Private printing. 1979. 175 pp.

> Guide to tracing your Swiss-born ancestor back to Switzerland and extending this line in Switzerland. Many photo examples.

Martina Wermes. *Important Addresses and Telephone Numbers for Genealogical Research for the Five New (Eastern) States of the Federal Republic of Germany and Berlin*, 2nd. ed. [partially translated, adapted and supplemented for English-language users by Edward Reimer Brandt]. Minneapolis: translator. 1994. 20 pp.

> Current addresses of religious institutions, archives (state, branch, city), libraries and genealogical organizations, with explanations and supplementary sources of information.

Martina Wermes, Renate Jude, Marion Bahr and Hans-Jürgen Voigt. *Bestandsverzeichnis der Deutschen Zentralstelle für Genealogie.* [Index to the Holdings of the German Central Office for Genealogy]. Vol. I: *Die Kirchenbuchunterlagen der östlichen Provinzen Posen, Ost- und Westpreussen, Pommern und Schlesien.* [The Parish Registers of the Eastern Provinces of Posen, East and West Prussia, Pomerania and Silesia]. Vol II: *Die archivalischen und Kirchenbuchunterlagen deutscher Siedlungsgebiete im Ausland: Bessarabien, Bukowina, Estland, Lettland und Litauen, Siebenbürgen, Sudetenland, Slowenien und Südtirol.* [The Parish Registers of the German Settlements in Other Areas: Bessarabia, Bukovina, Estonia, Latvia and Lithuania, Transylvania, the Sudetenland, Slovenia and South Tyrol]. Vol. III: *Die Kirchenbuchunterlagen der Länder und Provinzen des Deutschen Reiches.* [The Parish Registers of the States and Provinces of the German Empire]. Neustadt/Aisch: Verlag Degener & Co. 1991-94. Vol. I: 1991. 182 pp. Vol II: 1992. 189 pp. Vol. III: 1994. 217 pp.

> Bilingual introductory material. The rest is in list form.

> Volume I lists the archives' original or microfilmed parish registers for the German eastern provinces within the borders of 1905 but excluding East Brandenburg.

Volume II lists microfilms of parish registers and other archival records for (1) North Bukovina (only those that arrived via Danzig, Bromberg, Posen and other places, since the 1940 Hitler-Stalin Pact prohibited the transfer of such registers); (2) South Bukovina (where Romania sanctioned the transfer of such records to Germany); (3) Bessarabia (from which the transfer of records was prohibited, but where all German repatriates received pedigree charts prior to their departure); (4) the Transylvanian districts of Mediasch, Schelk, Reps and Schässburg, which were in the archives at Kronstadt (Brasov), but not those for other districts; (5) the Baltic countries (but mostly Latvia); (6) South Tyrol (archival records in Bozen [Bolzano] and Brixen, plus a few Catholic parishes); and (7) Bohemia and Moravia, i.e., the Czech Republic (but the original microfilms suffered a loss of damage in World War II, so comparatively few records still exist).

Volume III deals with Berlin, Schleswig-Holstein, Thuringia, Baden, Bavaria, Brandenburg (including the part now in Poland), Hamburg, Hanover, Hesse, Mecklenburg, the Rhine province, the Kingdom of Saxony, the Prussian Province of Saxony, Westphalia, Anhalt, Brunswick, Hesse-Nassau, Lippe, Oldenburg, the Saarland, Schaumburg-Lippe, and Württemberg.

Dr. Franz Wilhelm & Dr. Josef Kallbrunner. *Quellen zur deutschen Siedlungsgeschichte in Südosteuropa.* [*Sourcebook for Histories of German Settlements in Southeast Europe*]. Part of the series: *Schriftenreihe der Deutschen Akademie* [*Series by the German Academy*]. Munich, Germany: Verlag von Ernst Reinhardt. 1938. Recently reprinted by the Helmut Scherer Verlag, Berlin.

Very extensive lists of Germans who migrated to Southeast Europe between 1749 and 1803, showing places of emigration and general area of immigration; maps and tables; has numerous errors, mostly with respect to two or more places having the same name.

Oren Windholz. *Bohemian Germans in Kansas: A Catholic Community from Bukovina.* Hays, KS: author. 1993. 50 pp.

Illustrated history of the migration of Germans from the Bohemian Forest to the Bukovina and America.

Don Yoder, ed. *Rhineland Emigrants: Lists of German Settlers in Colonial America.* Baltimore: Genealogical Publishing Co. 1981; reprinted 1985. 170 pp.

European origins of Pennsylvania Germans, with references to church, parish and provincial records in southwest German archives, and some corresponding Pennsylvanian records. Collection of 24 articles, most of them translated from the German originals. Extensive index.

Gary J. Zimmerman and Marion Wolfert. *German Immigrants: Lists of Passengers Bound from Bremen to New York, with Places of Origin.* Baltimore, MD: Genealogical Publishing Co., Inc. 1985-93 and ongoing. Volume 1: 1847-1854 (1985, 1993). Volume 2: 1855-1862 (1986, 1993). Volume 3: 1863-1867 (1988). Volume 4 (by Marion Wolfert): 1868-1871 (1993).

The original lists of emigrants departing from the Bremen port were destroyed either by policy or remainder both before and during World War II. This series has reconstructed these records from official United States sources of arrival records rather than departure records. Only those passengers listing a specific place of origin are noted in the manifests. Immigrants' names are arranged in alphabetical order, with family members grouped together. Includes age, place of origin, date of arrival and name of ship, with citations to original source material.

PERIODICALS AND INDEXES TO PERIODICALS

The following publications are arranged alphabetically by the name of the publication.

E. Welsch, J. Danyel and T. Kilton. *Archives and Libraries in a New Germany*. New York: Council for European Studies, Columbia University. 1994/5.
> Focuses on changes in the five new eastern states of Germany. Comprehensive subject matter.

The Augustan Society Omnibus. P.O. Box P, Torrance, CA 90504-0210.
> Multi-ethnic, including German, coverage.

Sallyann Amdur Sack, ed. *Avotaynu: International Review of Jewish Genealogy*. 155 N. Washington Ave., Teaneck, NJ 07621.
> Independent Jewish periodical, with worldwide coverage.

Jo Ann Kuhr, ed. *Clues*. Published by the American Historical Society of Germans from Russia.
> Annual 100-page publication comprised of a surname exchange list for Germans from Russia and supplementary genealogical data, such as passenger lists. Now also includes a chapter on Latin America.

Dorot. Published quarterly by the New York Jewish Genealogical Society.

Denise Kolesar and Brian J. Lenius, eds. *East European Genealogist*. East European Branch, Manitoba Genealogical Society, P.O. Box 2536, Winnipeg, MB R3C 4A7, Canada.
> Strong German element. Greatest strength is Galicia.

Familienkundliche Nachrichten. [*Genealogical News*]. Neustadt (Aisch), Germany: Verlag Degener & Co. Often called *FaNa*. Six issues per year.
> Widely read German genealogical publication dealing with queries (see chapter II).

John C. Alleman, ed. *FEEFHS: Newsletter of the Federation of East European Family History Societies*. P.O. Box 21346, Salt Lake City, UT 84121.
> Multi-ethnic newsletter that covers all of Germany and Austria, but emphasizes the ex-Communist East European areas where Germans lived.

George B. Everton, Jr., ed. *The Genealogical Helper*. Published by The Everton Publishers, Inc., P.O. Box 368, Logan, UT 84321. Six issues per year.
> Contains general genealogical articles, queries and advertisements. Some German books, organizations and researchers are mentioned.

Larry O. Jensen, ed. *German Genealogical Digest*. Published by German Genealogical Digest, P.O. Box 700, Pleasant Grove, UT 84062.
> Quarterly publication with in-depth articles on German genealogical research and specialized areas. On-going indexes and specific help are available.

Elizabeth Nick, ed. and pub. *The Gottschee Tree*. c/o Liz Information Service, P.O. Box 725, Louisville, CO 80027-0725. Quarterly.
> Focuses on the former Gottschee German settlement (now Kocevje, Slovenia), 1330-1941.

Sophia Stalzer Wyant and Maria Wyant Cuzzo, eds. *The Gottscheer Connection*. Published by the Gottscheer Research & Genealogy Association, c/o Kate Loschke Pruente, 21534 American River Dr., Sonora, CA 95370-91112.

Heritage Quest. Historic Resources, Inc., P.O. Box 329, Bountiful, UT 84011-0329.
> Substantial number of articles on German-American genealogy by leading American and German experts.

Maajan— Die Quelle. [*Maajan—The Source*]. Published by the Schweizerische Vereinigung für jüdische Genealogie, Zurich, Switzerland.

Le Mar and Lois Zook Mast, eds. *Mennonite Family History*. 10 West Main St., Elverson, PA 19520-0171.
> Chief genealogical periodical in North America for Mennonites and closely related denominations, e.g., Amish and Brethren.

Mennonite Genealogist. Published by the California Mennonite Historical Society, Fresno Pacific College Archives, 4824 E. Butler Ave., Fresno, CA 93727
> Newsletter, recently started in 1995, of the Genealogical Project Committee.

Mennonite Historian. Published by the Mennonite Heritage Centre, 600 Shaftesbury Blvd., Winnipeg, MB R3P 0M4, Canada, and the Centre for Mennonite Brethren Studies, Winnipeg.
> Carries a substantial amount of genealogical information, especially for Mennonites in Western Canada.

Pathways and Passages. Polish Genealogical Society of the Northeast. 8 Lyle Road, New Britain, CT 06053-2104.
> The official publication of the Polish Genealogical Society of the Northeast

Periodical Source Index (PERSI). Published by Allen County Public Library Foundation, 900 Webster St., Box 2270, Fort Wayne, IN 46801-2270.
> An index to 2000 genealogical and local history periodicals published in the United States, covering 1847 to 1985, with subsequent annual supplements. The index is arranged by locality, subject matter and surname. See "Using PERSI in German Genealogy" in *Der Blumenbaum*, April-May-June 1995, for instructions.

Myron E. Gruenwald, ed. and pub. *Die Pommerschen Leute*. [*The Pomeranian People*]. 1280 Westhaven Dr., Oshkosh, WI 54904.
> An English-language specialty newsletter offering articles and queries to Pomeranian researchers.

Praktische Forschungshilfe. [*Practical Research Help*]. Germany: C. A. Starke Verlag, Postfach 1310, D-65549 Limburg/Lahn. Often called PraFo.
> Quarterly genealogy supplement to the Archiv für Sippenforschung (see chapter II).

Patricia A. Eames, ed. *RAGAS Newsletter*, Box 236, Glen Echo, MD 20812.
> Contains the latest information on archival research developments in the former Soviet Union, including articles on German, Jewish and other records.

Der Schlüssel. [*The Key*].
> A multi-volume index to German-Austrian-Swiss genealogical periodicals. Covers publications from 1870 to 1975 and includes the following registers: title index, place name register, register of subjects and surname index.The compilers, who devoted 40 years to this work, recently died, so the completion of the series beyond 1975 is in doubt. The Family History Library has the series, but not on microfilm.

Armand Bauer, ed. *Der Stammbaum*. [*The Family Tree*]. Published by the Germans from Russia Heritage Society, 1008 East Central Ave., Bismarck, ND 58501.
> Annual genealogical issue of the *Heritage Review*. Focuses especially on Germans who went from the western Black Sea region to the Dakotas. In English.

Maralyn A. Wellauer, ed. *The Swiss Connection*. 2845 North 72nd St., Milwaukee, WI 53120.

Ewald Wuschke, ed. and pub. *Wandering Volhynians: A Magazine for the Descendants of Germans from Volhynia and Poland*. Published by Ewald Wuschke, 3492 West 39th Ave., Vancouver, BC, Canada V6N 3A2.
> Chief publication concerning Volhynian Germans, with a Volhynia/Poland surname and village research list.

Chapter XIX

USEFUL ADDRESSES

This section shows addresses of many publishers, booksellers, map sources, libraries, information centers and genealogical societies that can be of help to people doing Germanic genealogical research. To find other toll-free "800" numbers, call 800-555-1212 for information and ask the operator for the number of a specific company.

PUBLISHERS AND BOOKSELLERS

AKB Publications
691 Weavertown Rd.
Myerstown, PA 17067-2642
(*Phone: 717-866-2300*)
(*refers to Annette K. Burgert, leading author/publisher on colonial emigration to Pennsylvania*)

Alice's Ancestral Nostalgia
P.O. Box 510092
Salt Lake City, UT 84151
Phone: 801-575-6510

Ancestry, Inc.
P.O. Box 476
Salt Lake City, UT 84110-0476
Phone: 800-531-1790

Association of Professional Genealogists
3421 M St. N.W., Suite 236
Washington, DC 20007

Avotaynu, Inc.
Box 900
Teaneck, NJ 07666
Phone: 800-866-1525
(*Book publishing address*)

Avotaynu, Inc.
155 N. Washington Ave.
Bergenfield, NJ 07621
Phone: 800-AVO-TAYN(U)
       (800-286-8298)
(*Jewish genealogy*)

Edna M. Bentz
13139 Old West Ave.
San Diego, CA 92129-2406
Phone: 619-484-1708

Böhlau Verlag GmbH & Co.
Theodor-Heuss-Str. 76
D-51149 Köln
Germany

R. R. Bowker & Co.
245 W. 17th St.
New York, NY 10011-5300
Phone: 800-521-8110 or 212-645-9700

Edward R. Brandt
13 - 27th Ave. S.E.
Minneapolis, MN 55414-3101

Calmar Publications
202 Wildwood Lane
Louisville, KY 40223
Phone: 502-425-0460
(*Genealogies of German Turner gymnastic group during Civil War*)

Clearfield Company, Inc.
200 E. Eager St.
Baltimore, MD 21202-3761
(*Phone: 410-625-9004*)
(*Branch of Genealogical Publishing Co.*)

CMBC Publications
600 Shaftesbury Blvd.
Winnipeg, MB R3P 0M4
Canada
(*Mennonite history*)

Martha Remer Connor
7754 Pacement Ct.
Las Vegas, NV 89117-5122
(*Hungarian German census transcripts*)

Council for European Studies
Box 44, Schermerhorn Hall
Columbia University
New York, NY 10027

Alfred A. Curran
119 Sefton Dr.
New Britain, CT 06053-2550
Phone: 203-827-8023

Randy Daitsch
820½ N. Detroit St.
Los Angeles, CA 90046
(*Shtetl gazetteer*)

Verlag Degener & Company
Nürnberger Strasse 27
Postfach 1360
D-91403 Neustadt/Aisch
Germany

Editions-Reliures Schortgen
43, rue Marie Muller-Tesch
L-4250 Esch-Alzettee
Luxembourg
(*Luxemburgers in America*)

The Everton Publishers, Inc.
P.O. Box 368
Logan, UT 84323-0368
Phone: 800-443-6325 or 801-752-6022

Facts on File, Inc.
460 Park Ave. S.
New York, NY 10016-7382
Phone: 800-322-8755

The Family Historian
12961 Lake Ave.
Lakewood, OH 44107-1533
(*Slovak German gazetteer*)

Family Tree Press
2912 Orchard Ave. N.
Minneapolis, MN 55422
Phone: 612-588-5824

Gale Research Inc.
835 Penobscot Bldg.
Detroit, MI 48226-4094
Phone: 800-521-0707 or 313-961-2242

Genealogical Publishing Co., Inc.
1001 N. Calvert St.
Baltimore, MD 21202-3897
Phone: 800-296-6687

Genealogists Bookshelf
Box 468
343 E. 85th St.
New York, NY 10028-4550

Genealogy House
3148 Kentucky Ave. S.
St. Louis Park, MN 55426-3471
Phone: 612-920-6990

Genealogy Unlimited, Inc.
(Genun Publishers)
P.O. Box 537
Orem, UT 84059-0537
Phone: 800-666-4363

Generation Press, Inc.
172 King Henry's Blvd.
Agincourt, Ontario, M1T 2V6
Canada

Germanic Genealogy Society
Branch of Minnesota Genealogical Society
P.O. Box 16312
St. Paul, MN 55116

Goodspeed's Book Shop
18 Beacon St.
Boston, MA 02108-3703

Hearthside Press
8405 Richmond Hwy., Suite H
Alexandria, VA 22309-2425
Phone: 703-360-6900
(*Genealogies of Shenandoah Valley, Virginia area Germans, Pennsylvania Germans*)

Hebert Publications
Rt. 2, Box 572
Church Point, LA 70525-9333
Phone: 318-873-6574
(*Genealogies of Louisiana Germans*)

Heimat Publishers
1 Lyme Regis Crescent
Scarborough, ON M1M 1E3
Canada
(*Danube Swabians*)

Heritage Books, Inc.
1540 Pointer Ridge Pl., Suite E
Bowie, MD 20716-1800
Phone: 800-398-7709

Heritage House
P.O. Box 39128
Indianapolis, IN 46239-0128
Phone: 317-862-3330

Heritage Quest
P.O. Box 40
Orting, WA 98360-0040
Phone: 800-442-2029

Hunterdon House
38 Swan St.
Lambertville, NJ 08530-1022
Phone: 609-397-2523
(*For Ontario, Canada, publications*)

Jesperson Press
26A Flavin St.
St. John's, Newfoundland A1C 3R9
Canada

Dr. Arta F. Johnson
153 Aldrich Rd.
Columbus, OH 43214-2625

Brian J. Lenius
Box 18, Grp. 4, R.R. 1
Anola, MB R0E 0A0
Canada
(*Galician gazetteer*)

The Linden Tree
1204 W. Prospect Ave.
Cloquet, MN 55720-1332
Phone: 218-879-5727

Macmillan of Canada
29 Birch Ave.
Toronto, Ontario M4V 1E2
Canada

Mary Keysor Meyer
5179 Perry Rd.
Mt. Airy, MD 21771

Monda Genealoga Ligo
P.O. Box 21346
Salt Lake City, UT 84121-0346

John D. Movius
P.O. Box 4327
Davis, CA 95617-4327
(*Resource Guide to East European
Genealogy*, *and other FEEFHS
publications*)

National Archives and Records Service
601 Penn. Ave. NW, Rm G9
Washington, DC 20004-2601
Phone: 202-724-0098
(*U.S. Government printing office for the
Library of Congress*)

Olde Springfield Shoppe
P.O. Box 171
Elverson, PA 19520-0171
(*Leading bookseller for Mennonite and
Amish genealogy*)

Oro Press
217 W. 1st Ave.
Denver, CO 80223-1507
Phone: 303-722-4425
(*Has tourist history of Germany and
Austria*)

Oxmoor House, Inc.
P.O. Box 2262
Birmingham, AL 35201-2262
Phone: 800-633-4712

Park Genealogical Book Co.
3601 - 78th Ave. N.
Brooklyn Park, MN 55443-2826
Phone: 612-560-9086

Picton Press
P.O. Box 1111
Camden, ME 04843-1111
Phone: 203-236-6565

Prairie Heritage Chapter, GRHS
P.O. Box 328
Bismarck, ND 58502-0328

Helmut Preussler Verlag
Rothenburger Str. 25
D-90443 Nürnberg
Germany
(*Sudeten Germans*)

Verlag Rautenberg
Postfach 19 09
D-26789 Leer
Germany
(*specialize in former German eastern
areas*)

Horst Reschke
3083 W. 4900 S.
Salt Lake City, UT 84118-2527
(*German military records*)

Roots International
Maralyn A. Wellauer
3239 N. 58th St.
Milwaukee, WI 53216-3123
Phone: 414-871-7421

K. G. Saur
Subsidiary of R. R. Bowker Co.
121 Chanlon Rd.
New Providence, NJ 07974-1541
(*American distributor for many German
publishers*)

Helmut Scherer Verlag
Boothstr. 21a
D-12207 Berlin
Germany

Scholarly Resources, Inc.
104 Greenhill Ave.
Wilmington, DE 19805-1897
Phone: 800-772-8937

George K. Schweitzer
Genealogical Sources, Unltd.
407 Ascot Court
Knoxvile, TN 37923-5807

Kenneth L. Smith
523 S. Weyant Ave.
Columbus, OH 43213-2275

C. A. Starke Verlag
Frankfurter Strasse 51-53
Postfach 1310
D-65549 Limburg/Lahn
Germany
(*Publishes Archiv für Sippenforschung
and Praktische Forschungshilfe - PraFo*)

Dr. Jacob Steigerwald
355 West 4th St.
Winona, MN 55987-2805
(*Romanian Germans*)

Suhrkamp Publishers New York, Inc.
175 Fifth Ave.
New York, NY 10010-7703
Phone: 212-460-1653
(*Distributor for German publishing houses*)

Ernest Thode (Thode Translations)
RR 7, Box 306, Kern Rd.
Marietta, OH 45750-9437
Phone: 614-373-3728

Charles E. Tuttle Co., Inc.
P.O. Box 541
28 S. Main St.
Rutland, VT 05701-0541
Phone: 800-526-2778 or 802-773-8229

University of Utah Press
University of Utah
101 University Services Bldg.
Salt Lake City, UT 84112
Phone: 800-444-8638

Westkreuz-Verlag Bonn/Berlin
Vühlenstr. 10-14
D-53902 Bad Münstereifel
Germany

Westland Publications
P.O. Box 117
McNeal, AZ 85617-0117
Phone: 602-642-3500

Who's Who in Genealogy & Heraldry
8944 Madison St.
Savage, MD 20763

Ye Olde Genealogie Shoppe
9605 Vandergriff Road
P.O. Box 39128
Indianapolis, IN 46239-0128
Phone: 317-862-3330

Zielke-Verlag
Stadtlohnweg 13 C407
D-48161 Münster
Germany
(*current East European German genealogy*)

MAP SOURCES

Genealogy House
3148 Kentucky Ave. S.
St. Louis Park, MN 55426-3471
Phone: 612-920-6990

Genealogy Unlimited, Inc.
P.O. Box 537
Orem, UT 84059-0537
Phone: 800-666-4363

International Maps
3930 - 69th St.
Des Moines, IA 50322-2608

Jensen Publications
P.O. Box 441
Pleasant Grove, UT 84062-0441

The Map Store
First Bank Place W.
120 S. 6th St.
Minneapolis, MN 55402-1800
Phone: 612-339-4117

The Map Store
World Trade Center
30 East 7th Street
St. Paul, MN 55101-4901
Phone: 612-227-6277

The Map Store
5821 Karric Square Drive
Dublin, OH 43017-4243
Phone: 800-332-7885

Jonathan Sheppard Books
Box 2020, Plaza Station
Albany, NY 12220-0020

Ernest Thode
RR 7, Box 306, Kern Rd.
Marietta, OH 45750-9437
Phone: 614-373-3728

Travel Genie
Books-Maps-Gifts
Lincoln Center
620 Lincoln Way
Ames, IA 50010-6900
Phone: 515-232-1070

Viking Penguin, Inc.
375 Hudson St., Floor #4
New York, NY 10014-3672
Phone: 800-631-3577

Ye Olde Genealogie Shoppe
3851 S. Post Rd.
Indianapolis, IN 46239-9382
Phone: 317-862-3330

LIBRARIES AND INFORMATION CENTERS

Allen County Public Library
900 Webster St.
P.O. Box 2270
Fort Wayne, IN 46802-2270
Phone: 219-424-7241

This library is second only to the LDS Family History Library for the extent of its genealogical holdings. Nationwide in scope with 128,000 volumes and 132,000 microtext items. Publishes *Periodical Source Index* (*PERSI*).

Family History Library
The Church of Jesus Christ of Latter-
    day Saints (Mormon)
35 North West Temple Street
Salt Lake City, UT 84150-1003

Main LDS library. See chapter III referring to local branches (over 200 in the United States, others in Canada and Europe).

German Information Center
410 Park Avenue
New York, NY 10022-4407

Publishes *The Week in Germany* and provides other informational services. Offers information, maps and posters.

Germans from Russia Heritage
    Collection
North Dakota Institute for Regional
    Studies
North Dakota State University
    Libraries
Fargo, ND 58105-5599

Largest historical collection on Germans from Russia in the U.S.

Max Kade Institute for German
    American Studies
University of Wisconsin - Madison
901 University Bay Drive
Madison, WI 53705-2269

German-American studies research center. Has a German gazetteer (prior to German unification in 1871) and other early historical works not readily available elsewhere.

Library of Congress
101 Independence Ave. S.E.
Washington, DC 20003-1001

Contains over 80 million items in 470 languages.

Mennonite Historical Library
Goshen College
Goshen, IN 46526-4794
Phone: 219-535-7000

History and index of names in Amish genealogies. Composite genealogy of all living married Amish persons.

National Archives & Records
    Administration
General Services Administration
Washington, DC 20004

Central repository for United States federal records. Also includes records of Nazi Germany and captured records.

Newberry Library
60 W. Walton St.
Chicago, IL 60610-3380
Phone: 312-943-9090

Private, non-circulating reference library in history and humanities. Large collection of local history and genealogy, especially for the Midwest. Famous for *The Genealogical Index of the Newberry Library* (4 vols.), a surname index to most personal names found in the Newberry Library's local history and genealogy collection, prior to 1918. Has microfilms of registers of 444 Catholic parishes of Archdiocese of Chicago prior to 1910.

Swiss National Tourist Office
608 - 5th Avenue, Rm. #202
New York, NY 10020-2342

Offers information and maps.

University of Texas
Barker Texas History Center
Austin, TX 78712-1104

Records for German-Wendish settlement in Texas, also maps.

State Historical Society of Wisconsin
816 State St.
Madison, WI 53706-1488
Phone: 608-264-6535

One of the largest genealogical collections in the United States. The scope of the collection pertains to all parts of the United States and Canada. Contains over one million items. Has a complete microfilm collection of all available censuses of the United States and Canada; the largest newspaper collection in the United States outside the Library of Congress; an extensive city directory and telephone book collection; passenger lists on microfilm for major ports, including Quebec (1865-1900) and Halifax (1890-1900); and vital records, census and biographical indexes for Wisconsin.

York County Historical Society
259 E. Market St.
York, PA 17403-2014

Has 10 volumes with indexes of Pennsylvania settlers, giving European origins.

LENDING LIBRARIES

Consult with your local library on the availability of interlibrary loans.

Genealogical libraries that have lending policies for their members are:

New England Historic Genealogical
   Society
101 Newbury St.
Boston, MA 02116-3087
Phone: 617-536-5740

Circulates 15,000 volumes. Specializes in historic New England, middle Atlantic states, the South, the Midwest, the West, Canada and Europe.

National Genealogical Society Library
4527 - 17th St. N.
Arlington, VA 22207-2399

Collection of published and non-published works.

American Genealogical Lending Library
P.O. Box 244
Bountiful, UT 84011-0244
Phone: 800-298-5358

Commercial lending library with microfilm and microfiche available for rental or for purchase. Covers United States and Canadian records.

SPECIAL RESOURCES IN AND NEAR MINNESOTA

Catholic Historical Society of St. Paul
2260 Summit Ave.
St. Paul, MN 55105-1094

Family History Centers in Minnesota

(*These are library locations, not mailing addresses.*)

Family History Centers in North Dakota

(*These are library locations, not mailing addresses.*)

Family History Centers in South Dakota

(*These are library locations, not mailing addresses.*)

Family History Centers in Iowa

(*These are library locations, not mailing addresses.*)

This office, as all others, can give you the name and address of the Diocese, Bishop, Archbishop or Cardinal in any area of Germany or the world.

2801 Douglas Drive, Crystal (*612-544-2479*) (largest in the area)

2140 Hadley Ave., Oakdale (*612-770-3213*)

2742 Yellowstone Blvd., Anoka (*612-442-9679*)

3033 NE Birchmont Dr., Bemidji (*218-751-9129*)

521 Upham Road, Duluth (*218-722-9508*)

1851 Marie Lane, North Mankato (*507-625-8342*)

1002 SE 16th St., Rochester (*507-282-2382*)

1420 - 29th Ave. N., St. Cloud (*612-252-4355*)

2006 Buffalo Hills Lane, Brainerd

Hwy. 25 N., Buffalo

2502 - 17th Ave. SW, Fargo (*701-232-4003*)

2814 Cherry St., Grand Forks (*701-746-6126*)

1500 Country West Rd, Bismarck (*701-222-2794*)

2025 Ninth St. NW, Minot (*701-838-4486*)

3900 S. Fairhall Ave., Sioux Falls (*605-361-1070*)

530 S. Mannston, Gettysburg (*605-765-9270*)

LDS Church, Rosebud (*605-747-2818*)

2822 Canyon Ln. Dr., Rapid City (*605-341-8572*)

1201 West Clifton, Sioux City (*712-255-9686*)

2524 Hoover, Ames (*515-232-3634*)

4300 Trailridge Rd. SE, Cedar Rapids (*319-363-9343*)

3301 Ashworth Rd., West Des Moines (*515-225-0416*)

4929 Wisconsin Ave., Davenport (*319-386-7547*)

Family History Centers in Wisconsin

(*These are library locations, not mailing addresses.*)

3335 Stein Blvd., Eau Claire (*715-834-8271*)

744 S. 6th, Barron

910 East Zingler, Shawano (*715-526-2946*)

1711 University Ave., Madison (*608-238-1071*)

9600 West Grange Ave., Hales Corner (*414-425-4182*)

Family History Centers in Manitoba and Western Ontario, Canada

(*These are library locations, not mailing addresses.*)

45 Dalhousie Dr., Winnipeg, MB (*204-261-4271*)

700 Third St. W., Fort Frances, ON (*807-274-9394*)

2255 Ponderosa Dr., Thunder Bay, ON (*807-939-1451*)

German Consulate
1100 First Bank Place West
120 S. 6th St.
Minneapolis, MN 55402-1814
Phone: 612-338-6559

Will answer questions about Germany's current status, customs, history and mailing information. Check other major cities for other German consulates.

Germanic Genealogy Society
Branch of Minnesota Genealogical
    Society
P.O. Box 16312
St. Paul, MN 55116

Library collection located at:
Concordia College
Buenger Memorial Library
275 N. Syndicate St.
St. Paul, MN 55104
Phone: 612-641-8237
(*Hamline Ave. & Marshall Street*)

Collection of hundreds of genealogical materials useful to those researching German-speaking ancestors. Has gazetteers including *Meyers Orts- und Verkehrs-Lexikon* gazetteer and *Glenzdorfs*, maps, passenger list indexes, periodicals as well as general and specific reference works. The Concordia library itself contains an extensive German Lutheran collection.

Minneapolis Public Library
300 Nicollet Mall
Minneapolis, MN 55401-1992
Phone: 612-372-6500

Has special genealogy room in the history department. Contents include *Deutsche Geschlechterbücher* (dozens of volumes of biographies of nobles and prominent burghers).

Minnesota Historical Society
Research Center
345 W. Kellogg Blvd.
St. Paul, MN 55102-1906
Phone: 612-296-2143

Library collects published sources of Minnesota life and Minnesota people. Has an extensive collection of Minnesota newspapers, local histories, city directories, photographs and family histories. Also has a good collection of historical and genealogical material relating to many eastern states. Archives and manuscripts center houses state and federal census records, and town and county records of Minnesota. Some examples are military and pension records, naturalization records, alien registration records, school records, court records, vital records, burial permits, tax and election records, church records, business and railroad records.

Consulate of Switzerland
Mr. Schurt Schneider
15500 Wayzata Blvd.
Wayzata, MN 55391
Phone: 612-449-9767

Will answer questions about Swiss customs, history, postal codes and mailing problems. Check other major cities for other Swiss consulates.

University of Minnesota
Wilson Library, West Bank
309 - 19th Ave. S.
Minneapolis, MN 55455-0414
Phone: 612-624-0303 (reference)
Phone: 612-624-4549 (map library)

Has over two million volumes and 250,000 maps, several thousand newspapers and over a million government documents. Borchert Map Library has an extensive collection of historical and contemporary maps for European and other countries. Very strong collection of German materials, including biographical and language dictionaries of Germans and Austrians, local and church histories of German areas, many German gazetteers including *Müllers Grosses Deutsches Ortsbuch*, and works on Pennsylvania German pioneers. The University of Minnesota has a Center for Austrian Studies and possibly the largest American library collection of books on the Hapsburg Empire.

GENEALOGY-RELATED GERMANIC SOCIETIES

A large number of German-American genealogical societies can be found in various directories. The most comprehensive one is probably Elizabeth Petty Bentley's, *The Genealogist's Address Book*, 3rd edition (Baltimore: Genealogical Publishing Co., 1995). In Part 3, listing "Ethnic and Religious Organizations and Research Centers," look under the Austrian, German, Luxembourg and Swiss categories, as well as under religious archives and organizations for groups that have retained a distinct religious identity (Jewish, Mennonite, Moravian), as well as for German mainstream churches. If your ancestors came from a non-Germanic country, look under that category, too, because many other societies (Czech, Hungarian, Polish, Slovak and Slovenian, for example) have a multiethnic scope.

The following is a selected list of the most prominent German-American genealogical societies, those specializing in certain particular areas, certain multi-purpose societies with relevant resources and the leading pertinent academic society. Many sell books.

For genealogy-related societies in countries outside the United States, check the chapters on the countries in question.

Alliance of Transylvanian Saxons
5393 Pearl Road
Cleveland, OH 44129-1597

American Historical Society of Germans
    from Russia
631 D Street
Lincoln, NE 68502-1199
(*about 60 chapters, mostly in western U.S. and Canada*)

American Historical Society of Germans
    from Russia
North Star Chapter of Minnesota
2523 E. 42nd St.
Minneapolis, MN 55406-3053

American/Schleswig Holstein Heritage
    Society
P.O. Box 313
Davenport, IA 52805-0313

Banat Listserver
c/o Bob Madler
1571 York Way
Sparks, NV 89431

The Bukovina Society of the Americas
P.O. Box 81
Ellis, KS 67637-0081

Danube Swabian Association
127 Route 156
Trenton, NJ 08620-1821

Galizien German Descendants
12367 S.E. 214th St.
Kent, WA 98031-2215

German-Acadian Coast Historical and
    Genealogical Society
P.O. Box 517
Destrehan, LA 70047-0517

German-American Research and
    Document Center
University of Wisconsin Foundation
702 Langdon St.
Madison, WI 53706-1487

German-Bohemian Heritage Society
P.O. Box 822
New Ulm, MN 56073-0822

German Genealogical Society of America
P.O. Box 291818
Los Angeles, CA 90029-1818
(*Street address:*
    2125 Wright Ave., Suite C-9
    La Verne, CA 91750-5814)

German Interest Group
    of Chicago Genealogical Society
c/o Ronald Otto
16828 Willow Lane Dr.
Tinley Park, IL 60477-2948

German Research Association, Inc.
P.O. Box 711600
San Diego, CA 92171-1600

German Society of Pennsylvania
611 Spring Garden St.
Philadelphia, PA 19123-3505

German-Texan Heritage Society
507 E. 10th St.
P.O. Box 684171
Austin, TX 78768-4171

Germanic Genealogy Society
Branch of Minnesota Genealogical Society
P.O. Box 16312
St. Paul, MN 55116-0312

Germans from Russia Heritage Society
1008 E. Central Ave.
Bismarck, ND 58501-1936
(*focuses on western Black Sea area; about 25 chapters in western U.S. and Canada, about 2/3 in the Dakotas*)

Glückstal Colony Research Association
1015 - 22nd St.
Santa Monica, CA 90403

Gottscheer Research & Genealogy
  Association
c/o Elizabeth Nick
174 S. Hoover Ave.
Louisville, CO 80027-2130

Illinois Mennonite Historical and
  Genealogical Society
P.O. Box 819
Metamora, IL 61548-0819

Immigrant Genealogical Society
P.O. Box 7369
Burbank, CA 91510-7369
(*major research service*)

The Lost Palatine
Gail Breitbard, Editor
Rt. 1, Box 1160
Estero, FL 33928-9801

Luxembourger Society of Wisconsin
P.O. Box 328
Port Washington, WI 53074

Mid-Atlantic Germanic Society
P.O. Box 2642
Kensington, MD 20892-2642

Orangeburg-German-Swiss Genealogical
  Society
c/o Mrs. T.L. Ulmer
3415 Pine Belt Rd.
Columbia, SC 29204-3128

Ostfriesian Genealogical Society
c/o Franklin Heibult, Pres.
R.R. 1
Ashton, IA 51232-9801

Palatines to America
P.O. Box 101
Capital University
Columbus, OH 43209-2394
(*focuses on colonial immigrants; 9 chapters, mostly between Illinois and New York*)

Pennsylvania German Research Society
R.R. 1, Box 478
Sugarloaf, PA 18249-9735

Die Pommerschen Leute
c/o Myron E. Gruenwald
1280 Westhaven Drive
Oshkosh, WI 54904-8142
(*publishes Die Pommerschen Leute*)

Pommerscher Verein Freistadt
P.O. Box 204
Germantown, WI 53022-0204

Sacramento German Genealogical Society
P.O. Box 660061
Sacramento, CA 95866-0061

Schwenkfeldian Exile Society
Pennsburg, PA 18073

Society of German-American Studies
c/o Professor LaVern J. Rippley
St. Olaf College
Northfield, MN 55057-1099

Swiss American Historical Society
216 E. 39th St.
Norfolk, VA 23504-1004

NON-GERMANIC AND MULTI-ETHNIC SOCIETIES
OF IMPORTANCE TO GERMANIC RESEARCH

Czechoslovak Genealogical Society
  International
P.O. Box 16225
St. Paul, MN 55116-0225
(*publishes Naše Rodina*)

Federation of East European Family
  History Societies
P.O. Box 21346
Salt Lake City, UT 84121-0346
(*multi-continental umbrella group*)

Hungarian/American Friendship Society
2811 Elvyra Way, Apt. # 236
Sacramento, CA 95821-5865
(*publishes Régí Magyarország: "Old
Hungary"*)

Hungarian Genealogical Society of
  America
124 Esther St.
Toledo, OH 43605-1435

East European Branch
Manitoba Genealogical Society
P.O. Box 2536
Winnipeg, Manitoba R3C 4A7
Canada
(*publishes East European Genealogist*)

Lithuanian American Genealogy Society
c/o Balzekas Museum of Lithuanian
  Culture
6500 Pulaski Road
Chicago, IL 60629-5136

Orphan Train Heritage Society of
  America
Route 4, Box 565
Springdale, AZ 72764

Polish Genealogical Society of America
984 N. Milwaukee Ave.
Chicago, IL 60622-4199
(*publishes Rodziny and Bulletin of PGSA*)

Polish Genealogical Society of Michigan
c/o Burton Historical Collection
Detroit Public Library
5201 Woodward St.
Detroit, MI 48202-4007
(*publishes The Eaglet*)

Polish Genealogical Society of the
  Northeast
8 Lyle Road
New Britain, CT 06053-2104
(*publishes Pathways and Passages*)

Wisconsin State Genealogical Society
P.O. Box 5106
Madison, WI 53705-0106
(*Street address:
2109 - 20th Ave,.Monroe, WI 53566*)

DATELINE OF GERMANIC HISTORY

This dateline emphasizes events of genealogical importance or interest. *Items in italics refer mostly to non-European countries*; those in regular type refer to Europe.

400-600 Angles and Saxons of Germany, and Jutes of Juteland in Denmark come to Britain. Angles and Saxons rule most of England after 600.

768-814 Charlemagne (Karl der Grosse) rules a large empire that becomes the Holy Roman Empire in 800. The empire includes today's France, Switzerland, Germany, Austria, the Benelux countries and northern Italy.

870-1648 Alsace is part of the Holy Roman Empire.

900-1350 Areas east of Hamburg-Halle-Northwest Czech line (including the Czech rimland), hitherto occupied by Slavs, become Germanicized through migration and assimilation. Lesser expansion since the Reformation, mostly in border areas east of the Oder River.

1000-1500 Jewish expulsions. During the Middle Ages large numbers of Jews are expelled from their homes throughout Europe, most going to Poland, Italy and the Ottoman Empire. Expulsions were from German areas (1000-1350), Hungary (1300s) and Austria (1400s).

1100-1300 German colonization of eastern parts of Lorraine and the Netherlands.

1100-1600 German merchants form the Hanse, resulting in powerful trading alliances between the most important ports in the Baltic and North Seas. The Hanseatic league dominates the foreign trade of Scandinavia and northern Germany. Its influence fades in the late 1400s. Surnames become common in Germany during this period.

1141-1181 "Saxons" (mostly Franks) are invited to settle in Transylvania to defend Hungary's eastern border. Also to *Zips* region (northern or Upper Hungary, today the Slovak Republic) at the same time for the same reasons, but lasting till 1340 after Mongol devastation of the area in 1240-42 required resettlement.

1224 Hungarian king issues the Andreanum ("golden patent"), guaranteeing Germans on crownland personal freedom, right to own land and local autonomy.

1241-49 Founding of the Hanseatic League.

1291-1648 Growth and independence of Switzerland and formation of the Schwyz League by the original cantons of Switzerland. Switzerland slowly gains its independence from the Holy Roman Empire and is officially recognized as independent in 1648.

1330 First settlement in Gottschee County, Slovenia, with immigration continuing until the 1790s.

1345-1918 Ottoman Empire of Turkey controls large portions of Europe, reaching its peak between 1400-1680. Gradually the Austrian Empire pushes it back. Modern-day European areas under Turkish rule at this time include Hungary, Serbia, Macedonia, Bulgaria, Romania, Greece and part of Ukraine.

1348-1365 Bubonic plague (also called the Black Death) threatens all of Europe. Over 25 million Europeans die in periodic outbreaks.

1419-36	Hussite wars for religious freedom in Bohemia. John Huss is leader of the reform movement. He is burned to death in 1415, causing his followers to demand more freedom.
1517	Martin Luther posts his theses disputing traditional religious doctrine of the Roman Catholic church.
1518-23	Ulrich Zwingli begins the Reformation in Switzerland, which leads to the formation of the Reformed (Calvinist) Church.
1524-25	Peasants' War, a mass uprising against secular authorities — inspired but repudiated by Luther — is crushed.
1526	Turkish defeat of Hungary at Battle of Mohacs soon leads to conquest of most of Hungary.
1530	Augsburg Confession (creed) adopted by Lutherans.
1530-1648	Non-Catholics subjected to extreme persecution during this period, including forcible conversion and expulsions and deaths in some areas. Areas dominated by Protestant rulers also persecute dissidents.
1545	Transylvanian Saxons and many Zipsers become Lutherans.
1555	Peace of Augsburg (between Catholics and Lutherans only) states subjects must adopt the religion of their local ruler.
1563	Catholic Counter-Reformation begins in Bavaria.
1568	Particularly notorious persecution of Protestants in the Spanish Netherlands (including Belgium) by the Duke of Alva. Large-scale flight of Walloon Calvinists, especially to the Palatinate, Hesse and Brandenburg, and Dutch-Flemish-Frisian Mennonites to the Danzig area, which is under the Polish crown (religious flight begins about 1530).
1582-85	Calendar reform is proposed by Pope Gregory XIII. The Gregorian calendar is adopted by most Catholic countries of Europe. It is adopted by Prussia in 1612, by most Protestant countries in 1700, by Great Britain in 1752 and by Russia in 1917.
1598	Edict of Nantes grants freedom of religion in France.
1600	Surnames are in common use throughout Germany (in some areas as early as 1100).
1617	John Calvin's works are published.
1618-48	Thirty Years' War. Many German areas are devastated and population drops from 15 million to 10 million. Peace of Westphalia grants Calvinists equal rights and gives subordinate German rulers more independence. Substantial migrations occur, especially Swiss to the Palatinate, to repopulate the most ravaged areas. Restrictive emigration laws make it difficult and expensive to leave certain areas, e.g. Württemberg. Sweden gains control of Western Pomerania and parts of northwestern Germany. France gains control of most of Alsace.
1622	January 1 is declared to be the beginning of the year in Germany (previously it was March 25).
1650-1750	Introduction of church records (baptisms, marriages and deaths) in most German areas (about 1525 in Switzerland already).
1677	Changing of surnames is forbidden in Bavaria.
1678-79	Alsace acquired by France by the Treaty of Nijmegen.
1683	*Start of German group immigration to North America.*

1683	Turks are defeated at the gates of Vienna. Austria acquires substantial Turkish territories in the Balkans by 1699 treaty, which leads to heavy migration from western Germanic areas to repopulate devastated lands.
1685	King Louis XIV of France revokes the Edict of Nantes, which had granted freedom of religion. Persecution and forcible conversion of Huguenots (French Protestants) causes hundreds of thousands to flee to Switzerland, Germany, the Netherlands, Great Britain and North America. Friedrich Wilhelm, the Great Elector, helps many immigrate to Brandenburg.
1687-88	Transylvania reconquered by Austria (recognized by treaty, 1699). Later becomes haven for Austrian Protestants.
1689-97	War of the League of Augsburg results in French burning down many towns in the Palatinate and mass flight of the population.
1701	Brandenburg becomes the Kingdom of Prussia.
1710-11	*First relatively large-scale immigration of Swiss and Palatines to the American colonies.*
1718	The Banat (lower Danube) reconquered by Austria; is Austrian crownland, 1718-99.
1731-38	*Expulsion of Salzburger Protestants from the Austrian Empire, some of whom come to America, most going to East Prussia and other European areas. Schwenkfelders and Moravian Brethren also come to America in 1733-41.*
1740	Freedom of worship decreed in Prussia.
1740-48	War of the Austrian Succession involves much of Europe, with Prussia gaining most of Silesia.
1744-72	Second phase of "Great Swabian Migration" to the Lower Danube. (First wave, 1718-37, was largely wiped out by Turkish border raids.)
1749-53	*Peak of Germanic immigration to colonial America, mostly from near the Rhine valley.*
1750	*First group immigration of Germans to Canada (via Rotterdam to Quebec).*
1750-1800	*Many German soldiers (mostly from North Germany) in the service of the Dutch East Indies Co. settle in South Africa (Cape Province).*
1756-63	Very destructive Seven Years' War, involving all major European powers, leads to prolonged Austrian-Prussian rivalry for German leadership.
1763	Catherine the Great's manifesto invites Germans to settle in Russia and grants them free land, freedom from military service and many special privileges.
1764-67	Heavy immigration of Germans to the Volga River region in Russia.
1767	Changing of surnames is forbidden in the Austrian Empire.
1768-1812	Three Russo-Turkish Wars open up newly acquired "South Russia" (Ukraine) to colonization.
1771	Decree ending use of patronymic surnames in Schleswig-Holstein.
1772-95	Partition of Poland by Russia, Prussia and Austria in three stages: 1772, 1793 and 1795. Poland disappears as an independent country until 1918.
1775	Austria gains the Bukovina from Turkey.
1775-83	*American Revolutionary War, with independence declared in 1776. Thirty thousand Hessian and other German mercenaries fight for Great Britain. Thousands remain in the United States and Canada after the war.*

1781	The Patent of Tolerance guarantees freedom of religion in Austria and opens the way for immigration of Protestants.
1781-1864	Serfdom is abolished in Northern Europe, but with steps toward it as early as 1718. Key dates: Austria (1781, again in 1848 after being reinstituted); France (1789); Prussia (1807); all German territory (by 1848); Hungary (1853-54); Russia (1861); Russian Poland and Romania (1864).
1782-87	Third wave of Danube Swabian migration, accompanied by migration to Galicia and the Bukovina.
1785-1844	Jews required to adopt family names in all Austrian-ruled lands except Hungary (1785-87), in France and Germany (1808-12), and in Russia and Poland (1844).
1786	*German Mennonites from Pennsylvania begin to emigrate to Ontario, more heavily after 1807.*
1789-1824	Heaviest German immigration to the Black Sea region of Russia (now Ukraine).
1789-1917	Jewish people are emancipated granting them equality by law in France (1789), Prussia (1850), Austro-Hungarian Empire (1867), Germany (1871), Switzerland (1874) and Russia (1917).
1792-1815	Wars against revolutionary France by Prussia, Austria and other countries. Napoleon forces the end of the Holy Roman Empire in 1806, with the Hapsburg family continuing to rule Austria, but no longer influential in Germany. Rhenish Confederation is founded in 1806. Civil registration is introduced in France and western Germany. In 1815, the Congress of Vienna establishes the German Confederation of 39 sovereign states, in which Prussia has considerable influence. Sweden loses the last of its territory in Germany.
1794	Changing of surnames is forbidden in Prussia.
1795-1835	Russia adopts laws establishing the Pale of Settlement (roughly Ukraine, Bessarabia, Belarus or White Russia, Poland and Lithuania), to which all new Jewish residents are restricted.
1798	Switzerland declares neutrality.
1810-24	*Most Latin American countries gain independence.*
1811	Decree ending use of patronymic surnames in Ostfriesland (East Frisia).
1814	*Cape Province ceded by the Netherlands to Great Britain.*
1816-17	*Crop failures and famine spark the first significant immigration from Germany and Luxembourg to the United States.*
1817	Lutherans and Reformed Churches are ordered to merge into the Evangelical Church in Prussia and merge elsewhere about the same time. Religious groups are ordered to maintain vital records in what is now Romania.
1822-1889	*Independent Empire of Brazil; changed to a republic after the 1888 abolition of slavery.*
1824-29	*Heavy German immigration to Brazil, especially from Rhineland-Palatinate and Hesse.*
1830	*Gradually increasing German emigration to the United States and Canada, coinciding with the beginning of the Industrial Revolution at home.*

1838-54	*Main wave of emigration of "Old Lutherans," who rejected the Evangelical merger, to New York, Wisconsin, Missouri, Michigan and Texas. About one third went to Australia (mostly South Australia) and some to Canada.*
1843	Polish uprisings against Prussia and Austria fail.
1843-59	*First large wave of German emigrants to the United States (1846-1857), especially from the Palatinate and the Rhineland. This emigration peaks in 1854 and is largely stopped by the Panic of 1857. Most German immigration to Texas occurs during this period. German colonization societies spring up. Public subsidies and even coercion cause many German paupers to go to the United States, and Brazil (1846-59). Others go to Canada and Chile (1846-66, especially 1852-57). Some, including Swiss, go to New Zealand (1843-45) and assisted farm laborers go to Australia (mostly New South Wales). Many leave Europe after the crop failures of 1845-47, which affects most of Europe and are accompanied by famine and cholera epidemics. Others escape after the 1848-49 revolutions are crushed throughout Germany and in other European countries. This coincides with a period of American boom.*
1848	National civil registration is adopted in Switzerland (by religious denomination until 1876) after a brief civil war. Prior registration was at the cantonal level.
1851 ff.	*Australian Gold Rush, especially in Victoria, attracts many Germans from South Australia, New Zealand and elsewhere.*
1857-58	*Depression in the United States (Panic of 1857).*
1857-59	*Large wave of German military and civilian immigrants to South Africa (British Kaffraria, i.e., eastern Cape Province).*
1861-65	*American Civil War.*
1861-1900	Heaviest immigration of Germans to Volhynia, mostly from Poland, sparked mostly by abolition of Russian serfdom and rising Polish nationalism.
1861-86	*Relatively strong immigration from diverse Germanic areas (many from Hanover, Polish and Czech areas) to New Zealand, sparked partly by discovery of gold on West Coast of South Island.*
1861-91	*Rapid increase in German immigration to Queensland (especially from Mecklenburg to Silesia and east), making it the Australian state with the most Germans.*
1862	*Morrill Act makes free land available in the United States.*
1863-64	Second Polish uprising against Russia.
1864	Austria and Prussia defeat Denmark.
1865	Changing of surnames is forbidden in Lippe.
1865-74	*Second large wave of German emigrants to the United States, peaking in 1873. Many people leave to avoid military service. Others emigrate because the Industrial Revolution destroys cottage industries.*
1866	Prussia defeats Austria. As a result, Austria is forced to share power with Hungary as the Austro-Hungarian Empire is established in 1867.
1867	*Dominion of Canada is created by the British North America Act as a self-governing confederation.*
1870-71	Prussia's victory over France leads to the creation of the (Second) German Empire, taking Alsace-Lorraine from France.

1871	Special privileges of Germans are revoked in Russia, sparking emigration to North and South America.
1871-85	*Heavy German and Swiss immigration to Argentina and Brazil.*
1871-1907	Over 500 killed and thousands made homeless in anti-Jewish pogroms in Russia, with a first serious wave in 1881-83 and a much worse one in 1903-07. This coincides with the forced relocation of all other Russian Jews to the Pale of Settlement in 1882-91, thus leading to emigration of half of the four million Jews, many of them to the United States. Jewish emigration resumes after World War I.
1873-79	*Depression in the United States (Panic of 1873).*
1874-76	Civil registration is required in Prussia (1874) and the rest of the German Empire (1876).
1874-1914	*Many Germans from Eastern Europe, especially Russia but also eastern parts of Austria-Hungary, immigrate to the Great Plains states, Canadian Prairie provinces and Argentina.*
1878	Much of the Ottoman Turkish Empire is broken up, with international recognition of Romanian independence, Russian acquisition of Bessarabian and Caucasus territory, and Austro-Hungarian control over Bosnia and Herzegovina, among other changes.
1878-79	*Last large German immigration to South Africa.*
1880-90	*Largest number of Luxembourg emigrants come to the United States.*
1880-93	*Third wave of German emigrants to the United States, with all-time peak in 1882. Coincides with American economic boom, briefly interrupted by the Depression of 1884.*
1881-88	*Large numbers of Swiss emigrants come to the United States.*
1882-89	*Relatively heavy German (mostly Protestant) immigration to Chile.*
1884-86	*Establishment of German colonies and protectorates in Africa and the Southwest Pacific. Limited immigration, mostly to Namibia (German South-West Africa).*
1890-1914	Heavy migration of Russian Germans into Siberia.
1890	*American frontier officially declared closed. German-Americans start emigrating to Western Canada in considerable numbers.*
1892	*Ellis Island opens as immigration receiving center in New York. Immigrants previously were processed at Castle Garden.*
1893-96	*Economic crisis in the United States ends large-scale immigration from Germany.*
1895	Civil registration adopted in Hungary. Pre-1895 church records collected by the government after World War I.
1901	*Various Australian colonies form Commonwealth of Australia.*
1907	*New Zealand becomes a dominion (had a constitution since 1852.)*
1909-10	*Peak of Transylvanian Saxon immigration to the United States.*
1910	*Union of South Africa is established, following the 1899-1902 Boer War.*
1910-20	*Largest number of Swiss emigrants come to the United States during this period.*
1912-13	First and Second Balkan Wars.

1914-18	World War I, involving almost all of Europe. Bolshevik Revolution of 1917, followed by civil war, causes emigration from Russia. Internment of many German-born residents of the United States and Australia. Hostility toward Germans in Canada.
1917	*Severe discrimination against German-Americans begins with American entry into World War I.*
1919	Transformation of former German possessions into mandates of various Allied powers.
1919-23	Peace of Paris, including the Treaties of St. Germain (with Austria) and Trianon (with Hungary), breaks up the Austro-Hungarian Empire, while the Treaties of St. Germain and Versailles (with Germany) require cession of German and Austrian border territories with a sizable number of Germans to Czechoslovakia, Poland, Italy, France, Belgium and Denmark, creation of the Free City of Danzig, followed by transfer of the Memel region to Lithuania in 1923. German colonies and protectorates become Allied mandates, nominally under supervision of the League of Nations.
1921-23	Germany endures extreme inflation ($1 = 4 billion marks).
1921-24	*Immigration is severely curtailed by new American laws.*
1923-30	*Immigration of Mennonite refugees from the Bolshevik Revolution in Russia to Canada and Latin America. Simultaneous emigration of Western Canadian Mennonites to Mexico and Paraguay. Catholic and Lutheran refugees from the Soviet Union settle in southern Brazil.*
1924-41	Autonomous Soviet Socialist Republic of Volga Germans is formed.
1929	Beginning of worldwide Great Depression, ended by World War II.
1932	Germany has 6 million unemployed.
1933-45	Adolf Hitler is the *Führer* (leader) of the Third Reich in Germany.
1934	*American immigration restrictions are eased somewhat to allow entry of political refugees from Nazi Germany. A large number go to all countries in the Americas, especially in and after 1938.*
1938	Hitler annexes Austria and the Sudetenland region of Czechoslovakia.
1939-45	World War II, with German casualties of 3.8 million civilians and 4 million soldiers. Nazis kill 12 million civilians, half of them Jews. Total war deaths are about 25 million; Russia, Germany, Poland and Yugoslavia have the greatest losses.
1939	Hitler-Stalin Pact provides for repatriation of Germans in Stalin's sphere of influence in Eastern Europe (but not in the Soviet Union itself) to the "homeland," mostly the Warta River region in German-occupied Western Poland.
1941-42	Deportation of most Germans living east of the Dnieper River to the Asian portion of the Soviet Union and other remote areas (with most families split apart), after Hitler attacks Russia. Most of those west of the Dnieper River are saved by the rapid advance of the German armies.
1944-48	Mass flight of Germans from Eastern Europe before the advancing Soviet armies, with expulsion of most of the remainder after the end of the war (1945-48), pursuant to the Potsdam Agreement. Many are killed or returned to Soviet control. Population of West Germany increases 25% as 14 million ethnic Germans arrive. Many displaced, stateless persons go on to North and South America and elsewhere.

1944-48	Many Romanian Germans sent to Russian slave labor camps (1944-45, some remaining until the 1950s); Germans in Yugoslavia in concentration camps there (1945-48).
1949	The democratic Federal Republic of Germany and the communist German Democratic Republic are formed.
1949 ff.	*Many Germans emigrate to the United States, Canada, Australia, and Latin America.*
1950s	*Heaviest immigration of Danube Swabians to the United States (Midwest, Northeast and California) and to many other countries, including Canada and Brazil.*
1953	Stalin dies. During the following thaw, Germans are released from slave labor camps, allowing families to re-unite, but not to return to their pre-war homes in the Volga and Black Sea regions. The new eastern German heartland is in Kazakhstan, other Muslim republics, and near the Trans-Siberian Railway.
1961	The Berlin Wall and other border barricades are built to prevent East Germans from fleeing the German Democratic Republic for the Federal Republic of Germany.
1980-85	Majority of Germans leave Romania for Germany, with many soon migrating all over the world (1983-85).
1987	*Glasnost* leads to emigration of many ethnic Germans and Jews from the Soviet Union, East Central Europe, and Southeast Europe. Those returning to Germany are known as *Aussiedler* (resettlers). This emigration is still continuing.
1989-1990	The Berlin Wall crumbles after East Germans flee to the West *en masse*. Democratic elections are held throughout East Central Europe, and Germany is reunified as the German Democratic Republic is dissolved and merges into the Federal Republic of Germany.
1991-92	Soviet Union collapses after failed coup. All non-Russian republics declare their independence. Loose Commonwealth of Independent States (excluding the Baltic countries) is established.

Appendix B

MAPS

This selection of maps shows the major areas of German, Austrian and Swiss settlement in Europe throughout modern history. These maps have been selected or created to help locate hard-to-find regions or provinces (not individual towns). The historical maps show some of the many boundary changes that have occurred in Europe.

The following list identifies each map and the page where it appears.

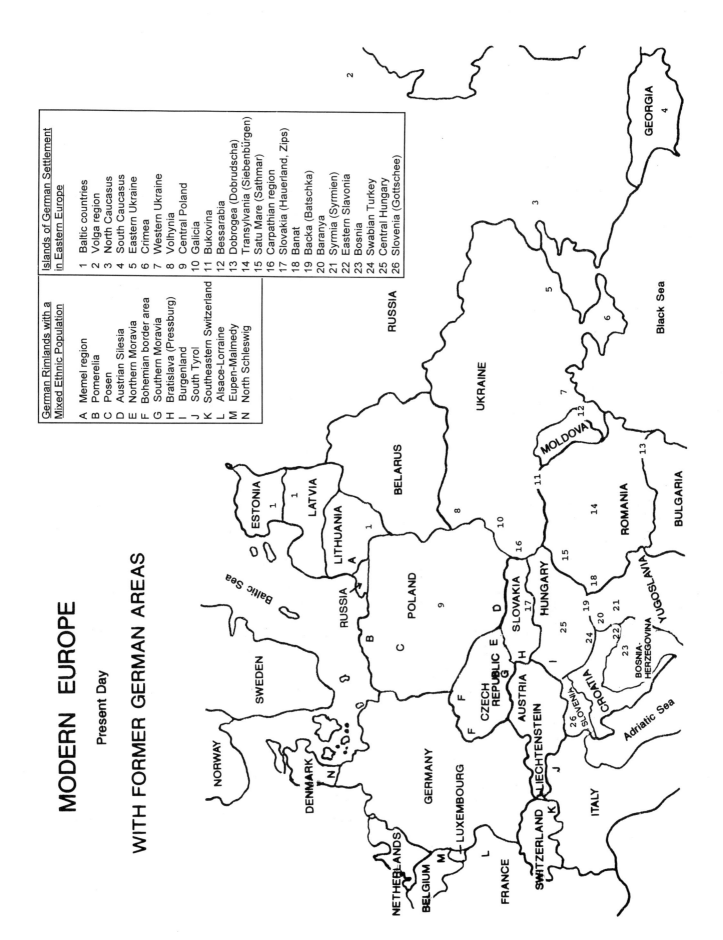

MODERN EUROPE

Present Day

WITH FORMER GERMAN AREAS

German Rimlands with a
Mixed Ethnic Population

A Memel region
B Pomerelia
C Posen
D Austrian Silesia
E Northern Moravia
F Bohemian border area
G Southern Moravia
H Bratislava (Pressburg)
I Burgenland
J South Tyrol
K Southeastern Switzerland
L Alsace-Lorraine
M Eupen-Malmedy
N North Schleswig

Islands of German Settlement
in Eastern Europe

1 Baltic countries
2 Volga region
3 North Caucasus
4 South Caucasus
5 Eastern Ukraine
6 Crimea
7 Western Ukraine
8 Volhynia
9 Central Poland
10 Galicia
11 Bukovina
12 Bessarabia
13 Dobrogea (Dobrudscha)
14 Transylvania (Siebenbürgen)
15 Satu Mare (Sathmar)
16 Carpathian region
17 Slovakia (Hauerland, Zips)
18 Banat
19 Backa (Batschka)
20 Baranya
21 Syrmia (Syrmien)
22 Eastern Slavonia
23 Bosnia
24 Swabian Turkey
25 Central Hungary
26 Slovenia (Gottschee)

CENTRAL and EASTERN EUROPE

After WW II - 1955

NORWAY

FINLAND

SWEDEN

ESTONIAN
S.S.R.

RUSSIAN S.F.S.R.

(includes Kaliningrad enclave)

DENMARK

Baltic Sea

LATVIAN S.S.R.

LITHUANIAN
S.S.R.

• Bremen

NETHERLANDS

EAST

Gdansk

• Kaliningrad

Szczecin

BYELORUSSIAN

S.S.R.

Hannover

W. • E.
Berlin

BELGIUM

WEST

GERMANY

POLAND

• Warsaw

• Frankfurt
am Main

• Leipzig

• Wroclaw

• Brest Litovsk

FRANCE

Strasbourg

GERMANY

• Prague

CZECHOSLOVAKIA

• Cracow

SWITZERLAND

2

Vienna

• Bratislava

MOLDAVIAN
S.S.R.

AUSTRIA

TRANSCARPATHIA

UKRAINIAN S.S.R.

HUNGARY

• Zagreb

ROMANIA

ITALY

Sarajevo •

YUGOSLAVIA

Adriatic Sea

• Bucharest

Black Sea

ALBANIA

BULGARIA

TURKEY

GREECE

—————— current boundaries

- - - - - pre-World War II
boundaries and
boundaries of
Soviet Republics

1. LUXEMBOURG

2. LIECHTENSTEIN

Germanic Genealogy Society

CENTRAL and EASTERN EUROPE

After WW I - 1924

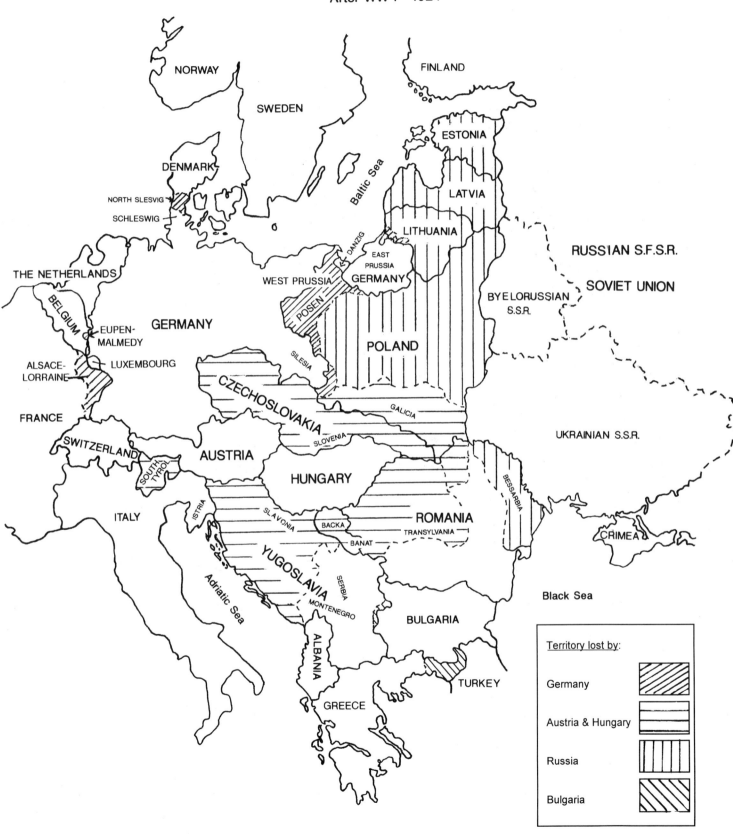

NORWAY

FINLAND

SWEDEN

ESTONIA

DENMARK

Baltic Sea

LATVIA

NORTH SLESVIG

SCHLESWIG

LITHUANIA

RUSSIAN S.F.S.R.

THE NETHERLANDS

DANZIG

EAST PRUSSIA

GERMANY

SOVIET UNION

WEST PRUSSIA

BELGIUM

BYELORUSSIAN S.S.R.

GERMANY

POSEN

EUPEN-MALMEDY

LUXEMBOURG

POLAND

ALSACE-LORRAINE

SILESIA

CZECHOSLOVAKIA

FRANCE

GALICIA

SLOVENIA

UKRAINIAN S.S.R.

SWITZERLAND

SOUTH TYROL

AUSTRIA

HUNGARY

ISTRIA

ITALY

BESSARABIA

SLAVONIA

ROMANIA

BACKA

TRANSYLVANIA

BANAT

CRIMEA

YUGOSLAVIA

SERBIA

Adriatic Sea

MONTENEGRO

Black Sea

BULGARIA

ALBANIA

TURKEY

GREECE

Territory lost by:

Germany

Austria & Hungary

Russia

Bulgaria

Germanic Genealogy: A Guide to Worldwide Sources and Migration Patterns   315

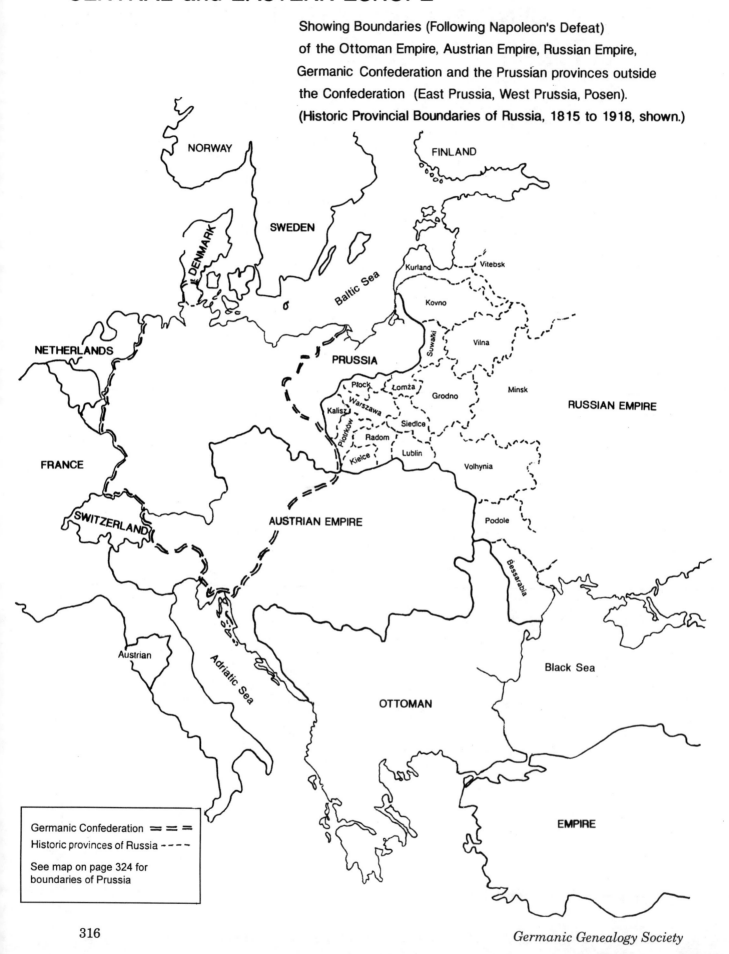

CENTRAL and EASTERN EUROPE – 1815

Showing Boundaries (Following Napoleon's Defeat)
of the Ottoman Empire, Austrian Empire, Russian Empire,
Germanic Confederation and the Prussian provinces outside
the Confederation (East Prussia, West Prussia, Posen).
(Historic Provincial Boundaries of Russia, 1815 to 1918, shown.)

NORWAY

FINLAND

SWEDEN

DENMARK

Baltic Sea

Kurland

Vitebsk

Kovno

NETHERLANDS

PRUSSIA

Suwałki

Vilna

Płock

Łomża

Grodno

Minsk

RUSSIAN EMPIRE

Kalisz

Warszawa

Siedlce

FRANCE

Piotrków

Radom

Lublin

Kielce

Volhynia

SWITZERLAND

AUSTRIAN EMPIRE

Podole

Bessarabia

Austrian

Adriatic Sea

Black Sea

OTTOMAN

EMPIRE

Germanic Confederation = = =
Historic provinces of Russia - - - -

See map on page 324 for
boundaries of Prussia

316

Germanic Genealogy Society

CENTRAL and EASTERN EUROPE - 1721

Showing the de facto Boundary of the Holy Roman Empire,
Habsburg Lands (Austria), Venice and Prussia

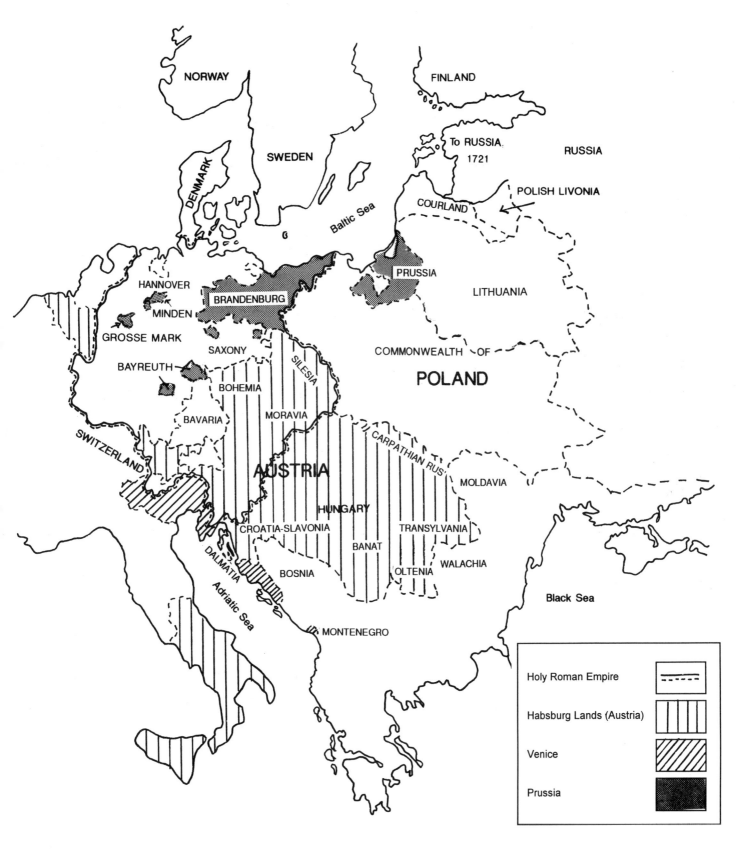

NORWAY

FINLAND

SWEDEN

To RUSSIA
1721

RUSSIA

DENMARK

Baltic Sea

COURLAND

POLISH LIVONIA

HANNOVER

PRUSSIA

BRANDENBURG

LITHUANIA

MINDEN

GROSSE MARK

SAXONY

COMMONWEALTH OF

BAYREUTH

SILESIA

POLAND

BOHEMIA

BAVARIA

MORAVIA

SWITZERLAND

CARPATHIAN RUS

MOLDAVIA

AUSTRIA

HUNGARY

CROATIA-SLAVONIA

TRANSYLVANIA

DALMATIA

BANAT

OLTENIA

WALACHIA

BOSNIA

Adriatic Sea

Black Sea

MONTENEGRO

Holy Roman Empire	
Habsburg Lands (Austria)	
Venice	
Prussia	

GERMAN DIALECTS

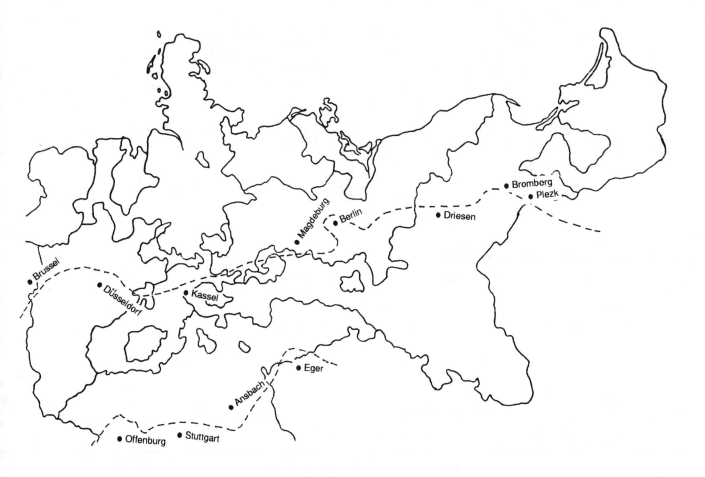

There was a fundamental difference between the German dialects spoken in the northern lowlands (hence the modifier "Low") where Low German served as a *lingua franea* from Flanders to the eastern Baltic, and the dialect spoken farther south. The distinction between the spoken German of Middle Germany and the High German dialects in the south was not as apparent. Since these lines were not entirely stable, depending upon which sounds are used as the criterion for drawing the lines, the map is only an approximation.

EUROPEAN RIVERS CONVERGING TO SEAPORTS

Used in Emigration

FEDERAL REPUBLIC OF GERMANY

(Present Day)

Kiel

SCHLESWIG-HOLSTEIN

Rostock

Lübeck

HAMBURG

MECKLENBURG-VORPOMMERN

Emden

Lüneburg

Oldenburg

Witten-berge

BREMEN

BRANDENBURG

LOWER SAXONY

BERLIN

Rheine

Branden-burg

Osnabrück

Potsdam

Frankfurt (Oder)

Hannover

Münster

Magdeburg

SAXONY-ANHALT

NORTHRHINE-WESTPHALIA

Kassel

Leipzig

Köln

Dresden

Aachen

Weimar

SAXONY

THURINGIA

HESSE

Koblenz

Frankfurt
am Main

Trier

Mainz

Würzburg

RHINELAND-PALATINATE

Darmstadt

SAARLAND

Nürnberg

Heidelberg

Regensburg

Karlsruhe

BAVARIA

Stuttgart

BADEN-WÜRTTEMBERG

Augsburg

München

Freiburg
im Breisgau

Rosenheim

Konstanz

FEDERAL REPUBLIC OF GERMANY

(West Germany)

1949-1990

SCHLESWIG-HOLSTEIN

BREMEN

Bremerhaven

HAMBURG

NIEDERSACHSEN (Lower Saxony)

WEST BERLIN

NORDRHEIN-WESTFALEN

(Northrhine-Westphalia)

HESSEN (Hesse)

RHEINLAND-PFALZ

(Rhineland-Palatinate)

SAARLAND

BAYERN (Bavaria)

BADEN-WÜRTTEMBERG

GERMAN DEMOCRATIC REPUBLIC
(East Germany)

1949-1990

BEZIRKE

450 Berlin (Ost)
451 Rostock
452 Schwerin
453 Neubrandenburg
454 Potsdam
455 Frankfurt
456 Cottbus
457 Magdeburg
458 Halle
459 Erfurt
461 Gera
462 Suhl
463 Dresden
464 Leipzig
465 Karl-Marx-Stadt

Kartographie: Institut für Landeskunde

Germanic Genealogy Society

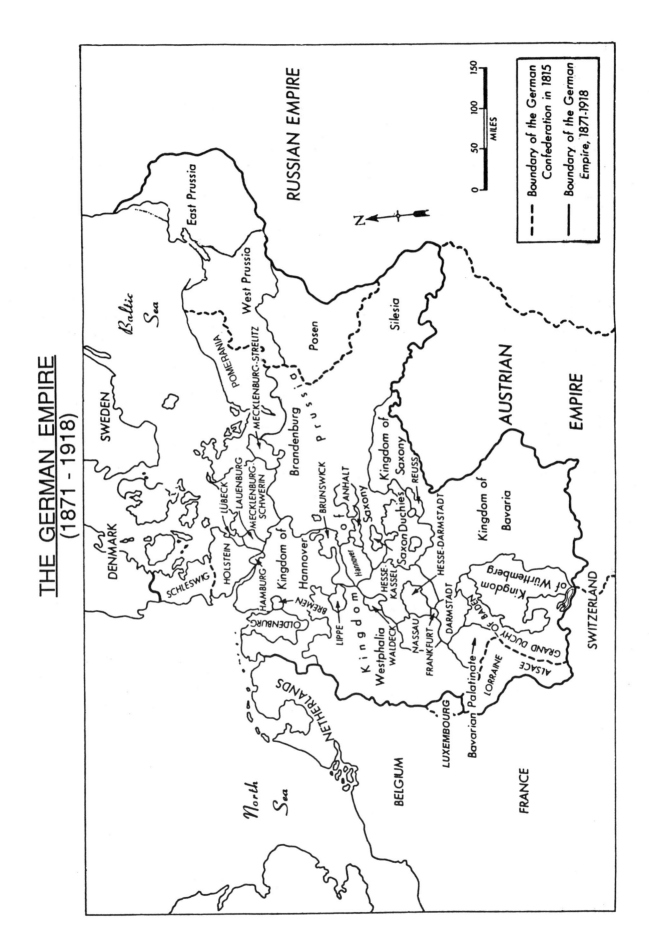

THE GERMAN EMPIRE
(1871 - 1918)

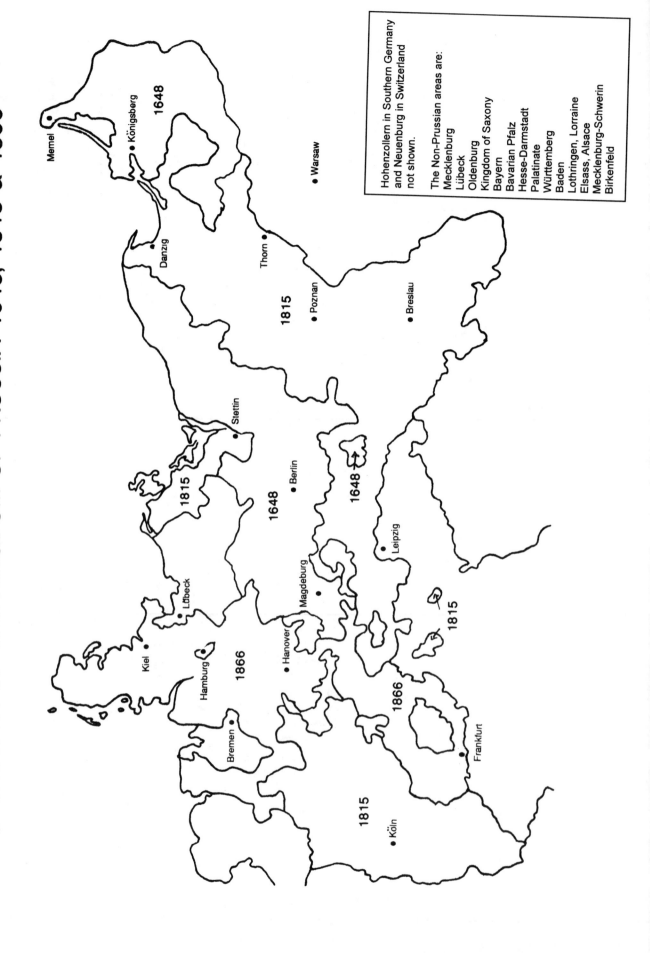

THE GROWTH OF THE KINGDOM OF PRUSSIA 1648, 1815 & 1866

Hohenzollern in Southern Germany
and Neuenburg in Switzerland
not shown.

The Non-Prussian areas are:
Mecklenburg
Lübeck
Oldenburg
Kingdom of Saxony
Bayern
Bavarian Pfalz
Hesse-Darmstadt
Palatinate
Württemberg
Baden
Lothringen, Lorraine
Elsass, Alsace
Mecklenburg-Schwerin
Birkenfeld

Memel

• Königsberg

1648

• Warsaw

Danzig

Thorn

• Poznan

1815

• Breslau

Stettin

1815

Berlin

1648

1648

• Leipzig

1815

Lübeck

1866

Magdeburg

Kiel

Hanover

Hamburg

1866

Bremen

1815

Frankfurt

1815

• Köln

Germanic Genealogy Society

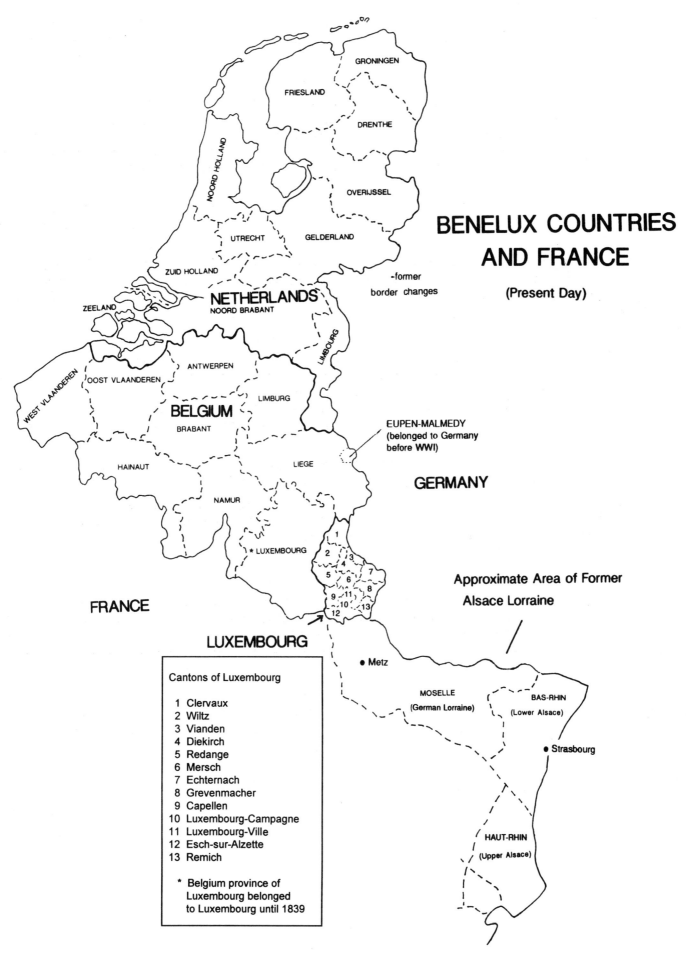

BENELUX COUNTRIES
AND FRANCE

(Present Day)

GRONINGEN

FRIESLAND

DRENTHE

NOORD HOLLAND

OVERIJSSEL

UTRECHT

GELDERLAND

ZUID HOLLAND

-former
border changes

NETHERLANDS

ZEELAND

NOORD BRABANT

LIMBOURG

WEST VLAANDEREN

OOST VLAANDEREN

ANTWERPEN

LIMBURG

BELGIUM

BRABANT

EUPEN-MALMEDY
(belonged to Germany
before WWI)

HAINAUT

LIEGE

GERMANY

NAMUR

* LUXEMBOURG

Approximate Area of Former
Alsace Lorraine

FRANCE

LUXEMBOURG

● Metz

MOSELLE
(German Lorraine)

BAS-RHIN
(Lower Alsace)

● Strasbourg

Cantons of Luxembourg

1 Clervaux
2 Wiltz
3 Vianden
4 Diekirch
5 Redange
6 Mersch
7 Echternach
8 Grevenmacher
9 Capellen
10 Luxembourg-Campagne
11 Luxembourg-Ville
12 Esch-sur-Alzette
13 Remich

* Belgium province of
  Luxembourg belonged
  to Luxembourg until 1839

HAUT-RHIN
(Upper Alsace)

SWITZERLAND and LIECHTENSTEIN
(Present - Day)

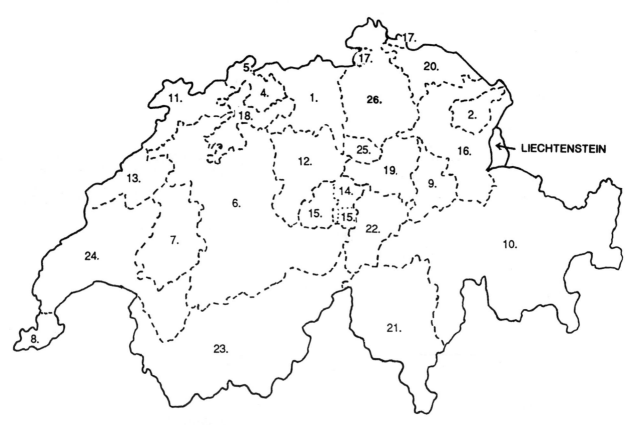

<u>Cantons of Switzerland</u> are listed below in 3 or 4 languages, the bold-faced ones indicating the principal language or languages spoken. Language is indicated by (Ger.) Swiss-German; (Fr.) French; (It.) Italian; and (Rom.) Romansch. Date indicates entry into Swiss Confederation.

1. **Aargau (Ger.)**, Argovie (Fr.), Argovia (It.)	1803
2. **Appenzell Inner-Rhoden (Ger.)**, Rhodes-Interieures (Fr.)	1513
3. **Appenzell Ausser-Rhoden (Ger.)**, Rhodes-Exterieures (Fr.)	1513
4. **Basel-Land (Ger.)**, Bâle-Campagne (Fr.), Basilea-Campagna (It.)	1501
5. **Basel-Stadt (Ger.)**, Bâle-Ville (Fr.), Basilea-Citta (It.)	1501
6. **Bern (Ger.)**, Berne (Fr.), Berna (It.)	1353
7. **Fribourg (Fr.), Freiburg (Ger.)**, Friborgo (It.)	1481
8. **Genève (Fr.)**, Genf (Ger.), Ginevra (It.)	1815
9. **Glarus (Ger.)**, Glaris (Fr.), Glarona (It.)	1352
10. **Graubünden (Ger.), Grischun (Rom.), Grigioni (It.)**, Grisons (Fr.)	1803
11. **Jura (Fr.)**, Jura (Ger.) *Separated from Bern Canton	*1974
12. **Luzern (Ger.)**, Lucerne (Fr.), Lucerna (It.)	1332
13. **Neuchâtel (Fr.)**, Neuenburg (Ger.), Neuchâtel (It.)	1815
14. **Nidwalden (Ger.)**, Nidwald (Fr.), Sottoselva (It.)	1291
15. **Obwalden (Ger.)**, Obwald (Fr.), Sopraselva (It.)	1291
16. **Sankt Gallen (Ger.)**, Saint Gall (Fr.), S. Gallo (It.)	1803
17. **Schaffhausen (Ger.)**, Schaffhouse (Fr.), Sciaffusa (It.)	1501
18. **Solothurn (Ger.)**, Soleure (Fr.), Soletta (It.)	1481
19. **Schwyz (Ger.)**, Schwyz (Fr.), Svitto (It.)	1291
20. **Thurgau (Ger.)**, Thurgovie (Fr.), Turgovia (It.)	1803
21. **Ticino (It.)**, Tessin (Ger., Fr.)	1803
22. **Uri (Ger., Fr., It.)**	1291
23. **Valais (Fr.), Wallis (Ger.)**, Vallese (It.)	1815
24. **Vaud (Fr.)**, Waadt (Ger.), Vaud (It.)	1803
25. **Zug (Ger.)**, Zoug (Fr.), Zugo (It.)	1352
26. **Zürich (Ger.)**, Zurich (Fr.), Zurigo (It.)	1351

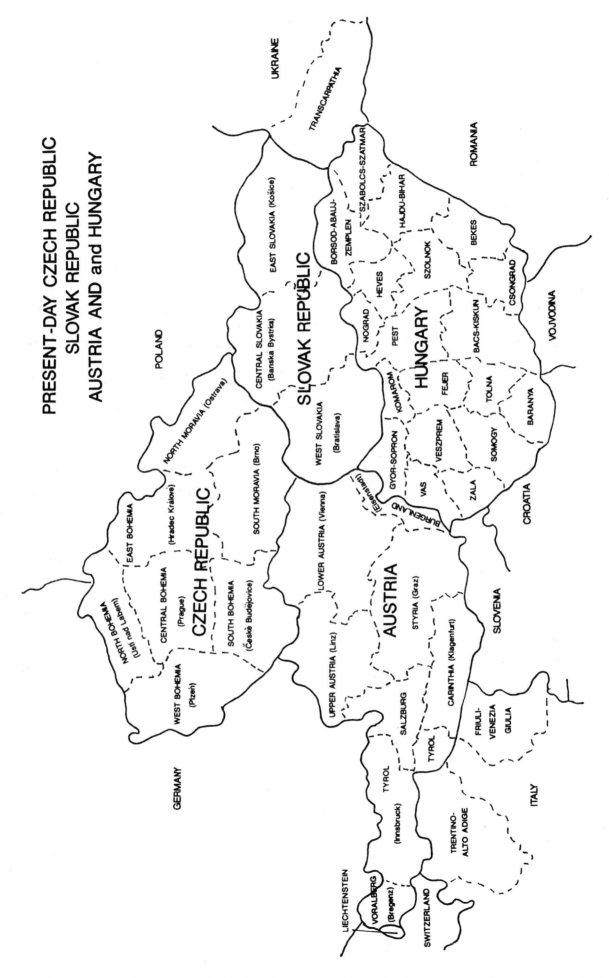

PRESENT-DAY CZECH REPUBLIC
SLOVAK REPUBLIC
AUSTRIA AND and HUNGARY

UKRAINE

TRANSCARPATHIA

ROMANIA

SZABOLCS-SZATMAR

BORSOD-ABAUJ-
ZEMPLEN

EAST SLOVAKIA (Košice)

HAJDU-BIHAR

SZOLNOK

POLAND

HEVES

BEKES

NOGRAD

CSONGRAD

CENTRAL SLOVAKIA
(Banská Bystrica)

SLOVAK REPUBLIC

PEST

BACS-KISKUN

VOJVODINA

NORTH MORAVIA (Ostrava)

HUNGARY

KOMAROM

FEJER

TOLNA

WEST SLOVAKIA
(Bratislava)

SOUTH MORAVIA (Brno)

GYOR-SOPRON

BARANYA

EAST BOHEMIA

(Hradec Králové)

VESZPREM

SOMOGY

(Eisenstadt)

CZECH REPUBLIC

CENTRAL BOHEMIA
(Prague)

VAS

ZALA

BURGENLAND

LOWER AUSTRIA (Vienna)

CROATIA

NORTH BOHEMIA
(Ústí nad Labem)

SOUTH BOHEMIA
(Českè Budějovice)

SLOVENIA

WEST BOHEMIA
(Plzeň)

STYRIA (Graz)

GERMANY

UPPER AUSTRIA (Linz)

AUSTRIA

CARINTHIA (Klagenfurt)

SALZBURG

FRIULI-
VENEZIA
GIULIA

TYROL

TYROL

ITALY

(Innsbruck)

TRENTINO-
ALTO ADIGE

LIECHTENSTEIN

VORALBERG
(Bregenz)

SWITZERLAND

GERMAN EASTERN REGIONS
and the Sudetenland 1918-1938

DENMARK AND NORTH SCHLESWIG

Legend:
- German border 1937
- Oder-Neisse-line and Polish-Soviet Demarcation line
- German border until 1918
- Sudetenland 1938
- Teschener Silesia
- Province boundaries
- Other boundaries

DENMARK (Present Day)

Approximate Area of Former Schleswig

Germanic Genealogy Society

GERMAN SETTLEMENTS IN THE AUSTRO-HUNGARIAN EMPIRE

1867 to 1918

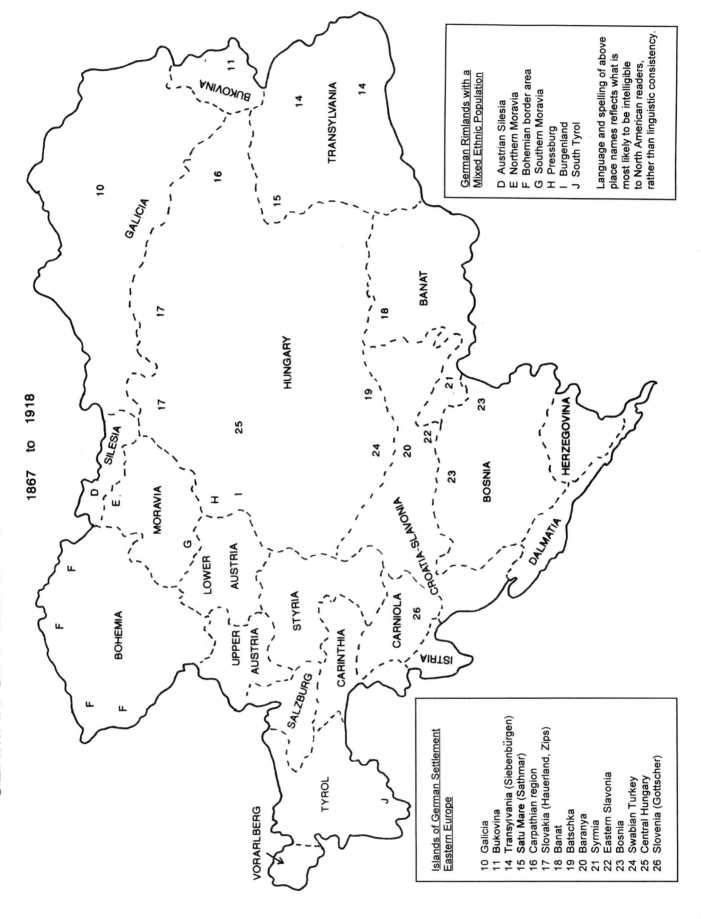

German Rimlands with a Mixed Ethnic Population

D Austrian Silesia
E Northern Moravia
F Bohemian border area
G Southern Moravia
H Pressburg
I Burgenland
J South Tyrol

Language and spelling of above place names reflects what is most likely to be intelligible to North American readers, rather than linguistic consistency.

Islands of German Settlement Eastern Europe

10 Galicia
11 Bukovina
14 Transylvania (Siebenbürgen)
15 Satu Mare (Sathmar)
16 Carpathian region
17 Slovakia (Hauerland, Zips)
18 Banat
19 Batschka
20 Baranya
21 Syrmia
22 Eastern Slavonia
23 Bosnia
24 Swabian Turkey
25 Central Hungary
26 Slovenia (Gottscher)

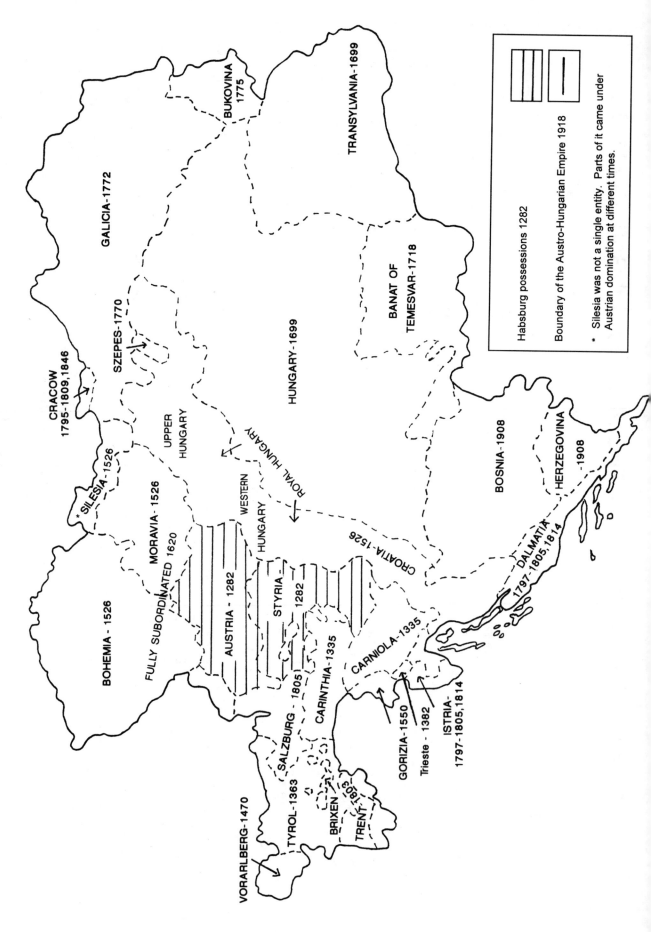

GROWTH OF THE AUSTRO-HUNGARIAN EMPIRE

with dates of annexation of various lands

Legend:

Habsburg possessions 1282

Boundary of the Austro-Hungarian Empire 1918

* Silesia was not a single entity. Parts of it came under Austrian domination at different times.

TRANSYLVANIA-1699

BUKOVINA 1775

GALICIA-1772

CRACOW 1795-1809,1846

SZEPES-1770

SILESIA-1526

BANAT OF TEMESVAR-1718

HUNGARY-1699

UPPER HUNGARY

MORAVIA-1526

FULLY SUBORDINATED 1620

WESTERN HUNGARY

ROYAL HUNGARY

BOHEMIA - 1526

AUSTRIA - 1282

STYRIA - 1282

CROATIA-1526

BOSNIA-1908

HERZEGOVINA -1908

CARNIOLA-1335

CARINTHIA-1335

DALMATIA 1797-1805,1814

SALZBURG - 1805

GORIZIA-1550

Trieste - 1382

ISTRIA- 1797-1805,1814

VORARLBERG-1470

TYROL-1363

BRIXEN 1803

TRENT-1803

DIVISION OF AUSTRO-HUNGARIAN EMPIRE

after World War I. 1918-1923

MOLDAVIA

BUKOVINA

ROMANIA

BULGARIA

WALACHIA

GALICIA

(To Poland)

(To Czechoslovakia)

Current Ukraine

CARPATHIAN RUTH.

RUTHENIA

TRANSYLVANIA

(To Romania)

POLAND

Current Slovak Republic

(To Czechoslovakia)

BANAT

SERBIA

HUNGARY

BACKA

YUGOSLAVIA

GERMANY

BOHEMIA (To Czechoslovakia)

Current Czech Republic

(To Yugoslavia)

Joint Imperial Rule

(To Yugoslavia)

BOSNIA-HERZEGOVINA

BURGENLAND

AUSTRIA

CARNIOLA

(To Yugoslavia)

(To Italy)

ISTRIA

DALMATIA

(To Yugoslavia)

VENETIA

SWITZERLAND

SOUTH TYROL

(To Italy)

ITALY

LOMBARDY

Hungarian areas given
to successor states

Austrian areas given
to successor states

Hungarian area
given to Austria

POLAND
(Present Day)

Black Sea

RUSSIA

LITHUANIA

SŁUPSK

GDAŃSK

ELBLĄG

SUWAŁKI

KOSZALIN

OLSZTYN

SZCZECIN

BYDGOSZCZ

PIŁA

TORUŃ

ŁOMŻA

OSTROŁĘKA

BIAŁYSTOK

GORZÓW WIELKOPOLSKI

WŁOCŁAWEK

CIECHANÓW

GERMANY

POZNAŃ

PŁOCK

KONIN

WARSZAWA

BELARUS

SIEDLCE

ZIELONA GORA

SKIERNIEWICE

ŁÓDŹ

BIAŁA PODLASKA

LESZNO

KALISZ

ZGORZELEC

LEGNICA

ZDUŃSKA WOLA

RADOM

WROCŁAW

PIOTRKÓW TRYBUNALSKI

LUBLIN

CHEŁM

KAMIENNA

GÓRA

OPOLE

CZĘSTOCHOWA

KIELCE

TARNOBRZEG

ZAMOŚĆ

CZECH REPUBLIC

KATOWICE

CRACOW

TARNÓW

RZESZÓW

PRZEMYŚL

BIELSKO BIAŁA

NOWY SĄCZ

KROSNO

UKRAINE

SLOVAK REPUBLIC

The northern, western and southwestern provinces (*voivodships*) of Poland once constituted parts of the German (Prussian) Provinces of East Prussia, West Prussia, Posen, Pomerania, Brandenburg and Silesia.

Germanic Genealogy Society

THE PARTITION OF POLAND
1772-1795

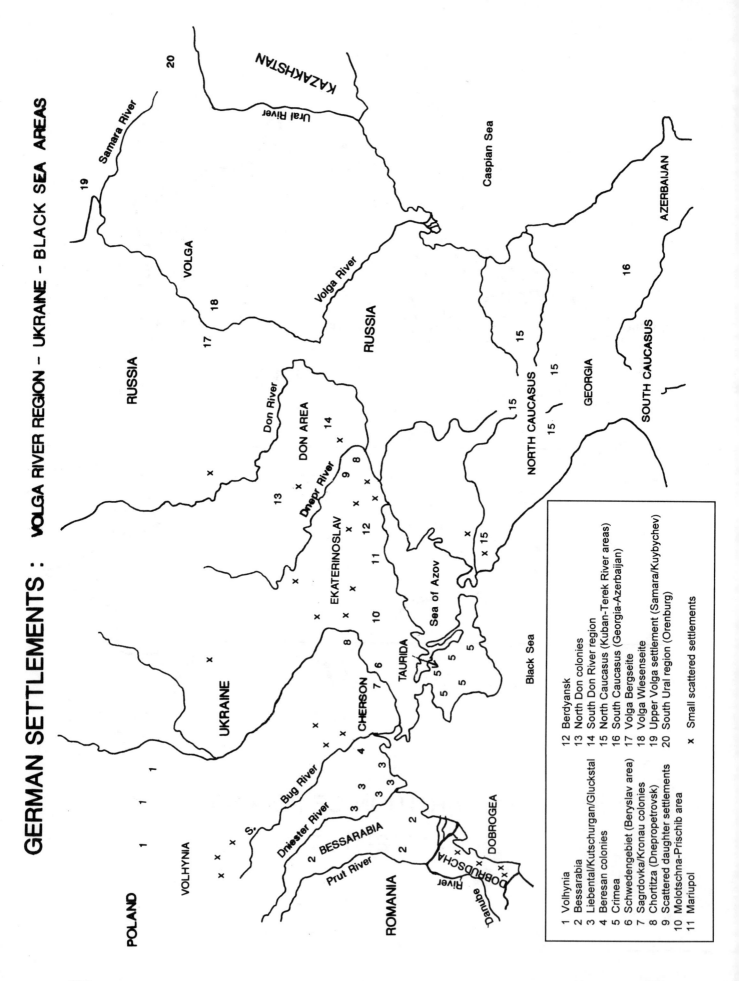

GERMAN SETTLEMENTS : VOLGA RIVER REGION – UKRAINE – BLACK SEA AREAS

KAZAKHSTAN

Samara River

Ural River

20

19

18

17

VOLGA

Caspian Sea

Volga River

RUSSIA

AZERBAIJAN

16

15

15

NORTH CAUCASUS

15

GEORGIA

SOUTH CAUCASUS

RUSSIA

Don River

DON AREA

14

13

Dnepr River

9   8

EKATERINOSLAV

12

11

15

10

Sea of Azov

15

8

TAURIDA

6

7   5

5   5

5

5

5

Black Sea

UKRAINE

CHERSON

4

Bug River

3   3

S.

3   3   3

Dniester River

3

BESSARABIA

2   2

2

Prut River

2

DOBRUDSCHA

DOBROGEA

ROMANIA

Danube River

POLAND

VOLHYNIA

1   1   1

1

1

1   Volhynia
2   Bessarabia
3   Liebental/Kutschurgan/Gluckstal
4   Beresan colonies
5   Crimea
6   Schwedengebiet (Beryslav area)
7   Sagrdovka/Kronau colonies
8   Chortitza (Dnepropetrovsk)
9   Scattered daughter settlements
10 Molotschna-Prischib area
11 Mariupol
12 Berdyansk
13 North Don colonies
14 South Don River region
15 North Caucasus (Kuban-Terek River areas)
16 South Caucasus (Georgia-Azerbaijan)
17 Volga Bergseite
18 Volga Wiesenseite
19 Upper Volga settlement (Samara/Kuybychev)
20 South Ural region (Orenburg)
x   Small scattered settlements

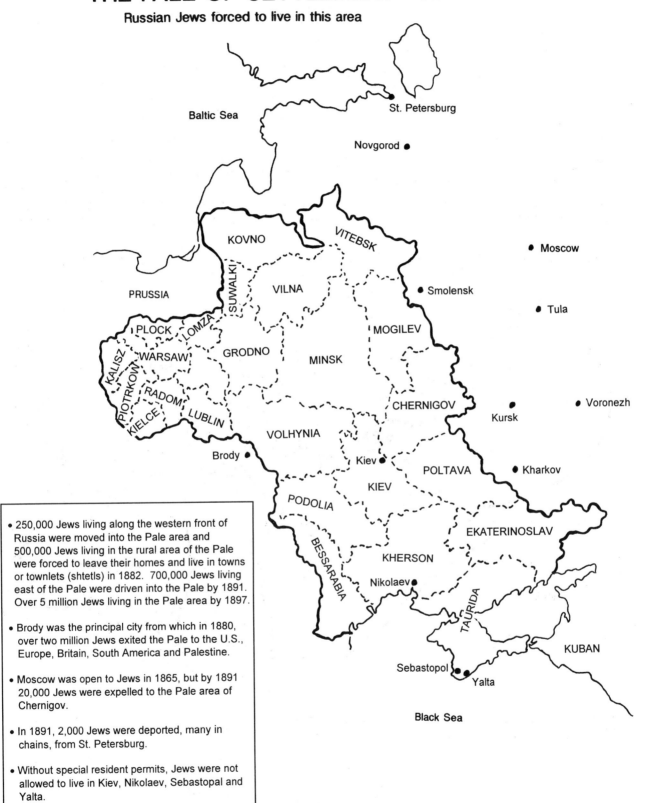

THE PALE OF SETTLEMENT 1835-1917

Russian Jews forced to live in this area

Baltic Sea

St. Petersburg

Novgorod •

KOVNO

VITEBSK

• Moscow

SUWALKI

VILNA

PRUSSIA

• Smolensk

PLOCK

LOMZA

MOGILEV

• Tula

KALISZ

WARSAW

GRODNO

MINSK

PIOTRKOW

RADOM

CHERNIGOV

LUBLIN

KIELCE

VOLHYNIA

• Voronezh

Kursk •

Brody •

Kiev •

POLTAVA

• Kharkov

KIEV

PODOLIA

EKATERINOSLAV

BESSARABIA

KHERSON

Nikolaev •

TAURIDA

KUBAN

Sebastopol •

• Yalta

Black Sea

- 250,000 Jews living along the western front of Russia were moved into the Pale area and 500,000 Jews living in the rural area of the Pale were forced to leave their homes and live in towns or townlets (shtetls) in 1882. 700,000 Jews living east of the Pale were driven into the Pale by 1891. Over 5 million Jews living in the Pale area by 1897.

- Brody was the principal city from which in 1880, over two million Jews exited the Pale to the U.S., Europe, Britain, South America and Palestine.

- Moscow was open to Jews in 1865, but by 1891 20,000 Jews were expelled to the Pale area of Chernigov.

- In 1891, 2,000 Jews were deported, many in chains, from St. Petersburg.

- Without special resident permits, Jews were not allowed to live in Kiev, Nikolaev, Sebastopal and Yalta.

SUCCESSOR STATES TO YUGOSLAVIA

(Present Day)

Vojvodina and Kosovo were autonomous provinces of Serbia. Slovenia, Croatia, Bosnia and Herzegovina, and Macedonia are now independent countries.

Map legend:
1 Belonged to the Austrian part of the Austro-Hungarian Empire.
2 Belonged to the Hungarian part of the Austro-Hungarian Empire.
3 Ruled by the Austro-Hungarian Empire after 1878 and annexed in 1908.
4 Independent prior to 1878.

SOUTH AMERICA AND CENTRAL AMERICA

'Showing Areas Settled by Germans from Russia

BELIZE

VENEZUELA

SURIANAME

GUYANA

F. GUIANA

COLOMBIA

ECUADOR

BRAZIL

PERU

Pacific Ocean

BOLIVIA

SANTA
CRUZ

GRAND CHACO

Rio De Janeiro

PARAGUAY

PARANA

Ponta Grossa

Sao Paulo

Atlantic Ocean

CHILE

MISIONES

Curitiba

CORRIENTES

RIO GRANDE DO SUL

SANTA CATARINA

1

ARGENTINA

2

Porto Alegre

CORDOBA

SANTA FE

ENTRE
RIOS

URUGUAY

Santiago

Montevideo

BUENOS

Buenos Aires

LA PAMPA

AIRES

Azul

Valdivia

1 Formosa
2 Chaco

AUSTRALIA

Showing Areas of German Settlement

WESTERN AUSTRALIA

NORTHERN TERRITORY

SOUTH AUSTRALIA

QUEENSLAND

Cairns

Townsville

Mackay

Rockhampton

Bundaberg

Maryborough

Brisbane

Lismore

Glen Innes

Tamworth

NEW SOUTH WALES

Broken Hill

Cudgegong

Newcastle

Forbes

Wagga Wagga

Albury

Goulburn

Sydney

VICTORIA

Mt. Gambier

Geelong

Melbourne

Port Pirie

Adelaide

Kalgoorlie

Perth

Katanning

German Settlements in Australia

1 Bendigo & Eaglehawk
2 Ballarat & Sebastopol
3 Bathurst
4 Horsham
5 Hamilton
6 Echuca

INDEX

Armgart, Martin, 187
Arndt, Karl J. R., 121, 123
Arndt, Karl R., 8, 14, 274
Arnstein, George, 125, 128
AROS, 200, 211. *See* Archives of
  Russia Society
Asia, 101, 201
Asia Minor, 168
Asian Muslim Republics (CIS), 85,
  104, 215, 311
  Researching in, 215
Assiniboia district, Northwest
  Territories, 279
Assisted Immigration Scheme (New
  Zealand), 160
Astrakhan, Russia, 204
Asunción, Paraguay, 36, 39
Auckland, New Zealand, 26, 46, 47,
  48, 161
Auerbach, Berthold, 128
Auerbacher, Moses Baruch, 128
Aufhausen, Germany, 130
Augsburg Confession, 305
Augsburg, Germany, 228
Aussiedler, 104, 207, 215, 311. *See
  also* Resettlers
Australasia, 244
Australia, 114, 120, 133, 169, 171,
  309
  Archives, 46
  Austrians In, 40
  Church records, 44
  Civil registers, 43
  Colonies, 309
  Gazetteers, 45
  Genealogical societies, 42
  German immigration, 124, 147,
    168, 308
  German language newspapers, 45
  German settlements, 154
  Jews In, 42
  Lutheran records, 44
  Map of, 312
  Marriage records, 44
  National library, 46
  Naturalization records, 45
  Newspapers, 45
  Other records, 45
  Passenger lists, 44
  State libraries, 46
  Swiss In, 40, 105
Australian Capital Territory,
  Australia, 43
Austria, 37, 76, 79, 109, 128, 129,
  160, 174, 192, 205, 220, 221, 290,
  304, 306, 307, 308, 310
  Archives, 284
  Church records, 118, 191, 284
  Civil records, 193, 219
  Emigration records, 194
  Family histories, 125
  Gazetteers, 65, 70, 72, 191
  Genealogical societies, 194, 284

Austria (*continued*)
  German emigration, 142, 143,
    148, 151, 153, 159, 160, 161,
    169
  History, 66, 77, 78, 84, 88, 90,
    92–99, 100, 106, 125, 138, 141,
    149, 191, 220, 222, 227, 230,
    232, 306, 307, 308
  Land cadasters, 224
  Map of, 312
  Microfilms, 16, 17
  Military records, 193
  Miscellaneous records, 193
  National archives, 193, 194
  Periodicals, 291
  Postal codes, 74, 287
  Provinces, 191
  Records, 118
  Religions, 116
  Researching in, 175, 191
  State archives, 225
  States, 83
  Treaty of St. Germain, 75
Austrian Empire, 112, 113, 125, 126,
  132, 133, 304, 306
  Gazetteers, 73
  History, 76, 89, 91, 92–99, 94, 98,
    140, 191, 219
  Religions, 306
  States, 76, 191
Austrian Military Border, 107
Austrian Protestants, 113
Austrian Silesia, 73, 76, 78, 84, 85,
  192
  German emigration, 152
  History, 95, 126, 217
  Researchers, 187
Austrians
  In Australia, 40
  In Brazil, 148
  In Chile, 151
  In New Zealand, 159
  In South Tyrol, 109
Austro-Hungarian Empire, 72, 114,
  117, 142, 202, 212, 275, 309, 310
  Atlases, 73
  Church records, 193
  German emigration, 144, 146,
    151, 161
  History, 77, 78, 84, 89, 92–99,
    140, 191, 193, 198, 219, 229,
    308
  Map of, 312
  Military records, 216
Azerbaijan, 85
  Researching in, 215

—B—

Bach, Adolf, 60, 63
Backa, 79, 85, 231. *See also* Bácska,
  Yugoslavia. *See also* Batschka
Bacs Bodrog, Hungary, 276

Bácska, Yugoslavia, 79, 192. *See
  also* Batschka. *See also* Backa
  History, 85, 97
Bad Buchau, Germany, 126
Bad Karlshofen, Germany, 189
Bade, James N., 137, 159, 160, 168
Baden, 19, 76, 77, 81, 90, 125, 130,
  134, 144, 166, 173, 176, 289
  Emigration, 284
  German emigration, 102, 140,
    144, 159, 164
  History, 98
  State archives, 178
Baden-Württemberg, 79, 81, 83, 112,
  125, 279
  Genealogical societies, 181
  History, 91
  Records, 126, 127
  State archives, 177
Baeck Institute. *See* Leo Baeck
  Institute
Baginsky, Paul Ben, 286
Bahia, Brazil, 147
Bahlow, Hans, 62, 64
Bahr, Marion, 199, 288
Bailliere, F. F., 45
Baisingen, Germany, 132
Baker, Zachary M., 132
Balch Institute of Ethnic Studies, 199
Balkan region, 93, 306
Balkan Wars, 309
Ballarat, Victoria, 158
Baltic countries, 84, 99, 100, 103,
  104, 207, 311. *See also* Lithuania.
  See also Latvia. *See also* Estonia
  Genealogical societies, 187
  German colonization, 99
  German emigration, 144
  Lutheran Consistories, 203
  Lutheran parishes, 203
  Microfilms, 16
  Records, 127
  Researchers, 199
Baltic Sea, 81
Baltimore, Maryland, 24, 25
Balzekas Museum of Lithuanian
  Culture, Chicago, 210
Bamberg, Bavaria, 82
Bamberger, Naftali Bar-Giori, 128
Banat, 66, 79, 97, 192, 231, 306
  Banat Listserver, 301
  Church registers, 284
  Gazetteers, 66
  German emigration, 98
  History, 78, 85, 93
Bangladesh, 56
Banja Luka, Bosnia, 97
Banská Bystrica, Slovak Republic,
  219
Baptist Brethren, 111, 121
  Records, 120
Baptists, 111, 144, 172, 205
  In Argentina, 145
  In Australia, 44, 159

Bohemian Germans (*continued*)
   In United States, 124, 149, 218, 281, 283, 289
   In Venezuela, 153
Böhmen, 192. *See also* Bohemia
Böhmerwald, 79
Bolivia, 152
   Civil registers, 36
   German immigration, 37, 146
   German settlements, 146
Bolotenko, George, 213
Bolshevik Revolution, 104, 114, 138, 310
Bolzano, Italy, 95, 221, 222, 289. *See also* Bozen, Italy
Bonjour, Edgar, 107
Bonn, Germany, 279
Bopfingen, Germany, 130
Bork, Inge, 284
Bornemann, Irma, 107
Borneo, 56
Borrie, W. D., 45, 154, 155, 156, 157, 158
Borussians, 99. *See also* Prussians
Bosnia, 93, 97, 192, 229, 309
   German immigration, 113
   History, 77, 78
Bosnia-Herzegovina, 192
   History, 229
   National archives, 230
   Researching in, 229
Bosnien, 192. *See also* Bosnia
Boston, Massachusetts, 24, 25, 143
Bounty land property, 9
Bovenizer, Austin, 236
Boyer, Carl, 24
Boys Town (Nebraska), 7
Bozen, Italy, 95, 221, 222, 289. *See also* Bolzano, Italy
   Records, 194
Brachwitz, Heike, 185
Brandenburg, 19, 76, 77, 81, 82, 83, 90, 112, 113, 116, 164, 166, 236, 274, 279, 282, 289, 305, 306, 331
   German emigration, 157, 161
   History, 78, 84, 89, 91, 242
   Records, 247
   Researchers, 187
   State archives, 178
Brandt, Bruce, 61, 225, 275
Brandt, Edward Reimer, 61, 194, 199, 225, 275
Brasov, Romania, 82, 289. *See also* Kronstadt
Bratislava, Slovak Republic, 85, 96, 219. *See also* Pressburg
Brauer, A., 45
Braun, Peter J., Molotschna Mennonite records collection, 205
Braunsberg, East Prussia, 80
Braunschweig, 19, 77. *See also* Brunswick
   State archives, 179

Brazil, 35, 38, 120, 133, 145, 148, 153, 159, 169, 170, 171, 215, 228, 307, 308, 309
   Census records, 37
   Civil registers, 36
   Genealogical societies, 40
   German immigration, 37, 95, 146, 147, 148, 149, 167, 274
   German settlements, 146
   History, 37
   Military records, 38
   National archives, 39, 149
   National library, 38
   Records at Family History Library, 35
   Southern, 35
Brechenmacher, Josef Karlmann, 64
Brecht, Samuel Kriebel, 121
Breimesser, H., 130
Breisgau, Germany, 79, 130
Bremen, Germany, 19, 24, 44, 76, 77, 83, 90, 91, 112, 141, 160, 170, 279
   Genealogical societies, 182
   German emigration, 159
   History, 242
   Passenger lists, 23, 24, 289
   State archives, 178
Brenham, Texas, 142
Brenner Pass, Austria/Italy, 96, 221
Breslau, Germany, 163, 243
Brest Litovsk, Belarus, 81
Brethren, 110, 111, 120, 172, 291
Brisbane, Queensland, 25, 43, 44, 155, 156, 157
Britain, 79, 304. *See also* Great Britain. *See also* United Kingdom
British, 49
British Columbia, Canada
   Civil records, 33
   Homesteading in, 31
   Provincial Archives, 32
British East Africa, 162, 165, 171. *See also* Kenya
British East India Company, 55, 56
British East Indies, 167
British Honduras, 146. *See also* Belize
British Kaffraria, Cape Province, South Africa, 164, 171
Brixen, Italy, 289
Brno, Czech Republic, 95. *See also* Brünn
   Church records, 218
Broken Hill, New South Wales, 42, 156
Bromberg, 187, 289. *See also* Bydgoszcz, Poland
Broome, Western Australia, 159
Brüder-Unität, 110. *See also* Unitas Fratrum
Bruhn, Elmar, 187
Brumbaugh, Gaius M., 277
Brumbaugh, Martin G., 123
Brunei, 56

Brünn, 95, 218. *See also* Brno, Czech Republic
Brunswick, 19, 76, 77, 289. *See also* Braunschweig
Brussels, Belgium, 112
   National archives, 232
Bubonic plague, 96, 115, 241, 304
Bucharest, Romania, 227
Buchau, Germany, 130
Buchenland, 85, 93. *See also* Bukovina
Bucuresti, Romania, 227
Budapest, Hungary, 85, 97, 191, 220
   Church records, 17
Budweis, 95. *See also* Cesky Budejovice, Czech Republic
Buëa, 167. *See* Buea, Cameroon
Buea, Cameroon, 167
Buenos Aires, Argentina, 38, 39, 40, 145, 146
   Arrival lists, 26
Buffalo, New York, 142
Bug River, Ukraine, 82, 101, 124, 214, 282
Bühl, Germany, 130
Bukke, Inger M., 273, 275
Bukovina, 107, 109, 114, 123, 148, 149, 153, 192, 212, 277, 281, 288, 289, 306
   Church records, 288
   German emigration, 40, 141, 143, 148, 149, 151, 153
   German immigration, 98, 149, 274, 307
   History, 77, 78, 85, 93, 95, 98, 99, 227
   Place names, 66
   Records, 127, 228
   Researchers, 186
Bukowina, 85, 192. *See also* Bukovina
Bukowina-Institut, 228
Bulgaria, 79, 107, 109, 192, 208, 274, 304
   Census records, 228
   History, 78, 85, 215
   Microfilms, 16
   Records, 176
   Researching in, 215
Bulletin board services, 133, 134, 135
Bundaberg, Australia, 157
Burgau Margravate, Germany, 125
Burgenland, 83, 94, 191, 192
   German emigration, 141, 143
   History, 77, 84, 191
   Jewish records, 221
   Researchers, 187
Burgert, Annette Kunselman, 168, 276
Burgher rolls, 174
Burgoyne, Bruce E., 276
Burgundian tribe, 105
Burgundy, 92, 106

Burgwedel, Germany, 189
Burma, 56
Butler, Reg, 41
Bydgoszcz, Poland, 214, 227. *See also* Bromberg
Byler, John M., 123
Bystricky, Vladimír, 218
Bytca, Slovak Republic, 219

—C—

Cadrilater, Bulgaria, 216. *See also* Dobruja
Cairo, Egypt, 53, 54
Calendar, 275, 283
    French Revolutionary, 234, 272, 273, 275
    Gregorian, 234, 270, 273, 275, 305
    Julian, 270, 273, 275
Calgary, Alberta, 30
California, 142, 143, 225, 311
Calvert, Albert F., 166, 167, 168
Calvin, John, 105, 110, 305
Calvinists, 88, 89, 110, 112, 114, 305. *See also* Reformed Church
    In Canada, 29
    In Germany, 234
    In Poland, 222
    In Prussia, 172
    In Ukraine, 102
Calw, Germany, 189
Camann, Eugene, 276
Cambodia, 20
Cameroon, 53, 162, 167
Canada, 34, 55, 107, 114, 117, 120, 133, 143, 205, 275, 281, 297, 306, 308, 311
    Canada West, 28
    Census, 144
    Church records, 28
    Civil records, 32
    Computerized Land Records Index, 28
    Consulates, 283
    Eastern Canada, 143, 144
    Genealogical societies, 30, 281
    German emigration, 146
    German immigration, 103, 124, 140, 143, 145, 149, 168, 274, 277, 287
    German settlements, 143
    History, 308
    Land grants, 31
    List of church archives, 116
    Lower Canada, 28
    National Archives, 25, 30, 31
    National Library, 30
    Niagara peninsula, 143
    Port cities, 141
    Prairie provinces, 103, 145, 309
    Provincial archives, 31
    Provincial libraries, 32
    Researching in, 28, 275

Canada (*continued*)
    Upper Canada, 28, 143
    Western Canada, 31, 103, 114, 119, 144, 215, 291, 309
Canberra, Australian Capital Territory, 45, 46
Canterbury, New Zealand, 26, 46, 48, 160, 161
Cape Archives Depot, South Africa, 51
Cape Colony, South Africa, 50, 164, 165, 171
Cape of Good Hope, 55
Cape Province, South Africa, 50, 51, 164, 165, 171, 306, 307, 308
Cape Town, South Africa, 26, 50, 51, 52, 165
Capellen canton, Luxembourg, 84
Carinthia, 76, 83, 92, 191, 192
    History, 77
Carniola, Slovenia, 76, 77, 85, 92, 97, 107, 109, 192, 230. *See also* Krain
Caroline Islands, 162
Carpatho-Ukraine, 97, 192, 212, 214, 220
    Gazetteers, 70, 73
    History, 78, 85, 216
    Researchers, 187
Caspian Sea region, 82, 102, 103, 215
Cassubia, 101
Castle Garden, New York, 141, 309
Castlemaine, Victoria, 158
Catherine the Great, 82, 101, 278, 306
Catholic Church. *See* Catholics
Catholic consistory
    Mogilev, Belarus, 204
    Saratov, Russia, 204
    Tiraspol, Ukraine, 204
Catholic Counter-Reformation. *See* Counter-Reformation
Catholic Historical Society of St. Paul, 298
Catholics, 110, 116, 118, 138, 144, 191, 196, 209, 220, 305
    Archives, 191
    Dissidents, 111
    Ecclesiastical census records, 36
    History, 95, 96, 98, 193
    In Alsace-Lorraine, 234
    In Argentina, 35, 145
    In Australia, 44, 159
    In Austria, 116, 191, 284
    In Austrian Silesia, 152
    In Belgium, 232
    In Black Sea region, 200, 204
    In Bohemia, 141, 217
    In Bosnia, 97
    In Brazil, 35, 147, 149, 310
    In Bukovina, 98, 117, 274
    In Canada, 29, 144
    In Chile, 152

Catholics (*continued*)
    In China, 55, 168
    In East Galicia, 213
    In Eastern Europe, 185
    In France, 234
    In Galicia, 124, 223, 224, 282
    In Germany, 88, 116
    In Latvia, 210
    In Liechtenstein, 197
    In Luxembourg, 106, 115
    In Minnesota, 230
    In Moravia, 141
    In Netherlands, 237
    In New Zealand, 48, 161
    In Norway, 237
    In Russian Empire, 204
    In Silesia, 152
    In Slovak Republic, 219
    In Soviet Union, 310
    In Sweden, 242
    In Switzerland, 105, 116, 195
    In Tanzania, 167
    In Ukraine, 102, 204, 279
    In Volga River region, 200, 203, 204
    In Volhynia, 124, 224, 282
    In Westphalia, 152
    In Württemberg, 152
    Naming practices, 62
    Records, 7, 16, 17, 18, 31, 37, 38, 118, 123, 172, 176, 185, 220
    Writing to local churches, 176
Caucasus region, 102, 201, 204, 207, 215, 309
    History, 101
    Researching in, 215
CD-ROM, 5, 13, 14, 19, 134, 135, 276. *See also under* Computers
Celestino, Ayrton Gonçalves, 40, 148, 149, 151, 153
Cemetery associations, 7
Cemetery records
    United States, 7
Census records, 174. *See also under each country*
    Latin America, 37
    State census, 12
    U. S. Soundex index, 11
    United States, 2, 11
Central America, 146, 171
    German settlements, 150
    Map of, 312
Central Archives for the History of the Jewish People, Jerusalem, 125
Central Europe, 70
Central Poland, 90, 99, 100, 101, 102, 188, 205, 224. *See also* Poland
    Genealogical societies, 188
    German emigration, 104
    Researchers, 187
Central Society of German Citizens of the Jewish Faith, 127

Centralverein deutscher Staatsbürger jüdischen Glaubens, 127

Cernauti, 98. *See also* Chernivsti, Ukraine

Cerny, Johni, 14, 15, 22, 26

Certified Genealogical Record Specialists, 6

Certified Genealogists, 6

Cesky Budejovice, Czech Republic, 95. *See also* Budweis

Ceylon, 56

Chaco, Argentina, 145

Chamness, Leigh Ann, 123

Charbin, 54, 168. *See also* Harbin, China

Charlemagne, 82, 87, 88, 92, 304

Charlottetown, Prince Edward Island, 34

Chechnya, 82, 215

Chelm, Poland, 84, 101

Chelmno, Poland, 80

Chernivtsi, Ukraine, 98

Cherson, Ukraine, 79. *See also* Kherson, Ukraine

Chicago, Illinois, 142, 143

Chihuahua, Mexico, 152

Children's Aid Society, 7

Chile, 35, 38, 145, 151, 168, 169, 171, 308, 309
  Census records, 37
  Civil registers, 36
  German immigration, 152
  German settlements, 151
  National archives, 39
  National library, 39
  Records at Family History Library, 35
  Research helps, 35

Chiloé province, Chile, 152

China, 20, 54, 167, 168
  German emigration, 149

Chlebowskiego, Bronislawa, 66, 73

Chortitza, Ukraine, 102, 207. *See also* Chortitz, Ukraine

Chorzempa, Rosemary A., 223

Chote, A. H., 168

Christchurch, New Zealand, 26, 46, 47, 160, 161

Christiania, 238. *See also* Oslo, Norway

Church of Jesus Christ of Latter-day Saints, 2, 16, 20, 121, 235, 276

Church of Scotland. *See also* Presbyterians
  In Canada, 29

Church of the Brethren, 120

Church of United Brethren, 244

Church records. *Check under individual countries and religions*

Cieszyn, Poland, 84, 95

Cigler, Michael, 40, 169

Cilli, Slovenia, 85

Cincinnati, Ohio, 129, 142, 287

CIS. *See* Commonwealth of Independent States (CIS)

Ciskei, South Africa, 164

Cis-Leithania, 93. *See also* Austria

City directories, 7, 174

Civic, Australian Capital Territory, 43

Civil records/civil registers, 173. *Check under individual countries*

Clasen, Armin, 168

Clervaux canton, Luxembourg, 84

Cleugh, James, 109

Cleveland, Ohio, 142, 143

Cloos, Patricia, 41, 168

Cobb, Sanford Hoadley, 276

Coburg, Germany, 77, 82

Cohen, Chester G., 70, 118, 135

Cohen, H. A., 43

Colenbringer, H. T., 163

Colmar, France, 235

Cologne, Germany, 243, 279

Colombia, 154

Colorado, 142, 143
  German immigration, 103

Commonwealth of Independent States (CIS), 54, 111, 199, 201, 202, 211, 213, 215, 311
  History, 104
  Researching in, 211, 283

Commonwealth of Poland and Lithuania, 99, 111, 115, 209

Communist Manifesto, 90

Compromise of 1867, 93

CompuServe, 13, 20. *See also* Electronic research

Computers, 13, 18, 129, 133, 134, 202, 227, 283. *See also* Electronic research
  Bulletin board services, 13
  CD-ROM, 5, 14. *See also* CD-ROM
  Family History Library, 17
  GEDCOM, 13, 17, 133
  Genealogy programs, 13, 17
  Map programs, 14
  On-line services, 20
  Software, 13

Concepcion, Chile, 38, 152

Congregationalists
  In Canada, 30
  In Latin America, 35

Congress of Vienna, 75, 100, 105, 307

Congress Poland, 82, 100, 222. *See also* Central Poland
  Church records, 124, 205, 224

Connecticut, 142

Connor, Martha Remer, 221, 276

Conrad Grebel College, 30, 144, 205

Consistory of Moscow (Lutheran), 203

Consistory of Saint Petersburg (Lutheran), 202

Consistory of Saratov (Lutheran), 203

Coolgardie, Western Australia, 159

Cope, J. P., 165, 169

Copenhagen, Denmark, 24

Cordoba, Argentina, 145

Corkhill, Alan, 41

Correspondence abroad, 246

Costa Rica, 151, 152
  Civil registers, 36, 37
  German immigration, 37

Cottbus, Germany, 83

Counter-Reformation, 88, 92, 111, 115, 242, 305

County atlases, 8

County histories, 15

County plat books, 8

Coupek, Milan, 218

Courland, 80, 99, 207
  Lutheran consistory, 203

Court records, 8, 173

Cracow, Poland, 80, 90, 223

Creglingen, Germany, 130

Crespo, Entre Rios, Argentina, 40

Crimea, 82, 113

Crimean peninsula, 80, 102

Crimean War, 56, 103, 164

Croatia, 79, 85, 97, 192, 230
  Emigration, 161
  German emigration, 160
  History, 77, 78, 98
  Microfilms, 16
  National Archives, 230
  Researching in, 230

Croats, 94

Crop failures
  Of 1816-17, 102, 105, 307
  Of 1846-47, 105, 140, 308
  Of 1880s, 105
  Of 1932-33, 104

Crowe, Elizabeth Powell, 14

Crown Land, Canada Company, 31

Crusius, Christian, 70

Cuba, 151

Curacao, 154

Curitiba, Brazil, 38, 40, 149, 150

Cuzzo, Maria Wyant, 290

Cyprus, 245

Czech Brethren, 110, 217. *See also* Moravian Brethren

Czech Republic, 72, 79, 80, 82, 85, 87, 94, 95, 116, 134, 142, 185, 187, 192, 216, 217, 218, 246, 271, 289
  Addresses, 218
  Archives, 217, 218
  Church records, 217
  Civil records, 218
  German emigration, 151
  History, 84, 89, 94, 95, 216, 217
  Jewish records, 218
  Jews, 216, 217
  Map of, 312
  Microfilms, 16

Fast, Henry N., 205
Father Flanagan's Boys Town
     (Nebraska), 7
Faust, Albert Bernhardt, 277
Federal Republic of Germany, 91,
     311. *See also* Germany
     History, 92
     Länder (states), 83
     Map of, 312
Federation of Micronesia, 162
FEEFHS. *See* Genealogical societies:
     Federation of East European
     Family History Societies
     (FEEFHS)
Fehlinger, Hans, 107, 227
Feigmanis, Aleksandrs, 210
Feldkirch, Austria, 191
Ferdinand II, 242
FHL. *See* Family History Library
FHLC, 19, 21. *See also* Family
     History Library Catalog
Fichtner R., 130
FIDOnet, 134, 135
Fiedler, Jiri, 126
Filby, P. William, 6, 15, 24, 26, 277,
     278
Finland, 241
     Emigration, 233
     German immigration, 233
     History, 233, 242
     Luheran records, 203
     National Archive, 233
     Researching in, 233
Finnell, Arthur, 119
Firchau, Otto, 187
Firth, Lester, 169
Fischer, Adolf, 187
Fiti tribe (Tanzania), 166
Fiume, 192
Flanders, Belgium, 96, 232
     History, 96, 232
Flemings (Belgians), 60, 89, 112,
     115, 232, 236
Flemish, 78. *See also* Flemings
     (Belgians)
Flemish language, 232, 236
Florianopolis, Brazil, 147
Florida, 114, 142, 143
Foisel, John, 107, 277
Formosa, Argentina, 145
Forty-Eighters, 139
France, 53, 79, 80, 87, 112, 115, 116,
     120, 133, 222, 304, 305, 306, 307,
     310. *See also* Lorraine. *See also*
     Alsace
     Church records, 234
     Civil records, 234
     Emigration records, 234
     Genealogical societies, 235
     German emigration, 25, 233
     History, 76, 77, 78, 84, 86, 88, 89,
          90, 91, 106, 141, 305, 307, 308
     Map of, 312
     Miscellancous rccords, 235

France (*continued*)
     National Archive, 235
     Place names, 67
     Records, 276
     Regional Archives, 235
     Researching in, 233
Franconia, 80, 90, 112, 113, 116,
     189, 283
     History, 88, 95, 96
Franco-Prussian War, 244
Frank, Jerry, 202, 208
Franken, 80. *See also* Franconia
Frankfurt am Main, Germany, 76,
     189, 277
Frankfurt an der Oder, Germany, 83
Frankfurt, Germany, 112, 115
Franklin district, Northwest
     Territories, 32
Franklin, Charles M., 123
Franks, 92, 304
Franschhoek, South Africa, 52
Franz, Eckhart G., 169, 277
Fraser, Lynn, 32
Fratautz, Bukovina, 281
Fredericton, New Brunswick, 33
Freeman, Margaret Zimmerman, 200
Freeman, Robert, 200
Freiburg canton, Switzerland, 83,
     148. *See also* Fribourg canton,
     Switzerland
Freiburg im Breisgau, Germany, 130
Freiburg, Germany, 79
Freiherr, Werner, 223
Fremantle, Western Australia, 25
French East India Company, 55
French Foreign Legion, 53, 137, 162
French language, 232
     Records, 234
French Reformed Church, 112. *See
     also* Huguenots
French Revolution, 147, 234
Fresno, California, 120
Friaul, 92, 222. *See also* Friuli, Italy
Fribourg canton, Switzerland, 83
Friederichs, Heinz F., 172, 278
Friesen, Nick, 55
Friesland, 112, 236. *See also* Frisia
Frisian language, 236
Frisians, 78, 236
Friuli, Italy, 92, 222
Froelke, Ruth, 284
Fulda River, Germany, 81
Fünfkirchen, 97. See also Pécs,
     Hungary
Funke, Alfred, 169
Furer, Howard B., 142, 169

—G—

Gade, John Allyne, 238
Galicia, 66, 80, 81, 98, 112, 114,
     119, 124, 134, 192, 205, 212, 225,
     290. *See also* Western Galicia. *See
     also* East Galicia

Galicia (*continued*)
     Catholic records, 223
     Church records, 223
     Civil records, 193, 225
     Colonization, 284
     Gazetteers, 66, 71, 74
     German emigration, 141, 144
     German immigration, 307
     History, 76, 77, 78, 93, 98, 125,
          222, 224
     Land cadasters, 224
     Land records, 224
     Records, 188, 205
     Researchers, 187
Galicja, 84. *See also* Galicia
Galizien, 81, 192. *See also* Galicia
Galveston, Texas, 24
Gardiner, Duncan B., 70, 97, 216,
     218
Garnsey, Heather E., 43, 46
Gay, Ruth, 135
Gazetteers, 69–74, 175
     Australia, 45
     Austria, 65, 191
     Banat, 66
     Galicia, 66
     German Empire, 74
     Germany, 5, 65, 66, 74
     Hungary, 66
     Poland, 66, 73
     Prussia, 65
     Soviet Union, 67
     Switzerland, 65
Gdansk, Poland, 24, 222. *See also*
     Danzig
     Archives, 226
     History, 84
     Records, 127
GEDCOM. *See under* Computers
Gedenkbuch (memorial book), 127
Geelong, Victoria, 158
Geheimes Staatsarchiv Preussischer
     Kulturbesitz, 186. *See* Prussian
     State Privy Archives, Berlin
Gemeinschaft unabhängiger Staaten,
     211. *See also* Commonwealth of
     Independent States
Genealogical institutes. *See*
     Genealogical societies
Genealogical libraries, 296–300
Genealogical periodicals, 8
     Archiv für Sippenforschung, 4
     Avotaynu, 117
     Die Pommerschen Leute, 185
     *Familienkundliche Nachrichten
          (FaNa)*, 4, 5
     German, 174
     List of, 290–91
     Mennonite Family History, 120
     Mennonite Genealogist, 120, 291
     *Praktische Forschungshilfe
          (PraFo)*, 4, 5
     RAGAS Newsletter, 212, 291
     The Gottschee Tree, 231

Genealogists (continued)
Professional, 6, 15
Generalgouvernement, Poland, 80,
285
Geneva, Switzerland, 54, 80, 83, 105,
110. *See also* Genf canton,
Switzerland
Genf canton, Switzerland, 83
GEnie, 13, 20. See also Electronic
research
Georgia (country), 85, 113, 124, 215
Researching in, 215
Georgia (U.S. state), 113, 123, 142,
189
German immigration, 140, 142
Georgia Salzburger Society, 122
Geppert, Karlheinz, 132
Gera, Germany, 83
German Bohemians, 283
German Central Office for
Genealogy. *See* Genealogical
societies: Deutsche Zentralstelle für
Genealogie. *See also* Genealogical
societies: Deutsche Zentralstelle für
Genealogie
German colonies, 45, 49, 53, 73, 75,
96, 97, 99, 103, 113, 145, 149,
150, 152, 157, 162, 203, 214, 220,
309, 310. *See also individual
territories*
German Confederation, 106, 307
States, 76
German Consulate, 299
German Customs Union, 90
German Democratic Republic, 91,
127, 288, 311
Bezirke, 83
Map of, 312
Records, 177
German East Africa, 53, 162, 166–
67, 168. *See also* Tanzania
German East Africa Company, 166
German emigration. *See under*
Germans. *See individual countries*
German Empire, 61, 72, 117, 142,
175, 279, 308
Atlases, 74
Church records, 288
German emigration, 145, 146
History, 75, 84, 87–92, 93, 138,
198, 234, 282, 309
Map of, 312
Records, 177, 184
Research, 277
States, 77
German Historical Institute (GHI)
London, 134
Washington, DC, 134
Genealogical societies, 234
German Information Center, 296
German language, 262
Cases, 262
Dialects, 59, 312

German language (continued)
Diseases, 269
Gender, 262
High German (Hochdeutsch), 59
Interchangeable letters, 57, 68
Jurisdictional terms, 264
Kinship terms, 264
Low German (Plattdeutsch), 59
Newspapers abroad, 4, 41
Nouns, 262
Numbers, 269
Occupations, 267
Records, 234
Time terminology, 268
Umlauts, 69, 263
Word list, 264
German names, 280, 285
German Poland, 160
German emigration, 161
German Reformed Church, 119
German script, 260. *See also* Gothic
script
German Solomon Islands, 162
German South-West Africa, 26, 53,
162, 165, 309. *See also* Namibia
German Wars of Unification, 138
German-American churches, 123
Germans
Aussiedler. *See* Aussiedler
Expellees (1945), 91, 101, 104
Expulsions of, 98, 115, 310
German emigration, 98
In Algeria, 137
In Alsace-Lorraine, 198, 233
In Argentina, 137, 145, 151, 154,
198
In Armenia, 215
In Asia, 101
In Asian Muslim republics, 104,
215
In Australia, 25, 40, 41, 137, 154,
155
In Austria, 198
In Austrian Empire, 94
In Austrian Silesia, 187
In Austro-Hungarian Empire, 92,
93, 94, 142, 230, 275
In Azerbaijan, 215
In Baltic countries, 100, 144, 207,
209
In Banat, 72, 194
In Belarus, 214
In Belgium, 198, 231, 232
In Bessarabia, 102, 107, 113, 187,
199, 214, 227
In Black Sea region, 102, 188,
206, 212, 288, 291, 307
In Bohemia, 74, 109, 143, 153,
187
In Bosnia, 97, 98
In Bosnia-Herzegovina, 229
In Brazil, 40, 137, 145, 148, 151,
154

Germans (continued)
In Bukovina, 74, 95, 98, 107, 123,
124, 143, 148, 149, 151, 153,
186, 199, 227, 277, 281, 288
In Bulgaria, 215
In Burgenland, 187
In Canada, 25, 137, 143, 151, 198,
281
In Carpatho-Ukraine, 187, 220
In Caucasus, 101, 113, 203, 215
In Central America, 151
In Central Poland, 187, 225
In Chile, 137, 151, 152, 153
In China, 54
In Commonwealth of Independent
States, 211
In Croatia, 220, 230
In Czech Republic, 217
In Czechoslovakia, 108, 198, 220
In Denmark, 198, 232
In Dobruja, 107, 109, 216, 227
In Dutch Guiana, 153
In Eastern Europe, 114, 115, 140,
144, 145, 148, 149, 175, 177,
184, 186, 197, 198, 220, 274,
290
In Eastern Poland, 225
In Egypt, 137
In England, 244
In Estonia, 198, 199, 209
In Finland, 233
In France, 198, 233
In French Foreign Legion, 137
In Galicia, 98, 108, 187, 191, 194,
225, 226
In Georgia (country), 215
In German Empire, 142
In Great Britain, 198, 243
In Guatemala, 35
In Hungary, 109, 187, 198, 219,
220, 277
In Ireland, 235
In Italy, 109, 198, 221
In Latin America, 26, 137, 198
In Latvia, 198, 199, 209
In Liechtenstein, 198
In Lithuania, 198, 199, 209, 210
In London, 78
In Luxembourg, 106, 198
In Mexico, 35, 38, 137, 152
In Michigan, 287
In Moldova, 214, 227
In Moravia, 109, 187
In Morocco, 137
In Namibia, 26, 137
In Netherlands, 198, 236
In New York, 236
In New Zealand, 25, 40, 137, 160
In North America, 198
In Norway, 237, 238
In Ottoman Turkish Empire, 106
In Paraguay, 35, 137, 151, 153
In Peru, 153

Great Depression, 310
Great Dividing Range, Australia, 157
Great Lakes, 26
Great Nordic War, 100
Great Poland (early duchy), 80, 82
Grebel, Conrad, 110
Greece, 245, 304
Greenslopes, Queensland, 42
Greenwood, Val D., 15
Greifswald, Germany, 185, 223
Grevenmacher canton, Luxembourg, 84
Greytown, New Zealand, 160
GRHS, 202, 208. *See also* Genealogical societies: Germans from Russia Heritage Society
Grimm, J. A., 131
Grisons canton, Switzerland, 83
Grodno, 81, 208. *See also* Hrodna, Belarus
    Archives, 203
Grosspolen, 80. *See also* Great Poland
Grothe, Hugo, 108
Grovedale, Victoria, 158
Gruenwald, Myron E., 291
Guam, 49, 162
Guatemala, 150
    Civil registers, 36
    Records at Family History Library, 35
Guild books, 174
Guild records, 176
Guise, Jacques de, 23
Gulf of Mexico, 26
Günzburg, Germany, 125
GUS. *See also* Commonwealth of Independent States. *See also* Gemeinschaft unabhängiger Staaten
Gustavus Adolphus, 242
Gut, B., 131
Gutenberg, 88
Guzik, Estelle M., 15, 132, 135
Gypsies, 94

—H—

Haardt, 80, 82
Hagin, Mathias, 148
Hahn, Joachim, 130
Hahndorf, South Australia, 41, 45, 157
Haigerloch, Germany, 129, 130
Halifax, Nova Scotia, 25, 30, 32, 33, 141, 143, 144, 297
Hall, Charles M., 24, 44, 71, 279
Halle, Germany, 83, 304
Haller, Charles R., 279
Halychyna, 85. *See also* East Galicia
Hamar, Norway, 240
Hamburg, Germany, 19, 41, 44, 45, 76, 77, 83, 87, 90, 141, 150, 151, 160, 164, 187, 279, 289, 304

Hamburg, Germany (*continued*)
    Genealogical societies, 182
    German emigration, 147, 159
    History, 91
    Passenger lists, 23, 37, 173, 276
    State Archives, 127, 178
Hamilton, Ontario, 29
Hamilton, Victoria, 42
Handwriting, 283
Hannover, 19, 60, 77. *See also* Hanover
Hanover, 19, 76, 77, 90, 176, 244, 289. *See also* Hannover
    German emigration, 159, 160, 161, 164, 308
    History, 76, 79
Hanover/Steinbach Historical Society (Manitoba), 153
Hanseatic League, 78, 87, 88, 109, 160, 233, 237, 238, 241, 243, 304
Hansen, Miriam Hall, 203
Hapsburg Empire, 70, 88, 92, 94, 95, 98, 99, 108, 110, 113, 236, 284, 307
    History, 89, 141
Harbin, China, 54, 55, 168, 215
Harmonie Associates, 121
Harmonists, 114, 121. *See also* Rappists
Harmony Society, 121
Harmony, Pennsylvania, 114, 121
Harms, Wilmer, 54
Harmstorf, Ian, 40, 41, 169
Harz region, Germany, 241
Harzgebirge, 80
Hauerland, Slovak Republic, 85, 96, 219
Hauländereien, 100
Haut-Rhin department, France, 234, 235. *See also* Alsace
Hawkes Bay province, New Zealand, 161
Haymarket, New South Wales, 43
Hebrew names, 133
Hebrew Union College, 129
Hechingen, Germany, 130, 132
Heebner, Balthasar, 124
Heese, J. A., 52, 53
Hehe tribe (Tanzania), 166
Heidelberg, Germany, 127, 189, 276
Height, Joseph S., 146, 279, 286
Heike, Otto, 108
Heilbronn-Sontheim, Germany, 131
Heilongjiang province, China, 168
Heimatarchiv der Deutschen aus Mittelpolen und Wolhynien, 188
Heimatortskarteien, 188, 216, 283, 286
Heintze, Albert, 64
Heinzmann, Franz, 58, 174, 279
Helmbold, F. Wilbur, 2
Hemsbach, Germany, 131
Henning, Eckart, 58, 63, 64, 175, 273, 283

Heraldry, 283
Herdecke, Germany, 188
Herder-Institut, 186. *See also* Johann-Gottfried-Herder-Institut
Hermannstadt, 82. *See also* Sibiu, Romania
Herrero tribe (Namibia), 165
Herrnhut, Germany, 113, 122
Herrnhuter, 110, 113, 122, 163, 217. *See also* Moravian Church. *See also* Moravian Brethren
Herzegovina, 93, 98, 192, 229, 309
    History, 77, 78
Herzegowina, 192. *See also* Herzegovina
Herzog, Hertha, 141
Hesse, 19, 77, 81, 82, 83, 90, 112, 116, 147, 150, 164, 176, 189, 279, 289, 305, 307. *See also* Hessen
    German emigration, 102, 140, 144, 160, 276
    History, 76, 79, 89, 91
    State archives, 178
Hesse-Cassel, 76, 277
    History, 76
Hesse-Darmstadt, 76
    German emigration, 144
Hessen, 19, 77. *See also* Hesse
    Genealogical societies, 182
Hesse-Nassau, 19, 77, 289. *See also* Hessen-Nassau
    History, 76, 98
    State archives, 178
Hessen-Nassau, 19, 77. *See also* Hesse-Nassau
Hessian soldiers, 138, 169, 244, 306
HETRINA, 169
Heusser, J. Christian, 148, 153
Hexel, Ernst, 188
High German (Hochdeutsch), 59
Hill, Roscoe R., 39
Hiller, Georg, 145, 169
Hillsboro, Kansas, 119
Himka, John-Paul, 225
Himly, Francois J., 235
Hinke, William John, 285
Historical dateline, 304
Historical societies
    Canadian Moravian Historical Society, 122
    Historic Harmony/Harmony Museum, 121
    Historical Society of Tanzania, 167
    Illinois Mennonite Historical and Genealogical Society, 120
    Institute for Historic Family Research, 194
    Lancaster Mennonite Historical Society, 120
    Manitoba Mennonite Historical Society, 120
    Mennonite Archives of Ontario, 120

—I—

Japan, 167
Java, 56
Jebenhausen, Germany, 128, 130, 131
Jekaterinoslav, Ukraine, 80. *See also* Ekaterinoslav, Ukraine
Jelgava, Latvia, 210. *See also* Mitau
Jenner, Margaret, 41, 156
Jensen, Larry O., 5, 67, 71, 108, 172, 175, 234, 270, 272, 273, 279, 290
Jerusalem, Israel, 125
Jeske, Gerhard, 177
Jewish Genealogical Family Finder, 133
Jewish genealogical societies, 118
Jewish Genealogy Echo/Conference, 133, 134, 135
Jewish records, 17
Jews, 62, 72, 98, 111, 112, 113, 114, 125–36, 125, 138, 172, 220, 222, 290, 307, 310, 311
  Archives, 193
  Computer research, 133, 134
  Exhibits and memorials, 128
  Expulsions of, 115, 128, 304
  Family names, 126, 283
  Genealogical resources, 133
  Genealogical societies, 42, 133
  Genealogy research, 283
  History, 71, 94, 108, 125
  In Alsace, 116
  In Alsace-Lorraine, 116
  In Australia, 42, 114, 155
  In Austria, 116, 284
  In Austrian Silesia, 126
  In Austro-Hungarian Empire, 116, 117, 144, 307
  In Baden, 116
  In Bavaria, 116
  In Belarus, 275
  In Berlin, Germany, 116
  In Bohemia, 108, 126, 217
  In Brazil, 147
  In Budapest, Hungary, 117
  In Bukovina, 70, 98, 108, 117
  In Canada, 29, 30, 114, 117, 144
  In China, 55
  In Czech Republic, 117, 126, 216, 217
  In Danube Swabian settlements, 117
  In East Galicia, 213
  In Eastern Europe, 69, 115, 138, 140, 199
  In France, 127, 307
  In Galicia, 70, 98, 108, 117, 144, 224
  In German Empire, 117
  In Germany, 116, 124, 139, 143, 285, 307
  In Hamburg, Germany, 116
  In Hapsburg Empire, 117
  In Hesse, 116
  In Hesse-Nassau, 116

Jews (*continued*)
  In Hohenzollern, 127
  In Holland, 127
  In Hungary, 97, 108, 117
  In Israel, 114, 127
  In Latin America, 37, 114
  In Latvia, 70, 210, 275
  In Lithuania, 70, 275
  In Lodz, Poland, 117
  In Lower Austria, 116
  In Mannheim, Germany, 116
  In Moldova, 205, 215, 275
  In Moravia, 126
  In Netherlands, 237
  In North America, 117, 140
  In Poland, 62, 64, 101, 111, 115, 117, 205, 222, 275
  In Posen, 116
  In Prussia, 307
  In Romania, 117
  In Russian Empire, 62, 64, 113, 114, 117, 146, 205, 275, 307, 312
  In Slovak Republic, 117, 126, 216
  In South Africa, 164
  In Soviet Union, 115
  In Switzerland, 117, 129, 307
  In Trieste, Italy, 108, 117
  In Ukraine, 205, 213, 275
  In United States, 30, 114, 115, 117, 127, 143, 284
  In Vienna, Austria, 108, 116
  In Volhynia, 224
  In Western Europe, 114
  In World War I, 127
  In Württemberg, 127
  Lineage car files, 184
  Museums, 128
  Near Main River, Germany, 116
  Near Moselle River, 116
  Near Rhine River, 116
  Pogroms, 113, 114, 309
  Publications, 133
  Records, 16, 17, 117, 118, 126, 191, 218, 220
  Relations with Christians, 114
  Surnames, 62, 64, 275
JGC. *See* Jewish Genealogy Echo/Conference
Jiaozhou, China, 55, 168
Jiganoff, V. D., 55
Jihlava, Czech Republic, 95
Johann-Gottfried-Herder-Institut, 186
Johansson, Carl-Erik, 243
Johnson, Arta F., 61, 64, 111, 116, 118, 119, 120, 121, 122, 123, 280
Johnson, Keith A., 280
Johnson, Margaret, 202
Jonasson, Eric, 34, 144
Jones, George Fenwick, 62, 64, 123, 280
Jones, Henry Z., Jr., 139, 235, 276, 280
Judaism, 122, 205. *See* Jews

Judak, Margit, 221
Jude, Renate, 199, 288
Jura canton, Switzerland, 80, 83
Jutland, 238, 242

—K—

Kabardino-Bulkaria, 215
Kaemmerer, M., 71
Kaerger, K., 169
Kaffraria, 164, 165. *See also* British Kaffraria
Kagan, Joram, 135
Kahn, Bruce, 135, 211
Kaiserslautern, Germany, 37, 188
Kaiser-Wilhelms-Land, 162
Kalgoorlie, Western Australia, 159
Kaliningrad, Russia, 99. *See also* Königsberg, East Prussia
Kalisch, 100. *See also* Kalisz, Poland
Kalisz, Poland, 100, 101
Kallbrunner, Josef, 61, 109, 225, 289
Kalmar, Sweden, 241
Kaminkow, Marion J., 15, 280, 281
Kaniki, H. H. Y., 167, 169
Kann, Robert A., 108
Kansas, 119, 123, 124, 142, 143, 152, 277, 289
Kaps, J., 123
Karasek, A., 108
Karl der Grosse, 88, 92. *See also* Charlemagne
Karl Marx-Stadt, German Democratic Republic, 83. *Same as* Chemnitz, Germany
Karlsruhe, Germany, 284
Kärnten, 83, 92, 191, 192. *See also* Carinthia
Karpato-Ukraine, 85, 192. *See also* Carpatho-Ukraine
Kaschau, 97, 219. *See also* Kosice, Slovak Republic
Kashubs, 100
Käsmark, 96. *See also* Kezmarok, Slovak republic
Katanning, Western Australia, 159
Katzman, Harry, 134
Kauder, Viktor, 108
Kaukasus, 215. *See also* Caucasus region
Kaunas, Lithuania, 81
Kavel, A. L. C., 41, 45
Kazakhstan, 85, 103, 104, 215, 311
Kazmierczak, Wiktor, 109
Keewatin district, Northwest Territories, 32
Kei River, 164
Keiskama River, 164
Keller, Hanzheinz, 147
Kemp, Thomas Jay, 15, 32, 35, 280
Kenawa, Western Australia, 159
Kennedy, Patricia Grimsted, 200
Kenya, 162, 166, 167. *See also* British East Africa

Kerry county, Ireland, 235
Kessler, W., 108
Ketsch, Germany, 132
Kezmarok, Slovak Republic, 96
KGB (Russian secret police), 208
Kharkiv, Ukraine, 201, 212. *See also*
  Kharkov
Kharkov. *See* Kharkiv, Ukraine
Kherson, Ukraine, 79, 201, 204
Khmel'nyts'kyi, Ukraine, 81
Kiautschou, 168. *See* Jiaozhou,
  China
Kiefner, Theo, 189
Kiel, Germany, 233
Kiev, Ukraine, 201
  Archives, 212, 213
  Records, 205, 214
Killion, Martyn C. H., 43, 46
Kilton, T., 290
King's German Legion (English), 56,
  164, 244
King William's Town, South Africa,
  52, 165
King, Susan, 135
Kingdom of Bavaria, 125
Kingdom of Poland, 135
Kingdom of Prussia, 306
Kingdom of Württemberg, 125
Kinzig River, 82
Kirkham, E. Kay, 15
Kirlibaba, Bukovina, 98
Kitchener, Ontario, 30, 143, 144
Klagenfurt, Austria, 191
Klaipeda, Lithuania, 210
Klaube, Manfred, 108
Klein, Borys, 208
Kleinpolen, 80. *See also* Little
  Poland
Klemzig, South Australia, 45, 157
Klippenstein, Lawrence, 120
Kneifel, Eduard, 123
Knittle, Walter Allen, 280
Koblenz, Germany, 37, 82
Kocevje, Slovenia, 85, 97, 230, 290
Koger, Marvin Vastine, 283
Kohl, Waltraut, 131
Kolesar, Denise, 290
Köln, Germany, 243
Kolo, Poland, 82, 84
Kongsberg, Norway, 238
Königsberg, East Prussia, 80, 99. *See
  also* Kaliningrad, Russia
Konin, Poland, 82, 84
Koop, Gerhard S., 146, 169
Kopittke, Eric, 25, 44
Kopittke, Rosemary, 25, 44
Korean War, 20
Körner, Karl Wilhelm, 170
Kosice, Slovak Republic, 97, 219
Kosiek, Rolf, 108
Kosovo (Serbia), 231, 336
Koss, David H., 111, 123
Kossmann, Oskar, 100, 101, 108
Kowallis, Otto K., 71

Kowallis, Vera N., 71
Kraichgau, Germany, 276
Krain, 85, 92, 192, 230. *See also*
  Carniola, Slovenia
Krainburg, 230. *See also* Kranj,
  Slovenia
Krajnska, Slovenia, 85. *See also*
  Carniola, Slovenia
Krakow, 109. *See* Cracow, Poland
Krallert, Wilfried, 71
Kranj, Slovenia, 230
Krasnodar, Russia, 103
Kredel, Otto, 66, 71, 198
Krefeld, Germany, 113, 119, 139
Kreider, Rachel W., 123, 278
Kremnica, Slovak Republic, 85, 96
Kremnitz, 85, 96. *See also* Kremnica,
  Slovak Republic
Krewson, Margrit Beran, 124, 175,
  280
Kriebel, Reuben, 124
Krippner, Mrs. C., 49
Kristensen, Peter K., 273, 275
Kroatien, 192. *See also* Croatia
Kroeker, Irene Enns, 153, 169
Kronstadt, 82, 289. *See also* Brasov,
  Romania
Krushel, Howard, 202, 214
Kuban River, 80
Kuban, Caucasus, 80, 201
Kubijovic, Wolodymyr, 71
Kucher, W., 131
Kuhlberg, Ivan
  Lists of settlers, 208, 212
Kuhn, Heinrich, 71
Kuhn, Walter, 71
Kühner, J., 130
Kuhn-Rehfus, Maren, 132
Kuhr, Jo Ann, 208, 290
Kujawien, 80. *See also* Kuyavia,
  Poland
Kulm, 80. *See also* Chelmno, Poland
Kulmerland, Poland, 80
Kulturkampf, 97, 113, 229
Kung, Hugo, 169
Kur-, 80
Kurhessen, Germany, 80
Kurland, 80, 99. *See also* Courland
Kurpfalz, Germany, 80
Kurzweil, Arthur, 117, 136, 280
Kutschurgan, Ukraine, 102
Kuyavia, Poland, 80
Kuybyshev, 103. *See also* Samara,
  Russia
Kvikne, Norway, 238
Kyrgyzstan, 215

—L—

La Frontera province, Chile, 152
La Pampa, Argentina, 145
La Plata, Argentina
  Arrival lists, 26
Labadists, 114

Labrador, Canada, 33
Lackey, Richard S., 2
Lahn River, Germany, 276
Laibach, 85, 97, 230. *See also*
  Ljubljana, Slovenia
Lake Constance, Switzerland, 129
Lake Llanquique (Chile), 151
Lake Nyasa (Tanzania), 167
Lake Peipus, 80
Lake Tanganyika, 166
Lampe, Karl H., 273
Lancaster County, Pennsylvania, 123
Land cadasters, 213, 225
Land grants
  Canada, 31
Land records, 173
  United States, 9
Lande, Peter, 135
Ländl, Austria, 80, 113
Lange Hermann, 261
Lange, Henry, 169
Lange, Herrmann, 69
Languages, 273
  Arabic, 54
  English, 38
  French, 54
  German, 38, 253
  Latin, 38, 253
  Portuguese, 38
  Spanish, 38
  Table of, 246, 270
Laos, 20
Latin America, 35, 38, 39, 104, 215,
  290, 307, 311, 372
  Census records, 37
  Church and cemetery records, 35
  Civil registers, 36
  Family History Library holdings,
    35
  Gazetteers, maps and atlases, 38
  German immigration, 37, 145–54,
    168
  German settlements, 145
  Land records, 37
  Language of records, 38
  Military records, 38
  Passenger lists, 26
  Probate and notarial records, 37
  Published records, 38
  Repositories, 38
  Useful addresses, 40
  Writing to, 39
"Latin farmers", 138
Latin language, 221
  Records, 234
Lattermann, Alfred, 22
Latvia, 80, 81, 84, 207, 289
  Archive of Vital Records, 210
  Church records, 186, 288
  German colonization, 99
  German emigration, 144, 163
  Lutheran parishes, 203
  Researching in, 209
  State Historical Archive, 210

Lauenburg, Germany, 232
Laupheim, Germany, 131
Laurentzsch, U., 130
Lausitz, Germany, 81. *See also*
    Lusatia
Law, Hugh T., 235
LBI. *See also* Leo Baeck Institute
LDS, 2, 5, 18, 19, 22, 276, 296. *See
    also* Church of Jesus Christ of
    Latter-day Saints
LDS Library. *See* Family History
    Library
Le Havre, France, 141, 234
    Passenger lists, 23, 234, 235
League of Nations, 54
Learned, Marion Dexter, 175
Lehmann, Heinz, 34, 144, 145, 281
Leipzig, Germany, 83, 209, 223, 231,
    247, 277
    Deutsche Zentralstelle für
        Genealogie, 127
    Estonian records, 209
    German emigration, 163
Leitha River, 93
Leitmeritz, 218
Lemberg, Austria, 80, 108, 125, 205,
    212, 224. *See also* L'viv, Ukraine.
    See also L'vov, Russia
Lemieux, Victoria, 32
Leningrad. *See* Saint Petersburg,
    Russia
Lenius, Brian J., 31, 66, 71, 213,
    223, 224, 290
Leo Baeck Institute, 30, 117, 126,
    128, 129
Leonard, David, 32
Lesser Antilles, 171
Lesson, Daniel N., 136
Lettland, 209. *See also* Latvia
Letzeburgesch dialect, 106
Leutschau, 96, 219. *See also* Levoca,
    Slovak Republic
Levi, Kate Everest, 281
Levoca, Slovak Republic, 96, 219
Libau, 24, 210. *See also* Leipäja,
    Latvia
Library of Congress, 28, 31, 128, 135
    Address, 296
    Bibliography of German sources,
        280
    Card catalog, 14
    Genealogies, 280, 281
    German-American genealogical
        sources, 175
    Local Histories, 15
    Polish consular records, 55
Lich, Glen E., 281
Liebental, Ukraine, 102
Liechtenstein, 84, 116, 169
    Church records, 197
    Civil records, 197
    History, 106
    Map of, 312
    National archives, 197

Liechtenstein (*continued*)
    Postal codes, 74, 287
    Researching in, 175, 197
Liège, Belgium, 231
Liepäja, Latvia, 24, 210
Ligett, Don, 175
Limerick county, Ireland, 235
Lincoln, Nebraska, 54
Lind, Marilyn, 71, 76, 281
Linder, Erich Dieter, 72, 281
Lindi, Tanzania, 166
Lineage card files, 184
Lineage societies, 190. *See also*
    Genealogical societies
Linz, Austria, 191
Lipno, Poland, 84
Lippe, 19, 57, 76, 77, 279, 289
    Genealogical societies, 183
    History, 76, 308
    State archives, 179
    Surnames, 308
Liptak, Eva, 221
Litauen, 99, 210. *See also* Lithuania
Lithuania, 81, 84, 100, 289, 310
    Atlases, 70
    Church records, 203, 210, 223,
        288
    German colonization, 99
    German emigration, 144
    History, 67, 77, 91, 99, 220, 222,
        307
    Memel River region, 84
    National archives (LVIA), 210
    Place names, 67
    Researching in, 210
Litomerice, Czech Republic
    regional archives, 218
Little Poland, 80
Liverpool, England, 23, 44, 141, 244
Livland, 81, 99. *See also* Livonia
Livonia, 81, 99, 100
    Lutheran consistory, 203
Ljubljana, Slovenia, 85, 97, 230, 231
Llanquique province, Chile, 151, 152
Lobethal, South Australia, 45
Local histories, 8, 174
    In Library of Congress, 15
Lodewyckx, Augustin, 169
Lodge records, United States, 7
Lodomeria, 81, 93
Lodomerien, 81. *See* Lodomeria
Lodz, Poland, 81, 84, 90, 100, 101
Loeb, Rene, 196
Loewen, Abram J., 55
Lohrbächer, A., 132
Lombard, R. T. J., 26, 49, 52, 53
Lombardy, 76, 221
Lome, Togo, 53
Lomza, Poland, 81, 134
London, England, 243, 244
    Great Fire of 1666, 243
Lorraine, 116, 304. *See also* France
    Genealogical societies, 235
    German emigration, 97

Lorraine (*continued*)
    History, 76, 88, 89, 234
    Map of, 312
    Regional archive, 235
Louis the German, 92
Louisiana
    German immigration, 142
Low German (Plattdeutsch), 59, 163
Low German surnames, 64
Lower Austria, 83, 191
Lower Danube, 306
Lower Hungary, 220
Lower Hutt, New Zealand, 47
Lower Saxony, 80, 81, 83
    History, 91
    State archives, 179
Lower Silesia
    German emigration, 124
Lowrey, Joan, 13, 15
Lubaczów, Poland, 213
    Roman Catholic archdiocese, 224
Lübeck, Germany, 19, 76, 77, 241
Lubetzky, R., 170
Lublin, Poland, 222
Lucerne canton, Switzerland, 83, 117
Lück, K., 108
Ludwig the German, 87. *See also*
    Louis the German
Ludwigsburg, Germany, 131
Luft, Edward David, 72, 216
Luneburg Heath, 81
Lüneburg, Germany, 81
Lüneburger Heide, 81. *See* Luneburg
    Heath
Lunenburg, Nova Scotia, 143
Lunow, Germany, 161
Lusatia, 81, 87. *See also* Lausitz,
    Germany
    German emigration, 157
Lütge, Wilhelm, 170
Luther, Martin, 60, 88, 93, 110, 305
Lutheran Church. *See* Lutherans
Lutheran Church of Australia, 44
Lutheran Consistory
    Moscow, Russia, 203
    Others in Russia, 203
    Saint Petersburg, Russia, 202
    Saratov, Russia, 203
Lutheran-Reformed merger, 114. *See
    also* Lutherans *and* Reformed
Church
Lutherans, 88, 99, 102, 114, 116,
    118, 144, 172, 305
    Church records, 185, 186, 202
    History, 98, 123, 202
    In Alsace-Lorraine, 234
    In Argentina, 35, 145
    In Australia, 41, 44, 45, 155, 159
    In Austria, 284
    In Black Sea region, 203, 277
    In Brazil, 35, 147, 149
    In Bukovina, 123
    In Canada, 29, 30, 41, 144, 279
    In Caucasus region, 203

Lutherans (*continued*)
  in Central Poland, 101
  In Chile, 35
  In China, 54
  In Denmark, 232
  In East Prussia, 203
  In Estonia, 209
  In Finland, 203
  In France, 234
  In Galicia, 224
  In Germany, 110, 285
  In Latin America, 36
  In Latvia, 210
  In Lower Silesia, 41
  In Michigan, 308
  In Missouri, 308
  In Netherlands, 237
  In New York, 308
  In New Zealand, 48, 160, 161
  In North America, 123
  In Norway, 237, 239
  In Poland, 123
  In Pomerania, 41
  In Russia, 102
  In Russian Empire, 202, 277
  In Saint Petersburg region, 203
  In Slovak Republic, 219
  In South Africa, 50, 163, 164, 165
  In South Australia, 45, 308
  In Soviet Union, 310
  In Sweden, 242
  In Tanzania, 167
  In Texas, 308
  In Transylvania, 96
  In Ukraine, 279
  In United States, 41, 54
  In Volga River region, 203
  In Volhynia, 224, 277
  In Wisconsin, 308
  In Württemberg, 203
  Merger with Reformed Church,
    105, 111, 114, 116, 154, 172,
    202, 307
  Missouri Synod, 147
  Records, 7, 16, 18, 118, 124, 172,
    176
  Writing to local churches, 176
Luxembourg, 76, 80, 304, 309
  Cantons, 84
  Census records, 197
  Church records, 196
  Civil records, 196
  Emigration, 278, 307
  Gazetteers, 72
  German emigration, 25, 143
  History, 76, 84, 88, 94, 96, 106,
    140
  Language, 106
  Map of, 312
  Microfilms, 17
  Researching in, 196
  State archives, 196
Luxembourg province, Belgium, 232

Luxembourg-Campagne canton,
  Luxembourg, 84
Luxembourg-Ville canton,
  Luxembourg, 84
Luzern canton, Switzerland, 83, 143.
  See also Lucerne canton,
  Switzerland
LVIA, 210. *See* Lithuania: National
  archives
L'viv, Ukraine, 80. *See also* L'vov,
  Russia. *See also* Lemburg, Austria
  Archives, 203, 212, 213, 225
  History, 125
  Records, 205, 214
  Roman Catholic archdiocese, 224
L'vov, Russia, 80. *See also* L'viv,
  Ukraine. *See also* Lemburg, Austria
Lwów, Poland, 80, 125, 224
Lyng, J., 45, 154, 155, 156, 157
Lynnwood Manor, South Africa, 52
Lyons, France, 110

—M—

Macartney, C. A., 94, 108
Macedonia, 304, 336
Mackay, Australia, 157
Mackenzie district, Northwest
  Territories, 32
Madison, Wisconsin, 142, 239, 240
MADU, 213. *See* Main Archival
  Directorate of Ukraine
Mafra, Brazil, 148, 149
Magdeburg, Germany, 79, 83, 112
  German emigration, 159
Magocsi, Paul Robert, 72, 117
Magyars, 89, 93, 96
Mähren, 192. *See also* Moravia
Mährisch-Ostrau, 95. *See also*
  Ostrava, Czech Republic
Mährisch-Trübau, 95. *See also*
  Moravská Trebová, Czech
  Republic
Main Archival Directorate of Ukraine
  (MADU), 213
Main River, Germany, 81, 82
Mainz, Germany, 81, 98, 115
Maji Maji rebellion, Tanzania, 166
Malay Archipelago, 55, 56
Malay Peninsula, 55, 56
Malaysia, 56
Malbork, Poland, 99. *See also*
  Marienburg
Mallee district, Victoria, 158
Malmedy, Belgium, 72, 84, 91, 231
Malta, 245
Manchuria, 54, 168, 215. *See also*
  Harbin *and* Charbin, China
Mändle, Max I., 126
Manifesto of 1763 (Russian), 101
Manitoba, Canada, 119, 144, 152
  Civil records, 33
  Homesteading in, 31
  Provincial Archives, 31, 32

Mannheim, Germany, 98
Maps, 175, 312. *See also under*
  individual countries
  Europe, 312
  U.S. Army maps of Eastern
    Europe, 68
Marburg, Germany, 186, 190
Marburg, Queensland, 44
Marburg, Slovenia, 85, 97, 230. *See
  also* Maribor, Slovenia. *See also*
  Maribor, Slovenia
Mariana Islands, 49, 162
Maribor, Slovenia, 85, 97, 230. *See
  also* Marburg, Slovenia
Marienburg, 99. *See also* Malbork,
  Poland
Mariupol, Ukraine, 103
Marschalck, Peter, 170
Marshall Islands, 49, 162
Marten, New Zealand, 161
Marx, Karl, 90, 147
Maryborough, Australia, 157
Maryland, 142, 225
  German immigration, 139
Masowien, 81. *See also* Mazovia,
  Poland
Massachusetts, 142, 225
Massier, Erwin, 281
Mast, Le Mar, 291
Mast, Lois Zook, 291
Masurien, 81. *See also* Mazuria,
  Poland
Mauelshausen, Carl, 124
Max Kade Institute for German
  American Studies, 296
Mazovia, Poland, 81
Mazuria, Poland, 81
McBride, J., 40
McCagg, William O., Jr., 108, 136
McEvedy, Colin, 72
Mecklenburg, 19, 76, 81, 174, 233,
  236, 243, 279, 289
  Genealogical societies, 182
  German emigration, 144, 160,
    164, 282, 308
  History, 89, 138, 236
  State archives, 179
  Surnames, 64
Mecklenburg-Schwerin, 77, 150
  German emigration, 146
Mecklenburg-Strelitz, 77
Mecklenburg-Vorpommern, 82, 83,
  92
Medessen, Germany, 186
Mediasch district, Transylvania, 289
Mehr, Kahlile B., 202, 203, 204, 206,
  228
Melbourne, Victoria, 25, 43, 45, 155,
  156, 158
Melchior, Wilfried, 224
Melville, Western Australia, 158
Memel River region, 67, 87, 91, 209,
  210, 310
Memel, Richard, 108

Memelland, 84, 108. *See* Memel River region
Mennicken-Cooley, Mary, 41, 159, 170
Mennonists, 110. *See* Mennonites
Mennonite Historical Centre, 205
Mennonites, 62, 102, 110, 111, 112, 113, 114, 118, 120, 121, 123, 138, 139, 143, 144, 167, 168, 169, 170, 171, 172, 174, 213, 214, 275, 287, 291. *See also* Templer Mennonites
Dutch, 89, 100, 144, 156, 305
Flemish, 89, 305
Frisian, 89, 305
German, 307
History, 98
In Alberta, 146
In Argentina, 145
In Australia, 156
In Belize, 146, 151, 152
In Bolivia, 146, 152, 153
In Brazil, 149
In Canada, 30, 114, 119, 151, 152, 153, 310
In China, 54, 149
In Chortitz, Ukraine, 119
In Costa Rica, 152
In Danzig, 119, 305
In Elbing (Elblag, Poland), 119
In France, 234
In Galicia, 119, 224
In Gdansk, Poland, 119
In Germany, 113, 119, 144
In Hamburg, Germany, 112, 119
In Kansas, 152
In Latin America, 114, 310
In Manitoba, 152
In Mexico, 35, 38, 146, 151, 152, 153, 310
In Molochna, Ukraine, 119
In Netherlands, 119, 144, 151, 156, 236, 237
In Oklahoma, 152
In Ostfriesland, 112
In Palestine, 156
In Paraguay, 35, 152, 153, 310
In Poland, 119, 222
In Prussia, 124, 151, 156
In Russia, 151
In Russian Empire, 102, 119, 124, 144, 152, 156, 204, 310
In Saskatchewan, 152
In Schleswig-Holstein, 112
In Soviet Union, 149
In Spanish Netherlands, 124
In Switzerland, 105, 119, 195
In Ukraine, 119, 207
In United States, 119, 152, 153
In Volhynia, 205, 224
In West Prussia, 236
Lineage card files, 184
Old Order, 146
Records, 119, 124

Meran, 96, 221. *See also* Merano, Italy
Merano, Italy, 96, 221
Mercenaries, 140
Merriman, Brenda Dougall, 28, 34, 281
Mersch canton, Luxembourg, 84
Merseburg, Germany, 177
Meter, Ken, 218, 281
Methodists, 111, 172
German-American, 122
In Canada, 29, 30
In Germany, 111, 114
In Switzerland, 111, 114
In United States, 111
Records, 122
Metz, France, 235
Mexico, 25, 26, 38, 151, 152, 170, 372
Census records, 37
Civil registers, 36
German emigration, 146
German immigration, 37
German settlements, 152
Mennonite church books, 119
México City, 39
National archives, 39
National library, 39
Records at Family History Library, 35
Research helps, 35
Meyer, Mary Keysor, 6, 15, 277, 281
Michels, John M., 66, 72, 108
Michigan, 143
German-Bohemians, 218, 281
Micronesia, 49, 162
Middle Ages, 88, 96, 106, 110, 111, 115, 234
Migration to Eastern Europe, 78
Middle Kingdom, 87
Midwest. *See also under* United States
Mies county, Czech Republic, 161
Military Death Index, 20
Military records, 174
United States, 10
Military service, 138
Miller, Betty, 120
Miller, J. Virgil, 120
Miller, Michael M., 208, 215, 281
Miller, Olga Katzin, 26, 170, 281
Milwaukee, Wisconsin, 142
Minden, Germany, 279
Minneapolis, Minnesota, 239
Public Library, 299
Minnesota, 142, 143, 225, 282, 287
German-Bohemians, 218, 281, 283
Minnesota Historical Society Research Center, 299
Minsk, Belarus
Archives, 203, 214
Minson, Marian, 159, 160
Misiones, Argentina, 145

Mississippi, 143
Mississippi River, 24
Mitau, 210. *See also* Jelgava, Latvia
MITEK Information Services, 212
Mitgliederverzeichnis, 186
Mittelmark, Germany, 81
Mittelpolen, 100. *See also* Congress Poland
Mogilev, Belarus, 204
Catholic consistory, 204
Mohn, J., 130
Mokotoff, Gary, 72, 133, 136
Moldau, 81, 214. *See also* Moldova *and* Moldavia
Moldavia, 81, 93. *See also* Moldau *and* Moldova
Records, 228
Moldova, 81, 82, 85, 201, 202, 208. *See also* Moldau *and* Moldavia
History, 93, 222
Researching in, 214
Möller, Hilde, 187
Molochansk, Ukraine, 102
Molochna, Ukraine, 205
Molotschna, Ukraine, 102, 205. *See also* Molochna, Ukraine
Monaco, 245
Mönchengladbach, Germany, 188
Mongols, 96, 304
Montbéliard, France, 112, 234
Montenegro, 78, 85, 229, 231
Montevideo, Uruguay, 36, 39
Arrival lists, 26
Montreal, Quebec, 25, 141
Moorhead, Minnesota, 239
Moors, 107
Moos, Mario von, 282
Moravia, 73, 76, 85, 94, 192, 289
Archives, 218
Church records, 218
Gazetteers, 73
German emigration, 141, 151, 160, 161
History, 77, 78, 84, 88, 91, 93, 94, 95, 110, 125, 126, 141, 216, 217
Religious dissidents, 111
Researchers, 187
Moravian Brethren, 88, 110, 113, 122, 124, 158, 163, 165, 167, 202, 217, 285, 306. *See also* Moravian Church
Archives, 122
In Argentina, 145
In Australia, 159
In Palatinate, 122
In United States, 122
In Volga River region, 122, 203
Records, 122
Moravian Church, 110, 122. *See also* Moravian Brethren
In England, 244
Moravians, 144, 172, 306
In United States, 113

Moravská Trebová, Czech Republic, 95
Moresnet, Belgium, 231
Moreton Bay district, New South Wales, 43, 157
Moreton Bay, Queensland, 25
Moritz, Eduard, 170
Mormons, 121. *See also* Church of Jesus Christ of Latter-day Saints
Morocco, 54, 162
Morogoro, Tanzania, 167
Morrill Act of 1862 (Homestead Act), 9, 140, 308
Morris, Pauline J., 160
Mortuary records, 7
Möschle, S., 131
Moscow, Russia, 102, 207, 211
    "German Suburb", 101
    City archive, 203
    Lutheran Consistory, 203
Moselle department, France, 234, 235
Moselle River, 80, 96, 106
Moshi, Tanzania, 167
Mosquito Coast. *See* Nicaragua *and* Honduras
Movius, John D., 73, 176, 184, 200, 282
Mukachevo, Ukraine, 214. *See also* Munkatsch
Mulhall, Michael George, 170
Müller, Friedrich, 72
Müller, Fritz Ferdinand, 166, 170
Müller, Martha, 233, 282
Müller, Sepp, 108
Munich Agreement of 1938, 95
Munkatsch, 214. See also Mukachevo, Ukraine
Münster, Germany, 110
Münsterites, 110
Munz, G., 131
Murray River, Australia, 156
Musat, Ing. George, 228
Museum and Documents Center of the Jews of Latvia, 210
Museum of Waldensian Heritage, 119
Muslims, 112
Mussolini, Benito, 230
Mutzelburg, Owen B., 40, 46
Myanmar, 56, 167

—N—

Nahe River, Germany, 80
Nama tribe (Namibia), 165
Names, 57–64
    Changes in English-speaking countries, 63
    Given, 62
    Meaning, 62
    Surnames. *See under* Surnames
Namibia, 49, 53, 162, 165, 309
    Passenger lists, 26

Nancy, France, 235
Nanjing, China, 55
Nansen International Office for Refugees, 54
Napoleon, 90, 100, 102, 105, 125, 222, 224, 231, 244, 307
Napoleonic Wars, 75, 93
Narew River region, Poland, 81
Narewgebiet, Poland, 81. *See* Narew River region
Nassau, 76. *See also* Hesse-Nassau
    History, 76
Natal, South Africa, 165, 171
National archives. *Check under each country*
National Archives and Records Administration, 25, 27, 296
National Archives and Records Service, 15
National Archives of Canada, 25, 31, 213
National Archives Volunteer Association (NAVA), 211
National Genealogy Conference, 13
National Huguenot Society, 119
National libraries. *Check under each country*
National Library of Australia, 45
National Library of Canada, 31
Nationalism, 138
Naturalization records, 11
Naugard County, Pomerania, 185
NAVA. *See* National Archives Volunteer Association
Nazareth, Pennsylvania, 122
Nebraska, 119, 142, 143
Neckar River, Germany, 81
Neisse River, 161
Nelson, New Zealand, 160, 161
Netherlands, 105, 112, 120, 133, 287, 304, 305, 306, 307
    Census records, 237
    Church records, 237
    Civil records, 237
    Genealogical societies, 236, 237
    German emigration, 124, 139
    Guild records, 237
    History, 56, 78, 86, 88, 89, 92, 93, 105, 106, 123, 231, 236, 241
    Map of, 312
    Military records, 237
    Religion, 112
    Researching in, 236
    State Archive, 237
Netze River region, 81, 82, 90, 100, 101, 223. *See also* Notec River region, Poland
Netzeland, 282
Neubrandenburg, Germany, 83
Neuchâtel canton, Switzerland, 83, 117
Neuenburg, 83. *See also* Neuchâtel canton, Switzerland
Neuman, Ron, 68

Neumann, Kurt, 186
Neumark, 81, 282. *See also* East Brandenburg
    History, 100
    Researchers, 187
Neu-Ostpreussen, 81. *See also* New East Prussia
Neurussland, 81. *See also* New Russia. *See also* Black Sea region
Neusatz, 231. *See also* Novi Sad, Yugoslavia
Neusohl, 219. *See also* Banská Bystrica, Slovak Republic
Neutra, 219. *See also* Nitra, Slovak Republic
New Brunswick, Canada
    Civil records, 33
New East Prussia, 81, 100
New Economic Policy (1921-28), Russian, 104
New England, 142, 143, 297
"New Germany", 147, 151, 153
New Guinea, 49, 162
New Hampshire, 142
New Harmony, Indiana, 114
New Jersey, 142, 143, 276
    German immigration, 280
New Netherlands, 139, 236. *See also* New York
New Orleans, Louisiana, 24, 25, 141
New Philadelphia, Ohio, 122
New Russia, 81, 102. *See also* Black Sea region
New South Wales, Australia, 26, 41, 43, 154, 155, 156, 157, 168, 308
"new tribes", 87
New York, 139, 142, 143, 225, 236, 276
    German immigration, 139, 280
New York Children's Aid Society, 7
New York, New York, 24, 25, 141, 143, 145, 309
    Passenger arrival lists, 23
New Zealand, 26, 155, 156, 158, 168, 308, 309
    Archives, 47
    Books and other publications, 48
    Church records, 48
    Civil registers, 47
    Genealogical societies, 46
    German immigration, 95, 308
    German settlements, 159
    Land records, 48
    Map of, 312
    Passenger lists, 47
    Swiss in, 105
Newberry Library, 296
Newcastle, New South Wales, 25, 156
Newfoundland, Canada, 33
    Civil records, 33
Newspapers, 8
    Directory of, 274
    German-language, 8

Niagara peninsula, 143. *See also under* Canada
Nicaragua, 146
    Mosquito Coast, 150
Nick, Elizabeth, 231, 290
Nidwalden canton, Switzerland, 83
Nied, Victoria, 97
Niederösterreich, 83, 191. *See also* Lower Austria
Niedersachsen
    Genealogical societies, 182
    State archives, 179
Nigeria, 162, 167
Nitra, Slovak Republic, 219
Nitrianske Pravno, Slovak Republic, 85, 96
Nizhny Novgorod, Russia, 203
Nord Slesvig, Denmark, 84. *See also* Schleswig
Nordrhein-Westfalen
    Genealogical societies, 182
    State archives, 179
Nordstetten, Germany, 128, 131
North Adelaide, South Australia, 44
North Africa, 107
North America, 306, 310
    German immigration, 94, 103, 140, 244, 305, 309
    Swiss immigration, 105
North American Baptist College Archives, Edmonton, Alberta, 121
North Bukovina, 85, 212. *See also* Bukovina
North Carolina, 113, 142, 143, 276
    German immigration, 140, 142, 280
North Caucasus, 80, 82, 85, 103, 215
North Dakota, 66, 72, 107, 108, 113, 121, 142, 143, 288, 291
    German immigration, 103
North Dakota Institute for Regional Studies, 170, 215, 281
North Island, New Zealand, 161
North Newton, Kansas, 119
North Sea, 81
North Sydney, Quebec, 25
Northern Bessarabia, 85
Northern Territory, Australia, 43, 154, 155
Northfield, Minnesota, 239
Northrhine-Westphalia, 80, 83, 96, 279
    History, 91
    State archives, 179
Northwest Territories, Canada, 32, 33, 279
    Civil records, 33
Norway
    Church records, 239
    Civil records, 239
    Community history books, 239
    Genealogical societies, 239
    Geography, 238
    German immigration, 237

Norway (*continued*)
    History, 86, 241, 242
    Language, 238
    Names, 238
    National Archives, 240
    Researching in, 237
Nösner Zipser, 96
Notec River region, Poland, 82. *See also* Netze River region
Nova Santa Rosa, Brazil, 40
Nova Scotia, Canada, 143, 144
    Civil records, 33
    Provincial Archives, 32
Novi Sad, Serbia, 231
Nunavut, Canada, 32, 33
Nuremberg, Germany, 80. *See* Nürnberg, Germany
Nürnberg, Germany, 80
Nuthack, Joachim O. R., 198, 218
Nyeko, Balan, 165, 168

—O—

O'Connor, Patrick, 236
Oberdorf (am Ipf, Bopfingen), Germany, 131
Oberösterreich, 83, 191. *See also* Upper Austria
Oberpfalz, 128
Oberwihl, nr. Waldshut, Germany, 130
Obwalden canton, Switzerland, 83
Odenwald, Germany, 81
Oder River, Germany-Poland, 81, 157, 161, 304
Oder-Neisse River line, 75, 91, 141, 223
Odessa, Ukraine, 79, 82, 102, 107, 113, 205, 214, 279
    Archives, 208, 212, 213
    German immigration, 102
Offenburg, Germany, 131
Ohaupo, New Zealand, 48
Ohio, 143, 225
Oklahoma, 143, 152
    German immigration, 103
Old Catholics, 111
    Records, 193
Old Economy, Pennsylvania, 114
Old High German language, 115
Old Lutherans, 41, 45, 111, 114, 124, 138, 147, 155, 172, 276, 285, 308
    In Australia, 45
Old Order Mennonites, 146, 153. *See also* Mennonites
Oldenburg, 19, 60, 76, 77, 289
    Genealogical societies, 182
Oledry, 78. *See also* Holländerein
Olinyk, Dave, 68, 72
Olmütz, 85, 95, 218. *See also* Olomouc, Czech republic
Olomouc, Czech Republic, 95
    Archives, 218
Olson, May, 8, 14, 274

Olzog, Günter, 72, 281
Ontario, Canada, 28, 119, 143, 144, 145, 307
    Abstract records, 31
    Civil records, 33
    Provincial Archives, 31, 32
    Research helps, 281
Opava, Czech Republic, 218
Orange Free State, South Africa, 165
Orange Walk, Belize, 146
Oranienbaum, Russia, 208
Ore Mountains, 80
Oregon, 142
Orenburg, Russia, 84, 103
Orphanage records, 7
Ortssippenbücher, 5, 58, 64, 181, 279. *See also* Village genealogies
Ösel
    Lutheran consistory, 203
Oslo, Norway, 238
Ossetia, 215
Österreich, 92, 192. *See also* Austria
Österreichisch-Schlesien, 85, 192. *See also* Austrian Silesia
Ostfriesland, 57, 58, 236. *See also* East Frisia
    Genealogical societies, 182
    History, 307
    State archives, 179
Ostgalizien, 85. *See also* East Galicia
Ostmark, 92. *See also* Austria
Ostpreussen, 19, 77, 288. *See also* East Prussia
Ostrava, Czech Republic, 95
Ostsee, 81. *See also* Baltic Sea
Otago, New Zealand, 26, 160, 161
Ottawa, Ontario, 31
Otto I, the Great, 88, 92
Ottoman Archives, 228, 229
Ottoman Nufüs census records, 228
Ottoman Turkish Empire, 92, 113, 228, 304, 309
    History, 79, 93, 106–7, 216, 220, 222, 228
Ottoman Turks, 80
Oure River, 106
Ovambo tribe (Namibia), 165

—P—

Pacific states, 142, 143
Packer, D. R. G., 154
Paikert, Géza C., 108
Pakistan, 56, 167
Palatinate, 19, 76, 77, 81, 89, 105, 111, 112, 113, 116, 119, 122, 189, 276, 279, 305, 306. *See also* Pfalz
    Card index file, 188
    German emigration, 102, 139, 140, 153, 163, 287, 306, 308
    History, 79, 89, 98, 105, 137, 235
    Immigration, 305
    State archives, 179
Palatines, 139, 236, 244, 245, 280

Schmidt, Josef, 109, 284, 286
Schmidt-Pretoria, Werner, 163, 164, 170
Schmiedehaus, Walter, 152, 170
Schneider, Ludwig, 225, 284
Schnell, E. L., 163, 164, 165, 171
Schön, Th., 131
Schonfeld, Louis, 134
Schönhengst, 85, 95. *See also* Hrebec, Czech Republic
Schrader-Muggenthaler, Cornelia, 196, 234, 284
Schreiber, Hermann, 109
Schreiner-Yantis, Netti, 280
Schroeder, William, 153, 171
Schubert, David A., 41
Schulz, Karin, 284
Schurz, Carl, 138
Schwaben. *See also* Swabia. *See also* Swabians. *See also* Alamanni
Schwäbisch Gmünd, Germany, 131
Schwäbische Türkei, 85, 192. *See also* Swabian Turkey
Schwabs, 100. *See* Swabians
Schwarz, Ernst, 71, 109
Schwarzburg-Rudolstadt, 19, 77
Schwarzburg-Sondershausen, 19, 77
Schweitzer, George Keene, 175, 226, 284
Schwenkfelders, 111, 113, 124, 172, 306
    Records, 121
Schwerin, Germany, 83
Schwetzingen, Germany, 132
Schwierz, Israel, 130
Schwyz canton, Switzerland, 83
Scotland, 105
    Germanicized Scots, 243
    History, 78
Scottish mercenaries, 243
Sea of Azov, 80, 85, 102
Seenplatte, 81
Semgallen, 81. *See also* Semgalia. *See also* Zemgalia
Semigalia, 81
Semipalatinsk, Russia, 103
Sending money abroad, 247
Senekovic, Dagmar, 284
Senz, Josef Volkmar, 109, 286
Separatist (Lutherans), 113, 202, 203
    In Volga River region, 203
Serbia, 192, 304
    History, 78, 85
    Researching in, 231
Serbs, 94
Seven Weeks' War, 93
Seven Years' War, 93, 101, 137, 306
Seventh-Day Adventists, 122, 172
    In Brazil, 147
    In Latin America, 35
Shandong peninsu, China, 168
Shanghai, China, 55
Shea, Jonathan D., 273, 285
Sheehan, Colin Gordon, 41

Ship arrival lists, 11
Shipyard, Belize, 146
Shtetls, 113
Siberia, 54, 85, 103, 104, 215, 309
Sibiu, Romania, 82
Siebenbürgen, 82, 85, 96, 106, 187, 192, 220. *See also* Transylvania
Sieg River, Germany, 81
Sielemann, Jürgen, 127
Silesia, 19, 62, 71, 76, 77, 82, 113, 116, 166, 274, 331. *See also* Schlesien
    Church records, 218, 288
    Gazetteers, 73
    Genealogical societies, 188
    German emigration, 45, 124, 152, 157, 159, 164, 308
    History, 77, 78, 84, 90, 91, 93, 95, 101, 126, 216, 217, 306
    Place names, 68
    Protestants, 217
    Records, 247
    Researchers, 187
    Surnames, 64
Silverman, Marlene, 134
Simons, Menno, 110
Singapore, 56
Sino-Judaic Archives of the Hoover Institution, 55
Skender, L. Edward, 97, 109
Skrzypinski, Henryk, 214, 227
Slask, 84. *See also* Silesia
Slavonia, 97, 192, 230
    History, 76, 77, 85
Slavs, 87, 93, 95, 197, 304
Slawonien, 85, 192. *See also* Slavonia
Slovak Republic, 72, 93, 134, 216, 217, 220, 271, 304. *See also* Slovakia
    Church records, 219
    Embassy, 219
    Gazetteers, 70
    History, 96, 126, 216
    Jewish records, 219
    Jews, 216
    Land records, 219
    Map of, 312
    Microfilms, 16, 17
    Military records, 216
    National Archives, 219
    Researchers, 187
    Researching in, 219
Slovakia, 214. *See* Slovak Republic
    Gazetteers, 73
    German emigration, 141
    History, 78, 96, 216
Slovaks, 94, 96
Slovenes, 94
Slovenia, 79, 82, 85, 94, 97, 192, 222, 230
    Church records, 288
    History, 78
    Microfilms, 16

Slovenia (*continued*)
    National Archive, 231
    Records, 128
    Researching in, 230
Smelser, Ronald, 285
Smith, Anna Piszczan-Czaja, 118, 124, 136, 285
Smith, Clifford Neal, 23, 37, 41, 44, 114, 118, 124, 136, 150, 157, 285
Smith, Frank, 239
Smith, Kenneth L., 64, 123, 173, 273, 285
Smith, Leonard H., Jr., 34
Smith, Norma H., 34
Sobotik, Robert, 73
Social Security Death Index, 20, 134
Socinians. *See also* Unitarians
    In Poland, 111, 222
Sofala, South Africa, 164, 171
Solomon Islands, 49, 162
Solothurn canton, Switzerland, 83, 117, 143, 284
Sondershausen, Germany, 190
Sons of the American Revolution, 112
Sorbs, 81. *See also* Lusatia
Soshnikov, Vladislav Yevgyenevich, 200, 206, 207, 211, 212, 214
Soundex index to U. S. census records, 11
South Africa, 26, 51, 53, 55, 56, 113, 162, 163, 164, 165, 168, 169, 171, 306, 308, 309
    Archives, 52
    Boer War, 309
    Church records, 50
    Civil registers, 51
    Genealogical societies, 52
    German settlements, 162, 163
    Immigration and naturalization records, 51
    King's German Legion. *See* King's German Legion (English)
    Land records, 51
    Military records, 51
    Other Records, 51
    Passenger lists, 26
    South African-German Cultural Association, 52
    Swiss in, 105
    Wills, probate and orphan records, 51
South African War
    Veterans records, 31
South America, 310
    Colonization, 169
    German immigration, 103, 309
    Map of, 312
    Swiss in, 105
South Asia, 55
South Australia, 25, 26, 41, 43, 45, 46, 154, 155, 156, 157, 158, 159, 161, 170, 308

South Australia (*continued*)
German immigration, 41
State library, 41
South Bessarabia
History, 85
South Brazil, 169, 171
South Bukovina, 289
South Carolina, 142, 143, 276
German immigration, 140, 142
South Caucasus, 85, 102, 113, 215
South Dakota, 113, 121, 143, 291
South Island, New Zealand, 46, 49, 158, 160, 161, 308
South Prussia, 82
South Russia, 55, 81, 82, 102, 119, 205, 215, 306. *See also* New Russia. *See also* Südrussland. *See also* Ukraine
Researching in, 215
South Tyrol, Italy, 95, 109, 221, 289
Archive, 222
Church records, 288
History, 84, 95
Records, 128
Southeast Europe, 61, 108, 200, 219, 220, 225, 311. *See also* Eastern Europe
Genealogical societies, 188
Researchers, 187
Southern Trunk Railway (New Zealand), 160
Southhampton, England, 23
Southland, New Zealand, 160, 161
South-West Africa, 165
Southwest Pacific
German colonies, 309
Soviet Union, 54, 67, 91, 114, 116, 200, 310, 311
Gazetteers, 67
German emigration, 149
History, 78, 84, 91, 96, 97, 104, 207, 216
Maps of German settlements in, 67
Place names, 67
Researchers, 199
Researching in former, 283. *See under each country*
Spain, 89, 112, 113, 115, 117, 236, 241
History, 86, 88, 92, 106
Spalek, John M., 171, 175
Spanish Inquisition, 112
Spanish Lookout, Belize, 146
Spanish Netherlands, 105, 123, 287, 305
Spanuth, Johannes, 164
Spessart, Germany, 82
Spis, Slovak Republic, 85, 96. *See also* Zips, Slovak Republic
Srem, Yugoslavia, 82, 85, 192, 231. *See also* Syrmia. *See also* Syrmien
Sri Lanka, 56, 167

Staatsarchiv. *See* Germany: State archives
Stache, Christa, 124, 136, 285
Stadtarchiv. *See* Germany: City Archives
Stalin, 67, 310, 311
Stalingrad, Battle of, 104
Standesamt. *See* Germany: Civil Registry Offices
State archives. *Check under individual countries*
State census records, 12
Stebelska, H., 226
Steiermark, 83, 191, 192. *See also* Styria
Steigerwald, Germany, 82
Steigerwald, Jacob, 98, 109, 145, 149, 153, 155, 285
Stein, Neithard von, 187
Stern, Malcolm H., 136
Stettin. *See also* Szczecin, Poland
Archives, 226
Stiefvater, O., 131
Stirling, Western Australia, 158
Stockholm, Sweden, 241, 243
Stoeckl, Michael, 187, 228
Stoffel, Gertraut Maria, 160
Stoffel, Hans-Peter, 160
Strasbourg, France, 234, 235
Strassburger, Ralph Beaver, 285
-strasse, 82
Strasse, 82
Strauss, Peter, 136
Studienstelle ostdeutsche Genealogie der Dorschungsstelle Ostmitteleuropa, 188
Stumpp, Karl, 62, 64, 67, 73, 109, 213, 286
Stuttgart, Germany, 127, 134, 188, 216
Styria, 76, 83, 92, 94, 191, 192
History, 77
Subcarpathian Rus', 85, 96, 212, 214, 216
History, 97
Sub-Carpathian Ukraine, 214
Sub-Saharan Africa, 107
Suceava, Romania, 98
Süd-Bessarabien, 85. *See also* South Bessarabia
Suderman, Jim, 120
Sudeten Germans, 95, 98
Researchers, 218
Sudetengebirge, 82
Sudetenland, 82, 95, 116, 310
Church records, 288
Genealogical societies, 187
History, 78, 84, 91, 141
Map of, 312
Records, 128
Researchers, 187
Sudhaus, Fritz, 171
Südpreussen, 82. *See also* South Prussia

Südrussland, 81, 82. *See also* South Russia. *See also* Ukraine. *See also* New Russia
Südtirol, 221. *See also* South Tyrol, Italy
Records, 194
Suess, Jared H., 61, 65, 66, 196, 273, 286
Suhl, Germany, 83
Sulimierskiego, Filipa, 66, 73
Sulz, Austria, 129
Sulzbach-Rosenberg, Germany, 128
Sulzer, Salomon, 128
Surnames
Americanicized, 62
Changes in English-speaking countries, 61
Derived from locations, 59
Descriptive, 59
Dialectic, 59
Double, 60
French, 60
German, 57
Italian, 60
Lithuanian, 60
Matronymic, 57
Occupational, 58
Patronymic, 57, 126, 206, 238, 242, 306, 307
Polish, 60
Slavic, 60
Spelling variations, 57
Sutschawa, Bukovina, 98. *See also* Suceava, Romania
Suwalk, Lithuania, 134
Svitavy, Czech Republic, 95
Swabia, 117, 125, 220, 283
Danube Swabians, 97
History, 88, 98
Swabian Turkey, 97, 109, 192
History, 85
Swabians, 81, 102, 108, 306. *See also* Alamanni
Swakopmund, Namibia, 26
Swan River district, Western Australia, 159
Sweden, 99, 100, 184, 238
Census records, 243
Church records, 242
Court records, 243
Emigration records, 243
History, 79, 89, 233, 241, 305
Immigration, 233
Land records, 243
Lutherans, 242
Military records, 243
Names, 242
Researching in, 241
Swedish Pomerania, 242, 243
Swedenborgians, 144
Swedish East India Company, 55
Swiss, 79
In Argentina, 146
In Australia, 40, 105, 155

Transylvania (*continued*)
  History, 77, 85, 227
  Records, 228
  Researchers, 187
Transylvanian Saxons, 96, 98, 106,
  109, 113, 141, 142, 191, 220, 277,
  287, 305, 309
  Records, 228
Trappist Catholics, 165
Treaty of Kiel, 238
Treaty of Lübeck, 242
Treaty of Nijmegen, 305
Treaty of St. Germain, 75, 310
Treaty of Trianon, 75, 310
Treaty of Versailles, 75, 310
Trebon, Czech Republic
  Regional archives, 218
Trent, Italy, 95, 192, 221
  History, 77
  State Archives, 222
Trento, 95, 221. *See also* Trent, Italy
Tribbeko, John, 287
Trient, 95, 192, 221. *See also* Trent,
  Italy
Trier, Germany, 37, 147, 150, 167
Triest, 192. *See also* Trieste, Italy
Trieste, Italy, 24, 92, 192, 230
Triple Frisia, 236
Troppau, 218. *See also* Opava, Czech
  Republic
Trujillo, 37
Tunkers, 111
Turkey, 54, 55, 167, 168, 191, 215,
  306
  Archives, 229
  Census records, 228
  History, 86, 227
  Researching in, 228
  State Library, 229
Turkish Wars, 97
Turkmenistan, 215
Turks, 81, 82, 89, 97, 107, 113, 305,
  306
Turner, Eugene James, 142, 274
Tvedt, Kevin, 60, 64
Twigden, Liz, 41, 42, 154, 157, 171
Tyrol, 76, 83, 191, 192
  German emigration, 153
  History, 77, 92, 93, 95, 97

—U—

Uckermark, Germany, 82, 276
Uecker River, 82
Ueckermark, Germany, 82
Uetrecht, E., 65, 74
Ufa, Russia, 103
Uganda, 171
Ukraina, 212. *See also* Ukraine
Ukraine, 82, 85, 90, 102, 103, 104,
  112, 113, 134, 192, 200, 201, 202,
  205, 207, 212, 213, 275, 287, 304,
  306, 307. *See also* Südrussland.

Ukraine (*continued*)
  See also South Russia. *See also*
    New Russia
  Archives, 203
  Atlases, 70
  Church records, 223
  German immigration, 102, 124
  History, 66, 88, 101, 125, 222,
    307
  Land records, 225
  Map of, 312
  Microfilms, 16, 17
  Researchers, 187
  Researching in, 212
Ukrainians, 94, 223
Ulbrich, Heinz, 187
Ullman, Robert, 95
Ulm, Germany, 97, 131
Ungarn, 192. *See also* Hungary
Union of Kalmar, 242
Union of South Africa, 309. *See also*
  South Africa
Unitarians, 111
  In Poland, 222
Unitas Fratrum, 110, 217. *See also*
  Moravian Church
United Brethren in Christ
  In Canada, 30
United Church of Canada, 30
United Church of Christ
  In Latin America, 35
United Empire Loyalists, 31, 112
United Kingdom, 120. *See also*
  Northern Ireland. *See also* Britain.
  See also Great Britain
  Researching in, 243
United States, 114, 119, 120, 133,
  145, 306, 308, 309, 311
  Atlantic states, 297
  Bounty land property, 9
  Cemetery associations, 7
  Cemetery records, 7
  Census records, 2, 11
  Church records, 7, 282
  Civil War, 160
  Consulates, 283, 287
  County histories, 15
  Court records, 8
  Customs Service arrival records,
    26
  Depression, 308
  Genealogical helps, 284, 285
  Genealogical societies, 281
  German immigration, 24, 90, 95,
    97, 124, 139, 140, 142, 144,
    146, 148, 149, 160, 169, 170,
    171, 233, 274, 276, 277, 278,
    279, 280, 281, 287, 307, 308,
    309, 310
  German settlements, 142
  German-language newspapers, 8
  Great Plains states, 103, 142, 309
  Homestead property, 9
  Immigration, 233, 310

United States (*continued*)
  Immigration and Naturalization
    Service, 26
  Land records, 9
  Library of Congress, 72
  List of church archives, 116
  Lodge records, 7
  Midwest states, 119, 141, 142,
    143, 287, 296, 297
  Military Death Index, 20
  Military records, 10
  Mortuary records, 7
  National Archives, 15, 25, 28
  Naturalization, 278
  Naturalization records, 11
  Orphanage records, 7
  Port cities, 141
  Private school records, 7
  Professional associations, 7
  Reasons for immigration, 137
  Research helps, 280, 286
  Ship arrival lists, 11
  Social Security Death Index, 20
  Southern states, 143, 297
  Tax records, 9
  Vital records, 2, 9
  Western states, 297
Unity of Brethren, 110. *See also*
  Unitas Fratrum
University of Minnesota, 300
University of Texas, 297
University of Toronto, 205
University student lists, 174
Unruh, Benjamin Heinrich, 124, 204,
  207, 208, 213, 236, 287
Unterwalden canton, Switzerland, 83
Upper Austria, 83, 97, 191
Upper Canada, 143. *See also under*
  Canada
Upper Hungary, 93, 96, 219, 304.
  See also Slovak Republic
Upper Palatinate, 128
Upper Silesia, 77
Ural Mountains, 84, 103
Uri canton, Switzerland, 83
Uruguay, 36, 38, 120, 145, 149, 153
  Census records, 37
  Civil registers, 36
  National archives, 39
  National library, 39
  Research helps, 35
Usambara highlands, Tanzania, 166
Utah, 142
Uzhhorod
  Archives, 214

—V—

Vaduz, Liechtenstein, 197
Valais canton, Switzerland, 83
Valdese, North Carolina, 119
Valdivia province, Chile, 151, 152
Valparaiso, Chile, 152
  Arrival lists, 26

Vancouver, British Columbia, 145
Vanderhalven, F., 74
Vasmer, Max, 74
Vatican City, 245
Vaud canton, Switzerland, 83
Venetia, Italy, 222
    History, 76
Venezuela, 153
Ventspils, Latvia, 210
Verdenhalven, Fritz, 273
Vianden canton, Luxembourg, 84
Victoria, Australia, 26, 43, 154, 155,
    156, 157, 158, 161, 308
Victoria, British Columbia, 32, 33
Victoria, Cameroon, 167
Vienna, Austria, 83, 115, 191, 193,
    194, 306. *See also* Wien
    City archives, 193
    Military Archives, 216
Vietnam, 20
Vietnam War, 20
Village genealogies, 181. *See also*
    Dorfsippenbücher *and*
    Ortssippenbücher
Vilnius, Lithuania, 210
Vine Hill, Nick, 25, 40, 42, 44, 45,
    46, 49
Virginia, 142, 143, 276, 287
    German immigration, 139, 142
Visby, Sweden, 241
Vistula River region, Poland, 80, 84,
    100, 101
Vistula-Nogat delta area
    History, 77
Vital records. *See under each country*
Vogesen, 82. *See* Vosges Mountains
Vogtland, Germany, 82
Voigt, Hans-Jürgen, 199, 288
Voigt, Karl, jun., 65
Vojvodina (Serbia), 79, 80, 82, 97,
    220, 231, 276, 336
    Archives, 231
    History, 78, 85, 192, 229
Volga German Republic, 104
Volga River region, Russia, 40, 54,
    102, 103, 104, 122, 145, 148, 188,
    206, 207, 208, 212, 310, 311
    Map of, 312
    Records, 203
    Settlements, 84
    Settler lists, 208
Volhynia, 81, 90, 101, 103, 104, 112,
    124, 188, 201, 202, 204, 205, 206,
    207, 212, 213, 291, 308. *See also*
    Zhitomir
    Church records, 124, 223
    Genealogical societies, 188
    Genealogical sources, 225
    German emigration, 145, 153
    History, 78, 85
    Researchers, 187
Volhynian Germans, 149
Völkerwanderung, 87, 110. *See also*
    Great Barbarian Migrations

von Blom, D., 153
von der Porten, Edward, 109
von Moos, Mario, 282
von Poellnitz, G., 165
von Stein, Neithard, 187
von Tiesenhausen, Berend, 171
Vondra, Josef, 41
Vorarlberg, Austria, 83, 92, 125, 129,
    191, 192
    History, 77
Vorderösterreich, 125
Vosges Mountains, 82
Vysov, Czech Republic, 95

—W—

Waadt, 83. *See also* Vaud canton,
    Switzerland
Wagemann, Ernst, 35
Wagenpfeil, H., 131
Wagner, Ernst, 109, 287
Waibola Township, New Zealand,
    160
Walachei, 82. *See also* Walachia
Walachia, 82
    Records, 228
    Religious dissidents, 111
Waldeck, 19, 76, 77, 276
    History, 76
Waldensians, 88, 110, 119, 189
    In Germany, 188
    In Italy, 112, 222
    Records, 118
    Resource centers, 188
Waldo, Peter, 88, 110
Waldus, Peter, 110. *See* Peter Waldo
Walker, Mack, 138, 146, 147, 148,
    151, 153, 171
Wallis, 83. *See also* Valais canton,
    Switzerland
Wallonia, Belgium, 232
Walloons (Belgians), 89, 112, 232,
    305
    In Germany, 188
    Records, 118, 119, 123
    Resource centers, 188
Wandler, Diane J., 2, 288
Wanneroo, Western Australia, 158
Wappäus, Johann, 171
War of the League of Augsburg, 306
Ward, Robert, 174, 199
Wardale, Carol, 41, 156
Warmia, East Prussia, 116. *See also*
    Warmia, Poland
Warmia, Poland, 80, 116
Wars of Liberation (German), 90
Wars of Unification (German), 75, 91
Wars of Unification (Italian), 93
Warsaw, Poland, 80, 81, 82, 90, 101,
    109, 205, 213, 222, 226
    Archives, 226
    History, 100
    Records, 205

Warta River region, Poland, 82, 84,
    99, 101, 104, 310
Warthe River, 84. *See also* Warta
    River region, Poland
Warthegau, 82, 99. *See also* Warta
    River region, Poland
Washington (state), 142, 143
Washington, DC, 143
Waterloo County, Ontario, 34, 143
Waterloo, Ontario, 30, 205
Webster, J. B., 165, 168, 171
Wecken, Ernst, 283
Wegemer, B., 130
Wegmann, Susanne, 40
Weichsel River region, 84. *See also*
    Vistula River region, Poland
Weidlein, Johann, 109
Weikel, Sally A., 288
Weimar Republic
    History, 84
Weiner, Miriam, 117, 136, 205, 215,
    288
Weinstrasse, 82
Weisser, Charles, 205
Welisch, Sophie A., 66, 74, 98, 109,
    288
Wellauer, Maralyn A., 171, 270, 288,
    291
Wellington County, Ontario, 34
Wellington, New Zealand, 26, 47, 48,
    161, 162
Welsch, E., 290
Welte, Thomas, 132
Wends, 81, 82
Wermes, Martina, 199, 288
Werner, Manuel, 132
Werner, Otto, 132
Werra River, 81
Weser River, 81
West Frankish Kingdom, 87
West Indies, 146, 278
West Prussia, 19, 76, 77, 112, 113,
    274, 279, 331. *See also*
    Westpreussen
    Church records, 288
    Genealogical societies, 187, 188
    German emigration, 103
    History, 76, 77, 78, 84, 89, 90, 91,
        100, 102, 125, 140, 152
    Name index files, 188
    Place names, 68
    Records, 247
West Volhynia, 124
Western Australia, 41, 42, 43, 154,
    155, 157, 158, 159, 168, 170
Western Canada, 144. *See also under*
    Canada
Western Galicia, 84, 98, 223. *See
    also* Galicia
Western Pacific Islands, 162
Western Samoa, 162
Western Ukraine, 213
Westerwald, 82

GERMANIC GENEALOGY SOCIETY MEMBERSHIP

NAME _____

ADDRESS _____

PHONE _____

APPLICATION _____ RENEWAL _____

MEMBERSHIP NUMBER _____

Membership is open to anyone interested in Germanic genealogy. A member is encouraged to become a member of the MINNESOTA GENEALOGICAL SOCIETY.

Dues are $5.00 per year payable in March.

Make check payable to Germanic Genealogy Society.

Mail to: GERMANIC GENEALOGY SOCIETY
P.O. BOX 16312
ST. PAUL, MN 55116-0312

11/95

* * * * * * * * * * * * *

MINNESOTA GENEALOGICAL SOCIETY MEMBERSHIP

NAME _____

ADDRESS _____

NATIONALITIES OF INTEREST _____

INDIVIDUAL $18 _____ FAMILY $22 _____

APPLICATION _____ RENEWAL _____

MEMBERSHIP NUMBER _____

Make check payable to Minnesota Genealogical Society.

Mail to: MINNESOTA GENEALOGICAL SOCIETY
P.O. BOX 16069
ST. PAUL, MN 55116

HISTORY OF THE ORGANIZATION

The GERMAN INTEREST GROUP was started in December, 1979 and by-laws were officially adopted in September, 1980. The name GERMANIC GENEALOGY SOCIETY was officially adopted at the November 1992 Annual Meeting. It became a branch of the MINNESOTA GENEALOGICAL SOCIETY on January 10, 1981. On November 21, 1992 the name was officially changed to Germanic Genealogy Society

PURPOSES OF THE ORGANIZATION

The purposes are exclusively educational, more specifically to:

1) provide an association of those interested in genealogy;

2) provide opportunity for exchange of ideas relating to genealogical practices and experiences;

3) hold meetings for the instruction and interest of its members;

4) foster and increase an interest in Germanic genealogy;

5) collect, and when practicable, publish genealogical biographical and historical material relating to Minnesota families of German descent and their forbears;

6) encourage the establishment of German genealogical resources in genealogical departments in libraries throughout the State of Minnesota.

SALES MATERIAL

Germanic Genealogy: A Guide to Worldwide Sources & Migration Patterns.

The Lutherans of Russia, Vol. 1, Parish Index to Church Books of the Evangelical Lutheran Church of St Petersburg, 1833-1885.

Die Ahnenstammkartei des Deutschen Volkes, An Introduction and Register. How to access a collection of pedigree charts and family group records & card index of 2.7 million names at the German Center for Genealogy in Leipzig.

A Translation of Abbreviations Found in *Müllers Grosses Deutsches Ortsbuch*

Using the *Meyers Orts - und Verkehrslexikon*

Guide to Pennsylvania Archives

Library Holdings of the Germanic Genealogy Society at Concordia Library

Blank Family Group Sheets & Ancestor Charts (English, German)

A complete list is available in the newsletter or on request with a S.A.S.E. from GGS.

MEMBERSHIP COMMITTEE - keeps an updated list of the membership. The committee processes membership applications and renewals and prepares the address labels for the newsletter. A welcome packet will be sent to all new members.

PROGRAM COMMITTEE - obtains locations for meetings, arranges for speakers, prepares meeting sites and forwards this information to the newsletter.

SPRING CONFERENCE COMMITTEE - plans annual spring conference meeting, arranges for keynote speaker, location and luncheon.

RESEARCH COMMITTEE - provides information to members by writing or publishing genealogical research articles, answering queries, providing translators, and keeping a bibliography of resources and addresses to aid in Germanic research.

LIBRARY COMMITTEE - purchases and catalogs our group's books and materials, which are housed at the Concordia College Library in St. Paul . Also maintains clipping file, newsletter and quarterly collection.

REGIONAL RESOURCE COMMITTEE - gives ideas and assistance to various small study groups concentrating on a particular area. Plans Fall Workshop meeting which concentrates on specific Germanic regions.

NEWSLETTER COMMITTEE - issues an informative newsletter 4 times a year featuring German research hints, book reports, special articles, members' queries, as well as announcements and information about upcoming meetings. The committee writes, prints and mails this newsletter to Germanic Genealogy Society members. In addition, newsletters are exchanged with other genealogy groups.

SALES COMMITTEE - publishes various forms and research information helpful to Germanic Research.

In addition to the above Standing Committees, Special Committees are often established to carry out specific purposes in the interest of the Society. Such committees might be:

By-Laws Review Committe	Telephone Committe
Cemetery Recording Committee	Auditing Committee
Nominating Committee	Archives Committee
Research Book Committee	

All GGS members are eligible to serve on these committees and are encouraged to do so according to their interests.

GGS Special Publications

Germanic Genealogy: A Guide to Worldwide Sources and Migration Patterns
Germanic Genealogy Society

Your best Guide for German Research: comprehensive 370 page How-to Handbook for the family history researcher. Help for beginners through advanced. Includes:
- Country by country guide to the sources
- Useful addresses for archives and societies • Current German postal codes • Worldwide Germanic migration patterns
- Jewish, Catholic, Lutheran, Mennonite history and sources • Historical and modern maps, including boundary changes • Annotated list of gazetteers • German word list + language hints • German naming patterns and place names • Extensive, annotated bibliography

Tells how to:
- Get started on your research
- Find your ancestor's place of origin
- Use church and civil records • Get the most from passenger departure and arrival lists • Read German script • Correspond abroad • Use the resources of the Family History Library and its Centers.
- And much, much more!
- Well indexed, up-to-date, easy-to-use.

Softbound. 370 pages, 1995.

$24.00 plus $3.00 P&H

GGS Special Publications Order Form

Mail to:

**GGS Book Orders
PO Box 16312 Dept B511
St. Paul, MN 55116-0312**

- Germanic Genealogy:
A Guide to Worldwide Sources and Migration Patterns
........$24.00* plus P&H
- Register to the Ahnenstammkartei des Deutschen Volkes
........$20.00* plus P&H
- The Lutherans of Russia Volume 1, 1833-1885
........$30.00* plus P&H

Register to the Ahnenstammkartei des Deutschen Volkes
Thomas K. Edlund

The Deutsche Zentralstelle für Genealogie (German Central Office for Genealogy) located in Leipzig, Germany has collected family histories of Germanic & Central European people since 1922. Their primary collection consists of "Ahnentafeln" or pedigree charts and family group sheets and family history manuscripts. The collection also contains a card index of 2.7 million names.

Since re-unification these records have been microfilmed by the FHL in Salt Lake City. However, the collection is organized phonetically with similar sounding surnames filed together, regardless of their spelling. This makes access to the collection of 1,200 rolls difficult to use without a register.

Mr. Edlund has compiled a register for use as a finding aid to the films. It allows you to determine the correct microfilm number for each surname you are researching. This register lists the grouping by family name, including spelling variations. The 140 page "Register" is a detailed directory of the microfilm contents, but is <u>NOT</u> an every name index (which would take thousands of pages). The register contains an introduction to and explanation of the Ahnenstammkartei and an index to the microfilm. This register will ensure that you order the correct microfilm for each of the surnames you are researching. A valuable finding aid for all German research facilities. Paperbound, 140 pages, perfect binding, 1995.

$20.00 plus $3.00 P & H

The Lutherans of Russia Volume 1, Parish Index to the Church Books of the Evangelical Lutheran Consistory of St. Petersburg 1833-1885
Thomas K. Edlund

Finally there is quick access to these valuable records! This microfilm collection has been very difficult to use because it is arranged by year instead of parish, and was recorded in the order received from each of the 199 parishes. Mr. Edlund and staff at the FHL in Salt Lake City spent over a year preparing this finding aid.

This volume is organized by parish for easy use. It is your key to the church books. Each parish is listed by year, giving film number, item number, and page number references. Includes a "see also" listing for many villages which were not parishes and a Russian to German parish name cross reference. This 383 page volume lists town names in German and Russian (Cyrillic).

In the introduction, Mr. Edlund provides the historical background of German settlements in the former Imperial Russian Empire. He also describes the Lutheran Church development in the Russian Empire. The St. Petersburg Consistory covered a huge geographic area stretching both northeast from the city of St. Petersburg and south to the Black Sea including 18 provinces of imperial Russia. Paperbound, 383 pages, perfect binding, 1995.

$30.00 plus $3.00 P & H

**Postage & Handling: each book $3.00 within U.S.;
$5.00 for surface mail to foreign countries.**

*Minnesota residents please add 6.5% sales tax per book.
Give complete return address information when ordering.

- Enclosed is a check or money order for.

$_____

HERE'S WHAT OTHERS ARE SAYING ABOUT
GERMANIC GENEALOGY!

"When the *Research Guide to German-American Genealogy* was first published a few years ago, I was impressed with its scholarly, yet easy-to-use format. Now we are fortunate to have a new edition with the revised title *Germanic Genealogy: A Guide to Worldwide Source and Migration Patterns* and what I thought to be a near perfect handbook to the Germanic researcher, has yet been improved and expanded. This book answers a multitude of questions the beginner encounters in the struggle with the complexities of Germanic genealogy. But it also contains a wealth of information for the more seasoned researcher. We owe a debt of gratitude to the dedicated authors who created this great research tool."

Horst A. Reschke, Editor of the Q&A column,
"Questions on Germanic Ancestry," Heritage Quest Magazine

"While most guides to doing German research center on the present boundaries of Germany, this book deals with German speaking persons who emigrated throughout the world. ... This book is probably the most comprehensive guide available for persons doing research in German ancestry."

Immigrant Genealogical Society Newsletter

"Make space on your shelf for *Germanic Genealogy*. ... Loaded with useful information ... contains 130 more pages than the first version. ... German history buffs will discover sections of the book that are especially intriguing to them. ... the 32-page index makes this vast pool of information readily useful to the researcher. ... Definitely a book to keep at one's side."

Der Blumenbaum, Sacramento German Genealogy Society

"This is an excellent resource for beginners and more advanced researchers, with a well-presented format showing the procedure to find those German-speaking ancestors. ... This book is highly recommended to all who are engaged in research for German-speaking ancestors."

The Palatine Immigrant, Palatines to America

"The 370 page book is indexed and is the first ever published which deals with the genealogy of German-speakers and their descendants in about sixty countries."

Olmsted County [Minnesota] Genealogical Society

"Retitled and dramatically enlarged since its 1991 debut ... contains a wealth of information for genealogical researchers at all levels. ... This guide is of value to people with European and Eastern European roots and extends itself to Asians, South Africans, and other ethnicities which may have been affected by Germany. The first few chapters are devoted to novice genealogists. ... The remainder of the book is invaluable to the more sophisticated genealogist. ... All in all, *Germanic Genealogy* will be a welcome addition to the most popular genealogy collections ... Public libraries may want to consider purchasing reference and circulating copies, since the price is right."

Booklist, American Library Association

MORE REVIEWS OF
GERMANIC GENEALOGY!

"Other books describe genealogical research in Germany, but what makes *Germanic Genealogy* especially valuable is its emphasis on how to do research on German-speaking individuals who live (or once lived) in other parts of Europe, North America, Latin America, South Africa, Australia, New Zealand, etc. This permits the reader to locate sources in countries about which he may have little information. For many years, I have been seeking possible sources of information in Chile, where an uncle emigrated from Germany in the late 1920s. Now I can contact the library and archive listed in the book. ...

"Bibliographic citations in each chapter and at the end of the book are very useful. ... Scattered references to Jewish records are found throughout the book, and much of the general information applies to the Jewish researcher as well as to anyone else. In addition, however, the chapter, 'Genealogical Resources for German-Jewish Ancestry,' by George Arnstein, is most welcome. ...

"In brief, *Germanic Genealogy* is a book that anyone conducting research on German-speaking families located anywhere in the world will wish to consult."

Avotaynu: The International Review of Jewish Genealogy

"Wer an der Völkerwanderungen und Familienforschung interessiert ist, wird die kürzliche Neuerscheinung: *Germanic Genealogy* der amerikanischen Germanic Genealogy Society als hilfreiche Info-Quelle schätzen. Über 370 Seiten lang befaßt sich dieses Buch mit Menschenbewegungen in 60 Ländern der Welt, zehn Seiten davon sind ausschließlich den Schicksalen der deutschen Auswanderer nach Afrika — vorzugsweise Südafrika und früheren deutschen Kolonien und Protektoraten — gewidmet."

Afrika-Kurier, Murrayfield, South Africa

"The Germanic Genealogy Society's previous book, *Research Guide to German-American Genealogy*, was a highly rated resource... But, this new edition is even better! It is so greatly expanded that it deserves the entirely new title it was given.

"The strength of the previous edition, dealing with resources in areas of German settlement outside today's Germany, is even further enhanced to the extent that the entire name of the work has changed to reflect that — it deals with <u>Germanic</u>, not merely German, genealogy; and it deals with <u>worldwide</u> sources and migration patterns. ...

"The unique and most helpful sections deal with the history of the 'German-speaking people in Europe,' including migration patterns, and instructions for researching Germanic families in European records, country by country. ...

"This is an excellent reference work for beginners and experienced researchers alike. Each genealogical and public library should have a copy for reference, and most GTHS members will want their own copies. Even those not particularly interested in genealogical research will benefit from the background on history and geography."

German-Texan Heritage Society